Lecture Notes in Computer Sc

Edited by G. Goos, J. Hartmanis and J. va

T0238820

Springer
Berlin
Heidelberg
New York
Barcelona
Hong Kong
London
Milan
Paris
Singapore
Tokyo

Mark Aagaard   John Harrison (Eds.)

Theorem Proving in Higher Order Logics

13th International Conference, TPHOLs 2000
Portland, OR, USA, August 14-18, 2000
Proceedings

Springer

Series Editors

Gerhard Goos, Karlsruhe University, Germany
Juris Hartmanis, Cornell University, NY, USA
Jan van Leeuwen, Utrecht University, The Netherlands

Volume Editors

Mark Aagaard
John Harrison
Intel Corporation
5200 NE Elam Young Parkway
Hillsboro, OR 97124, USA
E-mail: {johnh,maagaard}@ichips.intel.com

Cataloging-in-Publication Data applied for

Die Deutsche Bibliothek - CIP-Einheitsaufnahme

Theorem proving in higher order logics : 13th international conference ;
proceedings / TPHOLs 2000, Portland, OR, USA, August 14 - 18, 2000.
Mark Aagaard ; John Harrison (ed.). - Berlin ; Heidelberg ; New York ;
Barcelona ; Hong Kong ; London ; Milan ; Paris ; Singapore ; Tokyo :
Springer, 2000
  (Lecture notes in computer science ; Vol. 1869)
  ISBN 3-540-67863-8

CR Subject Classification (1998): F.4.1, I.2.3, F.3.1, D.2.4, B.6.3

ISSN 0302-9743
ISBN 3-540-67863-8 Springer-Verlag Berlin Heidelberg New York

Springer-Verlag Berlin Heidelberg New York
a member of BertelsmannSpringer Science+Business Media GmbH
© Springer-Verlag Berlin Heidelberg 2000
Printed in Germany

Typesetting: Camera-ready by author, data conversion by PTP-Berlin, Stefan Sossna
Printed on acid-free paper   SPIN: 10722303   06/3142   5 4 3 2 1 0

Preface

This volume is the proceedings of the *13th International Conference on Theorem Proving in Higher Order Logics (TPHOLs 2000)* held 14–18 August 2000 in Portland, Oregon, USA. Each of the 55 papers submitted in the full research category was refereed by at least three reviewers who were selected by the program committee. Because of the limited space available in the program and proceedings, only 29 papers were accepted for presentation and publication in this volume.

In keeping with tradition, TPHOLs 2000 also offered a venue for the presentation of work in progress, where researchers invite discussion by means of a brief preliminary talk and then discuss their work at a poster session. A supplementary proceedings containing associated papers for work in progress was published by the Oregon Graduate Institute (OGI) as technical report CSE-00-009.

The organizers are grateful to Bob Colwell, Robin Milner and Larry Wos for agreeing to give invited talks. Bob Colwell was the lead architect on the Intel P6 microarchitecture, which introduced a number of innovative techniques and achieved enormous commercial success. As such, he is ideally placed to offer an industrial perspective on the challenges for formal verification. Robin Milner contributed many key ideas to computer theorem proving, and to functional programming, through his leadership of the influential Edinburgh LCF project. In addition he is known for his work on general theories of concurrency, and his invited talk brings both these major themes together. Larry Wos was the developer of many of the fundamental approaches to automated proof in first order logic with equality. He also led the way in applying automated reasoning to solving open mathematical problems, and here he discusses some achievements of this project and future prospects.

The TPHOLs conference traditionally changes continent each year in order to maximize the chances that researchers all over the world can attend. Starting in 1993, the proceedings of *TPHOLs* or its predecessor have been published in the following volumes of the Springer-Verlag *Lecture Notes in Computer Science* series:

1993 (Canada)	780	1997 (USA)	1275
1994 (Malta)	859	1998 (Australia)	1479
1995 (USA)	971	1999 (France)	1690
1996 (Finland)	1125		

The 2000 conference was organized by a team from Intel Corporation and the Oregon Graduate Institute. Financial support came from Compaq, IBM, Intel, Levetate, Synopsys and OGI. A generous grant from the National Science Foundation allowed the organizers to offer student bursaries covering part of the cost of attending TPHOLs. The support of all these organizations is gratefully acknowledged.

May 2000   *Mark Aagaard, John Harrison*

Conference Organization

Mark Aagaard (General Chair)
Kelly Atkinson
Robert Beers
Nancy Day
John Harrison (Program Chair)
Naren Narasimhan
Tom Schubert

Program Committee

Mark Aagaard (Intel)
Flemming Andersen (IBM)
David Basin (Freiburg)
Richard Boulton (Glasgow)
Gilles Dowek (INRIA)
Harald Ganzinger (Saarbrucken)
Ganesh Gopalakrishnan (Utah)
Mike Gordon (Cambridge)
Jim Grundy (ANU)
Elsa Gunter (Bell Labs)
John Harrison (Intel)
Doug Howe (Ottawa)
Warren Hunt (IBM)

Bart Jacobs (Nijmegen)
Paul Jackson (Edinburgh)
Steve Johnson (Indiana)
Sara Kalvala (Warwick)
Tom Melham (Glasgow)
Paul Miner (NASA)
Tobias Nipkow (München)
Sam Owre (SRI)
Christine Paulin-Mohring (INRIA)
Lawrence Paulson (Cambridge)
Klaus Schneider (Karlsruhe)
Sofiene Tahar (Concordia)
Ranga Vemuri (Cincinnati)

Invited Speakers

Bob Colwell (Intel Corporation)
Robin Milner (University of Cambridge)
Larry Wos (Argonne National Laboratory)

Additional Reviewers

Abdelwaheb Ayari, Stefan Berghofer, Witold Charatonik, Roy L. Crole, Paul
Curzon, Nancy Day, Hans de Nivelle, Jean-Christophe Filliatre, Thomas For-
ster, Stefan Friedrich, M. J. Gabbay, Raj Goré, Roope Kaivola, Felix Klaedtke,
Skander Kort, Nazanin Mansouri, Yassine Mokhtari, Naren Narasimhan, Mal-
colm Newey, Claire Quigley, Rajesh Radhakrishnan, Harald Ruess, Hassen Saidi,
Gerhard Schellhorn, M. K. Srivas, Elena Teica, Luca Vigano, Burkhart Wolff

Contents

Fix-Point Equations for Well-Founded Recursion in Type Theory

Antonia Balaa and Yves Bertot

INRIA Sophia-Antipolis
http://www-sop.inria.fr/lemme/{Antonia.Balaa,Yves.Bertot}

1 Introduction

Inductive type theories, as used in systems like Coq or Lego [11,14,4], provide a systematic approach to program recursive functions over inductive data-structures and to reason about these functions. Recursive computation is described by reduction rules, included in the type system under the name ι-*reduction*. If t is an element of a recursive type, f is a recursive function over that type and v is the value of $f(t)$, then the equality $f(t) = v$ is a simple tautology, because $f(t)$ and v are equal modulo ι-reduction.

In practice, the inductive data-structures on which recursive functions may be defined are not restricted to simple concrete data-types, such as term algebras or finite-branching trees. Infinite branching is also allowed, so that some inductive types are powerful enough to describe the more complicated notions of terminating functions [9]. The intuitive notion is that of well-founded orders, for which there exists no infinite descending chain. If we describe a function such that recursive calls are performed only on terms that are smaller than the initial argument for some well-founded order, then we are sure there cannot be an infinite sequence of recursive calls.

For a user intending to describe complex programs, this is good news: it becomes possible to write algorithms without having to follow a tedious encoding using primitive structural recursion. Pleasant and efficient descriptions of complex algorithms become possible, for example, algorithms for computing Gröbner bases, as described by Théry [16] and Coquand and Persson [5].

In practice, using a function defined by well-founded recursion can also be unwieldy. In some sense, these functions are also defined by structural recursion, but the recursion follows the structure of the proof that there is no infinite descending chain starting from the function's argument. To actually use the reduction rules, one needs a full description of how the proof was constructed and it is not enough to simply know that such a proof exists.

This work provides a fix-point equality theorem that represents the reduction rule and can be used without any knowledge of the proofs' structure. The first motivation is practical in nature. Without a fix-point equality, it is hard to collect information about a function. In a system like Coq, the fix-point equation is only a consequence of the encoding based on generalized inductive data-types. With our work to generate this equality automatically, it becomes simpler to reason about well-founded recursive functions in Coq.

J. Harrison and M. Aagaard (Eds.): TPHOLs 2000, LNCS 1869, pp. 1–16, 2000.

1.1   Related Work

This work draws its theoretical and practical background from all the work done around inductive definitions in mathematics and computer based theorem proving tools. From the theoretical point of view, the main entry point may be the work by P. Aczel [1]. The immersion of inductive definitions in type theory based systems was mostly studied in the 1980 decade, for instance by Constable and Mendler in [3,2]. The flavor we use in this paper is mostly described by Coquand, Pfenning, and Paulin-Mohring in [14,4,11]. General use of well-founded recursion in Martin-Löf's intuitionistic type theory was studied by Paulson in [12], who shows that reduction rules can be obtained for each of several means to construct well-founded relations from previously known well-founded relations. By comparison with Paulson's work, our technique is to obtain reduction rules that are specific to each recursive function. The introduction of well-founded recursion using an accessibility principle as used in this paper was described by Nordström in [9].

Inductive definitions and inductive types also appear in proof systems based on simply-typed higher-order logic, such as HOL [6] or Isabelle [13]. Camilleri and Melham provide a package to systematize the definition of inductive relations in the HOL system [8], but this is not powerful enough to describe the notion of accessibility used in this paper. Harrison [7] provides a more practical tool, powerful enough to describe the necessary elements for well-founded recursion as described in this paper. In particular, the transfer theorem described below in section 3.1 is also described in Harrison's work. Konrad Slind [15] also gives a package to ease the definition of recursive functions based on well-founded induction, making sure his package will be general enough to be used with two different proof systems. The work of Harrison and Slind is also gives solutions to the question of constructing fix-point equations (they are called *recursion equations* in [15]), but the main question here is whether the logical foundations of type-theory, with constructivity and without extensionality, is sufficient to recover these equations. Harrison and Slind do not cover this question, using extensionality and non-constructive features freely.

2   Detailed Description of the Problem

In this section, we describe the inductive objects of type theory as used in CC^{ind} [11]. We show the differences that exist between structural recursive functions and well-founded recursive functions.

In type theory, types are used to represent both propositions and datatypes. To distinguish between these, *sorts* are provided, that are used to denote the types of types. The sort *Set* will be used to type the types representing datatypes, while the sort *Prop* will be used for the types representing propositions. Inductive definitions can be used to construct inductive datatypes, for instance the type of natural numbers given below, or to construct inductive propositions, for instance the proposition of accessibility given below. Types can be returned by functions. When the returned value is in *Prop*, a function is actually a proposition, will shall used the letter P to range over such propositions. When the returned value is in *Set*, a function denotes a dependent type. We shall use the letter B to range over such functions.

An inductive type is specified by giving a name, a type, and the name and type of its constructors. For instance, the *nat* for natural numbers is constructed using an inductive definition with two constructors 0 and S.

Inductive nat : Set :=

$$0 : nat$$
$$|S : nat \rightarrow nat.$$

It is possible to define structurally recursive functions over an inductive type. For a given function, the user needs to provide values for the constructors that are not really recursive and functions that compute the final value from the values of recursive calls of sub-terms belonging to the inductive type for the other constructors. For natural numbers, there exists an operation *nat_rec* whose behavior is described by the following two reduction rules (we use the notation $(f\ x_1\ x_2)$ to represent the application of f to two arguments):

$$(nat\_rec\ t\ V_0\ f\ 0) \leadsto V_0$$

$$(nat\_rec\ t\ V_0\ f\ (S\ x)) \leadsto (f\ x\ (nat\_rec\ t\ V_0\ f\ x))$$

The term *nat_rec* is a plain object of the typed calculus, its type takes into account the fact that one may define a function with a dependent type B. The Π notation is used to express that the type of the value returned by a function depends on the value received as argument by this function. When the type is used as a proposition, we will replace the Π notation with a more intuitive $\forall$.

nat_rec :
$\Pi\ B : nat \rightarrow Set.$
$\quad (B\ 0) \rightarrow$
$\quad (\Pi x :\ nat\ (B\ x) \rightarrow (B\ (S\ x))) \rightarrow (\Pi\ x :\ nat.B(x)).$

Inductive types may be more general. Consider the notion of *accessibility*, as described in [9], and defined as follows: given a binary relation R over a set A, an element $a \in A$ is accessible if every element smaller than a (we use a terminology where R is used as an order, but it does not even need to be transitive) is accessible. In particular, all minimal elements are accessible. The notion of accessibility can be defined with the following inductive definition:

Inductive Acc[A : Set; R : A → A → Prop] : A → Prop :=
Acc_intro $: \forall x : A.(\forall y : A.(R\ y\ x) \Rightarrow (Acc\ A\ R\ y)) \Rightarrow (Acc\ A\ R\ x).$

To make the notation easier, we shall assume that we work with a fixed relation, which we shall denote $<$ instead of R. Here, the recursion operation is described by a single reduction rule:

$(Acc\_rec\ t\ \Phi\ x\ (Acc\_intro\ x\ h)) \leadsto$
$$(\Phi\ x\ h\ \lambda y : A.\lambda p : y < x.(Acc\_rec\ t\ \Phi\ y\ (h\ y\ p)))$$

Acc_rec takes the following type:

$Acc\_rec : \Pi B : A \to Set.$
$\quad (\Pi x : A.$
$\qquad (\forall y : A.y < x \Rightarrow (Acc\ y)) \to$
$\qquad (\Pi y : A.y < x \to (B\ y)) \to (B\ x)) \to$
$\quad \Pi x : A.(Acc\ x) \to (B\ x)$

We often omit the first argument of Acc_rec, represented here by the formal parameter B of type: $A \to Set$. The function Φ must have the following type:

$\Phi : (\Pi x : A.(\forall y : A.y < x \Rightarrow (Acc\ y)) \to$
$\qquad (\Pi y : A.y < x \to (B\ y)) \to (B\ x))$

The function Φ takes three values as arguments, an object x, a proof that all elements smaller than x are accessible, and a function that can only be called on objects that are smaller than x. The reduction rule expresses that when computing the value $(Acc\_rec\ t\ \Phi\ x\ q)$, you can unroll the recursion one step, replacing it with a call to Φ on the right arguments, but you can perform this step only when q is of the form $(Acc\_intro\ x\ h)$.

Accessibility describes those elements from which one cannot start an infinite descending chain. A relation is well-founded when the accessibility predicate is verified for all elements of the type. There is then a theorem $wf_<$ that states $wf_< : \forall x : A.(Acc\ x)$. With a well-founded relation, it is possible to construct a new function $Rec_{wf_<}$ with the following value:

$(Rec_{wf_<}\ F\ x) =$
$\quad (Acc\_rec\ (\lambda z : A.\lambda h : (\forall y : A.y < z \Rightarrow (Acc\ z)).(F\ z))\ x\ (wf_<\ x))$

The function F must have the following type:
$F : \Pi x : A.(\Pi y : A.y < x \to (B\ y)) \to (B\ x).$

This function $Rec_{wf_<}$ is used to define functions by well-founded recursion. But does it have a reduction behavior that is similar to a recursion operator? At first sight no, since the proof that x is accessible is of the form $(wf_<\ x)$, not an instance of Acc_intro, the form that would be needed to use the ι-reduction of Acc_rec. Under closer scrutiny however, it is possible to prove that every object of an inductive type is obtained by applying one of the constructors of this type to proper arguments. Here there is only one constructor to the type Acc and one can deduce there exists a hypothesis h stating $\forall y : A.y < x \Rightarrow (Acc\ x)$ such that the proof $(wf_<\ x)$ is equal to $(Acc\_intro\ x\ h)$. Based on this equality, we have the following rule (with some type information omitted):

$$(Rec_{wf_<}\ F\ x) \rightsquigarrow (F\ x\ \lambda y : A.\lambda p : y < x.(Acc\_rec(\lambda x \lambda p'.(F\ x))\ y\ (h\ y\ p'))) \quad (1)$$

What is unfortunate with this rule is the presence of Acc_rec instead of $Rec_{wf_<}$ in the right hand side. Certainly, a rule of the following form would be preferable:

$$(Rec_{wf_<}\ F\ x) \rightsquigarrow (F\ x\ \lambda y : A.\lambda p : y < x.(Rec_{wf_<}\ F\ y)) \quad (2)$$

It is the objective of this work to provide a systematic method to provide rule 2 as an equality theorem.

3   Producing the Fix-Point Equation

We can break down the problem into two parts. The first part shows that proving the fix-point equation can be reduced to proving a specific property of the function F. The second part describes a method to prove that property for a class of functions.

3.1   Reducing to the Step Hypothesis

The crux of fix-point equation proofs is to show that the values of proofs really are irrelevant. For any value x in A, there exists a term T obtained by a certain number n_x of unrollings of F, such that $(Acc\_rec\ \lambda y.\lambda h.(F\ y)\ x\ h) = (T\ x)$. Thus, if F does not use the actual value of proof arguments, $(Acc\_rec\ \lambda y.\lambda p.(F\ y)\ x\ h)$ does not either. Since the term h in this expression is a proof, its value is not used and it does not matter whether h is of the form $(wf_<\ x)$ or $(h'\ x\ h'')$.

The transfer theorem has the following statement:
$$\forall F : \Pi x : A.(\Pi y : A.y < x \to (B\ y)) \to (B\ x).$$
$$(\forall x : A.\forall f : (\Pi y : A.(B\ y)).\forall g : (\Pi y : A.y < x \to (B\ y)).$$
$$(\forall y : A.\forall h : y < x.(g\ y\ h) = (f\ y))$$
$$\Rightarrow (F\ x\ \lambda y : A.\lambda h : (y < x).(g\ y\ h)) =$$
$$(F\ x\ \lambda y : A.\lambda h : (y < x).(f\ y)))$$
$$\Rightarrow \forall x : A.(Rec_{wf_<}\ F\ x) = (F\ x\ \lambda y : A\lambda p : y < x.(Rec_{wf_<}\ F\ y)).$$

The proof of this theorem proceeds by an induction over the accessibility of x with respect to the transitive closure of $<$. See appendix A for a Coq proof.

We shall call *step hypothesis* the only hypothesis of this transfer theorem.

3.2   Using Extensionality

The axiom of extensionality states that two functions are equal as soon as their values are equal on every possible argument. It has the following statement:

$$\forall A : Type.\forall B : A \to Set.\forall f, g : (\Pi x : A.(B\ x)).(\forall x : A.(f\ x) = (g\ x)) \Rightarrow f = g$$

Obviously, the step hypothesis is a direct consequence of extensionality. If this axiom is added, then the question of the fix-point equation is solved. The rest of this paper describes how one can avoid using extensionality.

4   A Syntactic Construction of the Step Hypothesis

For a given F, the step hypothesis has the following statement:
$$(\forall x : A.\forall f : (\Pi y : A.(B\ y)).\forall g : (\Pi y : A.y < x \to (B\ y)).$$
$$(\forall y : A.\forall h : y < x.(g\ y\ h) = (f\ y))$$

$$\Rightarrow (F\ x\ \lambda y : A.\lambda h : (y < x)(g\ y\ h)) =$$
$$(F\ x\ \lambda y : A.\lambda h : (y < x).(f\ y)))$$

Constructing a proof of this statement without using extensionality will be done by a structural analysis of F.

4.1   Some Notation

Given a set of sorts S (S will typically contain categories like $Prop$, Set, $Type$), a *term* is an element of the language T defined as follows:

$$T ::= \lambda x : T.T |(TT)| \Pi x : T.T |S| x.$$

This is the usual set of terms for type theory, see for example in section 2 in [11].

We will not describe the typing rules for this language here, but we shall assume we work in a context where a collection of inductive types has been defined and all the terms we manipulate are well-typed. In particular, for every inductive type ty we will assume there exists a function corresponding to a case operator, and a function corresponding to reasoning by cases, whose types are obtained systematically from the inductive definition following the methods in [11]. The case operator is a simplified instance of the recursion operator, where recursive values are not used, while the "reasoning-by-cases" operator is deduced similarly from the induction principle associated to the inductive type.

For instance, in the case of natural numbers, the case operator is the function nat_case with the following type:

nat_case :
   $\Pi B : nat \rightarrow Set.(B\ 0) \rightarrow (\Pi m : nat.(B\ (S\ m))) \rightarrow \Pi n : nat.(B\ n)$

The "reasoning-by-case" operation has the following type:

nat_case' :
   $\forall P : nat \rightarrow Prop.(P\ 0) \rightarrow (\forall m : nat.(P\ (S\ m))) \rightarrow \forall n : nat.(P\ n)$

For an arbitrary type ty, we will suppose it has k constructors

$$c_i : \Pi x_1 : t_{i,1} \ldots \Pi x_{n_i} : t_{i,n_i}.ty \qquad (1 \leq i \leq k).$$

The case operator for this inductive type will be denoted ty_case, with the following type:
$ty\_case : \Pi B : ty \rightarrow Set.$
   $(\Pi x_1 : t_{1,1} \ldots \Pi x_{n_1} : t_{1,n_1}.(B\ (c_1\ x_1 \ldots x_{n_1}))) \Rightarrow$
$\ldots$

   $(\Pi x_1 : t_{k,1} \ldots \Pi x_{n_k} : t_{k,n_k}.(B\ (c_k\ x_1 \ldots x_{n_k}))) \Rightarrow$
$\Pi x : ty.(B\ x)$
When considering a usage of ty_case, it will have the form

$$(ty\_case\ t\ l_1 \ldots l_k\ V)$$

Where each l_i will have the form:

$$l_i = \lambda x_1 : t_{i,1} \ldots \lambda x_{n_i} : t_{i,n_i}.b_i$$

and we shall sometimes abbreviate this expression as:

$$l_i = \lambda \overline{x_{(i)}}.b_i$$

For the type ty, we shall also assume there exists a term ty_case' with type

$ty\_case' : \Pi P : ty \rightarrow Prop.$
$\quad (\Pi x_1 : t_{1,1} \ldots \Pi x_{n_1} : t_{1,n_1}.(P\ (c_1\ x_1 \ldots x_{n_1}))) \Rightarrow$
$\ldots$

$\quad (\Pi x_1 : t_{k,1} \ldots \Pi x_{n_k} : t_{k,n_k}.(P\ (c_k\ x_1 \ldots x_{n_k}))) \Rightarrow$
$\Pi x : ty.(P\ x).$

This term ty_case' will be used to construct proofs instead of values.

We will also assume there exists two theorems eq_ind_r and eq_ind, with the following statements (types):

$$eq\_ind\_r : \forall A : Set.\forall x : A.\forall P : A \rightarrow Prop.(P\ x) \Rightarrow \forall y : A.y = x \Rightarrow (Py),$$

$$eq\_ind : \forall A : Set.\forall x : A.\forall P : A \rightarrow Prop.(P\ x) \Rightarrow \forall y : A.x = y \Rightarrow (Py),$$

and a theorem $refl\_equal$ with the following statement:

$$refl\_equal : \forall A : Set.\forall x : A.x = x.$$

On several occasions, we will consider *contexts* which are expressions with a hole in them, to be filled with some value. A context will be denoted $C[\cdot; \ldots; \cdot]$ and the same contexts where holes have been filled in with values will be denoted $C[x_1; \ldots; x_n]$. We will also consider the operation of substituting all occurrences of a term with another. This operation will be denoted $C[g := h]$. This term is equal to $C[h; \cdots; h]$, where $C[\cdot; \ldots; \cdot]$ is the context such that $C[g; \ldots; g] = C$ and g does not occur free in $C[\cdot; \ldots; \cdot]$.

4.2 Constructing the Proof in Absence of Bound Variables

For some values of X, computing $(F\ X\ g)$ may lead to some term where g occurs. Let us say it is convertible to

$$T = C[(g\ T'\ H)],$$

such that all variables occurring in the terms T' and H are free in T. Suppose we have an hypothesis H_{eq}

$$H_{eq} : \forall y : A.\forall h : y < x.(g\ y\ h) = (f\ y).$$

Let $C' = C[g := \lambda y : A.\lambda h : y < x.(fy)]$, we can reduce the task of proving $C[(g\ T'\ H)] = C'$ to the task of proving $C[(f\ T')] = C'$ using eq_ind_r and H_{eq}. If p is a proof of $C[(f\ T')] = C'$, then

$$(eq\_ind\_r\ (B\ T')\ (f\ T')\ (\lambda n.C[n] = C')\ p\ (g\ T'\ H)\ (H_{eq}\ T'\ H))$$

is a proof of $C[(g\ T'\ H)] = C'$. We can repeat this process until there is no more instance of g in the left-hand side, and conclude using $refl\_equal$. Note the constraint about free variables in T' and H that must also be free in $C[(g\ T'\ H)]$. If this constraint is not respected the proof term will not be well typed.

4.3   Handling Case Operators

Bound variables are introduced when one uses the case operator of some inductive type. Intuitively, the case operators perform some form of pattern matching on values in an inductive type. This pattern matching makes several cases appear, corresponding to the various constructors of the inductive type. Most constructors carry values and the λ-abstractions are used in the case operators to give access to these values, like pattern-matching rules in functional programming.

For instance, let us consider a well-founded definition of a discrete logarithm function:

$(F_{log}\ x) =$
  $(nat\_case\ \lambda x : nat.\Pi f : (\Pi y : nat.(y < x) \to nat).nat$
      $\lambda f : (\Pi y : nat.(y < 0) \to nat).0$
        $\lambda\ n : nat.\lambda f : (\Pi y : nat.(y < (S\ n)) \to nat).(S\ (f\ (div2\ (S\ n))\ (th\ n)))$
$log = (Rec_{wf<}\ F_{log})$

This definition assumes we are given a function $div2$ that divides a number by 2 and a theorem $th : \forall n : nat.(div2\ n) < (S\ n)$. The second and third arguments of nat_case describe the computation to perform in two different cases. This is where λ-abstractions occur. The bound variable n represents the predecessor of the function argument in the case where this argument is non-zero.

The idea for this part of our work is to follow the same structure of pattern matching, not to compute the value returned by the function, but to construct a different proof of equality in each case. The recursive analysis of F is decomposed into two phases. The first phase corresponds to the subterms of F that have a functional type, receiving a function as argument. The second part is the part where the function argument is already received. One switches from the first phase to the second when crossing a λ-abstraction.

First phase : sub-terms of F with a functional argument. The expression F has type $\Pi x : A.(\Pi y : A.y < x \to (B\ y)) \to (B\ x)$. It is a function that can receive (at least) two arguments. We shall always assume that F is of the form $\lambda x.F'$.

The expression F' must be well typed in a context where x has type A and F' must have the type:

$$\Pi y : A.y < x \rightarrow (B\ y)) \rightarrow (B\ x).$$

In a more general setting, the problem is the following one: given a type environment Γ, a term X well-typed in Γ, and composed only of applications of constructors to other constructors and variables occurring in Γ, given a variable f declared in Γ with type $f : \Pi y : A.(B\ y)$, prove the following equality:

$$\forall g : (\Pi y : A.y < X \rightarrow (B\ y)).(\forall y : A.\forall h : y < X.(g\ y\ h) = (f\ y)) \Rightarrow$$
$$(F'\ \lambda x : A.\lambda h : y < X.(f\ y)) = (F'\ \lambda x : A.\lambda h : y < X.(g\ y\ h)$$

F' should be a function, but it would be too restrictive to assume that F' should be a λ-abstraction. In fact we shall consider two cases:

1. it is a λ-abstraction, $F' = \lambda g.T$, in this case we can switch to the second phase for T, after having added in the context $g : \Pi y : A.y < X \rightarrow (B\ y)$ and $H_{eq} : \forall y : A.\forall h : y < X.(g\ y\ h) = (f\ y)$. If this yields a proof p, then

$$\lambda g : \Pi y : A.y < X \rightarrow (B\ y).\lambda H_{eq} : \forall y : A.\forall h : y < X.(g\ y\ h) = (f\ y).p$$

   is the requested proof.

2. it is built with a *case* expression, that is, F' has the following form:

$$F' = (ty\_case\ t\ l_1\ \ldots l_k\ V).$$

   where t, l_1, $\ldots$, l_k are formed as described in section 4.1. Because of the type of F', the term t should have the following form:

$$t = \lambda x : ty.\Pi g : (\Pi y : A.y < X[x] \rightarrow (B\ y)).t'$$

   where $X[\cdot]$ is a context such that $X[V] = X$ and t' is some arbitrary type. Note that $X[\cdot]$ may have no hole when V does not occur in X.
   Recall the terms l_i are such that $l_i = \overline{\lambda x_{(i)}}.b_i$, we can recursively address the problem of finding a proof for formulas:

$$\forall g : (\Pi y : A.\Pi h : y < X[(c_i\ x_1 \ldots x_{n_1})].(B\ y)).$$
$$(\forall y : A.\forall h : y < X[(c_i\ x_1 \ldots x_{n_i})].(g\ y\ h) = (f\ y)) \Rightarrow$$
$$(b_i\ \lambda y : A.\lambda h : y < X[(c_i\ x_1 \ldots x_{n_i})](f\ y)) = (b_i\ g)$$

   now with the term X being replaced with $X[(c_i\ x_1 \ldots x_{n_i})]$, a new type environment Γ' modified so that the new variables x_1, $\ldots$, x_n have been added with type $x_j : t_{i,j}$. Let us suppose this yields k proofs called p_i. We can then construct a proof for the whole equality with the following shape:

$$(ty\_case'$$
$$\lambda x : ty.\forall g : (\Pi y : A.y < X[x] \rightarrow (B\ y)).$$
$$(\forall y : A.\forall h : y < X[x].(g\ y\ h) = (F\ y)) \Rightarrow$$
$$(ty\_case\ t\ l_1 \ldots l_k\ x\ \lambda y : A.\lambda h : y < X[x].(g\ y\ h)) =$$

$$\frac{(ty\_case\ t\ l_1 \ldots l_k\ x\ \lambda y : A.\lambda h : y < X[x].(f\ y))}{\lambda \overline{x_{(1)}}.p_1}$$

$$\ldots$$

$$\ldots$$

$$\frac{}{\lambda \overline{x_{(k)}}.p_k}$$
$$V\ g\ H_{eq})$$

Second phase: sub-terms of F where g occurs. In the second phase, the variable g, corresponding to the function that may be called to represent recursive calls, has a special status, and we are looking at a sub-term of F where g may occur free. We want to provide the equality of this term with another term where all free occurrences of g are replaced by $\lambda y : A.\lambda h.y < X.(f\ y)$.

We reduce the problem to the following one: given a type environment Γ, a term X well-typed in Γ, and composed only of application of constructors to other constructors and variables occurring in Γ, given three variables f, g, and H_{eq} declared in Γ with types $f : \Pi y : A.(B\ y)$, $g : \Pi y : A.\Pi h : y < X.(B\ y)$, and $H_{eq} : \forall y : A.\forall h : y < X.(g\ y\ h) = (f\ y)$, given an expression C, well typed in Γ where f does not occur, construct a proof for the equality:

$$C = C[g := \lambda y.\lambda h : y < X.(f\ y)].$$

We only consider the following cases:

1. if C falls in the case described in section 4.2, then apply the corresponding method,
2. if $C = (g\ T\ H)$, compute recursively a proof p for

$$T = T[g := \lambda y.\lambda h : y < X.(f\ y)],$$

then the following expression is a good candidate for the requested proof:

$$(eq\_ind\ A\ T\ [n : A](g\ T\ H) = (f\ n)\ (H_{eq}\ T\ H)$$
$$T[g := \lambda y.\lambda h : y < X.(f\ y)]\ p)$$

However, this expression may be untypable. The type of this expression is supposed to be $(g\ T\ H) = (f\ T')$, but this expression is well-typed if its type is well-typed. For an equality to be well-typed, both sides must have the same type. The type of $(g\ T\ H)$ is $(B\ T)$ and the type of $(f\ T')$ is $(B\ T')$. If these two expressions are not $\beta\iota$-convertible, our method will fail.

3. if $C = (C'\ g)$ and g does not occur in C', then switch back to the first phase to find a proof of:

$$\forall g : (\Pi y : A.(y < X).(B\ y)).(\forall y : A.\forall h : (y < X).(g\ y\ h) = (f\ y)) \Rightarrow$$
$$(C'\ g) = (C'\ \lambda y : A.\lambda h : y < X.(f\ y)),$$

then apply this proof to the current g and H_{eq}.

4. if $C = (ty\_case \; t \; l_1 \ldots l_k \; V)$ and $ty, l_1, \ldots, l_k$ are described as in section 4.1, let us suppose we are recursively able to find a proof p_0 of

$$V = V[g := \lambda y.\lambda h : y < X.(f \; y)]$$

in the same context Γ, for the same value X, and the same f, g, and H_{eq}, and let us suppose we are recursively able to find k proofs p_i for the following statements:

$$b_i = b_i[g := \lambda y.\lambda h : y < X'_i.(f \; y)]$$

where X'_i is $X[V := (c_i \; x_1 \ldots x_k)]$, with new typing contexts Γ_i such that declarations have been added for each of the variables $x_1 : t_{i,1}, \ldots, x_{n_i} : t_{i,n_i}$ (modulo a renaming of variables to make sure the new variables are distinct from variables already present in Γ), and where the two variables g, H_{eq} have their type changed in Γ_i to

$$g : \lambda y : A.y < X'_i \to (B \; y) \qquad H_{eq} : \lambda y : A.\lambda h : y < X'_i.(g \; y \; h) = (f \; y).$$

Writing l'_i for the terms $\overline{\lambda x}_{(i)}.b_i[g := \lambda y.\lambda h : y < X'_i.(f \; y)]$, the term

$p = (ty\_case'$
$\qquad \lambda x : ty.\forall g : (\Pi y : A.y < X[V := x] \to (B \; y)).$
$\qquad\qquad \forall H_{eq} : \forall y : A.\forall h : y < X[V := x].(g \; y \; h) = (f \; y).$
$\qquad\qquad\qquad (ty\_case \; t \; l_1 \ldots l_k \; x) = (ty\_case \; t \; l'_1 \ldots l'_k \; x)$
$\qquad \lambda x_1 : t_{1,1}.\ldots.\lambda x_{n_1} : t_{1,n_1}.\lambda g : (\Pi y : A.y < X'_1 \to (B \; y)).$
$\qquad\qquad \lambda H_{eq} : (\forall y : A.\forall h : y < X'_1 \Rightarrow (f \; y) = (g \; y \; h)).p_1$
$\qquad \ldots$
$\qquad \lambda x_1 : t_{k,1}.\ldots.\lambda x_{n_k} : t_{k,n_k}.\lambda g : (\Pi y : A.y < X'_k \to (B \; y)).$
$\qquad\qquad \lambda H_{eq} : (\forall y : A.\forall h : y < X'_k \Rightarrow (f \; y) = (g \; y \; h)).p_k$
$\qquad V \; g \; H_{eq})$

is a proof of:

$$(ty\_case \; t \; l_1 \ldots l_k \; V) = (ty\_case \; l'_1 \ldots l'_k \; V)$$

and

$(eq\_ind\_r \; ty$
$\qquad V$
$\qquad \lambda x : ty.(ty\_case \; t \; l_1 \ldots l_k \; V) = (ty\_case \; l'_1 \ldots l'_k \; x)$
$\qquad p$
$\qquad V[g := \lambda y.\lambda h : y < X.(f \; y)]$
$\qquad p_0)$

is a proof of $C = C[g := \lambda y.\lambda h : y < X.(f \; y)]$.

4.4   The Class of Acceptable Functions

We put several restrictions on the form of functions for which our method will work. These restrictions can be summarized as follows: the function F must be well-typed and must only use its functional argument in two possible ways:

1. The functional argument is fully applied
2. The functional argument is itself passed as argument to a case construct, that is, a function of the form ty_case.

In particular, this precludes situations where F would pass its functional argument to an auxiliary function. Attempting to summarize these constraints as a formal language description we have the following result:

$$\mathcal{T}' = \lambda x : \mathcal{T}.\mathcal{T}_1$$
$$\mathcal{T}_1 = \lambda f : (\Pi y : \mathcal{T}.\Pi h : (R\ y\ x).\mathcal{T}).\mathcal{T}_{2,f} \mid (ty\_case\ \lambda\overline{x_{(1)}}.\mathcal{T}_1 \cdots \lambda\overline{x_{(k)}}.\mathcal{T}_1\ \mathcal{T})$$
$$\mathcal{T}_{2,f} = (\mathcal{T}_1\ f) \mid (f\ \mathcal{T}_{2,f}\ \mathcal{T}_{2,f}) \mid (\mathcal{T}_{2,f}\ \mathcal{T}_{2,f}) \mid \lambda x : \mathcal{T}.\mathcal{T}_{2,f} \mid$$
$$(ty\_case\ \lambda\overline{x_{(1)}}.\mathcal{T}_{2,f} \cdots \lambda\overline{x_{(k)}}.\mathcal{T}_{2,f}\ \mathcal{T}_{2,f})$$

The notation $\mathcal{T}_{2,f}$ is used to stress the fact that the functional argument must really be used in F in a more restrictive manner than any other λ-term. In particular, no instance of $\mathcal{T}_{2,f}$ may be f, and f may not occur free in $\mathcal{T}_1$ in the case $(\mathcal{T}_1\ f)$ of $\mathcal{T}_{2,f}$.

5   Usage in the Coq System

In the Coq system, the type Acc is defined exactly as it is described in this paper. The function Rec_{wf} is represented by a function named $well\_founded\_definition$. This function takes as parameters the input type (corresponding to A throughout this paper), the relation on this type ($<$), the theorem stating that this relation is well-founded ($wf_<$), a function mapping elements of the input type to sets (B), and a function (F).

This method to define well-founded recursive function is specially supported in the syntax of the **Program** tactic, that makes it possible to describe an algorithm without giving a complete justification that it is well defined, the necessary proofs being left as side conditions. Because the extraction mechanism provided by Coq uses the sort mechanism to delete proof arguments in functions, well-founded recursive function are naturally extracted as recursive functions that can be used to compute in Caml or a lazy programming language.

Programmers in Coq do not use the ty_case operators to write down their algorithms. Instead, the Coq system provides a pattern matching construct that is equivalent to ty_case or ty_case' constructs, the distinction being done automatically depending on the type of the result. An advantage of this approach is that the same pattern matching construct is used to describe the function and the proof. A drawback is that a single pattern matching construct may expand into a large number of ty_case constructs if the patterns occurring on the left hand side of pattern-matching rules are deep.

Also, pattern-matching constructs can be much simpler to write than ty_case constructs when the types of all cases are equal. In this case, the user does not need to provide this type, which is computed automatically by the proof system from the type of the first branch. In this case, we will say that the pattern-matching construct becomes simply typed.

We have used our method to construct by hand fixpoint equalities for a small variety of functions including Ackermann's function, well-founded encodings of factorial, remainder, a list-based quicksort, and some auxiliary function working on lists for a Java byte-code verifier. In all the cases treated so far, the functions defined by well-founded recursion had a non-dependent type, so that the problem raised in the second phase (case 2) did not occur.

Based on our method, we are constructing a procedure to generate the equality automatically when it is possible. This procedure will be provided in Coq with the following syntax:

```
Wf_Definition f A B order th_wf F.
```

Where f is the name of the new recursive function to be defined, A is the input type, B is the function that computes the output type from the input value, order is a binary relation on A, th_wf a proof that order is well-founded, and F the value of the functional that describes the function being defined (the functional of which f will be the fix-point, so to say). This command defines the function f and the theorem f_fxp_eqn whose statement is :

$$\forall x : A.(f\ x) = (F\ x\ \lambda y : A.\lambda h : (order\ y\ x).(f\ y))$$

For instance, here is how our tool is to be used to define the log function.

```
Section define_rem.
Parameters div2 : nat -> nat; th : (n:nat)(lt (div2 n) (S n)).

Wf_Definition log nat [_:nat]nat lt lt_wf
  [x:nat]<[x:nat](f:(y:nat)(lt y x)->nat)nat>Cases x of
      0 => [f:?](0)
    | (S n) => [f:?](S (f (div2 (S n))(th n)))
  end.
```

The fixpoint equation we obtain is:

```
log_fxp_eqn :
 (x:nat) (log x)
   =(<[x0:nat]((y:nat)(lt y x0)->nat)->nat>
       Cases x of
         0 => [_:((y:nat)(lt y (0))->nat)](0)
        |(S n) =>
          [f:((y:nat)(lt y (S n))->nat)](S (f (div2 (S n))(th n)))
       end [y:nat; _:(lt y x)](log y))
```

But it is easy to obtain a simpler formulation, where dependently typed case expressions become simply typed:

```
Theorem log_simple_equation :
  (x:nat)(log x) =
     (Cases x of 0 => (0) | (S n) => (S (log (div2 (S n))))) end).
Intros x;Rewrite log_fxp_eqn;Case x;Simpl;Auto.
Qed.
```

6 Conclusion

The practical result of this work is a tool to generate an equation that is usually difficult to obtain. In its simplest form, the equation can be as simple as the function definitions that can be obtained with the Program tactic, where proof information also disappears [10].

The desire to produce proofs of fix-point equalities without using extensionality looks very much like a theoretic rather than pragmatic question. As mere users of a type-theory based proof system, we do not know how well or how badly the axiom of extensionality interferes with other aspects of the logic we use. The theoretical result brought by this paper is that we do not need to answer this question for a reasonable class of functions.

In future work, we would like to study how this method can be extended to handle functions containing recursion operators and mutual recursion. We also want to provide a simplified version of the fix-point equation where proof arguments do not appear, following the example of log_simple_equation. This improvement can be implemented by a simple partial evaluation. It should also be possible to re-use the results of Parent [10] and Slind [15] towards the support of plain functional programming in proof systems.

References

1. Peter Aczel. An introduction to inductive definitions. In J. Barwise, editor, *Handbook of Mathematical Logic*, volume 90 of *Studies in Logic and the Foundations of Mathematics*, 1977.
2. Robert Constable, S. F. Allen, H. M. Bromley, W. R. Cleaveland, J. F. Cremer, R. W. Harber, D. J. Howe, T. B. Knoblock, N. P. Mendler, P. Panangaden, J. T. Sasaki, and S. F. Smith. *Implementing mathematics with the Nuprl proof development system*. Prentice-Hall, 1986.
3. Robert L. Constable and Nax P. Mendler. Recursive definitions in type theory. In Rohit Parikh, editor, *Logics of Programs*, volume 193 of *LNCS*, pages 61–78. Springer Verlag, June 1985.
4. Thierry Coquand and Christine Paulin-Mohring. Inductively defined types. In P. Martin-Löf and G. Mints, editors, *Proceedings of Colog'88*, volume 417 of *Lecture Notes in Computer Science*. Springer-Verlag, 1990.
5. Thierry Coquand and Henrik Persson. Gröbner bases in type theory. In *Types'98*, volume 1658 of *Lecture Notes in Computer Science*. Springer-Verlag, 1998.
6. Michael J. C. Gordon and Thomas F. Melham. *Introduction to HOL : a theorem proving environment for higher-order logic*. Cambridge University Press, 1993.

7. John Harrison. Inductive definitions: Automation and application. In P. J. Windley, T. Schubert, and J. Alves-Foss, editors, *Higher Order Logic Theorem Provoing and Its Applications: Proceedings of the 8th International Workshop*, volume 971 of *Lecture Notes in Computer Sciences*. Springer-Verlag, 1995.
8. Thomas F. Melham. A package for inductive relation definitions in HOL. In *Proceedings of the 1991 International Workshop on the HOL Theorem Proving system and its Applications*, pages 350–357. IEEE Computer Society Press, 1992.
9. Bengt Nordström. Terminating general recursion. *BIT*, 28, 1988.
10. Catherine Parent. Synthesizing proofs from programs in the Calculus of Inductive Constructions. In *Mathematics of Program Construction*, volume 947 of *Lecture Notes in Computer Science*. Springer-Verlag, July 1995.
11. Christine Paulin-Mohring. Inductive Definitions in the System Coq - Rules and Properties. In M. Bezem and J.-F. Groote, editors, *Proceedings of the conference Typed Lambda Calculi and Applications*, number 664 in Lecture Notes in Computer Science, 1993. LIP research report 92-49.
12. Lawrence C. Paulson. Constructing recursion operators in intuitionistic type theory. Technical report 57, University of Cambridge, Computer Laboratory, October 1984.
13. Lawrence C. Paulson and Tobias Nipkow. *Isabelle : a generic theorem prover*, volume 828 of *Lecture Notes in Computer Science*. Springer-Verlag, 1994.
14. Frank Pfenning and Christine Paulin-Mohring. Inductively defined types in the Calculus of Constructions. In *Proceedings of Mathematical Foundations of Programming Semantics*, volume 442 of *Lecture Notes in Computer Science*. Springer-Verlag, 1990. technical report CMU-CS-89-209.
15. Konrad Slind. Function definition in higher order logic. In *Theorem Proving in Higher Order Logics*, volume 1125 of *Lecture Notes in Computer Science*. Sprinter Verlag, August 1996.
16. Laurent Théry. A certified version of Buchberger's algorithm. In *Automated Deduction (CADE-15)*, volume 1421 of *Lecture Notes in Artificial Intelligence*. Springer-Verlag, July 1998.

A   Proof of the Transfer Theorem

This text can be checked mechanically using Coq Version 6.3.1.

```
Scheme Acc_ind2 := Induction for Acc Sort Prop.
Transparent well_founded_induction.
Variables A:Set; R:A -> A -> Prop;
  R_wf:(well_founded A R); B:A -> Set;
  F:(x : A) ((y : A) (R y x) -> (B y)) -> (B x).
Definition f := (well_founded_induction A R R_wf B F).

Inductive Trans  : A -> A -> Prop :=
  Tc1: (x, y : A) (R x y) -> (Trans x y)
| Tc2: (x, y, z : A) (R x y) -> (Trans y z) -> (Trans x z).
Hints Resolve Tc1 Tc2 ex_intro.
```

```
Theorem trans_balance:
  (x, y, z : A) (R x y) -> (Trans y z)
    -> (Ex [t : A] (Trans x t) /\ (R t z)).
Intros x y z H H0; Generalize x H; Clear H x; Elim H0;EAuto.
Intros x y0 z0 H H1 H2 x0 H3; Elim (H2 x); Auto.
Intros x1 H4; Exists x1;Elim H4;EAuto. Qed.
```

```
Theorem well_founded_ind2:
 (P : A -> Prop)
   ((x : A)((y : A)(Trans y x) -> (P y)) -> (P x)) -> (a : A)(P a).
Intros P H a; Apply H; Cut ((y : A)(Trans y a) -> (P y)) /\ (P a).
Intros H0; Elim H0; Auto.
Elim a using (well_founded_ind A R R_wf).
Intros x H0; Split. Intros y H1; Inversion H1. Elim (H0 y); Auto.
Elim trans_balance with 1 := H2 2 := H3.
Intros x1 H7; Elim H7; Intros H8 H9. Elim (H0 x1); Auto.
Apply H; Intros y H1; Generalize H0; Inversion H1.
Intros H5; Elim (H5 y); Auto.
Elim trans_balance with 1 := H2 2 := H3.
Intros x1 H6 H7; Elim H6; Intros H8 H9.
Elim H7 with y := x1; Auto.  Qed.
```

```
Theorem is_trans:
  (x, y, z : A) (Trans x y) -> (R y z) -> (Trans x z).
Induction 1; EAuto.
Qed.
Hints Resolve is_trans.
```

```
Theorem wf_transfer:
  ((x : A) (f' : (y : A)  (B y))
            (g : (y : A) (R y x) -> (B y))
              ((y : A) (h : (R y x))  (g y h) = (f' y))
     -> (F x [y : A] [h : (R y x)]   (g y h)) =
        (F x [y : A] [_ : (R y x)]   (f' y)))
  -> (x : A)  (f x) = (F x [y : A] [h : (R y x)] (f y)).
Unfold f; Intros H x; Elim x using well_founded_ind2; Intros x'.
Unfold 3 well_founded_induction.
Elim (R_wf x') using Acc_ind2; Simpl.
Intros x'' accessible H_rec_acc H_rec_well_founded.
Apply H with
  g := [y : A] [h : (R y x'')]
        (Acc_rec A R B [x0 : A]
          [_ : (y1 : A) (R y1 x0) -> (Acc A R y1)]
          [g' : (y1 : A) (R y1 x0) -> (B y1)]
          (F x0 g') y (accessible y h)).
Intros y h; Rewrite H_rec_well_founded; EAuto. Qed.
```

Programming and Computing in HOL

Bruno Barras

University of Cambridge
Computer Laboratory
New Museums Site
Pembroke Street
Cambridge CB2 3QG
United Kingdom
Bruno.Barras@cl.cam.ac.uk

Abstract. This article describes a set of derived inference rules and an abstract reduction machine using them that allow the implementation of an interpreter for HOL terms, with the same complexity as with ML code. The latter fact allows us to use HOL as a computer algebra system in which the user can implement algorithms, provided he proved them correct.

1 Introduction

This article describes another step towards using HOL [10] as a programming language. In order to preserve consistency, most logical systems forbid non-terminating functions. In HOL, library `bossLib` provides an automated and uniform mechanism for the definition of recursive functions. Termination proofs are handled by another library, `tfl` [15]. What we provide here is a tool to *evaluate* HOL expressions seen as programs of an ML-like language.

The ability to compute normal form of expressions efficiently has many applications. One of the most obvious is to solve numerical equations that only require calculations. For instance, we would not say that proving $1 + 2 = 3$ needs reasoning. We can simply assign an algorithm to $+$ that performs addition. Then, the above theorem is proven simply by running the algorithm with arguments 1 and 2, which shall return 3.

In some logical formalisms, this notion of computation is even considered essential. This is particularly obvious with type theoretic systems, such as Pure Type Systems [2,3], where the conversion rule asserts that two statements equal with respect to β-conversion have the same proofs. As a consequence, $1 + 2 = 3$ would be proven by reflexivity (assuming β-conversion is extended with rules to compute with natural numbers).

However, in HOL, only α-convertible terms are identified and, following LCF's idea [11], every theorem must be produced by using the basic inference rules, such as reflexivity of equality or Modus Ponens. The goal is to build the theorem $\vdash 1 + 2 = 3$ (an equality derivation) given the expression $1 + 2$. According to LCF's terminology, this is a conversion [13,14].

J. Harrison and M. Aagaard (Eds.): TPHOLs 2000, LNCS 1869, pp. 17–37, 2000.

Let us illustrate our idea of computing within the logic on a very simple example. Assuming we represent natural numbers with 0 and a successor function S, we can use the following theorems to compute with addition:

$$0 + m = m \qquad S(n) + m = S(n + m)$$

Each of them corresponds to one step of simplification. Using transitivity of equality, we can build simplification paths of arbitrary length; the goal we set is to build a reduction path from the original term to its normal form. If m and n are two canonical numbers (built only upon 0 and S), then these equations allow us to compute the canonical representation of the sum of m and n. This is done of course the same way as running the following ML program:

```
datatype num = 0 | S of num;
fun  0    + m = m
  | (S n) + m = S(n+m);
> val + = fn : num * num -> num
```

The idea is to interpret equations as clauses defining an ML program, and we mimic the way ML programs are evaluated. Put in another way, we follow the algorithm of an ML interpreter, the term to be reduced being equivalent to the state of this interpreter.

An essential point is to produce proofs of such theorems as efficiently as possible. We will show that this leads to new proof techniques, where computation is not only used to evaluate numerical expressions, but is applied to symbolic computations. This establishes a connection between theorem proving and computer algebra systems.

A last motivation we give here for computing within the logic is testing the specifications. One can check on some examples that what is specified actually behaves as intended when formalized. As a simple example, one can define EVEN with

$$\text{EVEN } 0 = T \qquad \text{EVEN } 1 = F \qquad \text{EVEN } (S(S(n))) = \text{EVEN } n$$

One can then try to run the specification and check that EVEN 127 computes to F, etc. It may be useful in the case of more elaborate specification.

The structure of the paper is the following: we first comment why the existing tools of HOL are unable to solve our problem in the general case. Then, we introduce abstract machines as a way of implementing reduction functions for pure λ-calculus and then λ-calculus with constants. Section 4 shows how to tailor derived inference rules in order to make the reduction function return a derivation instead of the mere normal form. Summarizing all this leads to the abstract machine we implemented in HOL (section 5). We finally test our conversion on examples of various sizes and remark it has the same asymptotic complexity as ML code.

2   Comments on the Strategy

The task discussed above can be done by already existing tools, such as conversion REWRITE_CONV. The latter, given a list of theorems, repeatedly performs rewrites on a term, until this is not possible anymore. Free variables may be instantiated so that the left hand side of a theorem becomes equal to the current term. For more details, see [13]. There are several other conversions (the most powerful being simpLib) that can perform higher order matching or conditional rewriting. However, using these conversions for the evaluation of expressions may fail for various reasons. This section details why they do not work properly, and how we suggest to fix these problems. Let us first recall that officially, HOL terms are λ-terms with constants. This means terms are either variables, constants, application or abstraction:

$$\text{Term} := x \mid c \mid T_1 \, T_2 \mid \lambda x. \, T$$

Bottom-Up Evaluation

Since a term may contain several redexes, we have to choose a strategy determining the order following which they are reduced.

HOL's rewriters use a top-down rewriting strategy. That is, they first try to make simplifications at the top of the term. When all simplifications at the top have been done, the sub-expressions are simplified recursively. Since this can create redexes at the top of the term, one then has to simplify the whole expression.

This strategy is not bad for symbolic computations since it tries first to simplify the largest expressions, which may make subterms disappear without wasting time reducing them. The drawback of this strategy is that it applies the same simplifications several times at the same subterm. Moreover, some simplification rules may duplicate some arguments (and all the redexes in them). Therefore, we may make the same computation several times, as in a *call-by-need* strategy.

The idea of computation is rather to evaluate with a bottom-up strategy, putting first the sub-expressions in a given canonical form (its value), which creates redexes at the upper level. This is closer to the situation of programming languages such as ML, which implement a *call-by-value* strategy.

We exclude lazy strategies as they are generally implemented with side effects. And since the primitive rules of HOL are purely applicative, we cannot reuse all the work done in compilation of lazy languages.

Laziness for Conditional and Elimination Constants

Another problem with the strategy of HOL's casual rewriting strategies appears with the conditional, which is defined by the clauses

$$\vdash \text{COND T} \, t_1 \, t_2 = t_1 \qquad \text{and} \qquad \vdash \text{COND F} \, t_1 \, t_2 = t_2.$$

The condition *and* both branches are all simplified, and then depending on the value of the boolean one or the other branch is dropped. This is particularly inefficient in the case of recursive functions. It can even make the simplification process loop.

As an example, consider the power function. It can be defined by primitive recursion over the exponent, and we can use the following theorem as a definition:

```
pow x n = if n = 0 then 1 else x * pow x (n-1)
```

Let us look at the successive steps REWRITE_CONV (and actually any simple bottom-up strategy) would do, omitting uninteresting steps:

```
pow 10 0
= if 0 = 0 then 1 else 10 * pow 10 (0-1)
= if T then 1 else 10 * if (0-1) = 0 then 1 else pow 10 ((0-1)-1)
```

In the first step, we simply use the definition of power. This produces a conditional whose first argument is neither T nor F, thus a top-down strategy will simplify all three arguments before trying to simplify again the conditional. In the second step, we can see that the condition reduces to T, but we still have to simplify the other two arguments. Furthermore, the else branch contains a recursive call, and the definition of power can be expanded again. It is obvious this will never terminate.

HOL's reduceLib library was designed to (among others) avoid this problem and allow to compute efficiently usual boolean and numerical expressions. However, this mechanism is not general in the sense that it cannot deal with other user-defined constants, and the same effort will have to be done whenever we introduce constants such as datatype destructors. Consider for instance the option type. In the expression option_case e f (SOME x), which reduces to f x, we would like to avoid computing the canonical form of e (the case for NONE). Again, this may dramatically slow down the evaluation process, and even make it loop.

Thus, we definitely want to avoid wiring in the simplifier special handling for a given constant. On the other hand, we prefer providing a more general feature, where the user has a simple way of declaring which arguments of a constant must be evaluated lazily. Most ML programmers will feel more familiar with this kind of analysis than "hacking" his own conversion. This contradicts our first intention of implementing a *call-by-value* strategy. Thus, we make a distinction between reductions associated to a constant done by pattern-matching, where arguments need to be evaluated eagerly, and β-reduction, which we will reduce with a *call-by-need* strategy. Thanks to that, one can control eagerness of evaluation by choosing one or the other of these two equivalent forms:

$$\vdash M \; x = N \quad \Leftrightarrow \quad \vdash M = \lambda x. N$$

where x does not appear free in M. In the first case, the argument of M will be evaluated eagerly, while in the second one, M is reduced on the spot, returning a λ-abstraction that will evaluate its argument only if needed.

In the case of the conditional, the following reduction specification is to be preferred to the one given earlier:

$$\vdash \text{COND}\, T = \lambda t_1. \lambda t_2. t_1 \qquad \vdash \text{COND}\, F = \lambda t_1. \lambda t_2. t_2$$

Weak Reduction

A weak reduction (no reduction under abstractions) is more desirable. As the example below shows, evaluating the body of an abstraction may have serious effects on efficiency:

```
fun pow2 0 = 1
  | pow2 n = let val y = pow2 (n-1) in y+y end;
```

The partially evaluated form has terrible performance, since the time complexity of the algorithm evaluated with a call-by-value strategy becomes exponential[1].

```
fun pow2 0 = 1
  | pow2 n = (pow2 (n-1))+(pow2 (n-1));
```

We prefer let the user decide which form is the most efficient and then interpret a function under the form provided. Experienced users of strict functional languages will make this optimization by hand very easily.

On the other hand, it would be annoying not being able to compute an expression just because it is hidden by, say, an universal quantification. So, we implement a strong reduction, but the latter is used only when necessary, that is, when we know the abstraction will not be applied any more.

All these remarks will be be summarized when describing the transitions of the abstract machine. Now, we explain how a reduction function can be implemented by an abstract machine and adapted to produce a theorem.

3 Abstract Machines

In this section, we describe how normalization functions can be implemented with abstract reduction machines, such as Krivine's abstract machine (KAM, see [7]). To describe an abstract machine we give ourselves a set of states and a transition relation between these states. Then, the normalization process is the following:

$$t \xrightarrow{\text{inj}} S_i \xrightarrow{T^*} S_f \xrightarrow{\text{proj}} \text{nf}(t)$$

Given a term t, we inject it into an initial state. Applying all transitions possible on this state, the abstract machine reaches a final state S_f, and a projection method (not necessarily the inverse of injection) gives back a term, which should be the normal form of t.

There are several good properties we can expect from an abstract machine. Firstly, if computing the next step is an atomic operation (in the sense that

---

[1] With a call-by-need strategy, both are exponential.

its execution time can be bounded independently of the size of its input), then studying the number of steps to the normal form gives us the time complexity of the interpreter[2]. Secondly, it can be implemented by a tail-recursive function, which ensures that the size of the input it can deal with is limited only by the size of the process, and not the fixed (small) size allocated to the execution stack.

Terms with Focus

We introduce terms with focus. The focus is a subterm we can mutate easily. We will write the focused term between square brackets (e.g. $(\lambda x.\,[f\,x])\,y)$, and $C(t)$ simply denotes a term which admits t as a subterm. We can consider several operations on these terms with focus (we will consider other operations later on):

$$
\begin{array}{lrcl}
\text{Zoom in:} & C[a\,b] & \longrightarrow & C([a]\,b) \\
\text{Zoom out:} & C([a]\,b) & \longrightarrow & C[a\,b] \\
\text{Beta:} & C[(\lambda x.\,m)\,b] & \longrightarrow & C[m\{b/x\}]
\end{array}
$$

These operations are of two kinds: *Beta* actually reduces the term, whereas *Zoom in* and *out* simply move the focus within the term.

An easy algorithm to put a term in head normal form is the following:

- if the focus is an application, then zoom in and resume;
- if the focus is an abstraction, then zoom one step out, reduce and resume.
- otherwise, zoom out completely and stop.

The injection function is simply $(t \mapsto [t])$, and the projection is the last step above. The machine stops when a variable applied to arguments or a non-applied abstraction is found: this is a head normal form.

Let us remark that *Beta* is not atomic, because of the substitution. We now show an abstract machine that solves this problem by using *closures*.

Krivine's Abstract Machine

The KAM is a very simple machine that computes the weak head normal form of a pure λ-terms (without constants), which means we only have to look for redexes in the left subterm of applications. Therefore, we can represent our terms with focus by a pair of the focused term and its arguments: $[t]\,ts$ can be represented by $\langle t, ts \rangle$, which is the pair of a term t and a list of terms ts.

If we want the steps to be atomic, we must be able to delay substitution, because of the β step. Hence the idea of replacing terms with closures, a pair of an environment e and a term t. The environment itself is a list of closures[3], and

---

[2] This requirement is not necessary: this is just a methodological constraint that urges the designer to split the expensive transitions and think how he can factorize them, but does not solve the problem per se.

[3] As in the literature, we use the de Bruijn indices [9] for bound variables. A name-carrying presentation might have been given, in which case an environment would be a mapping from variables names to closures, see [8].

maps any de Bruijn index into a closure, acting as a delayed substitution, which is propagated as the code (the term) is executed.

The transitions of the KAM are given below:

$$
\text{KAM} \left[
\begin{array}{rcl}
\langle e,\ a\ b,\ S\rangle & \longrightarrow & \langle e,\ a,\ (e,b)::S\rangle \\
\langle e,\ \lambda m.,\ C::S\rangle & \longrightarrow & \langle e.C,\ m,\ S\rangle \\
\langle e.\,(e',t),\ 0,\ S\rangle & \longrightarrow & \langle e',\ t,\ S\rangle \\
\langle e.C,\ (n+1),\ S\rangle & \longrightarrow & \langle e,\ n,\ S\rangle
\end{array}
\right.
$$

There are three kinds of transitions: the first rule moves the focus in search of a new redex, the second one actually reduces the term, and the other ones propagate substitutions.

Extension to Strong Reduction

Crégut [7] extends this machine to KN, to perform strong reductions. But this is still a *call-by-need* strategy. If we want to reduce the argument of a constant, we must be able to focus on it. Hence we cannot represent our terms with focus the same way. Instead of a list of terms, the second component of the state will be a *stack*, following the syntax

$$
S := [\,]\ |\ @_L(t).S\ |\ @_R(t).S\ |\ \lambda(x).S
$$

where t is a term and x a variable.

It describes a path in the term, from the occurrence to the top, keeping track of the other sons of a node. The first constructor means we are at the top of the term. The next two are used when going under an application (respectively left and right), and the last one to cross abstraction and do strong reductions.

For instance, term $(\lambda x.\,[f\ x])\ y$ would be represented by $\langle f\ x,\ \lambda(x).@_L(y).[\,]\rangle$.

Computing with Constants (Pattern-Matching)

The KAM deals with β-reduction. But we also want to rewrite theorems defining the computational behavior of the constants. The simplest kind of rewrites we can use is a mere definition, i.e. a theorem showing that a constant c is equal to its definition. We interpret a theorem $\vdash c = M$ as introducing the reduction rule $c \triangleright M$.

Mathematicians and ML programmers are used to define functions using patterns, assigning the result for all the inputs that *match* these patterns. A function is generally totally defined by giving a finite set of clauses. The example of addition given in the introduction is an illustration of that way of defining functions by pattern-matching. For instance, a theorem $\vdash \forall x.\, c\ x = M$ will be interpreted as rule $c\ N \triangleright M\{N/x\}$. It differs slightly from $c \triangleright \lambda x.\, M$ because, in the former case, reduction can occur only when c is applied to at least one argument.

Furthermore, one can define a function whose domain is a recursive type by giving a clause for every constructor. For instance, a function over naturals is totally and uniquely defined if by giving two clauses: one for 0 thanks to a theorem of the form $\vdash c\ 0 = P$ and another one for the successor case with a theorem like $\vdash c\ (S\ n) = Q$.

We see that we need to guess how to instantiate the free variable of the left hand side of the equation we rewrite. This operation is called *pattern-matching*. Not any form should be allowed for the left hand sides (the pattern). Since our intent is to emulate a language like ML, we adopt the same kind of restrictions than ML patterns. That is, they should follow a restricted syntax:

$$\text{Pattern} := x \mid c\ p_1 \ldots p_n \qquad \text{where } p_1, \ldots, p_n \in \text{Pattern}.$$

Left hand sides must be patterns not reduced to a variable. Note that unlike ML we do not restrict to linear patterns. The same variable may occur in the pattern, and matching succeeds if the corresponding terms are α-equivalents[4]. There is no restriction on the right hand side. However, free variables not occurring in the pattern will not be instantiated.

We have to extend the transition rules of the KAM in order to take constants into account. As usual, arguments of applications are stored in the stack. When a constant is found, we look in the simplification database whether the term can be rewritten on the spot. If it can be simplified, we resume reduction on the residue. Otherwise, arguments in the stack are (weakly) reduced one by one and applied to the constant. Every time an argument is applied, we check out if it can be rewritten by a theorem of the database.

4   The Inference Rules

If we want to be able to build a theorem corresponding to any reduction path, we could use rules that correspond to the usual definition: $\beta\eta$-reduction is the smallest reflexive, transitive and congruent (with respect to application and abstraction) containing the rules β and η. Thus, the rules REFL, TRANS (reflexivity and transitivity of equality), MK_COMB, ABS (equality is congruent with respect to application and abstraction), BETA_CONV and ETA_CONV (one step β and η conversions) are enough to fulfill our goal.

However, they are not the best choice of atomic rules to build a derivation, because they perform useless operations such as type-checking and α-conversion tests: the one-step rules BETA_CONV, ETA_CONV and REFL compute the type of their input term and TRANS performs an α-conversion test. In principle, we should be able to avoid completely type-checking because of the subject-reduction property (the reduct of a well-typed term is a well-typed term with same type). The idea to avoid these redundancies is to start from the empty reduction path (yielded by reflexivity) and then the rules simply add steps to the current path or access to the subterms. According to this, transitivity would not be necessary any more,

---

[4] But since we only perform weak reduction on the arguments of a constant, we may miss some simplifications. $\lambda x.\ (\lambda y.\ y)\ x$ and $\lambda x.\ x$ would not be identified

but we keep it to extend the current path with an arbitrary theorem in order to do rewrites regarding constants, as for the addition example of the introduction.

In figure 1, we propose a new set of inference rules more convenient for building derivations. Let us first explain the unusual form of rules Mk_comb and Mk_abs. Rule Mk_comb can be read in another way, similar to a tactic:

$$\frac{\Gamma \vdash t = a\,b}{\vdash a = a \qquad \vdash b = b \qquad R_t \equiv \left[\frac{\Gamma_1 \vdash a = a' \qquad \Gamma_2 \vdash b = b'}{\Gamma \cup \Gamma_1 \cup \Gamma_2 \vdash t = a'\,b'}\right]}$$

That is, given a derivation ending on an application (the goal), rule Mk_comb returns two empty derivations starting from the subterms (these are the sub-goals), and a rule R_t that completes the initial derivation from the completed derivations of the subterms (this is the validation). The presentation of the figure respects the shape of the final derivation and the ellipses are the parts still to be built.

$$(\text{Trans}) \quad \frac{\Gamma \vdash t_1 = t_2 \qquad \Gamma' \vdash_{\text{HOL}} t_2 = t_3}{\Gamma \cup \Gamma' \vdash t_1 = t_3}$$

$$(\text{Mk\_comb}) \quad \frac{\Gamma \vdash t = a\,b \qquad \Gamma_1 \vdash a = a' \qquad \Gamma_2 \vdash b = b'}{\Gamma \cup \Gamma_1 \cup \Gamma_2 \vdash t = a'\,b'}$$

where the subderivations of $\vdash a = a$ and $\vdash b = b$ are indicated by vertical ellipses.

$$(\text{Mk\_abs}) \quad \frac{\Gamma \vdash t = \lambda x.\,m \qquad \Gamma' \vdash m = m'}{\Gamma \cup \Gamma' \vdash t = \lambda x.\,m'} (x \notin \text{FV}(\Gamma'))$$

where the subderivation of $\vdash m = m$ is indicated by a vertical ellipsis.

$$(\beta) \quad \frac{\Gamma \vdash t = (\lambda x.\,m)\,b}{\Gamma \vdash t = m\{b/x\}} \qquad (\eta) \quad \frac{\Gamma \vdash t = \lambda x.\,m\,x}{\Gamma \vdash t = m} (x \notin \text{FV}(m))$$

$$(\text{Refl}) \quad \frac{}{\vdash t = t} \qquad (\text{Accept}) \quad \frac{\Gamma \vdash t = t'}{\Gamma \vdash_{\text{HOL}} t = t'}$$

Fig. 1. Derived rules used by the conversion

An important remark is that we introduced a new ML datatype to represent derivations. It is close to HOL's theorems. Notation $\vdash$ is used to represent our theorems and $\vdash_{\text{HOL}}$ for HOL's. This new datatype is also abstract and values can be built only using a small set of inference rules (those of fig. 1). However, the goal is to build a HOL theorem in the end (the projection step of abstract machines), hence the Accept rule. Apart from these rules, we only need a function to access the right hand side of a theorem. The latter represents the end of the current reduction path and is used to decide which is the next step to perform.

Note that the rules are trivially derivable in HOL's logic, so that ⊢ can be implemented by ⊢$_{HOL}$. As a first step, one can forget this distinction. However, we will show that for efficiency reasons, it may be useful to consider alternative representations for ⊢. For instance, we already noticed that the transitivity rule of HOL performs an α-conversion test that would make this rule non-atomic. We achieved making these rules atomic for ⊢$_{HOL}$ by implementing several derived rules more efficiently, and changing the internal representation of terms.

Using Pointer Equality

The "validations" of rules MK_COMB and MK_ABS have to check their inputs to be reduction paths starting from the subterms. Usual HOL rules would test for α-convertibility, which ruins the constant time requirement. Instead of this, we test for pointer equality.

Terms with Explicit Substitutions

β-reduction has to perform a substitution, which takes as much time as the size of the function body. We proposed to implement λ-terms using explicit substitutions. However, they are not mentioned in the interface: terms are still used as simple λ-terms with constants. This is essential for compatibility reasons, and because we consider delaying substitution more as a requirement for the efficiency of the implementation than as a fundamental construction (one can already delay atomic substitution thanks to the LET constant).

In our proposition (implemented in the last release of HOL), the internal representation of terms uses de Bruijn indices (as before) *and* explicit substitutions. A term is either a bound variable, a free variable, a constant, an application, an abstraction or a closure:

$$t := n \mid x \mid c \mid t_1\ t_2 \mid \lambda x.\,t \mid [e]t$$
$$\text{Env} := \text{id} \mid e.t \quad \text{where } e \in \text{Env}$$

Abstractions bear a variable to record a printable name, and also give a type for the domain. Equality modulo substitution propagation is called σ. Terms are therefore identified modulo βσ-conversion.

We provide a new β-reduction function that uses explicit substitutions (it simply issues an explicit substitution instead of actually performing it). The propagation is performed lazily as the term is decomposed, but it is also possible to force all the substitutions in a term. This modification has no cost for those who do not use these new functions.

We are not going to describe in detail the implementation of explicit substitutions. As a hint, one can think substitutions as either the identity, or the parallel composition of a substitution with a new binding, as the above definition suggests. The de Bruijn representation does require other constructors to deal with lifting of indices.

Technically, let us just mention that it implements a particular strategy of $\lambda\sigma$ [1] that avoids non termination (see [12]) by eagerly doing substitution composition (thus we do not need any explicit composition operator in the syntax of substitutions).

A relevant point is that it allows a β-reduction in constant time, for it simply introduces a substitution operator. As a further benefit, substitutions can be composed. The point of substitution composition appears, when reducing a term with many β-redexes, the substitution is done in the body only when all the arguments have been provided. For instance, in the following reduction path, each steps takes constant time:

$$\vdash (\lambda x\,y\,z.\,m)\,a\,b\,c$$
$$\vdash ([a]\lambda y\,z.\,m)\,b\,c$$
$$\vdash ([a.b]\lambda z.\,m)\,c$$
$$\vdash [a.b.c]m$$

And then we can propagate the compound (parallel) substitution in m. The usual approach would yield three successive substitutions in m. But there is even worse than that: the first step would substitute a for x in m. Then, in the second step, we would substitute b for y, including in the occurrences of a that appeared in m during the first step. This is useless since we know y cannot occur in a. As we will make more precise later on, this has a major impact on the complexity.

Note that an n-ary β-reduction step would still not solve the problem since the inner redexes may result from arbitrary complex reductions, as in

$$(\lambda x.\,\text{id}\,(\lambda y\,z.\,m))\,a\,b\,c$$

where id is the identity function. As a first step, only the redex on x can be reduced. Then, redexes on y and z appear from the reduction of id.

5   The Abstract Machine of computeLib

Description of the Machine

The state of the machine is a "theorem with focus", that is the pair of a theorem and a stack. The difference with the datatype of stack presented in section 3 is that it contains theorems instead of terms.

The injection simply maps a term into the empty derivation (thanks to the REFL rule):

$$t \mapsto \langle \vdash t = t, [\,] \rangle$$

Here, we assume the transitions (to be described in the next subsections) will eventually lead to a state where the stack is $[\,]$ again, so that the projection step is the first projection. As we said when discussing the strategy, we favor weak reductions. This is achieved by having two sets of transitions W and S. The first one only does weak reductions, and the second one makes strong reductions whenever no weak reductions are possible.

Convention of the Transition Rules

One crucial point for an efficient implementation of a call-by-value strategy is that values appearing in environments are already evaluated. Hence, we need to make a clear distinction between $[t]0$ where we know t is already fully evaluated, and $[\text{id}]t$ where t may still contain redexes.

The idea is to have a convention such that terms without closures represent evaluated forms and $[e]t$ denotes the unevaluated program t in environment e. Thus, the exact injection function is:

$$\text{inj} \stackrel{\text{def}}{=} (t \mapsto \langle \vdash [\text{id}]t = [\text{id}]t, [ ] \rangle)$$

We can define strong and weak normal forms and closures as subsets of terms:

$$\text{Snf} := n\,v \mid x\,v \mid c\,v \mid \lambda x.\,v$$
$$\text{Wnf} := n\,w \mid x\,w \mid c\,w \mid [e]\lambda x.\,m$$
$$\text{Clos} := n\,w \mid x\,w \mid c\,w \mid \lambda x.\,v \mid [e]t$$

with v (resp. w) a list of elements of Snf (resp. Wnf), t contains no substitution, and in Snf and Wnf, no rules matches $c\,v$ or $c\,w$.

An invariant of the machine will be that any term appearing in the state belongs to Clos and has no unbound de Bruijn indice (the closure operator being a binder). This is true for the initial state, and every transition preserves this invariant.

But since explicit substitutions where hidden, the term manipulation primitives only allow us to access to its fully substituted form t, and we cannot discriminate the two states above. In the implementation, every theorem carries an external information about the actual form of the right hand side. For every transformation we apply to theorems, we are able to do the same on the annotation, so that it is always consistent. Thanks to that, we can do as if we could access the internal representation. This duplicates the operations, but improves considerably portability since it makes less assumption on the exact datatype of the theorem prover.

As an informal notation, we will write theorems using the internal syntax of terms (section 4). In fact, the datatype used in the implementation is not exactly the same. For instance, it has a n-ary representation of application, to access faster to the head of an application, and constant are annotated with the set of rewrites that apply to it, avoiding lookups during the reduction.

Transitions for Weak Reduction

The transitions in figure 2 are adapted from the KAM. Considering only right hand sides of theorems, the first four rules look very similar to the KAM. Note that in rule 2, theorem $\vdash t' = [e.u']m$ is obtained by applying R_t to theorems $\vdash a = [e]\lambda x.\,m$ and $\vdash b = b'$, which builds $\vdash t = ([e]\lambda x.\,m)\,b'$. Then, applying rule β yields $\vdash t = [e.b']m$.

The next two rules show that substitutions operate only on de Bruijn indices. Rule 7 is the one that actually performs rewriting, since it replaces a term matching the left hand side of a rewrite with the right hand side instantiated. We define Match as a partial function mapping any term t to a rewrite of Σ and a substitution that identifies t with the left hand side of the equation:

$$\mathrm{Match}_{\Sigma}(t) \stackrel{\mathrm{def}}{=} (\vdash l = r, e) \text{ if } \vdash l = r \in \Sigma \wedge [e]l =_{\alpha\sigma} t$$

This matching side-condition can be considered atomic since its time complexity only depends on the size of the rewrite set, but not on the size of the term to be reduced. Proposition $\mathrm{NoMatch}_{\Sigma}(t)$ is true whenever the above partial function has no result.

The next two rules start reducing the next argument of a partially applied variable or constant, when no reduction is possible. This is achieved by simply swapping the head and the argument (and $@_L$ becomes $@_R$). The last rule applies when this argument has been weakly normalized, in which case it is applied to the head appearing in the stack. One simply has to use R_t.

$$\langle \vdash t = [e](a\ b), S \rangle \longrightarrow \langle \vdash [e]a = [e]a, @_L(\vdash [e]b = [e]b, R_t).S \rangle$$
$$\langle \vdash a = [e]\lambda x.\, m, @_L(\vdash b = b', R_t).S \rangle \longrightarrow \langle \vdash t = [e.b']m, S \rangle$$
$$\langle \vdash t = [e.a]0, S \rangle \longrightarrow \langle \vdash t = a, S \rangle$$
$$\langle \vdash t = [e.a]n+1, S \rangle \longrightarrow \langle \vdash t = [e]n, S \rangle$$
$$\langle \vdash t = [e]x, S \rangle \longrightarrow \langle \vdash t = x, S \rangle$$
$$\langle \vdash t = [e]c, S \rangle \longrightarrow \langle \vdash t = c, S \rangle$$
$$\langle \vdash t = c\ w, S \rangle \longrightarrow \langle \vdash t = [e]r, S \rangle$$
$$\text{when } \mathrm{Match}_{\Sigma}(c\ w) = (\vdash l = r, e)$$
$$\langle \vdash a = x\ w, @_L(\vdash b = b', R_t).S \rangle \longrightarrow \langle \vdash b = b', @_R(\vdash a = x\ w, R_t).S \rangle$$
$$\langle \vdash a = c\ w, @_L(\vdash b = b', R_t).S \rangle \longrightarrow \langle \vdash b = b', @_R(\vdash a = c\ w, R_t).S \rangle$$
$$\text{when } \mathrm{NoMatch}_{\Sigma}(c\ w)$$
$$\langle \vdash b = b', @_R(\vdash a = a', R_t).S \rangle \longrightarrow \langle \vdash t = a'\ b', S \rangle \qquad \text{when } b' \in \mathrm{Wnf}$$

Fig. 2. Weak transitions of the machine (W)

Several rules have side-conditions. Actually checking a condition like $b' \in$ Wnf would make the step non-atomic because the complexity of this operation is at least linear with the size of b'. We avoid this costly operation by ordering the rules: we first apply the upper rules but the last one. If none of these rule apply, this means we have a weak normal form and the last rule of figure 2 can be applied without actually checking the side-condition.

Applying all the rules of figure 2 leads to a state with an empty stack and where the right hand side of the theorem belongs to Wnf.

Transitions for Strong Reduction

This subsection describes the strong normalization. The goal of this second machine is to reduce redexes appearing under an abstraction. The first rule of figure 3 shows that we can always make weak reductions. Notation $W(\vdash t = t')$ stands for the first component (a theorem) of the state reached by applying all the transitions of W on $\langle \vdash t = t', [] \rangle$.

Rule 2 starts reducing under an abstraction when the weak reduction returned an unapplied abstraction. A fresh name x' has to be found to avoid captures. This side-condition is indeed costly and we could not find a way to avoid it. Note that this problem would not arise in a real de Bruijn setting.

The next two rules start reducing in the head of an application by pushing the last argument in the stack.

The other rules try to rebuild the normal form when the head term is normalized. We have to look at the stack: if we find λ, the abstraction is rebuilt; for $@_L$, we start normalizing the next argument on the stack; and for $@_R$, we have normalized both subterms, so the application can be rebuilt.

Let us explain how we avoid checking side-conditions (the problem of rule 2 has already been explained): rule 1 is applied once every time a step of S may produce a term with redexes (this is the case only for rule 2); the last three rules are dealt with as for W, since applying repeatedly the other rules yields a state where the right hand side is a strong normal form.

As with W, applying all the rules of figure 3 leads to a state with an empty stack and where the right hand side of the theorem belongs to Snf. This is the strong normal form. To summarize our conversion is simply the composition of ACCEPT and S with the injection function: $\text{CBV\_CONV} \stackrel{\text{def}}{=} \text{ACCEPT} \circ S \circ \text{inj}$.

$$\langle \vdash t = t', S \rangle \longrightarrow \langle W(\vdash t = t'), S \rangle \qquad \text{when } t \notin \text{Wnf}$$
$$\langle \vdash t = [e]\lambda x.\, m, S \rangle \longrightarrow \langle \vdash [e.x']m = [e.x']m, \lambda(x', R_t).S \rangle$$
$$\text{when } x' \notin \text{FV}([e]\lambda x.\, m)$$
$$\langle \vdash t = x\ w\ b, S \rangle \longrightarrow \langle \vdash x\ w = x\ w, @_L(\vdash b = b, R_t).S \rangle$$
$$\langle \vdash t = c\ w\ b, S \rangle \longrightarrow \langle \vdash c\ w = c\ w, @_L(\vdash b = b, R_t).S \rangle$$
$$\langle \vdash m = m', \lambda(x, R_t).S \rangle \longrightarrow \langle \vdash t = \lambda x.\, (m'\{0/x\}), S \rangle \qquad \text{when } m' \in \text{Snf}$$
$$\langle \vdash a = a', @_L(\vdash b = b', R_t).S \rangle \longrightarrow \langle \vdash b = b', @_R(\vdash a = a', R_t).S \rangle \qquad \text{when } a' \in \text{Snf}$$
$$\langle \vdash b = b', @_R(\vdash a = a', R_t).S \rangle \longrightarrow \langle \vdash t = a'\ b', S \rangle \qquad \text{when } b' \in \text{Snf}$$

Fig. 3. Strong reduction of the machine (S)

6   Computing Within the Logic: Some Examples

The machine described in the previous section was implemented in HOL as library computeLib. It contains functions to create simplification sets from theorems, and a conversion CBV_CONV which normalizes its input term.

The first application of computeLib was to replace reduceLib. It was actually straightforward to implement since we only had to collect the theorems used by reduceLib without taking care of the order in which rewrites should be applied[5]. Moreover, this new version appears twice as fast as the former reduceLib.

Now we describe two other applications of computeLib. The first one tests our claim that we can program *and* compute within the logic as we do in ML. We chose sorting because this is a recurrent problem in algorithm complexity analysis.

Merge Sort

We can define all the functions involved in merge sort, and HOL manages to prove automatically all the termination proofs (they are primitive recursive functions). So, the development in HOL is a mere translation of the ML program.

It is interesting to notice how computeLib interacts well with bossLib: starting from the initial simplification set (which defines the computational behavior of many the standard functions on booleans, numerals and lists), one simply has to add the theorems returned by bossLib and get a simplification set rws to use with CBV_CONV:

```
CBV_CONV rws (--' merge_sort L38400 '--);
```

where L38400 is a list of 38400 natural numbers between 0 and 4.

We measured the execution times of this algorithm on lists of various length. We compared several execution models: using HOL's rewriter, CBV_CONV, or ML. Indeed, we compared three instantiations of our abstract theorems. Figure 4 is a table reporting execution times. The description of the rewriters is the following:

rewriter: using HOL's rewriter REWRITE_CONV. Other simplifiers may be a bit faster, but the complexity is not better.
without ES: atomic rules are implemented using usual HOL inference rules (without explicit substitutions and with redundant typing).
with ES: the kernel is implemented with explicit substitutions.
unsafe: the type of theorems is a mere triple (assumptions, lhs and rhs).
Moscow ML: the algorithm is expressed directly in the implementation language.

The first three rewriters are considered safe as they only use features provided by the current release of HOL98 (which includes explicit substitutions of section 4 in the kernel). The fourth is said "unsafe" because the rules of ⊢ are implemented without checking the preconditions (for instance in the transitivity rule the right

---

[5] The division and modulo operations were implemented by a special conversion that resorts to an oracle that computes in ML the quotient and modulo, and then simply checks the result. We could reproduce this by providing the possibility to add a conversion to our simplification set. One simply has to specify the name and arity of the constant the conversion works for.

hand side of the first theorem and the left hand side of the second one are not checked to be equal). A bad usage of these rules would allow the derivation of a paradox. However, the conversion has so far shown to use them in a safe way, but this has not been proven yet.

Size of the list	Rewriter	Without ES	With ES	Unsafe	Moscow ML
4	0.06s	0.03s			
12	3.4s	0.11s	0.09s	0.08s	
20	900s	0.30s	0.24s	0.18s	
40		0.89s			
100		3.5s	2.04s	1.3s	
200		11.7s	4.9s	3.2s	
400			11.7s	7.5s	
1200		377s	41.6s	27s	0.043s
19200			996s	629s	1.57s
38400			2090s	1370s	4.3s

Fig. 4. Timing of several implementations of merge sort

We can notice that explicit substitution play a crucial role: they make the complexity $N. \log N$ instead of N^2. Comparing the safe version (with ES) with MoscowML, we have a slow down factor of 990 for a size of 1200 and 490 for size 38400. Indeed, our implementation has a better complexity on huge examples, probably because memory allocation represent most of the overall time in the case of the execution in ML.

With the unsafe version, more than half of the time is spent in the function that does matching and instantiation of theorems, precisely a part of code that still could be improved a lot.

As a final remark, non tail recursive functions fail (due to a stack overflow) on the example of size 38400, because the number of recursive calls exhausts the memory space allocated for the execution stack With a tail recursive implementation, the interpreter needs a constant amount of memory on the stack. Instead, the "stack" component of the state plays the role of the execution stack, but is allocated in the heap.

Various Representations for Theorems

We instantiated the type of theorems with several different implementations. This resulted in differences in efficiency. One can implement it with the classical HOL theorems, or a lazier variant that does theorem decompositions only when a step has actually been done. This is the approach of Boulton's lazy theorems [5].

One can also try a more efficient representation of equations using a triple (assumptions, left hand side, right hand side), which allow an even more efficient implementation of the rules. But a problem arises when implementing ACCEPT.

One can either trust the implementation of these rules and ACCEPT would produce a theorem without resorting to primitive rules, just as we produce theorems read from disk, or create a new tag that would mark all the theorems that rely on our implementation.

On the other hand, one could imagine an even safer representation of theorems, that would carry an explicit representation of derivations. ACCEPT would just consist of dropping the derivation part.

Application: A Decision Procedure on Polynomials

We also developed a theory of rings, and adapted the tactic originally written by Boutin to normalize polynomial expressions [6] in Coq [4].

Let us assume we have a type α and a ring structure (i.e. $0, 1, +, -, *$ with the expected properties of commutativity and associativity).

It consists in defining a datatype α polynom representing polynomial expressions syntactically:

$$Pol := \mathrm{Var}(i) \mid \mathrm{Cst}(v) \mid P_1 \oplus P_2 \mid P_1 \otimes P_2 \mid \ominus P$$

Having a syntactic representation of a polynomial expression in the logic allows us to write within the logic a function that can analyze the polynomial.

We define an interpretation function that relates the syntactic polynomial to assigns a value of type α (the target ring) to every syntactic polynomial expression (of type α polynom) in a valuation ρ.

$$[\mathrm{Var}(i)]_\rho = \rho(i)$$
$$[\mathrm{Cst}(c)]_\rho = c$$
$$[P_1 \oplus P_2]_\rho = [P_1]_\rho + [P_2]_\rho$$
$$[P_1 \otimes P_2]_\rho = [P_1]_\rho.[P_2]_\rho$$
$$[\ominus P]_\rho = -[P]_\rho$$

Then, we write a HOL function F of type α polynom $\rightarrow$ α polynom that returns a simplified version of a syntactic polynomial given as argument. The simplifications performed are:

- expanding and ordering of monomials in a canonical order,
- erasing monomials with null coefficient.

At last, we prove the correctness of our function, i.e. the interpretation of our syntactic polynomial by assigning values to every variable is preserved by our function.

$$\forall P \rho. \ [P]_\rho = [F(P)]_\rho$$

This is true for any ring. This proof showed a need for tools to write theories parameterized by assumptions, such as sections in Coq or locales in Isabelle.

Our problem is now to find a polynomial P and a valuation ρ such that $[\![P]\!]_\rho$ is equal to our initial expression. Such function analyses the head constructor of a HOL term: if it's an addition, multiplication, or unary negation, then the corresponding syntactic operator is built and the respective subterms are translated; there is also a predicate to recognize canonical elements of the ring; all the other expressions are abstracted, that is a new variable is created (unless this expression was already found), and ρ is updated so that it maps it to the corresponding expression.

Deciding the equality of two expressions simply consists of applying the simplification procedure described above to the two hand sides, and comparing the resulting polynomials (we must find two polynomials in the same valuation, because the way we order monomials depends on the way the valuation is computed).

Note that we cannot do the same conversion with real numbers, since equality is not decidable, which precludes the simplification of monomials with coefficient 0.

We tested this procedure on a quite large example: the 8 squares problem (stated in [6]). This is a result similar to the binomial equality $(a + b)^2 = a^2 + 2ab + b^2$, but we have to simplify a polynomial consisting of the sum of 8 squares of polynomials, each one being the sum of 8 monomials. Once fully developed, we have a sum of 512 monomials, and we must sort it to merge and simplify monomials of same power. Using the method described above, it took 41s to solve.

This problem could be solved using REWRITE_CONV, and a conversion dealing with associative-commutative theory thanks to a variable ordering. This a bit tricky to implement and our attempts resulted in execution times higher than with computeLib. The fundamental reason is that such rewriters will most of the time perform elementary permutations, swapping two adjacent monomials, which makes sorting quadratic. On the other hand, by abstracting the problem of sorting, the reflection technique allows us to use an algorithm with better complexity.

Running the same example on a computer algebra system, say Maple, takes far less than a second, but the comparison is quite unfair:

- We can trust the result[6], since it has been produced only using a very small number of well-principled inference rules.
- The algorithm we used is at the least straightforward: almost no effort was spent on improving the algorithm. We are of course limited by the fact we must produce an applicative algorithm. This precludes the use of hash-consing.
- We compare a program compiled in native code (Maple) with an interpreter for the λ-calculus, ran by the bytecode interpreter of Moscow ML, which is compiled in native code. A slow down factor of 100 would not be surprising only for these two levels of interpretation.

---

[6] In Maple, sqrt('-x'^2) and sqrt(''-x''^2) simplify to expressions of opposite signs!

7   Further Work

There is still much space for improvements. It was designed to be simple so that we can test it, and modify it easily. The directions for further work are manifold.

Improving the Implementation

There are very few optimizations of datastructures. For instance, the database of rewrites does not resort to discrimination nets. It is a hash-table which keys are pairs of constant names and arity, and results are simply lists of rewrites.

Adding More Features

Here, we discuss how we can extend the class of theorems we are able to rewrite with:

- Support conditional rewriting (i.e. equations with preconditions). This is equivalent to "when" clauses in Objective Caml.
- Support an aliasing construction. In program

    fun f 0 = 1 | f n = n+n;

    the second branch cannot be read as an equation because it overlaps with the first one, which has higher priority. The theorem we get is rather $\vdash \forall k.\, f\,(S(k)) = S(k) + S(k)$. It would be nice to avoid multiple reconstruction of a constructor using a kind of aliasing:

$$\vdash \forall n\, k.\,(n = S(k)) \implies (f\,n = n + n)$$

    which can be read as the ML pattern branch **f (n as S(k)) = n+n**. This is not really conditional rewriting because the value of k is not constrained by the left hand side.

The difficulty with these extensions is that they make pattern-matching and reduction itself mutually dependent.

Ensure Termination and Canonicity

In the introduction we said that the idea was to put arguments of defined functions in canonical form before reducing, but the system does not make any difference between these classes of constants. It could be handy to check for the user that he provided rewrites for all the possible inputs (exhaustive pattern-matching), ensuring that we will eventually reduce to a canonical expression.

Similarly, we do not check termination of the set of rewrites. Adding theorem $\vdash c = c$ trivially breaks termination.

Extraction

Now we have the expected complexity, we could try to reduce the large constant factor by optimizing the datastructures, but we will never cut it down drastically. Instead of interpreting the program, we could try to compile it, for instance by translating our rewrites into an ML program. This way, we would reduce the number of interpretation levels.

This scheme has several serious limitations. One is that CBV_CONV still accepts a too wide range of theorems. For instance, in ML, patterns must be linear, but we can deal with non-linear patterns. More problematic is the fact that we can assign to a polymorphic constant different algorithms depending on the way type variables are instantiated (we have a kind of overloading). This is not possible in ML since we do not have types at runtime. Finally, only closed ML programs (without free variable) can be executed.

8   Conclusion

We designed and implemented a rewriting strategy that allows the specification of algorithm in a style similar to a purely applicative ML, and furthermore provide an interpreter with the same asymptotic complexity as the corresponding ML code. It allows the evaluation of expressions without taking extra care, but it is also a qualitative improvement in the sense that computational problems of medium and large size could not be dealt with by REWRITE_CONV. We showed it was usable (and already used by several enthusiastic HOL developers!) by running a very classical example of algorithmic, and much faster than the usual tools of HOL such as REWRITE_CONV. However, we claim the contribution of computeLib is not only regarding efficiency but strengthens the vision of HOL as a programming language and as a tool for software verification. For the moment, this is still modest, but seems promising. The idea of extraction could bring a major speed up.

The second aspect of this work is its generality, based on an abstract notion of theorems and a small number of inference rules. This made it very easy to adapt it to Isabelle's meta-logic. The resulting conversion is not yet as efficient as with HOL, since the kernel is not implemented with explicit substitutions. It is yet slower than Isabelle's optimized simplifier, but could be improved since about half of the time is spent only instantiating rewrites, operation which has not been optimized in section 4. Another asset of this abstractness is the possibility to trade safety for efficiency, depending on the way it is implemented.

Acknowledgements

I would like to thank Mike Gordon and Larry Paulson for their warm welcome in their team. All along this work, I have been helped and encouraged by the interest Konrad Slind and Michael Norrish showed to my project. They made possible the smooth integration of the abstract machine in the current release of

HOL. My acknowledgements also goes to Joe Hurd for the stimulating discussions we had at tea time.

References

1. M. Abadi, L. Cardelli, P.-L. Curien, and J.-J. Lévy. Explicit substitutions. In *Conference Record of the Seventeenth Annual ACM Symposium on Principles of Programming Languages, San Francisco, California*, pages 31–46. ACM, January 1990. Also Digital Equipment Corporation, Systems Research Center, Research Report 54, February 1990.
2. H. Barendregt. Lambda Calculi with Types. Technical Report 91-19, Catholic University Nijmegen, 1991. In Handbook of Logic in Computer Science, Vol II.
3. B. Barras. *Auto-validation d'un système de preuves avec familles inductives*. Thèse de doctorat, Université Paris 7, November 1999.
4. B. Barras, S. Boutin, C. Cornes, J. Courant, J.-C. Filliâtre, E. Giménez, H. Herbelin, G. Huet, C. Muñoz, C. Murthy, C. Parent, C. Paulin, A. Saïbi, and B. Werner. The Coq Proof Assistant Reference Manual version 6.1. Technical Report 0203, Projet Coq-INRIA Rocquencourt-ENS Lyon, August 1997.
5. R. J. Boulton. Lazy techniques for fully expansive theorem proving. *Formal Methods in System Design*, 3(1/2):25–47, August 1993.
6. S. Boutin. Using reflection to build efficient and certified decision procedures. In Martin Abadi and Takahashi Ito, editors, *TACS'97*, volume 1281. LNCS, Springer-Verlag, 1997.
7. P. Crégut. An abstract machine for λ-terms normalization. In Gilles Kahn, editor, *Proceedings of the ACM Conference on LISP and Functional Programming*, pages 333–340, Nice, France, June 1990. ACM Press.
8. Pierre-Louis Curien, Thérèse Hardin, and Jean-Jacques Lévy. Confluence properties of weak and strong calculi of explicit substitutions. *Journal of the ACM*, 43(2):362–397, March 1996.
9. N.J. De Bruijn. Lambda-calculus notation with nameless dummies, a tool for automatic formula manipulation, with application to the church-rosser theorem. *Indag. Math.*, 34 (5), pp. 381–392, 1972.
10. M. J. C. Gordon and T. F. Melham. *Introduction to HOL: A theorem proving environment for higher order logic*. Cambridge University Press, 1993.
11. M.J. Gordon, R. Milner, and C. Wadsworth. *Edinburgh LCF*. LNCS 78. Springer-Verlag, 1979.
12. P.-A. Melliès. Typed λ-calculi with explicit substitutions may not terminate. In M. Dezani-Ciancaglini and G. Plotkin, editors, *Proceedings of the International Conference on Typed Lambda Calculi and Applications*, Edinburgh, Scotland, April 1995. Springer-Verlag LNCS 902.
13. Lawrence C. Paulson. A higher-order implementation of rewriting. *Science of Computer Programming*, 3:119–149, 1983.
14. Lawrence C. Paulson. *Logic and Computation: Interactive proof with Cambridge LCF*. Cambridge University Press, 1987.
15. K. Slind. Function definition in higher order logic. In J. von Wright, J. Grundy, and J. Harrison, editors, *Theorem Proving in Higher Order Logics: 9th International Conference, Turku, Finland*, volume 1125, pages 381–397. LNCS, Springer-Verlag, August 1996.

Proof Terms for Simply Typed Higher Order Logic

Stefan Berghofer* and Tobias Nipkow

Technische Universität München, Institut für Informatik
http://www.in.tum.de/~berghofe/
http://www.in.tum.de/~nipkow/

Abstract. This paper presents proof terms for simply typed, intuitionistic higher order logic, a popular logical framework. Unification-based algorithms for the compression and reconstruction of proof terms are described and have been implemented in the theorem prover Isabelle. Experimental results confirm the effectiveness of the compression scheme.

1 Introduction

In theorem provers based on the LCF approach, theorems can only be constructed by a small set of primitive inference rules. Provided the implementation of these rules is correct, all theorems obtained in this way are sound. Hence it is often claimed that constructing an explicit proof term for each theorem is unnecessary. This is only partially true, however. If the core inference engine of a theorem prover is relatively large, correctness is difficult to ensure. Being able to verify proof terms by a small and independent proof checker helps to minimize the risks. Moreover, a precise notion of proof terms facilitates the exchange of proofs between different theorem proving systems. Finally, proof terms are a prerequisite for proof transformation and analysis or the extraction of computational content from proofs. Probably the most prominent application these days is proof-carrying code [5], a technique that can be used for safe execution of untrusted code. For these reasons we have extended Isabelle [9] with proof terms. However, apart from the actual implementation, our work is largely independent of Isabelle and most of this paper deals with the general topic of proof terms for simply typed, intuitionistic higher order logic (abbreviated to λHOL below), Isabelle's meta logic. Because other logics (e.g. full HOL) can be encoded in this meta logic, this immediately yields proof terms for those logics as well.

We start with a disclaimer: the idea of proof terms based on typed λ-calculus has been around for some time now and is the basis of a number of proof assistants for type theory, for example Coq [2]. Even more, with the advent of "pure type systems" and the λ-cube [1], it became clear what proof terms for λHOL look like in principle (although this seems to have had little impact on the HOL world). What we have done is to re-introduce the strict syntactic separation between terms, types, and proofs to make it more amenable to readers from a simply typed background. Thus our presentation of proof terms can be seen as a

* Supported by DFG Graduiertenkolleg *Logic in Computer Science*

J. Harrison and M. Aagaard (Eds.): TPHOLs 2000, LNCS 1869, pp. 38–52, 2000.

partial evaluation of the corresponding pure type system, i.e. separating the layers. Things are in fact a bit more complicated due to the presence of schematic polymorphism in our term language.

The main original contribution of the paper is a detailed presentation of proof compression. A naive implementation of proof terms results in proofs of enormous size because with every occurrence of a proof rule the instantiations for its free variables are recorded. Thus it is natural to try and leave out some of those terms and to reconstruct them by unification during proof checking. Necula and Lee [6] have presented a scheme for proof compression in LF, another logical framework based on type theory. They analyze the proof rules of the object logic statically to determine what can be reconstructed by a weak form of unification. In contrast, we do a dynamic analysis of each proof term to determine what can be dropped. Reconstruction of missing information by unification is also available in other systems, e.g. Elf [12,11], but none of them offers an automatic dynamic compression algorithm.

There has also been work on recording proofs in the HOL system [3,14], but it is firmly based on a notion of proof that directly reflects the implementation of inferences as calls to ML functions. These proof objects lack the conciseness of λ-terms and it is less clear how to compress them other than textually.

We start by presenting the logical framework (§2) and its λ-calculus based proof terms (§3). In order to shrink the size of proofs we introduce partial proofs (§4), show how to collect equality constraints from a (partial) proof (§4.1), how to solve these constraints (§4.2) (to check that the proof is correct), and how to generate partial proofs from total ones, i.e. how to compress proofs (§4.3).

2   The Logical Framework

In a nutshell, Isabelle's meta logic [9,8] is the minimal higher order logic of implication and universal quantification over simply typed λ-terms including schematic polymorphism. Thus types are first order only, which makes type reconstruction decidable. A type τ is either a variable α or a compound type expression $(\tau_1, \ldots, \tau_n)tc$, where tc is a type constructor and n is its arity. The (infix) constructor $\rightarrow$ for function types has arity 2. We assume implicitly that all types are well-formed, i.e. every type constructor is applied to the correct number of arguments. The set t of terms is defined in the usual way by

$$t = x \mid c \mid \lambda x :: \tau.\, t \mid t\, t$$

Formulae are terms of the primitive type prop. The logical connectives are:

universal quantification	$\bigwedge$ ::	$(\alpha \rightarrow \text{prop}) \rightarrow \text{prop}$
implication	$\Longrightarrow$ ::	$\text{prop} \rightarrow \text{prop} \rightarrow \text{prop}$

Now we show how an object logic is formalized in this meta logic. As an example we have chosen a fragment of HOL. First we introduce new types and constants for representing the connectives of this logic:

Tr	::	$\text{bool} \rightarrow \text{prop}$	$\forall$	::	$(\alpha \rightarrow \text{bool}) \rightarrow \text{bool}$
$\longrightarrow$	::	$\text{bool} \rightarrow \text{bool} \rightarrow \text{bool}$	$\exists$	::	$(\alpha \rightarrow \text{bool}) \rightarrow \text{bool}$

Here, bool is the type of object level propositions. The function Tr establishes a connection between meta level and object level truth values: the expression Tr P should be read as "P is true". The application of Tr is occasionally dropped when writing down formulae. The inference rules for the meta logic consist of the usual introduction and elimination rules and are shown in §3.1 below.

Inference rules of object logics are usually written like this:

$$\frac{\phi_1 \quad \cdots \quad \phi_n}{\psi}$$

In our meta logic they become nested implications:

$$\phi_1 \Longrightarrow \cdots \Longrightarrow \phi_n \Longrightarrow \psi$$

Here are some examples:

impl   : $\bigwedge A\ B.$ $(\text{Tr } A \Longrightarrow \text{Tr } B) \Longrightarrow \text{Tr } (A \longrightarrow B)$

impE   : $\bigwedge P\ Q\ R.$ $\text{Tr } (P \longrightarrow Q) \Longrightarrow \text{Tr } P \Longrightarrow (\text{Tr } Q \Longrightarrow \text{Tr } R) \Longrightarrow \text{Tr } R$

allI   : $\bigwedge P.$ $(\bigwedge x.\ \text{Tr } (P\ x)) \Longrightarrow (\text{Tr } (\forall x.\ P\ x))$

allE   : $\bigwedge P\ x\ R.$ $\text{Tr } (\forall x.\ P\ x) \Longrightarrow (\text{Tr } (P\ x) \Longrightarrow \text{Tr } R) \Longrightarrow \text{Tr } R$

exI   : $\bigwedge P\ x.$ $\text{Tr } (P\ x) \Longrightarrow \text{Tr } (\exists x.\ P\ x)$

exE   : $\bigwedge P\ Q.$ $\text{Tr } (\exists x.\ P\ x) \Longrightarrow (\bigwedge x.\ \text{Tr } (P\ x) \Longrightarrow \text{Tr } Q) \Longrightarrow \text{Tr } Q$

Note that the introduction rules impl and allI are for object level implication and universal quantification are expressed by simply referring to the meta level counterpart of these connectives. The expression $\bigwedge x.\ \phi$ is just an abbreviation for $\bigwedge (\lambda x.\ \phi)$, and similarly for $\forall$ and $\exists$.

3   Proof Terms

3.1   Basic Concepts

The set of proof terms p is defined as follows:

$$p = h \mid c_{\overline{[\tau_n/\alpha_n]}} \mid \lambda h : \phi.\ p \mid \lambda x :: \tau.\ p \mid p\ p \mid p\ t$$

The letters h, c, x, t, ϕ and τ denote proof variables, proof constants, term variables, terms of arbitrary type, terms of type prop and types, respectively. Note that terms, types and proof terms are considered as separate concepts. This is in contrast to type theoretic frameworks, where these concepts are identified. We will write $\Gamma \vdash p : \phi$ for "p is a proof of ϕ in context Γ", where ϕ is a term of type prop, representing the logical proposition proved by p. The context Γ associates a proof variable with a term representing the proposition whose proof it denotes, and a term variable with its type. We require each context to be well-formed, i.e. every variable is associated with at most one term or type. Proof constants correspond to axioms or already proved theorems. The environment Σ maps proof constants to terms representing propositions. Our language of proof terms allows abstraction over proof and term variables, as well as application of proofs to proofs and terms. The abstractions correspond to the introduction of $\bigwedge$ and $\implies$, while applications correspond to the elimination of these connectives. In contrast to polymorphic λ-calculi, no explicit application and abstraction is provided for types. To achieve a certain degree of polymorphism, we allow $\Sigma(c)$ to contain free type variables and introduce the notation $c_{[\tau_n/\alpha_n]}$ to specify a suitable instantiation for them. The notion of provability can now be defined inductively as follows:

$$\frac{}{\Gamma, h : \phi, \Gamma' \vdash h : \phi} \qquad \frac{\Sigma(c) = \phi}{\Gamma \vdash c_{[\tau_n/\alpha_n]} : \phi[\tau_n/\alpha_n]}$$

$$\frac{\Gamma, h : \phi \vdash p : \psi \quad \Gamma \vdash \phi :: \mathsf{prop}}{\Gamma \vdash (\lambda h : \phi.\ p) : \phi \implies \psi} \qquad \frac{\Gamma, x :: \tau \vdash p : \phi}{\Gamma \vdash (\lambda x :: \tau.\ p) : \bigwedge x :: \tau.\ \phi}$$

$$\frac{\Gamma \vdash p : \phi \implies \psi \quad \Gamma \vdash q : \phi}{\Gamma \vdash (p\ q) : \psi} \qquad \frac{\Gamma \vdash p : \bigwedge x :: \tau.\ \phi \quad \Gamma \vdash t :: \tau}{\Gamma \vdash (p\ t) : \phi[t/x]}$$

The judgement $\Gamma \vdash t :: \tau$ used above expresses that the term t has type τ in context Γ. We will not give a formal definition of this judgement here, since it is well-known from simply typed lambda calculus.

3.2 Representing Backward Resolution Proofs

This section explains how proof terms are constructed for proofs that are built up backwards by higher-order resolution as described by Paulson [8] and implemented in Isabelle. Although Isabelle also has LCF-like functions for forward proofs corresponding to the above inference rules, most proofs are constructed backwards without recourse to the forward rules. We now show how to augment these backward steps by proof terms. Thus the functions for backward resolution proofs need no longer be part of the trusted kernel of Isabelle.

In Isabelle, proof states are represented by theorems of the form

$$\psi_1 \implies \cdots \implies \psi_n \implies \phi$$

where ϕ is the proposition to be proved and ψ_1, ..., ψ_n are the remaining subgoals. Each subgoal is of the form $\bigwedge \overline{x}.\ \overline{A} \implies P$, where $\overline{x}$ and $\overline{A}$ is a context of parameters and local assumptions.

Resolution

A proof of a proposition ϕ starts with the trivial theorem $\phi \implies \phi$ whose proof term is $\lambda v : \phi.\ v$. The initial proof state is then refined successively using the resolution rule

$$\frac{\dfrac{P_1 \ \ldots \ P_m}{C}\ R}{\dfrac{P_1' \ \ldots \ P_i' \ \ldots \ P_{m'}'}{C'}\ R'} \quad \longmapsto \quad \theta\left(\frac{P_1' \quad \ldots \quad P_{i-1}' \quad P_1 \quad \ldots \quad P_m \quad P_{i+1}' \quad \ldots \quad P_{m'}'}{C'}\right)$$

$$\text{where} \quad \theta\ C = \theta\ P_i'$$

until a proof state with no more premises is reached. When refining a proof state having the proof term R' using a rule having the proof term R, the proof term for the resulting proof state can be expressed by

$$\theta \; (\lambda \overline{q_{i-1}} \; \overline{p_m}. \; R' \; \overline{q_{i-1}} \; (R \; \overline{p_m}))$$

where θ is a unifier of C and P_i'. The first $i - 1$ abstractions are used to skip the first $i - 1$ premises of R'. The next m abstractions correspond to the new subgoals introduced by R.

Proof by assumption
If the formula P_j in a subgoal $\bigwedge \overline{x_k}. \; \overline{P_n} \Longrightarrow P_j$ of a proof state having the proof term R equals one of the assumptions in $\overline{P_n}$, this subgoal trivially holds and can therefore be removed from the proof state

$$\frac{Q_1 \; \ldots \; Q_{i-1} \quad \bigwedge \overline{x_k}. \; \overline{P_n} \Longrightarrow P_j \quad Q_{i+1} \; \ldots \; Q_m}{C} \quad R \quad \longmapsto \quad \frac{Q_1 \; \ldots \; Q_{i-1} \quad Q_{i+1} \; \ldots \; Q_m}{C}$$

$$\text{where} \quad 1 \leq j \leq n$$

The proof term of the new proof state is obtained by supplying a suitable projection function as an argument to R:

$$\lambda \overline{q_{i-1}}. \; R \; \overline{q_{i-1}} \; (\lambda \overline{x_k} \; \overline{p_n}. \; p_j)$$

Lifting rules into a context
Before a subgoal of a proof state can be refined by resolution with a certain rule, the context of both the premises and the conclusion of this rule has to be augmented with additional parameters and assumptions in order to be compatible with the context of the subgoal. This process is called *lifting*. Isabelle distinguishes between two kinds of lifting: lifting over assumptions and lifting over parameters. The former simply adds a list of assumptions $\overline{Q_n}$ to both the premises and the conclusion of a rule:

$$\frac{P_1 \; \ldots \; P_m}{C} \quad R \quad \longmapsto \quad \frac{\overline{Q_n} \Longrightarrow P_1 \; \ldots \; \overline{Q_n} \Longrightarrow P_m}{\overline{Q_n} \Longrightarrow C}$$

The proof term for the lifted rule is

$$\lambda \overline{r_m} \; \overline{q_n}. \; R \; (\overline{r_m \; \overline{q_n}})$$

where the first m abstractions correspond to the new premises (with additional assumptions) and the next n abstractions correspond to the additional assumptions.

Lifting over parameters replaces all free variables a_i in a rule $R \, [\overline{a_k}]$ by new variables a_i' of function type, which are applied to a list of new parameters $\overline{x_n}$. The new parameters are bound by universal quantifiers.

$$\frac{P_1 \, [\overline{a_k}] \; \ldots \; P_m \, [\overline{a_k}]}{C \, [\overline{a_k}]} \quad R \, [\overline{a_k}] \quad \longmapsto \quad \frac{\bigwedge \overline{x_n}. \; P_1 \, [\overline{a_k' \; \overline{x_n}}] \; \ldots \; \bigwedge \overline{x_n}. \; P_m \, [\overline{a_k' \; \overline{x_n}}]}{\bigwedge \overline{x_n}. \; C \, [\overline{a_k' \; \overline{x_n}}]}$$

The proof term for the lifted rule looks similar to the one in the previous case:

$$\lambda \overline{r_m} \; \overline{x_n}. \; R \left[\overline{a_k' \; \overline{x_n}} \right] \; (\overline{r_m \; \overline{x_n}})$$

3.3 Constructing an Example Proof

We will now demonstrate how a proof term can be synthesized incrementally while proving a theorem in backward style. A proof term corresponding to a proof state will have the general form

$$\lambda(g_1 : \phi_1) \ldots (g_n : \phi_n). \ldots (g_i \; \overline{x^i} \; \overline{h^i}) \ldots$$

where the bound variables g_1, ..., g_n stand for proofs of the current subgoals which are still to be found. The $\overline{x^i}$ and $\overline{h^i}$ appearing in the proof term $(g_i \; \overline{x^i} \; \overline{h^i})$ are parameters and assumptions which may be used in the proof of subgoal i. As an example, the construction of a proof term for the theorem

$$(\exists x. \; \forall y. \; P \; x \; y) \longrightarrow (\forall y. \; \exists x. \; P \; x \; y)$$

will be shown by giving a proof term for each proof state. The parts of the proof terms, which are affected by the application of a rule will be underlined. Initially, the proof state is the trivial theorem:

step 0, remaining subgoal: $(\exists x. \; \forall y. \; P \; x \; y) \longrightarrow (\forall y. \; \exists x. \; P \; x \; y)$

$$\lambda g : ((\exists x. \; \forall y. \; P \; x \; y) \longrightarrow (\forall y. \; \exists x. \; P \; x \; y)). \; g$$

We first apply rule impl. Applying a suitable instance of this rule to the trivial initial proof term yields

$$\lambda g : (\exists x. \; \forall y. \; P \; x \; y) \Longrightarrow (\forall y. \; \exists x. \; P \; x \; y).$$
$$\underbrace{(\lambda g' : ((\exists x. \; \forall y. \; P \; x \; y) \longrightarrow (\forall y. \; \exists x. \; P \; x \; y)). \; g')}_{} \quad \} \text{ proof term from step 0}$$
$$\underbrace{(\text{impl} \; (\exists x. \; \forall y. \; P \; x \; y) \; (\forall y. \; \exists x. \; P \; x \; y) \; g)}_{\text{instance of impl}}$$

and by $\beta\eta$ reduction of this proof term we obtain

step 1, remaining subgoal: $(\exists x. \; \forall y. \; P \; x \; y) \Longrightarrow (\forall y. \; \exists x. \; P \; x \; y)$

$$\text{impl} \; (\exists x. \; \forall y. \; P \; x \; y) \; (\forall y. \; \exists x. \; P \; x \; y)$$

We now apply alll to the above proof state. Before resolving alll with the proof state, its context has to be augmented with the assumption $\exists x. \; \forall y. \; P \; x \; y$ of the current goal. The resulting proof term is

$$\lambda g : (\bigwedge y. \; \exists x. \; \forall y. \; P \; x \; y \Longrightarrow \exists x. \; P \; x \; y).$$
$$\text{impl} \; (\exists x. \; \forall y. \; P \; x \; y) \; (\forall y. \; \exists x. \; P \; x \; y) \qquad \} \text{ proof term from step 1}$$
$$((\lambda h_2 : (\exists x. \; \forall y. \; P \; x \; y \Longrightarrow \bigwedge y. \; \exists x. \; P \; x \; y).$$
$$\lambda h_1 : (\exists x. \; \forall y. \; P \; x \; y).$$
$$\text{alll} \; (\lambda y. \; \exists x. \; P \; x \; y) \; (h_2 \; h_1)) \qquad \qquad \Big\} \text{ lifted instance of alll}$$
$$(\lambda h_3 : (\exists x. \; \forall y. \; P \; x \; y)$$
$$\lambda y :: \beta. \; g \; y \; h_3)) \qquad \Big\} \text{ rearranging quantifiers}$$

as before, we apply β reduction, which yields

step 2, remaining subgoal: $\bigwedge y.\ \exists x.\ \forall y.\ P\ x\ y \Longrightarrow \exists x.\ P\ x\ y$

$\lambda g : (\bigwedge y.\ \exists x.\ \forall y.\ P\ x\ y \Longrightarrow \exists x.\ P\ x\ y).$
  impl $(\exists x.\ \forall y.\ P\ x\ y)\ (\forall y.\ \exists x.\ P\ x\ y)$
   $(\lambda h_1 : (\exists x.\ \forall y.\ P\ x\ y).$
    allI $(\lambda y.\ \exists x.\ P\ x\ y)\ (\lambda y :: \beta.\ \underline{g\ y\ h_1}))$

By eliminating the existence quantifier using exE we get

step 3, remaining subgoal: $\bigwedge y\ x.\ \forall y.\ P\ x\ y \Longrightarrow \exists x.\ P\ x\ y$

$\lambda g : (\bigwedge y\ x.\ \forall y.\ P\ x\ y \Longrightarrow \exists x.\ P\ x\ y).$
  impl $(\exists x.\ \forall y.\ P\ x\ y)\ (\forall y.\ \exists x.\ P\ x\ y)$
   $(\lambda h_1 : (\exists x.\ \forall y.\ P\ x\ y).$
    allI $(\lambda y.\ \exists x.\ P\ x\ y)$
     $(\lambda y :: \beta.\ \text{exE}\ (\lambda x.\ \forall y.\ P\ x\ y)\ (\exists x.\ P\ x\ y)\ h_1\ (\underline{g\ y})))$

Applying the introduction rule exI for the existential quantifier results in

step 4, remaining subgoal: $\bigwedge y\ x.\ \forall y.\ P\ x\ y \Longrightarrow P\ (?x\ y\ x)\ y$

$\lambda g : (\bigwedge y\ x.\ \forall y.\ P\ x\ y \Longrightarrow P\ (?x\ y\ x)\ y).$
  impl $(\exists x.\ \forall y.\ P\ x\ y)\ (\forall y.\ \exists x.\ P\ x\ y)$
   $(\lambda h_1 : (\exists x.\ \forall y.\ P\ x\ y).$
    allI $(\lambda y.\ \exists x.\ P\ x\ y)$
     $(\lambda y :: \beta.\ \text{exE}\ (\lambda x.\ \forall y.\ P\ x\ y)\ (\exists x.\ P\ x\ y)\ h_1$
      $(\lambda x :: \alpha.$
       $\lambda h_2 : (\forall y.\ P\ x\ y).$
        exI $(\lambda x.\ P\ x\ y)\ (?x\ y\ x)\ (\underline{g\ y\ x\ h_2}))))$

We now eliminate the universal quantifier using allE, which yields

step 5, remaining subgoal: $\bigwedge y\ x.\ P\ x\ (?y\ y\ x) \Longrightarrow P\ (?x\ y\ x)\ y$

$\lambda g : (\bigwedge y\ x.\ P\ x\ (?y\ y\ x) \Longrightarrow P\ (?x\ y\ x)\ y).$
  impl $(\exists x.\ \forall y.\ P\ x\ y)\ (\forall y.\ \exists x.\ P\ x\ y)$
   $(\lambda h_1 : (\exists x.\ \forall y.\ P\ x\ y).$
    allI $(\lambda y.\ \exists x.\ P\ x\ y)$
     $(\lambda y :: \beta.\ \text{exE}\ (\lambda x.\ \forall y.\ P\ x\ y)\ (\exists x.\ P\ x\ y)\ h_1$
      $(\lambda x :: \alpha.$
       $\lambda h_2 : (\forall y.\ P\ x\ y).$
        exI $(\lambda x.\ P\ x\ y)\ (?x\ y\ x)$
         (allE $(P\ x)\ (?y\ y\ x)\ (P\ (?x\ y\ x)\ y)\ h_2\ (\underline{g\ y\ x}))))))$

We can now prove the remaining subgoal by assumption, which is done by substituting the projection function $\lambda(y :: \beta)\ (x :: \alpha).\ \lambda h_3 : (P\ x\ y).\ h_3$ for g:

step 6, no subgoals

  impl $(\exists x.\ \forall y.\ P\ x\ y)\ (\forall y.\ \exists x.\ P\ x\ y)$
   $(\lambda h_1 : (\exists x.\ \forall y.\ P\ x\ y).$
    allI $(\lambda y.\ \exists x.\ P\ x\ y)$
     $(\lambda y :: \beta.\ \text{exE}\ (\lambda x.\ \forall y.\ P\ x\ y)\ (\exists x.\ P\ x\ y)\ h_1$
      $(\lambda x :: \alpha.$
       $\lambda h_2 : (\forall y.\ P\ x\ y).$
        exI $(\lambda x.\ P\ x\ y)\ x$
         (allE $(P\ x)\ y\ (P\ x\ y)\ h_2\ (\lambda h_3 : (P\ x\ y).\ h_3)))))$

4   Partial Proof Terms

Proof terms are large, contain much redundant information, and need to be compressed. The solution is simple: leave out everything that can be reconstructed. But since we do not want to complicate reconstruction too much, it should not degenerate into proof search. Thus we have to keep the skeleton of the proof. What can often be left out are the ϕ, τ and t in $\lambda h{:}\phi.\ p$, $\lambda x{::}\tau.\ p$ and $(p\ t)$.

Since we will have to reconstruct the missing information later on, it is conceptually simpler to model the missing information by *unification variables*. These are simply a new class of free (term and type) variables, syntactically distinguished by a leading "?", as in $?f$ and $?\alpha$. We will sometimes write $?f_\tau$ to emphasize that $?f$ has type τ. *Substitutions* are functions that act on unification variables, e.g. $\theta = \{?f \mapsto \lambda x.x, ?\alpha \mapsto \tau\}$.

In the remainder of this section we work with *partial* proofs, where terms and types may contain unification variables, as in $(p\ ?f)$. Note that term unification variables that occur within the scope of a λ need to be "lifted" as in $\lambda x{::}\tau.\ (p\,(?f\,x))$. Because of this lifting, this partial information may take up more space than it saves. Therefore an actual implementation is bound to introduce separate new constructors for proof trees, e.g. $\lambda h{:}\_.\ p$, $\lambda x{::}\_.\ p$ and $(p\ \_)$, where $\_$ represents the missing information. This is in fact what Necula and Lee describe [6]. However, it turns out that our partial proofs are easier to treat mathematically, not far from the "$\_$"-version, and also allow to drop only part of a term (although we will not make use of this feature).

Of course, we cannot check partial proofs with the rules of §3.1. In fact, we may not be able to check them at all, because too much information is missing. But we can collect equality constraints that need to hold in order for the proof to be correct. Such equality constraints are of the form $T_1 =^? T_2$, where T_1 and T_2 are either both terms or both types. A substitution *solves* a constraint if the two terms become equal modulo $\beta\eta$-conversion, or if the two types become identical. Sets of such equality constraints are usually denoted by the letters C and D. To separate C into term and type constraints, let C_t denote the term and C_τ the type part. The subscripts t and τ do *not* refer to variable names but are simply keywords.

We will now show how to extract a set of constraints from a partial proof; how to solve those constraints is discussed later on.

4.1   Collecting Constraints

The relation $\Gamma \vdash p \rhd (\phi,\ C)$ is a partial function taking Γ and a partial proof p and producing a formula ϕ (which may contain unification variables) and a set of constraints C. The function will be defined such that, if θ solves C, then $\theta(p)$ proves $\theta(\phi)$. The notation $\overline{V_\Gamma}$ denotes the list of all term variables declared in

Γ, and $\overline{\tau_\Gamma}$ denotes the list of their types, i.e. $\overline{V_\Gamma} = x_1 \ldots x_n$ and $\overline{\tau_\Gamma} = \tau_1 \ldots \tau_n$ for $\Gamma = x_1 :: \tau_1 \ldots x_n :: \tau_n$.

$$\frac{}{\Gamma', h : \phi, \Gamma \vdash h \triangleright (\phi, \emptyset)} \qquad \frac{\Sigma(c) = \phi}{\Gamma \vdash c_{\overline{[\tau_n/\alpha_n]}} \triangleright (\phi[\overline{\tau_n/\alpha_n}], \emptyset)}$$

$$\frac{\Gamma, h : \phi \vdash p \triangleright (\psi, C) \quad \Gamma \vdash \phi \triangleright (\tau, D)}{\Gamma \vdash (\lambda h{:}\phi.\ p) \triangleright (\phi \Longrightarrow \psi, C \cup D \cup \{\tau =^? \mathsf{prop}\})}$$

$$\frac{\Gamma, x :: \tau \vdash p \triangleright (\phi, C)}{\Gamma \vdash (\lambda x{::}\tau.\ p) \triangleright (\bigwedge x :: \tau.\ \phi, \{\lambda x :: \tau.\ r =^? \lambda x :: \tau.\ s \mid (r =^? s) \in C_t\} \cup C_\tau)}$$

$$\frac{\Gamma \vdash p \triangleright (\phi, C) \quad \Gamma \vdash q \triangleright (\psi, D)}{\Gamma \vdash (p\ q) \triangleright (?f_{\overline{\tau_\Gamma} \to \mathsf{prop}}\ \overline{V_\Gamma}, \{\phi =^? (\psi \Longrightarrow ?f_{\overline{\tau_\Gamma} \to \mathsf{prop}}\ \overline{V_\Gamma})\} \cup C \cup D)}$$

$$\frac{\Gamma \vdash p \triangleright (\phi, C) \quad \Gamma \vdash t \triangleright (\tau, D)}{\Gamma \vdash (p\ t) \triangleright (?f_{\overline{\tau_\Gamma} \to \tau \to \mathsf{prop}}\ \overline{V_\Gamma}\ t, \{\phi =^? \bigwedge x :: \tau.\ ?f_{\overline{\tau_\Gamma} \to \tau \to \mathsf{prop}}\ \overline{V_\Gamma}\ x\} \cup C \cup D)}$$

As usual, the unification variables $?f$ must be "new" in each case.

The above rules follow those in §3.1 very closely. For example, the intuition behind the rule for the application $(p\ q)$ is the following: if p proves proposition ϕ, then ϕ must be some implication and the proposition ψ proved by q must be the premise of this implication. Moreover, the proposition proved by $(p\ q)$ is the conclusion of the implication. The set of constraints for $(p\ q)$ is the union of the constraints for p and q, plus one additional constraint expressing that ϕ is a suitable implication. One point to note is the judgement $\Gamma \vdash t \triangleright (\tau, D)$ used in two premises of the constraint collection rules. It corresponds to $\Gamma \vdash t :: \tau$ just like $\Gamma \vdash p \triangleright (\phi, C)$ corresponds to $\Gamma \vdash p :: \phi$, i.e. D is a set of type constraints whose solvability implies that t has type τ. The rules for $\Gamma \vdash t \triangleright (\tau, D)$ are not given because they are well-known: both from the literature about type inference for simply typed terms and because they closely resemble the rules above, just one level down. In a setting where types, terms and proofs are not syntactically distinguished, we would only have one judgement $.\vdash.\triangleright(.,.)$.

We introduce the notation $(\phi, C) = collect(\Gamma, p)$ as a functional variant of $\Gamma \vdash p \triangleright (\phi, C)$.

Example 1. Let $p = \lambda x :: ?\alpha_1.\ \lambda h_1 : (?f_{?\alpha_2}\ x).\ \lambda y :: ?\alpha_3.\ \lambda h_2 : (?f'_{?\alpha_4}\ x\ y).\ h_1\ h_2\ y$
Then

$$collect([],p) = (\bigwedge x :: ?\alpha_1.\ ?f_{?\alpha_2}\ x \Longrightarrow \bigwedge y :: ?\alpha_3.\ ?f'_{?\alpha_4}\ x\ y \Longrightarrow$$
$$?g'_{?\alpha_1 \to ?\alpha_3 \to ?\alpha_3 \to \mathsf{prop}}\ x\ y\ y,$$

$$\{\lambda x :: ?\alpha_1.\lambda y :: ?\alpha_3.\ ?f_{?\alpha_2}\ x =^?$$
$$\lambda x :: ?\alpha_1.\lambda y :: ?\alpha_3.\ ?f'_{?\alpha_4}\ x\ y \Longrightarrow ?g_{?\alpha_1 \to ?\alpha_3 \to \mathsf{prop}}\ x\ y,$$
$$\lambda x :: ?\alpha_1.\lambda y :: ?\alpha_3).\ ?g_{?\alpha_1 \to ?\alpha_3 \to \mathsf{prop}}\ x\ y =^?$$
$$\lambda x :: ?\alpha_1.\lambda y :: ?\alpha_3).\ \bigwedge z :: ?\alpha_3.\ ?g'_{?\alpha_1 \to ?\alpha_3 \to ?\alpha_3 \to \mathsf{prop}}\ x\ y\ z,$$
$$?\alpha_2 =^? ?\alpha_1 \to ?\beta_1, ?\beta_1 =^? \mathsf{prop}$$
$$?\alpha_4 =^? ?\alpha_1 \to ?\alpha_3 \to ?\beta_2, ?\beta_2 =^? \mathsf{prop}\})$$

where $?g$, $?g'$ and $?\beta_i$ are new variables generated during constraint collection.

Theorem 1. *(Soundness and completeness)*

1. *If $\Gamma \vdash p \rhd (\phi', C)$ and θ solves C then $\theta(\Gamma) \vdash \theta(p) : \theta(\phi')$.*
2. *If $\Gamma \vdash p : \phi$ and $\Gamma \vdash p \rhd (\phi', C)$ then $C \cup \{\phi =^? \phi'\}$ is solvable.*

This theorem shows the advantage of working with partial proofs as opposed to proofs containing "_": we can produce the full proof by instantiation from the partial one.

Thus there are two possible system architectures for checking partial proofs:

- either constraint collection $\Gamma \vdash p \rhd (\phi', C)$ and constraint solving are part of the trusted kernel and $\theta(\phi')$ is accepted as the correct answer;
- or, for the security conscious, neither collecting nor solving is part of the trusted kernel and their result is checked by checking $\theta(\Gamma) \vdash \theta(p) : \theta(\phi')$.

4.2   Solving Constraints

Our constraints are a mixture of term and type constraints. Type constraints can be solved by first-order unification and thus do not need to be discussed here: they can be solved at any time in any order. Therefore we concentrate on term constraints in this subsection.

Since higher-order unification is undecidable, we restrict to unification of so called (higher-order) *patterns* [4], i.e. λ-terms where each occurrence of a unification variable is applied only to distinct bound variables. For example $\lambda xy.?F\,y\,x$ is a pattern, whereas $\lambda x.?F\,x\,x$ and $?Fa$ are not patterns. The set of all patterns is denoted by $\mathcal{P}at$. For us, the key property of patterns is that their unification is decidable and that solvable pattern unification problems have most general unifiers [4,12,7,13]. Thus we may assume a function mgu taking two patterns as arguments and either failing or returning the most general unifier of its arguments.

Since the constraints C generated by $\Gamma \vdash p \rhd (\phi, C)$ may contain non-patterns, we have to delay solving those constraints until (hopefully) they are turned into patterns by the solution of other pattern constraints. Of course, in the worst case C may not contain any patterns at all, in which case we have to give up. Thus we have to take care when constructing partial proofs to make sure the complete proof can be reconstructed by pattern unification.

Example 2. The first constraint in $\{?f\,?z =^? ?z,\ \lambda xy.?f\,x =^? \lambda xy.?f\,y\}$ is not a pattern constraint, but if the second constraint is solved first, it yields the substitution $?f \mapsto \lambda x.?u$, which turns the first constraint into the trivial $?u =^? ?z$.

We say that a set of equality constraints C *can be solved by pattern unification* if $C \longrightarrow^* \emptyset$, where $\longrightarrow$ is defined by the rewrite rule

$$C \cup \{s =^? t\} \longrightarrow \theta(C)$$

where s and t are patterns and $mgu(s, t)$ returns the unifier θ. Note that the choice of which pair $s =^? t$ to solve at which point is immaterial because $\longrightarrow$ is confluent. This is well-known for first-order terms, and holds for patterns as well because of the existence of most general unifiers and the following easy results:

Lemma 1. *1. If $s,t \in \mathcal{P}at$ and $mgu(s,t)$ returns θ then $\mathcal{R}an(\theta) \subseteq \mathcal{P}at$.*
2. If $\mathcal{R}an(\theta) \subseteq \mathcal{P}at$ and $u \in \mathcal{P}at$ then $\theta(u) \in \mathcal{P}at$.

4.3   Compressing Proof Terms

The basic idea here is straightforward: given a proof term, remove all of the information that can be reconstructed by unification. If our meta logic were Prolog (i.e. proof terms contain no λs), we could drop all terms t in an application $(p\ t)$, because first-order unification can reconstruct them. In our setting we require that pattern unification should be able to reconstruct the missing terms.

Compression is performed in three phases. First, all terms and types in the proof are replaced by suitably lifted unification variables. A substitution reversing the term abstractions is constructed as well.

$$
\begin{aligned}
varify(\overline{x},\overline{\tau},\lambda v{:}\phi.\ p) &= \text{let } (p',\theta) = varify(\overline{x},\overline{\tau},p) \\
&\quad\ \text{in } (\lambda v{:}(?f_{\overline{\tau}\to\text{prop}}\ \overline{x}).\ p',\ \theta \cup \{?f \mapsto \lambda\overline{x}.t\}) \\
varify(\overline{x},\overline{\tau},\lambda y{::}\tau.\ p) &= \text{let } (p',\theta) = varify(\overline{x}y,\overline{\tau}\ ?\alpha,p) \\
&\quad\ \text{in } (\lambda y{::}?\alpha.\ p',\ \theta) \\
varify(\overline{x},\overline{\tau},(p\ q)) &= \text{let } (p',\theta) = varify(\overline{x},\overline{\tau},p);\ (q',\theta') = varify(\overline{x},\overline{\tau},q) \\
&\quad\ \text{in } ((p'\ q'),\theta \cup \theta') \\
varify(\overline{x},\overline{\tau},(p\ t)) &= \text{let } (p',\theta) = varify(\overline{x},\overline{\tau},p) \\
&\quad\ \text{in } ((p'\ (?f_{\overline{\tau}\to?\beta}\ \overline{x})),\ \theta \cup \{?f \mapsto \lambda\overline{x}.t\}) \\
varify(\overline{x},\overline{\tau},c_{\overline{[\tau_n/\alpha_n]}}) &= (c_{\overline{[?\alpha_n/\alpha_n]}},\emptyset)
\end{aligned}
$$

Thus $varify(\overline{x},\overline{\tau},p) = (p',\theta)$ does not quite imply $\theta(p') = p$ because θ does not reverse the type abstractions: types are first-order and thus they can be reconstructed uniquely by unification.

Then the constraints are extracted from the resulting partial proof: $(\phi',C) = collect(\Gamma,p')$. Finally we compute (with the help of function *solves*) a minimal set of term variables $V \subseteq \mathcal{D}om(\theta)$ such that $\theta(C)$ can be solved by pattern unification. Thus the overall algorithm for compressing a proof p is

$$
\begin{aligned}
compress(p,\phi) = \text{ let } &(p',\theta) = varify([],[],p) \\
&(\phi',C) = collect([],p') \\
&V = solves(C \cup \{\phi =^? \phi'\},\theta) \\
\text{in}\quad &\theta|_V(p')
\end{aligned}
$$

where $\theta|_V$ is the restriction of θ to V. Function $solves(D,\theta)$ returns $V \subseteq \mathcal{D}om(\theta)$ such that $\theta|_V(D)$ is solvable by pattern unification. The details are explained below.

The main correctness theorem expresses that compression does not lose any information in the following sense: the constraints collected from the compressed version of a valid proof are solvable by pattern unification and any solution yields a proof of the original formula.

Theorem 2. *Let ϕ be ground. If $\vdash p : \phi$, $q = compress(p,\phi)$ and $(\psi,C) = collect([],q)$ then*

1. $C \cup \{\phi =^? \psi\}$ *is solvable by pattern unification and*
2. *if θ solves $C \cup \{\phi =^? \psi\}$ then $\vdash \theta(q) : \phi$.*

The second part of the theorem follows directly from the soundness of *collect* (part 1 of Theorem 1) because ϕ is ground, i.e. $\theta(\phi) = \phi$.

The fact that $C \cup \{\phi =^? \psi\}$ is solvable by pattern unification is a bit more subtle. From $q = compress(p, \phi)$ it follows by definition of *compress* that there are p', θ, ϕ', C' and V such that $(p', \theta) = varify([], [], p)$, $(\phi', C') = collect([], p')$, $V = solves(C' \cup \{\phi =^? \phi'\}, \theta)$ and $q = \theta|_V(p')$. Because $(\psi, C) = collect([], q) = collect([], \theta|_V(p'))$ and $(\phi', C') = collect([], p')$ it can be shown that $\psi = \theta|_V(\phi')$ and $C = \theta|_V(C')$. Thus $C \cup \{\phi =^? \psi\} = \theta|_V(C' \cup \{\phi =^? \phi'\})$. It can be shown that $\theta(C' \cup \{\phi =^? \phi'\})$ is solvable by pattern unification. Appealing to Theorem 3 below, it follows that so is $C \cup \{\phi =^? \psi\}$.

Theorem 3. *If $\theta(C)$ is solvable by pattern unification, then $solves(C, \theta)$ terminates successfully with a set of variables V such that $\theta|_V(C)$ is solvable by pattern unification.*

This can be viewed as a specification of *solves* or as its main correctness theorem. Of course there are trivial implementations of *solves* that simply return $\mathcal{D}om(\theta)$. What we want is a minimal set V with the stated property. Note that in general there is no least such V:

Example 3. Let $C = \{\lambda x.?f(?g(x)) =^? \lambda x.f(x)\}$ and $\theta = \{?f \mapsto f, ?g \mapsto \lambda x.x\}$. Then $\theta(C)$, $\theta|_{\{?f\}}(C)$ and $\theta|_{\{?g\}}(C)$ are solvable by pattern unification.

Therefore *solves* nondeterministically computes a minimal set of variables by simulating the process of solving the constraints by pattern unification. Every time the process gets stuck, i.e. no more pattern constraints are left, a minimal set of additional variables is instantiated.

The main complication is that pattern unification may introduce new variables. Thus we need to keep track of where they came from, i.e. which original variable needs to be instantiated in order to ensure that the new variable becomes instantiated. Again, there may be a choice:

Example 4. Let $C = \{\lambda xyz.?f z x =^? \lambda xyz.?g x y\} \cup C'$ and let $\theta = \{?f \mapsto \lambda xy.f y, ?g \mapsto \lambda xy.f x\} \cup \theta'$. Solving the first constraint in C yields the substitution $\sigma = \{?f \mapsto \lambda xy.?h y, ?g \mapsto \lambda xy.?h x\}$. Now we need to compute the value of $?h$ (in case it is required later on in order to continue) and we need to record that $?h$ depends on either $?f$ or $?g$, i.e. instantiating $?f$ or $?g$ will instantiate $?h$. We can chose to record either dependency.

In the algorithm below, this dependency relation is stored in a partial function D mapping new variables to old ones they depend on.

Finally we introduce some terminology to select those variables that occur in non-pattern positions: given an equality constraint st, $\mathcal{NPVars}(st)$ is the set of variables $?f$ that occur in subterms of the form $?f \, \bar{u}$ in st, such that $\bar{u}$ is not a list of distinct bound variables.

Now we can describe $solves(C, \theta)$ as an imperative algorithm. As long as there are pattern problems left in C, we solve them and propagate the solution. Once we are left only with non-pattern problems, we pick one such that values for all its non-pattern variables are known (via θ). All those variables are then instantiated and recorded in V. If there is no such non-pattern problem either, the algorithm fails. Luckily, Theorem 3 tells us that this will not happen in the cases we are interested in.

$V := \emptyset; D := \{?f \mapsto ?f \mid ?f \in Var(C)\}$
while $C \neq \emptyset$ do
    if there is a pattern problem $(s =^? t) \in C$
    then $\sigma := mgu(s, t); C := \sigma(C - \{s =^? t\});$
           forall $(?f \mapsto t) \in \sigma$ do
               $\delta := mgu(\theta(?f), \theta(t));$
                  $D := D \cup \{?h \mapsto D(?f) \mid ?h \in \mathcal{D}om(\delta)\}$
           od
    else pick some $st \in C$ such that $\mathcal{NPV}ars(st) \subseteq \mathcal{D}om(\theta);$
           $V := V \cup \{D(?f) \mid ?f \in \mathcal{NPV}ars(st)\};$
           $C := \theta|_{\mathcal{NPV}ars(st)}(C);$
od;
return V

Note that the else-case does not necessarily compute a minimal V: if $st = (\lambda xy.?f\, x\, (?g\, y\, y) =^? \lambda xy.x\}$ and $\theta(?f) = \lambda xy.x$ and $\theta(?g) = \lambda xy.x$ then it suffices to instantiate either $?f$ or $?g$, whereas above both are added to V. The above algorithm can be refined by instantiating st stepwise from the top and normalizing the result each time.

5   Implementation

The algorithms for compression and reconstruction of proofs have been implemented in ML as a part of the theorem prover Isabelle. During the proof of a theorem, the corresponding proof term is built up incrementally. Since this may slow down the execution of proof scripts, the generation of proof terms can be switched on and off as needed: during the interactive development of a proof this feature may be switched off. When the proof is completed, the proof script may be re-run with proof generation switched on and the resulting proof term could be exported.

We have tested the implementation on several proofs of theorems in Pelletier's collection [10], which were generated by Isabelle's tableau prover. The following table summarizes some results[1]. It shows the number of terms (i.e. terms such as ϕ and t in $\lambda h{:}\phi.\ p$ and $(p\, t)$) occurring in the uncompressed proof term, as well as the number of terms occurring in the compressed proof term (i.e. terms not replaced by placeholders "_", as explained in §4). In all cases, the compression

---

[1] These measurements were done on a Pentium II with 400 MHz and 512 MB RAM

ratio was more than 90%. The compression rate reported by Necula and Lee [6] appears to be a little better, but that is probably because we counted only the number of terms, not their size: our dynamic compression scheme should drop at least as much as Necula and Lee's static scheme.

number of terms			reconstruction
uncompressed	compressed	compression	time [s]
52	4	92.3%	0.030
116	6	94.8%	0.120
170	9	94.7%	0.190
316	16	94.9%	0.360
425	31	92.7%	0.710
1948	142	92.7%	5.220
2345	153	93.5%	5.950

The following diagram shows the correspondence between the number of terms in the uncompressed proof term and the time needed for reconstruction.

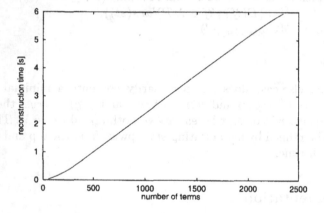

A crucial point is the efficient handling of large sets of constraints: when having computed a unifier for a constraint, one possibility is to apply this unifier to all the remaining constraints. Another possibility is to accumulate the unifiers and only apply them when needed. The first solution can be rather slow when having a large number of constraints, while the second solution—which has been chosen in our implementation—requires efficient data structures for storing substitutions. To speed up reconstruction, our implementation of function *collect* described in §4.1 tries to solve newly introduced constraints immediately, instead of collecting all constraints first and then solving them at the end.

6   Conclusion

We have given a first presentation of proof terms for simply typed intuitionistic higher-order logic, an important logical framework. We hope that by unfolding the underlying type theory and explicitly isolating the simply typed components familiar to users of Isabelle or HOL, this may popularize the λ-calculus view of proofs in those quarters as well. We have also presented what appears to be a novel compression scheme for proofs. Hence our work provides a new and promising basis for exchanging proofs in simply typed logics, in particular HOL, both among theorem provers (especially automatic and interactive) and in the realm of proof carrying code.

References

[1] H. P. Barendregt. Lambda calculi with types. In S. Abramsky, D. Gabbay, and T. Maibaum, editors, *Handbook of Logic in Computer Science*, volume 2, pages 118–309. Oxford University Press, 1992.

[2] B. Barras, S. Boutin, C. Cornes, J. Courant, Y. Coscoy, D. Delahaye, D. de Rauglaudre, J.-C. Filliâtre, E. Giménez, H. Herbelin, G. Huet, H. Laulhère, C. Muñoz, C. Murthy, C. Parent-Vigouroux, P. Loiseleur, C. Paulin-Mohring, A. Saïbi, and B. Werner. The Coq proof assistant reference manual – version 6.3.1. Technical report, INRIA, 1999.

[3] M. J. C. Gordon, J. M. J. Herbert, R. W. S. Hale, J. Harrison, W. Wong, and J. von Wright. Self-checking prover study – final report. Technical report, SRI, 1995. Available at http://www.csl.sri.com/reports/postscript/proofchecker.ps.gz.

[4] D. Miller. A logic programming language with lambda-abstraction, function variables, and simple unification. *Journal of Logic and Computation*, 1(4):497–536, 1991.

[5] G. C. Necula. Proof-carrying code. In *Conference Record of POPL '97: The 24th ACM SIGPLAN-SIGACT Symposium on Principles of Programming Languages*, pages 106–119. ACM Press, New York, 1997.

[6] G. C. Necula and P. Lee. Efficient representation and validation of proofs. In *13th IEEE Symp. Logic in Computer Science (LICS'98)*, pages 93–104. IEEE Computer Society Press, 1998.

[7] T. Nipkow. Functional unification of higher-order patterns. In *8th IEEE Symp. Logic in Computer Science*, pages 64–74. IEEE Computer Society Press, 1993.

[8] L. C. Paulson. The foundation of a generic theorem prover. *Journal of Automated Reasoning*, 5:363–397, 1989.

[9] L. C. Paulson. *Isabelle: A Generic Theorem Prover*, volume 828 of *LNCS*. Springer, 1994.

[10] F. J. Pelletier. Seventy-five problems for testing automatic theorem provers. *Journal of Automated Reasoning*, 2:191–216, 1986.

[11] F. Pfenning. Logic programming in the LF Logical Framework. In G. Huet and G. Plotkin, editors, *Logical Frameworks*, pages 66–78. Cambridge University Press, 1991.

[12] F. Pfenning. Unification and anti-unification in the calculus of constructions. In *6th IEEE Symposium on Logic in Computer Science*, pages 74–85. IEEE Computer Society Press, 1991.

[13] Z. Qian. Unification of higher-order patterns in linear time and space. *Journal of Logic and Computation*, 6:315–341, 1996.

[14] W. Wong. Recording and checking HOL proofs. In E. Schubert, P. Windley, and J. Alves-Foss, editors, *Higher Order Logic Theorem Proving and Its Applications. 8th International Workshop*, volume 971 of *LNCS*, pages 353–68. Springer-Verlag, Berlin, 1995.

Routing Information Protocol in HOL/SPIN

Karthikeyan Bhargavan, Carl A. Gunter, and Davor Obradovic

University of Pennsylvania
bkarthik@saul.cis.upenn.edu, gunter@cis.upenn.edu,
davor@saul.cis.upenn.edu

Abstract. We provide a proof using HOL and SPIN of convergence for
the Routing Information Protocol (RIP), an internet protocol based on
distance vector routing. We also calculate a sharp realtime bound for this
convergence. This extends existing results to deal with the RIP standard
itself, which has complexities not accounted for in theorems about abstract versions of the protocol. Our work also provides a case study in
the combined use of a higher-order theorem prover and a model checker.
The former is used to express abstraction properties and inductions, and
structure the high-level proof, while the latter deals efficiently with case
analysis of finitary properties.

1 Introduction

The high connectivity on which the Internet relies is enabled by scalable and
robust protocols that enable routers connecting different physical networks to
forward packets toward destinations described in a uniform addressing system.
The first Internet routing protocols were based on distance vector routing, which
uses information about distance and direction to a destination to route packets.
The first such protocol standardized by the Internet Engineering Task Force
(IETF) was the Routing Information Protocol (RIP), and this protocol remains
in widespread use today. Although the correctness of distance vector routing has
been proved for theoretical versions of the algorithm, the RIP standard itself
has never been proved to have some of the properties it is expected to possess.
Since there exist non-trivial differences between the abstract version and the
standard itself, proofs of some key properties of the standard are worthwhile.
In this paper we carry out the proof of convergence using a combination of
the HOL [5,9] higher-order theorem prover and the SPIN model checker [10,17].
The automated assistance reduces the burden of case analysis in parts of the
standard where manual analysis would prove tedious. Moreover, the HOL/SPIN
proof provides high confidence for RIP and insights into the techniques needed
to address other routing protocols, most of which are more complex than RIP.

Routing protocols are meant to be robust with respect to failures of links and
routers. If there is a failure then the routers communicate this information and
routing tables are updated to route around the failed link or router. This process
takes some time since routers cannot possess instantaneous global knowledge
of network characteristics. They therefore pass information that is incomplete

J. Harrison and M. Aagaard (Eds.): TPHOLs 2000, LNCS 1869, pp. 53–72, 2000.

and, if the protocol has the right characteristics, they eventually *converge* on a suitable set of alternative routes. We have two results: we show that the RIP protocol will converge after a failure, and we calculate a sharp realtime bound on the time this will take as a function of the radius of the network. Both results are based on assumptions about network reliability and timing assumptions specified in the RIP protocol.

The first proof concerns the convergence of the asynchronous distributed Bellman-Ford protocol as specified in the IETF RIP standard [8,12]. The classic proof of a 'pure' form of the protocol is given in [1]. Our result covers additional features included in the standard to improve realtime response times (*e.g.* split horizons and poison reverse). These features add additional cases to be considered in the proof, but the automated support reduces the impact of this complexity. Adding these extensions makes the theory better match the standard, and hence also its implementations. Our proof also uses a different technique from the one in [1], providing some noteworthy properties about network stability.

Our second proof provides a sharp realtime convergence bound on RIP in terms of the radius of the network around its nodes. In the worst case, the Bellman-Ford protocol has a convergence time as bad as the number of nodes in the network. However, if the maximum number of hops any source needs to traverse to reach a destination is k (the radius around the destination) and there are no link changes, then RIP will converge in k timeout intervals for this destination. From our first proof of convergence, it is easy to see that this occurs within $2 \cdot (k - 1)$ intervals, but the proof of the sharp bound of k is complicated by the number of cases that need to be checked: we show how to use automated support to do this verification, based on the approach developed in the previous case study supplemented by a new invariant. Thus, if a network has a maximum radius of 5 around each of its destinations, then it will converge in at most 5 intervals, even if the network has 100 nodes. Assuming the timing intervals in the RIP standard, such a network will converge within 15 minutes if there are no link changes.

The basis of our verification is the RIP standard. Early implementations of distance vector routing were incompatible, so all of the routers running RIP in a domain needed to use the same implementation. Users and implementors were led to correct this problem by providing a specification that would define precise protocols and packet formats, leading to the first version of the standard [8]. In time this standard was revised to a second version [12]. At the level of abstraction we use here, our proof is applicable to both of these versions.

There have been a variety of successful formal studies of communication protocols. However, most of the studies to date have focused on *endpoint* protocols (that is, protocols between pairs of hosts) using models that involve two or three processes (representing the endpoints, or the endpoints and an adversary, for instance). Studies of routing protocols must have a different flavor since a proof that works for two or three routers is not interesting unless it can be generalized. Routing protocols generally have the following attributes which influence the way formal verification techniques can be applied:

1. An (essentially) unbounded number of replicated, simple processes execute concurrently.
2. Dynamic connectivity is assumed and fault tolerance is required.
3. Processes are reactive systems with a discrete interface of modest complexity.
4. Real time is important and many actions are carried out with some timeout limit or in response to a timeout.

Most routing protocols have other attributes such as latencies of information flow (limiting, for example, the feasibility of a global concept of time) and the need to protect network resources. These attributes sometimes make the protocols more complex. For instance, the asynchronous version of the Bellman-Ford protocol is much harder to prove correct than the synchronous version [1], and the RIP standard is still harder to prove correct because of the addition of complicating optimizations intended to reduce latencies.

Following this introduction we give a description of the Routing Information Protocol as specified in its standard. We then describe our formalization of RIP in HOL and SPIN. In the fourth and fifth sections we show the convergence of RIP and derive a sharp realtime bound for the convergence. In the sixth section we provide some analysis of our methodology including a discussion of the benefits of automation and some crude measurements of the complexity of the proofs as viewed by the automated tools and the person carrying out the verification respectively. Our final section summarizes the conclusions.

2   Routing Information Protocol

The RIP protocol specification is given in [8,12] and a good exposition can be found in [11]. We start by describing the general networking environment and the task of a routing protocol. Then we give a brief description of the RIP protocol, including its pseudocode (Appendices A.1, A.2). Finally, we discuss differences between the standard and the underlying theory and the way they affect protocol requirements.

2.1   Routing in Internetworks

An *internet* is a family of *networks* connected by *routers*. Figure 1 illustrates an internetwork with four networks (shown as clouds) and four routers (shown as black squares). The goal of the routers is to forward packets between hosts (shown as circles) that are attached to the networks. The routers use *routing tables* which they develop through running a distributed *routing protocol*. Packets from hosts travel in *hops* across networks linked by routers. Each router chooses a link on which to forward the packet based on the packet's destination address and other parameters. In order to be able to make good forwarding decisions, routers need to maintain partial topology information in the routing tables.

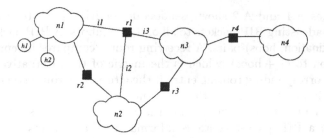

Fig. 1. An Internet

The aim of a routing protocol is to establish a procedure for updating these tables. In most cases, routing information can be exchanged only *locally* (i.e. between neighboring routers). However, the overall goal of a routing protocol is to establish good *global* paths (between distant hosts on the internet). An *interface* is the link between a router and a network. In this example, router $r1$ has interfaces $i1$, $i2$ and $i3$, which connect it to the networks $n1$, $n2$ and $n3$ respectively. Hosts $h1$ and $h2$ belong to the network $n1$. Routers are said to be *neighbors* if they have interfaces to a common network. In our example, all routers are neighbors of $r1$, but $r2$ and $r4$ are not neighbors.

2.2 Routing Information Protocol

Each RIP router maintains a routing table. A routing table contains one entry per destination network, representing the current best route to the destination. An entry corresponding to destination d has the following fields:

- hops: number of hops to d (i.e. total number of routers that a message sent along that route traverses before reaching the network d - this includes the router where this entry resides). This is sometimes called a *metric* for d.
- nextR: next router along the route to d.
- nextIface: the interface that will be used to forward packets addressed to d. It uniquely identifies the next network along the route.

Routers periodically *advertise* their routing tables to their neighbors. Upon receiving an advertisement, the router checks whether any of the advertised routes can be used to improve current routes. Whenever this is the case, the router updates its current route to go through the advertising neighbor. Routes are compared exclusively by their length, measured in the number of hops.

The value of hops must be an integer between 1 and 16, where 16 has the meaning of *infinity* (a destination with hops attribute set to 16 is considered unreachable). Hence, RIP will not be appropriate for internets that contain a router and a destination network that are more than 15 hops apart from each other.

Appendices A.1 and A.2 show pseudocode for RIP. A router advertises its routes by broadcasting RIP packets to all of its neighbors. A RIP packet contains a list of (destination, hops)-pairs. A receiving router compares its current metric for destination to (1 + hops), which is the metric of the alternative route, and updates the corresponding routing entry if the alternative route is shorter. There is one exception to this rule—if the receiving router has the advertising router as nextR for the route, it adopts the alternative route regardless of its metric.

Normally, a RIP packet contains information that reflects the advertising router's own routing table. This rule has an exception too—routers do not advertise routes on the interfaces through which they had been learned. Precisely, if a route is learned over the interface i, it should be advertised on that interface with hops set to 16 (infinity). This rule is called *split horizon with poisoned reverse* and its purpose is to prevent creation of small routing loops.

Each routing table entry has a timer expire associated with it. Every time an entry is updated (or created), expire is re-set to 180 seconds. Routers try to advertise every 30 seconds, but due to network failures and congestion some advertisements may not get through. If a route has not been refreshed for 180 seconds, the router will assume that there was a link failure, the destination will be marked as unreachable and a special garbageCollect timer will be set to 120 seconds. If this timer expires before the entry gets updated, the route is expunged from the table.

2.3 Standard vs. Theory

The mathematical theory behind RIP is described in [1] as the Asynchronous Distributed Bellman-Ford Algorithm (ADBF). In the ADBF model, at every point in time, a router is either idle, sending an advertisement, or receiving an advertisement. The routing table is updated upon receiving an advertisement. Details of the proof that ADBF finds shortest routes are presented in [1].

An interesting question is: 'Can we use (essentially) the same proof to show that RIP protocol converges to the set of shortest routes?' It turns out that the answer is quite certainly 'no'. Although motivated by the ADBF, RIP standard [8,12] differs from it in several important details:

- ADBF has 'more powerful bookkeeping'. In RIP, routers keep track of only one (current best) route to each destination. On the other hand, ADBF nodes keep, for each destination, the most recent routes *through each of the neighbors*. Correspondingly, this would be reflected in the pseudocode (Appendices A.1, A.2) by all subscript indices becoming *(dest,neighbor)*, instead of just *dest*. This makes ADBF more flexible, which comes at the expense of maintaining a larger data structure.
- RIP has 'blind' updates. As a consequence of the previous difference, RIP routers need to separately handle the case when an advertisement is received from a neighbor which is already nextR for the route. In this case, the receiving router can do nothing better than blindly accept the advertised route, regardless of its length. ADBF does not have this special case.

– RIP's route length is bounded. RIP can handle routes of at most 15 hops. Distances of 16 or more hops are all considered equivalent to infinity. This is a practical optimization intended to balance the tradeoff between quicker loop elimination and greater range for routing information propagation.
– RIP has the *split horizon with poisoned reverse* rule. This is another engineering optimization, not present in ADBF.

The first of the above gaps alone would be enough to make proofs of convergence requirements for RIP substantially different from proofs for ADBF. Besides matching the RIP setting closely, our proof technique also gives useful insights about the speed of propagation of updates, which can be used for establishing timing bounds for convergence.

3 Formal Specification of RIP

In the previous section, we gave a short description of the RIP standard along with its pseudo-code. In this section, we present a formal specification of the protocol that can be analyzed by HOL90 and SPIN. First, we make some simplifications of the protocol:

1. We observe that RIP (Appendices A.1, A.2) operates independently for every destination, with no interaction between the state or events associated with different destinations. This means that we need to specify and prove the protocol only for a single destination and the result will hold for the general version as well.
2. We only analyze the protocol *in between* topology changes. When the protocol starts, it may have *any* sound state to begin with. However, once it has started, one must give the protocol a reasonable period of time to converge. So we assume that there are no topology changes in the lifetime of the analysis. Under this assumption, the protocol indeed converges as we show in Section 4. Moreover, in Section 5, we precisely characterize the time period for which there must be no topology changes to guarantee convergence.
3. We abstract away from actual timing constraints. If topology changes are ruled out, routes cannot be expired ($expire_{dest}$) or deleted ($garbageCollect_{dest}$). So the only timing constraint left is the time interval between periodic broadcasts of advertisements. We model this by (a) enabling a router to broadcast advertisements at any time (a safe abstraction), and (b) adding a fairness assumption to the broadcast sequence.

We next specify RIP in HOL for analysis in the HOL90 theorem prover. Then we model the protocol in Promela, the specification language for the SPIN model-checker. The Promela modeling is straight-forward: it simply involves rewriting the pseudo-code in terms of Promela's C-like syntax, and SPIN's event semantics. The HOL specification is more involved, since we need to transform the pseudo-code into a functional specification.

3.1   RIP in HOL

For a RIP router, the universe $\mathcal{U}$ is a bipartite, connected graph whose nodes are partitioned into *networks* and *routers*, connected through *interfaces*. Routers are always connected to at least two networks. We specify networks and routers using distinct uninterpreted type variables: 'network, 'router. Now any specific universe can be described simply by a function conn : 'router → 'network → bool, that describes the interfaces—which routers and networks are connected with each other. A function conn describes a *valid* universe $\mathcal{U}$ if (a) conn connects each router to at least 2 networks, and (b) conn describes a connected graph.

When the RIP protocol starts operating in a universe $\mathcal{U}$, it is given as input a valid conn function, describing the topology of $\mathcal{U}$, and an initial state s_0. The protocol then seeks to compute paths from each router to the destination d. We describe the HOL specification in three steps: (1) the state of the protocol, along with an initial state assumption, (2) the processes that change the state and pass messages to each other, and (3) the semantics of these processes in HOL, and typical properties they are expected to satisfy.

Protocol State   The goal of RIP is to compute an optimal path at each router r to the destination network d. The path is described by a *routing entry*: the number of hops to d, the next router (nextR) along this path, and the network between r and nextR (nextN). RIP only computes paths of length less than 16; destinations more than 16 hops away are considered unreachable.

The protocol state consists of a table of the current routing entries at each router r, which we call the routing table (rtable). A protocol state is defined as as a 3-tuple s : rtable whose components are hops : 'router → num and nextN : 'router → 'network and nextR : 'router → 'router. In addition, we want all protocol states to be *sound*, where soundness is defined as follows:

Definition 1 (Soundness). *A protocol state s = (hops, nextN, nextR) of a universe described by a valid conn is said to be sound with respect to d if*

1. $\forall r :$ 'router.conn r (nextN(r)) $\land$ conn (nextR(r)) (nextN(r))
2. $\forall r :$ 'router.$1 \leq$ (hops(r)) ≤ 16
3. $\forall r :$ 'router.(conn r d) $\Rightarrow$ (hops$(r) = 1$) $\land$ (nextN$(r) = d$) $\land$ (nextR$(r) = r$)
4. $\forall r :$ 'router.$\neg$(conn r d) $\Rightarrow$ (hops$(r) > 1$) $\land$ (nextN$(r) \neq d$) $\land$ (nextR$(r) \neq r$)

We stipulate that the *initial state* of the protocol, s_0, must be sound. Observe that soundness really has to do with the 'local' connections at a router, which are typically configured by mechanisms external to RIP. By stipulating that the initial state is sound, we require that the router is never deluded about its local topology, otherwise there is no guarantee that it will ever discover global path information. Put another way, if the system ever gets into an unsound state, convergence cannot be guaranteed. Note however, that we can only assume the initial state to be sound, we need to prove that all succeeding states will remain sound under RIP.

Processes We represent different event handlers in the protocol by different processes; they typically perform different kinds of actions and may do so in parallel. As a result, there are three kinds of processes in the universe: each router r has an *advertising process* (generating advertisements), and a *routing process* (handling packet reception), and at each network net there is a *network process* (performing broadcasts).

The advertising process persistently broadcasts route advertisements on each of its connected networks. Each such advertisement is a tuple (src, hopcount), saying that the broadcasting router src, knows of a path of length hopcount to the destination d. Suppose the protocol state is $s = $ (hops, nextN, nextR), then the hopcount advertised by src on net may have the following values:

- if net = nextN(src), then hopcount = 16 (Infinity);
- otherwise, hopcount = hops(src).

When an advertisement is to be broadcast on network net, it is handed over to the network process for net. The network process executes the broadcast by attempting to deliver the incoming advertisement to all routers rcv connected to the net. We do not assume that the network is reliable in any way, so it may not deliver the advertisement to any router, or it may deliver it to some of the routers in an arbitrary order. However, we make the following assumptions

- *Fairness*: the network cannot ignore a router forever. So in any execution of the network net, if a router src sends advertisements infinitely often, and rcv is another router connected to net, the network process must deliver src's advertisements to rcv infinitely often.
- *Zero Delay*: We assume that if the network does deliver an advertisement, it does so instantaneously.

We call the tuple (src, net, rcv, hopcount), corresponding to the delivery of an advertisement, an *advertisement event*. Observe that the unreliability of the networks in conjunction with the persistent broadcasts of the advertisement processes allows many possible sequences of advertisement events. In fact, the network and advertising processes can generate every possible sequence of (src, net, rcv) tuples in advertisement events, subject to the fairness assumption and the fact that src and rcv must both be connected to net. The only advertisement field that depends on the network state is the hopcount.

The third process in the system is the routing process at reach router. The routing process at router rcv reacts to incoming advertisements and updates the routing table entry, (hops(rcv), nextN(rcv), nextR(rcv)), at rcv. Essentially, if an advertisement, (src, hopcount), arriving at rcv through net, is such that hopcount + 1 < hops(rcv) or src = nextR(rcv) $\wedge$ net = nextN(rcv), then the routing table at rcv is updated so that hops(rcv) = hopcount + 1 and nextN(rcv) = net and nextR(rcv) = src. In HOL, we represent this process by a state update function, update : rtable $\rightarrow$ ('router $*$ 'network $*$ 'router $*$ num) $\rightarrow$ rtable, which, given a protocol state, (hops, nextN, nextR), and an advertisement event (src, net, rcv, hopcount), computes the new protocol state. The HOL code for the update function is given for illustration in Appendix A.3.

Trace Semantics The observable behavior of the network and advertising processes is essentially an infinite sequence of advertisement events. Therefore, we choose to express the semantics of these processes as an event trace—an infinite sequence of tuples $(\mathsf{src}_i, \mathsf{net}_i, \mathsf{rcv}_i)$, representing advertisement events. Such a trace is considered *valid* only if

- the trace is fair—$\forall r_1, r_2 : {}'\mathsf{router}.\forall i.\exists j > i.(\mathsf{src}_i = r_1) \land (\mathsf{rcv}_i = r_2)$, and
- the events are possible—$\forall i.(\mathsf{conn}\ \mathsf{src}_i\ \mathsf{net}_i) \land (\mathsf{conn}\ \mathsf{rcv}_i\ \mathsf{net}_i.)$

The hopcount field of the advertisement can be filled in as follows: Suppose that at the ith step (event) of the protocol, the state of the protocol is $s_i = (\mathsf{hops}, \mathsf{nextN}, \mathsf{nextR})$, then

- if $\mathsf{nextN}(\mathsf{src}_i) = \mathsf{net}_i$, then src_i sends an advertisement $(\mathsf{src}_i, 16)$ to rcv_i instantaneously via net_i;
- otherwise, src_i sends an advertisement $(\mathsf{src}_i, \mathsf{hops}(\mathsf{src}_i))$ to rcv_i instantaneously via net_i.

Given an event trace, the routing processes react to the events and update the protocol state. This produces an infinite state sequence of the protocol s_i defined as follows:

- s_0 is any sound state
- $s_{i+1} = \mathsf{update}\ s_i\ (\mathsf{src}_i, \mathsf{net}_i, \mathsf{rcv}_i, \mathsf{hopcount}_i)$, where the hopcount field is filled in as described above.

Thus the semantics of the update processes is the state sequence it can generate for a given event trace. All properties desired of the protocol are expressed and proved in terms of this state sequence. In particular, the convergence theorem states that, given any valid event trace, the states generated in the sequence must converge to the optimal routing table.

3.2   RIP in Promela

Promela [10,17] is a natural specification language for network protocols. In addition to C-like programming constructs, it supports non-determinism, dynamic processes, and synchronous/asynchronous channel communication between processes. We translate the pseudo-code given in Appendices A.1, A.2 into Promela. A fragment of the resulting Promela code corresponding to the routing process is shown in Appendix A.4.

As in the HOL specification, at each router, we have a routing process and an advertisement process. The advertisements process is a simple non-terminating while loop that keeps sending advertisement to all its neighboring networks. The routing process waits for input advertisements and processes them as before. Finally we have a network process for each network, which simply implements the broadcast mechanism by taking advertisements sent to the network and transporting them to the input buffers of all the routers connected to it. It is only the network processes that know the topology of the network, the routing and advertisement processes only know the networks they are directly connected to.

Once all the above Promela processes are in place, we use SPIN to simulate the protocol for sample topologies to check our model. We can also verify that the protocol works for small topologies. A point worth noting is that in varying the topologies, all we need to change is the encoding of the network processes. The routing and advertising processes operate above this connection layer. In effect, the network processes can pretend to have an arbitrary topology and the routing/advertisement processes will not know the difference. We use this property later in our SPIN proofs of convergence, where we fool a solitary update process to believe it is part of a larger network.

4   Convergence of RIP

In this section we present a proof of convergence for RIP. We prove that, in the absence of topology changes, RIP will find shortest routes to the destination d, from every router inside the range of 15 hops.

4.1   Proof Results

On the outermost level, our proof uses induction on distance from the destination. For each router r, *distance* to d is defined as

$$D(r) = \begin{cases} 1, & \text{if } (\text{conn } r\ d) \\ 1 + \min\{D(s) \mid s \text{ neighbor of } r\}, & \text{otherwise.} \end{cases}$$

For $k \geq 1$, the k-*circle* around d is the set of routers

$$C_k = \{r \mid D(r) \leq k\}.$$

The key notion in our proof is that of the k-stability:

Definition 2 (Stability). *For $k \geq 1$, we say that the universe is k-stable if both of the following properties hold:*

(S1) *Every router from the k-circle has its metric set to the actual distance to d. Moreover, if r is not connected to d, it has its nextR set to the first router on some shortest path to d:*

$$\forall r.\ r \in C_k \ \Rightarrow\ \mathsf{hops}(r) = D(r)\ \wedge\ (\neg \mathsf{conn}\ r\ d\ \Rightarrow\ D(\mathsf{nextR}(r)) = D(r) - 1)$$

(S2) *Every router outside the k-circle has its hops strictly greater than k:*

$$\forall r.\ r \notin C_k \ \Rightarrow\ \mathsf{hops}(r) > k.$$

Our goal is to prove that under any fair advertisement trace, the universe is guaranteed to become k-stable, for every $k < 16$. This proof will be carried out by induction on k.

Recall our stipulation that the universe starts in a sound state. It is easy to show that sound states are 1-stable, so this gives us the basis of induction:

Lemma 1. *The universe $\mathcal{U}$ is initially 1-stable.*   □

A key property of k-stability is that once it is achieved, it is preserved forever.This would not be true if our definition of stability did not contain condition S2. This condition strengthens the induction hypothesis enough that we can induct on k-stability.

Lemma 2 (Preservation of stability). *For any $k < 16$, if the universe $\mathcal{U}$ is k-stable at some point, then it remains k-stable after an arbitrary number of advertisements.*   □

Lemma 1 is easily proved in HOL using the definition of soundness. We also prove Lemma 2 in HOL, and it involves a significantly larger case analysis.

Progress from k-stability to $(k + 1)$-stability happens gradually—more and more routers start to conform to the conditions S1 and S2. This is why we need an additional, more refined, definition of stability which captures individual routers, rather than entire 'circles' of routers.

Definition 3. *Given a k-stable universe, we say that a router r at distance $k+1$ from d is $(k + 1)$-stable if it has an optimal route:*

$$\mathsf{hops}(r) = D(r) = k + 1 \quad \wedge \quad \mathsf{nextR}(r) \in C_k.$$

To prove that a k-stable universe eventually becomes $(k+1)$-stable, it suffices to show that *every router* at distance $(k + 1)$ eventually becomes $(k + 1)$-stable. This is the statement of the following lemma:

Lemma 3. *For any $k < 15$, and any router r such that $D(r) = k + 1$, if the universe $\mathcal{U}$ is k-stable at some point and the advertisement trace is fair, then r will eventually become $(k + 1)$-stable. Moreover, r then remains $(k + 1)$-stable indefinitely.*   □

One of the key facts used in the proof of this lemma is fairness of the advertisement trace. Without fairness, neighbors of r would be allowed to simply stop advertising to r at any point. This would keep r's routing table unchanged and hence prevent it from ever achieving $(k + 1)$-stability.

Observe that Lemma 3 only involves one router r at a distance $k + 1$ from d. Starting from a k-stable state, we need to show that r converges to the correct value. Moreover, since all future states of the system are guaranteed to be k-stable (Lemma 2), r will receive advertisements from only two kinds of neighbors—those within the k-circle, and those outside it. This leads us to a finitary abstraction of the system. We can then prove the lemma using SPIN, which performs an exhaustive state search to prove that r will converge to the right value.

However, we need to prove that the finitary abstraction is property-preserving. This proof is done in HOL, by induction on the length of fair advertisement traces. The abstraction proof is the crucial link that allows us to join the HOL and SPIN results, without loss of rigor. The abstraction proof itself is rather complex with a large case analysis. However, the effort is justified since the finitary abstraction can then be used for multiple proofs with minor modifications. This re-use can be seen in the proof statistics in Section 6 (Table 1). The abstraction proof is represented in the table as the HOL portion of the second proof of Stability Preservation (Lemma 2).

Finally, using the fact that there are only finitely many routers, we easily derive the Progress Lemma which proves our inductive step:

Lemma 4 (Progress). *For any $k < 15$, if the universe $\mathcal{U}$ is k-stable at some point, then $\mathcal{U}$ will eventually become and remain $(k + 1)$-stable indefinitely.*   □

The main result about the convergence of RIP is a corollary of the above inductive argument:

Theorem 1 (Convergence of RIP). *Starting from an arbitrary sound initial state, evolving under an arbitrary fair advertisement trace, the universe $\mathcal{U}$ eventually becomes and remains 15-stable.*   □

4.2 Significance of the Results

Our proof, which we call the *radius proof,* differs from the one described in [1] for the asynchronous Bellman-Ford algorithm. Rather than inducting on estimates for upper and lower bounds for distances, we induct on the the radius of the stable region around d. The proof has three attributes of interest:

1. *It states a property about the RIP protocol, rather the asynchronous distributed Bellman-Ford algorithm.*
2. *The radius proof is more informative.* It shows that correctness is achieved quickly close to the destination, and more slowly further away. It also implicitly estimates the number of advertisements needed to progress from k-stability to $(k + 1)$-stability. We exploit this in the next section to show a realtime bound on convergence.
3. *It uses a combination of theorem proving and model checking.* HOL is more expressive and serves as the main platform. SPIN is used to treat large case analyses.

5   Sharp Timing Bounds for RIP Stability

In the previous section we proved convergence for RIP conditioned on the fact that the topology stays unchanged for some period of time. We now calculate how big that period of time must be. To do this, we need to have some knowledge about the times at which certain protocol events happen. In the case of RIP, we use a single reliability assumption that describes the frequency of advertisements.

Fundamental Timing Assumption: There is a value Δ, such that during every topology-stable time interval of the length Δ, each router gets at least one advertisement from each of its neighbors.   □

RIP routers normally try to advertise every 30 seconds. However, because of congestion or some other condition, some packets may not go through. This is why the standard prescribes that a failure to receive an advertisement within 180 seconds is treated as a link failure. Thus, $\Delta = 180$ seconds satisfies the Fundamental Timing Assumption for RIP. Notice that the assumption implies fairness of the advertisement trace.

As before, we concentrate on a particular destination d. Our timing analysis is based on the notion of weak k-stability.

Definition 4 (Weak stability). *For $2 \leq k \leq 15$, we say that the universe $\mathcal{U}$ is weakly k-stable if all of the following conditions hold:*

(WS1) $\mathcal{U}$ *is $(k-1)$-stable.*
(WS2) $\forall r.\ D(r) = k \implies (r$ *is k−stable* $\vee$ $\mathsf{hops}(r) > k)$.
(WS3) $\forall r.\ D(r) > k \implies \mathsf{hops}(r) > k$.

Weak k-stability is stronger than $(k-1)$-stability, but weaker than k-stability. The second disjunct in WS2 is what distinguishes it from the ordinary k-stability. Similarly as before, we have the preservation lemma:

Lemma 5 (Preservation of weak stability). *For any $2 \leq k \leq 15$, if the universe $\mathcal{U}$ is weakly k-stable at some time t, then it is weakly k-stable at any time $t' \geq t$.* $\qquad\square$

This lemma and all of the subsequent results in this section are stated using real time. This is possible because of the Fundamental Timing Assumption, which provides a connection between discrete advertisement events and continuous time. Precisely, to show that some property P holds after a Δ time interval, it is enough to prove that P holds after each router receives at least one advertisement from each of its neighbors.

Now we show that the initial state inevitably becomes weakly 2-stable after RIP packets have been exchanged between every pair of neighbors:

Lemma 6 (Initial progress). *If the universe $\mathcal{U}$ is in a sound state and the topology does not change, $\mathcal{U}$ becomes weakly 2-stable after Δ time.* $\qquad\square$

The main progress property says that it takes one Δ-interval to get from a weakly k-stable state to a weakly $(k+1)$-stable state. This property is shown in two steps. First we show that condition WS1 for weak $(k+1)$-stability holds after Δ:

Lemma 7. *For any $2 \leq k \leq 15$, if the universe is weakly k-stable at some time t, then it is k-stable at time $t + \Delta$.* $\qquad\square$

Then we show the same for conditions WS2 and WS3. The following puts both steps together:

Lemma 8 (Progress). *For any $2 \leq k < 15$, if the universe is weakly k-stable at some time t, then it is weakly $(k+1)$-stable at time $t + \Delta$.* $\qquad\square$

Lemmas 5, 6, and 8 are proved in SPIN (Lemma 7 is contained in Lemma 8). The technique for doing the proofs in SPIN is the same as in the previous section. We find a finitary abstraction of the system starting from the time when the universe if weakly k-stable. This abstraction allows us to prove the Lemmas in SPIN for a single router.

The *radius* of the universe (around d) is the maximum distance from d:

$$R = max\{D(r) \mid r \text{ is a router}\}.$$

The main theorem describes convergence time for a destination in terms of its radius:

Theorem 2 (RIP convergence time). *A sound universe of radius R becomes 15-stable within $max\{15, R\} \cdot \Delta$ time, assuming that there were no topology changes during that time interval.*   □

The theorem is an easy corollary of the preceding lemmas and is proved in HOL. Consider a universe of radius $R \leq 15$. To show that it converges in $R \cdot \Delta$ time, observe what happens during each Δ-interval of time:

after Δ	weakly 2-stable	(by Lemma 6)
after $2 \cdot \Delta$	weakly 3-stable	(by Lemma 8)
after $3 \cdot \Delta$	weakly 4-stable	(by Lemma 8)
. . .	. . .	. . .
after $(R-1) \cdot \Delta$	weakly R-stable	(by Lemma 8)
after $R \cdot \Delta$	R-stable	(by Lemma 7)

R-stability means that all the routers that are not more than R hops away from d will have shortest routes to d. Since the radius of the universe is R, this includes *all* routers.

An interesting observation is that progress from k-stability to $(k+1)$-stability is not guaranteed to happen in less than $2 \cdot \Delta$ time (we leave this to the reader). Consequently, had we chosen to calculate convergence time using stability, rather than weak stability, we would get a worse upper bound of $2 \cdot (R-1) \cdot \Delta$. In fact, our upper bound is sharp: in a linear topology, update messages can be interleaved in such a way that convergence time becomes as bad as $R \cdot \Delta$.

Figure 2 shows an example that consists of k routers and has the radius k with respect to d. Router r_1 is connected to d and has the correct metric. Router r_2 also has the correct metric, but points in the wrong direction. Other routers have no route to d. In this state, r_2 will ignore a message from r_1, because that route is no better than what r_2 (thinks it) already has. However, after receiving a message from r_3, to which it points, r_2 will update its metric to 16 and lose the route. Suppose that, from this point on, messages are interleaved in such a way that during every update interval, all routers first send their update messages and then receive update messages from their neighbors. This will cause exactly one new router to discover the shortest route during every update interval. Router r_2 will have the route after the second interval, r_3 after the third, ..., and r_k after the k-th. This shows that our upper bound of $k \cdot \Delta$ is sharp.

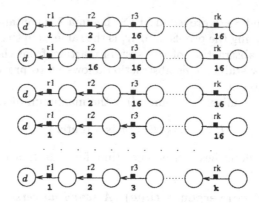

Fig. 2. Maximum Convergence Time

6   Analysis of Methodology

SPIN is extremely helpful for proving properties such as Lemma 8, which involve tedious case analysis. To illustrate this, assuming weak k-stability at time t, consider what it takes to show that condition WS2 for weak $(k + 1)$-stability holds after Δ time. (WS1 will hold because of Lemma 7, but further effort is required for WS3.) To prove WS2, let r be a router with $D(r) = k + 1$. Because of weak k-stability at the time t, there are two possibilities for r: (1) r has a k-stable neighbor, or (2) all of the neighbors of r have hops $> k$. To show that r will eventually progress into either a $(k+1)$-stable state or a state with hops $> k+1$, we need to further break the case (2) into three subcases with respect to the properties of the router that r points to: (2a) r points to $s \in C_k$ (the k-circle), which is the only neighbor of r from C_k, or (2b) r points to $s \in C_k$, but r has another neighbor $t \in C_k$ such that $t \neq s$, or (2c) r points to $s \notin C_k$. Each of these cases, branches into several further subcases based on the relative ordering in which r, s and possibly t send and receive update messages.

Doing such proofs by hand is difficult and prone to errors. Essentially, the proof is a deeply-nested case analysis in which *final* cases are straight-forward to prove—an ideal job for a computer to do! Our SPIN verification is divided into four parts accounting for different kinds of topologies. Each part has a distinguished process representing r and another processes modeling the environment for r. An environment is an abstraction of the 'rest of the universe'. It generates all message sequences that could possibly be observed by r. SPIN considered more cases than a manual proof would have required, 21,804 of them altogether for Lemma 8, but it checked these in only 1.7 seconds of CPU time. Even counting set-up time for this verification, this was a significant time-saver. The resulting proof is probably also more reliable than a manual one.

Table 1 summarizes some of our experience with the complexity of the proofs in terms of our automated support tools. The complexity of an HOL verification for the human verifier is described with the following statistics measuring things

Table 1. Protocol Verification Effort on RIP Convergence

Task	HOL	SPIN
Modeling RIP	495 lines, 19 defs, 20 lemmas	141 lines
Stability Preservation Once	9 lemmas, 119 cases, 903 steps	
Stability Preservation Again	29 lemmas, 102 cases, 565 steps	207 lines, 439 states
Stability Progress	Reuse Stability Preservation	285 lines, 7116 states
Weak Stability Preservation	Reuse Stability Preservation	216 lines, 1019 states
Initial Weak Stability	Reuse Stability Preservation	221 lines, 1139 states
Weak Stability Progress	Reuse Stability Preservation	342 lines, 21804 states

written by a human: the number of *lines* of HOL code, the number of *lemmas* and *definitions*, and the number of proof *steps*. Proof steps were measured as the number of instances of the HOL construct THEN. The HOL automated contribution is measured by the number of *cases* discovered and managed by HOL. This is measured by the number of THENL's, weighted by the number of elements in their argument lists. The complexity of SPIN verification for the human verifier is measured by the number of *lines* of Promela code written. The SPIN automated contribution is measured by the number of *states* examined and the amount of *memory* used in the verification. In our investigations we have found that SPIN is generally memory bound, that is, it runs out of memory in a relatively short period of time if the state space it must search is too large. For our final RIP proofs, however, each of the verifications took less than a minute and the time is generally proportional to the memory. Most of the lemmas consumed the SPIN-minimum of 2.54MB of memory, some required more. The figures were collected for runs on a lightly-loaded Sun Ultra Enterprise with 1016MB of memory and 4 CPU's running SunOS 5.5.1. The tool versions used were HOL90.10 and SPIN-3.24. We carried out parallel proofs of Lemma 2, the Stability Preservation Lemma, using HOL only and HOL together with SPIN.

It is important to observe that the SPIN figures were derived from *final* runs. The typical process was as follows: attempt to prove a result with SPIN, find that it is too costly, apply an abstraction that was proved in HOL, and try the SPIN proof again on the abstracted problem (which presumably has a smaller set of cases to check). This was repeated until we were happy with the size of the SPIN state space and the clarity of the abstractions. This use of SPIN was worthwhile even if the proof was eventually carried out entirely in HOL since SPIN provided a quick way to 'debug' our lemmas. We experimented with the question of whether to stop with a mixed HOL/SPIN proof or complete the entire proof in HOL. A proof entirely in HOL arguably provides more confidence since the relationship between the HOL and SPIN parts of a proof are treated manually in our study. We proved stability preservation twice, once using HOL/SPIN and again using only HOL. Table 1 indicates some associated statistics showing that the complexity of the HOL proof dropped by about 40% at the cost of writing

207 lines of SPIN code. In future work we may attempt to measure programmer months since this would provide a more complete indication of scalability.

7   Related Work

Combining model checking with theorem proving has long been recognized as a very promising direction in effective formal methods [2]. There are primarily two ways in which the methodologies can be combined. Systems like PVS [16] use model checking as a decision procedure to solve finitary sub-goals in a deductive proof. On the other hand, model checking can be used to prove a finitary abstraction of a system where the soundness of the abstraction can be proved in a theorem prover [13,14]. We use the latter methodology for our proofs—we carry out our induction and abstraction proofs in HOL90, while the induction step is proved for a finitary abstraction of the system in SPIN.

In recent years, a variety of protocol standards have been formally verified. Notable success has been achieved in verifying cache coherence protocols, bus protocols and endpoint communication protocols [2]. In the domain of routing protocols, there has been work on verifying ATM routing protocols [3], where the authors use SPIN to verify the absence of deadlock of the routing protocol for a few fixed configurations. An instance verification of an Active Network routing protocol has been carried out in Maude [18]. Formal testing support has been developed for multicast routing protocols [7]. Other work has been in the form of manual proofs of key safety properties [6,15,4,1].

8   Conclusion

This paper provides the most extensive automated mathematical analysis of an internet routing protocol to date. Our results show that it is possible to provide formal analysis of correctness for routing protocols from IETF standards and drafts with reasonable effort and speed, thus demonstrating that these technique can effectively supplement other means of improving assurance such as manual proof, simulation, and testing. Specific technical contributions include the f t proofs of the convergence of the RIP standard, and a sharp realtime bound for this convergence. We have also gained insight into strategies for combining a higher-order theorem prover such as HOL with a model checker such as SPIN in a unified methodology that leverages the expressiveness of the theorem prover and the high level of automation of the model checker to provide an efficient but high-confidence analysis.

Acknowledgments

We would like to thank the following people for their assistance and encouragement: Roch Guerin, Elsa L. Gunter, Luke Hornof, Sampath Kannan, and Insup Lee. This research was supported by NSF Contract CCR-9505469, DARPA Contract F30602-98-2-0198, and ARO Contract DAAG-98-1-0466.

References

1. Dimitri P. Bertsekas and Robert Gallager. *Data Networks*. Prentice Hall, 1991.
2. Edmund M. Clarke and Jeannette M. Wing. Formal Methods: State of the Art and Future Directions. *ACM Computing Surveys*, 28(4):626–643, December 1996. report by the Working Group on Formal Methods for the ACM Workshop on Strategic Directions in Computing Research.
3. D. Cypher, D. Lee, M. Martin-Villalba, C. Prins, and D. Su. Formal Specification, Verification, and Automatic Test Generation of ATM Routing Protocol: PNNI. In *Formal Description Techniques & Protocol Specification, Testing, and Verification (FORTE/PSTV) IFIP*, November 1998.
4. J.J. Garcia-Luna-Aceves and Shree Murthy. A Loop-Free Path-Finding Algorithm: Specification, Verification and Complexity. In *Proceedings of IEEE INFOCOM '95*, April 1995.
5. M. J. C. Gordon and T. F. Melham, editors. *Introduction to HOL: A theorem proving environment for higher order logic*. Cambridge University Press, 1993.
6. Timothy G. Griffin and Gordon Wilfong. An analysis of BGP convergence properties. In Guru Parulkar and Jonathan S. Turner, editors, *Proceedings of ACM SIGCOMM '99 Conference*, pages 277–288, Boston, August 1999.
7. Ahmed Helmy, Deborah Estrin, and Sandep Gupta. Fault-oriented Test Generation for Multicast Routing Protocol Design. In *Formal Description Techniques & Protocol Specification, Testing, and Verification (FORTE/PSTV) IFIP*, November 1998.
8. C. Hendrick. Routing information protocol. RFC 1058, IETF, June 1988.
9. Home page for the HOL interactive theorem proving system. http://www.cl.cam.ac.uk/Research/HVG/HOL.
10. Gerard J. Holzmann. *Design and Validation of Computer Protocols*. Prentice Hall, 1991.
11. Christian Huitema. *Routing in the Internet*. Prentice Hall, 1995.
12. G. Malkin. *RIP Version 2 Carrying Additional Information*. IETF RFC 1388, January 1993.
13. Abdel Mokkedem, Ravi Hosabettu, Michael D. Jones, and Ganesh Gopalakrishnan. Formalization and Analysis of a Solution to the PCI 2.1 Bus Transaction Ordering Problem. *Formal Methods in System Design*, 16(1):93–119, January 2000.
14. Olaf Müller and Tobias Nipkow. Combining model checking and deduction for i/o-automata. In *Proceedings of the Workshop on Tools and Algorithms for the Construction and Analysis of Systems*, May 1995.
15. Shree Murthy and J.J. Garcia-Luna-Aceves. An efficient routing protocol for wireless networks. *ACM Mobile Netowrks and Applications Journal*, October 1996. Special Issue on Routing in Mobile Communication Networks.
16. N. Shankar. PVS: Combining specification, proof checking, and model checking. In Mandayam Srivas and Albert Camilleri, editors, *Formal Methods in Computer-Aided Design (FMCAD '96)*, volume 1166 of *Lecture Notes in Computer Science*, pages 257–264, Palo Alto, CA, November 1996. Springer-Verlag.
17. Home page for the SPIN model checker. http://netlib.bell-labs.com/netlib/spin/whatispin.html.
18. Bow-Yaw Wang, José Meseguer, and Carl A. Gunter. Specification and formal verification of a PLAN algorithm in Maude. In *Proceedings of the International workshop on Distributed System Valdiation and Verification*, pages E:49–E:56. IEEE Computer Society Press, April 2000.

A   Code Samples

A.1   Pseudocode for RIP Declarations

process RIPRouter
state:

me	// ID of the router
interfaces	// Set of router's interfaces
known	// Set of destinations with known routes
$hops_{dest}$	// Distance estimate
$nextR_{dest}$	// Next router on the way to *dest*
$nextIface_{dest}$	// Interface over which the route advertisement was received
timer $expire_{dest}$	// Expiration timer for the route
timer $garbageCollect_{dest}$	// Garbage collection timer for the route
timer *advertise*	// Timer for periodic advertisements

events:
    receive RIP (router, dest, hopCnt) over iface
    timeout ($expire_{dest}$)
    timeout ($garbageCollect_{dest}$)
    timeout (advertise)

utility functions:
    broadcast(*msg, iface*)
    { Broadcast message *msg* to all the routers attached to the network on the other side
    of interface *iface*.
    }

A.2   Pseudocode for RIP Event Handlers

event handlers:
    receive RIP (router, dest, hopCnt) over iface

```
{
   newMetric ← min (1 + hopCnt, 16)
   if (dest ∉ known) then
   {
     if (newMetric < 16)
     {
       hops_dest ← newMetric
       nextR_dest ← router
       nextIface_dest ← iface
       set expire_dest to 180 seconds
       known ← known ∪ {dest}
     }
   } else
   { if (router = nextR_dest) or (newMetric < hops_dest)
     {
       hops_dest ← newMetric
       nextR_dest ← router
       nextIface_dest ← iface
       set expire_dest to 180 seconds
       if (newMetric = 16) then
       {
         set garbageCollect_dest to 120 seconds
       } else
       {
         deactivate garbageCollect_dest
} } } }
```

timeout ($expire_{dest}$)
```
{ hops_dest ← 16
  set garbageCollect_dest to 120 seconds
}
```

timeout ($garbageCollect_{dest}$)

```
{ known ← known − {dest}
}

timeout (advertise)
{
  for each dest ∈ known do
    for each i ∈ interfaces do
    {
      if (i = nextIface_dest) then
      {
        broadcast ([RIP(me, dest, hops_dest)], i)
      } else
      {
        broadcast ([RIP(me, dest, 16)], i)        // Split horizon with poisoned reverse
      }
    }
    set advertise to 30 seconds
}
```

A.3   HOL Code for Update Function

```
val update_DEF = new_definition
  ("update",
  --'!(src:'router) (net:'network) (rcv:'router) (hopcount:num)
    (hops:'router->num) (nextN:'router->'network) (nextR:'router->'router).
      update (hops,nextN,nextR) (src,net,rcv,hopcount) =
      let (nh,nn,nr) =
        (((nextR(rcv)=src) /\ (nextN(rcv)=net))  =>
                      (SUC hopcount,net,src)
                 | (((SUC hopcount) < hops(rcv)) =>
                                  (SUC hopcount,net,src)
                           | (hops(rcv),nextN(rcv),nextR(rcv))))
        in ((\r:'router.(r=rcv)=> nh | (hops(r))),
            (\r:'router.(r=rcv)=> nn | (nextN(r))),
            (\r:'router.(r=rcv)=> nr | (nextR(r))))'--);
```

A.4   Promela fragment for Routing Process

```
proctype Update(router ME){
        mesg adv;
        chan in = routerinput[ME];

        do
        :: atomic{in?adv ->
                  if
                  :: (adv.src == rtable[ME].nextR) &&
                     (adv.net == rtable[ME].nextN) ->
                          if
                          :: adv.hopcount >= INFINITY ->
                                  rtable[ME].hops = INFINITY
                          :: adv.hopcount < INFINITY ->
                                  rtable[ME].hops = adv.hopcount + 1
                          fi
                  :: adv.hopcount + 1 < rtable[ME].hops ->
                          rtable[ME].nextR = adv.src;
                          rtable[ME].nextN = adv.net;
                          rtable[ME].hops = adv.hopcount + 1
                  :: else -> skip
                  fi}
        od
}
```

Recursive Families of Inductive Types

Venanzio Capretta

Computing Science Institute, University of Nijmegen
Postbus 9010, 6500 GL Nijmegen, The Netherlands
venanzio@cs.kun.nl
telephone: +31+24+3652647, fax: +31+24+3553450

Abstract. Families of inductive types defined by recursion arise in the
formalization of mathematical theories. An example is the family of term
algebras on the type of signatures. Type theory does not allow the direct
definition of such families. We state the problem abstractly by defining
a notion, *strong positivity*, that characterizes these families. Then we investigate its solutions. First, we construct a model using wellorderings.
Second, we use an extension of type theory, implemented in the proof
tool Coq, to construct another model that does not have extensionality
problems. Finally, we apply the two level approach: We internalize inductive definitions, so that we can manipulate them and reason about
them inside type theory.

1 Introduction

In type theory we can define a new inductive type by giving its constructors (or
introduction rules). For example, we define the types of natural numbers, binary
trees, and lists over a type A as

$$\mathbb{N}: \quad \frac{}{0: \mathbb{N}} \quad \frac{n: \mathbb{N}}{(S\, n): \mathbb{N}}, \qquad \mathbb{T}: \quad \frac{}{\text{leaf}: \mathbb{T}} \quad \frac{x_1: \mathbb{T} \quad x_2: \mathbb{T}}{\text{node}(x_1, x_2): \mathbb{T}}, \quad \text{and}$$

$$\text{List}(A): \quad \frac{}{\text{nil}_A: \mathbb{N}} \quad \frac{a: A \quad l: \text{List}(A)}{\text{cons}_A(a, l): \text{List}(A)},$$

respectively.

Consider the family $T: \mathbb{N} \to *$ ($*$ indicates the type of all small types, or
sets) of inductive types indexed on the natural numbers:

$$T_0: \quad \frac{}{c_0: T_0}$$

$$T_1: \quad \frac{}{c_1: T_1} \quad \frac{x: T_1}{c_0(x): T_1}$$

$$T_2: \quad \frac{}{c_2: T_2} \quad \frac{x: T_2}{c_1(x): T_2} \quad \frac{x_1: T_2 \quad x_2: T_2}{c_0(x_1, x_2): T_2} \tag{1}$$

$$\vdots$$

J. Harrison and M. Aagaard (Eds.): TPHOLs 2000, LNCS 1869, pp. 73–89, 2000.
© Springer-Verlag Berlin Heidelberg 2000

Every new type in the family is defined by a new constant and by the constructors of the previous type in the hierarchy with an extra recursive argument. Intuitively T_n is the type of trees with branching degree at most n. In the standard formulation of inductive types this definition is not allowed: The constructors and their types must be given directly at the moment of definition of the inductive type, whereas the number of constructors of T_n and their types are defined by recursion on n.

Families of this kind have not only theoretical interest. They arise in the course of formalization of mathematics in a proof tool. I first encountered them when I was working on the formalization of Universal Algebra in Coq (see [6] and [7]). The family of term algebras on the type of signatures is one of them. The type of single-sorted signatures is $\mathsf{Sig} := \mathsf{List}(\mathbb{N})$. Given a signature $\sigma := [a_1, \ldots, a_n]$, the type of terms over σ is defined by

$$\mathsf{Term}_\sigma: \quad \frac{t_{11}: \mathsf{Term}_\sigma \ \cdots \ t_{1a_1}: \mathsf{Term}_\sigma}{(\mathsf{f}_1 \ t_{11} \cdots t_{1a_1}): \mathsf{Term}_\sigma} \ \cdots \ \frac{t_{n1}: \mathsf{Term}_\sigma \ \cdots \ t_{na_n}: \mathsf{Term}_\sigma}{(\mathsf{f}_n \ t_{n1} \cdots t_{na_n}): \mathsf{Term}_\sigma}.$$

(One of the a_i's must be 0, so that Term_σ is nonempty.) We cannot obtain the family $\mathsf{Term}: \mathsf{Sig} \to *$ directly with an inductive definition, because the number and arity of the constructors depend on the signature σ: They are not fixed for the whole family. The situation is even more complicated when we consider many-sorted signatures, which require families of mutual inductive types. In [6] we used Martin-Löf's W types to solve this instance of the problem. Here we formulate the general problem, we show that W types still provide a good model, but also propose a better solution (which, however, requires an extension of type theory). You can see the details of its application to many-sorted algebras in [7].

In Section 3 we formulate the general problem: We propose an extension of the notion of strictly positive operator, which is used to determine the admissibility of inductive definitions, using *positive type pointers*—that is, terms that specify the positive occurrence of parameters in recursive definitions.

In Section 4 we represent inductive types using Martin-Löf's type constructor for wellorderings (W types) (see [14,15] and chapter 15 of [18]), extending the work by Dybjer [10]. This solution has the disadvantage that structurally equal elements of a W-type are not always convertible, thus making the W-type representation only *extensionally* isomorphic to the desired inductive type.

Alternatively, we can exploit the extension of the positivity condition implemented in the system Coq and described by Gimenez in [12]. It allows an inductive definition to inherit a positive occurrence of a type variable from another inductive definition. To use this construction in our case, we need to give a translation of our recursive family of operators into an inductive family. In Section 5 we give such translation and we use it to solve our problem.

Finally, in Section 6 we use the two level approach (see [4], [5], [13] and [3]): Positivity is a metapredicate; that is, it is not expressed inside type theory but is an external syntactic property of type operators. This means that we cannot reason about positive operators and inductive definitions inside type theory. We internalize it by defining a type-theoretic predicate $\mathsf{Positive}$ expressing the metaproperty. We define also a type of codes for inductive types and associate a code to every proof of an instance of the predicate Positive. We define a function that associates a type to every code. Now we solve our problem by first, constructing a family of positive operators by recursion; second, proving their positivity inside type theory; third, obtaining the corresponding family of codes; finally, instantiating the codes to types. This last method has been completely formalized in the proof assistant Coq [2].

2   Inductive Types

We work in a type theory that is at least as expressive as the Pure Type System $\lambda P\bar{\omega}$ (see [1]): There are two sorts of types, $*$ for small types and $\square$ for large types. Sort $*$ is an element of $\square$. Moreover, we have sum and Σ types, which can be considered as special cases of inductive types, which we define later in this section. In $\lambda P\bar{\omega}$ every small type $T: *$ has an isomorphic version in $\square$. For simplicity we identify the two; in other words, we consider $*$ and $\square$ as the first two steps in a cumulative hierarchy of type universes. When we write type expressions that mix the two sorts, as $T \times *$ or $T + *$, the version of T in $\square$ is used. Note, however, that if $*$ is impredicative (for example, if we work in the Calculus of Constructions) not all elements of $*$ can have a representation in $\square$, because this would lead to Girard's paradox (see [8]). Only if impredicativity was not used in the definition of the type, we can consider it as an element of $\square$. When we use small types in $\square$ constructions we assume that this condition is satisfied without saying it (as supported by the Coq implementation).

We use the notation $t[x]$ to denote a term t in which a variable x may occur. Thus t and $t[x]$ denote the same term, but in the second expression we stress the dependence on x. Do not confuse this notation with $(f\ x)$, which denotes the application of a function f to x. If s is a term of the same type as x, $t[s]$ denotes the result of the substitution $t[x := s]$.

In *extensional* type theory inductive types can be implemented as fixed points of type operators (see [17]). We are working in *intensional* type theory, in which inductive types are recursively defined by constructors. Following [9], [19], [21] and [23] an inductive type I is defined by a list of constructors:

$$
\begin{aligned}
&\text{inductive } I\ [\overrightarrow{X : S}] : (z_1 : Q_1) \cdots (z_n : Q_n) * := \\
&\quad c_1\ :\ (x_1 : P_{11}) \cdots (x_{k_1} : P_{1k_1})(I\ M_{11} \cdots M_{1m}) \\
&\quad \vdots \\
&\quad c_n\ :\ (x_1 : P_{n1}) \cdots (x_{k_1} : P_{nk_1})(I\ M_{n1} \cdots M_{nm}) \\
&\text{end,}
\end{aligned}
\tag{2}
$$

where I does not occur in the Ss, Qs and Ms and occurs only strictly positively in the Ps. $\overrightarrow{X}$ is a list of general parameters of I (such as the parameter X in $\text{List}(X)$). See one of the cited references or chapter 4 of the Coq manual [2] for the definition of strict positivity and for the other rules.

If the types of the constructors do not use dependent product—that is, they are in the form $P_{i1} \to \cdots \to P_{ik_i} \to I$—we can use the alternative formulation of inductive types as fixed points of strictly positive type operators (see, for example, [10]). It is less intuitive but simpler for theoretical purposes, so we adopt it. Every strictly positive operator $X: * \vdash \Phi[X]: *$ has a functorial extension, which, for $X, Y: *$, maps every $f: X \to Y$ to a function $\Phi[f]: \Phi[X] \to \Phi[Y]$; preserving identities and composition (see [9] and [20]). This condition is sufficient to formulate the rules for inductive types (Matthes [16] gives an extension of *system F* in which this is the only condition required for inductive types). In the next sections we consider extensions of the positivity condition that still have the functorial property. The rules for inductive types are then the same as in the following definition, with the corresponding property replacing *strictly positive*.

Definition 1. Let $X: * \vdash \Phi[X]: *$ be a strictly positive operator. The inductive type $\mu_X(\Phi)$ is defined by the following rules (where we write I for $\mu_X(\Phi)$):

formation $I: *$

introduction $\dfrac{y: \Phi[I]}{(\mu\text{-intro } y): I}$

elimination $\dfrac{x: I \vdash (P\ x): * \qquad z: \Phi[(\Sigma\ I\ P)] \vdash u: (P\ (\mu\text{-intro } (\Phi[\pi_1]\ z)))}{(\mu\text{-ind } [z]u): (x: I)(P\ x)}$

conversion $(\mu\text{-ind } [z]u\ (\mu\text{-intro } y)) \rightsquigarrow u[(\Phi[[x]\langle x, (\mu\text{-ind } [z]u\ x)\rangle]\ y)]$

We use this formulation to define our inductive types, since they are all non-dependent, but we use the notation of Formula 2 when it is intuitively clearer and when we need to define types whose constructors belong to dependent product types.

If the elimination predicate P is a constant type T, we obtain the recursion principle; if, furthermore, the recursion term u does not depend on the induction arguments, we obtain the iteration principle:

$$\frac{T: * \quad z: \Phi[I \times T] \vdash u: T}{(\mu\text{-rec } [z]u): I \to T} \quad \text{and} \quad \frac{T: * \quad z: \Phi[T] \vdash u: T}{(\mu\text{-it } [z]u): I \to T}.$$

It is well known that the recursion and iteration principles are equivalent, whereas the full induction principle is a proper extension of them (see, for example, [11] or [20]).

The types of natural numbers, binary trees, and lists over a type A can be defined as $\mathbb{N} := \mu_X(\mathbb{N}_1 + X)$, where $\mathbb{N}_1$ is the type with only one element 0_1; $\mathbb{T} := \mu_X(\mathbb{N}_1 + X \times X)$; and $\mathsf{List}(A) := \mathbb{N}_1 + A \times X$, respectively. Their constructors can be defined in terms of the single constructor $\mu\text{-intro}$:

$$0 := (\mu\text{-intro } (\mathsf{inl}\ 0_1)), \qquad S := [n](\mu\text{-intro } (\mathsf{inr}\ n));$$
$$\mathsf{leaf} := (\mu\text{-intro } (\mathsf{inl}\ 0_1)), \quad \mathsf{node} := [x_1, x_2](\mu\text{-intro } (\mathsf{inr}\ \langle x_1, x_2 \rangle));$$
$$\mathsf{nil} := (\mu\text{-intro } (\mathsf{inl}\ 0_1)), \quad \mathsf{cons} := [a, l](\mu\text{-intro } (\mathsf{inr}\ \langle a, l \rangle)).$$

The problem that we consider here is: Given a family of type operators $\Phi: A \to (* \to *)$ such that every element of it is strictly positive, can we construct the corresponding family of inductive types? Observe that it is not possible to characterize such families in a decidable way. In fact, for every function $f : \mathbb{N} \to \mathbb{N}$ we can associate such a family:

$$\Phi: \mathbb{N} \to (* \to *)$$
$$(\Phi \, n \, X) = \begin{cases} X & \text{if } (f \, n) = 0 \\ X \to X & \text{otherwise.} \end{cases}$$

Deciding whether every element of this family is strictly positive is equivalent to deciding whether f is constantly 0. Since, in type theory, every primitive recursive function on the natural numbers is definable, we would be able to decide whether any such function is constantly 0, which is notoriously impossible.

The following section gives a decidable characterization of some of these families, which is wide enough for the examples that we are considering.

3   Families of Inductive Types Defined by Strong Elimination

Strong elimination is the elimination rule for inductive types in which the elimination predicate is allowed to be *big*; that is, we can have an elimination predicate $x: I \vdash (P \, x): \square$. If $*$ is impredicative, strong elimination results in inconsistency (see [8]). Nevertheless, it can still be admitted if the inductive type I is defined without the use of impredicativity—that is, as already mentioned, if there is a type in $\square$ isomorphic to it. In such a case we allow strong elimination. This form of strong elimination is supported in Coq. We use strong elimination only in the form of iteration over the type $*$:

$$\frac{Z: \Phi[*] \vdash W[Z]: *}{(\mu\text{-it } [Z]W): I \to *}.$$

We recast Example 1 as

$$X: * \vdash \Psi[X]: \mathbb{N} \to *$$
$$\Psi_0 \quad := \mathbb{N}_1$$
$$\Psi_{(S \, n)} := \mathbb{N}_1 + X \times \Psi_n.$$

To be completely formal, we must write

$$X: *, Z: \mathbb{N}_1 + * \vdash W[X, Z]: *$$
$$:= \text{Case } Z \text{ of}$$
$$(\text{inl } \_) \Rightarrow \mathbb{N}_1$$
$$(\text{inr } R) \Rightarrow \mathbb{N}_1 + X \times R$$
$$\text{end}$$
$$\overline{X: * \vdash \Psi[X] := (\mu\text{-it } [Z]W): \mathbb{N} \to *} \tag{3}$$

The desired family of inductive types is now specified by $T_n := \mu_X(\Psi_n)$. Unfortunately, this is not an allowed definition, since Ψ does not satisfy the strict-positivity condition: Although Ψ_n reduces to a strictly positive operator for each numeral n, Ψ_x does not if $x \colon \mathbb{N}$ is a variable. Therefore, we cannot define the family $T \colon \mathbb{N} \to *$, even if every member of it is individually definable.

The case of term algebras over single-sorted signatures is similar. The operator associated to a signature $\sigma := [a_1, \ldots, a_n]$ is $\Psi_\sigma[X] := X^{a_1} + \cdots + X^{a_n}$. We can define first a single component $(n \colon \mathbb{N}, X \colon * \vdash X^n \colon *)$ by strong elimination on the natural numbers and then Ψ_σ by strong elimination on $\mathsf{List}(\mathbb{N})$. The type of terms associated with the signature σ is then $\mathsf{Term}_\sigma := \mu_X(\Psi_\sigma)$. As in the previous example this definition is not allowed in the standard implementation of inductive types, because Ψ_σ does not satisfy the strict-positivity condition.

Our purpose is to find ways to define families of inductive types in type theory. The first step is a formal description of the problem—that is, an abstract characterization of the definitions we are looking for. If we consider the first of the preceding examples, we see that the reason why every single element of the family is strictly positive is that, in the recursive step of the definition, not only the type parameter X but the recursive call Ψ_n (or R in the formalized version) also occurs only strictly positively. It is enough to require that all such recursive calls occur strictly positively. Note, however, that, in the formal version of the definition, the recursive call is Z, not R, which is just a bound variable in the Case construction. It doesn't mean anything to say that Z occurs positively and the variable R does not actually occur in W (being bound). So we need a finer notion than strict positivity. The following concept of *positive type pointer* solves the problem. To understand it intuitively, consider a generic premise for a definition by strong elimination $(X \colon *, Z \colon \Theta[*] \vdash U[X, Z] \colon *)$ where Θ is a strictly positive operator. We want to define first the family of type operators $X \colon * \vdash \Psi[X] := (\mu\text{-it }[Z]U) \colon \mu_Y(\Theta[Y]) \to *$ and then the family of inductive types $x \colon \mu_Y(\Theta[Y]) \vdash \mu_X((\Psi\ x)) \colon *$. Imagine Z represented as a tree structure whose leaves are types representing recursive calls. We must require that each occurrence of a term pointing to such a leaf occurs only strictly positively in U.

Figure 1 is a depiction of type pointers. It shows how a type pointer can be constructed for each of the type constructors that build new strongly positive operators. If Z is in a product type (clause 3), it is a pair, represented by a binary node with a subtree for each branch. A positive type pointer first chooses one of the components and then uses a positive type pointer for that component. If Z is in a function type (clause 5), the situation is similar, but the number of components is equal to the cardinality of the domain type (possibly infinite). If Z is in a sum type (clause 4), then it is in one of the two forms specified by the component types. A positive type pointer must take into account both possibilities, so it prescribes a type pointer for each of the two components. Therefore, the picture for clause 3 shows two positive type pointers corresponding to the two components, whereas the picture for clause 4 shows only one positive type pointer that consists of two components. The picture for clause 8 shows how a positive type pointer is used in a recursive definition of a family of strongly

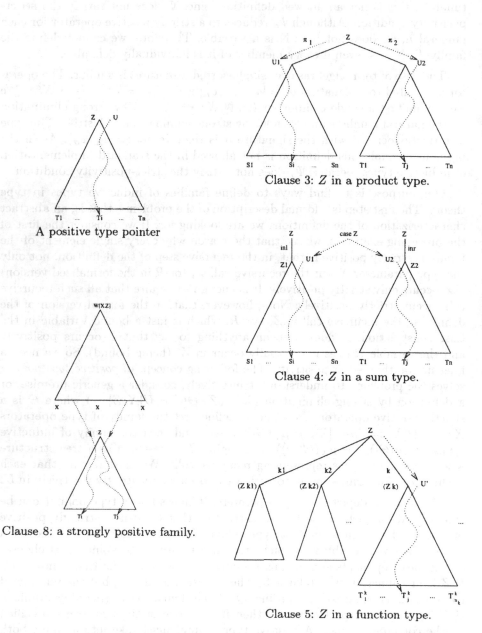

A positive type pointer

Clause 3: Z in a product type.

Clause 4: Z in a sum type.

Clause 8: a strongly positive family.

Clause 5: Z in a function type.

Fig. 1. Illustration of Definition 2: the use of positive type pointers in the definition of families of strongly positive operators.

positive operators. The term $W[X, Z]$ is the iterator of the recursive definition. It contains some direct occurrences of the variable X and some recursive calls, here indicated by the leaves T_i and T_j of the iteration variable Z. When T_i and T_j are replaced with the values of the recursive call, new occurrences of X appear. The requirement that $W[X, Z]$, besides being strongly positive in X, is also a positive type pointer in Z causes all the new occurrences of X to be strictly positive.

Definition 2. *A type operator $(X: * \vdash \Phi[X]: *)$ that can be lifted to kinds $(X: \square \vdash \Phi[X]: \square)$ is* strongly positive *and a term $(Z: \Phi[*] \vdash U[Z]: *)$ is a* positive type pointer *for Φ if they satisfy the following recursive clauses.*

1. *If K is a type that does not depend on X (that is, X does not occur free in K), then $\Phi[X] = K$ is strongly positive and $Z: K \vdash K: *$ is a positive type pointer for Φ.*
2. *If $\Phi[X] = X$ then Φ is strongly positive and $Z: * \vdash Z: *$ is a positive type pointer for Φ.*
3. *If $\Phi[X] = \Phi_1[X] \times \Phi_2[X]$ and Φ_1 and Φ_2 are strongly positive, then Φ is strongly positive and if $Z_1: \Phi_1[*] \vdash U_1[Z_1]: *$ and $Z_2: \Phi_2[*] \vdash U_2[Z_2]: *$ are positive type pointers for Φ_1 and Φ_2, respectively, then*

$$Z: \Phi_1[*] \times \Phi_2[*] \vdash (U_1 (\pi_1 Z)): * \quad and$$
$$Z: \Phi_1[*] \times \Phi_2[*] \vdash (U_2 (\pi_2 Z)): *$$

are positive type pointers for Φ.
4. *If $\Phi[X] = \Phi_1[X] + \Phi_2[X]$ and Φ_1 and Φ_2 are strongly positive, then Φ is strongly positive and if $Z_1: \Phi_1[*] \vdash U_1[Z_1]: *$ and $Z_2: \Phi_2[*] \vdash U_2[Z_2]: *$ are positive type pointers for Φ_1 and Φ_2, respectively, then*

$$Z: \Phi_1[*] + \Phi_2[*] \vdash \text{Case } Z \text{ of } (\text{inl } Z_1) \Rightarrow U_1[Z_1] \mid (\text{inr } Z_2) \Rightarrow U_2[Z_2] \text{ end}: *$$

is a positive type pointer for Φ.
5. *If $\Phi[X] = K \to \Phi'[X]$, where K is a type that does not depend on X, and Φ' is a strongly positive type operator, then Φ also is strongly positive and if $Z': \Phi'[*] \vdash U'[Z']: *$ is a positive type pointer for Φ', then, for every $k: K$,*

$$Z: K \to \Phi'[*] \vdash U'[(Z\ k)]: *$$

is a positive type pointer for Φ.
6. *Suppose $t: A_1 + A_2$ for types A_1 and $A_2: *$. If $\Phi[X] = (\text{Case } t \text{ of } (\text{inl } x_1) \Rightarrow \Phi_1[x_1, X] \mid (\text{inl } x_2) \Rightarrow \Phi_2[x_2, X] \text{ end})$ and Φ_1 and Φ_2 are strongly positive, then Φ also is strongly positive.*
7. *If Φ and Ψ are strongly positive operators and $Z: \Phi[*] \vdash U[Z]: *$ is a positive type pointer for Φ, then $Z: \Phi[*] \vdash \Psi[U[Z]]: *$ also is a positive type pointer for Φ.*
8. *If $Y: * \vdash \Theta[Y]: *$ is a strongly positive type operator, $I = \mu_Y(\Theta)$, and $X: *, Z: \Theta[*] \vdash W[X, Z]: *$ is a positive type pointer for Θ with respect to Z and is strongly positive with respect to X, then every element of the family $X: * \vdash \Phi[X] := (\mu\text{-it } [Z]W[X, Z]): I \to *$ is strongly positive; that is, for every $i: I$, $X: * \vdash (\Psi[X]\ i): *$ is a strongly positive type operator.*

Clause 7 may seem too restrictive because we do not consider the possibility that different positive type pointers for Φ may be used in Ψ. For example, if $\Psi[Y] = Y \times Y$, we may want to define the type pointer $X: * \vdash U_1[X] \times U_2[X]$ where U_1 and U_2 are different positive type pointers for Φ. In that case we should modify Φ such that it becomes an operator on two parameters, $Y_1, Y_2: * \vdash Y_1 \times Y_2$, and then apply clause 7 twice, the first type substituting $U_1[X]$ for Y_1, the second time substituting $U_2[X]$ for Y_2. This can be done in all similar situations.

We do not include a definition of positive type pointer corresponding to the strongly positive operator obtained in clause 8. This further complication is not necessary to define the families of types in which we are interested.

The definition of strongly positive type operator coincides with the definition of strictly positive type operator but for the last clause, which allows the definition of families of strongly positive type operators by recursion, using a positive type pointer as the recursion term.

For example, consider the family of type operators defined in Formula (3). We want to prove that $X: * \vdash (\Psi[X]\ n)$ is strongly positive for every $n: \mathbb{N}$. Since $\mathbb{N} = \mu_Y(\Theta[Y])$ with $\Theta[Y] = \mathbb{N}_1 + Y$, we can use clause 8 of Definition 2. We have to prove that $X: *, Z: \mathbb{N}_1 + * \vdash W[X, Z]: *$ is a strongly positive type operator with respect to X and a positive type pointer for Θ with respect to Z. The first property follows from clause 6 and the easily verifiable fact that the two branches of the Case definition are strongly positive with respect to X (they are actually strictly positive). The second follows from clause 4 with $\Phi_1[Y] = \mathbb{N}_1$ and $U_1[Z_1] = \mathbb{N}_1$ (positive type pointer by clause 1), $\Phi_2[Y] = Y$ and $U_2[Z_2] = \mathbb{N}_1 + X \times Z_2$ (positive type pointer by clause 7, with $\Psi[V] = \mathbb{N}_1 + X \times V$, and clause 2).

It follows that, in the system extended by Definition 2, we can define the family of inductive types $T := [n: \mathbb{N}]\mu_X(\Psi[X]\ n): \mathbb{N} \to *$.

Definition 2 does not add new inductive types to the system, but simply allows us to collect types in new families.

Theorem 1. *Every closed type $\mu_X(\Phi)$ definable by Definition 2 is definable by Definition 1 also.*

Proof We must prove that every strongly positive operator $X: * \vdash \Phi[X]: *$ in which no free variable except X occurs, is strictly positive (or, better, reduces to a strictly positive one). The proof is by induction on the number of times clause 8 of Definition 2 is used. We don't need to consider the other clauses, since they are the same in the definition of strict positivity. Suppose then that Φ has been obtained by clause 8—that is, $\Phi = (\Psi\ a)$, where Ψ is as in clause 8 and a is a closed term of type I. We assume that a is in normal form (otherwise we normalize it). We prove that $(\Psi\ a)$ is strictly positive by induction on the set of closed terms of I in normal form. (Note that this is structural induction external to type theory, and not an internal application of the elimination rule. This explains why a must be a *closed* term for it to work.) Suppose $a = (\mu\text{-intro}\ b)$

with $b: \Theta[I]$ closed. Then

$$
\begin{aligned}
(\Psi\ a) &= (\Psi\ (\mu\text{-intro } b)) \\
&= (\mu\text{-it } [Z]W[X, Z]\ (\mu\text{-intro } b)) \\
&\rightsquigarrow W[X, (\Theta[(\mu\text{-it } [Z]W[X, Z])]\ b)] \\
&= W[X, (\Theta[\Phi[X]]\ b)]
\end{aligned}
$$

The term $(\Theta[\Phi[X]]\ b)$ can be represented as a tree isomorphic to the structure tree of a and whose leaves are in the form $(\Psi\ c)$, with c an element of I structurally simpler than a. By induction hypothesis, for all recursive occurrences of elements of I in b (that is, the elements of I that are structurally simpler that a), the corresponding elements of the family Ψ are strictly positive. Since $(\Psi\ a)$ is strictly-positively constructed from such occurrences by the type pointer W (this is the main property of the notion of positive type pointer and can be proved straightforwardly for every clause of Definition 2), it is also strictly positive.
□

4   Wellorderings

In the previous section we proposed an extension of the notion of inductive type. We see now that, without extending type theory, we can encode the desired types and families as wellorderings. Wellorderings (also called W types) are types of trees specified by a type of nodes A and, for every element a of A, a type of branches $(B\ a)$. This means that every node labelled with the element a has as many branches as the elements of $(B\ a)$.

Wellorderings were introduced by Martin-Löf [14,15] and used by Dybjer [10] to encode all inductive types obtained from strictly positive operators. Here we extend Dybjer's construction to strongly positive operators.

Definition 3. *Let $A: *$ and $B: A \to *$. The type $W(A, B)$ is defined by the rules*

formation $W(A, B): *$

introduction $\dfrac{a: A \quad f: (B\ a) \to W(A, B)}{(\text{sup } a\ f): W(A, B)}$

elimination   *Let $P: W(A, B) \to *$, then*

$$
\dfrac{x: A, y: (B\ x) \to W(A, B), z: (u: (B\ x))(P\ (y\ u)) \vdash e[x, y, z]: (P\ (\text{sup } x\ y))}{(\text{W-ind } [x, y, z]e): (w: W(A, B))(P\ w)}
$$

conversion $(\text{W-ind } [x, y, z]e\ (\text{sup } a\ f))$
$\rightsquigarrow e[a, f, [u: (B\ a)](\text{W-ind } [x, y, z]e\ (f\ u))]$

Wellorderings can be realized in type theory with the standard implementation of inductive types. Using Formula 2 we can define the W constructor as

$$\text{inductive W } [A : *, B : A \to *]: * :=$$
$$\text{sup} : (x : A)((B\ x) \to \text{W}(A, B)) \to \text{W}(A, B)$$
$$\text{end.}$$

Dybjer showed in [10] that every strictly positive operator has an initial algebra constructed by a W type. This result holds if we take an extensional equality on the W type—that is, if we consider two elements (sup a_1 f_1) and (sup a_2 f_2) of $\text{W}(A, B)$ equal if a_1 and a_2 are convertible and if $(f_1\ b) = (f_2\ b)$ for every $b : (B\ a_1)$. In intensional type theory, which is the one we use, the second condition is not equivalent to the convertibility of f_1 and f_2. For this reason, when we use W types, we have to deal explicitly with extensional equality. They are, therefore, more cumbersome than direct inductive definitions. Once we have stressed this drawback, we can extend Dybjer's result to strongly positive operators.

Theorem 2. *For every strongly positive operator* $X : * \vdash \Phi[X] : *$ *there exist* $A : *$ *and* $B : A \to *$ *such that* $\text{W}(A, B)$ *is an initial algebra of* Φ. *(For a formal definition of initial algebras of type operators see, for example, [11] or [20].)*

Proof The proof is by induction on the structure of Φ as in Dybjer [10]. Our Definition 2 contains two extra clauses that are not present in Dybjer's definition: clauses 6 and 8. Let us see how Dybjer's proof can be extended to include them.

Clause 6 is easily treated by defining A and B by cases on the term t in the definition of Ψ and using the recursive results for the branches of the Case expression. (See the following example.)

If Ψ is obtained by clause 8 we define the families $A : I \to *$ and $B : (x : I)A_x \to *$ by recursion on I. Given $x = (\mu\text{-intro } y) : I$, we assume by inductive hypothesis that A and B are defined for all the recursive occurrences of elements of I in y. We define the new A_x and B_x, by using Dybjer's construction for the occurrences of X and of the recursive calls Z on $\text{W}[X, Z]$. Formally, using Dybjer's method recursively on the clauses of Definition 2, we can construct from W two families of operators W_A and W_B and then apply the iteration principle to obtain A and the induction principle to obtain B:

$$\frac{Z_A : \Theta[*] \vdash W_A[Z_A] : *}{A := (\mu\text{-it } [Z_A]W_A) : I \to *},$$

$$\frac{Z_B : \Theta[(\Sigma\ I\ [i : I]A_i \to *)] \vdash W[Z_B] : A_{(\mu\text{-intro } (\Theta[\pi_1]\ z))} \to *}{B := (\mu\text{-ind } [Z_B]W_B) : (i : I)A_i \to *}.$$

Note the difference with the proof of Theorem 1: The assumption that a closed term $a : I$ is used was essential to that proof. That was necessary because we were proving an external predicate. But here we are constructing families of types internal to type theory, therefore we can use the elimination rule of type I to construct A (with elimination predicate $P_A = [x : I]*$) and B (with elimination predicate $P_B = [x\colon I]A_x \to *$. Therefore A_x and B_x are defined also for a free variable $x\colon I$. □

This construction gives, in the case of the family of operators of Formula 3, the following families of As and Bs:

$$A\colon \mathbb{N} \to * \qquad\qquad B\colon (n\colon \mathbb{N})A_n \to *$$
$$A_0 \;:= \mathbb{N}_1 \qquad\qquad (B_0 \quad _- \quad) := \emptyset$$
$$A_{(S\ n)} := \mathbb{N}_1 + A_n \qquad (B_{(S\ n)}\ (\mathsf{inl}\ {_-}\,)) := \emptyset$$
$$(\cong \mathbb{N}_1 + \mathbb{N}_1 \times A_n) \qquad (B_{(S\ n)}\ (\mathsf{inr}\ a)) := \mathbb{N}_1 + (B_n\ a)$$

The W construction for terms over a signature in Sig is described in [6], where it is extended to many-sorted signatures.

5   Recursive vs. Inductive Families

We remarked that the W construction has the disadvantage that extensionally equal terms are not always convertible. This is unavoidable when we use transfinite types, but it could and should be avoided with finitary types. The solution proposed in this section exploits an extension of inductive types implemented in the proof tool Coq (see [12]). This consists in extending the notion of strict positivity to that of *positivity* by a clause that allows operators to inherit positive occurrences of a parameter X from inductive definitions.

Definition 4. *A type operator* $X\colon * \vdash \Psi[X]\colon *$ *is* positive *if it satisfies the clauses of the definition of strict positivity where we substitute "positive" for "strictly positive" everywhere, and the new clause*

X *is positive in* $(J\ t_1 \cdots t_m)$ *if* J *is an inductive type and, for every term* t_i, *either* X *does not occur in* t_i *or* X *is positive in* t_i, t_i *instantiates a general parameter of* J *and this parameter is positive in the arguments of the constructors of* J.

To apply this construction to our case we first need to replace the recursive definition of a family of type operators with an inductive one. We illustrate the method with the example of Formula 3. The family Ψ was defined by recursion on the natural numbers. Instead we use the following inductive definition

$$\text{inductive ind}(\Psi)[X\colon *]\colon \mathbb{N} \to * :=$$
$$\psi_0 \,:\ \text{ind}(\Psi)_0$$
$$\psi_1 \,:\ (n\colon \mathbb{N})\text{ind}(\Psi)_{(S\ n)}$$
$$\psi_2 \,:\ (n\colon \mathbb{N})X \to \text{ind}(\Psi)_n \to \text{ind}(\Psi)_{(S\ n)}$$
$$\text{end.}$$

(The constructors ψ_0 and ψ_1 could be unified in a single constructor ψ_{01}: $(n\colon \mathbb{N})\text{ind}(\Psi)_n$, but we keep them separate to keep the parallel with the definition of Ψ in Formula 3.) X is a general parameter of $\text{ind}(\Psi)$ and it is positive in the arguments of the constructors: It appears only as the type of the first argument of the constructor ψ_2. It follows from the clause in Definition 4 that $X: * \vdash (\mathsf{ind}(\Psi)\ X\ n)$ is a positive type operator for every $n: \mathsf{N}$. In the type system of Coq such positive operators can be used in the definition of inductive types, thus the family $T := [n]\mu_X((\mathsf{ind}(\Psi)\ X\ n)): \mathsf{N} \to *$ is admissible. Note that the condition expressed in clause 8 of Definition 2 by requiring W to be a positive type pointer corresponds to the fact that the recursive calls must occur positively in the definition of $\mathsf{ind}(\Psi)$. This translation can be done in general for every strongly positive operator.

Theorem 3. *For every strongly positive type operator* $X: * \vdash \Phi[X]: *$ *there exists a positive type operator* $X: * \vdash \mathsf{ind}(\Phi)[X]: *$ *such that, for every type* $X: *$, $\Phi[X] \cong \mathsf{ind}(\Phi)[X]$.

Proof As usual the relevant case is clause 8 of Definition 2. If $X: * \vdash \Psi[X]: I \to *$ is defined as in that clause, then we replace it with the inductive family

$$\mathsf{inductive\ ind}(\Psi)\ [X: *]: I \to *$$
$$\psi: (y: \Theta[I])W[X, (\Theta[\mathsf{ind}(\Psi)]\ y)] \to \mathsf{ind}(\Psi)_{(\mu\text{-intro}\ y)},$$
$$\mathsf{end}$$

which can be proved to be positive according to Definition 4, by induction on the proof that W is a positive type pointer. The general parameter X occurs only positively in the arguments of the constructor ψ because it occurs only positively in W (by induction hypothesis).

With this translation we get always inductive families with only one constructor. In practice it is intuitively easier to break it down into several constructors, as we did in the preceding example.   □

6   Applying the Two Level Approach to Inductive Types

The *two level approach* is a technique used for proof construction in type theory. A goal G is lifted to a syntactic level; that is, a term g, of a type $\mathsf{Goal}: *$ representing goals, is associated to G. Logical rules are reflected by functions or relations on Goal. To prove G we apply the functions or work with the relations on g. Once g is proved at the syntactic level, we can extract a proof of G.

The technique is described in [4] and in Ruys' thesis [22]. It was used by Boutin, who calls it *reflection*, to implement the Ring tactic in Coq [5]. Its furthest application consists in formalizing type theory inside type theory itself and use it to do metareasoning. This was partially done by Howe in [13] for Nuprl and by Barras and Werner in [3] for Coq.

We apply it to inductive definitions. First of all we define a type of codes for positive type operators PosOp. To every element $\phi: \mathsf{PosOp}$ we associate a positive type operator $(\mathsf{TypeOp}\ \phi): * \to *$ and an inductive type $(\mathsf{IndType}\ \phi): *$, using the technique of Section 5. Then we define an inductive predicate $\mathsf{Positive}$ on type operators, which is an internalization of the notion of strict positivity (note that we do not need to internalize strong positivity or positivity). We define a function that associates an element of PosOp to every operator $\Phi: * \to *$

and proof p: (Positive Φ). So we can define an inductive type by proving that the corresponding type operator is strictly positive. This can be done for the families of operators defined by recursion, hence solving our initial problem.

Definition 5. *The type* PosOp: $\Box$ *is defined by the following introduction rules:*

$$\frac{K:\ast}{(\text{op-const } K):\, \textsf{PosOp}} \qquad \frac{op_1:\,\textsf{PosOp} \quad op_2:\,\textsf{PosOp}}{(\text{op-prod } op_1\ op_2):\,\textsf{PosOp}} \qquad \frac{K:\ast \quad op:\,\textsf{PosOp}}{(\text{op-fun } K\ op)}$$

$$\frac{}{\text{op-id}:\,\textsf{PosOp}} \qquad \frac{op_1:\,\textsf{PosOp} \quad op_2:\,\textsf{PosOp}}{(\text{op-sum } op_1\ op_2):\,\textsf{PosOp}}.$$

We can associate an actual type operator to every element of PosOp, by recursion on it:

$$
\begin{aligned}
&\textsf{TypeOp}: \textsf{PosOp} \to \ast \to \ast \\
&\quad (\text{op-const } K) &&\Rightarrow [X:\ast]K \\
&\quad \text{op-id} &&\Rightarrow [X:\ast]X \\
&\quad (\text{op-prod } op_1\ op_2) &&\Rightarrow [X:\ast](\textsf{TypeOp}\ op_1\ X) \times (\textsf{TypeOp}\ op_2\ X) \\
&\quad (\text{op-sum } op_1\ op_2) &&\Rightarrow [X:\ast](\textsf{TypeOp}\ op_1\ X) + (\textsf{TypeOp}\ op_2\ X) \\
&\quad (\text{op-fun } K\ op) &&\Rightarrow [X:\ast]K \to (\textsf{TypeOp}\ op\ X).
\end{aligned}
$$

Unfortunately this approach leads us to a dead end, since the family of operators TypeOp is strongly positive but not positive, being obtained by recursion.

We apply instead the technique of Section 5 to transform TypeOp from a recursive family to an inductive one satisfying the positivity condition:

$$
\begin{aligned}
&\text{inductive } \textsf{IndOp}\ [X:\ast]: \textsf{PosOp} \to \ast \\
&\quad c_{\text{const}} \quad : \ (K:\ast)K \to (\textsf{IndOp}\ (\text{op-const } K)) \\
&\quad c_{\text{id}} \qquad : \ X \to (\textsf{IndOp}\ \text{op-id}) \\
&\quad c_{\text{prod}} \quad : \ (op_1, op_2:\textsf{PosOp})\,(\textsf{IndOp}\ op_1) \to (\textsf{IndOp}\ op_2) \\
&\qquad\qquad\qquad\qquad\qquad\qquad \to (\textsf{IndOp}\ (\text{op-prod } op_1\ op_2)) \\
&\quad c_{\text{sum,l}} \ : \ (op_1, op_2:\textsf{PosOp})(\textsf{IndOp}\ op_1) \to (\textsf{IndOp}\ (\text{op-sum } op_1\ op_2)) \\
&\quad c_{\text{sum,r}} \ : \ (op_1, op_2:\textsf{PosOp})(\textsf{IndOp}\ op_2) \to (\textsf{IndOp}\ (\text{op-sum } op_1\ op_2)) \\
&\quad c_{\text{fun}} \qquad : \ (K:\ast)(op:\textsf{PosOp})(K \to (\textsf{IndOp}\ op)) \to (\textsf{IndOp}\ (\text{op-fun } K\ op)) \\
&\text{end.}
\end{aligned}
$$

Lemma 1. *For every* op: PosOp, $X:\ast \vdash (\textsf{IndOp}\ X\ op)$ *is a positive operator.*

Proof Just check that the requirements of the new clause in Definition 4 are satisfied. $\qquad\qquad\qquad\qquad\qquad\qquad\qquad\qquad\qquad\qquad\qquad\qquad\qquad\qquad\square$

Thus, in the type system of Coq, we can associate an inductive type to every element of PosOp:

$$\textsf{IndType} := [op:\textsf{PosOp}]\mu_X(\textsf{IndOp}\ X\ op): \textsf{PosOp} \to \ast.$$

Whenever we have a family of type operators $X:\ast \vdash \Psi[X]: I \to \ast$ defined by recursion on an inductive type I, we can associate to it a function $f_\Psi: I \to \textsf{PosOp}$

and obtain the family of inductive types as $[x\colon I](\mathsf{IndType}\ (f_\Psi\ x))$. For example, the family Ψ from Formula 3 is translated into the function

$$f_\Psi\colon \mathbb{N} \to \mathsf{PosOp}$$
$$(f_\Psi\quad 0\quad) := (\mathsf{op\text{-}const}\ \mathbb{N}_1)$$
$$(f_\Psi\ (S\ n)) := (\mathsf{op\text{-}sum}\ (\mathsf{op\text{-}const}\ \mathbb{N}_1)\ (\mathsf{op\text{-}prod}\ \mathsf{op\text{-}id}\ (f_\Psi\ n)))$$

Moreover, we can avoid this translation by proving directly the positivity of the original operators inside type theory.

Definition 6. *The predicate* $\mathsf{Positive}\colon (* \to *) \to *$ *is inductively defined by the following rules:*

$$\frac{K\colon *}{(\mathsf{pos\text{-}const}\ K)\colon (\mathsf{Positive}\ [X\colon *]K)}$$

$$\frac{}{\mathsf{pos\text{-}id}\colon (\mathsf{Positive}\ [X\colon *]X)}$$

$$\frac{\Phi_1\colon * \to *\quad \Phi_2\colon * \to *\quad p_1\colon (\mathsf{Positive}\ \Phi_1)\quad p_2\colon (\mathsf{Positive}\ \Phi_2)}{(\mathsf{pos\text{-}prod}\ \Phi_1\ \Phi_2\ p_1\ p_2)\colon (\mathsf{Positive}\ [X\colon *](\Phi_1\ X) \times (\Phi_2\ X))}$$

$$\frac{\Phi_1\colon * \to *\quad \Phi_2\colon * \to *\quad p_1\colon (\mathsf{Positive}\ \Phi_1)\quad p_2\colon (\mathsf{Positive}\ \Phi_2)}{(\mathsf{pos\text{-}sum}\ \Phi_1\ \Phi_2\ p_1\ p_2)\colon (\mathsf{Positive}\ [X\colon *](\Phi_1\ X) + (\Phi_2\ X))}$$

$$\frac{K\colon *\quad \Phi\colon * \to *\quad p\colon (\mathsf{Positive}\ \Phi)}{(\mathsf{pos\text{-}fun}\ K\ \Phi\ p)\colon (\mathsf{Positive}\ [X\colon *]K \to (\Phi\ X))}$$

It is straightforward to define a function $\mathsf{pos\text{-}code}\colon (\Phi\colon * \to *)(\mathsf{Positive}\ \Phi) \to \mathsf{PosOp}$ by recursion on the proof of $(\mathsf{Positive}\ \Phi)$. In conclusion, given a recursive family of operators, we can prove by induction that every element of the family is positive and then obtain the recursive family of inductive types by composing $\mathsf{IndType}$ and $\mathsf{pos\text{-}code}$.

Lemma 2. *Every type operator* $\Phi\colon * \to *$ *such that* $(\mathsf{Positive}\ \Phi)$ *is provable, has an initial algebra.*

Finally we can apply this method to the strongly positive operators.

Theorem 4. *If* $X\colon * \vdash \Phi[X]\colon *$ *is a strongly positive operator, then there is a proof of* $(\mathsf{Positive}\ [X]\Phi[X])$.

Proof We just formalize the proof of Theorem 1. Since we are now developing the proof inside type theory, the requirement that no free variable except X appears in Φ is no longer necessary. Hence the result holds for every strongly positive operator. □

7   Conclusion

We have considered the problem of defining families of inductive types whose constructors are given by recursion. These families occur naturally in some developments of abstract mathematics in type theory. We characterized them with the notion of strong positive operator. We described a model of them in type theory that uses wellorderings. We showed that a more manageable model can be constructed in a type theory with an extended notion of inductive definition. Finally we generalized the later model to a complete internalization of inductive definitions. This last part was completely formalized in Coq.

8   Acknowledgements

I am indebted to Henk Barendregt and Herman Geuvers for their help. The first discussed the content of this article with me and provided many illuminating comments and suggestions. The second read a first draft of the paper and helped me improve it. But if there are still mistakes in it, the responsibility is solely mine.

References

1. H. P. Barendregt. Lambda calculi with types. In S. Abramsky, Dov M. Gabbay, and T. S. E. Maibaum, editors, *Handbook of Logic in Computer Science, Volume 2*, pages 117–309. Oxford University Press, 1992.
2. Bruno Barras, Samuel Boutin, Cristina Cornes, Judicaël Courant, Yann Coscoy, David Delahaye, Daniel de Rauglaudre, Jean-Christophe Filliâtre, Eduardo Giménez, Hugo Herbelin, Gérard Huet, Henri Laulhère, César Muñoz, Chetan Murthy, Catherine Parent-Vigouroux, Patrick Loiseleur, Christine Paulin-Mohring, Amokrane Saïbi, and Benjanin Werner. *The Coq Proof Assistant Reference Manual. Version 6.3.* INRIA, 1999.
3. Bruno Barras and Benjamin Werner. Coq in Coq. Draft paper, 2000.
4. G. Barthe, M. Ruys, and H. P. Barendregt. A two-level approach towards lean proof-checking. In S. Berardi and M. Coppo, editors, *Types for Proofs and Programs (TYPES'95)*, volume 1158 of *LNCS*, pages 16–35. Springer, 1995.
5. Samuel Boutin. Using reflection to build efficient and certified decision procedures. In Martín Abadi and Takayasu Ito, editors, *Theoretical Aspects of Computer Software. Third International Symposium, TACS'97*, volume 1281 of *LNCS*, pages 515–529. Springer, 1997.
6. Venanzio Capretta. Universal algebra in type theory. In Yves Bertot, Gilles Dowek, André Hirschowits, Christine Paulin, and Laurent Théry, editors, *Theorem Proving in Higher Order Logics, 12th International Conference, TPHOLs '99*, volume 1690 of *LNCS*, pages 131–148. Springer-Verlag, 1999.
7. Venanzio Capretta. Equational reasoning in type theory. http://www.cs.kun.nl/~venanzio, 2000.
8. Thierry Coquand. An analysis of Girard's paradox. In *Proceedings, Symposium on Logic in Computer Science*, pages 227–236, Cambridge, Massachusetts, 16–18 June 1986. IEEE Computer Society.
9. Thierry Coquand and Christine Paulin. Inductively defined types. In P. Martin-Löf, editor, *Proceedings of Colog '88*, volume 417 of *LNCS*. Springer-Verlag, 1990.
10. Peter Dybjer. Representing Inductively Defined Sets by Wellorderings in Martin-Löf Type Theory. *Theoretical Computer Science*, 176:329–335, 1997.

11. Herman Geuvers. Inductive and coinductive types with iteration and recursion. In Bengt Nordström, Kent Pettersson, and Gordon Plotkin, editors, *Proccedings of the 1992 Workshop on Types for Proofs and Programs, Båstad, Sweden, June 1992*, pages 193–217, 1992. ftp://ftp.cs.chalmers.se/pub/cs-reports/baastad.92/proc.dvi.Z.

12. Eduardo Giménez. A Tutorial on Recursive Types in Coq. Technical Report 0221, Unité de recherche INRIA Rocquencourt, May 1998.

13. Douglas J. Howe. Computational metatheory in Nuprl. In E. Lusk and R. Overbeek, editors, *9th International Conference on Automated Deduction*, volume 310 of *LNCS*, pages 238–257. Springer-Verlag, 1988.

14. Per Martin-Löf. Constructive mathematics and computer programming. In *Logic, Methodology and Philosophy of Science, VI, 1979*, pages 153–175. North-Holland, 1982.

15. Per Martin-Löf. *Intuitionistic Type Theory*. Bibliopolis, 1984. Notes by Giovanni Sambin of a series of lectures given in Padua, June 1980.

16. Ralph Matthes. Monotone (co)inductive types and positive fixed-point types. *Theoretical Informatics and Applications*, 33:309–328, 1999.

17. Paul Francis Mendler. *Inductive Definition in Type Theory*. PhD thesis, Department of Computer Science, Cornell University, Ithaca, New York, 1987.

18. Bengt Nordström, Kent Petersson, and Jan M. Smith. *Programming in Martin-Löf's Type Theory*. Clarendon Press, 1990.

19. C. Paulin-Mohring. Inductive Definitions in the System Coq - Rules and Properties. In M. Bezem and J.-F. Groote, editors, *Proceedings of the conference Typed Lambda Calculi and Applications*, volume 664 of *LNCS*, 1993. LIP research report 92-49.

20. Holger Pfeifer and Harals Rueß. Polytypic proof construction. In Yves Bertot, Gilleds Dowek, André Hirschowits, Christine Paulin, and Laurent Théry, editors, *Theorem Proving in Higher Order Logics, 12th International Conference, TPHOLs '99*, volume 1690 of *LNCS*, pages 54–72. Springer-Verlag, 1999.

21. F. Pfenning and C. Paulin-Mohring. Inductively defined types in the Calculus of Constructions. In *Proceedings of Mathematical Foundations of Programming Semantics*, volume 442 of *LNCS*. Springer-Verlag, 1990. technical report CMU-CS-89-209.

22. Mark Ruys. *Studies in Mechanical Verification of Mathematical Proofs*. PhD thesis, Computer Science Institute, University of Nijmegen, 1999.

23. Milena Stefanova. *Properties of Typing Systems*. PhD thesis, Computing Science Institute, University of Nijmegen, 1999.

Aircraft Trajectory Modeling and Alerting Algorithm Verification

Víctor Carreño[1] and César Muñoz[2]

[1] Assessment Technology Branch
Mail Stop 130, NASA Langley Research Center
Hampton, VA 23681-2199
v.a.carreno@larc.nasa.gov
[2] Institute for Computer Applications in Science and Engineering (ICASE)
Mail Stop 132C, 3 West Reid Street
NASA Langley Research Center
Hampton VA 23681-2199
munoz@icase.edu

Abstract. The Airborne Information for Lateral Spacing (AILS) program at NASA Langley Research Center aims at giving pilots the information necessary to make independent approaches to parallel runways with spacing down to 2500 feet in Instrument Meteorological Conditions. The AILS concept consists of accurate traffic information visible on the navigation display and an alerting algorithm which warns the crew when one of the aircraft involved in a parallel landing is diverting from its intended flight path. In this paper we present a model of aircraft approaches to parallel runways. Based on this model, we analyze the alerting algorithm with the objective of verifying its correctness. The formalization is conducted in the general verification system PVS.

1 Introduction

The Airborne Information for Lateral Spacing (AILS) [12,3,6] is a project being conducted at NASA Langley Research Center. Its objective is to reduce traffic delays and increase airport efficiency by enabling approaches to closely spaced parallel runways in Instrument Meteorological Conditions.

Approaches to parallel runways are currently limited to 4300 feet in Instrument Meteorological Conditions. Specially equipped airports with fast scan radars, high resolution monitoring systems, and approach-specific air traffic controllers can perform parallel approaches to 3400 feet [14,8]. The AILS project aims at shifting the responsibility of maintaining separation during parallel approaches from the air traffic controller to the aircraft crew. Via the AILS concept, approaches to parallel runways 2500 feet apart in Instrument Meteorological Conditions are expected.

AILS eliminates the delay inherent in the communication between air traffic controller and crew by displaying parallel traffic information in the cockpit. The degree of safety is enhanced by an alerting system which warns the crew when

J. Harrison and M. Aagaard (Eds.): TPHOLs 2000, LNCS 1869, pp. 90–105, 2000.

one of the aircraft involved in a parallel landing is deviating from the intended flight path. The alerting algorithm is a critical part of the AILS concept. Flaws in its logic could lead to non-alerted collision incidents. The algorithm has been extensively tested in simulators and in real flights.

The objective of this work is to conduct a formal analysis of the alerting algorithm in order to discover any possible errors that have not been detected during testing and simulation. In particular, we develop a formal model of parallel landing scenarios. Based on this model, we study the behavior of the AILS alerting algorithm with respect to collision incidents. In particular, we have found maximum and minimum times when an alarm will first sound prior to a collision. Indeed, we have proven that for any trajectory leading to a collision, an alarm is issued at least 4 seconds before the collision. Conversely, we have found that there exist trajectories leading to a collision where the alarm will not sound before 11 seconds. We believe that for all cases the largest time prior to a collision when the alarm will first sound is closer to 11 than to 4.

The paper is organized as follows. First, in section 2, we shortly review the alerting features which are integrated in the AILS concept. Next, in section 3, we describe in detail the AILS alerting algorithm. We model aircraft trajectories and collision scenarios in section 4. Section 5 contains the main properties that we have formally proven. Finally, we conclude with some remarks in section 6. The formalization presented in this paper has been developed in the general verification system PVS [11]. We use a stylized-LaTeX PVS concrete syntax and assume the reader is familiar with standard notations of higher-order logic.

2   System Description

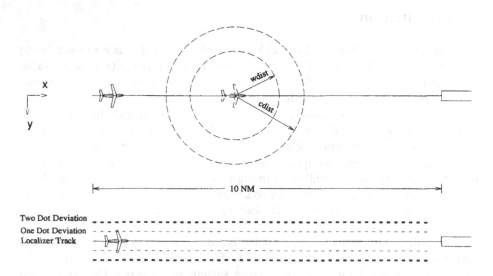

Fig. 1. Parallel runway approach

In a typical independent parallel approach, depicted in Figure 1, aircraft intersect their localizer track (longitudinal runway center) approximately 10 nautical miles from the runway threshold. During localizer intersection, aircraft have a 1000 feet vertical separation. After the aircraft are established in their localizer track, vertical separation is eliminated and aircraft start a normal glide path for landing.

The AILS alerting system starts operating when the aircraft are on their localizers. At this time the aircraft are approximately at the same altitude. As explained later, one aircraft is assumed to be the intruder and the other is assumed to be the evader. The scenario is then reversed. When the intruder aircraft deviates from its airspace, the AILS system provides 6 alert levels, depending on the severity of the deviation. Table 1 shows an alerting sequence as seen in the evader and intruder aircraft primary and navigation displays.

Table 1. Alerting sequence

	Evader	Intruder
1		Localizer alert (one dot deviation)
2		Localizer alert (two dot deviation)
3		Caution alert (traffic)
4	Caution alert (traffic)	
5		Warning alert (collision)
6	Warning alert (collision)	

All alerts in the intruder aircraft are expected to be followed by a corrective maneuver. The evader aircraft is not expected to perform an evasive maneuver until a warning alert is issued, at which time landing is aborted and an emergency escape maneuver is performed. Notice that the intruder aircraft always receives a caution or warning alert before the respective caution or warning alerts are issued to the evader.

An algorithm implementing the alerting features explained above runs independently on each aircraft. It runs twice every 0.5 seconds. The first time the algorithm assumes that the own-ship is the intruder aircraft and the adjacent aircraft is the evader. In the next iteration the algorithm assumes that the own-ship is the evader and the adjacent aircraft is the intruder.

Several assumptions were made by the AILS project researchers in the development of the alerting algorithm. These assumptions are justified by physical characteristics and operational constraints. They are as follows:

- Time is discrete and divided in increments of 0.5 seconds. In our model, we call this value `tstep`.
- The rate of turn is determined by the bank angle and ground speed.
- The speeds of the aircraft are constant. Henceforth, we use `intruderSpeed` and `evaderSpeed` as the constant speed values of the intruder and evader aircraft, respectively.

- The vertical separation between the aircraft is assumed to be 0 during a landing approach.
- Only the intruder aircraft will deviate from its path in a parallel approach. The evader aircraft is assumed to stay in its localizer with a heading angle of 0°.

It should be noted that the experimental AILS system, as currently designed, forms part of the Traffic Alert and Collision Avoidance System (TCAS) [13]. In this work, we assume that the AILS alerting algorithm is running in isolation from other aircraft components. In addition, we concentrate on the caution and warning alerting kernel of the AILS alerting system. The one dot and two dot deviation alerts present a simple scenario and can be easily added to our model by a separate function as it is done in the current implementation.

3 The AILS Alerting Algorithm

In this section we describe the alerting algorithm. We start in subsection 3.1 with a detailed, but informal, description of the actual algorithm. Then, in section 3.2, we abstract and formalize it in the PVS specification language.

3.1 Detailed Description

The alerting algorithm determines when an alarm will be triggered by calculating possible collision trajectories and comparing the future aircraft locations with predetermined time and distance thresholds. The algorithm is executed in two modes every **tstep** seconds: (1) the first mode assumes its own aircraft is a threat to the adjacent aircraft and the adjacent aircraft is following the localizer; (2) the second mode assumes the adjacent aircraft is a threat to its own and the own is following the localizer. In either mode, one aircraft is the intruder and one is the evader.

The algorithm considers two cases depending on whether the intruder is changing direction or not. When the intruder aircraft is not changing direction, i.e., its bank angle is 0, the algorithm determines if the two aircraft are diverging or converging and the point of closest separation. This is done by obtaining the derivative of the distance between the aircraft and solving for time when the derivative equals zero as follows.

$$\Delta_x(t) = x_{in}(t) - x_{ev}(t) \tag{1}$$

$$\Delta_y(t) = y_{in}(t) - y_{ev}(t) \tag{2}$$

$$\frac{d}{dt}\Delta_x(t) = \texttt{intruderSpeed} \times cos(\theta) - \texttt{evaderSpeed} \tag{3}$$

$$\frac{d}{dt}\Delta_y(t) = \texttt{intruderSpeed} \times sin(\theta) \tag{4}$$

$$R(t) = \sqrt{\Delta_x(t)^2 + \Delta_y(t)^2} \tag{5}$$

$$\frac{d}{dt}R(t) = \frac{\Delta_x(t) \times \frac{d}{dt}\Delta_x(t) + \Delta_y(t) \times \frac{d}{dt}\Delta_y(t)}{\sqrt{R(t)}} \tag{6}$$

For a time t, $(x_{in}(t), y_{in}(t))$ and $(x_{ev}(t), y_{ev}(t))$ are the coordinates of the intruder and evader aircraft, respectively, and θ is the heading angle of the intruder aircraft. When $\frac{d}{dt}R(t + \tau) = 0$, we get the time τ, relative to t, of the point of closest separation of the aircraft. Time τ has been calculated as

$$\tau(t) = -\frac{\Delta_x(t) \times \frac{d}{dt}\Delta_x(t) + \Delta_y(t) \times \frac{d}{dt}\Delta_y(t)}{\frac{d}{dt}\Delta_x(t)^2 + \frac{d}{dt}\Delta_y(t)^2} \tag{7}$$

Equations 3, 4, 6, and 7 were formally deduced by using the computer algebra tool MuPAD [4]. Notice that τ is undetermined when the aircraft are parallel and the ground speeds are equal. In this case, the alerting algorithm defines $\tau(t) = 0$ for any t. Since the evader aircraft is assumed to stay in its localizer with a heading angle of $0°$, it does not have a y-speed component. This is reflected in Equation 4.

For a time t, if $\tau(t)$ is negative or zero, the tracks are diverging or parallel, respectively. If $\tau(t)$ is greater than zero, the tracks are converging and $\tau(t)$ will be the time of closest separation (Figure 2). When tracks are diverging or parallel, the algorithm checks the aircraft separation at the present time against the threshold distance for warning or caution alert. When tracks are converging, the algorithm compares the time and distance of closest separation against time and distance thresholds, respectively. In either case, an alarm is triggered when the calculated time and distance are within the time and distance alert thresholds.

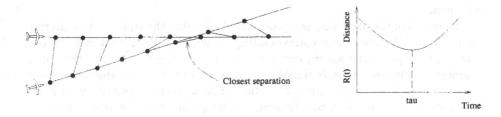

Fig. 2. Converging tracks

When the intruder aircraft is changing direction, i.e., its bank angle is not 0, the algorithm calculates the radius of the turn and the rate of change of direction. Tangential tracks are calculated from the arc path as to produce tangents which are 1.5° to 3° in angular separation (Figure 3). For each of these tangential tracks the algorithm determines whether the two aircraft tracks are diverging or converging and performs time and distance comparisons as explained above.

3.2 PVS Abstraction

The original AILS algorithm was written in FORTRAN at Langley Research Center. It has been revised several times and the latest version flown in the

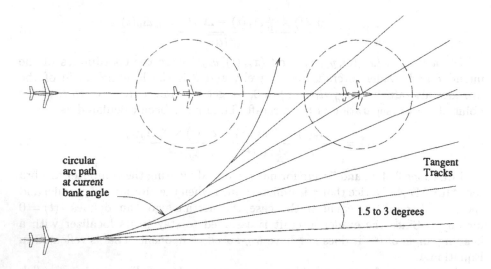

Fig. 3. Radial trajectory and tangential tracks

Boeing 757 experimental aircraft was provided by Honeywell. For the work presented in this paper, we created a high level abstract model of the alerting algorithm in the PVS language. The algorithm model uses the same strategy as the FORTRAN algorithm to determine if alarms are triggered, as explained above. All of the PVS declarations involved in the modeling of the algorithm can be seen in the theory file available at `http://shemesh.larc.nasa.gov/people/vac/ails.pvs`.

The model of the algorithm is a function which takes the states of the aircraft and returns a Boolean value corresponding to whether the alarm is triggered or not. The type of the alarm, caution or warning, depends on the threshold parameters. However, we only consider a generic type of alarm which abstracts from warning and caution alarms. The state of an aircraft is defined by a record with fields x, y: the position coordinates; heading: the angles between the flight path and the localizer track; and bank: the bank angle which range between −45° and 45° (type Bank). In PVS:

```
Bank : TYPE = {r:real | -45 ≤ r ≤ 45}

State : TYPE =
   [# x            : real,
      y            : real,
      heading      : real,
      bank         : Bank
   #]
```

Access to records can be written in PVS as function calls, i.e., if s is a State, x(s) refers to the field x of the state s.

The model of the alerting algorithm is given next.

```
larcalert(intruder,evader:State): bool =
  LET phi = bank(intruder) IN
  LET trkrate = g×(180/π)×tand(phi)/intruderSpeed IN
  IF trkrate = 0 THEN                      % Direction is not changing.
    chktrack(intruder,evader,0)            % Check strait tracks.
  ELSE                                     % Direction is changing
    LET arcrad =                           % Calculate arc radius.
      intruderSpeed²/(g×tand(phi)) IN
    LET idtrk =
      IF abs(trkrate) ≥ 3 THEN 1           % This determines
      ELSIF abs(trkrate) ≥ 1+1/2 THEN 2    % how often
      ELSIF abs(trkrate) ≥ 3/4 THEN 4      % tangential
      ELSE 8                               % tracks are
      ENDIF IN                             % calculated.
    arc_loop(intruder,evader,arcrad,trkrate,idtrk,0)
  ENDIF
```

where g is the gravitational acceleration constant (approx. 32.2 feet/seconds^2).

The first part of the function `larcalert` is exercised when the track rate (`trkrate`) is zero and there is no change in the intruder's heading. In that case, the function `chktrack` makes the calculation for converging or diverging tracks, according to Equations 1 to 7. If the tracks are diverging, the function `chkrange` is called to compare present locations against time and distance thresholds (`alertTime` and `alertRange`, respectively). If the tracks are converging, predicted locations at caution time or time of closest separation, whatever is smaller, are compared. An alarm is issued when calculated time and distance values are within the range of time and distance alert thresholds.

The structure of the definitions of `chkrange` and `chktrack` are given next.

```
chkrange(range,t:real): bool =
  range ≤ alertRange ∧ t ≤ alertTime

chktrack(intruder,evader:State,t:real): bool =
  LET range = R(t) IN
  LET tau = τ(t) IN
  IF tau ≤ 0 THEN                      % Tracks are diverging (or parallel).
    chkrange(range,t)                  % Check range at prediction time t.
  ELSE                                 % Tracks are converging.
    IF t+tau > alertTime THEN          % Closest separation beyond alert time.
      R(alertTime) ≤ alertRange        % Check range at alert threshold.
    ELSE                               % Closest separation within alert time.
      R(t+tau) ≤ alertRange            % Check range at time of
    ENDIF                              % closest separation.
  ENDIF
```

The second part of the function `larcalert` handles the case when the intruder is changing direction. The arc radius is calculated and the function `arc_loop` generates the tangential tracks from the arc trajectory. The function `arc_loop` is a recursive function modeling a DO-LOOP statement. It is used to iterate the function chktrack on tangential tracks every idtrk time steps. The actual definition of arc_loop is too long to be included in the paper and can also be seen in the theory file as pointed above. The structure of the function is:

```
arc_loop(intruder,evader,arcrad,trkrate,idtrk,iarc): RECURSIVE bool =
  IF iarc = MaxStep THEN FALSE
  ELSE
    calculate positions of aircraft
    IF  not time for a tangential track THEN
      IF chkrange(...) THEN    % Check range at that point.
        TRUE                   % Trigger an alarm.
      ELSE
        arc_loop(...,iarc+1)   % Go to new iteration.
      ENDIF
    ELSE                       % Time for tangential tracks.
      IF chktrk(...) THEN      % Check track at this point.
        TRUE                   % Trigger an alarm.
      ELSE
        arc_loop(...,iarc+1)   % Go to new iteration.
      ENDIF
    ENDIF
  ENDIF
```

Based on the idtrk argument and the step in the loop iarc, the function arc_loop determines if a tangential track is calculated or not. If a tangential track is not calculated, the function chkrange compares the distance between the calculated positions of the aircraft and the distance threshold. The function chktrk is used to check for collisions on all the tangential tracks in the loop. The function arc_loop terminates when one of the functions chkrange or chktrack triggers an alarm or when iarc has reached a constant MaxStep defined as alert_time/tstep.

In the PVS model, we are using an axiomatic definition of the square root function (sqrt, see section 5). Trigonometric functions (sind, cosd, and tand, for sine, cosine, and tangent of angles in degrees, respectively) are defined by series approximations. However, as we will see in section 5, we also provide axioms about trigonometric functions to facilitate the proofs.

As we have seen, the AILS algorithm considers a limited set of possible trajectories for the intruder aircraft, i.e., assuming a constant radius turn at the original bank angle, only tangent track escapes to the turn arc are considered. The developers of the algorithm state that this assumption is reasonable under normal circumstances, i.e., the intruder aircraft is not intentionally trying to collide with the evader aircraft. However, to evaluate the behavior of the algorithm in a wider range of possible landing scenarios, a more general model of trajectories for the intruder aircraft is necessary. In the next section, we develop such a model.

4   Parallel Landing Scenarios

According to the characteristics and assumptions of the AILS algorithm, we
propose a time-discrete model of trajectories with time increments of tstep
seconds. In that model, as in the case of the alerting algorithm, intrusion paths
are determined by the bank angle and ground speed of the intruder aircraft.
Given a ground speed $gs > 0$, a bank angle ϕ, the heading turn rate is given by

$$\text{trkrate}(gs, \phi) = \frac{\text{tand}(\phi) \times g \times 180}{gs \times \pi},$$

where g is the gravitational acceleration constant.

Although under normal operation the bank angle of a commercial aircraft
is limited to $-30°$ to $30°$, we allow the bank angle to range from $-45°$ to $45°$.
For a minimum ground speed of 180 feet per second, it means a maximum
heading turn rate of about $6°$ per second. These values produce very aggressive
blundering situations quite consistent with worst cases scenarios tested by the
AILS developing group. Incidentally, the function trkrate is well-defined for
bank angles in that range.

Definition 1 (Intruder trajectory). *An intruder trajectory of length n for
an aircraft with state s and ground speed gs is a sequence of states $in_0 \ldots in_n$
such that $in_0 = s$ and for $0 < i \leq n$,*

1. $|heading(in_i) - heading(in_{i-1})| = tstep \times trkrate(gs, bank(in_i))$,
2. $x(in_i) = x(in_{i-1}) + gs \times tstep \times cosd(heading(in_i))$, and
3. $y(in_i) = y(in_{i-1}) + gs \times tstep \times sind(heading(in_i))$.

In PVS, we define the next state of an intruder aircraft at state s and bank
angle ϕ by the function

```
next_intruder_state(s:State,φ:Bank): State =
  s WITH [
    x         := x(s) + intruderSpeed×tstep×cosd(heading(s)),
    y         := y(s) + intruderSpeed×tstep×sind(heading(s)),
    heading   := heading(s) + tstep×trkrate(intruderSpeed,bank(s)),
    bank      := φ
  ]
```

The notation WITH is the record (and function) overriding operator in PVS.

We model an intruder trajectory by a recursive function having as parameters
an initial state s, a bank angle assignment for each iteration step tr, and the
iteration step n, as follows

```
intruder_trajectory(s:State, tr:[posnat → Bank], n:nat):
  RECURSIVE State =
    IF n = 0 THEN s
```

```
    ELSE
      next_intruder_state(intruder_trajectory(s, tr, n-1),tr(n))
    ENDIF
    MEASURE n
```

For example, given an intruder aircraft at initial state s and bank angle equal to 0, a trajectory of length n such that the plane follows a straight line to its current heading angle is given by $in_0 \ldots in_n$, where $in_0 = s$ and for $0 < i \leq n$,

$$in_i = \text{intruder\_trajectory}(s, \lambda(n : \textbf{posnat}) : 0, i).$$

For the evader aircraft, we assume that it stays in its localizer with a constant speed and constant heading of $0°$. Heading and bank angles are irrelevant in the definition of an evader trajectory.

Definition 2 (Evader trajectory). *An evader trajectory of length n for an aircraft with state s and ground speed gs is a sequence of states $ev_0 \ldots ev_n$ such that $ev_0 = s$ and for $0 < i \leq n$,*

1. $x(ev_i) = x(ev_{i-1}) + gs \times tstep$ and
2. $y(ev_i) = y(ev_0)$.

For an initial state s of an aircraft, its state after n steps in a evader trajectory is defined by **evader_trajectory(s,n)** as follows

```
evader_trajectory(s:State, n:nat): State =
  (#
    x        := x(s) + evaderSpeed×tstep×n,
    y        := y(s),
    heading  := heading(s),
    bank     := bank(s)
  #)
```

We are interested in trajectories leading to collision incidents. Aircraft are said to be in *collision* if the distance between them is less than or equal to `collisionRange`. In our development, we consider 200 feet for `collisionRange`, which is approximately the wing span of a Boeing 747.

```
distance(s1,s2:State): real =
  sqrt((x(s2)-x(s1))² + (y(s2)-y(s1))²)
```

```
collision(s1,s2:State): bool =
  distance(s1,s2) ≤ collisionRange
```

Definition 3 (Collision scenario). *Given an intruder trajectory $in_0 \ldots in_n$ and an evader trajectory $ev_0 \ldots ev_n$, we said that they lead to a collision incident at step i, for $0 \leq i \leq n$, if collision(in_i,ev_i) holds.*

A collision scenario is defined in PVS as follows

```
collision_scenario(intruder,evader:State, tr:[posnat → Bank],
                    i:nat):bool =
  collision(intruder_trajectory(intruder,tr,i),
            evader_trajectory(evader,i))
```

We have implemented the model of trajectories, together with our high-level version of the alerting algorithm, in Java. The implementation, available in the same location as the PVS theory files, serves a double purpose. First, it allows us to graphically visualize all the collision trajectories for a given time and initial values of the intruder and evader aircraft. Trajectories are difficult to visualize in PVS given the huge amount of data generated as output by the model. Second and more importantly, by studying those trajectories, we were able to extract conjectures that we have then formally proven in PVS. Conversely, as we will mention later, we have rejected some conjectures by finding counter-examples via simulation of collision trajectories,

In the next section, we formally study in PVS the behavior of the alerting algorithm with respect to our model of collision trajectories.

5   Main Properties

The objective of this modeling and verification work is (1) to show that the method implemented in the algorithm to predict trajectories and trigger alarms is adequate and does not lead to dangerous situations, and (2) to explore possible trajectory scenarios which lead to unacceptable risk. To this effect we created models of the algorithm and aircraft trajectories in PVS, created simulations in JAVA to graphically visualize the behavior and characteristics of the landing scenario, and derived in the computer algebra tool MuPAD equations of section 3.

5.1   Axioms on Continuous Mathematics

Before stating the main properties, it should be said that most of the proofs require reasoning on continuous mathematics. We have assumed some uninterpreted functions and axioms in PVS, for instance

```
sqrt(x:real) : {z:real | z² = x and z ≥ 0}

sin_cos_sq_one : AXIOM
  ∀ (x:real): sind(x)² + cosd(x)² = 1
```

More involved properties, grounded on Equations 1 to 7, are also necessary, e.g.,

```
derivative_eq_zero_min : AXIOM
  ∀ (t1,t2:real): R(t1+τ(t1)) ≤ R(t1+t2)

decrease_zero_to_tau : AXIOM
  ∀ (t,t1,t2:real) :
    τ(t) ≥ 0 ∧ t2 ≤ τ(t) ∧ t1 ≤ t2
    ⇒
    R(t+t1) ≥ R(t+t2)

increase_tau_to_zero : AXIOM
  ∀ (t,t1,t2:real) :
    τ(t) ≤ 0 ∧ t2 ≥ τ(t) ∧ t1 ≥ t2
    ⇒
    R(t+t1) ≥ R(t+t2)
```

Axiom `derivative_eq_zero_min` states that at time t, $\tau(t)$ would be the time of closest separation between the aircraft. Axioms `decrease_zero_to_tau` and `increase_tau_to_zero` state that function R asymptotically decreases for times less than $\tau(t)$ and asymptotically increases for times greater than $\tau(t)$, respectively.

5.2   Finding a Time Prior to a Collision

Our intention is to show that for all aircraft trajectories which lead to a collision and all initial states[1], an alarm is issued *time* seconds before a collision. In our formal development, we have found maximum and minimum bounds for the values of *time*.

In first place, we have proven that an alarm (it can be caution or warning) is triggered when the distance between the aircraft is within the alerting range (`alertRange`). This property holds independently of the values of any other state variables of the aircraft.

```
alarm_when_alerting_distance : THEOREM
  ∀ (evader,intruder:State) :
    alerting_distance(evader,intruder) ⇒ larcalert(evader,intruder)
```

The theorem above establishes the largest lower bound on the elapsed time between an alert and a collision that we have found so far. For an alerting distance of 1400 feet and an intruder ground speed of 250 feet per second this results in an alarm at least 4 seconds before collision.

An effort to prove that a caution is issued for a value of (`alertTime`-1) (`alertTime` being defined as 19 seconds) failed. Indeed, we have found a collision trajectory which allows two aircraft to fly from a 2500 feet y-separation to a distance of less than 1900 feet, without triggering an alarm 11 seconds before the collision.

---

[1] Recall from section 2 that initial states are when the aircraft are on their localizers.

```
move_2500_to_1900_no_alarm_before_11_seconds : THEOREM
  ∃ (intruder,evader:State, tr:[posnat → Bank], n:nat) :
    collision_scenario(intruder,evader,tr,n+11/tstep) ∧
    abs(y(intruder)-y(evader)) = 2500 ∧
    distance(intruder_trajectory(intruder,tr,n),
            evader_trajectory(evader,n)) < 1900 ∧
  ∀ (i:[0...n]):
    ¬ larcalert(evader_trajectory(evader,i),
              intruder_trajectory(intruder,tr,i))
```

Intruder and evader trajectories that satisfy the above property are $in_0 \ldots in_n$, $ev_0 \ldots ev_n$, where

$$in_0 = (\text{\# x := 860, y := 0, heading := 3, bank := 0 \#})$$

$$ev_0 = (\text{\# x := 0, y := 2500, heading := 0, bank := 0 \#})$$

$$tr = \lambda(n : \text{posnat}) : \text{IF } n \leq 122 \text{ THEN } 0 \text{ ELSE } 45 \text{ ENDIF}$$

and for $0 < i \leq n$,

$$in_i = \text{intruder\_trajectory}(in_0, tr, i)$$

$$ev_i = \text{evader\_trajectory}(ev_0, i)$$

By combining these theorems, we can state that (1) there is a trajectory for which an alarm will not sound before 11 seconds and (2) for all trajectories an alarm will sound at least 4 seconds before a collision. We believe that for all cases the largest time prior to a collision when the alarm will first sound is closer to 11 than to 4.

5.3 Closing the Gap

In order to find a largest time prior to a collision, we need to find strong invariants on collision trajectories. Notice, for example, that for an intruder trajectory $in_0 \ldots in_n$ and an evader trajectory $ev_0 \ldots ev_n$, it cannot be the case that they lead to a collision incident at step n when $\text{distance}(in_0, ev_n) > R$, where

$$R = \text{collisionRange+intruderSpeed} \times \text{n} \times \text{tstep}.$$

Indeed, any intruder aircraft out of the circle of center $(\text{x}(ev_n), \text{y}(ev_n))$ and radius R, needs a larger time than $\text{n} \times \text{tstep}$ to reach any point of the circle of center $(\text{x}(ev_n), \text{y}(ev_n))$ and radio collisionRange. The property above can be expressed in PVS as follows.

```
collision_invariant : LEMMA
  ∀ (intruder,evader:State, tr:[posnat → Bank], n:nat) :
    collision_scenario(intruder,evader,tr,n)
    ⇒
  ∀ (i:[0...n]):
    distance(intruder_trajectory(intruder,tr,i),
            evader_trajectory(evader,n)) ≤
    collisionRange+intruderSpeed× (n-i)×tstep
```

The proof of the invariant above requires the following lemma.

```
distance_invariant : LEMMA
  ∀ (intruder,evader:State, tr:[posnat → Bank], n:nat) :
    distance(intruder_trajectory(intruder,tr,n),evader) ≤
    distance(intruder_trajectory(intruder,tr,n+1),evader) +
    intruderSpeed×tstep
```

Lemma distance_invariant states that with respect to a fix evader position, one step in a straight trajectory leads farther than one step in any other direction.

We intend to use the above invariant and lemmas, together with properties derived from the physical trajectories, to find a bound greater than 4 seconds for any collision scenario. Under the assumption that the intruder bank angle is zero, we have proven that an alarm is issued 19 seconds before a collision. That property is experessed in PVS as follows

```
alarm_before_19_seconds_to_collision : THEOREM
  bank(intruder) = 0 ∧
  collision_scenario(intruder,evader,straight_trajectory,m+38)
  ⇒
  (∀ (i:subrange(m,m+38)):
    larcalert(intruder_trajectory(intruder,straight_trajectory,i),
              evader_trajectory(evader,i)))
```

We are trying to generalize the proof for an arbitrary trajectory and a time of 9 seconds.

6   Conclusion

Several case studies have been performed on the application of hybrid automata to the modeling of systems which include continuous and discrete domains. In particular, a simplified TCAS system was modeled in [9] using hybrid automata. That work focuses on establishing a hybrid model of the closed loop system formed by several aircrafts flying under TCAS assumptions. Although it is claimed that the model is suitable for formal analysis, there is no explicit attempt to automate the proof process. On the other hand, state exploration techniques have been used to analyze the system requirements specification of TCAS II written in RSML [7]; we refer for instance to [5,2]. These works focus on the reactive aspect of the whole system.

In the work presented in this paper, we constructed a formal model of the kernel of an alerting algorithm and we studied its behavior with respect to a model of collision trajectories. We defer the integration of the alerting algorithm with rest of the system, for example TCAS, for future research.

An abstract model of the algorithm and its properties were developed in the general verification system PVS. We complemented the prover capabilities with computer algebra tools. Indeed, differential equations, resulting from physical phenomena, were mechanically verified in MuPAD. Models of the algorithm and collision trajectories were implemented in Java. The implementation allowed us to graphically explore collision scenarios before performing rigorous attempts to prove properties.

Although we have confidence in the conjectures that have been declared as axioms, work is being performed [10] in the development of a PVS library on transcendental functions which complements a previous work on mathematical analysis in PVS [1]. Hence, it might be possible in the near future to replace the axiomatic definitions with theorems.

Lower and upper bounds for a time when an alarm will be issued before a collision were found. Our immediate goal, in the verification of the AILS algorithm, is to prove certain facts about the characteristics of the aircraft trajectories. We hope that these facts allow us to prove the adequacy of the alerting algorithm for a time large enough to avoid any possible collision incident.

References

1. B. Dutertre. Elements of mathematical analysis in PVS. In J. Von Wright, J. Grundy, and J. Harrison, editors, *Ninth international Conference on Theorem Proving in Higher Order Logics TPHOL*, volume 1125 of *Lecture Notes in Computer Science*, pages 141–156, Turku, Finland, August 1996. Springer Verlag.
2. W. Chan, R. Anderson, P. Beame, and D. Notkin. Improving efficiency of symbolic model checking for state-based system requirements. Technical Report TR-98-01-03, University of Washington, Department of Computer Science and Engineering, January 1998.
3. T. Doyle and F. McGee. Air traffic and operational data on selected u.s. airports with parallel runways. Technical Report NASA/CR-1998-207675, NASA, May 1998.
4. B. Fuchssteiner. *MuPAD User's Manual*. John Wiley and Sons, Chichester, New York, first edition, March 1996. Includes a CD for Apple Macintosh and UNIX.
5. M.P.E. Heimdahl and N.G. Leveson. Completeness and Consistency Analysis of State-Based Requirements. In *Proceedings of the 17th International Conference on Software Engineering*, pages 3–14, April 1995.
6. S. Koczo. Coordinated parallel runway approaches. Technical Report NASA-CR-201611, NASA, October 1996.
7. N.G. Leveson, M.P.E. Heimdahl, H. Hildreth, and J.D. Reese. Requirements specification for process-control systems. Technical Report ICS-TR-92-106, University of California, Irvine, Department of Information and Computer Science, November 1992.
8. A.M. Lind. Two simulation studies of precision runway monitoring of independent approaches to closely spaced parallel runways. Technical Report AD-A263433 ATC-190 DOT/FAA/NR-92/9, NASA, March 1993.
9. J. Lygeros and N. A. Lynch. On the formal verification of the TCAS conflict resolution algorithms. In *Proceedings 36th IEEE Conference on Decision and Control*, San Diego, CA, pages 1829–1834, December 1997. Extended abstract.
10. U. Martin and H. Gottliebsen. Computational logic support for differential equations and mathematical modeling. Personal communication, 2000.

11. S. Owre, J. M. Rushby, and N. Shankar. PVS: A prototype verification system. In Deepak Kapur, editor, *11th International Conference on Automated Deduction (CADE)*, volume 607 of *Lecture Notes in Artificial Intelligence*, pages 748–752, Saratoga, NY, June 1992. Springer-Verlag.
12. L. Rine, T. Abbott, G. Lohr, D. Elliott, M. Waller, and R. Perry. The flight deck perspective of the NASA Langley AILS concept. Technical Report NASA/TM-2000-209841, NASA, January 2000.
13. RTCA. Minimum operational performance standards for traffic alert and collision avoidance system (TCAS) airborne equipment – consolidated edition. Guideline DO-185, Radio Technical Commission for Aeronautics, One McPherson Square, 1425 K Street N.W., Suite 500, Washington DC 20005, USA, 6 September 1990.
14. G. Wong. Development of precision runway monitor system for increasing capacity of parallel runway operations. *AGARD, Machine Intelligence in Air Traffic Management*, page 12, October 1993.

Intel's Formal Verification Experience on the Willamette Development

Bob Colwell and Bob Brennan

Intel Corporation,
RA2-401,
2501 NW 229th Avenue,
Hillsboro, OR 97124, USA

In some ways, microprocessor design quality has improved tremendously since the '70's and '80's. It was not uncommon in those days to have to respin silicon five or ten times before the device exhibited even basic functionality. Microprocessors were designed by circuit designers directly into schematics, with little pre-silicon functional testing. In the late '80's, register transfer level (RTL) descriptions of CPUs, such as the Intel® 486, processor were written, allowing useful pre-silicon validation to be performed. This validation was primarily black-box assembly tests written by humans, and it worked because the CPUs were simple designs that could be controlled and observed directly from such tests. Later CPUs required much more intensive pre-silicon efforts, including random code testing and massive amounts of simulation cycles, to get around human limitations on test writing productivity and insufficient imagination in knowing where to look for bugs. Modern designs ('90's until present) often run operating systems successfully on first silicon, despite having microarchitectures that are orders of magnitude more complicated than their predecessors.

That was the good news. The not-so-good news is that a confluence of negative trends are now threatening microprocessor designers. Because performance and clock rate have become the metric of choice for buyers, CPU designers are concentrating on delivering them, and designs are becoming extremely complex as a result. Intel's last three new IA32 microarchitectures were the Pentium® Processor, the Pentium Pro Processor (P6), and Willamette. As measured by lines of RTL code, these processors have increased in complexity by a factor of 2.5x per generation: the Pentium Processor weighed in at 100K lines, the Pentium Pro Processor at 250K lines, and the new Willamette processor at 800K. Two other plausible indicators of design complexity are the total project design effort and the number of design errata found in testing. Both of those metrics have also increased at the rate of 2.5x per generation.

Total volume shipments have risen dramatically, from a few million parts in the '80's to hundreds of millions today, and Intel's experience with the Pentium Processor Floating Point Divider (FDIV) flaw is a stark reminder of how expensive a single design errata can be — $475M for Intel to replace only 5M parts. Moreover, today's much higher volumes are shipped much earlier in the product cycle; where only a few hundred thousand parts might have been sold in the first year of a new microprocessor in the '80's, today we ship millions within that crucial time period, where overlooked errata are most likely to be detected.

J. Harrison and M. Aagaard (Eds.): TPHOLs 2000, LNCS 1869, pp. 106–107, 2000.

This raises the stakes for "getting it right in the first place", and yet that must somehow be accomplished on a shorter development schedule.

These trends were already becoming clear when we began planning for the Willamette processor development effort, a new Intel IA32 CPU expected to become a product in 2000. Two fundamental goals of the processor were higher performance and higher clock rate (those are not always the same), and we did not know how to achieve them without a more complicated microarchitecture. To compensate for this additional complexity we decided to develop and deploy new formal verification techniques that were just becoming feasible. We had little corporate experience with this new technology, so we did not give up on the usual dynamic simulation methods, but we did allocate approximately 20 project heads to FV out of the total pre-silicon validation allocation of 100 people.

We purposely did not charter the new FV team with errata detection, although we did hope they would find some (if for no other reason than to confirm the new technology was actually doing something useful!). Instead, guided by our scars with FDIV, we adopted the attitude that dynamic simulations would find the vast majority of pre-silicon errors, and when that set of techniques hit its marginal utility asymptote, FV might locate any remaining FDIV-like errata that might still be hiding in the rest of the design.

Willamette's FV team emphasis was primarily model-checking, with limited theorem-proving. One reason for this was that our structural RTL code was at a generally rather low-level of abstraction, and there were no usable specifications written by the architects or designers up-front. We did do theorem proving on IEEE floating point units due to the existence of a specification, and since the creation of the necessary specification could then be leveraged by many other chip developments within the company.

Our FV results have been very encouraging. On Willamette units that were formally verified, no silicon errata have been seen to date. Despite the learning curves and team-building overhead, the 20 FV engineers on Willamette managed to formally verify over 15% of the overall design. Based on this experience, we will do more extensive FV on future CPU developments. We do not expect to phase out dynamic simulation, however; we found over 8000 pre-silicon design errors with dynamic testing, and it remains a time- and labor-effective way to drive such errors out of hiding. Finding the best balance between these validation methods is the key. And even with both methods fully employed and balanced, we believe that future designs will have to begin taking product complexity into account at the architecture phase of the design if future products are to achieve the high quality necessary to keep the customers happy and the manufacturer out of trouble.

A Prototype Proof Translator from HOL to Coq

Ewen Denney

Dept. Computing Science, Hong Kong Baptist University,
Kowloon Tong, Hong Kong
ewen@comp.hkbu.edu.hk

Abstract. We describe a low-level proof format, which can be used for independent proof checking and as an intermediate language for translating proofs between systems. The checker is presented as a virtual machine and the proof format as the bytecode. We compare HOL and Coq with a view to designing this pivot language, and describe a prototype which converts recorded HOL proofs into this intermediate format, and then translates them into Coq.

1 Communication between Proof Assistants

There are several motives for wanting to enable communication between proof assistants. The most important is that users of one proof assistant might want to use proofs written with another. Another is using one system to check another. There is also an ecumenical interest in forging links between theorem proving communities.

There has been some work in providing a general framework for different logics. The MathWeb [AHJ+00] and Open Mechanized Reasoning Systems projects [GPT94] aim to provide such a framework. However, it seems there is still much to do at the level of getting individual proof assistants, with their different logics, to understand each other. In this article we will examine the specific case of translating HOL [GM93] proofs to a Coq [BBC+97] readable format.[1]

The translation between these two logics involves a number of non-trivial logical issues. Our approach is to represent proofs using a low-level intermediate proof format, which we use as an intermediate language. We have implemented a translator based on these ideas which accepts a wide variety of HOL proofs. We believe that the approach we have taken has potential for more general application.

In order to communicate proofs, there must be a proof representation, some form of *proof object* [Bar96,BD93]. The starting point for this work is [Won99], which describes an extension of HOL with the ability to record proofs in a particular internal format (as a sequence of inference steps). A different approach is taken by the logical framework, *LF* [HHP87], which uses the dependently typed lambda calculus to represent proofs. An improved representation which avoids some redundancy has been given by Necula and Lee [NL98]. There have

---

[1] We use HOL 98 (Athabasca 5) and Coq V6.1.

J. Harrison and M. Aagaard (Eds.): TPHOLs 2000, LNCS 1869, pp. 108–125, 2000.

also been some specific translations between systems. Boyer and Dowek [BD93] implemented a proof checker for the Calculus of Constructions in Nqthm. The closest work to ours is that of Felty and Howe [FH97], who gave a translation of HOL terms into Nuprl. This work is complementary to ours, in that they concentrate on translating terms and ignore proofs, whereas we translate proofs but tackle a limited collection of terms.

In Section 2, we look at the differences between HOL and Coq, in both the logics and the pragmatics of proof development. Then in Section 3, we describe the proof format as the bytecode which runs on an 'idealised' virtual machine. Although the checker has not been implemented, these ideas form the basis of a prototype translator which has been implemented. In Sections 4 and 5, we describe various features of the translation that have been implemented to date, and give an overview of the algorithm used to translate to and from this format. Finally, in Section 6, we discuss various ways in which our prototype system can be improved.

2 Comparison of HOL and Coq

Although HOL and Coq are both implementations of a form of higher-order logic over a version of the lambda-calculus, there are significant differences in the details of the logic and in the pragmatics of proof development, so that it can be surprisingly difficult for users of one system to understand the mind-set of those of the other.

Zammit [Zam97] compares Coq and HOL, and we add some more details from the perspective of translation. We first compare the practicalities of proof construction, and then the details of the logics.

2.1 Proof Development

Proof Metalanguage HOL is an "LCF-style" theorem prover, meaning that the user uses the ML programming language directly within the proving session, in order to construct Hilbert-style proofs. Proof development is an interactive activity consisting of writing ML functions and invoking tactics, which is just evaluating ML expressions whose side-effects may alter the proof state.

This use of an external metalanguage is really quite alien to the Coq paradigm; an interactive proof session, and the saved proof script is entirely within the Coq proof language.

Proof Modes There are two modes in Coq: top-level and proof mode. In proof mode, we set a goal and interactively prove a theorem. At the top-level, when not actually proving a theorem, we can check the type of a term, and so on. In Coq terminology, all the commands which alter the proof state during a proof, in proof mode, are called tactics.

Although HOL also has two such modes, proofs are usually constructed at the top-level, which is just an ML session. There is an interactive goal-oriented facility but this is not primitive, and proofs constructed here are compiled down into combinations of forwards-style inference steps.

Proof Style HOL is fundamentally a forwards-style (bottom-up) theorem prover whereas Coq is backwards-style (top-down). Although, in practice, HOL tactics let proofs be carried out in a backwards style (top-down), this is just sugar for the forward inference steps. In fact, Coq also allows proof terms to be directly constructed in a forwards-style, but the interactive development language is backwards-style.

This directionality influences the treatment of contexts in the two systems. For example, the HOL rule of *modus ponens* is:

$$\frac{\Gamma_1 \vdash P \supset Q \quad \Gamma_2 \vdash P}{\Gamma_1 \cup \Gamma_2 \vdash Q}$$

The corresponding step[2] in Coq is the *cut rule*:

$$\frac{\Gamma \vdash P \supset Q \quad \Gamma \vdash P}{\Gamma \vdash Q}$$

The point is that in HOL, we start with two judgements with arbitrary contexts, and so must combine these contexts in the conclusion. In Coq, since we work backwards, the single context is just duplicated.

Tactics, Inference Rules, and Theorems In HOL terminology, the result of each inference step is a "theorem". When working forwards, at each step there is well-defined statement that's been proven at that point. These theorems are represented internally as the elements of a datatype thm, where a theorem is a list of assumptions and a conclusion.

When developing a proof interactively in HOL, since the user must use ML to construct the proof, a tactic can not be invoked directly. Rather, the user must type e(the_TACTIC), where e will evaluate the_TACTIC, and as a side-effect, change the proof state. Otherwise, a 'proof' is given directly, by defining a theorem via the inferences that prove it. For example,

```
val TWOREFLS = CONJ (REFL (Term '1:num')) (REFL (Term '2:num'));
```

binds the ML term TWOREFLS to a proof of $1 = 1 \wedge 2 = 2$. The functions REFL and CONJ return terms of type thm but are not datatype constructors; the proof cannot be reconstructed from the value of TWOREFLS.

The top-down notion of proof as a sequence of formulae, each of which is an axiom or follows from some previous members of the sequence using an inference rule, is not appropriate in a backwards style, since it does not really make sense to speak of having proved a theorem at each stage. Starting with a goal, and gradually destructing it until we reach True, say, we cannot directly[3] say that we have proven anything before the proof is finished.

---

[2] Although the HOL tactic IMP-RES-TAC corresponds more literally, in the sense that it works backwards and so duplicates the context, we make this correspondence since both are primitive at the level of proof abstraction we will work at.

[3] Of course, we have indirectly proven a conditional theorem.

In Coq, proofs are constructed interactively, or by loading the corresponding script from a file.

```
Theorem TwoRefls : (1=1) /\ (2=2).
 Split.
 Reflexivity.
 Reflexivity.
Qed.
```

This results in the identifier `TwoRefls` being bound to a proof object — a lambda term — but this definition could be done directly, as in HOL. Proofs are structured into various units (theorems, lemmas, definitions, *etc.*) each of which can be constructed directly or interactively. The intermediate states in the proofs of these units are not stored.

HOL tactics can do more than necessary, in the sense that many of the expanded primitive inferences are not used to construct the main theorem. User-defined tactics are used much more extensively in HOL than in Coq[4]. The user can define tactics, however, in Coq also, using basic tactics and tacticals. The Coq tactic language does not have powerful features such as recursion and pattern matching. If necessary, tactics can be written in Objective Caml and then linked to Coq's code. This does not seem to happen often, however!

Primitive Rules In HOL there is a well-defined set of *primitive* inference rules and axioms. Using these primitive rules and axioms, about 40 so-called *basic* rules are derived: introduction and elimination rules for the logical operators, congruence rules for equality, and so on. It is applications of these rules that are recorded in Wong's HOL proof format [Won99], and treated as though primitive. Proofs using HOL tactics compile down into basic rules.

This Hilbert-style approach is not really in the spirit of the Coq type-theoretic style of proof development. Although Coq is implemented in terms of about seven primitive tactics (Intro, Clear, Change, *etc.*), these have no special status in the language from the user's point of view. A proof is not thought of as being a sugared sequence of 'primitive' steps. The user just does whatever it takes to find an inhabitant t of a type τ in the calculus of constructions, at which point the system checks that t does indeed have type τ. The term t is retained as a proof object.

Contexts During Coq proofs, there is an explicit context, visible at all times. The context contains both variable declarations and propositional assumptions. In fact, propositions are just a special case of variables because to assume P is to assume a proof $H : P$. We can add an assumption using the command, `Variable n:nat`, for example. In HOL, however, the 'context' is a list of assumptions which can be open. Free term and type variables are not explicit.

---

[4] As pointed out in [Zam97], though, this is often more a measure of the low-level at which HOL proofs would otherwise be carried out.

2.2   Proof Language

Propositions In HOL, there is no distinction between booleans and propositions. Propositions are manipulated just like any other terms. A direct consequence of this is that extensionality of booleans corresponds to the law of the excluded middle.

In Coq, on the other hand, booleans `bool` are a type (with canonical closed terms `true` and `false`) in the (computational) universe `Set`, whereas propositions are more like types, but in the (non-computational) universe `Prop`. Thus terms can be 'typed' by propositions: if $t : P$, where P is a proposition, then t is a proof of P.

Logic HOL uses classical logic whereas Coq is intuitionistic. This is not a significant difference since proofs in Coq can be given as terms in either the `Set` or `Prop` universes, and the latter can consistently be assumed as classical, by adding a classical axiom.

Type Theory Coq uses a considerably more powerful type theory than HOL, the (inductive) calculus of constructions. The formulations of theorems and constructed objects are typically more complicated than in HOL. For example, HOL does not have dependent types, or full polymorphism. Expressing polymorphism with type variables rather than type quantifiers corresponds to Hindley-Milner polymorphism, rather than Girard-Reynolds. Inductive types are used extensively in Coq. Subset types (*e.g.* $\{n : nat \mid n > 0\}$) are a particular case of these. Moreover, Coq is Church-style (bindings must be explicitly typed), whereas HOL is Curry-style.

In Section 4, we will see how the translation copes with these differences. First, though, we describe an intermediate format.

3   Abstract Machine for Proof Checking

By *proof checker* we mean a tool which takes a proof and a proposition, and decides whether or not the proof is valid for this proposition. This is unlike a *proof assistant* which is a tool used to construct such a proof, by a combination of automatic search and user interaction. Many proof assistants (such as Coq) contain a checker at their core. Some authors consider a checker to take a proof script and produce a proof object, but we will identify proof objects and scripts here.

In this section, we discuss the possibilities for a low-level intermediate proof format, and then describe a proof checker which uses this format.

3.1   Proof Format

Proofs in HOL and Coq can be presented at several levels: in HOL, using tactics (which may invoke opaque decision procedures), as a sequence of basic inferences, as primitive inferences, or as the ML code which runs through the proof; in Coq, as (Coq style) tactics, as a sequence of internal manipulations to the proof state, or as a lambda-term. There is some choice, therefore, for the appropriate level at which to communicate proofs.

The LF approach is to encode proofs as terms in the lambda-calculus where the inference steps are primitive constants and use this as a universal proof format. The proof object produced by Coq is a lambda-term. Checking this proof amounts to checking it is well-typed. The type can be reconstructed and is not given explicitly in the proof object. It is not clear how HOL could directly produce such an object.

An alternative, however, is just to use the inference steps directly. This has the additional advantage of avoiding the mass of typing annotations that typically appear in LF representations. Also, to a certain extent, basic tactics are independent of the specific details of a logic, such as whether the terms are typed or not.

The next choice is whether the proofs should be in a backwards or forwards style. For reasons we will outline below, we adopt a backwards style, and show how to transform forwards-style HOL proofs. We start with a goal, which is then manipulated by the inferences. The proof is finished when we reach **Qed** and there are no more goals to prove.

To check a forwards-style proof, that is, a sequence of theorems each inferred from its predecessors, we would have to constantly check whether we had reached the desired goal.[5] At each stage, we would need to check that only proven theorems or axioms are used, or have two passes, where the first pass lists all the theorems, and the second checks their use. Either way, this is cumbersome. Also, it would be difficult to translate Coq's native low-level into a forwards style.

A backwards-style format offers two main advantages:

- Intermediate theorems do not need to be stored.[6] This reduces the size of proofs considerably, as well as the time needed to check a proof. It also reduces the complexity of the checker since, for each step, we just need to alter the proof state in a deterministic manner based on the current instruction, rather than check the validity of hypotheses, or compare theorems.
- There is less need for explicit arguments to rules, reducing the size of a proof further. For example, in forwards-style, the assumption rule is given as argument a proposition, P, and returns the theorem $P \vdash P$. Read backwards, the P is implicit; to prove the goal $P \vdash P$, we need just appeal to the assumption rule.

3.2   Abstract Machine

There is an analogy between running a program and checking a proof. We present a proof checker as a virtual machine, for which the inference steps are the bytecode.

---

[5] Or, with exactly one goal, have a convention that the given proof steps are all necessary, and compare the result when finished.

[6] Although it is possible to just record the application of inference rules used to construct a sequence of inferred theorems, checking this would have to be done backwards.

The idea is that the machine has a state that represents the proof checking as it proceeds, containing a stack of goals, the current context, the current proposition to be proven, and the list of steps to be followed. This is an alternative to requiring the proof format to carry such information. The machine will implicitly know what is required.

Following the virtual machine analogy, we will think of a proof file as consisting of a number of components. In the simplified prototype translator we will describe in the next two sections, we will just have axiom and theorem components. However, we also envisage signature and inference rule components, though these are not implemented in our prototype and are not formalised here.

The machine takes a collection of proofs, stored in the theorem component — an indexed collection of proofs. One of these will be the main theorem. The use of some other theorem corresponds to looking up the proof in the theorem component (like invoking a method), so there are no forward references. We place an ordering requirement to avoid circularity, by assigning each theorem a unique number. All proofs used are checked exactly once and there is a global state recording the checked status of each theorem. There is also an axiom component, listing the hypotheses on which the proofs are based.

We allow references to both internal and external theorems. External theorems must be taken from some named source and are considered to have been checked. The checker does not have access to their proofs. In the case of some theory library we could imagine that the proofs are publicly available. A theorem might also be proved by a BDD or computer algebra package, or a model checker, say, in which case there is no proof, but the appeal to this external source should still be listed in an external theory component, which lists the external theories which are used and assumed to be checked, or trusted.

A proof state consists of the current index, a list of goals to be proven, the current goal, that is, the current context and proposition, and a list of steps to be followed.

$$goal = context \times proposition$$
$$proof\_state = index \times list\ goal \times context \times proposition \times list\ step$$
$$context = list\ assumption$$
$$assumption = proposition\ |\ typed\ variable$$

We will allow the usual logical operators of predicate logic with equality, without specifying the term syntax beyond being a Church style lambda calculus with some notion of occurrence and substitution. A suitable formalism for doing this would be the XML-based OpenMath [CCC99] standard. We distinguish types, terms and propositions, however. The logic has the usual primitive logical operators, explicit contexts, and axioms for classical reasoning. We use the metavariables t for terms, occ for occurrences, x for variables, P for propositions, and thy for theory names

The machine is required to be able to check α-equivalence, inspect and replace subterms at given occurrences, and check that a formula has a particular form (e.g. an equality or a conjunction). We use the notations $\equiv^\alpha$, and subterm(occ, P), $P[occ := t]$, and $P[occs := t]$ for alpha equivalence, subterm at a given occurrence, and single and multiple substitution of terms at occurrences. We also use the notation $P[t/x]$ for the substitution of a term for a variable.

We will give transition rules for a minimal selection (we omit the rules for conjunction, disjunction and external theorems) of instructions:

$step ::=$ Ass | Thmit^* | Axiomit^* | Conj | LProj$P$ | RProj$P$ | Lor |
          Ror | OrElimPP' | Cut$P$ | Intro | Refl | Sym | Trans$t$ |
          Beta | Eta | Zeta | Absurd | Defxt | Unfoldocc | Fold$occt$ |
          Ext$thyit^*$ | Genocc^+ | Subst$occt$ | ExIntro$t$ | ExElimxt |
          App_cong

(use assumption in current context, use theorem i with arguments, use axiom i, conjunction introduction, conjunction eliminations, or introductions and elimination, cut, implication or quantification introductions, reflexivity, symmetry, transitivity, beta, eta and zeta (lambda-congruence) equality rules, reasoning from false, definition, unfold and fold a particular occurrence with respect to a definition, use external theorem i in theory thy, generalise at occurrences $occs$, substitution, existential elimination, application congruence).

The proof style used is closer to sequent calculus than Hilbert style. The code consists of low-level instructions for the various logical constructs, rewriting, and definitions. It differs from sequent calculus in its operational formulation, and in having explicit commands for definitions and the use of axioms and theorems.

There are instructions for the introduction and elimination of the various logical operators. Following Coq, the Intro instruction is introduction for both implication and quantification. The elimination rules for implication and quantification are Cut and Gen, respectively.

We distinguish two forms of substitution here:

$$\frac{x \vdash P}{P[t/x]} \qquad \frac{P[t/x] \quad t = t'}{P[t'/x]}$$

The first rule read backwards becomes generalisation, Gen occ^+. We indicate the term to generalise over by indicating the occurrence rather than giving the term to match against. We allow several arguments to Gen in order to generalise over several terms. However, we still need a substitution rule for the second rule.

We write simultaneous substitution of $t_1, \ldots, t_n$ for $x_1, \ldots, x_n$ in P as $P[t_k/x_k]$, where the range of the index $k = 1, \ldots, n$ is implicit. We write tuples using $\langle \rangle$ brackets. Context extension is indicated as $(\Gamma, x : \tau)$ and (Γ, P).

A selection of the transition rules is given in Figures 1 to 3. We write Thm$i$ for Thm$i[\,]$, and similarly for Axiom. We will write Qed as a synonym for True in the rules. The checking succeeds if the machine reaches Qed with no further goals to check. Otherwise, if we reach a state where no rule applies the checking fails.

When an axiom or theorem is invoked the machine does a lookup to see if it matches the current goal.

$$\texttt{lookup\_thm} : index \rightarrow proposition \times list\ step$$

$$\texttt{lookup\_axiom} : index \rightarrow proposition$$

If a theorem has been invoked, it then looks to see whether it has been checked or not. If it is unchecked, and its index is greater than the current index, then its proof is checked in the empty context. If this succeeds it is marked as checked. If it has already been checked, or is an axiom, the goal is proven immediately and replaced with any hypotheses. In either case, the goal is popped off the stack. We give separate rules for Axiom and Thm depending on whether or not any arguments are given.

The instruction Def $x\,t$ defines x to be t by adding the equality $x = t$ to the local context. The instructions Fold and Unfold make use of definitions in the local context.

4   Logical Aspects of the Translation

As mentioned above, in this simplified prototype, we will just have axiom and theorem components. We use the proof bytecode as a pivot language to translate between Coq and HOL. Translation from HOL to Coq is a two stage process.

1. HOL → Pcode: Translation to a syntactically neutral bytecode, representing top-down proofs.
2. Pcode → Coq: Conversion of bytecode to Coq commands.

It would, of course, have been possible to give a direct translation, but the two stages are a natural and modular split. The first stage involves manipulation of HOL terms and the extraction of relevant information, whereas the second involves the construction of Coq terms. This modularity would be more important if we gave translations to and from a third logic.

The input is a forwards-style HOL proof of the form:

$$HOL\_proof = goal \times inference\_step\ list$$
$$inference\_step = name \times argument\ list \times conclusion$$
$$argument = proposition\_in\_context \mid term \mid type$$
$$goal, conclusion = proposition\_in\_context$$
$$proposition\_in\_context = proposition\ list \times proposition$$

An example of the concrete syntax of an inference step in HOL (in the format of [Won99] is:

```
{Just = [REC_THM|- 1 = 1, REC_THM|- 2 = 2], Tag = "CJ",
        Thm = |- (1 = 1) /\ (2 = 2)}
```

Axioms and Theorems

$$\frac{\texttt{lookup\_thm}\,(j) = \langle P, S'\rangle \qquad \langle j, [\,], [\,], P, S'\rangle \longrightarrow \langle j, [\,], \Gamma', \texttt{Qed}, S''\rangle}{\langle i, G, \Gamma, P, \texttt{Thm}\,i :: S\rangle \longrightarrow \langle i, G, \Gamma, P, S\rangle} \quad \begin{cases} \neg checked\,(j), \\ i < j, \\ checked(j) := true \end{cases}$$

$$\frac{\begin{array}{c} \texttt{lookup\_thm}\,(j) = \langle \forall x_1 : \tau_1 \cdots x_n : \tau_n.P_1 \to \cdots \to P_m \to Q, S'\rangle \\ \langle j, [\,], [\,], \forall x_1 : \tau_1 \cdots x_n : \tau_n.P_1 \to \cdots \to P_m \to Q, S'\rangle \longrightarrow \\ \langle j, [\,], \Gamma', \texttt{Qed}, S''\rangle \end{array}}{\begin{array}{c} \langle i, G, \Gamma, Q[t_k/x_k], \texttt{Thm}\,j\,t_1 \cdots t_n :: S\rangle \longrightarrow \\ \langle i, \langle \Gamma, P_2[t_k/x_k]\rangle :: \cdots :: \langle \Gamma, P_m[t_k/x_k]\rangle :: G, \Gamma, P_1[t_k/x_k], S\rangle \end{array}} \quad \begin{cases} \neg checked\,(j), \\ i < j, \\ checked(j) := true \end{cases}$$

$$\frac{\texttt{lookup\_thm}\,(j) = \langle P, S'\rangle}{\langle i, G, \Gamma, P, \texttt{Thm}\,j :: S\rangle \longrightarrow \langle i, G, \Gamma, \texttt{Qed}, S\rangle} \quad \begin{cases} checked\,(j) \\ i < j \end{cases}$$

$$\frac{\texttt{lookup\_thm}\,(j) = \langle \forall x_1 : \tau_1 \cdots x_n : \tau_n.P_1 \to \cdots \to P_m \to Q, S'\rangle}{\begin{array}{c} \langle i, G, \Gamma, Q[t_k/x_k], \texttt{Thm}\,j\,t_1 \cdots t_n :: S\rangle \longrightarrow \\ \langle i, \langle \Gamma, P_2[t_k/x_k]\rangle :: \cdots :: \langle \Gamma, P_m[t_k/x_k]\rangle :: G, \Gamma, P_1[t_k/x_k], S\rangle \end{array}} \quad \begin{cases} checked\,(j) \\ i < j \end{cases}$$

$$\frac{\texttt{lookup\_axiom}(j) = P}{\langle i, G, \Gamma, P, \texttt{Axiom}\,j :: S\rangle \longrightarrow \langle i, G, \Gamma, \texttt{Qed}, S\rangle}$$

$$\frac{\texttt{lookup\_axiom}(j) = \forall x_1 : \tau_1 \cdots x_n : \tau_n.P_1 \to \cdots \to P_m \to Q}{\begin{array}{c} \langle i, G, \Gamma, Q[t_k/x_k], \texttt{Axiom}\,j\,t_1 \cdots t_n :: S\rangle \longrightarrow \\ \langle i, \langle \Gamma, P_2[t_k/x_k]\rangle :: \cdots :: \langle \Gamma, P_m[t_k/x_k]\rangle :: G, \Gamma, P_1[t_k/x_k], S\rangle \end{array}}$$

Definitions

$$\langle i, G, \Gamma, P, \texttt{Def}\,x\,t :: S\rangle \longrightarrow \langle i, G, (\Gamma, x : \tau, x = t), P, S\rangle$$

$$\frac{\texttt{subterm}(occ, P) = x}{\langle i, G, \Gamma, P, \texttt{Unfold}\,occ :: S\rangle \longrightarrow \langle i, G, \Gamma, P[occ := t], S\rangle} \quad (x = t \in \Gamma)$$

$$\frac{\texttt{subterm}(occ, P) = t}{\langle i, G, \Gamma, P, \texttt{Fold}\,occ\,c :: S\rangle \longrightarrow \langle i, G, \Gamma, P[occ := c], S\rangle} \quad (c = t \in \Gamma)$$

Substitution

$$\frac{\texttt{subterm}(occ, P) = t'}{\langle i, G, \Gamma, P, \texttt{Subst}\,occ\,t :: S\rangle \longrightarrow \langle i, \langle \Gamma, t = t'\rangle :: G, \Gamma, P[occ := t], S\rangle}$$

Fig. 1. Transition Rules

Equality Reasoning

$$\langle i, G, \Gamma, t \equiv^\alpha t', \mathtt{Refl} :: S \rangle \longrightarrow \langle i, G, \Gamma, \mathtt{Qed}, S \rangle$$

$$\langle i, G, \Gamma, t = t', \mathtt{Sym} :: S \rangle \longrightarrow \langle i, G, \Gamma, t' = t, S \rangle$$

$$\langle i, G, \Gamma, t_1 = t_2, \mathtt{Trans}\, t_3 :: S \rangle \longrightarrow \langle i, \langle \Gamma, t_3 = t_2 \rangle :: G, \Gamma, t_1 = t_3, S \rangle$$

Fig. 2. Transition Rules *cont.*

This will be translated simply to the instruction Conj.

In Section 2, we described differences between HOL and Coq that are significant for the representation of proofs. We now describe how these logical differences are handled by the translation.

Direction of Inference Translation between forwards and backwards styles is not a simple reversal since we must take account of dependencies introduced by subproofs (and definitions).

To do this, the sequence of HOL steps is converted into a DAG, where hypotheses are child nodes. Although the proof corresponds to a unique tree, during a HOL session the branches can be constructed in any order, and so can appear in any order in the list of proof steps. Hence we must match theorems to hypotheses. The nodes are the names of inference steps plus any arguments necessary for backwards proof. The underlying tree is traversed and output in infix order as a sequence of instructions.

Contexts The proof checking state uses an explicit context of variables and propositional assumptions. HOL inference steps which combine contexts in a specifically forwards style, such as CONJ and MODUS PONENS, can consistently be read backwards. Additional assumptions are propagated backwards automatically. The step ADD_ASSUM which adds an assumption to the context of a theorem can be ignored. For example, the HOL proof

$$\frac{\qquad\qquad \dfrac{}{B \vdash B}}{\dfrac{A \vdash A \quad B, C \vdash B}{A, B, C \vdash A \wedge B}}$$

will become

$$\frac{A, B, C \vdash A \quad A, B, C \vdash B}{A, B, C \vdash A \wedge B}$$

Prop and Bool It is fundamental to the classical nature of HOL that booleans are used as propositions. However, it would be inconsistent in Coq to identify equality of propositions and logical equivalence so equality of booleans is translated into an *iff*. In fact, since equality in HOL is extensional, unlike in Coq, we must also perform eta-expansion. Therefore, we translate all

---

Quantifications

$$\frac{}{\langle i, G, \Gamma, P, \mathtt{Gen}\ occ_1, \ldots, occ_n :: S\rangle \longrightarrow} \quad (x \notin \Gamma)$$
$$\langle i, G, \Gamma, \forall x : \tau . P[occ_1, \ldots, occ_n := x], S\rangle$$

$$\langle i, G, \Gamma, \forall x : \tau . P, \mathtt{Intro} :: S\rangle \longrightarrow \langle i, G, (\Gamma, x : \tau), P, S\rangle$$

Other Logical Rules

$$\frac{}{\langle i, G, \Gamma, P, \mathtt{Ass} :: S\rangle \longrightarrow \langle i, G, \Gamma, \mathtt{Qed}, S\rangle} \quad (P \in \Gamma)$$

$$\langle i, (\Gamma, P) :: G, \Gamma', \mathtt{Qed}, S\rangle \longrightarrow \langle i, G, \Gamma, P, S\rangle$$

$$\langle i, G, \Gamma, P, \mathtt{Absurd} :: S\rangle \longrightarrow \langle i, G, \Gamma, \bot, S\rangle$$

$$\langle i, G, \Gamma, Q \supset P, \mathtt{Intro} :: S\rangle \longrightarrow \langle i, G, (\Gamma, Q), P, S\rangle$$

$$\langle i, G, \Gamma, P, \mathtt{Cut}\ Q :: S\rangle \longrightarrow \langle i, (\Gamma, Q) :: G, \Gamma, Q \supset P, S\rangle$$

Fig. 3. Transition Rules *cont.*

equalities into an eta-expanded form, replacing equality on booleans with equivalence.

For example, if f and f' have type $\mathtt{num} \to \mathtt{bool}$, then $f = f'$ will be translated to

$$(x\_1385, x\_1386 : \mathtt{nat})x\_1385 = x\_1386 \to (fx\_1385) \leftrightarrow (f'x\_1386)$$

(the variables being generated automatically) and the HOL step

$$\frac{F = F' \quad a = a'}{Fa = F'a'}$$

will be translated to Cut a=a'; Generalize a a'. These Coq commands take the goal first from $Fa = F'a'$ to the subgoals $a = a' \to Fa = F'a'$ and $a = a'$, and then to $\forall x. \forall x'.x = x' \to Fx = F'x'$ and $a = a'$.

The HOL step 'equality modus ponens'

$$\frac{P = Q \quad P}{Q}$$

translates to the transition

$$\langle i, G, \Gamma, Q, \mathtt{Iff\_cut}\ P :: S\rangle \longrightarrow \langle i, (\Gamma, P) :: G, \Gamma, P \Longleftrightarrow Q, S\rangle.$$

In Coq, we represent this as the lemma

$$\texttt{iff\_impl} : (\texttt{P}, \texttt{Q} : \texttt{Prop})(\texttt{P} \leftrightarrow \texttt{Q}) \rightarrow (\texttt{P} \rightarrow \texttt{Q}).$$

The rules EQ_IMP_RULE_L, EQ_IMP_RULE_R, IMP_ANTISYM_RULE, and the associated axiom, IMP_ANTISYM_AX are translated similarly.

The other inferences to do with equality — reflexivity, symmetry, transitivity, congruence — also have propositional versions. This leads to complications, in particular, with the congruence rules (for example, the HOL rule MK_COMB and AP_TERM).

Theorems In HOL, a theorem is a list of hypotheses, paired with a conclusion. This is translated to a single proposition consisting of a quantification over free type and term variables and a nested implication from hypotheses to conclusions. Since HOL proofs work implicitly on the conclusion, each Coq proof must first Intro each of the assumptions.

We first explain how lemmas are used during a Coq proof. If the current goal is P, and lemma T directly proves P, then we can solve the goal immediately with the command Exact T. If T proves $A \rightarrow P$, then we can use the command Apply T, which will replace the goal with A. However, if the goal is B $\rightarrow$ C and we want to use the lemma A $\rightarrow$ B $\rightarrow$ C then Coq is unable to do the match. We have to first do an Intro, then apply the lemma, matching against C.

With either command, we can also 'pass' arguments to theorems. For example, if the goal is $P[t/x]$ and T proves $\forall x : \tau.P$, then we can use Exact $(T\, t)$.

Church-style type annotations Since Coq requires explicit quantification, we must add quantifiers over term and type variables wherever necessary. This means though that where a HOL proof would expect to be working on an unquantified proposition, the corresponding Coq proof must insert the appropriate number of Intro's. In practice, this means that lemma proofs must begin by introducing all the 'extra' quantifications, that is, the free variables, and the hypotheses.

5   Translation Algorithm

We have implemented a prototype translator in about 750 lines of ML, which accepts a subset[7] of HOL proofs and outputs a Coq readable file. The basic idea of the algorithm is to first represent the proof as a DAG, where each node corresponds to a theorem, in the HOL sense, and children are hypotheses. Then any shared hypotheses can be factored out as lemmas, and leaf nodes will become axioms. This gives the architectural organisation of the proof. As for translating

---

[7] Apart from a few basic inference steps [GM93] that we have just not got round to implementing (type instantiation, negation rules, and a few others), the main omissions are the steps for axioms and definitions. These are used by the definitional packages for making recursive function and type definitions, and treatment of this is the main topic of [FH97].

individual steps, there is some choice for how much detail can be put in the bytecode, and how much can be taken for granted. At one extreme, we could write a tactic in Coq, HolTac say, that mimicked HOL, and simply translate proofs to a single application of HolTac. Instead, we translate the proof, step by step, as it is.

We do not use the instruction set of Section 3.2 directly, but modify it for ease of implementation. There are two main differences from the virtual machine described above. The first is that we use HOL terms. This simplifies the implementation considerably since we can rely on the HOL system to manipulate terms. The second comes from the fact that certain inference steps in HOL correspond to several steps in the pivot language, and in Coq. However, we have not implemented the inference rule component. Thus, instead of writing the lemmas in the pivot, we translate them directly into Coq lemmas and (more generally) tactics. We extend the instruction set with a number of ad hoc instructions, such as Iff_sym (symmetry of *iff*) and AE_EX (application congruence for ∃). The generated Coq proofs must first load a file with Coq code (lemmas and tactics) for these instructions. For example, the instruction Iff_sym will be translated to an application of the lemma iff_sym, where

$$\text{iff\_sym} : (P, Q : Prop)(P \leftrightarrow Q) \rightarrow (Q \leftrightarrow P).$$

There are extra arguments to Intro1 and Zeta, giving the variables which these steps introduce to the local context. If the translator also implemented a checker these variables would be implicit. Similarly, the application congruence instructions, App_cong1 and App_cong2 (one for when the function terms are the same, and one for when they differ) also need extra arguments, for subterms that would be implicit. We do not need to pass arguments to axioms and theorems.

The datatype of bytecode instructions is:

```
datatype instr = Ass | Thm of int | Axiom of int | Conj |
LProj of term | RProj of term | Lor | Ror |
OrElim of (term*term) | Cut of term | Intro |
Intro1 of term | Refl | Sym | Trans of term | Beta | Eta |
Zeta of term | Absurd | Def of (term*term) |
Unfold of occurrence | Fold of (occurrence*term) |
Ext of (string*int) | Gen of occurrence |
Subst of (occurrence*term) | ExElim of term*term | ExIntro of term |
Iff_cut of term | App_cong1 of (term*term) | App_cong2 of term*term |
Nop | Genterm of (term*term) | Genterm_I of (term*term*term) |
Error of string | Iff_refl | Iff_sym | Iff_trans of term |
AE_FA of (term*term*term) | AE_EX of (term*term*term) |
MC_FA of (term*term*term) | MC_EX of (term*term*term);
```

The translation consists of four passes, of which we combine the first two. The input to the algorithm is the list of proof steps output by the HOL proof recorder. The first phase uses HOL functions, for example, for finding the types of terms. Since the bytecode uses HOL terms, the second phase must also use HOL functions but, in principle, it should be independent of HOL.

Conversion of individual steps to bytecode The   function   `trans_step` translates a HOL inference step, consisting of hypotheses, arguments, theorem concluded, and name of the inference rule, into a bytecode instruction. In general, most of the information is discarded. For example, modus ponens is translated as follows:

```
"MP" => let val _::h2::[] = hyps in Cut (concl h2) end
```

Here, `hyps` is the list of hypotheses for this step.

Creation of proof DAG The list of HOL inference steps is converted into a DAG format. Nodes represent either unproven theorems, or inference steps linked to their hypotheses.

```
datatype label = COUNT of int | LEMMA of int;
datatype node =
    THM of Thm.thm |
    INF of (string * dag ref ref list * arg list * Thm.thm)
and
dag = DAG of node * label;
```

Each node of the DAG is given a label. During the creation of the DAG, the label keeps a count of how many parents a node has (that is, how often it is used as a hypothesis). The steps are processed from top to bottom. The first step, which is assumed to conclude the main theorem, gives the root of the DAG. At any stage there is a list of global hypotheses. This is initialised to the list of hypotheses of the first step. The conclusions of subsequent steps are then matched against the list of global hypotheses. If there is no match the step is discarded. Otherwise, a new node is created for this step and the matched hypotheses are made to point to this node. The matches are removed from the list of global hypotheses, and the hypotheses of this step are added.

We assume that the first step encountered will be the one that concludes the main theorem. Since the top-down ordering will be respected by the HOL proof recorder, it follows that if a step cannot be added to the current proof DAG, then it is not needed in the proof of the main theorem.

Creation of proof lists The DAG is traversed from the root upwards, reading off steps into the current lemma. If the count label is greater than one, then a new lemma is created, the label is changed to Lemma n, where n is the current lemma number, and the traversal continues from there. Finally, theorem nodes without hypotheses are translated to axioms. Hypotheses are traversed from left to right, with one exception: the hypotheses of the HOL inference step `CHOOSE` are in the opposite order from those in the corresponding step of Coq.

Conversion of bytecode proofs to Coq The axioms are first converted, and then each of the lemmas. We use two mutually recursive translation functions `coqpp` and `expand_equiv`, which pretty-print terms and equalities, respectively, in a Coq-readable format. These are called, in turn, by `instr2coq` and `prop2coq`. The function `instr2coq` is the core of this stage of the conversion, and incorporates the specific Coq tactics which correspond to each bytecode instruction. For example,

```
Cut t => (dup (); "Cut " ^ (prop2coq t))
```

The function `prop2coq` displays a proposition, stored as a HOL term, by displaying quantifiers for the type and term variables, and then calling `coqpp`. Only those variables which would be free at this point in the proof should be quantified over. This means that we have to keep track of the variable context. In fact, there is a stack of contexts, initially set to empty for each lemma. The function `instr2coq` will alter the stack depending on the instruction processed. If the instruction performs an `Intro1 x`, then `x` is pushed onto the stack, that is, is added to the head of the top context on the stack. If the instruction solves the current goal, then the stack is popped. If, like `Cut`, the instruction splits the current goal into two subgoals, then the top element is duplicated.

6   Conclusion

We have presented a compact proof format which can be used both for independent proof checking, and as an intermediate language for the translation between HOL and Coq. We obtain small proofs, comparable with the results of [NL98], and which place minimal requirements on a checker.

The proof format is used for translation from HOL to Coq but is fairly independent of either format. In general, there is not a one-to-one correspondence between instructions and proof steps in either HOL or Coq.

Most appeals to classical reasoning in HOL proofs are translated to axioms in Coq proofs. The major difference between Coq and HOL turned out to be HOL's representation of propositions as booleans, and its associated use of equality reasoning. As commented on in [Zam97], in contrast to HOL, Coq offers little support for the 'equality-like' nature of *iff*. In consequence, the translation generates quite ugly proofs, and better results could perhaps be obtained by translating at a higher level.

We have not yet reached the ideal system outlined in Section 3. The main task is to make the bytecode independent of HOL by having its own notion of term, and adding an inference rule component. The OpenMath standard [CCC99] could be used for term syntax.

As well as only translating a subset of HOL proofs, it is possible that the generated proofs might fail because they rely on a term matching that Coq cannot manage. Rather than pessimistically add as much detail as could be needed, the translator could open a dialogue with Coq (such as suggested in [BSBG98]) in which Coq is asked if it can perform a certain matching; if not, sufficient detail is added until it can. Another problem is that a HOL lemma which is an equality may be used both as a 'true' equality, and as an equivalence. Since we translate all booleans to propositions, our algorithm will only produce one of these forms. Some mechanism of tagging 'true' booleans in the original proof could be used.

We have not given any correctness result. Formalising this would involve, at least, giving a translation from Coq into the bytecode, so that translation between HOL and Coq could be judged correct if it commutes with the respective translations into the bytecode. However, if we are satisfied that a proposition has been translated correctly, then it does not matter whether we have established in advance that a proof will be correctly translated. This is guaranteed if the translated proof is accepted by Coq.

We gave a classical translation into the non-computational Prop universe of the Calculus of Constructions. An alternative translation could be given which aimed to translate existentials to the computational form whenever possible.

We claimed that the bytecode can be used both for proof translation, and for proof checking, but the checker has not been implemented, although this would be straightforward. Since we need to keep track of the context as the proof is being translated anyway, it would make sense to combine the two.

A significant extension would be to write a translation in the reverse direction, that is, from (a suitable subset of) Coq to HOL. Since Coq has true proof objects, we could start with either the lambda terms, or the proof script. In either case, since Coq is top-down, we would need to run the machine in order to generate information that is implicit, and necessary for HOL's bottom-up style. An even greater challenge would be to give translations to and from a third proof assistant.

Acknowledgements
Thanks to Laszlo Nemeth and Wai Wong for reading drafts.

References

[AHJ+00] A. Franke A, S.M. Hess, G.Ch. Jung, M. Kohlhase, and V. Sorge. Agent-oriented integration of distributed mathematical services. *Journal of Universal Computer Science*, 5, 2000.

[Bar96]   Henk Barendregt. The quest for correctness. *Images of SMC research*, pages 39–58, 1996. At `ftp://ftp.cs.kun.nl/pub/CompMath.Found/quest.ps.Z`.

[BBC+97] Bruno Barras, Samuel Boutin, Cristina Cornes, Jean-Christophe Filliatre, Eduardo Giménez, Hugo Herbelin, Gerard Huet, Cesar Muñoz, Chetan Murthy, Catherine Parent, Christine Paulin-Mohring, Amokrane Saibi, and Benjamin Werner. The Coq Proof Assistant Reference Manual: Version 6.1. Technical Report RT-0203, Inria, May 1997.

[BD93]   Robert S. Boyer and Gilles Dowek. Towards checking proof-checkers. In *Workshop on Types for Proofs and Programs (Type '93)*, 1993.

[BSBG98] R. Boulton, K. Slind, A. Bundy, and M. Gordon. An interface between CLAM and HOL. In J. Grundy and M. Newey, editors, *Proceedings of the 11th International Conference on Theorem Proving in Higher Order Logics (TPHOLs'98)*, volume 1479 of *Lecture Notes in Computer Science*, pages 87–104, Canberra, Australia, September/October 1998. Springer-Verlag.

[CCC99]   O. Caprotti, D.P. Carlisle, and A.M. Cohen.   Draft of the Open Math standard.   *The Open Math Society*, 1999. http://www.nag.co.uk/projects/openmath/omsoc/.

[FH97]   A. P. Felty and D. J. Howe. Hybrid interactive theorem proving using Nuprl and HOL. In William McCune, editor, *Proceedings of the 14th International Conference on Automated deduction*, volume 1249 of *LNAI*, pages 351–365, Berlin, July 13–17 1997. Springer-Verlag.

[GM93]   M. J. C. Gordon and Thomas F. Melham, editors. *Introduction to HOL: A theorem proving environment for higher order logic*. Cambridge University Press, 1993.

[GPT94]   Fausto Giunchiglia, Paolo Pecchiari, and Carolyn Talcott. Reasoning theories: Towards an architecture for open mechanized reasoning systems. Technical Note CS-TN-94-15, Stanford University, Department of Computer Science, December 1994.

[HHP87]   Robert Harper, Furio Honsell, and Gordon Plotkin. A framework for defining logics. In *Symposium on Logic in Computer Science, Ithaca, NY*, pages 194–204. IEEE, June 1987.

[NL98]   Necula and Lee. Efficient representation and validation of proofs. In *LICS: IEEE Symposium on Logic in Computer Science*, pages 93–104, 1998.

[Won99]   Wai Wong. Validation of HOL proofs by proof checking. *Formal Methods in System Design: An International Journal*, 14(2):193–212, March 1999.

[Zam97]   Vincent Zammit. A comparative study of Coq and HOL. In Elsa L. Gunter and Amy Felty, editors, *Proceedings of the 10th International Conference on Theorem Proving in Higher Order Logics, TPHOLs'97, Murray Hill, NJ, USA*, volume 1275 of *Lecture Notes in Computer Science*, pages 323–337. Springer-Verlag, August 1997.

Proving ML Type Soundness Within Coq

Catherine Dubois

Université d'Évry Val d'Essonne, CNRS EP738, LaMI. F-91025 Évry Cedex, France
dubois@lami.univ-evry.fr

Abstract. We verify within the Coq proof assistant that ML typing is sound with respect to the dynamic semantics. We prove this property in the framework of a big step semantics and also in the framework of a reduction semantics. For that purpose, we use a syntax-directed version of the typing rules: we prove mechanically its equivalence with the initial type system provided by Damas and Milner. This work is complementary to the certification of the ML type inference algorithm done previously by the author and Valérie Ménissier-Morain.

1 Introduction

The piece of work presented in this paper supplements the certification laid out in [6] whose purpose was to verify in Coq the soundness and the completeness of the ML type inference algorithm with respect to the typing rules. We now connect the typing rules with the dynamic semantics and verify that the type system ensures a strong typing: a well-typed program cannot then produce type errors during its execution or, according to Milner's slogan [13], *Well-typed programs do not go wrong*. Thus the whole formal development presented in both this paper and [6] constitutes a machine-checked certification of the different aspects related to the ML typing discipline. More precisely we provide for a functional kernel of the ML language a formalization of the type system in the Calculus of Inductive Constructions and also a formalization of the type inference algorithm well-known in the literature as the algorithm $\mathcal{W}$. We prove within the Coq tool that $\mathcal{W}$ is correct and complete with respect to the typing rules. Completeness means here that if an expression is well-typed according to the typing rules then $\mathcal{W}$ succeeds and computes the principal type of the expression. The formal development contains also the definition of the dynamic semantics and establishes the soundness property. In this study, we consider a syntax-directed version of the typing rules. This version is often used in the ML community but it is not the one proposed initially by Damas and Milner [13]. Thus we formalize within Coq the initial version and prove mechanically the equivalence of both type systems. As far as we know, no publication does mention such a complete mechanized certification of ML typing aspects ([16,8,22] are only related to the type soundness, [15] is another certification of $\mathcal{W}$ in Isabelle/HOL).

The formulation and the proof of the type soundness property are intimately bound to the formulation of the dynamic semantics of the language. For example,

J. Harrison and M. Aagaard (Eds.): TPHOLs 2000, LNCS 1869, pp. 126–144, 2000.

for ML, Milner used a denotational semantics, Tofte used a big step semantics, Wright and Felleisen a reduction semantics. Machine-checked proofs of type soundness are often based upon a big step semantics or a reduction semantics. For instance, Syme [19] considers a reduction semantics to prove Java type soundness whereas Nipkow and von Oheimb [14] refer to a big step semantics. About ML, Terrasse in [21] uses a big step semantics but deals with the monomorphic case (Coq), Michaylov and Pfenning in [16] uses also a big step semantics but takes into account the polymorphic typing by substituting expressions (Elf). Lastly, in [3], A. Bove uses a reduction semantics but in the restricted monomorphic case (ALF). As far as we are aware, our machine-checked proof of ML type soundness is the first published one that deals with the notion of type scheme.

The rest of the paper is organized as follows. Section 2 presents the formalization of the ML kernel we consider together with its type system (and the involved notions e.g. substitutions). This part is another presentation (less detailed and less technical) of the sections 3, 4 and 5 of [6]. Consequently, the choices done for verifying W, particularly the fact to stick to a functional implementation of W, impact on the type soundness part. Then our paper deals with type soundness, first in the framework of an evaluation semantics (big step) and then in the context of a reduction semantics (small step). The last section connects our formalization with the type system provided by Damas and Milner.

We assume here familiarity with the Calculus of Inductive Constructions. We use version 6.1 of the Coq proof assistant [1]. In order to make this paper more readable, we adopt sometimes a pseudo-Coq syntax which differs slightly from the usual Coq syntax. Our paper provides the definitions of most concepts, the key lemmas but almost no proofs. The complete development is accessible on the Internet via http://www.univ-evry.fr/labos/lami/specif/dubois.

2   The Type System

2.1   The Kernel of the ML Language

The expressions we consider are natural number constants, identifiers (x), λ-abstraction ($\lambda x.e$), application ($e\ e'$), let binding (let $x = e$ in e') and recursive functions (Rec $f\ x.e$).

These expressions are described in Coq as an inductive data type (expr) with constructors for each kind of expressions. The type ident is the type of the identifiers. It does not matter what it is exactly provided that the equality of two identifiers is decidable.

```
Inductive expr: Set :=
   Const: nat -> expr          | Variable: ident -> expr
 | Lam: ident -> expr -> expr  | Rec: ident -> ident -> expr -> expr
 | App: expr -> expr -> expr   | Let_in: ident -> expr -> expr -> expr
```

2.2   Types and Type Schemes

Types consist only of the basic type *nat*, type variables denoted as usual with Greek letters α, β ... and functional types $\tau \to \tau'$ (where τ and τ' are types too). It is encoded in Coq as:

```
Inductive type: Set :=
   Nat: type | Var: stamp -> type | Arrow: type -> type -> type
```

The type variables, whose type is `stamp`, are essentially natural numbers. It is also a choice close to implementations. In the following, Coq terms like (`Arrow t1 t2`) are sometimes written `t1` $\to$ `t2`.

In order to express parametric polymorphism, it is necessary to specify type schemes : a type scheme, of the form $\forall \alpha, \alpha_1, \ldots \alpha_n.\tau$, is a type with some quantified type variables. The quantified variables are called the *generic variables* of the type scheme. A type scheme without generic variables is called a *trivial* type scheme and written as $\forall.\tau$.

In order to simplify the manipulation of free and bound variables, we distinguish syntactically free and bound variables in a type scheme. Consequently we define inductively the type `type_scheme` with two different constructors for variables, `Gen_var` for bound ones and `Var_ts` for the free ones.

```
Inductive type_scheme: Set :=  Nat_ts: type_scheme
 | Gen_var: stamp -> type_scheme | Var_ts: stamp -> type_scheme
 | Arrow_ts: type_scheme -> type_scheme -> type_scheme
```

According to this definition, the type scheme $\forall \alpha.\alpha \to \beta$ is represented by the Coq term (`Arrow_ts (Gen_var alpha) (Var_ts beta)`) where `alpha` and `beta` are the stamps associated to α and β respectively. We may also write this Coq term as (`Gen_var alpha`) $\to^\sigma$ (`Var_ts beta`) in a pseudo-Coq syntax.

The choice of this representation for type schemes has an important impact on the formal development. It allows to define with case analysis many operations on type schemes and to proceed by induction in a lot of proofs. However this choice gives no help when α-conversion is concerned. In order to smooth away this difficulty, it would be interesting to use higher order abstract syntax [5] to represent variable bindings in type schemes. But this representation does not admit induction (for the moment): this is a damning drawback for us.

2.3   Type Environments

The type information about the free identifiers of an expression is contained in a type environment (environment for short when there is no ambiguity) denoted in the rest of the paper by Γ or `env`. Because of polymorphism, environments contain type schemes. Thus an environment can be considered as a partial function from identifiers to type schemes. In Coq we represent an environment as a list of associations between identifiers and type schemes. Thus the type of environments, `type_env`, is defined as `list (ident * type_scheme)`.

The operation `assoc_ident_in_env` that finds the type scheme associated to an identifier (it is also written informally as $\Gamma(x)$) may fail. Thus this operation has the type `ident -> type_env -> (option type_scheme)` where the type `option` defined below allows to simulate the exception mechanism.

```
Inductive option [A : Set] : Set :=
    None : (option A) | Some : A -> (option A)
```

The extension of an environment is done by the operation `add_env` implemented as a simple list addition (a classical *cons*). We use also the informal notation $\Gamma \oplus x : \sigma$ (where x is an identifier and σ a type scheme).

2.4 Substitutions and Instances

The literature provides different definitions for the notion of substitution, which are not all equivalent (see [11] for a survey). We consider a substitution to be a function s from the set of type variables to the set of types, such that the domain, that is $\{x : \mathtt{stamp} \mid s(x) \neq x\}$, is finite : then s behaves like the identity anywhere else.

Substitutions are undeniably fundamental objects in our mechanized verification, but in fact they are brought indirectly by two instance relations: the instance relation between two types (type instance) and the instance relation between a type and a type scheme (generic instance).

The type τ is a type instance of the type τ' if there exists a substitution s such that $s\tau' = \tau$.

The type τ is a generic instance of the type scheme $\forall \alpha_1, \ldots, \alpha_n.\tau'$ if there exists a substitution s whose domain is $\{\alpha_1, \ldots, \alpha_n\}$ such that $s\tau' = \tau$.

Consequently we distinguish two kinds of substitutions:

– the so-called *free substitutions* (or substitutions), that can work only on the free variables of a type, a type scheme or an environment.
– the so-called *generic substitutions* that can work only on the generic variables of a type scheme.

The first ones are represented in Coq as association (between type variable and type) lists. The generic substitutions are represented by type vectors, without any reference to the names of the variables they are concerned with. They are used with the requirement that the type of the ith generic variable is located at the ith position in the vector.

Many operations come with the definition of substitutions: application of a substitution on a type variable, a type, a type scheme, composition of substitutions, domain, range, free variables of a substitution ... These operations are specified in Coq in a functional style and are very close to their ML implementation.

The choice of representing substitutions as association lists make some operations (e.g. the composition) complex. The proof that the composition does really what it is expected is quite clumsy (about 600 lines).

We could also represent substitutions (both kinds) by Coq abstractions of type `stamp -> type`. The application of a substitution to a variable, the composition of two substitutions are then operations got for free. This kind of representation is very attractive and often chosen in proof assistants based on λ-calculus. It is essentially the representation chosen by Naraschewski and Nipkow [15]. However the functional representation makes the implementation of some operations (e.g. the computation of the domain) impossible. And we need such an operation !

The notion of generic instances induces an ordering between type schemes: a type scheme σ_1 is said to be *more general* than a type scheme σ_2 and written $\sigma_1 \succ \sigma_2$ or in Coq (`more_general` σ_1 σ_2), if and only if any arbitrary generic instance of σ_2 is also a generic instance of σ_1. For example, $\forall \alpha\beta.\alpha \to \beta$ is more general than $\forall \alpha.\alpha \to \alpha$.
The translation in Coq is straightforward:

```
Definition more_general: type_scheme -> type_scheme -> Prop :=
[ts1, ts2 : type_scheme]
  (∀ t: type, (is_gen_instance t ts2) -> (is_gen_instance t ts1))
The Coq notation [x: T]e binds the identifier x of type T in e
```

This ordering induces in turn a partial order between environments: Γ_1 is said to be more general than the environment Γ_2 ($\Gamma_1 \succ \Gamma_2$) if and only if Γ_1 and Γ_2 are relative to the same identifiers[1] $x_1, x_2 \ldots x_n$ and $\forall i \in [1, n]$, $\Gamma_1(x_i) \succ \Gamma_2(x_i)$.

2.5   Type Generalization

The `let` construct is the only one that may introduce true polymorphic types[2] in the environment. This is done by the operation of generalization `gen_type` which builds a type scheme from a type τ and an environment Γ: it turns into generic variables those variables appearing free in τ but not in Γ.

$$\mathbf{gen\_type} \ \tau \ \Gamma = \forall \alpha_1 \ldots \alpha_n.\tau$$

with $\alpha_i \in (\mathtt{FV\_type} \ \tau) - (\mathtt{FV\_env} \ \Gamma)$ (as indicated by its name, `FV_env` computes the list of free variables of an environment).

The most natural Coq implementation that follows from the representations of types and type schemes is a function (see below) defined by case analysis according to the type to be generalized.

---

[1] we impose without any loss of generality the same order for the identifiers in both environments

[2] that is, non trivial type schemes

```
Fixpoint gen_type:= [t: type] [env: type_env]
  Cases t of
  Nat -> Nat_ts
| (Var v) ->  if v ∈ (FV_env env) then (Var_ts v) else (Gen_var v)
| (Arrow t1 t2) -> (Arrow_ts (gen_type t1 env) (gen_type t2 env))
  end.
```

However we do not implement the generalization exactly in this way. The implemented algorithm shares the same structure but incorporates a linear encoding of generic variables: any occurrence of the generic variable α is encoded as (Gen n) if α is the nth generic variable discovered during the generalization. Thus the generalization of the type $(\alpha \to \beta) \to (\beta \to \alpha)$ with respect to the empty environment is the type scheme ((Gen_var 0) $\to^\sigma$(Gen_var 1)) $\to^\sigma$((Gen_var 1) $\to^\sigma$(Gen_var 0)).

This encoding provides us with the following property: two type schemes obtained by generalization, identical up to the renaming of the generic variables, are represented by two terms (of type type_scheme) *syntactically equal*. Nevertheless the price for this is high: because of the encoding, the lemmas involving generalization have an inductive step not very natural, close to an invariant (see [6] for more details).

2.6 The Typing Rules and Some of Their Properties

The typing rules are given in the Natural Semantics style [10] (see figure 1). They are described as inference rules expressing how to derive typing sequents of the form $\Gamma \vdash e : \tau$. Such a sequent is read *the expression e has type τ under the environment Γ*.

The typing rules are encoded in Coq as clauses of the inductive relation type_of, the translation is quite obvious here. Here is a fragment of the Coq specification:

```
Inductive type_of: type_env -> expr -> type -> Prop :=
  type_of_const: ∀ env: type_env, ∀ n: nat, (type_of env (Const n) Nat)
| type_of_var: ∀ env: type_env, ∀ x: ident,
  ∀ t: type, ∀ ts: type_scheme,
  (assoc_ident_in_env x env)=(Some ts)  ->
    (is_gen_instance t ts) -> (type_of env (Variable x) t)
| type_of_lam: ∀ env: type_env, ∀ x: ident, ∀ e: expr, ∀ t, t': type,
  (type_of (add_env env x (type_to_type_scheme t)) e t') ->
    (type_of env (Lam x e) (Arrow t t'))
...
```

An important property, that appears as a key property for many other properties, states that the relation type_of is stable under substitution.

```
Theorem typing_is_stable_under_substitution:
  ∀ e: expr, ∀ t: type, ∀ env: type_env, ∀ s: substitution,
  (type_of env e t) ->
    (type_of (apply_subst_env env s) e (apply_subst_type s t))
```

$$(\text{CST})\ \Gamma \vdash n : nat$$

$$(\text{ID})\ \frac{\Gamma(x) = \sigma, \quad \tau \text{ is a generic instance of } \sigma}{\Gamma \vdash x : \tau}$$

$$(\text{ABS})\ \frac{\Gamma \oplus x : \forall.\tau \vdash e : \tau'}{\Gamma \vdash \lambda\, x.e : \tau \to \tau'}$$

$$(\text{REC})\ \frac{\Gamma \oplus x : \forall.\tau \oplus f : \forall.\tau \to \tau' \vdash e : \tau'}{\Gamma \vdash \mathbf{Rec}\ f\ x.e : \tau \to \tau'}$$

$$(\text{APP})\ \frac{\Gamma \vdash e : \tau \to \tau', \quad \Gamma \vdash e' : \tau}{\Gamma \vdash e\ e' : \tau'}$$

$$(\text{LET})\ \frac{\Gamma \vdash e : \tau, \quad \Gamma \oplus x : (\mathbf{gen\_type}\ \tau\ \Gamma) \vdash e' : \tau'}{\Gamma \vdash \mathbf{let}\ x = e\ \mathbf{in}\ e' : \tau'}$$

Fig. 1. The typing rules

Our Coq verification of this theorem deals explicitly with α-conversion. It requires for example to formalize the notion of renaming substitution and to verify mechanically under what conditions a type and a renamed version of it are generalized in the same type scheme. In that sense, our proof is fundamental because we really formalize and verify informal proofs that often become a little bit nebulous as soon as they deal with renaming. For details, see [6].

Some other properties about the typing rules are also required in different points in our whole development, for example the following property connecting typing sequents together with the ordering $\succ$ between environments:

```
Theorem typing_in_a_more_general_env:
∀ e: expr, ∀ Γ₁, Γ₂: type_env, ∀ τ: type,
Γ₁ ≻ Γ₂ -> (type_of Γ₂ e τ) -> (type_of Γ₁ e τ)
```

3 Big Step Dynamic Semantics

The big step dynamic semantics gives a meaning to the expressions of the language by defining their evaluation. Again we chose to specify it in the style of Natural Semantics. Let us first describe the possible values and then the inference rules.

3.1 Semantic Values and Evaluation Environments

The values we consider here are numbers and functional values also called closures. The value of an expression depends on the values of its free variables. These values are recorded in an evaluation environment (environment for short when there is no ambiguity), written Δ or c in the following.

Values and environments are mutually recursive notions. In effect, a closure is a pair composed of a functional expression and an environment. Two kinds of closures are distinguished: recursive closures $<<_@ \text{Rec } f\ x.e, \Delta >>$ and non recursive closures $<< \lambda\ x.e, \Delta >>$. This discrimination is also introduced by Boutin in his ML compiler certification [2]. We could also consider opaque closures (closures whose contents cannot be inspected): these are the values associated to predefined operations. They can be ignored without any loss of generality.

Within Coq, values and environments are specified by two mutually inductive types val and eval_env (isomorphic to lists of pairs *(identifier, value)*). [3]

```
Mutual Inductive val: Set := Num: nat -> val
   | Clos: ident -> expr -> eval_env -> val
   | Rec_clos: ident -> ident -> expr -> eval_env -> val
with  eval_env : Set := Cnil: eval_env
                    | Ccons: ident*val -> eval_env -> eval_env
```

Structurally the evaluation environments are very similar to the typing environments. Consequently we use similar notations: $\Delta(x)$ (in Coq, assoc_ident_in-_eval), $\Delta \oplus y : v$.

3.2 The Dynamic Semantics

The inference rules that describe the dynamic semantics are detailed in the figure 2. The evaluation sequent $\Delta \vdash_{eval} e \hookrightarrow v$ is read *the expression e evaluates to the value v in the environment Δ*.

The inference rules implements a call by value semantics. The distinction between the recursive and non recursive closures implies the definition of two inference rules for the application: (APP1) when a non recursive function is applied and (APP2) when a recursive function is applied.

The inference rules in figure 2 are translated into the inductive predicate val_of (a constructor per inference rule):

```
Inductive val_of: eval_env -> expr -> val -> Prop:=
 Val_of_num: ∀ n: nat,∀ c: eval_env, (val_of c (Const n) (Num n))
|Val_of_ident: ∀ c: eval_env, ∀ i: ident, ∀ v: val,
   (assoc_ident_in_eval i c) = (Some v) -> (val_of c (Variable i) v)
|Val_of_lambda: ∀ c: eval_env, ∀ i: ident, ∀ e: expr,
   (val_of c (Lam i e) (Clos i e c))
```

---

[3] We use here a separate type for environments and not the predefined lists : this choice is due to a limitation of the Coq version V6.1 we used.

```
|Val_of_app1: ∀ c,c1: eval_env, ∀ e1,e2,e: expr, ∀ i: ident,
      ∀ u,v: val, (val_of c e1 (Clos i e c1)) -> (val_of c e2 u) ->
      (val_of (Ccons (i,u) c1) e v)-> (val_of c (App e1 e2) v)
  . . . .
```

(CST) $\Delta \vdash_{eval} n \hookrightarrow n$

(ID) $\Delta \vdash_{eval} x \hookrightarrow \Delta(x)$

(ABS) $\Delta \vdash_{eval} \lambda\, x.e \hookrightarrow\, <<\lambda\, x.e, \Delta >>$

(REC) $\Delta \vdash_{eval} \mathbf{Rec}\, f\, x.e \hookrightarrow\, <<_{@} \mathbf{Rec}\, f\, x.e, \Delta >>$

(APP1) $$\frac{\Delta \vdash_{eval} e \hookrightarrow\, <<\lambda\, x.e_f, \Delta_f >>\, ,\quad \Delta \vdash_{eval} e' \hookrightarrow v,\quad \Delta_f \oplus x : v \vdash_{eval} e_f \hookrightarrow v'}{\Delta \vdash_{eval} e\, e' \hookrightarrow v'}$$

(APP2) $$\frac{\Delta \vdash_{eval} e \hookrightarrow\, <<_{@} \mathbf{Rec}\, f\, x.e_f, \Delta_f >>\, ,\quad \Delta \vdash_{eval} e' \hookrightarrow v,\quad \Delta_f \oplus x : v \oplus f : <<_{@} \mathbf{Rec}\, f\, x.e_f, \Delta_f >> \vdash_{eval} e_f \hookrightarrow v'}{\Delta \vdash_{eval} e\, e' \hookrightarrow v'}$$

(LET) $$\frac{\Delta \vdash_{eval} e \hookrightarrow v,\quad \Delta \oplus x : v \vdash_{eval} e' \hookrightarrow v'}{\Delta \vdash_{eval} \mathbf{let}\, x = e\ \mathbf{in}\ e' \hookrightarrow v'}$$

Fig. 2. Big step dynamic semantics

3.3   Typing Soundness or the *Subject Reduction* Theorem

The proved property is that any well-typed expression of type τ whose evaluation terminates has a value of type τ. This formulation shows that we need to formalize the notion of type for a value. It is immediate for a natural number constant but not for a closure because it is not an object of the language. Consequently we specify an inductive predicate called "semantic typing" (`type_of_val` in Coq) that links a value to its type: we write $\Vdash v : \tau$ to indicate that *the value v has the type τ*.

Furthermore the typing/evaluation connection can only be done if the typing environment and the evaluation environment agree (we write $\Gamma \vdash \Delta$ to denote that property, the corresponding Coq predicate is `eval_type_env_match`).

It means the value associated to an identifier in Δ has the type (more precisely the type scheme) indicated in the typing environment Γ.

A value v is assigned the type scheme σ ((sem_gen v σ) in Coq) if v has some type obtained as a generic instance of σ.

To define the semantic typing predicate, we follow Tofte's approach reformulated by Leroy in [12]. Thus we use the typing rules to type a closure. Informally, it means that the value $<< \lambda\, x.e, \Delta >>$ has the type $\tau_1 \to \tau_2$ if there exists a typing environment Γ that agrees with the evaluation environment Δ ($\Gamma \vdash \Delta$) and such that the typing sequent $\Gamma \vdash \lambda\, x.e : \tau_1 \to \tau_2$ can be derived.

The Coq formalization (given below) of the previous predicates raises no particular problem. Their definitions are mutually inductive. Let us notice that our Coq definition for $\Gamma \vdash \Delta$ adds a constraint about the order of the identifiers in both Δ and Γ: it must be the same. This constraint simplifies the formulation and the proof but is not restrictive at all.

```
Mutual Inductive type_of_val: val -> type -> Prop :=
  type_num: ∀ n: nat, (type_of_val (Num n) Nat)
|type_closure: ∀ i: ident, ∀ e: expr, ∀ c: eval_env,
    ∀ env: type_env, ∀ t1, t2 : type,
    (eval_type_env_match c env) ->
     (type_of env (Lam i e) (Arrow t1 t2)) ->
     (type_of_val (Clos i e c) (Arrow t1 t2))
|type_rec_closure:  similar to the previous clause

with  eval_type_env_match: eval_env -> type_env -> Prop :=
      match_nil: (eval_type_env_match Cnil nil)
     |match_cons: ∀ c: eval_env, ∀ env: type_env, ∀ i: ident,
       ∀ ts: type_scheme, ∀ v: val,
       (sem_gen v ts) -> (eval_type_env_match c env) ->
          (eval_type_env_match (Ccons (i,v) c)  (cons (i,ts) env))

with sem_gen: val -> type_scheme -> Prop  :=
     sem_gen_def: ∀ v: val, ∀ ts: type_scheme,
        (∀ t: type,  (is_gen_instance t ts) -> (type_of_val v t)) ->
          (sem_gen v ts)
```

The formulation of the typing soundness theorem in pseudo-Coq is as follows:

```
Theorem subject reduction:
 ∀ e: expr, ∀ v: val, ∀ Δ: eval_env, ∀ Γ : type_env, ∀ τ : type,
    Δ ⊢_eval e ↪ v -> Γ ⊢ e : τ ->
         Γ ⊢ Δ -> ⊩ v : τ
```

The proof proceeds by induction on $\Delta \vdash_{eval} e \hookrightarrow v$. Not surprisingly, the let step is the most difficult one. It requires the following lemma: if a value u has the type τ, then it also has the type scheme resulting from the generalization of τ.

```
Lemma sem_gen_gen_type: ∀ u: val, ∀ τ: type, ∀ Γ: type_env,
  (type_of_val u τ)  ->  (sem_gen u (gen_type τ Γ)).,
```

Proving this lemma consists in establishing that for any generic instance τ' of (gen_type τ Γ), the value u has the type τ'. The generic instance τ' can be written as a type instance of τ (according to a lemma required in the certification of $\mathcal{W}$). The end of the proof rests upon the property type_val_stable_subst close to the stability of typing by substitutions: if u has the type τ then u has also the type $s\tau$ for any substitution s.

```
Lemma type_val_stable_subst: ∀ v: val, ∀ τ: type, ∀ s: substitution,
   (type_of_val v τ)  ->  (type_of_val v (extend_subst_type s τ))
```

To verify this last property, we need to use a mutual induction scheme (between evaluation environments and values) generated automatically by Coq. In fact we prove simultaneously a similar property about the typing/evaluation environments connection: if $\Gamma \vdash \Delta$ then $s\Gamma \vdash \Delta$ for any substitution s.
Here again we use the property of preservation of the typing sequents by substitution.

The formalization of the big step semantics together with the proof of the type soundness require about thirty supplementary definitions and a hundred new lemmas with respect to the certification of $\mathcal{W}$. It is very little compared with the 7500 lines (91 definitions and 322 lemmas) for verifying $\mathcal{W}$.

4   Reduction Dynamic Semantics

The dynamic semantics presented in the previous section is called big step semantics because it gives no information about the computation. It only considers the possible values resulting from the evaluation of an expression. It follows that the big step semantics cannot deal with non terminating programs. The reduction semantics, also called small step semantics, specifies the elementary steps of the computation and consists of a bunch of rewriting rules. Consequently we can observe the reduction of an expression step by step (through a derivation) either for ever (if it is a non terminating expression) or until an expression in normal form is obtained (if the initial expression terminates). In our case, an expression in normal form also called a value is a constant or an abstraction (recursive or not).

Using a reduction semantics to establish type soundness for languages à la ML has been popularized by Wright and Felleisen in [23] and again afterwards by other researchers, for example Rémy and Vouillon when they specified the semantics of Objective ML [18]. With such an approach a type error is modelled as a locked reduction, that is the impossibility to further reduce a non value expression. In this context, establishing type soundness consists in verifying two properties: the preservation of the type by reduction (also called the subject reduction theorem) and the non-locking of well typed programs.

In this section we present the Coq formalization of the reduction semantics and prove the preservation of the type by reduction. We have also proved the non-locking property by establishing that any well-typed program that cannot reduce anymore is a value. This last part, not developed here by lack of space, does not raise any specific difficulty.

The Coq theories relative to this section add a dozen definitions and about thirty five lemmas.

4.1 The Coq Specification of the Reduction Semantics

The formalization of the reduction semantics is modular, it consists of three steps:

- the definition of the subset of the expressions that are values,
- the definition of the evaluation contexts that indicate where the reductions are allowed. A context is an expression that contains a hole written •. The notation $C[e]$ denotes the expression obtained by placing an expression e in the hole of C.

  The contexts are described by the following grammar

  $$C ::= \bullet \mid C\ e \mid v\ C \mid \text{let } x = C \text{ in } e$$

  where v and e are respectively a value and an expression.

  Defining such contexts amounts to imposing a reduction strategy. For instance, the right hand side of an application can be reduced only if the left hand side is a value.
- the definition of the reduction relation $\longrightarrow_r$ that specifies the elementary reductions.

These different steps are modelled within Coq as follows:

values The subset of the expressions which are values is described as the set of expressions such that the predicate is_value is proved to be satisfied:

```
Inductive is_value: expr -> Prop :=
  Cst_val : ∀ n: nat, (is_value (Const n))
 |fun_val : ∀ i: ident, ∀ e: expr, (is_value (Lam i e))
```

contexts One originality of our work is that we explicitly formalize the notion of evaluation context. In fact, if many Coq contributions about λ-calculus use a reduction relation, few of them formalize the notion of context.

We have chosen to represent a context (of type context) as a function on expressions. Then context is synonymous with expr -> expr. Consequently $C[e]$ is translated to the application (c e) where c is the functional representation of C. The following inductive definition is_MLcontext describes the allowed contexts.

```
Inductive is_MLcontext: context -> Prop :=
  hole : (is_MLcontext ([x:expr]x))
 |app_left :  ∀ e: expr, (is_MLcontext ([x: expr] (App x e)))
 |app_right :  ∀ v: expr, (is_value v) ->
               (is_MLcontext ([x: expr] (App v x )))
 |let_left :  ∀ e: expr, ∀ i: identifier,
               (is_MLcontext ([x: expr] (Let_in i x e)))
```

the reduction relation $\longrightarrow_r$ It contains 3 rules that express β-reduction and a fourth one which specifies the relation $\longrightarrow_r$ is context compatible.

$$
\begin{array}{ll}
(\beta_1) & (\lambda x.e)v \longrightarrow_r e[v/x] \\[2ex]
(\beta_2) & (\text{Rec } fx.e)v \longrightarrow_r e[v/x, \text{Rec } fx.e/f] \\[2ex]
(\beta_3) & \text{let } x = v \text{ in } e \longrightarrow_r e[v/x] \\[2ex]
(\text{CONTEXT}) & \dfrac{e_1 \longrightarrow_r e_2}{C[e_1] \longrightarrow_r C[e_2]}
\end{array}
$$

The formalization of the relation $\longrightarrow_r$ requires the preliminary specification of the following notions:

- free/bound identifier (inductive predicate free_ident)
- substituting an expression e' for x in an expression e: this operation is not allowed when free identifiers may be captured (we do not implement automatic renaming). The easiest way to implement a partial operation in Coq [4] is to switch to a relational version defined inductively, subst_expr. Thus (subst_expr e x e' e'') means e'' is the expression obtained by replacing in the expression e all the free occurrences of the identifier x by the expression e' ($e'' = e[e'/x]$).

The relation $\longrightarrow_r$ is written in Coq as an inductive predicate red with four constructors corresponding to the rules (β_1), (β_2), (β_3) and (CONTEXT).

```
Inductive red: expr -> expr -> Prop :=
  beta1: ∀ i: ident, ∀ e1,v,er: expr,
      (is_value v) -> (subst_expr e i v er) ->
      (red (App (Lam i e) v) er)
| beta2, beta3  follow a similar construction
| context: ∀ e1,e2: expr, ∀ ctx: context,
      (red e1 e2) -> (is_MLcontext ctx) -> (red (ctx e1) (ctx e2))
```

4.2   Subject Reduction Theorem

The subject reduction property states that reductions preserve the type of expressions. It is given below in the case of an elementary reduction step (it can be easily extended to the closure of $\longrightarrow_r$).

```
Theorem reduction_preserves_types: ∀ e1,e2: expr,
    (e1  ⟶r  e2) ->
        (∀ τ: type, ∀ Γ: type_env, Γ ⊢ e1 : τ -> Γ ⊢ e2 : τ)
```

---

[4] The Coq functions are incurably total functions (see [7] and [17] about encoding partial functions).

The proof proceeds by case analysis according to the reduction $e_1 \longrightarrow_r e_2$. In the step corresponding to the context compatibility, we finish the proof by case analysis on the form of the context.

For reductions involving β-reduction a substitution lemma is the key to showing type preservation.

```
Lemma substitution:
  ∀ e,e₁,e₂: expr, ∀ τ,τ₁: type, ∀ Γ: type_env, ∀ i: ident,
    Γ ⊢ e : τ ->
    Γ⊕i:(gen_type τ Γ) ⊢ e₁ : τ₁ ->
    (subst_term e₁ i e e₂)  ->  Γ ⊢ e₂ : τ₁
```

First of all, let us notice the formulation of the **substitution** lemma. Usually in the literature the typing hypothesis about e_1 assigns to the identifier i the type scheme $\forall \alpha, \alpha_1, \ldots \alpha_n.\tau$ where $\alpha, \alpha_1, \ldots \alpha_n$ are type variables not free in Γ. Thus the lemma we prove in our formalization can be seen as a specialization of the usual one. However it suffices to establish the type soundness and furthermore a lot of technical lemmas about **gen_type** were already available.

To verify this lemma, we proceed by induction on the expression e. The heaviest induction step concerns the abstraction because renaming of type variables is required. However numerous required properties have been established for verifying the property of preservation of typing sequents by substitution.

More generally, the proof makes an intensive use of the relation $\succ$ and the connected properties as for example the lemma **typing_in_a_more_general_env** (displayed in section 2.6). It remains to establish several supplementary lemmas about the type system as for example the extension lemma (see below). This lemma states that adding (or removing) in the environment a type information about an identifier non free in the expression has no impact on the conclusion of a typing sequent.

```
Lemma env_extension :
  ∀ e: expr, ∀ x: ident, ∀ τ: type, σ: type_scheme, ∀ Γ: type_env,
    ¬(is_free x e)  ->  ((Γ⊕x:σ) ⊢ e : τ <-> Γ ⊢ e : τ)
```

The proof of this lemma is based on a very specific equivalence relation between environments, $\Gamma \approx \Gamma'$, used nowhere else. Mainly this equivalence is built on the two following clauses:

$$\Gamma \approx \Gamma' -> (i:\sigma)(i:\sigma')\Gamma \approx (i:\sigma)\Gamma'$$
$$\Gamma \approx \Gamma' -> (i:\sigma)(j:\sigma')\Gamma \approx (j:\sigma')(i:\sigma)\Gamma' \text{ when } i \neq i'$$

The first clause removes a useless information, the second one swaps the information for two distinct identifiers. An important lemma about that notion states that if the typing sequent $\Gamma \vdash e : \tau$ is valid then we can also derive the sequent $\Gamma' \vdash e : \tau$ when $\Gamma \approx \Gamma'$.

5   Equivalence of Type Systems

All the work presented until now uses a syntax-directed presentation (called DM' in the paper) of the type system. Although this version is commonly used, it is not the initial version (called DM in the paper) given by Damas and Milner. This last one is not syntax-directed. We have chosen to use the presentation DM' because it is closer to W than DM and it is deterministic. This feature makes many proofs easier.

The systems DM and DM' are equivalent. We can find a paper proof in [9] but according to us, no formal and mechanized proof exists. We prove this equivalence with Coq, more precisely the soundness and completeness of DM' with respect to DM. It requires seventeen supplementary definitions and seventy lemmas.

5.1   Formalization of the Damas-Milner Type System DM

The DM typing rules are given in the figure 3: the typing sequent is now $\Gamma \vdash_{DM} e : \sigma$ (a type scheme is used instead of a type). We follow here the presentation given in [4] by Clément et al. We use also our favorite notations (e.g. a trivial type scheme (a type) is written $\forall.\tau$).

The rules (CST), (ABS), (REC), (APP) are identical in both systems: in DM, they handle trivial type schemes, likened to types. The rule (TAUT) related to identifiers is very simple : it only extracts the type information from the environment. The (LET) rule does no generalization at all, but on the other hand the rule (GEN) may introduce some supplementary quantified variables in a type scheme. The rule (INST) may weaken the type scheme of an expression.

The inductive predicate type_of_DM, illustrated partly below, formalizes the DM system in Coq. The relationship with the inference rules is again straightforward, except for the constructor type_of_DM_gen that quantifies a list of variables instead of a unique variable in the rule (GEN). The function bind_list implements the binding of variables in a type scheme. Its definition is very close to the definition of the function gen_type: it introduces a similar linear encoding of the generic variables.

```
Inductive type_of_DM: type_env -> expr -> type_scheme -> Prop :=
  type_DM_taut: ∀ env: type_env, ∀ x: ident, ∀ ts : type_scheme,
      (assoc_ident_in_env x env)=(Some ts) ->
        (type_of_DM env (Variable x) ts)
| type_DM_inst: ∀ env: type_env, ∀ e: expr, ∀ ts,ts': type_scheme,
      (type_of_DM env e ts) -> ts ≻ ts' -> (type_of_DM env e ts')
| type_DM_gen: ∀ env: type_env, ∀ e: expr, ∀ ts: type_scheme,
      (type_of_DM env e ts) ->
          ∀ l : (list stamp)(are_disjoints l (FV_env env)) ->
            (type_of_DM env e (bind_list l ts))
  ...
| type_DM_let_in: ∀ env: type_env, ∀ e,e': expr,
    ∀ x: ident, ∀ ts,ts': type_scheme
      (type_of_DM env e ts) ->
        (type_of_DM (add_env env x ts) e' ts') ->
          (type_of_DM env (Let_in x e e') ts')
```

$$(\text{CST}) \quad \Gamma \vdash_{DM} n : \forall.nat$$

$$(\text{TAUT}) \, \Gamma \vdash_{DM} x : \Gamma(x)$$

$$(\text{INST}) \quad \frac{\Gamma \vdash_{DM} x : \sigma, \quad \sigma \succ \sigma'}{\Gamma \vdash_{DM} x : \sigma'}$$

$$(\text{GEN}) \quad \frac{\Gamma \vdash_{DM} x : \sigma, \quad \alpha \notin FV(\Gamma)}{\Gamma \vdash_{DM} x : \forall \alpha.\sigma}$$

$$(\text{ABS}) \quad \frac{\Gamma \oplus x : \forall.\tau \vdash_{DM} e : \forall.\tau'}{\Gamma \vdash_{DM} \lambda\, x.e : \forall.\tau \rightarrow \tau'}$$

$$(\text{REC}) \quad \frac{\Gamma \oplus x : \forall.\tau \oplus f : \forall.\tau \rightarrow \tau' \vdash_{DM} e : \forall.\tau'}{\Gamma \vdash_{DM} \text{Rec } f\, x.e : \forall.\tau \rightarrow \tau'}$$

$$(\text{APP}) \quad \frac{\Gamma \vdash_{DM} e : \forall.\tau \rightarrow \tau', \quad \Gamma \vdash_{DM} e' : \forall.\tau}{\Gamma \vdash_{DM} e\, e' : \forall.\tau'}$$

$$(\text{LET}) \quad \frac{\Gamma \vdash_{DM} e : \sigma, \quad \Gamma \oplus x : \sigma \vdash_{DM} e' : \sigma'}{\Gamma \vdash_{DM} \text{let } x = e \text{ in } e' : \sigma'}$$

Fig. 3. The DM type system

5.2 Soundness of DM' with Respect to DM

We demonstrate the soundness of DM' with respect to DM by showing that if we can prove with the DM' typing rules that e has type τ then we can prove with the DM typing rules that e has also the type τ (or the trivial type scheme $\forall.\tau$). All that is done with the same environment.

```
Lemma soundness_DM'_wrt_DM: ∀ e: expr, ∀ Γ: type_env, ∀τ: type,
    Γ ⊢ e : τ -> Γ ⊢_DM e : ∀.τ
```

The proof is done by induction on the expression e. Most cases are established by applying the corresponding rule in DM and the induction hypothesis. The case where e is an identifier requires to successively apply the rules (TAUT) and (INST). The let case needs more effort, in particular we have to rewrite (bind_list (gen_vars τ Γ) $\forall.\tau$) as (gen_type τ Γ). Intuitively, this rewriting means that binding (in one time) all the variables of τ not free in Γ (computed by (gen_vars τ Γ)) gives exactly the same result as generalizing τ with respect to Γ. We have here a syntactic equality because of the encoding encapsulated in both bind_list and gen_type.

5.3   Completeness of DM' with Respect to DM

The completeness theorem states that if we can prove with the DM typing rules that e has the type scheme σ then we can establish with the DM' typing rules that e has a type τ whose generalization provides a type scheme at least as general as σ.

> Lemma completeness_DM'_wrt_DM:
> $\forall$ e: expr, $\forall$ Γ: type_env, $\forall$ σ: type_scheme,
> $\qquad$ $\Gamma \vdash_{DM}$ e : σ -> $\exists$ τ. $\Gamma \vdash$ e : τ $\wedge$ (gen_type τ Γ) $\succ$ σ

The proof requires an induction on $\Gamma \vdash_{DM} e : \sigma$ and is based on numerous lemmas about the $\succ$ relation. For example:

$\sigma_1 \succ \sigma_2$ -> $s\sigma_1 \succ s\sigma_2$ where s is a substitution

(are_disjoints l (FV_env Γ)) ->
  (gen_type τ Γ) $\succ$ σ -> (gen_type τ Γ) $\succ$ (bind_list l σ)

(bind_list l σ) $\succ$ σ and (gen_type τ Γ) $\succ$ $\forall.\tau$

The proofs of these lemmas are clumsy and technical: most require to exhibit generic substitutions.

6   Conclusion

In this paper, we have specified in the Calculus of Inductive Constructions the abstract syntax, the type system and the dynamic semantics of a polymorphic functional fragment of the core ML language. We have verified one of the more fundamental properties, that is ML typing is sound. We have experimented two kinds of semantics: evaluation and reduction.

The ML language and its type system were often extended, mainly with the aim of offering more flexibility to the programmer: extensible records, mutable values, objects, overloading ... Thus in order to validate these modifications, our formal development may be considered as a basis to investigate the properties of the new language (does it preserve or violate the properties established initially?). Beyond the necessary checking step by step, our objective is to develop a formal framework (based on the Calculus of Inductive Constructions and Coq) that allows to define type systems à la ML and to reason about them. Intuitively, it requires at the same time the construction of a library of formal components and a methodology for composing and re-using formal pieces.

Acknowledgements We thank Karim Berkani for his collaboration in the earlier verification of the reductions_preserve_types lemma in the monomorphic case. The polymorphic case presented in this paper has built on his work. Furthermore we thank the anonymous referees for their helpful comments.

References

1. B. Barras et al. The Coq Proof Assistant, Reference Manual, Version 6.1. INRIA, Rocquencourt, December 1996.
2. Samuel Boutin. Proving Correctness of the Translation from Mini-ML to the CAM with the Coq Proof Development System. Research report RR-2536, INRIA, Rocquencourt, April 1995.
3. Ana Bove. A Machine-assisted Proof that Well Typed Expressions Cannot Go Wrong. Chalmers University of Technology and Göteborg University, May 1998.
4. D. Clement, J. Despeyroux, T. Despeyroux, and G. Kahn. A simple Applicative Language: Mini-ML. In *Proceedings of the ACM Conference on Lisp and Functional Programming*, August 1986. also available as research report RR-529, INRIA, Sophia-Antipolis, May 1986.
5. J. Despeyroux, F. Pfenning, C. Schürmann. Primitive Recursion for Higher-Order Abstract Syntax. In *Proc. of TLCA '97*, LNCS 1210, Springer Verlag, 1997.
6. C. Dubois, V. Ménissier-Morain. Certification of a type inference tool for ML: Damas-Milner within Coq. Journal of Automated Reasoning, Vol 23, nos 3-4, 319-346, 1999.
7. C. Dubois, V. Viguié Donzeau-Gouge. A step towards the mechanization of partial functions : domains as inductive predicates. Workshop *Mechanization of partial functions*, CADE'15, Lindau, Germany, July 1998.
8. J. Frost. A Case Study of Co-induction in Isabelle. Technical Report 359, University of Cambridge, Computer Laboratory, February 1995.
9. R. Harper. Systems of polymorphic type assignment in LF. Technical Report CMU-CS-90-144, Carnegie Mellon University, Pittsburgh, Pennsylvania, June 1990.
10. G. Kahn. Natural semantics. In *Proceedings of the Symposium on Theoretical Aspects of Computer Science*, Passau, Germany, 1987. Also available as a Research Report RR-601, Inria, Sophia-Antipolis, February 187.
11. H.P. Ko, M.E. Nadel. Substitution and refutation revisited. In K. Furukawa, editor, *Proc. 8th International Conference on Logic Programming*, 679-692, the MIT Press, 1991.
12. X. Leroy. Polymorphic typing of an algorithmic language. Research report 1778, INRIA, 1992 (French original also available).
13. L. Damas, R. Milner. Principal type-schemes for functional programs. In *Proceedings of the 15'th Annual Symposium on Principles of Programming Languages*, pages 207-212. ACM, 1982.
14. T. Nipkow, D. von Oheimb. Java$_{light}$ is Type-Safe - Definitely. In *Proc. 25th ACM Symp. Principles of Programming Languages*, ACM Press, 1998, 161-170.
15. W. Naraschewski, T. Nipkow. Type Inference Verified: Algorithm W in Isabelle/HOL. Journal of Automated Reasoning, Vol 23, nos 3-4, 299-318, 1999.
16. S. Michaylov, F. Pfenning. Natural Semantics and some of its meta-theory in Elf. In Lars Halln, editor, *Proceedings of the Second Workshop on Extensions of Logic Programming*, Springer-Verlag LNCS, 1991. Also available as a Technical Report MPI-I-91-211, Max-Planck-Institute for Computer Science, Saarbrucken, Germany, August 1991.

144   C. Dubois

17. O. Müller, K. Slind. Treating Partiality in a Logic of Total Functions. *The Computer Journal*, 40(10), 1997.
18. D. Rémy, J. Vouillon. An effective object-oriented extension to ML. Theory And Practice of Object Systems, 4(1):27-50, 1998.
19. D. Syme. Proving Java type soundness. Technical Report 427, University of Cambridge, Computer Laboratory, 1997.
20. D. Terrasse. Encoding Natural Semantics in Coq. In *Proceedings of the Fourth International Conference on Algebraic Methodology and Software Technology (AMAST'95)*, LNCS 936. Springer-Verlag, July 1995.
21. D. Terrasse. Vers un Environnement d'Aide au Développement de Preuves en Sémantique Naturelle Thèse de Doctorat, Ecole Nationale des Ponts et Chaussées, 1995.
22. M. VanInwegen. Towards type preservation for core SML. University of Cambridge Computer Laboratory, 1997.
23. A. Wright, M. Felleisen. A Syntactic Approach to Type Soundness. Information and Computation, 115(1), pp.38-94, 1994.

On the Mechanization of Real Analysis in Isabelle/HOL

Jacques D. Fleuriot

Division of Informatics – University of Edinburgh
80 South Bridge, Edinburgh EH1 1HN
jdf@dai.ed.ac.uk

Abstract. Our recent, and still ongoing, development of real analysis in Isabelle/HOL is presented and compared, whenever instructive, to the one present in the theorem prover HOL. While most existing mechanizations of analysis only use the classical ϵ and δ approach, ours uses notions from both Nonstandard Analysis and classical analysis. The overall result is an intuitive, yet rigorous, development of real analysis, and a relatively high degree of proof automation in many cases.

1 Introduction

The development of analysis in Isabelle/HOL [10] is based on both the reals and the hyperreals of Robinson's Nonstandard Analysis (NSA) [12]. The real numbers, $\mathbb{R}$, are constructed in the theorem prover using the Dedekind cuts method [5] and then extended to give the hyperreals (denoted by $\mathbb{R}^*$) by means of the ultrapower construction [13,4]. Thus, when working in the hyperreals, $\mathbb{R}$ can be viewed as a proper subfield of $\mathbb{R}^*$, with the latter also containing new non-standard numbers such as infinitesimals and infinite numbers. By contrast, the development of analysis in HOL, for example, rests purely on the real numbers constructed using a variant of Cantor's method developed by Harrison [6].

Our approach follows the HOL methodology and proceeds strictly through definitions. This ensures that all theory extensions are conservative, thereby guaranteeing consistency. Such an approach is especially suitable for a rigorous development of infinitesimals, as many of the attacks on these numbers in the past have been due to inconsistent axiomatizations. In the next sections, we give an overview of the various types of numbers available in Isabelle/HOL, and of the mechanization of some real analysis in the theorem prover.

2 Nonstandard Numbers

An immediate consequence of our decision to formalize nonstandard rather than standard analysis is the extra amount of work spent on number constructions. The ultrapower construction of the hyperreals, for example, first required proving Zorn's Lemma and developing a theory of filters and ultrafilters for Isabelle/HOL. We have described details of the construction elsewhere [4], and so will only outline a few of the aspects relevant to this paper in what follows.

J. Harrison and M. Aagaard (Eds.): TPHOLs 2000, LNCS 1869, pp. 145–161, 2000.

2.1 On the Construction

The construction of the hyperreals resembles to some extent that of the reals
from the rationals using equivalence classes induced by Cauchy sequences. In
this case, however, a free ultrafilter $U_{\mathbb{N}}$ over the natural numbers is used to
partition the set of all sequences of real numbers into equivalence classes. The
free ultrafilter $U_{\mathbb{N}}$, whose existence is proved using Zorn's Lemma, is a collection
of subsets of $\mathbb{N}$ with the following properties (amongst others):

$$\emptyset \notin U_{\mathbb{N}} \text{ and } \mathbb{N} \in U_{\mathbb{N}} \qquad X \in U_{\mathbb{N}} \Longrightarrow \neg\, \mathrm{finite}\; X$$
$$X \in U_{\mathbb{N}} \wedge Y \in U_{\mathbb{N}} \Longrightarrow X \cap Y \in U_{\mathbb{N}} \qquad X \in U_{\mathbb{N}} \Longleftrightarrow -X \notin U_{\mathbb{N}}$$
$$X \in U_{\mathbb{N}} \wedge X \subseteq Y \Longrightarrow Y \in U_{\mathbb{N}}$$

In Isabelle, the following equivalence relation on sequences of real numbers is
then defined:

$$\mathbf{hyprel} :: ((\mathbf{nat} \Rightarrow \mathbf{real}) * (\mathbf{nat} \Rightarrow \mathbf{real}))\,\mathbf{set}$$
$$\mathbf{hyprel} \equiv \{p.\ \exists rs.\ p = (r,s) \wedge \{n.\ r(n) = s(n)\} \in U_{\mathbb{N}}\}$$

The set of equivalence classes, that is the quotient set, arising from **hyprel** is
used to define the new type **hyprel** denoting the hyperreals:

$$\mathbf{hypreal} \equiv \{x::(\mathbf{nat} \Rightarrow \mathbf{real}).\mathrm{True}\}/\mathbf{hyprel}$$

Thus, it follows from the definition of **hyprel** that for two hyperreals to be
equal, the corresponding entries in their equivalence class representatives must
be equal at an infinite number of positions. This is because $U_{\mathbb{N}}$ cannot contain
any finite set. Once the new type has been introduced, Isabelle provides coercion
functions — the abstraction and representation functions — that enable the basic
operations to be defined. In this particular case, the functions

$$\mathbf{Abs\_hypreal} :: (\mathbf{nat} \Rightarrow \mathbf{real})\,\mathbf{set} \Rightarrow \mathbf{hypreal}$$
$$\mathbf{Rep\_hypreal} :: \mathbf{hypreal} \Rightarrow (\mathbf{nat} \Rightarrow \mathbf{real})\,\mathbf{set}$$

are added to the theory such that **hypreal** and $\{x::\ \mathbf{nat} \Rightarrow \mathbf{real}.\ \mathrm{True}\}/\mathbf{hyprel}$
are isomorphic by **Rep_hypreal** and its inverse **Abs_hypreal**.

The familiar operations (addition, subtraction, multiplication, inverse) and
the ordering relation on the new type **hypreal** are then defined in terms of pointwise operations on the underlying sequences. For example, let $[\langle X_n \rangle]$ denote the
equivalence class (i.e. hyperreal) containing $\langle X_n \rangle$ then multiplication is defined
by

$$[\langle X_n \rangle] \cdot [\langle Y_n \rangle] \equiv [\langle X_n \cdot Y_n \rangle] \tag{1}$$

or, more specifically, in Isabelle as:

$$P \cdot Q \equiv \mathbf{Abs\_hypreal}\ (\bigcup X \in \mathbf{Rep\_hypreal}(P).$$
$$\bigcup Y \in \mathbf{Rep\_hypreal}(Q).\, \mathbf{hyprel}\hat{\ }\hat{\ }\{\lambda n.\ X\,n \cdot Y\,n\})$$

where

$$\bigcup x \in A.\, B[x] \equiv \{y.\, \exists x \in A.\, y \in B\} \text{ (union of family of sets)}.$$

$$r\,\hat{}\,\hat{}\,s \equiv \{y.\, \exists x \in s.\, (x,y) \in r\} \text{ (image of set } s \text{ under relation } r).$$

Equation (1) above is in fact proved as a theorem. All the expected field properties of the hyperreals are easily proved since they follow nicely from the corresponding properties of the reals. We define an embedding of the reals in the hyperreals by having the following map in Isabelle:

> hypreal_of_real :: real ⇒ hypreal
> hypreal_of_real r ≡ Abs_hypreal (hyprel`^`^`$\{\lambda n\!::\!\mathrm{nat}.\, r\}$)

In other words, we represent each real number r in $\mathrm{I\!R}^*$ by the equivalence class $[\langle r, r, r, \ldots \rangle]$. The properties of the embedding function, with respect to multiplication, addition and so on, follow trivially since they are just special cases of the operations on the hyperreals. In what follows, we will denote an embedded real r by $\underline{r}$ unless we use the Isabelle embedding function explicitly.

2.2 Numbers Big and Small

The embedding function enables us to define the set of embedded reals SReal explicitly, and prove that it is a proper subfield of $\mathrm{I\!R}^*$. The proof shows that the well-defined hyperreal $[\langle 1, 2, 3, \ldots \rangle]$ (denoted by ω) cannot be equal to any of the embedded reals as no singleton set is allowed in $U_{\mathrm{I\!N}}$. Once the embedding is defined and various of its properties proved, we formalize the definitions characterizing the various types of numbers that make up the new extended field:

> Infinitesimal ≡ $\{x.\, \forall r \in \mathrm{SReal}.\, 0 < r \rightarrow \mathrm{abs}\ x < r\}$
> Finite ≡ $\{x.\, \exists r \in \mathrm{SReal}.\, \mathrm{abs}\ x < r\}$
> Infinite ≡ −Finite

With this done, a number of theorems are proved, including:

$$\frac{x \in \mathsf{Infinitesimal} \quad y \in \mathsf{Infinitesimal}}{x\ \mathsf{op}\ y \in \mathsf{Infinitesimal}} \qquad \frac{x \in \mathsf{Finite} \quad y \in \mathsf{Finite}}{x\ \mathsf{op}\ y \in \mathsf{Finite}}$$

where op is $+$, $-$, or $\times$ (i.e. both sets are subrings of $\mathrm{I\!R}^*$). Other Isabelle theorems proved include amongst many others:

$$\frac{x \in \mathsf{Infinitesimal} \quad y \in \mathsf{Finite}}{x \times y \in \mathsf{Infinitesimal}} \qquad \frac{z \in \mathsf{Infinitesimal} \quad \underline{x} < \underline{y}}{\underline{x} + z < \underline{y}}$$

In all, we prove over 250 theorems describing the properties of the hyperreals and their inter-relationships. In addition, we use our free ultrafilter to extend the natural numbers and construct the *hypernatural* numbers, $\mathrm{I\!N}^*$. This additional type of nonstandard numbers provides us with infinitely large numbers greater than all the members of $\mathrm{I\!N}$. The set of infinite hypernaturals is denoted by HNatInfinite in Isabelle. We also define the function hypnat_of_nat, an embedding of the natural numbers into the hypernaturals [4].

3   Important Concepts from Nonstandard Analysis

Before we can mechanize any proofs from elementary analysis, we need to define a few more important concepts that will provide us with an adequate framework. Firstly, we define the crucial *infinitely close* relation $\approx$:

$$x \approx y \equiv x - y \in \text{Infinitesimal}$$

This is an equivalence relation about which we prove a number of properties such as:[1]

$$[|a \approx b; c \approx d|] \Longrightarrow a + c \approx b + d$$

$$[|s \in \text{SReal}; b \in \text{SReal}|] \Longrightarrow (a \approx b) = (a = b)$$

$$s \in \text{Finite} \Longrightarrow \exists! r.\ r \in \text{SReal} \land s \approx r \qquad (2)$$

$$[|a \approx b; b \in \text{Finite}|] \Longrightarrow a \in \text{Finite} \qquad (3)$$

Theorem (2) above is known as the *Standard Part Theorem* and is especially important as it enables us to formalize the notion of *standard part*. The standard part of a finite nonstandard number is defined as the unique real number infinitely close to it. The actual definition in Isabelle uses the Hilbert operator ϵ:

$$\text{st} :: \text{hypreal} \Rightarrow \text{hypreal}$$
$$\text{st}\ x \equiv (\epsilon r.x \in \text{Finite} \land r \in \text{SReal} \land r \approx x)$$

This definition would be sufficient if we were only working in the hyperreals. However, since we are concerned with the formalization of real analysis, and want to give both the standard *and* nonstandard definitions of various concepts, we define a second version of the standard part operation. This is used to return a number of type **real** rather than an embedded real:

$$\text{str} :: \text{hypreal} \Rightarrow \text{real}$$
$$\text{str}\ x \equiv (\epsilon r.x \in \text{Finite} \land \text{hypreal\_of\_real}\ r \approx x)$$

All the important properties of the standard part operator are proved. These include, for example:

$$\frac{x \in \text{SReal}}{\text{st}\ x = x} \qquad \frac{x \in \text{Finite}}{\text{st}\ x \approx x} \qquad \frac{x \in \text{Finite} \quad y \in \text{Finite}}{(x \approx y) = (\text{st}\ x = \text{st}\ y)}$$

3.1   Nonstandard Extensions

Nonstandard extensions provide systematic ways through which sets and functions defined on the reals are extended to the hyperreals (a process sometimes known as the ∗-transform [8]).

---

[1] $\exists! x.\ P$ stands for the unique existence quantifier while the Isabelle notation $[|\phi_1; \ldots; \phi_n|] \Longrightarrow \psi$ abbreviates the nested implication $\phi_1 \Longrightarrow (\ldots \phi_n \Longrightarrow \psi \ldots)$.

In particular, if f is a function from $\mathbb{R}$ to $\mathbb{R}$, then it can be extended to a function f^* from $\mathbb{R}^*$ to $\mathbb{R}^*$ by the following rule: $x = [\langle X_n \rangle] \in \mathbb{R}^*$ maps into $y = [\langle Y_n \rangle] = f^*(x) \in \mathbb{R}^*$ if and only if $\{n \in \mathbb{N}.\ f(X_n) \in Y_n\} \in U_{\mathbb{N}}$. In Isabelle, this is rendered as:

```
*f* :: (real ⇒ real) ⇒ hypreal ⇒ hypreal
*f* f x ≡ Abs_hypreal (⋃X ∈ Rep_hypreal(x). hyprel^^{λn. f(Xn)})
```

Thus, the nonstandard extension operator provides a generic way through which, given a function taking standard arguments, we can define an analogous one that accepts nonstandard arguments. In what follows, we will denote the nonstandard extension of a given real function f either by f^* or by its equivalent Isabelle notation (`*f*f`). We prove this important simplification theorem:

$$(\texttt{*f* } f)\ (\texttt{Abs\_hypreal (hyprel^^}\{\lambda n.\ Xn\}))) = $$
$$(\texttt{Abs\_hypreal (hyprel^^}\{\lambda n.\ f(Xn)\})))$$

In other words, we have that $f^*[\langle X_n \rangle] = [\langle f(X_n) \rangle]$. This is useful as it allows us to formalize definitions and prove properties of nonstandard functions by couching them in terms of the corresponding real functions and our free ultrafilter. We easily prove a number of theorems about nonstandard extensions such as $f^*(\underline{r}) = \underline{f(r)}$ and $f^*(x) + g^*(x) = (\lambda u.\ f(u) + g(u))^*(x)$. We will come across others as we further outline our formalization of analysis.

We also extend functions from $\mathbb{N}$ to $\mathbb{R}$: given such a function s, its $*$-transform is the function $s^* : \mathbb{N}^* \to \mathbb{R}^*$ where $s^*([\langle X_n \rangle]) = [\langle s(X_n) \rangle]$ for any $[\langle X_n \rangle] \in \mathbb{N}^*$. In Isabelle, the nonstandard extension is denoted by (`*fNat* s`) and is useful in the formalization of sequences, for example (see Section 5.1).

4   Nonstandard Versus ϵ and δ Formalization

In general, one of the main advantages of the nonstandard approach is the way in which it simplifies the statement of many concepts from analysis. Nonstandard definitions tend to reflect the intuitive understanding that one has of particular concepts. For example, the standard formulation of uniform continuity:

$$\forall \epsilon.\ (0 < \epsilon \longrightarrow \exists \delta.\ (0 < \delta \wedge \forall xy.\ (0 < |x - y| < \delta \longrightarrow |f(x) - f(y)| < \epsilon)))$$

can be contrasted with the corresponding nonstandard one:

$$\forall xy.\ x \approx y \longrightarrow f^*(x) \approx f^*(y).$$

The second definition is not only concise and simple, but it also provides a rigorous, yet geometrically intuitive, characterization of the behaviour of a uniformly continuous function. The ϵ and δ definition, however, not only lacks an intuitive reading but also leads to more complicated proofs since one has to deal with the existential quantifier.

Our work shows that the use of NSA benefits the mechanization of analysis: the formalization is often simpler and shorter, and the proofs benefit from a higher degree of automation since the alternating quantifiers of the ϵ and δ approach are avoided. In our mechanization of analysis, we introduce for each concept both its standard and nonstandard definitions. In each case, we prove the equivalence of the two definitions, thereby providing us with a theorem with which we can re-cast properties that we are trying to prove in terms of equivalent nonstandard notions.

5   Mechanized Theories

Our mechanization process in Isabelle/HOL has been influenced significantly by that of Harrison in HOL [6]. Indeed, the substantial and highly focused formalization of elementary analysis in HOL has often provided us with guidance during our mechanization process. Moreover, it has also given us some means of analyzing, albeit rather roughly, the benefits that the use of NSA brings to the mechanization of analysis. We next give an overview of some of theories mechanized in Isabelle/HOL.

5.1   Sequences and Series

We follow Harrison's approach in HOL, and provide a relational definition for the limit of a sequence which we denote by $\longrightarrow$. Thus, in Isabelle, $X \longrightarrow l$ stands for X tends to l and has the following standard definition:

$$X \longrightarrow l \equiv \forall \epsilon.\, (0 < \epsilon \longrightarrow (\exists N.\, \forall n.\, N \leq n \longrightarrow \mathsf{abs}\,(Xn - l) < \epsilon))$$

It might not be immediately obvious that this definition is intended to capture the idea that terms "far enough" along the sequence can get arbitrarily close to l. Our formalization, however, also provides a nonstandard definition of limit, denoted by $\underset{NS}{\longrightarrow}$, that immediately captures the intuition. It is defined by the following simpler statement which does not involve any existential quantifiers:

$$X \underset{NS}{\longrightarrow} l \equiv (\forall N \in \mathsf{HNatInfinite}.\, (\ast \mathsf{fNat}\ast X)N \approx \underline{l})$$

Our first task, as is the case each time we introduce a new concept from analysis, is to prove that the two definitions are equivalent. We will not elaborate on the details of the proof here, but simply remark that for all of the equivalence proofs formalized, it is usually trickier to prove that the nonstandard definition implies the standard one — in each case, this requires the use of the Axiom of Choice, for example. This remark leads to another important point worth mentioning: all the equivalence proofs follow the same general pattern. This is not a coincidence and is related to one of the central features of NSA, known as the **Transfer Principle** which provides a context in which true statements about $\mathbb{R}$ are transformed into statements about $\mathbb{R}^*$ [8,7]. Details about the mechanization of the equivalence proofs, and other related remarks, can be found in the author's PhD thesis [4].

Once this important proof is mechanized, we can formally justify using nonstandard methods to prove standard theorems of elementary analysis. As for the properties of sequential limits, the following theorems, for example, are all proved *automatically* since there is no need to instantiate any existential variables:

$$
\frac{X \xrightarrow[NS]{} a \quad Y \xrightarrow[NS]{} b}{(\lambda n.\, X\,n + Y\,n) \xrightarrow[NS]{} a + b}
\qquad
\frac{X \xrightarrow[NS]{} a \quad Y \xrightarrow[NS]{} b}{(\lambda n.\, X\,n \cdot Y\,n) \xrightarrow[NS]{} a \cdot b} \tag{4}
$$

$$
\frac{X \xrightarrow[NS]{} a}{\lambda n.\, -X\,n \xrightarrow[NS]{} -a}
\qquad
\frac{X \xrightarrow[NS]{} a \quad X \xrightarrow[NS]{} b}{a = b}
$$

Theorem (4), for instance, is easily proved using (3) and a theorem about the preservation of multiplication across *-transforms:

$$
(*\mathtt{fNat}*\ f)N \cdot (*\mathtt{fNat}*\ g)N = (*\mathtt{fNat}*\ (\lambda x.\ fx \cdot gx))N
$$

Surveying the development of formalized analysis in HOL, Harrison observes that theorems about Cauchy sequences are the crucial ones [6]. As expected, these are also the important ones in our development. As in the case of sequential limits, we formalize a standard definition:

$$
\begin{aligned}
&\mathtt{Cauchy} :: (\mathtt{nat} \Rightarrow \mathtt{real}) \Rightarrow \mathtt{bool} \\
&\mathtt{Cauchy}\ X \equiv \forall \epsilon.\ (0 < \epsilon \longrightarrow (\exists M.\ (\forall mn.\ M \leq m \wedge M \leq n) \\
&\qquad\qquad\qquad\qquad \longrightarrow \mathtt{abs}\ (Xm - Xn) < \epsilon))
\end{aligned}
$$

and a nonstandard one:

$$
\begin{aligned}
&\mathtt{NSCauchy} :: (\mathtt{nat} \Rightarrow \mathtt{real}) \Rightarrow \mathtt{bool} \\
&\mathtt{NSCauchy}\ X \equiv \forall M \in \mathtt{HNatInfinite}.\ \forall N \in \mathtt{HNatInfinite}. \\
&\qquad\qquad (*\mathtt{fNat}*\ X)M \approx (*\mathtt{fNat}*\ X)N
\end{aligned}
$$

The equivalence of the two definitions is proven and, with this done the main theorem relating Cauchy sequences to convergence:

$$
\exists l.\ X \longrightarrow l \Longleftrightarrow \mathtt{Cauchy}\ X
$$

is easily mechanized, since we can replace $\longrightarrow$ by the equivalent $\xrightarrow[NS]{}$ and then unfold the nonstandard definition.

Proof Outline:
$\Rightarrow$ part:

$$
X \xrightarrow[NS]{} l \Longrightarrow X_n^* \approx \underline{l} \approx X_m^* \text{ for all } n, m \in \mathtt{HNatInfinite}
$$
$$
\Longrightarrow \mathtt{Cauchy}\ X
$$

$\Leftarrow$ part:[2]

$$\text{Cauchy } X \implies \text{NSBseq } X$$

$$\implies X^*_\Omega \in \text{Finite} \quad \text{where } \Omega \text{ is the infinite hypernatural } [\langle n \rangle]$$

$$\implies X^*_\Omega \approx \underline{l} \qquad \text{for some real number } l; \text{ by theorem (2)}$$

$$\implies X^*_\Omega \approx \underline{l} \approx X^*_n \quad \text{for all infinite } n$$

$$\implies X \xrightarrow[NS]{} l$$

The mechanization of this proof compares favourably with the one formalized by Harrison in HOL [6]. Both of them need the lemma stating that every Cauchy sequence is bounded but, otherwise, differ significantly in their formalization. Aside from dealing with the inherent difficulties associated with ϵ and δ proofs, Harrison needs to define the concept of a subsequence and several other auxiliary notions. He then proves the more or less involved theorem that every sequence contains a monotonic subsequence. One might argue that all this diverts attention from what is actually being proved; our formalization, by contrast, is direct and intuitive: the mechanized proof is only 7 steps long.

Series

In classical analysis, despite the notation $\sum_{i=0}^{\infty} a_i$, one does not try to interpret the expression literally as an infinite sum. Instead, one considers the sums of finitely many of the terms of the series, and examines the behaviour of such sums as an increasingly large, but still finite, number of terms are allowed [7]. In other words, an infinite series is defined as the limit of $\sum_{i=0}^{n} a_i$ as $n \to \infty$. Using our framework, however, it is possible to use the nonstandard criterion for sequential convergence to define *literally* infinite sums.

We first define, using Isabelle's primitive recursion package, the standard notion of finite sum ($\sum_{i=m}^{n-1} f_i$):

```
consts  sumr :: [nat, nat, (nat ⇒ real)] ⇒ real
primrec
sumr m 0 f = 0
sumr m (Suc n) f = if n < m then 0 else sumr m n f + f(n)
```

Isabelle automatically checks whether the reduction rules for sumr satisfy a primitive recursive definition, and then adds them to the simplifier. Thus, the **primrec** package provides a safe way of defining primitive recursion on datatypes in Isabelle/HOL [11]. All the expected theorems about finite sum are proved, mostly using induction followed by simplification. We will not expand on these here but instead consider how to define the nonstandard extension of sumr.

The nonstandard extension of the finite sum operation cannot be obtained by applying the *fNat* operator directly since this can only extend functions of a single variable. This is not a problem, however, as we can define the extension

---

[2] The NSA formulation of boundedness NSBseq $X \equiv \forall n \in \text{HNatInfinite}. X(n) \in \text{Finite}$, as proved in Isabelle, is used in this part of the mechanization.

in the same way that multiplication and addition, for example, were defined on the hyperreals:

sumhr :: (hypnat * hypnat * (nat ⇒ real)) ⇒ hypreal
sumhr $p \equiv (\lambda(M, N, f).$Abs_hypreal$(\bigcup X \in$ Rep_hypnat $M.$
      $\bigcup Y \in$ Rep_hypnat $N.$hyprel$^{\wedge\wedge}\{\lambda n.$ sumr $((Xn), (Yn), f)\})) p$

Without showing the coercion functions explicitly, this definition is simply asserting that

$$\text{sumhr } ([\langle X_n \rangle], [\langle Y_n \rangle], f) \equiv [\langle \text{sumr } X_n \ Y_n \ f \rangle] \tag{5}$$

This enables us to have possibly infinite hypernatural limits. Theorem (5) above is proved and is useful to the simplifier. We also mechanize various theorems which show that sumhr preserves the behaviour of finite summation [4]. Other interesting theorems include:

$$\text{sumhr } (0, M, f) \approx \text{sumhr } (0, N, f) \Longrightarrow \text{abs } (\text{sumhr } (M, N, f)) \approx 0$$

and an important theorem about the convergence of series in terms of the non-standard Cauchy criterion:

$\exists s. \ \lambda n. \ \text{sumr } 0 \ n \ f \longrightarrow s \Longleftrightarrow$
$(\forall M \in \text{HNatInfinite}. \ \forall N \in \text{HNatInfinite. abs } (\text{sumhr } (M, N, f)) \approx 0)$

This last theorem makes it trivial to prove that the terms of a convergent series tends to zero i.e.

$$\exists s. \ \lambda n. \ \text{sumr } 0 \ n \ f \longrightarrow s \Longrightarrow f \longrightarrow 0$$

In HOL, a functional definition is available that returns the limit sum to which an infinite series converges [6]. We follow the same approach and define a standard function suminf:

$$\text{suminf } f \equiv \epsilon s. \ \lambda n. \ \text{sumr } (0 \ n \ f) \longrightarrow s$$

which stands for $\sum_{i=0}^{\infty} f_i = s$. However, we can exploit the fact that our framework offers a literal interpretation for the sum of an infinite series and prove the following theorem:

$$\text{suminf } f = \text{str } (\text{sumhr } (0, \Omega, f)) \tag{6}$$

where Ω is the infinite hypernatural $[\langle n \rangle]$ defined in Isabelle. Of course, any infinite hypernatural can be used in the theorem above: Ω is just one of the simplest to define.

The nonstandard form of suminf provides a nice device which will be useful to define the transcendental functions in Isabelle. With this aim in mind, and following Harrison's approach in HOL, we also prove two of the most important convergence tests for series: the comparison and ratio tests. In both cases, the proofs formalized in Isabelle are purely standard although some of their steps use theorems derived by nonstandard means. The formalization in HOL now becomes a valuable guide to us: it indicates what lemmas need to be proved to bring our mechanization of the theorems through.

5.2 Continuity and Differentiation

The first crucial concept defined is that of pointwise limit. Once again, we provide both the traditional ϵ and δ formulation:

$$f \xrightarrow{\ a\ } l \equiv \forall \epsilon.\, 0 < \epsilon \longrightarrow (\exists \delta.\, 0 < \delta \wedge$$
$$(\forall x.\, 0 < \mathtt{rabs}\,(x-a) \wedge \mathtt{rabs}\,(x-a) < \delta \longrightarrow \mathtt{rabs}\,(f\,x - l) < \epsilon))$$

and a nonstandard one:

$$f \xrightarrow[NS]{\ a\ } l \equiv \forall x.\, x \neq \underline{a} \wedge x \approx \underline{a} \longrightarrow (\ast\mathbf{f}\ast\, f)\, x \approx \underline{l}$$

and prove their equivalence. Both $f \xrightarrow{\ a\ } l$ and $f \xrightarrow[NS]{\ a\ } l$ stand for f having limit l as x approaches a. We prove properties that are similar to those of sequential limits and once more with a high degree of automation. We carry out a simple experiment in which we compare purely ϵ and δ proofs of limit properties with the corresponding nonstandard ones in Isabelle [4]. The nonstandard proof of the product of limits, for example, is automatic while its standard proof is about 15 steps long, requires a case split due to the linearity of the reals, and explicit instantiation of the ϵ and δ properties.

Continuity

Once the properties of pointwise limits have been formalized, they can be used to provide the standard definition of continuity:

$$\mathtt{isCont}\, f\, a \equiv (f \xrightarrow{\ a\ } f\,a)$$

This states that a function f is continuous at a real point a if $f(x)$ tends to $f(a)$ as x tends to a. This motivates the following nonstandard definition:

$$\mathtt{isNSCont}\, f\, a \equiv (\forall x.\, x \approx \underline{a} \longrightarrow (\ast\mathbf{f}\ast\, f)\, x \approx \underline{f(a)})$$

An important point to note is that the formalization makes it explicit that the definition is referring to the embedded copies of the reals a and $f(a)$ in the hyperreals. The equivalence of the two definitions follows immediately from that of standard and nonstandard limits. We prove automatically that the sum, product, and division of continuous functions are also continuous. All these are direct consequences of the corresponding theorems for pointwise limits.

However, we have a second method for proving them: the theorems are all simple algebraic consequences of the nonstandard formulation of continuity. This provides a uniform approach that bypasses the limit results and provides simple, intuitive proofs. Moreover, it has the added advantage that, unlike the approach based on limits, it can easily prove that the composition of continuous functions is continuous i.e.,

$$[\![\mathtt{isCont}\, f\, a;\, \mathtt{isCont}\, g\, (f\,a)]\!] \implies \mathtt{isCont}\, (g \circ f)\, a$$

Proof. If $x \approx \underline{a}$ then $f^*(x) \approx \underline{f(a)}$, and so it follows that $g^*(f^*(x)) \approx \underline{g(f(a))}$.

□

This result is proved in one step by Isabelle's automatic tactic. Its formalization can be contrasted with the corresponding one in HOL, which required unfolding the limit definition and instantiating ϵ and δ properties since the theorem cannot be derived from limit properties [6]. This hints at another useful, and powerful aspect of nonstandard methods in theorem proving: their simple algebra enables them to deal uniformly with a wide range of theorems. An analogous problem, easily avoided with NSA, can be noticed if the standard treatment is used to mechanize the chain rule of differentiation.

Differentiation

We now give a brief outline of the development of differentiation which builds upon the theories already described. The standard formulation states that a function f has a derivative d at a point x if $(f(x + h) - f(x))/h \to d$ as $h \to 0$. In Isabelle, we formalize a relational definition $\text{DERIV}(x)\ f :> d$ meaning 'the derivative of f at x is d' as

$$\text{DERIV}(x)\ f :> d \equiv (\lambda h.\ (f(x + h) - f(x))/h) \xrightarrow{\quad 0 \quad} d$$

and a corresponding nonstandard one:

$$\text{NSDERIV}(x)\ f :> d \equiv \forall h \in \text{Infinitesimal} - \{0\}.\ \frac{f^*(\underline{x} + h) - \underline{f(x)}}{h} \approx \underline{d} \quad (7)$$

where the real point x becomes an embedded value and h a non-zero infinitesimal. The nonstandard definition simply reflects the intuition behind the Leibnizian notation $\frac{df}{dx}$ and treats differentiation as a quotient operation. We prove that the nonstandard definition has an equivalent statement in terms of limits, and hence that it is equivalent to the standard definition. We also prove another nonstandard characterization for the differentiability of a function f at a real point x:

$$\text{NSDERIV}(x)\ f :> d \iff \forall y.\ y \approx x \wedge y \neq x \longrightarrow \frac{f^*(y) - \underline{f(x)}}{y - \underline{x}} \approx \underline{d} \quad (8)$$

We easily mechanize all the expected properties about the differentiation of simple functions and their combination. The task is simple as we can avoid limits in favour of simple algebraic manipulations of infinitesimals.

Reporting on his formalization of derivatives in HOL, Harrison remarks that the formalization of the chain rule is not as straightforward as it might seem [6]. Indeed, when using the standard definition, the property cannot be derived using limits since these cannot be composed. This forces a direct and rather cumbersome proof that can potentially complicate mechanization. Using NSA, however, the chain rule

$$[\![\text{NSDERIV}(a)\ g :> e; \text{NSDERIV}((g\,a))\ f :> d]\!] \implies \text{NSDERIV}(a)\ (f \circ g) :> d \cdot e$$

admits a straightforward mechanization since it has the following simple, algebraic proof relying on equivalence theorem (8):

$$\frac{f^*(g^*(x)) - f(g(a))}{x - a} = \frac{f^*(g^*(x)) - f(g(a))}{g^*(x) - g(a)} \; \frac{g^*(x) - g(a)}{x - a} \approx d \cdot e$$

Our mechanization, as one sees, is a direct rendering of the classical notation used to denote the chain rule:

$$\frac{df}{dx} = \frac{df}{dg} \frac{dg}{dx}$$

and should be contrasted to the one in HOL, where Harrison has to formalize the Carathéodory derivative to provide the machinery necessary for simple derivation of the chain rule. In our work, we next use the chain rule to provide nice algebraic proofs of the theorems about the inverse and quotient of functions [4].

Overall our theories dealing with continuity and differentiation have been influenced quite significantly by the corresponding formalization in HOL. We also reproduce, for example, the HOL theorem for proof by bisection [6]. The lemmas set up by Harrison to prove the theorem act as an invaluable guide to the corresponding mechanization in Isabelle. Proof by bisection is often used in standard analysis to prove important theorems such as the Intermediate Value Theorem; it is a useful tool to have, even in a framework like ours that uses a combination of standard and nonstandard techniques, as this allows us an extra amount of flexibility when proving important theorems.

Indeed, apart from proof by bisection, we can use the fact that many fundamental results of standard real analysis have intuitively appealing proofs using NSA to carry out alternative formalizations in Isabelle. For example, the Intermediate Value Theorem:

$$[\![\, a \leq b; f(a) \leq y; y \leq f(b); \forall x.\, a \leq x \wedge x \leq b \longrightarrow \text{isCont } f \; x \,]\!]$$
$$\implies \exists x.\, a \leq x \wedge x \leq b \wedge f(x) = y$$

and the Extreme Value Theorem both have nice infinitesimal geometric proofs that rely on the notion of a partition [8,7,9]. This concept is formalized explicitly in Isabelle and, essentially, involves splitting a closed interval into infinitely many subintervals of equal infinitesimal lengths. The construction of partitions provides a particularly useful tool in infinitesimal calculus: it can also be used, with a slight modification, to provide a nonstandard treatment of the Riemann integral, for example [9]. We will not expand further on this, and simply mention that the other significant theorems formalized in the theory include Rolle's theorem and the Mean Value Theorem.

5.3   Power Series and Transcendental Functions

The development of power series and transcendental functions in Isabelle is to a large extent carried out through standard rather than nonstandard processes.

One of the reasons for this decision is that NSA does not seem, at first sight, to bring much in terms of simplification to the theory: the same techniques (e.g. convergence tests) are used in many cases for both standard and nonstandard proofs [7]. Our Isabelle development treats the HOL formalization as a useful blueprint; this enables us to focus on getting the main results that we want, namely the transcendental functions.

We prove similar results to Harrison in HOL [6], with the same main theorem about the term by term differentiation of power series from Burkill and Burkill [3]. On the formalization of the theorem in HOL, Harrison notes that this is "perhaps the most difficult single proof in the whole development of analysis". So, it is probably not surprising to note that this theorem produces the longest, and definitely the most complex, proof of our own development (the proof is 90 steps long!).

Once the basic properties of power series are established, we proceed to define a few of the well-known and fundamental transcendental functions. These include the exponential and trigonometric functions, as well as their inverses. The exponential function is of central importance and is defined as the function sum of the power series [7]:

$$\exp(x) \equiv \sum_{i=0}^{\infty} x^n/n!$$

The formulation of the exponential function thus requires the factorial function, which easily formalized using Isabelle's `primrec` package, and denoted by `fact`. We use the nonstandard equivalence theorem (6) to define the exp function:[3]

$$\text{exp} :: \text{real} \Rightarrow \text{real} \qquad\qquad (9)$$
$$\text{exp } x \equiv \text{str } (\text{sumhr } (0, \Omega, \lambda n.\ x^n/(\text{fact } n)))$$

The ratio test is used to show the convergence, and hence boundedness, of the infinite sum used to define exp. With the help of theorem:

$$\text{NSBseq } X \implies \text{Abs\_hypreal } (\text{hyprel}\,\widetilde{}\,\{X\}) \in \text{Finite} \qquad (10)$$

which states that every bounded real sequence defines a finite hyperreal, we deduce that:

$$\text{sumhr } (0, \Omega, \lambda n.\ x^n/(\text{fact } n)) \in \text{Finite}$$

which means that the infinite sum (9) given above is well-defined and does produce, by the Standard Part Theorem, a real-value as result. Theorem (10) reflects the close relationship existing between sequences and hyperreal numbers: it holds because the development of the hyperreals is based on the use of sequences of real numbers. This relation is further illustrated by the next theorems, also formalized in Isabelle:

---

[3] For clarity, we omit to show the embedding function `real_of_nat` used to embed the natural number returned by `fact` in the reals.

- If $\langle a_n \rangle$ converges to zero then $[\langle a_n \rangle]$ is an infinitesimal.
- If $\langle a_n \rangle$ is an unbounded sequence then $[\langle a_n \rangle]$ is an infinite hyperreal.

Returning to our exposition, termwise differentiation of the exponential function shows that

$$\frac{d}{dx}\, exp(x) = \mathtt{str}\ (\mathtt{sumhr}\ (1, \Omega, \lambda x.\ x^{n-1}/(\mathtt{fact}\ (n-1))))$$
$$= \mathtt{str}\ (\mathtt{sumhr}\ (0, \Omega, \lambda x.\ x^n/(\mathtt{fact}\ n))) = exp(x)$$

We prove the various properties of the exponential function, such as the addition theorem $exp(x) \cdot exp(y) = exp(x + y)$ and that $exp(0) = 1$. We also define cos and sin in Isabelle. The latter is defined as follows:

$$\sin x \equiv \mathtt{str}\ (\mathtt{sumhr}\ (0, \Omega, \lambda n.\ (\mathtt{if\ even}\ n\ \mathtt{then}\ 0$$
$$\mathtt{else}\ ((-1)^{(n-1)\ \mathtt{div}\ 2})/(\mathtt{fact}\ n)) \cdot x^n))$$

The power series for the trigonometric functions are straightforwardly shown to converge by means of the comparison test. Properties like $sin(0) = 0$ and $cos(0) = 1$, and the derivative results for sin and cos are all easily proved with the help of Isabelle's simplifier.

The way the properties of the various transcendental functions and their respective inverses are mechanized is very much through a re-construction of the HOL proofs in Isabelle. We even make use of a technique invented by Harrison to prove identities of the form $\forall x.\ f(x) = g(x)$ [6] and derive the results that we need. We ease our mechanization by implementing a simple tactic that tries to solve goals involving derivatives of functions automatically through backward proof steps followed by simplification.

The formalization of this last theory takes the formal development of analysis in Isabelle to a stage which, we hope, makes it suitable for interesting applications. We still have much of the theory of integration to develop, and the nonstandard approach promises to be useful for this. In what follows, we describe a few further aspects of our work that become possible because we have a formalization of NSA rather than purely standard analysis.

6   Infinitesimal and Infinite Reasoning

As expected, NSA in Isabelle provides a nice framework in which one can prove theorems involving the infinitely small rigorously. Very often, one sees in textbooks statements such as

$$\sin(\theta) = \theta \ \ where\ \theta\ is\ infinitely\ small$$

This is rarely given any further justification: the reader needs to rely on her knowledge of the sine function and on her intuition about what infinitely small means to see that the statement is indeed plausible. In NSA, however, an infinitely small number becomes a well-defined entity which can be manipulated like other more familiar types of numbers. As a result, many statements, including the one above, can then be proved in a rigorous yet intuitive way. We now give a brief proof of the statement, as mechanized in Isabelle.

Using the nonstandard formulation of derivative formalized by theorem (7), and the standard results that

$$\cos(0) = 1, \; \sin(0) = 0, \; \text{and } \text{DERIV}(x) \; \lambda x. \; \sin(x) :> \cos(x),$$

we can easily prove that $\sin^*(\theta) \approx \theta$ for all infinitesimal θ.

Proof:

if $\theta = 0$: This is trivial since $\approx$ is reflexive.

else if $\theta \neq 0$: Since $\text{DERIV}(x) \; \lambda x. \; \sin(x) :> \cos(x)$, for all x, we have that

$$\text{DERIV}(0) \; \lambda x. \; \sin(x) :> \cos(0)$$

$$\Rightarrow \forall h \in \textbf{Infinitesimal} - \{0\}. \; \frac{\sin^*(0+h) - \sin(0)}{h} \approx 1$$

$$\Rightarrow \frac{\sin^*(0+\theta) - \sin(0)}{\theta} \approx 1$$

$$\Rightarrow \frac{\sin^*(\theta)}{\theta} \approx 1$$

$$\Rightarrow \sin^*(\theta) \approx \theta$$

One important point to note is that we made use of theorem (3) to reach the final step. In a similar fashion, we also prove that $\cos^*(\theta) \approx \exp^*(\theta) \approx 1$ and, interestingly, that $\tan^*(\pi/2 + \theta) \in \textbf{Infinite}$, for all infinitesimal θ.

The above is just one possible example of formal reasoning about the infinitely small. The framework also enables us to investigate infinite processes, and check that their (asymptotic) results are infinitely close to the (ideal) ones expected. We can illustrate this point with an example.

Newton's iteration method for root approximation can be used to define the square-root operation on positive reals greater than zero. In Isabelle, assuming that real $a > 0$, we define the following function:

```
consts  square_root :: [nat, real] ⇒ real
primrec
square_root 0 a = a + 1
square_root (Suc n) a = (square_root n a + a/square_root n a)/2
```

The square-root function defined above is expected to produce closer and closer approximations to the desired square root, that is, the sequence of values computed should converge towards the square root. Cast within our nonstandard framework, this means that the value computed by the function after an infinite number of steps is infinitely close to the square root. This motivates the following definition in Isabelle:

```
sqrt :: real ⇒ real
sqrt a ≡ str ((*fNat* (λn. square_root n a)) Ω)
```

The square root function is said to be defined as the *hyperfinite* approximation of the Newton method iteration: we make use of the infinite hypernaturals and consider the value computed at the infinite step Ω.

It is easy to prove that the sequence $\lambda n.\, \texttt{square\_root}\ n\ a$ is bounded for a given a (e.g., by $a+1$), and hence, that $*\texttt{fNat}*\ (\lambda n.\, \texttt{square\_root}\ n\ a)$ returns a finite hyperreal at the Ω step which, by the Standard Part Theorem, is infinitely close to the real result required. We show that our formalization does define the square root function by proving that:

$$0 < a \implies ((*\texttt{fNat}*\ (\lambda n.\, \texttt{square\_root}\ n\ a))\Omega)^2 \approx \texttt{hypreal\_of\_real}\ a$$

that is:

$$0 < a \implies \texttt{sqrt}\ a \cdot \texttt{sqrt}\ a = \texttt{hypreal\_of\_real}\ a$$

The various properties of the square root function are all easily proved using the definition. This formalization was done as an experiment in Isabelle. The main formalization of square root is carried out as a special case of n-th roots, whose existence is one of the important theorems in our theory of sequences.

7   Conclusion

The automated theorem proving community has shown some rather limited interest in NSA so far. Ballantyne and Bledsoe implemented a prover using non-standard techniques in the late seventies [1]. Their work basically involved substituting (without proof) any theorem in the reals $\mathbb{R}$ by its analogue in the extended reals $\mathbb{R}^*$ and proving it in this new setting. Even though the prover had many limitations, and the work was just a preliminary investigation, the authors argued that through the use of nonstandard analysis, they had brought some new and powerful mathematical techniques to bear on the problem. More recently, Beeson developed a restricted axiomatic version of NSA using the logic of partial terms and used it to ensure the correctness of symbolic computations in his calculus system *Mathpert* [2]. In both work, the properties of the infinitely close relation, standard parts, infinitesimals and so on are asserted as axioms. Our strictly definitional approach to the mechanization of NSA, in effect, verifies the axioms that were built into both Ballantyne and Bledsoe's prover and Beeson's Mathpert.

In this work, we always formalize both the standard and nonstandard definitions of concepts and then prove their equivalence as theorems. These equivalence results are essential because they allow us to provide legitimate nonstandard proofs of familiar properties. In current mathematical practice, the standard definitions are the ones that are in widespread use, so having just nonstandard definitions without any justification might be viewed as objectionable. However, with the success and widening acceptance of NSA, it may be that in the future the so-called nonstandard definitions will become the established ones.

One of the main considerations during our formalization was to provide theories that would be on a par to those developed in HOL. The extensive HOL development has provided much of the initial motivation and subsequent drive necessary for our own work. Our theory of transcendental functions is the one that owes most to Harrison's salient work, as it stands almost wholly on the shoulders of HOL.

Our hope is for Isabelle to become a powerful framework for the mechanization of non-trivial problems involving continuous mathematics. The nonstandard numbers, just like the reals, have application in floating point error analysis, for example. Indeed, NSA has been used to develop theoretical techniques — the so-called asymptotic methods — for the formal verification of mathematical software [14]. With the advanced framework now established in Isabelle, this is an interesting and promising area of application which we hope to investigate next.

As a final note, we remark that the effort of formalizing both standard and nonstandard tools is not simply an exercise: potential users will have the freedom either to stick with classical (standard) techniques, use nonstandard ones, or a combination of both. We hope that they will experience the benefits that we feel infinitesimals and other nonstandard numbers can bring to mechanization.

References

1. A. M. Ballantyne and W. W. Bledsoe. Automatic proofs of theorems in analysis using non-standard techniques. Journal of the Association of Computing Machinery, vol. 24 (1977), 353—374.
2. M. Beeson. Using nonstandard analysis to ensure the correctness of symbolic computations. International Journal of Foundations of Computer Science, vol. 6 (1995), 299—338.
3. J. C. Burkill and H. Burkill. A Second Course in Mathematical Analysis. Cambridge University Press. 1970.
4. J. D. Fleuriot. A combination of Nonstandard Analysis and geometry theorem proving, with application to Newton's Principia. Author's PhD thesis available as University of Cambridge, Computer Laboratory Technical Report No. 469, 1999.
5. A. M. Gleason. Fundamentals of Abstract Analysis. Addison-Wesley, 1996.
6. J. Harrison. Theorem Proving with the Real Numbers. Springer-Verlag, 1998.
7. R. F. Hoskins. Standard and Nonstandard Analysis. Ellis Horwood Limited, 1990.
8. A. E. Hurd and P. A. Loeb. An Introduction to Nonstandard Real Analysis, Pure and Applied Mathematics, Volume 118. Academic Press Incorporated, 1985.
9. H. J. Keisler. Foundations of Infinitesimal Calculus. Prindle, Weber & Schmidt, Incorporated, 1976.
10. L. C. Paulson. Isabelle: A Generic Theorem Prover. *Lecture Notes in Computer Science*, vol. 828. Springer, 1994.
11. L. C. Paulson. Isabelle's object-logics. Technical Report 286, Computer Laboratory, University of Cambridge, February 1998.
12. A. Robinson. Non-standard Analysis. North-Holland, 1980.
13. K. D. Stroyan and W. A. J. Luxemburg. Introduction to the Theory of Infinitesimals. Academic Press, 1976.
14. D. Sutherland. Formal Verification of Mathematical Software. NASA-CR-172407, 1984.

Equational Reasoning via Partial Reflection

H. Geuvers, F. Wiedijk, and J. Zwanenburg

Department of Computer Science, Nijmegen University, the Netherlands
{herman,freek,janz}@cs.kun.nl

Abstract. We modify the reflection method to enable it to deal with partial functions like division. The idea behind reflection is to program a tactic for a theorem prover not in the implementation language but in the object language of the theorem prover itself. The main ingredients of the reflection method are a syntactic encoding of a class of problems, an interpretation function (mapping the encoding to the problem) and a decision function, written on the encodings. Together with a correctness proof of the decision function, this gives a fast method for solving problems. The contribution of this work lies in the extension of the reflection method to deal with equations in algebraic structures where some functions may be partial. The primary example here is the theory of fields. For the reflection method, this yields the problem that the interpretation function is not total. In this paper we show how this can be overcome by defining the interpretation as a relation. We give the precise details, both in mathematical terms and in Coq syntax. It has been used to program our own tactic 'Rational', for verifying equations between field elements.

1 Introduction

We present a method for proving equations between field elements (e.g. real numbers) in a theorem prover based on type theory. Our method uses the *reflection method* as discussed in [6,5]: we encode the set of syntactic expressions as an (inductive) data type, together with an interpretation function $[\![-]\!]$ that maps the syntactic expressions to the field elements. Then one writes a 'normalization' function $\mathcal{N}$ that simplifies syntactic expressions and one proves that this function is correct, i.e. if $\mathcal{N}(t) = q$, then the interpretations of t and q ($[\![t]\!]$ and $[\![q]\!]$) are equal in the field. Now, to prove an equality between field elements a and b, one has to find syntactic expressions t_1 and t_2 such that $\mathcal{N}(t_1) = \mathcal{N}(t_2)$ and $[\![t_1]\!]$ is a and $[\![t_2]\!]$ is b. This method has been applied successfully [2] to ring expressions in the theorem prover Coq, where it is implemented as the 'Ring tactic': when presented with a goal $a = b$, where a and b are elements of a ring, the Ring tactic finds the underlying syntactic expressions for a and b, executes the normalization function and checks the equality of the normal forms.

The application of the reflection method to the situation of fields poses one big extra problem: syntactic expressions may not have an interpretation, e.g. $\frac{1}{0}$. So, there is no interpretation function from the syntactic expressions to the actual field ($[\![-]\!]$ would be partial). The solution that we propose here is to write an

J. Harrison and M. Aagaard (Eds.): TPHOLs 2000, LNCS 1869, pp. 162–178, 2000.

interpretation *relation* instead: a binary relation between syntactic expressions and field elements. Then we prove that this relation is a partial function. The precise way of using this approach is discussed below, including the technical details of its implementation in Coq. For the precise encodings in Coq see [4].

The Reflection Method in General

Reflection is the method of 'reflecting' part of the meta language in the object language. Then meta theoretic results can be used to prove results from the obejct langauge. Reflection is also called *internalization* or the *two level approach*: the *meta language level* is *internalised* in the object language. The reflection method can (and it has, see e.g. [7]) be used in general in situations where one has a specific class of problems with a decision function. It is also not just restricted to the theorem prover Coq. If the theorem prover allows (A) user defined (inductive) data types, (B) writing executable functions over these data types and (C) user defined tactics in the meta language, then the reflection method can be applied. The classes of problems that it can be applied to are those where (1) there is a syntactic encoding of the class of problems as a data type, say via the type Problem, with (2) a decoding function $[\![-]\!]$: Problem $\rightarrow$ Prop (where Prop is the collection of propositions in the language of our theorem prover), (3) there is a decision function Dec : Problem $\rightarrow \{0, 1\}$ such that (4) one can prove $\forall p$:Problem$((\text{Dec}(p) = 1) \rightarrow [\![p]\!])$. Now, if the goal is to verify whether a problem P from the class of problems holds, one has to find a p : Problem such that $[\![p]\!] = P$. Then Dec(p) (together with the proof of (4)) yields either a proof of P (if Dec$(p) = 1$) or it 'fails' (if Dec$(p) = 0$ we obtain no information about P). Note that if Dec is complete, i.e. if $\forall p$:Problem$((\text{Dec}(p) = 1) \leftrightarrow [\![p]\!])$, then Dec$(p) = 0$ yields a proof of $\neg P$. The construction of p (the syntactic encoding) from P (the original problem) can be done in the implementation language of the theorem prover. Therefore it is convenient that the user has access to this implementation language; this is condition (C) above. If the user has no access to the meta language, the reflection method still works, but the user has to construct the encoding p himself, which is very cumbersome.

In this paper we first explain the reflection method by looking at the example of numbers with multiplication. We point out precisely which are the essential ingredients. Then we extend the example by looking at numbers with multiplication and division. Here the partiality problem arises. We explain how the reflection method can be applied to this example. This is an illustration of what we have implemented in Coq: a tactic for solving equations between elements of a field (a set with multiplication, division, addition, subtraction, constants and variables). The tactic has been applied successfully in a formalization of real numbers in Coq that we are currently working on.

2   Equational Reasoning Using the Reflection Method

We explain the reflection method by the simple example of numbers with multiplication. Suppose we have F : Set, $\cdot$: $F \rightarrow F \rightarrow F$, 1 : F and an equivalence relation $=_F$ on F (either a built-in equality of the theorem prover or a user defined relation) such that

(i) $=_F$ is a congruence for $\cdot$ (i.e. if $a =_F b$ and $c =_F d$, then $a \cdot c =_F b \cdot d$),
(ii) $\cdot$ is associative and commutative,
(iii) 1 is the unit with respect to $\cdot$.

Phrased differently, $\langle F, \cdot, 1 \rangle$ is an Abelian monoid. When dealing with F, we will want to prove equations like

$$(a \cdot c) \cdot (1 \cdot (a \cdot b)) =_F (a \cdot a) \cdot (b \cdot c) \tag{1}$$

where a, b, c are arbitrary elements of F. To prove this equation in a theorem prover each of the properties (i)–(iii) above has to be used (several times). It is possible to write a 'tactic' in the theorem prover that does just that:

Apply each of the steps (i)–(iii) to rewrite the left and right hand side of equation (1) until the two sides of the equation are literally the same.

Obviously this is not a very smart tactic (e.g. it does not terminate when the equality does not hold) and of course we can do better than this by applying (i)–(iii) in a clever order. For the case of Abelian monoids, this can be done by rewriting all terms into a normal form which has the shape

$$a_1 \cdot (a_2 \cdot (\ldots \cdot (a_n \cdot 1) \ldots))$$

where $n \geq 0$ and $a_1, \ldots, a_n$ are elements of F that can not be decomposed, listed in alphabetic order. So a_i may be a variable of type F or some other term of type F, that is not of the form $- \cdot -$ or 1. A tactic, which is written in the meta language, has access to the code of a_i, hence it can order the a_i according to some pre-defined total order, say the lexicographic one. (Note that a normal form as above can not be achieved via a term rewrite system, because we have to order the variables.) So, a more clever tactic does the following.

Rewrite the left and right hand side of equation (1) to normal form and check if the two sides of the equation are literally the same.

Following [5], there are three ways to augment the theorem prover with this proof technique for equational reasoning.

1. Add it to the primitives of the theorem prover,
2. Write (in the meta language) a tactic, built up from basic primitive steps, that performs the normalization and checks the equality.
3. Write a normalization function in the language of the theorem prover itself and prove it correct inside the theorem prover; use this as the core of the tactic.

The first is obviously undesirable in general, as it gives no guarantee that the method is correct (one could add any primitive rule one likes). The second and third both have their own pros and cons, which are discussed extensively in [5]. It is our experience (and of others, see [2]) that especially for theorem provers based on type theory, the third method is the most convenient one if one wants to verify a large numbers of problems from one and the same class. We will motivate why.

Reflection in Type Theory

We still work with the Abelian monoid $\langle F, \cdot, 1 \rangle$ from before and we want to verify equation (1). The equality on this monoid will be denoted by $=_F$, which may be user defined or not, as long as it is an equivalence relation and a congruence for $\cdot$. Note that there is also the definitional equality, built-in into Coq. This is usually denoted as $=_{\beta\delta\iota}$, as it is generated from the literal (α-) equality by adding the computation steps β, δ (for unfolding definitions) and ι (for recursion). Definitional equality is decidable and built into the type checker; it is included in the equality $=_F$ (if two terms are definitionally equal, they are equal in any respect).

We introduce an inductive type of *syntactic expressions*, E, by

$$E ::= V \mid C \mid E * E$$

where V is the type of variables, let's take

$$V ::= \mathbf{N}$$

and C is the type of constant expressions, containing in this case just one element, u. In type theory (using Coq syntax) the definition of V and E would be as follows.

```
Definition V : Set := nat.

Inductive E : Set :=
    evar  : V->E
|  eone  : E
|  emult : E->E->E.
```

To define the semantics of an expression $e : E$, we need a valuation $\rho : V \to F$ to assign a value to the variables. The interpretation function connecting the level of the syntactic expressions E and the semantics F is then defined as usual by recursion over the expression.

$$[\![-]\!]_\rho : E \to F$$

In Coq syntax the interpretation function I is defined as follows, given the Abelian monoid `<F, fmult, fone>`:

```
Variable rho : V->F.

Fixpoint I [e:E] : F :=
  Cases e of
     (evar v)       => (rho v)
  |   eone          => fone
  |  (emult e1 e2)  => (fmult (I e1) (I e2))
  end.
```

Now we write a 'normalization function':

$$\mathcal{N} : E \to E$$

that sorts variables, removes the unit (apart from the tail position) and associates brackets to the left. We don't give its encoding N : E -> E in Coq, but give the following examples.

$$\mathcal{N}((v_0 * u) * (v_1 * v_2)) =_{\beta\delta\iota} (v_0 * (v_1 * (v_2 * u))),$$
$$\mathcal{N}((v_2 * v_0) * v_1) =_{\beta\delta\iota} (v_0 * (v_1 * (v_2 * u))).$$

The equality $=_{\beta\delta\iota}$ is the internal (computational) equality of the theorem prover: no proof is required for its verification; a verification of such an equality is performed by the type checker.

We prove the following key lemma for the normalization function.

$$normcorrect : \quad [\![e]\!]_\rho =_F [\![\mathcal{N}(e)]\!]_\rho$$

In Coq terminology: we construct a proof term

normcorrect : (rho: V -> F)(e:E)((I rho e) = (I rho (N e))).

The situation is depicted in the following diagram; *normcorrect* states that the diagram commutes.

Solving equation $f =_F f'$ with f and f' elements of F now amounts to the following.

- Find (*by tactic*) e, e' and ρ with

$$[\![e]\!]_\rho =_{\beta\delta\iota} f \text{ and } [\![e']\!]_\rho =_{\beta\delta\iota} f'$$

- Check (*by type checker*) whether

$$\mathcal{N}(e) =_{\beta\delta\iota} \mathcal{N}(e')$$

The proof of $f =_F f'$ is then found by

$$f =_{\beta\delta\iota} [\![e]\!]_\rho =_F [\![\mathcal{N}(e)]\!]_\rho =_{\beta\delta\iota} [\![\mathcal{N}(e')]\!]_\rho =_F [\![e']\!]_\rho =_{\beta\delta\iota} f'$$

from *normcorrect* for e and e' and *trans* of $=_F$. In a diagram:

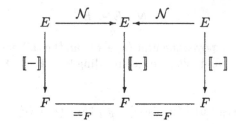

In Coq this means that we have to construct a proof term of type

```
f = f'
```

This is done from **normcorrect** using the proofs of symmetry and transitivity of $=_F$, **sym** and **trans**.

```
sym   : (x,y:F)   (x = y) -> (y = x).
trans : (x,y,z:F) (x = y) -> (y = z) -> (x = z).
```

The crucial point is that

```
(normcorrect rho e)    : ((I rho e)  = (I rho (N e))).
(normcorrect rho e')   : ((I rho e') = (I rho (N e'))).
```

can *only* be fitted together using **trans**, when (N e) and (N e') are $\beta\delta\iota$-convertible. In that case we find that (I rho (N e)) is $\beta\delta\iota$-convertible with (I rho (N e')) as well, so if we call that g by defining:

```
g := (I rho (N e))
```

then we find that:

```
(normcorrect rho e)    : (f = g).
(normcorrect rho e')   : (f' = g).
```

So using this, we can construct a proof term

```
(trans f g f' (normcorrect rho e) (sym f' g (normcorrect rho e')))
: f = f'.
```

The important points to note here are
(1) This proof term of an equality has a relatively small size, compared to a proof term that is spelled out completely in terms of congruence (of $=_F$ w.r.t. ·) and reflexivity, symmetry and transitivity (of $=_F$). The terms **refl**, **sym**, **trans**, and **normcorr** are just defined constants. The terms **rho**, **e** and **e'** are generated by the tactic; **rho** being of size linear in **f** and **f'** with a rather small constant. A proof term that is completely spelled out has a polynomial size in **f** and **f'**.
If we unfold the definitions, we observe that the bulk of the proof term is in normcorr. This will be rather large but it only has to be extended with a part

of – roughly – the size of the input elements themselves. So, then the proof term is still linear in the size of the input terms.

(2) *Checking* this proof term (i.e. verifying whether it has the type f = f') can in general take rather long. This is because type checking now involves serious computation, as we use the language of the theorem prover as a small programming language. The bulk of the work for the type checker is in verifying whether (N e) and (N e') are $\beta\delta\iota$-convertible.

We compare this to the approach of using a tactic that is written completely in the meta laguage. This tactic will do roughly the same thing as our reflection method: reduce expressions to normal form and generate step by step a proof term that verifies that this reduction is correct. Checking such a proof term will take about the same time. Some increase in speed may only be gained if we check a *user generated* proof term, because this will (in general) avoid reducing to full normal form (assuming the user sees the possible 'shortcuts').

(3) *Generating* the proof term is very easy, both for the reflection method as for the tactic written in the meta language. The tactics generate the full proof term without further interaction. Note that a completely user generated proof term of an equality (which may be fastest to type check, see above), is not realistic.

Here we also see why the reflection approach is particularly appealing for theorem provers based on type theory: one has to construct a proof term, which remains relatively small using reflection. Moreover, these theorem provers provide the required programming language to encode the normalization and interpretation functions in.

Looking back at the example from the beginning, encoded in Coq, we have as goal

```
Goal
((fmult (fmult a c) (fmult fone (fmult a b)))
                        = (fmult (fmult a a) (fmult b c))).
```

Now the tactic generates

```
(emult (emult (evar 0) (evar 2))
       (emult eone (emult (evar 0) (evar 1)))).
(* the e : E *)
(emult (emult (evar 0) (evar 0)) (emult (evar 1) (evar 2))).
(* the e' : E *)
```

and a function rho : V -> F which is defined in such a way that

```
(rho (evar 0)) = a
(rho (evar 1)) = b
(rho (evar 2)) = c
```

Then it constructs a term as above,

```
(trans f g f' (normcorrect rho e) (sym f' g (normcorrect rho e')))
```

where g is (I rho (N e)). Note that (I rho (N e)) $=_{\beta\delta\iota}$ (I rho (N e'))
$=_{\beta\delta\iota}$

(I rho (emult (evar 0) (emult (evar 0)
              (emult (evar 1) (emult (evar 2) eone)))))

$=_{\beta\delta\iota}$ (fmult a (fmult a (fmult b (fmult c fone)))). This term is given to
the type checker. If it type checks with as type the goal, the tactic succeeds (and
it has constructed a proof term proving the goal); if the type check fails, the
tactic fails.

3   Reflection with Partial Operations

We explain partial reflection by adapting the example to include division. We
view division as a ternary operation:

$$a \div b \mathbin{/\!/} p \text{ with } p \text{ a proof of } b \neq_F 0.$$

This is very much a type theoretic view. One may alternatively write

$$a \div b \text{ for } b \in \{z \mid z \neq_F 0\},$$

but note that this also requires a proof of $b \neq_F 0$, before $\div$ can be applied to it.

As a side remark, we note that we use the principle of *irrelevance of proofs*
when extending the equality on F to expressions of the form $a \div b \mathbin{/\!/} p$. That is,
if p and p' are both proofs of $b \neq_F 0$, then $(a \div b \mathbin{/\!/} p) =_F (a \div b \mathbin{/\!/} p')$. In our
encoding in Coq, this is achieved by representing $\{z \mid z \neq_F 0\}$ by the type Pos
of pairs $\langle b, p \rangle$ with $p : (b \neq_F 0)$ *with the equality on* Pos *the one inherited from*
F. Then we let $\div$ be a function from $F \times$ Pos to F.

If we extend our structure with a zero element and a division operator, like
in fields, we encounter the problem of undefined elements. These cause trouble
in various places. First of all, there is the question of which syntactic expression
one allows: if 1/0 is accepted, which interpretation does it have (one has to
choose one). This is of course related to the question whether the theorem prover
allows to write down $\frac{a}{0}$ (whatever its meaning may be). The second problem is
that a naive normalization function might rewrite $0/(0/v)$ to v (just because
$x/(x/v) = x/x * v = 1 * v = v$). But then, $\frac{0}{\frac{0}{a}} = a$, which is undesirable. Note that
the 'division by 0' problem can occur in a more disguised form, e.g. in $\frac{y}{\frac{y}{a}} = a$,
with y a variable, which is correct under the *side-condition* that $y \neq_F 0$. So,
it seems that, when normalizing an expression e, one would have to take the
interpretation $[\![e]\!]_\rho$ into account (and the interpretation of subexpressions of e)
to verify that the normalization steps are correct.

We have solved the problems just mentioned by

- Allowing syntactic expressions (like 1/0) that have no interpretation. So
  $[\![-]\!]_\rho$ is defined as a relation, for which it has to be *proved* that it is a partial
  function.
- Writing the normalization function N in such a way that, if expression e has
  an interpretation, then expression $N(e)$ has the same interpretation as e.

Syntactic expressions We now define the inductive type of *syntactic expressions*, E, by

$$E ::= V \mid C \mid E * E \mid E/E$$

where V is again the type of variables, for which we take $V ::= \mathbf{N}$ again. C is the type of constant expressions, now containing a zero, z, and a one expression, u. In type theory (using Coq syntax):

```
Inductive E : Set :=
    evar  : V->E
  | eone  : E
  | ezero : E
  | emult : E->E->E
  | ediv  : E->E->E.
```

Note that E doesn't depend on F and ρ; we have 'light' syntactic expressions (without any semantic information). This implies that $1/0$ is allowed in E: it is a well-formed expression.

Interpretation relation The semantics of an expression is now not given by a function but an *interpretation relation*:

$$\mathbb{I}_\rho \subseteq E \times F$$

Again, we need a valuation $\rho : V \to F$ to assign a value to the variables. The interpretation relation can then be defined inductively as follows.

$$v_n \mathbb{I}_\rho f \text{ iff } \rho(n) =_F f,$$
$$u \mathbb{I}_\rho f \text{ iff } f =_F 1,$$
$$z \mathbb{I}_\rho f \text{ iff } f =_F 0,$$
$$(e_1 * e_2) \mathbb{I}_\rho f \text{ iff } \exists f_1, f_2 \in F \ (e_1 \mathbb{I}_\rho f_1) \wedge (e_2 \mathbb{I}_\rho f_2) \wedge (f =_F f_1 \cdot f_2),$$
$$(e_1/e_2) \mathbb{I}_\rho f \text{ iff } \exists f_1, f_2 \in F \ (e_1 \mathbb{I}_\rho f_1) \wedge (e_2 \mathbb{I}_\rho f_2) \wedge (f_2 \neq_F 0) \wedge (f =_F f_1 \div f_2).$$

In Coq let there be given a structure <F, fmult, fdiv, fone, fzero>, with

```
fdiv: (x,y:F)(~(y =_F fzero))->F
```

and the other operations and the equality as expected. The inductive definition of $\mathbb{I}_\rho$ is as follows.

```
Inductive I : E->F->Prop :=
    ivar  : (n:V)(f:F) ((rho n) = f) -> (I (evar n) f)
  | ione  : (f:F)      (fone = f)    -> (I eone f)
  | izero : (f:F)      (fzero = f)   -> (I ezero f)
  | imult : (e,e':E)(f,f',f'':F)
            ((fmult f f') = f'') -> (I e f) -> (I e' f')
```

```
                                         -> (I (emult e e') f'')
| idiv  : (e,e':E)(f,f',f'':F)(nz:~(f' = fzero))
  ((fdiv f f' nz) = f'') -> (I e f) -> (I e' f')
                                         -> (I (ediv e e') f'').
```

Note that we do not just let `ione : (I eone fone)`, but take `fone` modulo the equality on F, and similarly for the constant, the variables and the two operators. This is because I should be a partial function *modulo* the equality on F. In more technical terms: correctness of normalization can only be proved with this version of I.

Normalization and correctness The 'normalization function':

$$\mathcal{N} : E \to E$$

now brings the expressions that have an interpretation in one of the following two normal forms

$$(v_1 * (v_2 * \ldots (v_n * \mathsf{u}) \ldots)) / (w_1 * (w_2 * \ldots (w_m * \mathsf{u}) \ldots)),$$
$$\mathsf{z} / \mathsf{u},$$

with $v_1, \ldots, v_n, w_1, \ldots w_m$ variables and the two lists $v_1, \ldots, v_n$ and $w_1, \ldots w_m$ disjoint. So, $\mathcal{N}$ creates two mutually exclusive lists of sorted variables, one representing the enumerator and one representing the denominator. The sorting of these lists is the same as for multiplicative expressions. In case $\mathcal{N}$ encounters a z in the enumerator, the whole expression is replaced by z/u (which has interpretation 0). For the expressions that do not have an interpretation (those $e \in E$ for which there are no $\rho : V \to F, f \in F$ with $e \rrbracket_\rho f$), the normalization function can return anything.

We don't give the encoding `N : E -> E` in Coq, but restrict ourselves to some examples.

$$\mathcal{N}(v_0/(v_1/v_3)) * v_1 =_{\beta\delta\iota} (v_0 * (v_3 * \mathsf{u}))/\mathsf{u},$$
$$\mathcal{N}((v_0/(v_1 * v_2))/(v_3/v_2)) =_{\beta\delta\iota} (v_0 * \mathsf{u})/(v_1 * (v_3 * \mathsf{u})).$$

We can understand the way $\mathcal{N}$ actually works as follows.

1. From an expression e, two sequences of variables and constants are created s_1 and s_2, the first representing the enumerator and the second the denominator. The intention is that, if e has an interpretation, then s_1/s_2 has the same interpretation.
2. These two sequences are put in normal form, following the normalization procedure for multiplicative expressions.
3. Variables that occur both in s_1 and s_2 are canceled, units are removed and s_1 is replaced by z if it contains a z.

Note that we tacitly identify a sequence s_1 with the expression that arises from consecutively applying $*$ to all its components. This is also the way we have implemented it in Coq: we do not use a separate list data structure, but encode it via $*$ and u. On these lists, we define an 'append' operation, which we denote by @. So, if s_1 and s_2 denote two expressions in multiplicative normal form, $s_1 @ s_2$ is the multiplicative normal form of $s_1 * s_2$. As a matter of fact, $\mathcal{N}$ doesn't do each of these steps sequentially, but in a slightly smarter (and faster) way.

In proving the correctness of $\mathcal{N}$, one has to preserve the property that all denominators are $\neq_F 0$. In that, the first step is the crucial one. (The second step is only a reordering of variables; one has to prove that this reordering preserves the $\neq_F 0$ property, which is easy. In the third step one has to prove that $\neq_F 0$ is preserved under cancellation, which is the case: if $a \cdot b \neq_F 0$, then $a \neq_F 0$.) The first step has a nice recursion: if $\mathcal{N}(e) = (s_1, s_2)$ and $N(e') = (s'_1, s'_2)$, then

$$\mathcal{N}(e * e') := (s_1 @ s'_1, s_2 @ s'_2),$$
$$\mathcal{N}(e/e') := (s_1 @ s'_2, s_2 @ s'_1).$$

Now, if $e * e'$ has an interpretation, then (by induction) s_2 and s'_2 have an interpretation different from 0 and hence the interpretation of $s_2 @ s'_2$ is different from 0. Similarly, if e/e' has an interpretation, then (by induction) s_2, s'_1 and s'_2 have an interpretation different from 0 and hence the interpretation of $s_2 @ s'_1$ is different from 0.

This is also how the correctness proof of $\mathcal{N}$ works: $\mathcal{N}$ itself doesn't have to bother about the interpretation of the expressions it operates on, because it is written in such a way that, the fact that e has an interpretation implies (in a rather simple way, sketched above) that $\mathcal{N}(e)$ has an interpretation (which is the same as for e).

Again we note that $\mathcal{N}$ cannot be found as a term rewriting system, for one because it orders variables, but more importantly because it only works properly for expressions that have an interpretation. We can use this information, because the expression we start from is derived from an existing $f : F$, which is well-defined (otherwise we couldn't write it down in the theorem prover). So, we already know that the first e has an interpretation (namely f) and by virtue of the construction of $\mathcal{N}$, this property is preserved.

We prove the following key lemmas.

$$normcorrect : \qquad e \, [\![_\rho f \qquad \Rightarrow \mathcal{N}(e) \, [\![_\rho f$$
$$extensionality : \quad (e \, [\![_\rho f) \wedge (e \, [\![_\rho f') \Rightarrow f =_F f'.$$

Extensionality states that $[\![_\rho$ is really a partial function (w.r.t. the equality $=_F$).

Reflection The reflection method for solving $f =_F f'$ is now:

− find (*by tactic*) e, e' and ρ with

$$e \, \rrbracket_\rho \, f \text{ and } e' \, \rrbracket_\rho \, f'$$

− construct (*see below*) proof terms for these two statements
− check (*by type checker*) whether

$$\mathcal{N}(e) =_{\beta\delta\iota} \mathcal{N}(e')$$

$(=_{\beta\delta\iota}$ means $\beta\delta\iota$-*convertible*)

The proof of $f =_F f'$ is then found by:

$$\left. \begin{array}{l} e \, \rrbracket_\rho \, f \ \Rightarrow \mathcal{N}(e) \, \rrbracket_\rho \, f \\[2mm] e' \, \rrbracket_\rho \, f' \Rightarrow \mathcal{N}(e') \, \rrbracket_\rho \, f' \end{array} \right\} \Rightarrow f = f'$$

from *normcorrect* (applied to (e, f) and (e', f'), respectively) and *extensionality* (applied to $(\mathcal{N}(e), f, f')$).

Just as in the case for reflection in Section 2, a precise proof term can be constructed, which type checks with type $f =_F f'$ if and only if these terms are can be shown to be equal in the equational theory. In the next Section we will exhibit such a proof term. The main work in type checking this proof term lies in the execution of the algorithm $\mathcal{N}$ (but this is done by the type checker).

One problem remains. As we now have an interpretation *relation*, there arise some *proof obligations*: it is not just enough to *find* encodings e and e' of f and f'; we have to *prove* that they are encodings indeed. That is, we have as new goals

$$e \, \rrbracket_\rho \, f \text{ and } e' \, \rrbracket_\rho \, f'$$

Of course, we don't want the user to have to take care of these goals; the tactic should solve them. This problem is dealt with in the next Section.

4   Proof Loaded Syntactic Objects

At the second step of the partial reflection method, we need proofs of $e \, \rrbracket_\rho \, f$. One way is to let the tactic construct these; so from $f : F$, the tactic extracts both $e : E$ and ρ and a proof term p with $p : e \, \rrbracket_\rho \, f$. This is possible, but it is not what has been implemented. We have chosen to have one data type for both expressions and proofs. The strategy for doing so (and which fits very well with the type theoretic approach) is to create *syntactic expressions with proof objects inside*

$$\bar{E}$$

with a *forgetful function* $| - |$ and an *interpretation function* $[\![-]\!]_\rho$,

$$| - | : \bar{E} \to E$$
$$[\![-]\!]_\rho : \bar{E} \to F$$

The key property to be proved is then

$$\lvert \bar{e} \rvert \, \rrbracket_\rho \, \llbracket \bar{e} \rrbracket_\rho$$

But note that $\bar{E}$ depends on F and ρ (it should 'know' about semantics), so $\bar{E}$ is a type of 'heavy' syntactic expressions (including proof terms). This can only work if we let $\bar{E}$ be a *dependent* type over F:

$$\bar{E}_f$$

which in Coq terms is defined as:

```
Inductive xE : F -> Set :=
    xevar  : (i:V)(xE (rho i))
  | xeone  : (xE fone)
  | xezero : (xE fzero)
  | xemult : (f,f':F)(e:(xE f))(e':(xE f'))(xE (fmult f f'))
  | xediv  : (f,f':F)(e:(xE f))(e':(xE f'))(nz:~(f' = fzero))
                (xE (fdiv f f' nz)).
```

The type $\bar{E}_f$ represents the type of 'heavy' syntactic expressions whose interpretation is f. The interpretation function is now

$$\llbracket - \rrbracket_\rho : \bar{E}_f \to F$$

for which it should hold that

$$\llbracket \bar{e} \rrbracket_\rho =_{\beta\delta\iota} f$$

so $\llbracket - \rrbracket_\rho$ is constant on its domain. In Coq terms we define:

```
xI := [f:F][e:(xE f)]f  : (f:F)(xE f) -> F.
```

Note that we do not define the interpretation by induction on $e : (xEf)$, but we just return f (the *intended* interpretation). The obligation is now to prove that the underlying 'light' syntactic expression has indeed f as interpretation. The forgetful function, extracting the 'light' syntactic expression, now is

$$\lvert - \rvert : \bar{E}_f \to E$$

It maps the 'heavy' syntactic expressions to the 'light' ones. In Coq terms:

```
Fixpoint xX [f:F; e:(xE f)] : E :=
  Cases e of
    (xevar i)              => (evar i)
  | xeone                  => eone
  | xezero                 => ezero
  | (xemult f' f'' e' e'') => (emult (xX f' e') (xX f'' e''))
  | (xediv f' f'' e' e'' p) => (ediv (xX f' e') (xX f'' e''))
  end.
```

which is defined by induction over $(\mathrm{xE}\ f)$. The maps $[\![-]\!]_\rho$ and $|-|$ 'extract' the two components (syntactic expression and semantic element) from the 'heavy' encoding. The key result now is that the second extraction is an interpretation of the first:

$$extractcorrect: \quad \forall x \in \bar{E}_f(|x|\ [\![_\rho\ [\![x]\!]_\rho)$$

which is just $\forall x \in \bar{E}_f(|x|\ [\![_\rho\ f)$.

The tactic now works as follows, given a problem $f =_F f'$.

– find (*by tactic*) $\bar{e} \in \bar{E}_f$, $\bar{e}' \in \bar{E}_{f'}$ and ρ with

$$|\bar{e}|\ [\![_\rho\ f \text{ and } |\bar{e}'|\ [\![_\rho\ f'$$

– obtain (*from extractcorrect*) proof terms for these two statements
– check (*by type checker*) whether

$$\mathcal{N}(|\bar{e}|) =_{\beta\delta\iota} \mathcal{N}(|\bar{e}'|)$$

So, the tactic creates e, e' of type E indirectly by creating $\bar{e}, \bar{e}'$ of types $\bar{E}_f, \bar{E}_{f'}$. In a diagram the situation is now as follows.

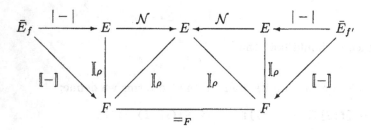

The outside triangles commute due to *extractcorrect*; the large middle triangle commutes due to *extensionality*; the other two triangles commute due to *normcorrect*. If we make the proof term given by this method explicit, it is

```
(extensionality rho ne f f'
    (normcorrect rho e  f  (extractcorrect rho f  xe ))
    (normcorrect rho e' f' (extractcorrect rho f' xe')))
: f = f'
```

where xe and xe' correspond to $\bar{e}$ and $\bar{e}'$, and where we have defined

```
e   := (xX f  xe).
e'  := (xX f' xe').
ne  := (N e).
```

This term is only well-typed when (N e) is $\beta\delta\iota$-convertible with (N e').

Normalizing Proof Loaded Objects

In presence of the type $\bar{E}_f$, we could do without the type E all-together. Then we would define a normalization function $\bar{\mathcal{N}}$ to operate on the 'heavy' syntactic expressions of type $\bar{E}_f$. This is possible (and it yields a simpler diagram), but it is not desirable, because then the computation (reducing $\bar{\mathcal{N}}(\bar{e})$ to normal form) becomes much heavier. Moreover, it would be more difficult to program $\bar{\mathcal{N}}$ (having to take all the proof terms into account) and the two levels in the reflection approach would be less visible, therefore slightly blurring the exposition.

Nevertheless, for reasons of completeness we have also constructed (see [4]) the function $\bar{\mathcal{N}}$ together with proofs that it is correct. Ideally, this would amount to the following diagram

$$\bar{E}_f \xrightarrow{\quad\bar{\mathcal{N}}\quad} \bar{E}_f \xleftarrow{\quad\bar{\mathcal{N}}\quad} \bar{E}_f$$

$$\downarrow [\![-]\!] \qquad\qquad \downarrow [\![-]\!] \qquad\qquad \downarrow [\![-]\!]$$

$$F \qquad\qquad\qquad F \qquad\qquad\qquad F$$

However, $\bar{\mathcal{N}}$ can not have the dependent type $\bar{E}_f \to \bar{E}_f$ (for $f : F$), because the value (in F) of the output of the normalization function is not *literally* the same as its input value, but only *provably* equal to it. So, we can *not* construct $\bar{\mathcal{N}}$ as a term xN : (z:F) (xE z) -> (xE z). Instead we construct xN : fE -> fE, where fE is the type of pairs < f, e >, with f : F and e : (xE f). (In type theoretic terms, this is the Σ-*type* of *dependent pairs* $\langle f, e \rangle$ with $f : F$ and $e : \bar{E}_f$.) Then we have to prove that if $\bar{\mathcal{N}}(\langle f, e \rangle)$ yields $\langle f', e' \rangle$, then f and f' are (provably) equal in F.

If we cast this in purely mathematical terms, the situation is as follows. Define $\bar{E} := \Sigma f{:}F.\bar{E}_f$ and let wf be the predicate on syntactic expressions stating that it has an interpretation (it is *well-formed*). It is defined as follows (for $e : E$).

$$\mathrm{wf}\,(e) := \exists f{:}F(e [\![\,]\!]_\rho f).$$

Now there are maps lift : $\{e : E \mid \mathrm{wf}\,(e)\} \to \bar{E}$ and $|-| : \bar{E} \to \{e : E \mid \mathrm{wf}\,(e)\}$. Furthermore, we can construct a proof-object

$$normwf \quad : \quad \forall e{:}E(\mathrm{wf}\,(e) \to \mathrm{wf}\,(\mathcal{N}(e)))\}.$$

Then we can read off the normalization function $\bar{N} : \bar{E} \to \bar{E}$ from the following diagram.

$$\bar{E} \dashrightarrow^{\bar{\mathcal{N}}} \bar{E}$$

$$|-| \Big\downarrow \Big\uparrow \mathrm{lift} \qquad\qquad |-| \Big\downarrow \Big\uparrow \mathrm{lift}$$

$$\{e : E \mid \mathrm{wf}\,(e)\} \xrightarrow[\quad\mathcal{N}\quad]{} \{e : E \mid \mathrm{wf}\,(e)\}$$

The proof term *normwf* shows that $\mathcal{N}$ is indeed a function from the set of well-formed expressions to itself. The correctness of $\bar{\mathcal{N}}$ is given by

$$normcorrect \quad : \quad \forall \bar{e} : \bar{E}(\llbracket \bar{e} \rrbracket =_F \llbracket \bar{\mathcal{N}}(\bar{e}) \rrbracket).$$

Here $\llbracket - \rrbracket : \bar{E} \to F$ is the interpretation function mapping (heavy) syntactic expressions to elements of F. (As a matter of fact, it is just the first projection.)

5   Partial Reflection in Practice

The approach of partial reflection is successfully used in our current FTA project (Fundamental Theorem of Algebra). First of all, we have a tactic called Rational for proving equalities. This tactic is implemented as outlined above.

But often we do not just want to prove an equality, but rather to use an equality to *rewrite* a goal in a different form. In order to explain how we have implemented rewrite tactics, we first say something about the equality in the FTA project. Our equality is just a congruence relation, respected by operations (such as + and *) and certain predicates (such as <). This means we cannot just replace equals by equals in *any* expression, but only those built-up from terms respecting our equality. (This stands in contrast to the standard Leibniz-equality in Coq; Leibniz-equals may be replaced in any proposition.) For instance, we have the following lemma:

```
less_wd_left : (a,b,c:F)(a=b) -> (b<c) -> (a<c).
```

Hence, we have defined rewriting tactics for each important predicate that respects our equality. For instance, the tactic Step_less_left t applies to a goal p<q: it lets Rational solve the equation t=p and returns the new goal t<q. It is defined for each t as

```
(Apply less_wd_left with b:=t) ;
[ Rational | (* Use Rational tactic to prove equality *)
  Idtac ]    (* Do nothing with new inequality *)
```

The following example illustrates its use. (Note that 1/z//H2 denotes 1 divided by z with as proof of the side condition z#0 – $z \neq_F 0$ – the variable H2.)

```
  H1 : 0 < z
  H2 : z # 0
  H3 : x*z < y*z
  ===============
  x < y
< Step_less_left x*z*(1/z//H2)
  H1 : 0 < z
  H2 : z # 0
  H3 : x*z < y*z
  ===============
  x*z*(1/z//H2) < y
```

6 Conclusion

We have extended the reflection method to include partial functions. The power of the method lies in the fact that no new proof obligations arise. So, if the user wants to prove a simple equation involving partial functions, the system does not (have to) generate a new set of goals (in order to prove that all partiality side conditions are fulfilled). That the necessary side conditions are fulfilled is already proven by the correctness of the normalization function. Phrased differently: normalization preserves well-definedness. The other crucial point is the fact that, although some syntactic expressions may be undefined, the ones that our tactic generates never are, for the simple reason that they are encodings of *well-defined* semantic objects in the theorem prover. So, the normalization function starts off from a syntactic expression that is well-defined (for the simple reason that the semantic object is its interpretation) and the well-definedness is preserved under normalization.

As a side remark, we point out that the fact that *the encoding always yields a well-defined syntactic expression* is a statement on the meta-level. As the encoding function is a meta-function we can not expect to state this literally in the theorem prover. We can state $\forall f : F \exists e : E \exists \rho(e \, [\![_\rho \, f)$, but this does not capture what we want to say: it is trivially true, taking a variable v for e and $\rho(v) = f$, and it does not say anything about the encoding function.

The actual implementation of the method as a tactic for solving equations between field elements has shown that this is a very useful technique. We believe it is very generally applicable in situations where partiality occurs.

Acknowledgements We thank Henk Barendregt for the many useful discussions on the subject and the anonymous referees for their comments on the paper.

References

1. G. Barthe, M. Ruys and H. Barendregt (1996), A Two-Level Approach towards lean Proof-Checking.
2. S. Boutin, Using reflection to build efficient and certified decision procedures. In Martin Abadi and Takahashi Ito, editors, TACS'97, volume 1281. LNCS, Springer-Verlag, 1997.
3. G. Huet et al. (1997), The Coq Proof Assistant, Reference Manual, Version 6.1, INRIA-Rocquencourt — CNRS-ENS Lyon.
4. The "Fundamental Theorem of Algebra" Project, Departmet of Computer Science, University of Nijmegen, the Netherlands. See http://www.cs.kun.nl/gi/projects/fta/
5. J. Harrison (1995), Meta theory and Reflection in Theorem Proving: a Survey and Critique, Technical Report CRC-053, SRI International Cambridge Computer Science Research Center.
6. D. Howe (1988) Computational Meta theory in Nuprl, The Proceedings of the Ninth International Conference of Automated Deduction, eds. E. Lusk and R. Overbeek, LNCS 310, pp. 238–257.
7. M. Oostdijk and H. Geuvers (2000), Proof by Computation in Coq, to appear in TCS.

Reachability Programming in HOL98 Using BDDs

Michael J.C. Gordon

University of Cambridge Computer Laboratory,
New Museums Site, Pembroke Street, Cambridge CB2 3QG, U.K.
mjcg@cl.cam.ac.uk, http://www.cl.cam.ac.uk/~mjcg

Abstract. Two methods of programming BDD-based symbolic algorithms in the Hol98 proof assistant are presented. The goal is to provide a platform for implementing intimate combinations of deduction and algorithmic verification, like model checking. The first programming method uses a small kernel of ML functions to convert between BDDs, terms and theorems. It is easy to use and is suitable for rapid prototying experiments. The second method requires lower-level programming but can support more efficient calculations. It is based on an LCF-like use of an abstract type to encapsulate rules for manipulating judgements $\rho\ t \mapsto b$ meaning "logical term t is represented by BDD b with respect to variable order ρ". The two methods are illustrated by showing how to perform the standard fixed-point calculation of the BDD of the set of reachable states of a finite state machine.

1   Background and Motivation

Theorem proving and model checking are complementary. Theorem proving can be applied to expressive formalisms (such as set theory and higher order logic) that are capable of modelling complex systems like complete processors. However, theorem proving systems require skilled manual guidance to verify most properties of practical interest. Model checking is automatic, but can only be applied to relatively small problems (e.g. fragments of processors). It can also provide counter-examples of great use in debugging.

The ideal would be to be able to automatically verify properties of complete systems (and find counter-examples when the verification of properties fail). This is not likely to be practical in the foreseeable future, so various compromises are being explored, for example

(i) adding a layer of theorem proving on top of existing model checkers, to enable large problems to be deductively decomposed into smaller pieces that can be checked automatically [12,2];

(ii) adding checking algorithms to theorem provers so that subgoals can be verified automatically [15] and counter-examples found.

J. Harrison and M. Aagaard (Eds.): TPHOLs 2000, LNCS 1869, pp. 179–196, 2000.

These two approaches differ in the starting point: (i) starts from a model checker and (ii) starts from a theorem prover. The goal is the same: combine the best of model checking and theorem proving. This paper concerns approach (ii).

The Prosper project[1] is currently undertaking research into making HOL98 the basis of a tool integration platform. Part of this work has resulted in the definition and implementation of a mechanism for enabling external tools to be 'plugged-in' to HOL98. This supports the easy implementation of the kind of linking of theorem proving and model checking done in pioneering studies with PVS [15] and falls under (ii) above.

This paper describes some experiments in adding simple model checking infrastructure to the HOL98 theorem prover and so also falls under (ii). However, it differs from the PVS and Prosper approaches because it aims to provide secure and general programming infrastructure to allow users to implement *their own* bespoke BDD-based verification algorithms and then to tightly integrate them with existing HOL98 tools like the simplifier. Sometimes it is appropriate to use an existing off-the-shelf tool and sometimes it is appropriate to build one's own bespoke solution. This paper concerns the latter.

The HOL98 system is based on Milner's LCF proof assistant [5]. In such systems arbitrary terms are values of a type *term* and can be freely constructed. However, theorems are represented as values of an abstract type *thm* whose primitive operations are axioms and rules of inference. Being an abstract type, values of type *thm* (i.e. theorems) can only by constructed using combinations of the primitive operations provided for the type *thm* – i.e. by proof. Theorem proving tools such as decision procedures, proof search strategies and simplifiers are implemented by composing together the primitive operations (i.e. axioms and inference rules) using programs in the ML programming language.

The goal of the research described in this paper is to extend the classical LCF-approach so that efficient symbolic calculations, like model checking, can also be implemented. This involves generalising the notion of theorem to include certain data representation judgements.

2 Overview

Let $\mathcal{M}$ be a finite state machine whose state is a vector $(v_1, \ldots, v_n)$ of boolean variables $v_1, \ldots, v_n$. Let P be some property of interest of states of $\mathcal{M}$ and let S be defined so that S i $(v_1, \ldots, v_n)$ is true if $(v_1, \ldots, v_n)$ is a state reachable in i or fewer steps from an initial state of $\mathcal{M}$.

Any boolean term with boolean free variables can be represented by a binary decision diagram (BDD) [3]. An example of such a term is:

$$\forall i.\ S\ i\ (v_1, \ldots, v_n) \Rightarrow P(v_1, \ldots, v_n)$$

This is true if all reachable states of $\mathcal{M}$ satisfy P. Note that although this term and all its free variables are boolean, it contains a bound variable i ranging over natural numbers, so the standard BDD algorithms cannot construct

---

[1] http://www.dcs.gla.ac.uk/prosper

its BDD. However, symbolic model checking algorithms provide ways of computing the BDDs of such terms. These algorithms can also compute the BDDs corresponding to much more complex properties of the execution of finite state machines (e.g. properties expressed in temporal logic).

In order to provide a platform for experimenting with programming model checking algorithms in the HOL98 proof assistant, and for combining them with deductive theorem proving, the BuDDy package[2] has been interfaced[3] to Moscow ML[4] so that BDDs can be manipulated as ML values of a type *bdd* and the various BuDDy operations are linked to ML functions.

In this paper, the evolution of an initial simple style of programming with BDDs into a more efficient one is described. The computation of the set of reachable states is used as a running example (more detailed examples are described elsewhere [6,7]). Note that

$$\forall i.\ \mathsf{S}\ i\ (v_1, \ldots, v_n) \Rightarrow \mathsf{P}(v_1, \ldots, v_n)$$

is equivalent to

$$(\exists i.\ \mathsf{S}\ i\ (v_1, \ldots, v_n)) \Rightarrow \mathsf{P}(v_1, \ldots, v_n)$$

The set of reachable states is represented by the term $\exists i.\ \mathsf{S}\ i\ (v_1, \ldots, v_n)$.

The first method is described in Section 3 and is based on a validity-critical kernel of three ML functions:

    termToBdd   : *term* → *bdd*
    addEquation : *thm* → *term* × *bdd*
    bddOracle   : *term* → *thm*

As long as these are implemented correctly (which includes BuDDy being correct) then the system is sound. The use of these functions to compute the BDD of $\exists i.\ \mathsf{S}\ i\ (v_1, \ldots, v_n)$ is described in Section 3.1.

The second method uses an abstract type *termbdd* that represents 'judgements' $\rho\ t\ \mapsto\ b$ that mean "HOL98 term t is represented by BDD b with respect to variable order ρ". An LCF-like approach to 'proving' such judgements is implemented: the type *termbdd* implements judgements just like the type *thm* implements theorems. A fragment of the calculus of BDD representation judgements is presented in Section 4.1 (with some planned extensions in Section 4.3). The ML functions implementing rules of inference for judgements are given in boxes following the rules. The calculation of $\exists i.\ \mathsf{S}\ i\ (v_1, \ldots, v_n)$ using judgements is described in Section 4.2.

Some related work is discussed in Section 5.

3   Representing Terms as BDDs

The interface from BuDDy to Moscow ML provides an ML type *bdd* together with ML functions corresponding to the C functions in the BDD package. Using

---

[2] http://www.itu.dk/research/buddy/
[3] http://www.itu.dk/research/muddy/
[4] http://www.dina.kvl.dk/~sestoft/mosml.html

these, it is easy to implement a function that maps any quantified boolean formula[5] to a BDD. Such a function has ML type $term \rightarrow bdd$ and is defined by a simple recursion over the structure of terms.[6]

Two approaches to supporting BDD calculation in HOL98 are described here. The first one is described in this section and is based on a global table that stores pairs (t, b), where t is a term and b the BDD representing it. The second approach is described in Section 4.

The HOL98 library `HolBddLib` uses the Moscow ML interface to ML to implement BDD tools for HOL98 [7]. This library predefines the following ML function for adding entries to the BDD table

`addEquation` : $thm \rightarrow term \times bdd$

Evaluating `addEquation`($\vdash t_1 = t_2$) computes a BDD, b_2 say, of the term t_2 and then stores the association (t_1, b_2) in the BDD table. The pair (t_1, b_2) is also returned.[7]

Using the BDD table, the BDDs of boolean terms that contain defined constants can be computed. For example, suppose the constant Foo is defined by

$\vdash$ Foo$(x, y) = \langle large\ QBF\ involving\ x\ and\ y \rangle$

then the BDDs of terms such as $\exists z.$ Foo$(x, (y \vee z)) \wedge$ Foo$(z, (x \Rightarrow y))$ can be computed in two ways: (i) by expanding out the definition of Foo to get a QBF; and (ii) by using the precomputed BDD of Foo(x, y) stored in the table.

The choice between (i) and (ii) depends on whether it is more efficient to separately recompute the BDDs of Foo$(x, (y \vee z))$ and Foo$(z, (x \Rightarrow y))$ from scratch or to get the BDDs by applying BuDDy operations to the BDD of Foo(x, y). An ML function `termToBdd` of type $term \rightarrow bdd$ is provided by `HolBddLib` that uses the second method (ii) to convert a term to a BDD. This works by deductively transforming terms to a form in which subterms correspond to entries in the BDD table. For example, applying `termToBdd` to $\exists z.$ Foo$(x, (y \vee z)) \wedge$ Foo$(z, (x \Rightarrow y))$ first uses a HOL98 conversion to prove the theorem

$\vdash (\exists z.$ Foo$(x, (y \vee z)) \wedge$ Foo$(z, (x \Rightarrow y))$

$=$

$(\exists z. (\exists y_1. (y_1 = y \vee z) \wedge$ Foo$(x, y_1)) \wedge \exists y_1. (y_1 = x \Rightarrow y) \wedge$ Foo$(z, y_1))$

The BDD of the left hand side of this equation can then be computed by computing the BDD of the right hand side, in which all applications of Foo have been transformed to be applied to sequences of distinct variables. The BDD of such

---

[5] A quantified boolean formula (QBF) is a term build out of boolean variables and constants (T, F) using boolean operators ($\neg$, $\wedge$, $\vee$, $\Rightarrow$, $=$ etc.) and quantification over boolean variables.

[6] The recursion needs to take into account BDD operations that optimise certain combinations of boolean constructions. For example, the BDD of a term $Qv_1 \cdots v_n.\ t_1\ \text{op}\ t_2$, where Q is a quantifier and op a binary operator, can be efficiently constructed from the BDDs of t_1 and t_2 in a single step. First constructing the BDD of $t_1\ \text{op}\ t_2$ and then doing n quantifications would be inefficient.

[7] An exception is raised by `addEquation` if it is not applied to an equation or if the computation of the BDD of t_2 fails.

applications can be obtained by a simple replacement operation on the BDD of $Foo(x, y)$ and so the BDD of the large term on the right hand side of the definition of Foo does not need to be recomputed, just tweaked.

The BDD representing a term is determined by an ordering of the variables. The variable order used by termToBdd can be explicitly declared, but if no order is declared, then variables get the order in which they are first encountered.

The creation of HOL98 theorems via BDD calculation is provided by a single ML function bddOracle : $term \rightarrow thm$ which maps a term t to the theorem $\vdash t$ if $termToBdd(t)$ is the BDD TRUE and raises an exception otherwise.

3.1 Computing Reachable States Using First Method

Suppose constants B and R are defined to represent, respectively, a set of initial states of a machine and its transition relation:

B_def $= \ \vdash B(v_1, \ldots, v_n) = \cdots$

R_def $= \ \vdash R((v_1, \ldots, v_n), (v'_1, \ldots, v'_n)) = \cdots$

The predicate S i repesenting the set of states reachable in i or fewer steps is then defined recursively by

S_def $= \ \vdash (S\ 0\ v = B\ v)$
$$\wedge$$
$$\forall i.\ S\ (i{+}1)\ v = (S\ i\ v\ \vee\ (\exists u.\ S\ i\ u\ \wedge\ R(u, v)))$$

where the variables u and v range over n-tuples of booleans and so can be specialised to tuples of boolean variables $(u_1, \ldots, u_n)$ and $(v_1, \ldots, v_n)$, respectively, and then separate base and step cases derived as theorems S_0 and S_suc, where

S_0 $\quad = \ \vdash S\ 0\ (v_1, \ldots, v_n) = B\ (v_1, \ldots, v_n)$

S_suc $= \ \vdash \forall i.\ S\ (i{+}1)\ (v_1, \ldots, v_n) =$
$$S\ i\ (v_1, \ldots, v_n)$$
$$\vee$$
$$\exists u_1 \cdots u_n.\ S\ i\ (u_1, \ldots, u_n)\ \wedge\ R((u_1, \ldots, u_n), (v_1, \ldots, v_n))$$

To compute the BDD of the set of reachable states, first add the definitions of B and R to the BDD table:

addEquation B_def;

addEquation R_def;

next compute the BDDs of S $0\ (v_1, \ldots, v_n)$, S $1\ (v_1, \ldots, v_n)$, S $2\ (v_1, \ldots, v_n)$ etc. Note from S_suc that the compution of of the BDD of S $(i{+}1)\ (v_1, \ldots, v_n)$ needs the BDD of S $i\ (v_1, \ldots, v_n)$, thus the order in which BDDs are added to the table is important. The $\forall$-quantified variable i in S_suc can be successively specialised to 0, 1, 2 etc. with the HOL98 inference rule SPEC (evaluating SPEC t_1 ($\vdash \forall i.\ t_2(i)$) specialises i to t_1 to deduce $\vdash t_2(t_1)$). To then reduce the numeral i+1, the function SimpNum can be used (SimpNum reduces arithmetical combinations of numerals, e.g. simplifies occurrences of "2+1" to "3").

addEquation S_0;

addEquation (SimpNum(SPEC "0" S_suc));

addEquation (SimpNum(SPEC "1" S_suc));

addEquation (SimpNum(SPEC "2" S_suc));

After these six applications of **addEquation**, the BDD table will consist of

$(B(v_1, ..., v_n), b_1)$

$(R((v_1, ..., v_n), (v'_1, ..., v'_n)), b_2)$

$(S \ 0 \ (v_1, ..., v_n), b_3)$

$(S \ 1 \ (v_1, ..., v_n), b_4)$

$(S \ 2 \ (v_1, ..., v_n), b_5)$

$(S \ 3 \ (v_1, ..., v_n), b_6)$

where, in fact, $b_1 = b_3$. Note that an evaluation of

   addEquation (SimpNum(SPEC "i" S_suc));

uses **termToBdd** to compute the BDD of the right hand side of **S_suc** with i specialised to i. Since the BDDs of S i $(v_1, ..., v_n)$ and $R((v_1, ..., v_n), (v'_1, ..., v'_n))$ are already in the BDD table their BDDs can be reused.

Since the state space is finite and the sets of states represented by S i increases as i increases, it follows that for some particular i, say $i = $ i, that eventually

$$S \ i \ (v_1, ..., v_n) \ = \ S \ (i{+}1) \ (v_1, ..., v_n)$$

which can be tested for at each stage by evaluating:

   bddOracle "S i $(v_1, ..., v_n)$ $=$ S $(i{+}1)$ $(v_1, ..., v_n)$"

This will either raise an exception (fixed-point not yet reached) or return a theorem $\vdash$ S i $(v_1, ..., v_n)$ $=$ S $(i{+}1)$ $(v_1, ..., v_n)$. When this theorem is proved, the BDD of the set of reachable states is clearly the BDD of S i $(v_1, ..., v_n)$ (see the theorem FpTh below).

The fixed-point is easily computed by an ML function that makes use of the auxiliary functions described in the following table.

ML function	ML type	Explanation
intToTerm	$int{\to}term$	intToTerm n = "n"
concl	$thm{\to}term$	concl($\vdash t$) = "t"
lhs	$term{\to}term$	lhs "$t_1{=}t_2$" = "t_1"
rhs	$term{\to}term$	rhs "$t_1{=}t_2$" = "t_2"
LeftDisjunct	$term{\to}term$	LeftDisjunct "$t_1 \vee t_2$" = "t_1"
mk_eq	$term{\times}term{\to}term$	mk_eq("t_1", "t_2") = "$t_1{=}t_2$"

In the function definition below, ML comments are enclosed between (* and *).

```
fun iterateToFixedPoint S_suc i =
  let val i_tm = intToTerm i
      val Sth  = SimpNum(SPEC i_tm S_suc)
      val S1   = LeftDisjunct(rhs(concl Sth)) (* S i (...)      *)
      val S2   = lhs(concl Sth)               (* S (i+1) (...) *)
  in
    addEquation Sth;   (* adds BDD of S (i+1) (...) to BDD table *)
    (bddOracle(mk_eq(S1,S2)), i_tm)
     handle oracleError => iterateToFixedPoint S_suc (i+1)
  end
```

The function `iterateToFixedPoint` just iterates `S_suc` until a fixed-point is reached and then, if the fixed-point is reached after i iterations, returns a pair whose second component is "i" and whose first component is the theorem:

$$\vdash \mathsf{S}\ i\ (v_1, ..., v_n)\ =\ \mathsf{S}\ (i{+}1)\ (v_1, ..., v_n)$$

The following fixed-point theorem is straightforward to prove

$$\mathsf{FpTh}\ =\ \vdash \forall i.\ (\forall v_1 \cdots v_n.\ \mathsf{S}\ i\ (v_1, ..., v_n)\ =\ \mathsf{S}\ (i{+}1)\ (v_1, ..., v_n))$$
$$\Rightarrow$$
$$(\forall v_1 \cdots v_n.\ \mathsf{S}\ i\ (v_1, ..., v_n)\ =\ \exists i.\ \mathsf{S}\ i\ (v_1, ..., v_n))$$

The function `ComputeReachableStates` defined below computes a pair, returned by **addEquation**, whose first component is the term $\exists i.\ \mathsf{S}\ i\ (v_1, ..., v_n)$ and whose second component is the BDD of this term. The definition of the function uses Modus Ponens, which is represented by the ML function MP (evaluating MP $(\vdash t_1 {\Rightarrow} t_2)$ $(\vdash t_1)$ returns the theorem $\vdash t_2$). The definition also uses GEN_ALL, which proves the universal closure of a theorem (i.e. universally quantifies all free variables), and SYM, which reverses an equation (evaluating SYM$(\vdash t_1 = t_2)$ returns the theorem $\vdash t_2 = t_1$).

```
fun ComputeReachableStates B_def R_def S_0 S_suc =
  (addEquation B_def;
   addEquation R_def;
   addEquation S_0;
   let val (th,i_tm) = iterateToFixedPoint S_suc 0
   in
    addEquation(SYM(MP (SPEC i_tm FpTh) (GEN_ALL th)))
   end)
```

The theorems S_0 and S_suc are just consequences of the definition of S, so could be computed from B_def and R_def. Thus `ComputeReachableStates` only needs to take B_def and R_def as parameters [6].

Note that executing `ComputeReachableStates B_def R_def S_0 S_suc` involves computing the BDD of $R((v_1, ..., v_n), (v'_1, ..., v'_n))$, which may be large.

Instead, it may be possible to derive an equation, S_simp_suc say, that expresses $\mathsf{S}\ (i{+}1)\ (v_1, ..., v_n)$ in terms of $\mathsf{S}\ i\ (v_1, ..., v_n)$ in a way that avoids having to compute the BDD of the transition relation. This can be achieved, for example, by disjunctive partitioning[8] [10, page 79]. In this case, the calculation of reachable states can be done just with

```
fun ComputeReachableStates B_def R_def S_0 S_simp_suc =
  (addEquation B_def;
   addEquation S_0;
   let val (th,i_tm) = iterateToFixedPoint S_simp_suc 0
   in
    addEquation(SYM(MP (SPEC i_tm FpTh) (GEN_ALL th)))
   end)
```

---

[8] Disjunctive partitioning is called 'early quantification' by some authors [13, page 45] and also called 'miniscoping' in the context of theorem proving.

Note that in this definition of `ComputeReachableStates` the argument `R_def` is not used.

Disjunctive partitioning can be done automatically using the HOL98 simplifier. To illustrate this nice example of synergy between HOL98 and BuDDy consider the transition relation R that corresponds to the interleaving of three assignments $v_1' = E_1(v_1, v_2, v_3)$, $v_2' = E_2(v_1, v_2, v_3)$ and $v_3' = E_3(v_1, v_2, v_3)$

$$R((v_1, v_2, v_3), (v_1', v_2', v_3')) =$$
$$(v_1' = E_1(v_1, v_2, v_3) \ \wedge \ v_2' = v_2 \ \wedge \ v_3' = v_3) \ \vee$$
$$(v_1' = v_1 \ \wedge \ v_2' = E_2(v_1, v_2, v_3) \ \wedge \ v_3' = v_3) \ \vee$$
$$(v_1' = v_1 \ \wedge \ v_2' = v_2 \ \wedge \ v_3' = E_3(v_1, v_2, v_3))$$

If $\overline{u}$, $\overline{v}$ abbreviate (u_1, u_2, u_3), (v_1, v_2, v_3), repectively, then S $(i{+}1)$ $\overline{v}$ is given by

$$S \ (i{+}1) \ \overline{v} \ = \ S \ i \ \overline{v} \ \vee \ (\exists \overline{u}. \ S \ i \ \overline{u} \ \wedge \ R(\overline{u}, \overline{v}))$$

Disjunctive partitioning is the following simplification of the right disjunct:

$$\exists \overline{u}. \ S \ i \ \overline{u} \ \wedge \ R(\overline{u}, \overline{v})$$
$$= \ \exists \overline{u}. \ S \ i \ \overline{u} \ \wedge \ ((v_1 = E_1\overline{u} \ \wedge \ v_2 = u_2 \ \wedge \ v_3 = u_3) \ \vee$$
$$(v_1 = u_1 \ \wedge \ v_2 = E_2\overline{u} \ \wedge \ v_3 = u_3) \ \vee$$
$$(v_1 = u_1 \ \wedge \ v_2 = u_2 \ \wedge \ v_3 = E_3\overline{u}))$$
$$= \ (\exists \overline{u}. \ S \ i \ \overline{u} \ \wedge \ v_1 = E_1\overline{u} \ \wedge \ v_2 = u_2 \ \wedge \ v_3 = u_3) \ \vee$$
$$(\exists \overline{u}. \ S \ i \ \overline{u} \ \wedge \ v_1 = u_1 \ \wedge \ v_2 = E_2\overline{u} \ \wedge \ v_3 = u_3) \ \vee$$
$$(\exists \overline{u}. \ S \ i \ \overline{u} \ \wedge \ v_1 = u_1 \ \wedge \ v_2 = u_2 \ \wedge \ v_3 = E_3\overline{u})$$
$$= \ ((\exists u_1. \ S \ i \ (u_1, v_2, v_3) \wedge v_1{=}E_1(u_1, v_2, v_3)) \ \wedge$$
$$(\exists u_2. \ v_2{=}u_2) \ \wedge$$
$$(\exists u_3. \ v_3{=}u_3)) \ \vee$$
$$((\exists u_1. \ v_1{=}u_1) \ \wedge$$
$$(\exists u_2. \ S \ i \ (v_1, u_2, v_3) \wedge v_2{=}E_2(v_1, u_2, v_3)) \ \wedge$$
$$(\exists u_3. \ v_3{=}u_3)) \ \vee$$
$$((\exists u_1. \ v_1{=}u_1) \ \wedge$$
$$(\exists u_2. \ v_2{=}u_2) \ \wedge$$
$$(\exists u_3. \ S \ i \ (v_1, v_2, u_3) \wedge v_3{=}E_3(v_1, v_2, u_3)))$$
$$= \ (\exists u_1. \ S \ i \ (u_1, v_2, v_3) \ \wedge \ v_1 = E_1(u_1, v_2, v_3)) \ \vee$$
$$(\exists u_2. \ S \ i \ (v_1, u_2, v_3) \ \wedge \ v_2 = E_2(v_1, u_2, v_3)) \ \vee$$
$$(\exists u_3. \ S \ i \ (v_1, v_2, u_3) \ \wedge \ v_3 = E_3(v_1, v_2, u_3))$$

Thus the BDD of $\exists \overline{u}. \ S \ i \ \overline{u} \ \wedge \ R(\overline{u}, \overline{v})$ can be computed without ever computing the BDD of $R(\overline{u}, \overline{v})$ and also without performing the BDD operation corresponding to $\exists \overline{u}$ (which might be expensive if there are lots of state variables). It follows that the BDD of S $(i{+}1)$ $\overline{v}$ can be computed from the BDD of S $i \ \overline{v}$ without computing the BDD of $R(\overline{u}, \overline{v})$, just by combining small BDDs via boolean operations and single quantifications.

The usual implementation of disjunctive partitioning is by writing programs that directly construct the BDD of the simplified term. The logical transformations are thus encoded in BDD building code. The approach here is to deductively simplify the next-state relation. The advantage is that the simplification is easy to program (given good simplification tools) and is guaranteed to be sound. Similar deductive simplifications come up in computing the backward image of a transition relation when finding the shortest sequence of states to a counterexample. However, it remains to be seen if deductive simplification using HOL98 can lead to new techniques, rather than nice ways of implementing existing ones!

3.2 Discussion of First Method

The style of programming illustrated by the definition of `iterateToFixedPoint` has good and bad points. It is good in that it is easy to experiment with BDD calculations via HOL98 terms: for example, disjunctive partitioning is easy to implement using the HOL98 simplifier. However, as the BDD table accumulates entries, the runtime of `termToBdd` (and hence `addEquation`) slows down. Furthermore, on large terms the process of transforming subterms to enable previously computed BDDs to be reused gets slow. To try to alleviate such performance problems, the data structure representing the BDD table is quite complex, combining a hash table with a discrimination net (to find matches to terms that are not in the map, but are instances of terms that are [4]). The resulting structure and the associated code supporting it is complex and hard to maintain. Furthermore, `termToBdd` makes some fixed choices about how to invoke BuDDy operations that might not be sensible for some situations. For example, for historical reasons[9], a term $Foo(t_1, t_2)$, where t_1 and t_2 are boolean terms, will be transformed to $\exists v_1 \, v_2. \, (v_1 = t_1) \wedge (v_2 = t_2) \wedge Foo(v_1, v_2)$, and then the BDD of this is computed using BuDDy's operations for conjunction and quantification. This works, but it might well be more efficient to separately compute the BDDs of t_1 and t_2 and then to use BDD substitution rather than quantification. There is no problem upgrading `termToBdd` to use substitution, but as more and more changes are made to optimise the code, the result becomes a heuristic expert system whose performance is hard to predict or control.

Another problem concerns storage management. The Moscow ML and BuDDy garbage collectors are linked, but the BDD map will keep BDDs around and block their collection, even if they are no longer used. This can be managed by having a `deleteBdd` operation that removes entries from the BDD table, and then inserting calls to the function into programs. For example, modifying `iterateToFixedPoint` to

```
fun iterateToFixedPoint S_suc i =
  let val i_tm = intToTerm i
      val Sth  = SimpNum(SPEC i_tm S_suc)
      val S1   = LeftDisjunct(rhs(concl Sth))
      val S2   = lhs(concl Sth)
  in
    addEquation Sth;                         (* S1 now used     *)
    (bddOracle(mk_eq(S1,S2)), i_tm)
      handle oracleError => (deleteBdd S1;   (* delete S1 entry *)
```

---

[9] The first version of the BuDDy interface to Moscow ML did not support the operation that substitutes a BDD for a variable in another BDD.

iterateToFixedPoint S_suc (i+1))
    end

however, such explicit BDD management is hard to get right and it is easy to leave storage leaks.

In the next section a second syle of programming is described that enables tightly tuned algorithms to be implemented whose performance is predictable.

4 BDD Representation Judgements

In the LCF approach, theorems are represented by an abstract type whose primitive operations are the axioms and inference rules of a logic. Theorem proving tools are implemented by composing together the inference rules using ML programs.

This idea can be generalised to computing valid judgements that represent other kinds of information. In particular, consider judgements (ρ, t, b), where ρ represents a variable order, t is a boolean term all of whose free variables are boolean and b is a BDD. Such a judgement is valid if b is the BDD representing t with respect to ρ, and we will write $\rho\ t\ \mapsto\ b$ when this is the case.

The derivation of 'theorems' like $\rho\ t\ \mapsto\ b$ can be viewed as 'proof' in the style of LCF by defining an abstract type *termbdd* whose primitive operations correspond to the BDD functions provided by BuDDy. The type *termbdd* models judgements $\rho\ t\ \mapsto\ b$ analogously to the way the type *thm* models theorems $\vdash t$.

4.1 Rules for BDD Representations

BDD variables in BuDDy are represented by natural numbers and the ordering used is the standard one. A variable ordering ρ can thus be represented by a partial function, called a variable map, from logic variables (a subset of terms in HOL98) to numbers. An ML function Var of ML type *int→bdd* maps a number to the corresponding BDD variable.[10] Thus an inference rule for inferring valid triples $\rho\ v\ \mapsto\ b$, where v is a variable, is

$$\text{BddVar}\ \frac{\rho(v) = n}{\rho\ v\ \mapsto\ \text{Var}\ n}$$

The name of the ML function corresponding to this rule is BddVar, as indicated to the left of the rule. In what follows, the descriptions of the ML functions implementing the rules are given in easy-to-skip boxes. For example:

BddVar : *term→termbdd*

> BddVar(v) returns $\rho_G\ t\ \mapsto\ b$, where if v already has an associated BDD in the global map ρ_G, then $b = \text{Var}(\rho_G(v))$ and if v is not in the map, then ρ_G is extended so that $\rho_G(v) = n$, where n is the first unused BDD variable, and then $b = \text{Var}(n)$. In this case BddVar(v) has a side-effect on ρ_G.

---

[10] The names and description of functions have been simplified to improve the exposition. For example, the function called Var in this paper is actually called ithvar in HolBddLib. Furthermore, some functions described here have not yet been implemented at the time of writing. An example illustrating the programs described in this paper can be seen at http://www.cl.cam.ac.uk/~mjcg/BDD/TPHOLs2000Paper.ml.

The rules given in this section have the same variable map ρ in the hypotheses and conclusion. The current implementation assumes there is a single global variable map, ρ_G, held in an assignable (reference) variable, and the construction of BDDs is done with respect to this (see Section 4.3 for further discussion). The user may explicitly set up this map at the beginning of a session, or let it be built incrementally as needed. We will write $t \mapsto b$ to mean that t is represented by b with respect to the current global variable map, i.e. $\rho_G\ t\ \mapsto\ b$. Each rule is implemented by an ML function that takes values of type $termbdd$ representing any hypothesis judgements and also other parameters (e.g. a term v representing a variable, as in BddVar) and returns a value representing the conclusion. For example, BddNot below takes an ML value corresponding to a judgement that gives a BDD representation for a term t and returns a value corresponding to a judgement representing $\neg t$.

The HOL98 logical constants T and F (values of type $term$) denote truth and falsity, respectively, whereas the values TRUE and FALSE of ML type bdd are the corresponding BDDs. The function NOT: $bdd \rightarrow bdd$ creates the negation of a BDD.

BddT : $termbdd$, BddF : $termbdd$
    BddT and BddF are predefined to be T $\mapsto$ TRUE and F $\mapsto$ FALSE, respectively.

BddNot : $termbdd \rightarrow termbdd$
    BddNot($t \mapsto b$) returns $\neg t \mapsto$ NOT b.

The rules for propositional connectives are straightforward. The BuDDy binary operators AND, OR, IMP, BIIMP construct the conjunction, disjunction, implication and equivalence of BDDs.

$$\text{BddAnd}\ \frac{\rho\ t_1\ \mapsto\ b_1 \qquad \rho\ t_2\ \mapsto\ b_2}{\rho\ t_1 \wedge t_2\ \mapsto\ b_1\ \text{AND}\ b_2} \qquad \text{BddOr}\ \frac{\rho\ t_1\ \mapsto\ b_1 \qquad \rho\ t_2\ \mapsto\ b_2}{\rho\ t_1 \vee t_2\ \mapsto\ b_1\ \text{OR}\ b_2}$$

$$\text{BddImp}\ \frac{\rho\ t_1\ \mapsto\ b_1 \qquad \rho\ t_2\ \mapsto\ b_2}{\rho\ t_1 \Rightarrow t_2\ \mapsto\ b_1\ \text{IMP}\ b_2} \qquad \text{BddEq}\ \frac{\rho\ t_1\ \mapsto\ b_1 \qquad \rho\ t_2\ \mapsto\ b_2}{\rho\ t_1 = t_2\ \mapsto\ b_1\ \text{BIIMP}\ b_2}$$

BddAnd : $termbdd \times termbdd \rightarrow termbdd$
    BddAnd($t_1 \mapsto b_1, t_2 \mapsto b_2$) returns $t_1 \wedge t_2 \mapsto b_1$ AND b_2;
    BddOr($t_1 \mapsto b_1, t_2 \mapsto b_2$) returns $t_1 \vee t_2 \mapsto b_1$ OR b_2;
    BddImp($t_1 \mapsto b_1, t_2 \mapsto b_2$) returns $t_1 \Rightarrow t_2 \mapsto b_1$ IMP b_2;
    BddEq($t_1 \mapsto b_1, t_2 \mapsto b_2$) returns $t_1 = t_2 \mapsto b_1$ BIIMP b_2.

The functions `Forall` and `Exists` of type $(int\ list) \to bdd \to bdd$ quantify BDDs, thus

$$\text{BddForall} \quad \frac{\rho\ t \mapsto b \qquad \rho(v_1) = n_1 \qquad \cdots \qquad \rho(v_p) = n_p}{\rho\ \forall v_1 \cdots v_p.\ t \mapsto \text{Forall}[n_1, \ldots, n_p]\ b}$$

$$\text{BddExists} \quad \frac{\rho\ t \mapsto b \qquad \rho(v_1) = n_1 \qquad \cdots \qquad \rho(v_p) = n_p}{\rho\ \exists v_1 \cdots v_p.\ t \mapsto \text{Exists}[n_1, \ldots, n_p]\ b}$$

> `BddForall`, `BddExists` both of type $term\ list \to termbdd \to termbdd$
> `BddForall` $[v_1, \ldots, v_n]$ $(t \mapsto b)$ returns
> $\forall v_1 \cdots v_n.\ t \mapsto$ `Forall` $[\rho_G(v_1), \ldots, \rho_G(v_n)]\ b$;
> `BddExists` $[v_1, \ldots, v_n]$ $(t \mapsto b)$ returns
> $\exists v_1 \cdots v_n.\ t \mapsto$ `Exists` $[\rho_G(v_1), \ldots, \rho_G(v_n)]\ b$.
> If any of the variables $v_1, \ldots, v_n$ are not in the global variable map, then the
> map is extended. Thus `BddForall` and `BddExists` might side-effect ρ_G.

The BDDs of quantifications of conjunctions can be built by calling `AND` followed by `Forall` or `Exists`, but it is more efficient to use optimised algorithms `ForallAnd` and `ExistsAnd` provided by BuDDy.

$$\text{BddForallAnd} \quad \frac{\rho\ t_1 \mapsto b_1 \quad \rho\ t_2 \mapsto b_2 \quad \rho(v_1) = n_1 \quad \cdots \quad \rho(v_p) = n_p}{\rho\ \forall v_1 \cdots v_p.\ t_1 \wedge t_2 \mapsto \text{ForallAnd}\ [n_1, \ldots, n_p]\ b_1\ b_2}$$

$$\text{BddExistsAnd} \quad \frac{\rho\ t_1 \mapsto b_1 \quad \rho\ t_2 \mapsto b_2 \quad \rho(v_1) = n_1 \quad \cdots \quad \rho(v_p) = n_p}{\rho\ \exists v_1 \cdots v_p.\ t_1 \wedge t_2 \mapsto \text{ExistsAnd}\ [n_1, \ldots, n_p]\ b_1\ b_2}$$

> `BddForallAnd`, `BddExistsAnd` of type $term\ list \to termbdd \to termbdd \to termbdd$
> `BddForallAnd` $[v_1, \ldots, v_n]$ $(t_1 \mapsto b_1)$ $(t_2 \mapsto b_2)$ returns
> $\forall v_1 \cdots v_n.\ t \mapsto$ `ForallAnd` $[\rho_G(v_1), \ldots, \rho_G(v_n)]\ b_1\ b_2$;
> `BddExistsAnd` $[v_1, \ldots, v_n]$ $(t_1 \mapsto b_1)$ $(t_2 \mapsto b_2)$ returns
> $\exists v_1 \cdots v_n.\ t \mapsto$ `ExistsAnd` $[\rho_G(v_1), \ldots, \rho_G(v_n)]\ b_1\ b_2$.
> If any of the variables $v_1, \ldots, v_n$ are not in the global variable map, then the
> map is extended. Thus `BddForallAnd` and `BddExistsAnd` might side-effect ρ_G.

The next rule expresses the fact that logically equivalent terms have the same BDD.

$$\text{BddEqMp} \quad \frac{\vdash t_1 = t_2 \qquad \rho\ t_1 \mapsto b}{\rho\ t_2 \mapsto b}$$

> `BddEqMp` : $thm \to termbdd \to termbdd$
> `BddEqMp` $(\vdash t_1 = t_2)$ $(t_1 \mapsto b)$ returns $t_2 \mapsto b$.

Let $t\{v_1 \leftarrow v_1', \ldots, v_p \leftarrow v_p'\}$ denote the result of replacing distinct free variables $v_1, \ldots, v_p$ in a term t with distinct variables $v_1', \ldots, v_p'$, respectively, renaming any bound variables in t to avoid capture. Let $b\{n_1 \leftarrow n_1', \ldots, n_p \leftarrow n_p'\}$ denote the result of replacing distinct BDD variables $n_1, \ldots, n_p$ in a BDD b with distinct variables $n'_1, \ldots, n'_p$, respectively. Let $\mathrm{Domain}(\rho)$ denote the set of variables ρ is defined on (i.e. $\mathrm{Domain}(\rho) = \{v \mid \exists n.\ \rho(v) = n\}$).

$$\texttt{BddReplace} \ \frac{\rho\ t \mapsto b \qquad \{v_1, \ldots, v_p, v'_1, \ldots, v'_p\} \subseteq \mathrm{Domain}(\rho)}{\rho\ t\{v_1 \leftarrow v'_1, \ldots, v_n \leftarrow v'_n\} \ \mapsto \ b\{\rho(v_1) \leftarrow \rho(v'_1), \ldots, \rho(v_n) \leftarrow \rho(v'_n)\}}$$

> **BddReplace** : $(term \times term)list \rightarrow termbdd \rightarrow termbdd$
> **BddReplace** $[(v_1, v'_1), \ldots, (v_n, v'_n)]$ $(t \mapsto b)$ returns
> $t\{v_1 \leftarrow v'_1, \ldots, v_n \leftarrow v'_n\} \mapsto b\{\rho_G(v_1) \leftarrow \rho_G(v'_1), \ldots, \rho_G(v_n) \leftarrow \rho_G(v'_n)\}$.
> If any of the variables v'_i ($1 \leq i \leq n$) are not in the global variable map, then they are added if necessary. Thus ρ_G may be side-effected.

The function **bddOracle** described earlier converts a term t to a BDD using **termToBdd**, which might be slow, and then returns $\vdash t$ if the resulting BDD is TRUE. The rule **TermBddOracle** below just checks whether the BDD part of a judgement is TRUE and if so creates a theorem whose conclusion is the term part. It is thus very efficient.

$$\texttt{TermBddOracle} \ \frac{\rho\ t \mapsto \mathrm{TRUE}}{\vdash t}$$

> **TermBddOracle** : $termbdd \rightarrow thm$
> **TermBddOracle**$(t \mapsto b)$ returns the theorem $\vdash t$ if b is TRUE, otherwise an exception is raised.

The ML functions **bddOracle** and **TermBddOracle** are the only ways of creating theorems from BDDs using **HolBddLib**. Eventually it is expected that **bddOracle** will be defined in terms of **TermBddOracle**.

Finally, the function **termToTermBdd** provide a way of using the first method of programming with BDDS to get some values of $termbdd$ as a starting point for invoking the rules of the second method.

> **termToTermBdd** : $term \rightarrow termbdd$
> **termToTermBdd**(t) applies **termToBdd** to t to get b and then returns $t \mapsto b$.

4.2 Computing Reachable States Using Representation Judgements

Suppose **th** is an equational theorem $\vdash t_1 = t_2$, e.g. a definition. If the right hand side t_2 can be represented as a BDD b using **termToBdd**, then a BDD representation **tb** $= t_1 \mapsto b$ can be created by evaluating

```
val tb0 = BddEqMp (SYM th) (termToTermBdd(rhs(concl th)))
```

Define **BddDef** : $thm \rightarrow termbdd$ by

```
fun BddDef th = BddEqMp (SYM th) (termToTermBdd(rhs(concl th)))
```

Suppose constants B and R have been defined by theorems B_def and R_def, respectively, then BDD representation judgements

$$\text{tbB} \;=\; \text{B} \, (v_1, \ldots, v_n) \mapsto b_{\text{B}}$$
$$\text{tbR} \;=\; \text{R}((v_1, \ldots, v_n), (v_1', \ldots, v_n')) \mapsto b_{\text{R}}$$

are defined in ML by

```
val tbB = BddDef B_def
and tbR = BddDef R_def;
```

Suppose that S has been defined by S_def and for some particular value of i the BDD representation $\text{tbi} \;=\; \text{S i} \, (v_1, \ldots, v_n) \mapsto b_i$ has been computed, for example, for i = 0, tb0 is defined by

```
val tb0 = BddEqMp (SYM S_0) tbB
```

An important BDD to calculate is the image of S i under R:

$$\exists u_1 \, \cdots \, u_n. \; \text{S i} \, (u_1, \ldots, u_n) \;\wedge\; \text{R}((u_1, \ldots, u_n), (v_1, \ldots, v_n))$$

If this is directly converted to a BDD representation judgement, new BDD variables for $u_1, \ldots, u_n$ may be created, which could be inefficient. A better strategy is to reuse the existing variables $v_1', \ldots, v_n'$ by computing instead the BDD of

$$\exists v_1' \, \cdots \, v_n'. \; \text{S i} \, (v_1', \ldots, v_n') \;\wedge\; \text{R}((v_1', \ldots, v_n'), (v_1, \ldots, v_n))$$

A derived rule, BddImage : $termbdd{\rightarrow}termbdd{\rightarrow}termbdd$ is easily defined to compute the image of a set under a transition relation. If

$$\text{tbP} \;=\; \text{P} \, (v_1, \ldots, v_n) \mapsto b_{\text{P}}$$
$$\text{tbR} \;=\; \text{R}((v_1, \ldots, v_n), (v_1', \ldots, v_n')) \mapsto b_{\text{R}}$$

then

```
BddImage tbP tbR =
BddForallAnd
  [v1,...,vn]
  tbP
  (BddReplace [(v1,v1'),...,(vn,vn'),(v1',v1),...,(vn',vn)] tbR)
```

For example, since S (i+1) $(v_1, \ldots, v_n)$ is

$$\text{S i} \, (v_1, \ldots, v_n) \;\vee\; \exists v_1' \, \cdots \, v_n'. \; \text{S i} \, (v_1', \ldots, v_n') \;\wedge\; \text{R}((v_1', \ldots, v_n'), (v_1, \ldots, v_n))$$

the BDD representation of this is computed by BddOr(tbi, BddImage tbi tbR).

The ML function iterateToFixedPoint2 defined below takes the transitive closure of R until a fixed-point is reached, returning a triple (th,tb,i_tm) where th is $\vdash$ S (i+1) $(v_1, \ldots, v_n)$ = S i $(v_1, \ldots, v_n)$, tb is S i $(v_1, \ldots, v_n) \mapsto b_i$ (where b_i is the BDD computed) and i_tm is "i"

```
fun iterateToFixedPoint2 S_suc tbR tb i =
  let val i_tm = intToTerm i
      val tb' = BddEqMp
                  (SYM(SimpNum(SPEC i_tm S_suc)))
                  (BddOr(tb, BddImage tb tbR))
```

```
 in
  (TermBddOracle(BddEq(tb,tb'))), tb, i_tm)
    handle oracleError => iterateToFixedPoint2 S_suc tbR tb' (i+1)
 end
```

The representation judgement $(\exists i.\ S\ i\ (v_1, ..., v_n)) \mapsto b_i$ is computed by

```
let val (th,tb,i_tm) =
      iterateToFixedPoint2 S_suc (BddDef R_def) (BddDef S_0) 0
    val FpThi = SimpNum(SPEC i_tm FpTh)
 in
  BddEqMp (SPEC_ALL(MP FpThi (GEN_ALL th))) tb
 end
```

where SPEC_ALL strips off all outmost universal quantifiers (inverse of GEN_ALL). Note the combination of HOL98 deduction (SPEC, SPEC_ALL, GEN_ALL, MP) and BDD calculation (BddEqMp).

The function `iterateToFixedPoint2` is much more efficient on large examples than `iterateToFixedPoint`. For example, with `iterateToFixedPoint`, the calculation of the BDDs of the sets of reachable states of peg solitaire brings my 500MB Linux box to a halt thrashing after a couple of days, and only reaches about 15 steps. Using `iterateToFixedPoint2` instead, all 32 steps are completed in a few hours.

4.3 Future Possibilities

The rules given above all have the same variable map ρ in the hypotheses and conclusion. The following experimental rules, which are currently not implemented (and so are not given ML names), are not of this form.

Let $\mathbf{Frees}(t)$ denote the set of free variables in t. Write $\rho_1 \subseteq \rho_2$ if ρ_1 is a restriction of ρ_2 (i.e. $\mathbf{Domain}(\rho_1) \subseteq \mathbf{Domain}(\rho_2)$). The following rule then holds.

$$\frac{\rho_1\ t\ \mapsto\ b \qquad \rho_2 \subseteq \rho_1 \qquad \mathbf{Frees}(t) \subseteq \mathbf{Domain}(\rho_2)}{\rho_2\ t\ \mapsto\ b}$$

It may be the case that the BDD representing a term doesn't depend on some variables in the term. For example, if $\{\}$ denotes the undefined-everywhere function, then $\{\}\ t \vee \neg t \mapsto$ TRUE holds for any term t. Thus any entries in the variable map that map variables to numbers not occuring in the support of the BDD can be pruned. Let $\mathbf{Support}(b)$ be the set of BDD variables (i.e. numbers) in b and let $\mathbf{Range}(\rho)$ denote the range of ρ (i.e. $\mathbf{Range}(\rho) = \{n \mid \exists v.\ \rho(v) = n\}$). Then

$$\frac{\rho_1\ t\ \mapsto\ b \qquad \rho_2 \subseteq \rho_1 \qquad \mathbf{Support}(b) \subseteq \mathbf{Range}(\rho_2)}{\rho_2\ t\ \mapsto\ b}$$

Judgements with different variable maps can be combined if the maps are compatible. Define

$$\mathtt{Compatible}(\rho_1, \rho_2)\ =\ \forall v\ n_1\ n_2.\ (\rho_1(v) = n_1) \wedge (\rho_2(v) = n_2) {\Rightarrow} (n_1 = n_2)$$

Compatible maps ρ_1 and ρ_2 can be unambiguosly joined to form a map $\rho_1 \cup \rho_2$. Rules for combining judgements with compatible maps can be formulated, for example

$$\frac{\rho_1 \ t_1 \ \mapsto \ b_1 \qquad \rho_2 \ t_2 \ \mapsto \ b_2 \qquad \texttt{Compatible}(\rho_1, \rho_2)}{\rho_1 \cup \rho_2 \ t_1 \wedge t_2 \ \mapsto \ b_1 \ \texttt{AND} \ b_2}$$

The rules for other binary operators are similar.

The next major stage in the development of `HolBddLib` will be to support judgements with different variable orders: i.e. calculation with $\rho \ t \mapsto b$ with several different ρs in play, rather than just $\rho_G \ t \mapsto b$. This will enable different variable orderings to be used within a single session. It is also planned to extend the HOL98 theory management system so that judgements $\rho \ t \mapsto b$ can be saved to disk and later reloaded, just like theorems of higher order logic.

5   Related Work

The Voss system [16] has strongly influenced the ideas described here. Voss consists of a lazy ML-like functional language, called FL, with BDDs as a built-in datatype. Quantified boolean formulae can be input and are parsed to BDDs. The normal boolean operations $\neg$, $\wedge$, $\vee$, $\equiv$, $\forall$, $\exists$ are interpreted as BDD operations. Algorithms for model checking are easily programmed.

Joyce and Seger interfaced an early HOL system (HOL88) to Voss and in a pioneering paper showed how to verify complex systems by a combination of theorem proving deduction and symbolic trajectory evaluation (STE) [9]. The HOL-Voss system integrates HOL88 deduction with BDD computations. BDD tools are programmed in FL and can then be invoked by HOL-Voss tactics, which can make external calls into the Voss system, passing subgoals via a translation between the HOL88 and Voss term representations.

In later work Lee, Seger and Greenstreet [11] showed how various optimised BDD algorithms could be programmed in FL.

The early experiments with HOL-Voss suggested that a lighter theorem proving component was sufficient, since all that was really needed was a way of combining results obtained from STE. A system based on this idea, called VossProver, was developed by Carl Seger and his student Scott Hazelhurst. It provides operations in FL for combining assertions generated by Voss using proof rules corresponding to the laws of composition of the temporal logic assertions verified by STE [8]. VossProver was used to verify impressive integer and floating-point examples (see the DAC98 paper by Aagaard, Jones and Seger [1] for further discussion and references).

After Seger and Aagaard moved to Intel, the development of the Voss and VossProver systems evolved into a new system called Forte. Only partial details of this are in the public domain [14,2], but a key idea is that FL is used both as a specification language and as an LCF-style metalanguage. The connection between symbolic trajectory evaluation and proof is obtained via a tactic `Eval_tac` that converts the result of executing an FL program performing STE into a theorem in the logic. Theorem proving in Forte is used both to split goals into smaller subgoals that are tractable for model checking, and to transform formulae so that they can be checked more efficiently.

The combination of HOL98 and BuDDy described here provides a similar programming environment to Voss's FL (though with eager rather than lazy evaluation). BuDDy provides BDD operations corresponding to $\neg$, $\wedge$, $\vee$, $\equiv$, $\forall$, $\exists$ and the HOL98 term parser plus `termToBdd` provides a way of using these to create BDDs from logical terms. Voss enables efficient computations on BDDs using functional programming. So does `HolBddLib`. However, in addition it allows FL-like BDD programming in ML to be intimately mixed with HOL98 deduction, so that, for example, theorem proving tools (e.g. simplifiers) can be directly applied to terms to optimise them for BDD purposes (e.g. disjunctive partitioning). This is in line with future developments discussed by Joyce and Seger [9] and it appears that the Forte system has similar capabilities.

6   Acknowledgements

The implementation of the interface between Moscow ML and the BuDDy BDD package was done by Ken Friis Larsen with the support of EPSRC grant GR/K57343 entitled *Checking equivalence between synthesized logic and non-synthesizable behavioural prototypes*. Ken Friis Larsen also implemented a prototype HOL98 oracle that was the starting point for the work reported here. Special thanks go to Jørn Lind-Nielsen for making his BuDDy code freely available.

Michael Norrish and Konrad Slind have provided invaluable help with HOL98, which they are currently developing. Mark Aagaard provided some of the information on Voss and its successors described in Section 5.

This work was also supported by ESPRIT Framework IV LTR 26241 project entitled *Proof and Specification Assisted Design Environments* (PROSPER), EPSRC grant GR/L35973 entitled *A Hardware Compilation Workbench* and EPSRC grant GR/L74262 entitled *A uniform semantics for Verilog and VHDL suitable for both simulation and formal verification*.

References

1. Mark D. Aagaard, Robert B. Jones, and Carl-Johan H. Seger. Combining theorem proving and trajectory evaluation in an industrial environment. In *Design Automation Conference (DAC)*, pages 538–541. ACM/IEEE, July 1998.
2. Mark D. Aagaard, Robert B. Jones, and Carl-Johan H. Seger. Lifted-FL: A Pragmatic Implementation of Combined Model Checking and Theorem Proving. In *Theorem Proving in Higher Order Logics (TPHOLs99)*, number 1690 in Lecture Notes in Computer Science, pages 323–340. Springer-Verlag, 1999.
3. Randall E. Bryant. Symbolic boolean manipulation with ordered binary-decision diagrams. *ACM Computing Surveys*, 24(3):293–318, September 1992.
4. E. Charniak, C. K. Riesbeck, and D. V. McDermott. *Artificial Intelligence Programming*. Lawrence Erlbaum Associates, 1980.

5. M. J. C. Gordon, R. Milner, and C. P. Wadsworth. *Edinburgh LCF: A Mechanised Logic of Computation*, volume 78 of *Lecture Notes in Computer Science*. Springer-Verlag, 1979.

6. Mike Gordon. Programming combinations of deduction and BDD-based symbolic calculation. Technical Report 480, University of Cambridge Computer Laboratory, December 1999.

7. Mike Gordon and Ken Friis Larsen. Combining the Hol98 proof assistant with the BuDDy BDD package. Technical Report 481, University of Cambridge Computer Laboratory, December 1999.

8. Scott Hazelhurst and Carl-Johan H. Seger. Symbolic trajectory evaluation. In Thomas Kropf, editor, *Formal Hardware Verification*, chapter 1, pages 3-78. Springer-Verlag, 1997.

9. J. Joyce and C. Seger. The HOL-Voss System: Model-Checking inside a General-Purpose Theorem-Prover. In J. J. Joyce and C.-J. H. Seger, editors, *Higher Order Logic Theorem Proving and its Applications: 6th International Workshop, HUG'93, Vancouver, B.C., August 11-13 1993*, volume 780 of *Lecture Notes in Computer Science*, pages 185-198. Spinger-Verlag, 1994.

10. Edmund M. Clarke Jr. and Orna Grumberg. *Model Checking*. The MIT Press, 1999.

11. Trevor W. S. Lee, Mark R. Greenstreet, and Carl-Johan Seger. Automatic verification of asynchronous circuits. Technical Report UBC TR 93-40, The University of British Columbia, November 1993.

12. K. L. McMillan. A methodology for hardware verification using compositional model checking. Technical report, Cadence Berkeley Labs, April 1999. Available at http://www-cad.eecs.berkeley.edu/~kenmcmil/.

13. Kenneth L. McMillan. *Symbolic Model Checking*. Kluwer Academic Publishers, 1993.

14. John O'Leary, Xudong Zhao, Robert Gerth, and Carl-Johan H. Seger. Formally verifying IEEE compliance of floating-point hardware. *Intel Technology Journal*, First Quarter 1999. Online at http://developer.intel.com/technology/itj/.

15. S. Rajan, N. Shankar, and M.K. Srivas. An integration of model-checking with automated proof checking. In Pierre Wolper, editor, *Computer-Aided Verification, CAV '95*, volume 939 of *Lecture Notes in Computer Science*, pages 84-97, Liege, Belgium, June 1995. Springer-Verlag.

16. Carl-Johan H. Seger. Voss - a formal hardware verification system: User's guide. Technical Report UBC TR 93-45, The University of British Columbia, December 1993.

Transcendental Functions and Continuity Checking in PVS

Hanne Gottliebsen

University of St Andrews, Scotland
hago@dcs.st-and.ac.uk

Abstract. In this paper we present a library of transcendental functions such as exp, log, cos, sin and tan and also an automated continuity checker for real valued functions, both done using PVS. Our aim is to develop theorem proving support for computer algebra systems, and other applications which rely on mathematical analysis. The focus of the paper is on the actual development done in PVS.

1 Introduction

The purpose of this paper is to describe our recent work on developing theorem proving tools to support computer algebra systems such as MAPLE and Mathematica in doing symbolic computation of integrals and differential equations.

Many users of computer algebra systems are not in general concerned with developing mathematics, rather they take well-established theories for granted and want tools that are as approachable as the ones they are familiar with: Numerical packages like Simulink or the NAG library or symbolic computation systems like MAPLE or Mathematica. Clearly when handling parametric cases, using numerical tools is not an option unless one is content with an experimental answer. However, there are some areas, including integration and solving differential equations, that symbolic computation systems do not handle well. In this papers we discuss a tool supporting symbolic computation systems in these areas. Descriptions of some applications of our tool can be found in [1,2]

Harrison [4] developed a large library of real analysis in HOL-Light, constructing the reals by using Dedekind cuts. Harrison implemented the theory of convergence nets and used these to define and reason about convergence of both functions and sequences. This forms the basis for power series and leads on to transcendental functions such as exp, log, cos, sin and tan which were all implemented. Furthermore a large collection of properties of these functions were proved. In PVS Dutertre [3] did an implementation of basic real analysis building on the axiomatic definition of the reals provided in PVS. Dutertre's implementation includes definitions of convergence, continuity and differentiability of real-valued functions and all the usual theorems about these that can be found in mathematics text books.

Based on Dutertre's analysis library in PVS and using Harrison's HOL-Light library as a guide we have developed a theory of transcendental functions in

J. Harrison and M. Aagaard (Eds.): TPHOLs 2000, LNCS 1869, pp. 197–214, 2000.
© Springer-Verlag Berlin Heidelberg 2000

PVS. In high school mathematics, trigonometric functions such as cos, sin and tan are normally defined using triangles and angles, but they can also be defined by power series; this was the approach taken by Harrison [4] and we have also used this method.

As argued in [1] computer algebra systems do not handle definite integration with parameters well, and this is partly due to them not handling sideconditions such as continuity. We have developed a basic continuity checker based on Dutertre's real analysis library in PVS. The continuity checker uses general theorems such as *The sum of two continuous functions is continuous*. A high level of automation is vital if the checker is to fulfill its role of support to a computer algebra system used in applied mathematics, and with PVS we have obtained a checker which utilizes the type system of PVS and is completely automatic.

We begin by describing some of the features in PVS which are most important to our development, particularly that of the continuity checker. Section 3 gives an overview of our implementation of the transcendental functions. In Sect. 4 we discuss two different approaches to automating continuity checking in PVS. Finally we discuss some applications of our work (Sect. 5).

2   Types and Judgements in PVS

PVS [6,7,8,9] is a specification and verification tool based on higher order logic. It is strongly typed and supports subtypes and dependent types. PVS specifications are organized in *theories*, which may be parametric. This allows us to write theories about eg. functions defined on *some subset* of the reals without restricting the theory to a certain subset. In this section we outline the basic uses of the type system and how *judgements* are used to aid typechecking. We also briefly explain how one can use the PVS *strategy language* to direct proofs.

2.1   Types

PVS contains primitive types such as real numbers and booleans and the usual constructors for function, record, and tuple types. For example, [real, nat -> real] is the type of functions from pairs of reals and nats to reals. PVS also supports abstract datatypes [8].

PVS supports two different ways of declaring subtypes: either (i) using a boolean expression as in

negreal : TYPE = {x : real | x < 0}

which declares negreal to be the type of negative reals, or (ii) by declaring an uninterpreted subtype as in

s : TYPE from t

which declares s to be a subtype of t.

Since the user can give arbitrary boolean expressions in type declarations typechecking is undecidable. Therefore Type Correctness Conditions (TCCs) are generated during typechecking. Some of these might be discharged by PVS automatically, but others might be left for the user to prove. For example, typechecking the function definition

```
div1(x:negreal) : real = 1 / x
```

raises this TCC

```
div1_TCC1: OBLIGATION (FORALL (x: negreal): x /= 0)
```

This is because division is of the type [real, nzreal -> real] (where nzreal is the type of non-zero reals).

2.2 Judgements

Judgements are used to help the typechecker discharge some of the many TCCs that might occur when using subtyping. Considering again the function div1 from above, we need a judgement asserting that negreal is not only a subtype of real but indeed a subtype of nzreal. The following judgement (from PVSs real library) does just that:

```
negreal_is_nzreal: JUDGEMENT negreal SUBTYPE_OF nzreal
```

The judgement is then used by the typechecker, and so the user will not be asked to prove the TCC div1_TCC1.

The judgements are a powerful tool, since type correctness is essential for applying any theorems during automatic proving. In Sect. 4 we will give an example of how judgements are used in this way to check functions for continuity.

2.3 Overloading Operators

A useful feature of PVS is overloading of operators. Since PVS is strongly typed it is easy to determine which version of an operator is being used. For instance, + is defined on numbers but Dutertre [3] overloads this to be defined on functions too:

```
+(f1, f2) : [T -> real] = LAMBDA x : f1(x) + f2(x);
```

So + is defined on functions from the type T to the reals. However as no information about judgements is carried over from the existing operator, a full set of judgements for the new operator might be necessary. An example of this is explained in Sect. 4.3.

2.4 Strategies

The PVS prover contains high level proof commands but also supports a *strategy language* which allows users to write their own proof strategies [9].

Example 1.

```
bar  [ T : TYPE ] : THEORY
  BEGIN
  f : VAR [T -> T]
  bar-lemma : THEOREM
      *some theorem*
  END bar
```

This theory has the parameter T, which is then used in the declaration of the function f.

```
(defstep foo (foo-arg)
  (let (foo-lemma (format nil "bar-lemma[~a]" foo-arg))
        (TRY (lemma foo-lemma) (GRIND) (SKIP)))
  ''If bar-lemma[foo-arg] succeeds and produces sub-goal(s)
    then run grind otherwise skip''
  ''Tries to apply bar-lemma with the right theory instantiation'')
```

The name of this strategy is foo; it takes one argument foo-arg. If we want to apply the strategy when using functions of eg. type [bool -> bool] we must specify that we want the actual parameter of bar to be bool. This is handled by foo-arg, when the strategy is used as follows:

```
(foo ''bool'')
```

The first part of the let-expression names bar-lemma[bool] foo-lemma, the second part is an application of the built-in strategy TRY, which tries to apply the first argument to the current sub-goal, if successful it then applies the second argument to each new sub-goal, if not – it applies the third argument instead.

By writing application specific strategies it is possible to gain a very high level of control over proofs and keep them automatic at the same time. Mechanisms are in place for inspecting goals and use the information to determine what the next step within a given strategy should be [9]. However, in many cases the high level proof commands available in PVS are suitable on their own.

3 Library of Trigonometric Functions

PVS includes the real numbers as part of the provided system. Together with the definitions is a large collection of theorems about linear expressions of real numbers, including the usual lemmas about eg. commutativity and associativity and also cancellation rules for equations and inequalities. Whereas this collection includes most basic rules, such as $0 * x = 0$, $\frac{1}{x} < 0$ iff $x < 0$ and $x * y \leq z * y$ iff ($x \leq z$ and $y \geq 0$) or ($z \leq x$ and $y \leq 0$), it is still lacking similarly simple lemmas which are useful for doing analysis eg. $|c| < 1 \Rightarrow c * x < x$ where $x > 0$. However, there is enough of a foundation to enable the development of those lemmas.

PVS also has an exponentiation function. It is restricted to take non-negative integer powers of real numbers. With this definition there is a limited selection of theorems about the power function such as $x^n > 0$ for $x > 0$ and $x^n \neq 0$ for $x \neq 0$.

As we shall see later another useful existing type is that of the polymorphic sequence. This has all the usual operations such as first, rest, delete and insert.

3.1   Existing Analysis Library

PVS' definition of the reals forms the basis of Dutertre's library [3] for basic analysis. This library contains many basic definitions and theorems used in real analysis, including sequences of reals; convergence of functions and of sequences; continuity and differentiation. Below we briefly outline the contents of the library for each of these areas of real analysis.

Sequences of Reals. Proving theorems about sequences of reals such as increasing or decreasing, extracting a subsequence and how subsequences inherit properties such as boundedness. Also contains a theory defining convergence of sequences and gives various criteria for a sequence to be convergent. Finally the limits of the usual combinations of sequences are given, eg. the limit of $s_1(n) + s_2(n)$ is the sum of the limits of $s_1(n)$ and $s_2(n)$.

Limits of Functions. The limit of a real-valued function is defined by the usual ε–δ definition. Again lemmas are given for calculating limits of combinations of functions. Finally various bounds on limits are listed.

Continuous Functions. As with the limits, the ordinary ε–δ definition is used and we see which operations on functions preserve continuity. By considering a continuous function restricted to a subinterval of its domain further theorems are proved, eg. the intermediate value theorem.

Differentiation. Again Dutertre uses the standard definition using the Newton quotient: A function f is differentiable at x iff

$$\frac{f(x + \Delta x) - f(x)}{\Delta x} \tag{1}$$

has a limit as Δx tends to 0. The derivative is then defined wherever the function is differentiable; it takes the value of the limit. The fact that a differentiable function is continuous is established and again we have all the usual rules for combining functions and preserving differentiability, including the values of the derivatives. The value of the derivative at a maximum or a minimum is also given, as is the mean value theorem.

In addition to the analysis library Dutertre has also built a theory to handle roots. This implementation covers positive integer roots of nonnegative reals and provides a useful extension of the power functions native to PVS as it provides a way to handle rational powers.

3.2   The Extension

Dutertre's library supports *rational functions*, that is functions made up of the identity functions, constants and the combinators $+$, $-$ (unary as well as binary), $*$ and $/$. We want to provide support for functions such as exp, log, cos, sin and tan, which are called transcendental functions. Combinations of rational and transcendental functions are called elementary functions, eg.

$$f(x) = \frac{\cos(x)}{\exp(x+a)} \ . \tag{2}$$

In high school the trigonometric functions are described using triangles and angles, but one can also define them by certain power series. This allows for analytical treatment of them. Following the usual mathematical development of the transcendental functions as limits of certain power series, we first develop a theory of partial sums, then consider sequences of these to determine convergence criteria for series. Particularly useful for this extension is the theory of convergence of sequences already available in Dutertre's library. We then define transcendental functions by their power series and via the power series prove a collection of theorems about the functions.

In general our definitions and lemmas are equivalent to Harrison's, but as we use Dutertre's library as a basis and not Harrison's more general approach, using convergence nets, our implementation is not quite as extensive. However, for the domain of transcendental functions, the two implementations do correspond closely.

Below we describe the various definitions and properties in the extension. Many more properties of the functions have been proved, but space does not allow us to include them all here.

Partial Sums. Our definition of partial sums is a little unusual as sum(n,m)(f) is

$$\sum_{j=n}^{n+m-1} f(j) \ . \tag{3}$$

However, this definition proves to be more flexible than the usual one starting the summation from 0, allowing many theorems about partial sums to be more easily proved.

In PVS we define the sum-function using recursion:

```
sumc(n,m,f) : RECURSIVE real =
     IF m = 0 THEN 0
     ELSE sumc(n,m-1,f) + f(n+m-1)
     ENDIF
   MEASURE m
sum(n,m)(f) : real = sumc(n,m,f)
```

Major theorems useful in the further development include:

$$\left| \sum_{i=n}^{n+m-1} f(i) \right| \le \sum_{i=n}^{n+m-1} |f(i)| , \tag{4}$$

$$\sum_{i=n}^{n+m-1} (f(i) + g(i)) = \sum_{i=n}^{n+m-1} f(i) + \sum_{i=n}^{n+m-1} g(i) . \tag{5}$$

Series. A series converges if the sequence of its partial sums converges. In that case, the sum also has the value of the limit of the sequence.

```
sums(f,s) : bool
   = convergence(LAMBDA r : sum(0,r)(f),s)
summable(f) : bool = EXISTS s : sums(f,s)
suminf(f : {g|summable(g)}) : real = epsilon(LAMBDA s : sums(f,s))
```

The operator **epsilon** is the *choice* operator of PVS. Here it is used to extract the s such that sums(f,s) ie. to extract the value of a convergent series.

Amongst the main theorems proved in Harrison's work and also proved for our extension of Dutertre's library are:

$$\text{If } \sum_{i=0}^{\infty} f(i) \text{ converges then so does} \sum_{i=0}^{\infty} f(i + k) , \tag{6}$$

$$\text{If } f_0 = \sum_{i=0}^{\infty} f(i) \text{ and } g_0 = \sum_{i=0}^{\infty} g(i) \text{ then } \sum_{i=0}^{\infty} f(i) + g(i) = f_0 + g_0 . \tag{7}$$

Results similar to (7) also hold for subtraction, negation, and multiplication and division by a non-zero constant.

Convergence Criteria. With the foundations laid we can now go on to use these theorems. Without aid in determining convergence one would have to go back to the definition for each series. This would be an unreasonable burden to put on any user, so we develop the following convergence criteria for series:

Cauchy-type $\sum\limits_{i=0}^{\infty} f(i)$ is convergent iff

$$\forall \varepsilon > 0 \,.\, \exists N \,.\, \forall n \geq N \,\forall m \geq 0 \,.\, \left| \sum_{i=n}^{n+m-1} f(i) \right| < \varepsilon \,.$$

Comparison If $\sum\limits_{i=0}^{\infty} g(i)$ converges and $\exists N \,\forall n \geq N \,.\, |f(n)| \leq g(n)$ then $\sum\limits_{i=0}^{\infty} f(i)$ converges.

Ratio Test If $\forall f,\, N,\, c < 1,\, n \,\geq\, N \,.\, |f(n+1)| \,\leq\, c * |f(n)|$ then $\sum\limits_{i=0}^{\infty} f(i)$ converges.

Power Series. As we are particularly interested in power series, we prove some more theorems regarding convergence of them:

- $\sum\limits_{i=0}^{\infty} x^i = \frac{1}{1-x}$ for $|x| < 1$.
- If $\sum\limits_{i=0}^{\infty} f(i) * x^i$ converges and $|y| < |x|$ then $\sum\limits_{i=0}^{\infty} f(i) * y^i$ converges.

We also prove a theorem about differentiation of power series.

Finally we are ready to begin to define the power series describing transcendental functions.

exp and log. exp is defined in the following way:

$$\exp(x) = \sum_{i=0}^{\infty} \frac{1}{i!} x^i \,. \tag{8}$$

The convergence of exp is proved using the ratio test.

We can now prove that exp is differentiable with the expected results. From this follows also that it is continuous everywhere.

For both exp and log, there is a large collection of well known facts as can be found in many text books. We have proved a useful collection of these. Firstly about exp:

$$\exp(0) = 1 \,, \tag{9}$$

$$\forall x \,\forall y \,.\, \exp(x + y) = \exp(x) \exp(y) \,, \tag{10}$$

$$\forall y \,.\, 0 < y \Rightarrow \exists x \,.\, \exp(x) = y, \text{ where } x \text{ is unique (surjective on } \mathbb{R}_+) \,. \tag{11}$$

This leads us on to log, which is defined on the positive reals by using the choice operator epsilon in PVS

```
log(x) : real = epsilon(LAMBDA y : exp(y) = x)
```

So $\log(x)$ gives a y such that $\exp(y) = x$, and we know from the theorem above, that this y is unique.

There are a few theorems about log; we present just a couple of them:

$$\log(1) = 0 , \tag{12}$$

$$\forall x > 0 \, \forall y > 0 . \, \log(\frac{x}{y}) = \log(x) - \log(y) . \tag{13}$$

Trigonometric functions and π. We now define cos and sin by their power series. To prove convergence of these series we used the comparison test and the fact the power series for exp is convergent.

sin is defined in the following way:

$$\sin(x) = \sum_{i=0}^{\infty} \frac{(-1)^i}{(2i+1)!} x^{2i+1} . \tag{14}$$

And cos is defined in the following way:

$$\cos(x) = \sum_{i=0}^{\infty} \frac{(-1)^i}{(2i)!} x^{2i} . \tag{15}$$

We proved a large collection of standard facts about cos and sin; here are some of the theorems:

$$\sin(0) = 0 , \tag{16}$$

$$\cos(0) = 1 , \tag{17}$$

$$\forall x . \, \sin(x)^2 + \cos(x)^2 = 1 , \tag{18}$$

$$\forall x . \, -1 \leq \sin(x) \leq 1 , \tag{19}$$

$$\forall x . \, -1 \leq \cos(x) \leq 1 , \tag{20}$$

$$\forall x \, \forall y . \, \sin(x + y) = \sin(x)\cos(y) + \cos(x)\sin(y) , \tag{21}$$

$$\forall x . \, \sin(-x) = -\sin(x) . \tag{22}$$

Now we want to give a definition of π. We first prove that there is a unique x between 0 and 2, such that $\cos(x) = 0$. Then π is defined to be 2 times this x, again using the choice operator of PVS.

There are various lemmas relating cos, sin and π:

$$\pi > 0 \ , \tag{23}$$

$$\cos(\pi) = -1 \ , \tag{24}$$

$$\sin(\pi) = 0 \ , \tag{25}$$

$$\forall x \ . \ \sin(x) = \cos(\frac{\pi}{2} - x) \ , \tag{26}$$

$$\forall k \ . \ \sin(k\pi) = 0 \ , \tag{27}$$

$$\forall x \ . \ \cos(x) = 0 \ \text{iff} \ ((\exists \ \text{odd} \ k \ . \ x = k\frac{\pi}{2}) \vee (\exists \ \text{odd} \ k \ . \ x = -k\frac{\pi}{2})) \ , \tag{28}$$

$$\forall x \ . \ \sin(x) = 0 \ \text{iff} \ ((\exists \ \text{even} \ k \ . \ x = k\frac{\pi}{2}) \vee (\exists \ \text{even} \ k \ . \ x = -k\frac{\pi}{2})) \ . \tag{29}$$

The function $\tan(x)$ is undefined for the values of x where $\cos(x) = 0$, and we just proved that those xs are of the form $k\frac{\pi}{2}$ where k is an odd integer, therefore we define a new type, which will be the domain for tan:

```
x : VAR real
k : VAR int
cos_nz_type : NONEMPTY_TYPE
    = { x | FORALL k : x /= (2 * k + 1) * pi / 2 }
```

We can then define tan and prove some lemmas about it:

$$\forall x \ . \ \cos(x) \neq 0 \ \Rightarrow \ \tan(x) = \frac{\sin(x)}{\cos(x)} \ , \tag{30}$$

$$\tan(n\pi) = 0 \ , \tag{31}$$

$$\forall x \ . \ \cos(x) \neq 0 \ \Rightarrow \ \tan(-x) = -\tan(x) \ , \tag{32}$$

$$\forall x \ \forall y \ . \ (\cos(x), \cos(y), \cos(x + y) \neq 0) \ \Rightarrow \ \tan(x + y) = \frac{\tan(x) + \tan(y)}{1 - \tan(x)\tan(y)} \ . \tag{33}$$

If we want to differentiate a function which is not defined on the full set of the reals, with the current implementation we have to restrict the function to an interval around the point of interest, such that the function is defined on the whole of that interval. So we prove the two following theorems:

$$\forall x \ \exists k \ . \ k_1 < x < k_2 \wedge \tan|_{(k_1,k_2)}{}'(x) = \frac{1}{\cos(x)^2}, \ \text{for} \ k_1 = k\pi - \frac{\pi}{2}, k_2 = k\pi + \frac{\pi}{2} \ ,$$

$$\forall y \ \exists x \ . \ \cos(x) \neq 0 \wedge -\frac{\pi}{2} < x < \frac{\pi}{2} \wedge \tan(x) = y \wedge x \ \text{is unique} \ .$$

3.3   Example Proof

The proofs in this development seems to fall into two categories. Either they are small and quite easy, or they are more complicated and tend to get very long. Proofs about properties of finite series fall into the first category, as they tend to be simple induction proofs. As one might expect, also a great part of the theorems about properties of the trigonometric functions are quite simple. This is because once the basic tools are in place we no longer have to go back to the ε–δ definitions to prove convergence to certain values. Between these two extremes of the development is a part which in general requires a lot of work. We will here only consider one of the easier proofs.

We want to prove the following theorem:

```
sin_cos : THEOREM
     FORALL x : sin(x) = cos(pi / 2 - x)
```

These four lemmas are used in the proof:

```
cos_add : LEMMA
     FORALL x, y : cos(x + y) = cos(x) * cos(y) - sin(x) * sin(y)

cos_pi2 : LEMMA
     cos(pi / 2) = 0

sin_pi2 : LEMMA
     sin(pi / 2) = 1

sin_neg : LEMMA
     FORALL x : sin(-x) = -sin(x)
```

The proof is as follows:

```
(SKOLEM!)
(USE "cos_add" ("x" "pi/2" "y" "-x!1"))
(LEMMA "cos_pi2")
(LEMMA "sin_pi2")
(USE "sin_neg" ("x" "x!1"))
(ASSERT)
```

It applies lemma cos_add to pi/2 and -x to get

cos(pi / 2 - x) = cos(pi/2) * cos(-x) - sin(pi/2) * sin(-x)

Then we use lemma cos_pi2 and sin_pi2 to get

cos(pi / 2 - x) = 0 * cos(-x) - 1 * sin(-x)

And finally using sin_neg we get

sin(-x) = -sin(x)

And this completes the proof.

4   Automated Continuity Checking

In this section we describe how we can determine if a function $f : A \rightarrow \mathbb{R}$, where $A \subseteq \mathbb{R}$, is continuous. For simple functions, this is an easy task as we apply the basic rules about combining continuous functions using eg. addition. But considering more complicated functions, maybe using composition, it becomes a lot harder to control. This is one case where a theorem prover can provide support. Our aim is to have an automated continuity checker, in the sense that the user should be able to pose his problem and use just a single command to get some sort of answer. This would be useful in conjunction with eg. computer algebra systems [2].

4.1   General Idea

We use Dutertre's [3] `continuous_functions` theory as the basis for our implementation. It builds on the well known definition of continuity,

Definition 1. *Let $f : A \rightarrow \mathbb{R}$ and $a \in A$. We say that f is* continuous *at a if*
$$\forall \varepsilon \in \mathbb{R}_+ \exists \delta \in \mathbb{R}_+ : \forall x \in A : |x - a| < \delta \implies |f(x) - f(a)| < \varepsilon$$

When checking if a certain function is continuous at some point we consider the term describing it, eg. $x + 2x^2$. In this case it is a sum of two functions, and we know that if each of the two functions is continuous, then so is the sum. Similarly holds for subtraction, multiplication and division, although in the latter case we must also make sure the denominator is non-zero. It is clear that using this approach we can syntactically take the term apart, with the basic parts being constant functions and the identity function.

What is described here is clearly a very basic method, and by no means a complete one. For example, the function

$$f(x) = \frac{x + 1}{x + 1} \, . \tag{34}$$

is not defined at -1 as such, and with this representation PVS's typechecker would require $x \neq -1$. However it is clear that if we add to the definition of f so that $f(1) = 1$, it could be simplified to

$$f(x) = 1 \, . \tag{35}$$

And by using L'Hospital's rule on (8) we see that f is indeed continuous at -1. Cases like these are not yet provided for in our PVS implementation.

We want to use the PVS theory `continuous_functions` by Dutertre [3]. This theory contains theorems about conserving continuity under certain operations together with the base cases of constant functions and the identity function being continuous. The theory is parameterized with a type T, which is used as the domain-type for the functions.

Let $f1, f2 : T \rightarrow \mathbb{R}$ and $g : T \rightarrow \mathbb{R} \setminus 0$ be functions, let $x0 \in T$ and let $k \in \mathbb{R}$. We then use the following named theorems:

```
sum_continuous : THEOREM
    continuous(f1, x0) and continuous(f2, x0)
        implies continuous(f1 + f2, x0)

diff_continuous : THEOREM
    continuous(f1, x0) and continuous(f2, x0)
        implies continuous(f1 - f2, x0)

prod_continuous : THEOREM
    continuous(f1, x0) and continuous(f2, x0)
        implies continuous(f1 * f2, x0)

const_continuous : THEOREM
    continuous(k, x0)

scal_continuous : THEOREM
    continuous(f1, x0) implies continuous(k * f1, x0)

opp_continuous : THEOREM
    continuous(f1, x0) implies continuous(- f1, x0)

div_continuous : THEOREM
    continuous(f1, x0) and continuous(g, x0)
        implies continuous(f1/g, x0)

inv_continuous : THEOREM
    continuous(g, x0) implies continuous(1/g, x0)

identity_continuous : THEOREM
    continuous(I[T], x0)

abs_continuous : THEOREM
    continuous(f1,x) implies continuous(abs(f1),x)
```

We want to use these theorems in as automatic a way as possible, and so we have two options; either we write special strategies to direct the proof, or we provide enough information for PVS to match the theorems to the input. In Sect. 4.2 we outline how strategies might be used to solve the problem, then in Sect. 4.3 we see how even better results can be achieved by the use of judgements.

4.2 Using Strategies

In this section we describe a strategy which directs PVS in doing continuity checking. We will not give all the details, but rather give an overview of how the strategy works.

There are two parts to the strategy, one which is called from the prover and another which is internal and only meant to be called from the top level strategy.

The top level strategy is called cts, and it does not take any arguments. The first thing cts does is check if the current goal fits the strategy, in that it must be of the form continuous(f,x)

In fact we allow for some variation, such as

```
FORALL x : p(x) => continuous(f,x)
```

where p is some predicate, but since these variations do not change the behavior of the main elements of the strategy, we will omit them in this overview.

As the PVS theory used for continuity is parametric in the domain type of the function, we then work out what that type is. Because PVS is strongly typed, this information is obtainable from the goal itself and the strategy language provides means to extract it.

The next step, which is done by a recursive strategy, is to apply the theorems of Sect. 4.1 in the correct order using the appropriate instantiations. Again PVS provides mechanisms for checking if a term is an application and the number of arguments it takes – we have to distinguish between the unary and binary versions of $-$. Having identified the top level symbol $(+, -, *, /, |\cdot|$, identity or constant functions) we can then apply the appropriate theorem. For example, for $x \in \mathbb{R}_+$ consider continuous(LAMBDA x : x+2/x,3). Here "+" is the top symbol, and so we first apply sum_continuous. This then gives us two sub-goals:

```
continuous(LAMDBA x : x,3)
continuous(LAMBDA x : 2/x,3)
```

A Type Checking Condition (TCC) is also generated

```
FORALL (x : posreal) : x /= 0
```

But it is automatically discharged by PVS, so we do not have to handle it. In more complicated cases PVS might not be able to discharge the TCC automatically, so the strategy takes care of TCCs too.

Each of the two sub-goals can be handled by the inner strategy. The first one is proved in the next step by using identity_continuous, whereas the second needs a few more steps.

At present our strategy relies on PVS to work out the instantiation of the theorems, and whereas in simpler examples, such as

```
continuous(LAMBDA x : 1/(|x|+1) + 2/(|x|+2),y)
```

this works well, it is not too hard to confuse PVS. There is a way to get around this, and that is to not only have the strategy decide (based on examining the current goal) which theorem to use next, but also the instantiation of it. Again, this information *can* be extracted from the goal, but the more detail we need to extract from the goal the more involved is the strategy, so we have not yet done this.

4.3 Using JUDGEMENTS

Interaction with the PVS team suggested that rather than writing ever more complicated strategies for continuity checking we should be looking to provide the PVS typechecker with the judgements needed to do all the matching. This method turned out to be surprisingly simple with very good results.

By giving judgements, eg

```
negreal_minus_nnreal_is_negreal:
  JUDGEMENT -(nx:negreal, nny:nnreal) HAS_TYPE negreal
```

we tell PVS that a certain kind of expression has a certain type, in this case that a negative real minus a non-negative real gives a negative real as a result.

For PVS to automatically (eg. while using the high level command GRIND) apply the theorems, the typechecker must be able to decide that the arguments are of the appropriate type, eg. to apply div_continuous, it must know the divisor to be a non-zero function. If the right judgements are in place, this will happen.

The above judgement is concerned with the type of subtracting two real numbers, but what we need in order to use the theorems of continuous_functions is judgements about the the usual function combinations as higher order operators, eg. subtraction of two functions, so that

$$f(x) = \frac{1}{-(|x|+1)-3} \tag{36}$$

will be matched to div_continuous.

Dutertre [3] already defined the higher order versions of $+$, $-$ (unary and binary), $*$, $/$, and $|\cdot|$, but we have added the following declarations and judgements:

```
npfun : TYPE =  [T -> npreal]

ph, pg : VAR posfun
nh, ng : VAR negfun
nzh, nzg : VAR nzfun
nnh, nng : VAR nnfun
nph, npg : VAR npfun
```

```
npfun_plus_npfun_is_npfun:   JUDGEMENT +(nph, npg) HAS_TYPE npfun
npfun_minus_nnfun_is_npfun:  JUDGEMENT -(nph, nng) HAS_TYPE npfun
npfun_times_npfun_is_nnfun:  JUDGEMENT *(nph, npg) HAS_TYPE nnfun
npfun_div_posfun_is_npfun:   JUDGEMENT /(nph, pg)  HAS_TYPE npfun
npfun_div_negfun_is_nnfun:   JUDGEMENT /(nph, ng)  HAS_TYPE nnfun
minus_npfun_is_nnfun:        JUDGEMENT -(nph)      HAS_TYPE nnfun
```

We have also added similar judgements for nzfun, posfun, negfun, nnegfun, and judgements for the $|\cdot|$ and identity functions. These judgements are mainly generalisations of the ones for real numbers found in the PVS distribution, however we added a few other useful ones too.

By including these judgements we have used successfully proved continuity of functions such as:

$$\exp(x^2 + |1 - x|) \,, \tag{37}$$

$$\exp(\cos(x) + 1) \,, \tag{38}$$

$$\frac{1}{|x| + 1} + \frac{2}{|x| + 2} \,. \tag{39}$$

And defined only on the negative reals:

$$\frac{1}{x - |x|} \,. \tag{40}$$

These proofs could all be done using only GRIND with the appropriate theories added, however to help the user even further we wrote a new strategy. It simply inspects the goal to obtain the domain type of the functions to be proved continuous. It then instantiates all the parameterised theories correctly and calls GRIND.

Using judgements for this problem has solved much of it in a very nice way. The judgements are short and easy to understand compared with specialised strategies. However, it seems likely that it will cause considerable difficulty to generalise the judgements to cover yet more functions. We would like to be able to handle functions with say a division with a trigonometric functions such as cos or sin in the denominator. In some cases, this would be obtainable, like in

$$f(x) = \frac{1}{\cos(x) + 2} \,. \tag{41}$$

Here we might consider judgements saying that $\cos(s)$ is between -1 and 1 and that adding something strictly greater that 1 is positive. As the denominator can be arbitrarily complex, it is not clear that this is a viable solution in the more general case, but already the use of judgements by the typechecker has solved fairly complicated cases.

5   Applications

We have successfully used the library of trigonometric functions with DITLU [1], a table look-up for symbolic definite integrals. The table works on integrals of the form

$$\int_a^b f(x) \; dx \tag{42}$$

where both the limits and the function may include parameters. Dependent on the function and the values (or ranges) of the parameters the integral might be undefined or take a particular value. In the table this is represented as case-statements and we used PVS to eliminate the cases that could definitely not occur for a given query. For example, one of the entries in the table is

$$\int_b^c \frac{1}{p+qx}\,dx = \begin{cases} 0 & (b=c) \\ \hline undefined & (q \neq 0) \wedge (b \neq c) \wedge \\ & ((b = -\frac{p}{q}) \vee (c = -\frac{p}{q})) \\ \hline \frac{log|qc+p| - log|qb+p|}{q} & (q \neq 0) \wedge (b \neq c) \wedge \\ & (b \neq -\frac{p}{q}) \wedge (c \neq -\frac{p}{q})) \\ \hline \frac{c-b}{p} & (b \neq c) \wedge (p \neq 0) \wedge (q = 0) \\ \hline undefined & (b \neq c) \wedge (p = 0) \wedge (q = 0) \end{cases}$$

So with a query like

$$\int_{-a}^{a+1} \frac{1}{x}\,dx \tag{43}$$

we get the following match with the entry above:

$$b = -a, c = a+1, p = 0, q = 1 \ .$$

We see that dependent on the value of a the first three cases might occur, case 1 if $a = \frac{-1}{2}$ and cases 2 and 3 if $a = -1$. However, the last two cases will not occur with this query, since $q = 1$. So the result of the query is the first three cases only. We used PVS to check these sideconditions in order to remove the cases which can not occur.

We have used the continuity checker together with experimental MAPLE code [2] to provide safer solutions to differential equations. In general computer algebra systems do not check all the sideconditions of well-know theorems before applying them. One such example is the Fundamental Theorem of Calculus

Theorem 1. $\int_b^c f(x)\,dx = g(c) - g(b)$ where g is the antiderivative of f and f is continuous on [b,c].

Applying this theorem without checking that f is continuous on the interval can lead to errors. The experimental MAPLE code returns the usual results, but also conditions on the results, for instance that some function is continuous on some particular interval. We used our continuity checker to prove these sideconditions for examples such as

$$y'(x) + y/(2\sqrt{x-a}) = \log(b-x)\exp(-\sqrt{x-a}) \ .$$

6   Discussion

We have presented here the outline of our implementation of two different additions to PVS: a library of transcendental functions and an automatic continuity checker. The library of transcendental functions is similar to that of Harrison [4], although our implementation is not built on convergence nets but on the standard ε–δ definition of convergence. The library includes definitions of the functions exp, log, cos, sin, tan, $\cos^{-1}$, $\sin^{-1}$ and $\tan^{-1}$ and a large collection of theorems about properties of these functions.

The automatic continuity checker deals with continuity for a wide range of combinations of functions, including some from the library of transcendental functions. The drawback of relying on judgements and the built-in matching in PVS is that with more complicated expressions (eg. in the denominator of a division) more specialised types and so judgements might also be needed. It seems clear that a combination of strategies and judgements is the best approach to get even more general results. We are currently exploring this.

Of further interest would be to consider an implementation of complex analysis in PVS, as this would allow for proper treatment of phenomena like *branch cuts*. This would require a complete reworking of the analysis library, but would then support more aspects of analysis.

Acknowledgements

We acknowledge support of the UK EPRSC under grant number GR/L48256 and the advice of Ursula Martin, Steve Linton and Andrew Adams on the development of transcendental functions in PVS. We also thank Bruno Dutertre for allowing us to extend his code for the reals in PVS and for discussions about the main issues regarding it. We also thank the members of the PVS help mailing list for many and swift answers to problems with the development, and the PVS team at SRI in Menlo Park for suggesting improvements.

References

1. Adams, A., Gottliebsen, H., Linton, S., Martin, U.: VSDITLU: a verified symbolic definite integral table look-up. Proc CADE 16, LNAI **1632**, 112-126, Springer 1999
2. Martin, U., Gottliebsen, H.: Computational logic support for differential equations and mathematical modelling. In preparation
3. Dutertre, B.: Elements of Mathematical Analysis in PVS. Proc TPHOLS 9, LNCS **1125**. Springer 1996.
4. Harrison, J.: Theorem Proving with the Real Numbers. Springer 1998.
5. Harrison, J.: Floating point verification in HOL. Proc TPHOLS 8, LNCS **971**, 186-199, Springer 1995
6. Shankar, N., Owre, S.: The Formal Semantics of PVS. Computer Science Laboratory, SRI International 1997
7. Shankar, N., Owre, S., Rushby, J. M., Stringer-Calvert, D. W. J.: PVS System Guide. Computer Science Laboratory, SRI International 1999
8. Shankar, N., Owre, S., Rushby, J. M., Stringer-Calvert, D. W. J.: PVS Language Reference. Computer Science Laboratory, SRI International 1999
9. Shankar, N., Owre, S., Rushby, J. M., Stringer-Calvert, D. W. J.: PVS Prover Guide. Computer Science Laboratory, SRI International 1999

Verified Optimizations for
the Intel* IA-64 Architecture**

Jim Grundy

The Australian National University
Department of Computer Science, Canberra ACT 0200, Australia
Jim.Grundy@acm.org

Abstract. This paper outlines a formal model of the Intel IA-64 architecture, and explains how this model can be used to verify the correctness of assembly-level code optimizations. The formalization and proofs were carried out using the HOL Light theorem prover.

1 Introduction

Current microprocessors dynamically reorder the sequence of instructions being executed to extract greater performance. The IA-64 takes a different approach [3, 6]. By exposing architectural features that would ordinarily be hidden, IA-64 allows the compiler to reorder instructions prior to execution. By moving the burden of instruction reordering from hardware to software, resources are freed to increase performance in other ways.

Formal methods have been applied to instruction reordering hardware [7], but as the responsibility for reordering instructions moves from hardware to software, so does the obligation to ensure the reorderings preserve the meaning of the code. This paper proves the correctness of some of the instruction reorderings performed in software for the IA-64. The work described deliberately stops-short of tackling the open-ended difficulty of verifying general properties of IA-64 programs. Instead, the proofs are limited to checking equivalence between similar small programs; the kinds of proofs that typify verification of individual optimizing transformations. The purpose of the work is to investigate the extent to which such proofs can be automated. The formalization and proofs were carried out with the HOL Light theorem prover [5].

2 Examples: Control and Data Speculation

This paper will focus on two examples of instruction reordering. The first illustrates *control speculation*, where an instruction is executed even though the result is not known to be needed. The second example illustrates *data speculation*, where an instruction is executed using data not known to be accurate.

---

* All names and brands are the property of their respective owners.
** Research supported by the Intel Corporation and the Australian Research Council.

J. Harrison and M. Aagaard (Eds.): TPHOLs 2000, LNCS 1869, pp. 215–232, 2000.
© Springer-Verlag Berlin Heidelberg 2000

```
        original code                          optimized code

    (p1)br label                                   ld8.s r9 r5
        ld8 r9 r5                              (p1)br label
        add r2 r9 r3                               chk.s r9 reload
                              continue:            add r2 r9 r3

                              reload:              ld8 r9 r5
                                                   br continue
```

Fig. 1. Control speculation example

2.1   Control Speculation

The execution of most IA-64 instructions may be predicated on the value of a one-bit *predicate* register. If the nominated register holds true, the instruction executes normally; if not, it has no effect. Predicated instructions are written with the predicate register parenthesized to the left. An example can be seen in the first instruction of the 'original' code fragment in Fig. 1.

Consider the original code presented in Fig. 1. If p1 holds true, then control branches to label. If not, execution falls through to the next instruction, which loads the general purpose register r9 with 8 bytes from the address held in r5. The values held in r9 and r3 are summed, and the result stored in r2.

Load instructions take several cycles to complete, and in this program the load is followed by an add which depends upon the value loaded. The execution of the add must therefore stall, to allow the load to complete before it can execute. We would like hide the load latency by moving the load earlier in the instruction stream. Unfortunately, we cannot execute the load earlier as it appears immediately after a conditional branch; if the branch is taken the load should not be executed. It is tempting to think we could move the load before the branch and ignore the result if it is not needed; this would be a *control speculative* execution of the load. However, this could cause a fault if the load tried to access an invalid address. A correct, but unnecessary, load could also incur a performance penalty if it required nonresident memory to be swapped in.

On a traditional architecture the load would stay where it was, but the IA-64 offers a way around these problems. Every register has a corresponding one-bit tag called a *not a thing* (nat) bit. A control speculative version of the load instruction is provided, which quietly sets this bit rather than causing a fault (including a page fault). The nat bit can be checked to see if the load succeeded. Using this feature, the code can be optimized as shown in Fig. 1.

The optimized code begins with a control speculative load, which attempts to read data into r9. If the load fails, the nat bit of r9 is set. Later, the chk.s instruction checks if r9 contains valid data. If the nat bit is clear, the load succeeded and execution continues unaffected. If it is set, execution is transferred to the code labeled reload, where the load is retried. The second load will exhibit the true faulting behavior, perhaps causing nonresident memory to be swapped in so the load can complete. Both paths then execute the add instruction.

original code   optimized code

```
st2 r1 r2                                        ld4.a r3 r4
ld4 r3 r4                                        st2 r1 r2
                                                 chk.a r3 reload
                                continue:

                                reload: ld4 r3 r4
                                        br continue
```

Fig. 2. Data speculation example

2.2   Data Speculation

Figure 2 gives another example optimization. Consider the unoptimized code. The first instruction stores two bytes from r2 to the address held in r1. The second loads four bytes into r3 from the address held in r4. As before, we would like hide the load latency from any subsequent instructions by moving the the load earlier in the instruction stream. However, this would result in incorrect behavior if the memory region written by the store overlaps that read by the load. In most situations the regions will not overlap, but they might, so the load must remain after the store.

The IA-64 provides a way around this obstacle with a special data speculative *advanced* load instruction. The advanced load records the region of memory a register was loaded from. A test can be used to check if the region has been overwritten since the load. Using this feature, the code can be optimized as shown. The optimized code begins with an advanced load, followed by the store. Next, register r3 is checked to see if it was effected by the store. If it was, a branch is taken to the label reload, where it is reloaded with the correct data.[1]

3   A Model of the IA-64

Our aim is to describe an abstract model of an IA-64 machine that can be used to show that the optimized code fragments just presented have the same behavior as the corresponding unoptimized fragments. This section will describe each component of the IA-64 architectural state that needs to be modeled to verify these optimizations.

3.1   Data Memory

We make the simplifying assumption that the instruction and data memories can be modeled separately. The data memory is defined in terms of two types, *word* and *size*. The type *word* describes 64-bit words, which are used to hold both addresses and data. The type *size* describes the units in which memory is accessed: 1, 2, 4 or 8 bytes.

---

[1] Other IA-64 instructions can handle these simple examples more succinctly. Here we present only the most general forms of speculation and recovery.

$$word \stackrel{\text{def}}{=} \{n \mid n < 2^{64}\} \qquad\qquad size \stackrel{\text{def}}{=} \{1,2,4,8\}$$

The function zext takes a word w and a size s, and returns a new word with a zero-extended copy of the first s bytes of w.

$$\vdash^{\text{def}} \text{zext } w\ s = w \bmod 2^{8 \times s} \qquad\qquad\qquad [\text{zext\_def}]$$

A word (address) and a size together describe a *region* of memory. The predicate overlapped determines if two regions overlap.

$$\vdash^{\text{def}} \text{overlapped } a_1\ s_1\ a_2\ s_2 = \qquad\qquad [\text{overlapped\_def}]$$
$$(\exists x \cdot a_1 \le x \wedge x < a_1 + s_1 \wedge a_2 \le x \wedge x < a_2 + s_2)$$

The data memory is modeled as a function from words (addresses) to words (values). The mem_read and mem_write operations are described as follows:

$$\vdash^{\text{def}} \text{mem\_read } m\ a\ s = \text{zext } (m\ a)\ s \qquad\qquad [\text{mem\_read\_def}]$$

$$\vdash^{\text{def}} (\text{mem\_read } (\text{mem\_write } m\ a\ s\ w)\ a\ s = \text{zext } w\ s) \wedge \qquad [\text{mem\_write\_def}]$$
$$(\neg\text{overlapped } a_1\ s_1\ a_2\ s_2 \Longrightarrow$$
$$\text{mem\_read } (\text{mem\_write } m\ a_2\ s_2\ w)\ a_1\ s_1 = \text{mem\_read } m\ a_1\ s_1)$$

Note that the behavior of reads and writes that access overlapping, but not identical, regions of memory is unspecified. Accurate modeling of such accesses is not necessary to verify optimizations like the ones discussed here.

Not all regions of memory are valid sources or destinations, this includes those that extend outside the address space, but may include others as well.

$$\vdash^{\text{def}} \text{mem\_valid\_source } a\ s \Longrightarrow a + s \le 2^{64} \qquad [\text{mem\_valid\_source\_def}]$$

$$\vdash^{\text{def}} \text{mem\_valid\_dest } a\ s \Longrightarrow a + s \le 2^{64} \qquad [\text{mem\_valid\_dest\_def}]$$

Some, *sequential*, regions of memory should be accessed only in the order originally specified. If, for example, IO devices are mapped into the memory space, those regions will be sequential. We do not specify which regions of memory are sequential, only that some may be.

$$\vdash^{\text{def}} \text{mem\_seq } a\ s \Longrightarrow \top \qquad\qquad\qquad [\text{mem\_seq\_def}]$$

Not all regions of memory may be read speculatively. This includes invalid sources and sequential regions, but may include other regions as well. An obvious example is memory that is nonresident and would therefore need to be swapped in. The validity of speculatively accessing a memory region may change as the state of the machine changes. The mem_valid_spec_source predicate takes an extra parameter x to represent the abstract state of the machine. It is not necessary to specify how the value of mem_valid_spec_source depends on x, only that it may, and that the type of x is sufficiently large to encompass the state of the machine.

$$\stackrel{\text{def}}{\vdash} \text{mem\_valid\_spec\_source } x \; a \; s \implies \qquad\qquad \text{[mem\_valid\_spec\_source\_def]}$$
$$\text{mem\_valid\_source } a \; s \land \lnot\text{mem\_seq } a \; s$$

Memory Access Ordering: It is not always possible to reorder memory accesses as described in Sect. 2.2. Code to synchronize multiple processes may depend on the precise ordering of those accesses. Changes to the memory access ordering that appear correct when viewed from the perspective of an individual process, may not be correct when the collection of processes are considered as a whole. The IA-64 provides special variants of the load and store instructions, and a special 'memory fence' instruction for use in such routines. These instructions must respect the memory access ordering. The execution of the ordinary load and store instructions are not required to access memory in the order they were issued. The memory accesses may be reordered or even coalesced by the hardware, provided that the resulting access order satisfies read-after-write (RAW), write-after-write (WAW), and write-after-read (WAR) data dependencies [6]. The optimizations considered here use only the ordinary versions of the load and store instructions, and so the memory model presented does not address access ordering. Mike Gordon has described a more elaborate memory model that encompasses memory access ordering issues for the Alpha architecture [4].

3.2   General Purpose Registers

The IA-64 architecture defines 128 general purpose registers. Each register holds a 64-bit word and a one-bit tag called a *not a thing* (nat) bit. The role of the nat bit is to indicate when the data held in the register is invalid due to a failed control speculation. These bits are set by failing control speculative loads, and are propagated by operations that use invalid data as input. We will describe the contents of a register with a record type:[2]

$$\textit{register} \stackrel{\text{def}}{=} \triangleleft\text{val: } \textit{word}; \text{nat: } \textit{bool}\triangleright$$

These registers cannot necessarily all be accessed by the instructions of a particular routine. Each routine has access to a subset of the registers known as a *frame*. The current frame moves though the register file as subroutines are entered and exited. This is similar to the register window system of the SPARC architecture [9], except that IA-64 frames may be of variable size. Hardware automatically renames the registers so that the current frame appears at the start of the register file. Even though the optimizations described here do not involve subroutine calls, the description of the register frame mechanism cannot be completely ignored. Within a routine, attempts to write registers not in the current frame will cause a fault, while reading such registers will produce undefined results.

---

[2] The actual formalization uses tuples as records are not supported in HOL Light. Records, in the style of hol98 [8], have been used here to simplify the presentation.

A new type *grindex* is defined for the set of general purpose register indexes, and we define a constant sof (size of frame) of that type to model the size of the current frame. The actual value of sof is unimportant, except that all frames must contain at least 32 registers.[3]

$$grindex \stackrel{\text{def}}{=} \{n \mid n < 128\} \qquad\qquad \vDash^{\text{def}} 32 \leq \text{sof} \qquad [\text{sof\_def}]$$

We define predicates reg_valid_source and reg_valid_dest to indicate which registers may be read and written.

$$\vDash^{\text{def}} \text{reg\_valid\_source } i = i < \text{sof} \qquad\qquad [\text{reg\_valid\_source\_def}]$$

$$\vDash^{\text{def}} \text{reg\_valid\_dest } i = \text{reg\_valid\_source } i \wedge (i \neq 0) \qquad [\text{reg\_valid\_dest\_def}]$$

The definition of the read and write operations for registers is straight forward; the only complications being due to the under-determined value of invalid reads and the hard-wired value of register 0. Note that the parameter x, as before, is used to allow the result of an undefined read to depend on some abstract notion of the general machine state.

$$\vDash^{\text{def}} \text{reg\_valid\_source } i \Longrightarrow \qquad\qquad [\text{reg\_read\_def}]$$
$$\text{reg\_read } x \, f \, i = \text{if } i = 0 \text{ then } \lhd \text{val:} = 0; \text{nat:} = F \rhd \text{ else} f \, i$$

$$\vDash^{\text{def}} \text{reg\_write } f \, i \, v = (\lambda j \cdot \text{if } j = i \text{ then } v \text{ else } f \, j) \qquad [\text{reg\_write\_def}]$$

It was not necessary to under-specify the result of invalid writes, because IA-64 instructions raise a fault rather than attempt this operation.

The following basic theorems regarding register operations are necessary stepping stones to verifying the optimizations.

$$\vdash \text{reg\_read } x \, f \, 0 = \lhd \text{val:} = 0; \text{nat:} = F \rhd \qquad\qquad [\text{reg\_read\_zero\_thm}]$$

$$\vdash \text{reg\_valid\_dest } i \Longrightarrow \text{reg\_read } x \, (\text{reg\_write } f \, i \, v) \, i = v \qquad [\text{reg\_read\_eq\_thm}]$$

$$\vdash \text{reg\_valid\_source } i \wedge i \neq j \Longrightarrow \qquad\qquad [\text{reg\_read\_ne\_thm}]$$
$$\text{reg\_read } x \, (\text{reg\_write } f \, j \, v) \, i = \text{reg\_read } x \, f \, i$$

$$\vdash \text{reg\_write } (\text{reg\_write } f \, i \, v) \, i \, w = \text{reg\_write } f \, i \, w \qquad [\text{reg\_write\_eq\_thm}]$$

3.3   Predicate Registers

The IA-64 includes 64 one-bit predicate registers. These registers can be used to mask execution of individual instructions. If the execution of an instruction

---

[3] The size of frame (sof) is defined as a constant because its value is not changed by the instructions used in the examples presented here. In general, however, its value can change and is better modeled as part of the state space defined in Sect. 3.5.

is conditional on the value of a predicate register, then the instruction is said to be *predicated* on that register. The description of the predicate registers is simpler than that of the general purpose registers as there is no notion of frame, the predicate registers are always visible, and their contents are always valid. Strictly speaking, (almost) all IA-64 instructions are predicated, those which are to be executed unconditionally are predicated on register 0, which is hard-wired to true. Writes to predicate register 0 are allowed, but they have no visible effect on the state. The operators on the predicate registers are pred_read and pred_write, and their definitions are similar to those for reg_read and reg_write.

$$prindex \stackrel{\text{def}}{=} \{n \mid n < 64\}$$

$$\stackrel{\text{def}}{=} \text{pred\_read } f\, i = \text{if } i = 0 \text{ then } \mathsf{T} \text{ else } f\, i \qquad\qquad \text{[pred\_read\_def]}$$

$$\stackrel{\text{def}}{=} \text{pred\_write } f\, i\, b = (\lambda j\cdot \text{if } i \neq 0 \wedge j = i \text{ then } b \text{ else } f\, j) \qquad \text{[pred\_write\_def]}$$

Properties similar to those proved about reg_read and reg_write hold for pred_read and pred_write as well.

$$\vdash \text{pred\_read } f\, 0 = \mathsf{T} \qquad\qquad\qquad\qquad \text{[pred\_read\_0\_thm]}$$

$$\vdash i \neq 0 \implies \text{pred\_read } (\text{pred\_write } f\, i\, b)\, i = b \qquad\qquad \text{[pred\_read\_eq\_thm]}$$

$$\vdash i \neq j \implies \text{pred\_read } (\text{pred\_write } f\, j\, b)\, i = \text{pred\_read } f\, i \quad \text{[pred\_read\_ne\_thm]}$$

$$\vdash \text{pred\_write } (\text{pred\_write } f\, i\, b)\, i\, c = \text{pred\_write } f\, i\, c \qquad\qquad \text{[pred\_write\_eq\_thm]}$$

3.4   The ALAT

Data speculative, or advanced, load instructions must keep track of the integrity of data that has been loaded. Any subsequent stores overlapping the region loaded will invalidate the data. On the IA-64 this task is performed using an architectural feature called the *Advanced Load Address Table* (ALAT).

Ideally, the ALAT records the following information for each speculatively loaded register:

- Whether the data in the register is valid.
- If so, what region of memory the data was loaded from.

The ALAT entry for each register can be described as a record as follows:

$$alat\_entry \stackrel{\text{def}}{=} \triangleleft\text{valid: } bool; \text{ addr: } word; \text{ sz: } size\triangleright$$

The information recorded in the ALAT does not have to be completely accurate to ensure the correct behavior of IA-64 programs. If the ALAT records a register as holding valid data, then that data must be valid; but the ALAT may falsely record that the data in a register is invalid. Such inaccuracy could cause suboptimal performance as it may force valid data to be reloaded, but the functional behavior of the program should be unaltered. There are many reasons why a particular implementation of the ALAT might exhibit such inaccuracy. For example, the ALAT may have fewer entries than there are registers. In order to capture the full generality of potential ALAT implementations, the specification presented gives only those properties that must be honored to guarantee correct program execution. This specification allows the ALAT to lose information in a variety of controlled ways. Indeed, an empty table would trivially satisfy the specification, though it would make for inefficient execution.

An ALAT will be modeled as a function from register indices to ALAT entries. The simplest operation on the ALAT does nothing except allow the ALAT to forget about the validity of one or more registers. This operation is called leak.

$$\models^{\mathsf{def}} (\neg(t\ i).\mathsf{valid} \implies \neg(\mathsf{leak}\ t\ i).\mathsf{valid}) \land \qquad\qquad [\mathsf{leak\_def}]$$
$$((\mathsf{leak}\ t\ i).\mathsf{valid} \implies \mathsf{leak}\ t\ i = t\ i)$$

The first clause of the definition asserts that the leak operation will not cause an invalid register to become valid. The second clause states that any register still valid after the leak has the same ALAT entry it had before.

A more constructive operation attempts to add information to the ALAT. The function validate t i a s attempts to add to the ALAT t the fact that register i contains valid data loaded from the region with address a and size s. It might not succeed, and it may cause the ALAT to forget about other registers.

$$\models^{\mathsf{def}} (\neg(t\ j).\mathsf{valid} \implies \neg(\mathsf{validate}\ t\ i\ a\ s\ j).\mathsf{valid} \lor i = j) \land \qquad [\mathsf{validate\_def}]$$
$$((\mathsf{validate}\ t\ i\ a\ s\ i).\mathsf{valid} \implies$$
$$\mathsf{validate}\ t\ i\ a\ s\ i = \triangleleft\mathsf{valid} := \mathsf{T}; \mathsf{addr} := a; \mathsf{sz} := s\triangleright) \land$$
$$(i \neq j \land (\mathsf{validate}\ t\ i\ a\ s\ j).\mathsf{valid} \implies \mathsf{validate}\ t\ i\ a\ s\ j = t\ j)$$

The first clause of this definition asserts that validating a register i will not cause any other register to become valid. The second clause asserts that if after validating register i, it is indeed valid, then i has associated with it the address and size supplied. The final clause states that if any other register is valid after the operation, the entry associated with it is unchanged.

The expression invalidate_single t i represents invalidating an individual register i from an ALAT t. Using invalidate_single may also invalidate other registers.

$$\models^{\mathsf{def}} (\neg(t\ j).\mathsf{valid} \implies \neg(\mathsf{invalidate\_single}\ t\ i\ j).\mathsf{valid}) \land \quad [\mathsf{invalidate\_single\_def}]$$
$$((\mathsf{invalidate\_single}\ t\ i\ j).\mathsf{valid} \implies i \neq j \land \mathsf{invalidate\_single}\ t\ i\ j = t\ j)$$

The operation invalidate_multiple t a s has the effect of invalidating in ALAT t all those registers loaded from regions that overlap the region with address a and size s. Other entries may also be invalidated as a result of this operation.

$\vdash^{\text{def}}(\neg(t\ i).\text{valid} \implies$ \hfill [invalidate_multiple_def]

$\qquad \neg(\text{invalidate\_multiple}\ t\ a\ s\ i).\text{valid}) \land$

$\qquad ((\text{invalidate\_multiple}\ t\ a\ s\ i).\text{valid} \implies$

$\qquad \neg\text{overlapped}\ (t\ i).\text{addr}\ (t\ i).\text{sz}\ a\ s \land \text{invalidate\_multiple}\ t\ a\ s\ i = t\ i)$

Further ALAT Freedoms: An ALAT has the freedom to lie, in a conservative way, about the information it records. An ALAT may report that a register contains invalid data, even when it records that the data is valid. A subsequent query about the register may correctly answer that the data is valid. To model this behavior, we need another function to check the validity of a register.

$\vdash^{\text{def}}\text{check}\ x\ t\ i \implies (t\ i).\text{valid}$ \hfill [check_def]

The important features of check are as follows:

- If check reports that a register is valid, then it really is valid.
- The value returned by check depends, in an unspecified way, on a variable x that represents an abstraction of the entire machine state.

3.5   The Machine State

The whole machine is modeled as a record of the components described thus far:

$state \overset{\text{def}}{=} \triangleleft$ip: *num*; — instruction pointer
$\qquad$ mem: *word* $\rightarrow$ *word*; — data memory
$\qquad$ grfile: *grindex* $\rightarrow$ *register*; — general purpose register file
$\qquad$ prfile: *prindex* $\rightarrow$ *bool*; — predicate register file
$\qquad$ alat: *grindex* $\rightarrow$ *alat_entry*; — advanced load address table
$\qquad$ unknown: *ind*$\triangleright$ — other unknown state

Two components of the state record were not previously alluded to. The instruction pointer ip stores the location of the current instruction in a separate instruction memory. The unknown field represents an abstraction of the other aspects of the state of an IA-64 that are not modeled here. Its purpose is to serve as an argument to under-specified functions where the result may depend on things other than those components of the state that have been modeled concretely. The type *ind* is used for unknown because little is known about it, except that it is large enough to encode a representation of the complete machine state.

4   IA-64 Instruction Semantics

To verify the optimizations presented in Sect. 2 we need to model the effect of executing an IA-64 program until a particular point in the code is reached. We will model the outcome of doing this with a new type *outcome*.

$\vdash^{\mathrm{def}}$ld_a p s r_1 r_2 σ =
  let $addr$ = reg_read σ.unknown σ.grfile r_2 in
  let $data$ = mem_read σ.mem $addr$.val s in
    if ¬pred_read σ.prfile p then
      STATE σ
    else if ¬reg_valid_dest r_1 then
      FAULT ILLEGAL_OPERATION
    else if $addr$.nat then
      FAULT NAT_CONSUMPTION
    else if ¬mem_valid_source $addr$.val s then
      FAULT ILLEGAL_LOAD
    else if mem_seq $addr$.val s then
      STATE σ with
            ◁grfile: = reg_write σ.grfile r_1 ◁val: = 0; nat: = F▷;
            alat: = invalidate_single σ.alat r_1▷
    else
      STATE σ with
            ◁grfile: = reg_write σ.grfile r_1 ◁val: = $data$; nat: = F▷;
            alat: = validate σ.alat r_1 $addr$.val s▷

p: predicate
s: size of data to load
r_1: destination register
r_2: register with source address
σ: initial state

Fig. 3. Meaning of the advanced load instruction

$outcome \overset{\mathrm{def}}{=}$ STATE $state$ — reaches nominated state
         | FAULT$fault$ — faults before reaching nominated state
         | ⊥   — neither faults nor reaches nominated state

The type $fault$ describes IA-64 faults visible to applications programmers (i.e., page faults are not included).

$fault \overset{\mathrm{def}}{=}$ NAT_CONSUMPTION | ILLEGAL_OPERATION ...

The meaning of each IA-64 instruction can be specified as a function from an initial state to an outcome. An example giving the definition of the advanced load instruction can be found in Fig. 3. The form of the definition is similar to that of the C pseudo code that defines this instruction in the architecture guide [6]. A type encompassing all IA-64 instructions can now be defined.

$inst \overset{\mathrm{def}}{=}$ LD $prindex$ $size$ $grindex$ $grindex$
       | LD_A $prindex$ $size$ $grindex$ $grindex$
       | LD_S $prindex$ $size$ $grindex$ $grindex$
       | CHK_A $prindex$ $grindex$ num
       $\vdots$

Assuming that we have a complete set of instruction meanings in the style of Fig. 3, we can define a function mapping instructions to their meaning.

$$\vdash^{def} \llbracket LD\ p\ s\ r_1\ r_2 \rrbracket = ld\ p\ s\ r_1\ r_2 \wedge \qquad\qquad\qquad \text{[inst\_sem\_def]}$$
$$\llbracket LD\_A\ p\ s\ r_1\ r_2 \rrbracket = ld\_a\ p\ s\ r_1\ r_2 \wedge$$
...

Some actions are common to all instructions and are therefore factored out. In particular, each instruction should advance the instruction pointer and change the unknown component of the state in some unspecified way. We define a function to return the unknown component of the next state, based on the current state σ and the instruction i. This function is completely unspecified.

$$\vdash^{def} \text{next\_unknown}\ \sigma\ i = x \Longrightarrow T \qquad\qquad\qquad \text{[next\_unknown\_def]}$$

We can now define a function **step** to advance the execution of a program in an instruction memory p by one step. Should an instruction cause a fault, **step** will make no further progress.

$$\vdash^{def} \text{step}\ p\ (\text{STATE}\ \sigma) = \qquad\qquad\qquad\qquad\qquad \text{[step\_def]}$$
$$\llbracket p\ \sigma.ip \rrbracket (\sigma\ \text{with} \lhd ip := \sigma.ip + 1;$$
$$\text{unknown} := \text{next\_unknown}\ \sigma\ (p\ \sigma.ip) \rhd) \wedge$$
$$\text{step}\ p\ (\text{FAULT}\ f) = \text{FAULT}\ f$$

4.1 Execution Sequences

The examples presented in Sect. 2 compare two programs by posing the question: Is the effect of one program when executed until it reaches some nominated instruction the same as that of another program when it is executed until it reaches a nominated instruction? To answer this question, we need to formalize what it means to execute a program until a nominated instruction is reached.

The first thing to note is that some executions of a program will raise faults, and therefore never reach a particular target instruction. To be more precise then, we are interested in what it means to execute a program until some nominated instruction is reached or a fault is raised. If l is the location of the instruction we are interested in, then the predicate at_or_fault l describes those outcomes where we have reached our goal.

$$\vdash^{def} \text{at\_or\_fault}\ l\ (\text{STATE}\ \sigma) = (\sigma.ip = l) \wedge \qquad\qquad \text{[at\_or\_fault\_def]}$$
$$\text{at\_or\_fault}\ l\ (\text{FAULT}\ f) = T$$

A program may contain loops, so during its execution it may execute the same instruction many times. When we talk about executing a particular program until a given instruction is reached, we are interested in the *first* time that instruction is reached. It simplifies the formalization to introduce a binder function that captures the concept of being 'the first.' We introduce the notation '$\mathcal{E}_1 n\cdot P\ n$' to represent the first number for which P holds. For example, $(\mathcal{E}_1 n\cdot n > 10)$ is 11.

$$\vdash^{def} (\exists n\cdot P\ n) \Longrightarrow \qquad\qquad\qquad\qquad\qquad\qquad\qquad \text{[$\mathcal{E}_1$\_def]}$$
$$P\ (\mathcal{E}_1 n\cdot P\ n) \wedge (\forall m\cdot m < (\mathcal{E}_1 n\cdot P\ n) \Longrightarrow \neg P\ m)$$

Using $\mathcal{E}_1$, we can define the expression $(f\ \mathsf{until}\ P)\ o$ to represent repeatedly applying the function f to o until some desired outcome, characterized by P, is reached. This expression yields $\bot$ if the desired outcome can never be reached.

$$\vdash^{\mathsf{def}} (f\ \mathsf{until}\ P)\ o = \mathsf{if}\ (\exists n\cdot P\ (f^n\ o))\ \mathsf{then}\ f^{(\mathcal{E}_1 n\cdot P\ (f^n\ o))}\ o\ \mathsf{else}\ \bot \qquad [\mathsf{until\_def}]$$

We can now phrase as follows the meaning of 'executing the program in p until the instruction at l is reached.'

$$(\mathsf{step}\ p)\ \mathsf{until}\ (\mathsf{at\_or\_fault}\ l)$$

4.2   Reasoning about until

The following theorem allows us to reason about IA-64 programs using a form of symbolic simulation within the theorem prover. It allows us to take repeated steps in the program until we reach the desired outcome.

$$\begin{aligned}
\vdash ((\mathsf{step}\ p)\ \mathsf{until}\ (\mathsf{at\_or\_fault}\ l))\ (\mathsf{STATE}\ \sigma) = & \qquad [\mathsf{until\_step\_thm}]\\
&\mathsf{if}\ \sigma.\mathsf{ip} = l\ \mathsf{then}\\
&\quad \mathsf{STATE}\ \sigma\\
&\mathsf{else}\\
&\quad ((\mathsf{step}\ p)\ \mathsf{until}\ (\mathsf{at\_or\_fault}\ l))\ (\mathsf{step}\ p\ (\mathsf{STATE}\ \sigma))\ \wedge\\
&((\mathsf{step}\ p)\ \mathsf{until}\ (\mathsf{at\_or\_fault}\ l))\ (\mathsf{FAULT}\ f) = \mathsf{FAULT}\ f
\end{aligned}$$

The proof of this theorem follows from a more general property of $\mathcal{E}_1$.

$$\vdash \neg P\ 0 \wedge (\exists n\cdot P\ n) \Longrightarrow (\mathcal{E}_1 n\cdot P\ n) = (\mathcal{E}_1 n\cdot P\ (n+1)) + 1 \qquad [\mathsf{first\_suc\_thm}]$$

5   Equivalent Behavior

We now need to consider what it means for two programs to be equivalent. It may be too strong a requirement to insist that the behavior of an optimized program be identical to that of the original code. For example, consider the two programs presented in Fig. 2. If the address in register r1 is not a valid destination, then both these programs will raise an ILLEGAL_STORE fault. Similarly, if the address in register r4 is not a valid source, then both will raise an ILLEGAL_LOAD fault. If both these conditions hold then the unoptimized code will raise an ILLEGAL_STORE fault and the optimized code will raise an ILLEGAL_LOAD fault. Nevertheless, we might still consider these programs to be equivalent. More precisely, we will consider the behavior of two programs to be equivalent when they both raise faults, without insisting that they raise the same fault. Equivalence of behavior will therefore be defined on outcomes rather than simply being defined on states.

The programs shown in Fig. 1 are even more problematic. In the case where predicate register p1 holds false then their behavior is the same, but when p1 holds true then the optimized code writes data to register r9 where the unoptimized code does not. This will be a problem unless r9 is a scratch register, the contents of which are not of ongoing interest. Assuming that is the case, our notion of equivalence needs to be broadened to encompass programs with identical behavior across a nominated set of interesting registers.

We begin by defining an equivalence relation on register files that holds if some initial region of the register files are the same.

$$\models^{\mathsf{def}}(f_1 \cong_n f_2) = \hspace{4cm} \text{[grfile\_eq\_def]}$$
$$n \leq \mathsf{sof} \wedge (\forall i\, x_1\, x_2 {\cdot} i < n \Longrightarrow \mathsf{reg\_read}\, x_1\, f_1\, i = \mathsf{reg\_read}\, x_2\, f_2\, i)$$

The following properties are important when reasoning about register files.[4]

$$\vdash f \cong_n f \hspace{6cm} \text{[grfile\_eq\_refl\_thm]}$$

$$\vdash (i \geq n) \Longrightarrow \hspace{5cm} \text{[grfile\_eq\_above\_thm]}$$
$$((\mathsf{reg\_write}\, f_1\, i\, v) \cong_n f_2) = (f_1 \cong_n f2) \wedge$$
$$(f_2 \cong_n (\mathsf{reg\_write}\, f_2\, i\, v)) = (f_1 \cong_n f2)$$

Having defined an equivalence relation on register files, we can now define one on execution outcomes.

$$\models^{\mathsf{def}}(\mathsf{STATE}\, \sigma_1 \cong_n \mathsf{STATE}\, \sigma_2) = \hspace{3cm} \text{[outcome\_eq\_def]}$$
$$(\sigma_1.\mathsf{mem} = \sigma_2.\mathsf{mem} \wedge \sigma_1.\mathsf{grfile} \cong_n \sigma_2.\mathsf{grfile} \wedge \sigma_1.\mathsf{prfile} = \sigma_2.\mathsf{prfile}) \wedge$$
$$(\mathsf{STATE}\, \sigma \cong_n \mathsf{FAULT}\, f) = \mathsf{F} \wedge$$
$$(\mathsf{STATE}\, \sigma \cong_n \bot) = \mathsf{F} \wedge$$
$$(\mathsf{FAULT}\, f \cong_n \mathsf{STATE}\, \sigma) = \mathsf{F} \wedge$$
$$(\mathsf{FAULT}\, f_1 \cong_n \mathsf{FAULT}\, f_2) = \mathsf{T} \wedge$$
$$(\mathsf{FAULT}\, f \cong_n \bot) = \mathsf{F} \wedge$$
$$(\bot \cong_n \mathsf{STATE}\, \sigma) = \mathsf{F} \wedge$$
$$(\bot \cong_n \mathsf{FAULT}\, f) = \mathsf{F} \wedge$$
$$(\bot \cong_n \bot) = \mathsf{T}$$

6   Example Proof

We can now return to a formal examination of the examples given in Sect. 2. We will consider only the example using data speculation, as its proof is the more challenging. We begin by specifying two instruction memories containing the original and optimized versions of the code from Fig. 2. Note that all instructions in these programs are unconditional, and hence predicated on register 0.

$$\models^{\mathsf{def}}\mathsf{original}\ 1000 = \mathsf{ST}\ 0\ 2\ 1\ 2 \wedge \hspace{3cm} \text{[original\_def]}$$
$$\mathsf{original}\ 1001 = \mathsf{LD}\ 0\ 4\ 3\ 4$$

---

[4] The equivalence relation $\cong_n$ is also symmetric and transitive as expected, but these properties are not used in the proofs described here.

$\vdash^{def}$optimized 2000 = LD_A 0 4 3 4 ∧   [optimized_def]
    optimized 2001 = ST 0 2 1 2 ∧
    optimized 2002 = CHK_A 0 3 4000 ∧
    optimized 4000 = LD 0 4 3 4 ∧
    optimized 4001 = BR 0 2003

The problem can now be stated as follows:

(STATE $\sigma_1 \cong_5$ STATE σ_2) ∧
reg_valid_source 1 ∧ reg_valid_source 2 ∧ reg_valid_source 4 ∧
σ_1.ip = 1000 ∧ σ_2.ip = 2000 $\Longrightarrow$
    (step original) until (at_or_fault 1002) (STATE σ_1) $\cong_5$
    (step optimized) until (at_or_fault 2003) (STATE σ_2)

Note that equivalence between the executions can be proved only when the source registers are valid, as reading invalid registers returns unspecified results. Note also that the problem has been phrased using constant register names. We could also use variables to model symbolic register names, provided we add further assumptions asserting that the variables hold distinct values.

To start the proof, we substitute concrete records for the states σ_1 and σ_2. The assumptions allow us to select records with many common fields. We then separate out those assumptions that remain of interest, yielding the goal below:

- $r_1 \cong_5 r_2$
- reg_valid_source 1 • reg_valid_source 2 • reg_valid_source 4

(step original) until (at_or_fault 1002)
    (STATE ◁ip: = 1000; mem: = m; grfile: = r_1;
            prfile: = p; alat: = a_1; unknown: = x_1▷) $\cong_5$
(step optimized) until (at_or_fault 2003)
    (STATE ◁ip: = 2000; mem: = m; grfile: = r_2;
            prfile: = p; alat: = a_2; unknown: = x_2▷)

The records in this goal describe the symbolic state for both programs before any instructions have executed. Since neither program has reached its target instruction, we can use the theorems until_step_thm, step_def and inst_sem_def (see Sect. 4) to progress the symbolic execution of both programs as follows:

. . .

(step original) until (at_or_fault 1002)
    ((st 0 2 1 2) (STATE ◁ip: = 1001; mem: = m; grfile: = r_1;
            prfile: = p; alat: = a_1; unknown: = x_3▷)) $\cong_5$
(step optimized) until (at_or_fault 2003)
    ((ld_a 0 4 3 4) (STATE ◁ip: = 2001; mem: = m; grfile: = r_2;
            prfile: = p; alat: = a_2; unknown: = x_4▷))

The values of the two unknown fields in the goal are actually expressions involving the next_unknown, the instruction, and the previous state. Since these fields contain no useful information, it is clearer if we generalize the proof by replacing them with fresh variables, as shown above.

The next step is to expand the definitions of st and ld_a. The definition of ld_a was presented in Fig. 3. These, and other, IA-64 instructions are defined as a selection among possible outcomes. We can use case analysis to reduce the resulting complex goal, that compares two conditionally defined outcomes, to a collection of simpler goals in which outcomes are compared under different premises. This step generates twenty subgoals, of which the following is among the most interesting.[5]

- $r_1 \cong_5 r_2$
- reg_valid_source 2
- reg_valid_dest 3
- $\neg$(reg_read x_3 r_2 2).nat
- mem_valid_dest (reg_read x_3 r_2 1).val 2
- mem_valid_source (reg_read x_4 r_2 4).val 4
- $\neg$(mem_seq (reg_read x_4 r_2 4).val 4)

- reg_valid_source 1
- reg_valid_source 4
- $\neg$(reg_read x_3 r_2 1).nat
- $\neg$(reg_read x_4 r_2 4).nat

(step original) until (at_or_fault 1002)
  (STATE ◁ip = 1001;
       mem: =
       mem_write m (reg_read x_3 r_2 1).val 2 (reg_read x_3 r_2 2)
       grfile: = r_1;
       prfile: = p;
       alat: = invalidate_multiple a_1 (reg_read x_3 r_2 1).val 2;
       unknown: = x_3▷) $\cong_5$
(step optimized) until (at_or_fault 2003)
  (STATE ◁ip: = 2001;
       mem: = m
       grfile: =
         reg_write r_2 3 ◁val: = mem_read m (reg_read x_4 r_2 4).val 4;
                     nat: = F▷;
       prfile: = p;
       alat: = validate a_2 3 (reg_read x_4 r_2 4).val 4;
       unknown: = x_4▷)

Here the execution of both programs has progressed by one instruction, without encountering a fault. The goal has also accumulated a number of assumptions that will reduce the number of case splits needed for successive symbolic simulation steps. We repeat this process until each outcome in every goal is reduced to either FAULT or a STATE where the instruction pointer has reached the target. Each goal can then be reduced using outcome_eq_def (see Sect. 5). Because of the trivial equivalence of any two faulting outcomes, only four goals remain unsolved by this process.

Of the four subgoals that remain after symbolic simulation, two can be discharged by conditional rewriting with theorems about reading and writing registers and memory (see Sect. 3). This could be done as part of each symbolic

---

[5] The assumption $r_1 \cong_5 r_2$ has been used so that all reads refer to register file r_2.

simulation step, but it is faster if done just once at the end. The two remaining goals capture the heart of the problem, they hinge on the behavior of the ALAT.

In the first goal we see both programs have written data to register 3. The original program wrote the result of a read from memory, but the optimized program wrote the value zero. This must be the result of the advanced load having failed, causing a zero to be written, and the second load not having been performed. This should not happen, and indeed there is a contradiction in the assumptions. We have assumed that a check on register 3 in the ALAT succeeds, which is not possible since we have performed the operation invalidate_single on that register. This goal can be solved with the HOL Light model elimination procedure, MESON_TAC, using the ALAT definitions (see Sect. 3.4).

> $\cdots$
> - check x'
> $$\frac{\text{(invalidate\_multiple (invalidate\_single } a_2\ 3)\ (\text{reg\_read } x_3\ r_2\ 1).\text{val } 2)\ 3}{\text{reg\_write } r_1\ 3\ \lhd\text{val:} = \text{mem\_read} \ldots (\text{reg\_read } x_3\ r_2\ 2)\ 4;\text{nat:} = F\rhd \cong_5}$$
>   reg_write r_2 3 $\lhd$val: = 0; nat: = F$\rhd$

In the second case, both programs have loaded register 3 with four bytes read from memory at the address held in register 2. However, the loads have been performed on different memories. In the unoptimized code, the memory was first modified by writing two bytes to the address held in register 1. The values loaded to register 3 will be the same provided the memory regions read and written do not overlap. This fact is embodied in an assumption of the goal.

> $\cdots$
> - check x''
> $$\frac{\begin{array}{l}(\text{invalidate\_multiple (validate } a_2\ 3\ (\text{reg\_read } x_4\ r_2\ 4).\text{val } 4)\\ (\text{reg\_read } x_3\ r_2\ 1\ ).\text{val } 2)\ 3\end{array}}{\begin{array}{l}\text{reg\_write } r_2\ 3\\ \quad \lhd\text{val:} = \text{mem\_read}\\ \qquad\qquad (\text{mem\_write } m\ (\text{reg\_read } x_3\ r_2\ 1).\text{val } 2\ (\text{reg\_read } x_3\ r_2\ 2).\text{val})\\ \qquad\qquad (\text{reg\_read } x_4\ r_2\ 4).\text{val } 4;\\ \quad \text{nat:} = F\rhd \cong_5\\ \text{reg\_write } r_2\ 3\ \lhd\text{val:} = \text{mem\_read } m\ (\text{reg\_read } x_4\ r_2\ 4).\text{val } 4;\text{nat:} = F\rhd\end{array}}$$

The assumption shown states that register 3 was set valid and associated with the memory region that was read. An invalidate_multiple operation was then performed, invalidating all registers with data read from regions overlapping the region of memory that was written. A check of register 3 then asserts that it is still valid, from which we can deduce that the regions of memory read and written do not overlap. We can prove this lemma using MESON_TAC on the definitions of the ALAT operations. Once proved, we can use it and the definition of mem_write (see Sect. 3.1) to solve the goal.

Both the examples presented in this paper were proved using HOL Light, as have other small examples using data speculation and transforming branching code into straight-line code using predication. All the proofs had the same form as the one just presented, in which the majority of the proof is completed by symbolic simulation and rewriting. None required any more user interaction to complete than was needed for the proof just presented.

7 Conclusion

This paper described a formal model for a significant portion of Intel's forthcoming IA-64 architecture. Theorems were proved about the model that allowed a symbolic simulator to be built using the HOL Light theorem prover. This system can be used to largely automate simple optimization proofs for assembly-level IA-64 code.

The scope of this research is intentionally limited. The problems considered are small, staying at the level of individual optimizing transformations rather than proofs about entire programs. Likewise the properties proved are modest, checking only for equivalence between two similar programs rather than attempting to prove general correctness properties. By limiting the scope of the problem it was possible to find a solution that is largely automated. Indeed, the proofs could likely be more automated than they already are. The motivation for this approach comes from hardware verification where automated techniques with limited scope, like equivalence checking, have found industrial markets where more general interactive techniques have fared less well.

8 Future Work

One class of optimization not addressed by the work described here is software pipelining of loops. In these optimizations the original loop is transformed into a new loop where each cycle of the transformed loop executes instructions that correspond to steps within the execution of several successive iterations of the original loop. The transformation reduces data dependencies between instructions within the loop, thereby hiding the latency of the slower instructions. The term 'software pipelining' derives from an analogy with hardware pipelining, where each cycle executes steps from several successive instructions. The IA-64 includes several features that actively support the software pipelining of loops. We believe we can attack the problem of verifying transformations that pipeline a loop by building on the framework presented here using techniques analogous to those used to verify the equivalence of unpipelined and pipelined hardware implementations [1].

9 Related Work

In this paper we have demonstrated a system for verifying optimizing transformations to IA-64 assembly code. Perhaps the most closely related work is that of the Refinement Calculator project, which has built a general system to support program transformation and refinement in HOL [2,10]. The work here differs from that in the following ways:

- Here we have worked with an unstructured assembly-level language, where as the Refinement Calculator (and similar transformation systems) manipulates structured programs.
- The work here has pursued a high degree of automation using symbolic simulation, where as systems like the Refinement Calculator usually focus on supporting a user-guided interactive style of reasoning.

Acknowledgements

This research was performed while the author was visiting the Microcomputer Software Laboratory of the Intel Corporation. Financial support was supplied by the Intel Corporation and the Australian Research Council. The author would like to thank John Harrison for his encouragement, support in visiting Intel, and his help with using HOL Light. Valuable feedback was provided by the anonymous referees.

References

1. Jerry R. Burch and David L. Dill. Automatic verification of pipelined microprocessor control. In David L. Dill, editor, *Computer Aided Verification: Proceedings of the 6th International Conference (CAV'94)*, volume 818 of *Lecture Notes in Computer Science*, pages 68–80, Stanford, California, June 1994. Springer-Verlag.
2. Michael Butler, Jim Grundy, Thomas Långbacka, Rimvydas Rukšėnas, and Joakim von Wright. The refinement calculator: proof support for program refinement. In Lindsay Groves and Steve Reeves, editors, *Formal Methods Pacific'97: Proceedings of FMP'97*, Discrete Mathematics and Theoretical Computer Science, pages 40–61, Victoria University of Wellington, New Zealand, March 1997. Springer-Verlag.
3. Carole Dulong. The IA-64 architecture at work. *Computer*, 31(7):24–32, July 1998.
4. Mike Gordon. A formalization of a simplified subset of the Alpha shared memory model. http://www.cl.cam.ac.uk/Research/HVG/FTP/FTP.html#papers.
5. John Harrison. *The HOL Light Manual*. University of Cambridge, Computer Laboratory, New Museums Site, Pembroke Street, Cambridge CB2 3QG, England, edition 1.0, May 1998.
6. Intel. IA-64 application developer's architecture guide. Order number 245188, Intel Corporation, Santa Clara CA, USA, May 1999.
7. Robert Brent Jones. *Applications of Symbolic Simulation to the Verification of Microprocessors*. PhD thesis, Stanford University, Department of Electrical Engineering, 161 Packard, 350 Serra Mall, Stanford CA 94305, USA, August 1999.
8. Michael Norrish and Konrad Slind. *The HOL System Description*. University of Cambridge, Computer Laboratory, New Museums Site, Pembroke Street, Cambridge CB2 3QG, England, hol98 Taupo-2 edition, February 2000.
9. SPARC International. *The SPARC Architecture Manual*. Prentice-Hall, New Jersey, 8th edition, 1992.
10. Joakim von Wright and Kaisa Sere. Program transformations and refinements in HOL. In Myla Archer, Jeffrey J. Joyce, Karl N. Levitt, and Phillip J. Windley, editors, *The HOL Theorem Proving and its Applications: International Workshop*, pages 231–239, University of California at Davis, August 1991. ACM-SIGDA, IEEE Computer Society Press.

Formal Verification of IA-64 Division Algorithms

John Harrison

Intel Corporation, EY2-03
5200 NE Elam Young Parkway
Hillsboro, OR 97124, USA

Abstract. The IA-64 architecture defers floating point and integer division to software. To ensure correctness and maximum efficiency, Intel provides a number of recommended algorithms which can be called as subroutines or inlined by compilers and assembly language programmers. All these algorithms have been subjected to formal verification using the HOL Light theorem prover. As well as improving our level of confidence in the algorithms, the formal verification process has led to a better understanding of the underlying theory, allowing some significant efficiency improvements.

1 Introduction

IA-64 is a new 64-bit computer architecture jointly developed by Hewlett-Packard and Intel, and the Intel Itanium™ processor is its first silicon implementation. We will summarize below the details of the IA-64 instruction set architecture (ISA) necessary for the present paper. A more complete description may be found in the IA-64 Application Developer's Architecture Guide, available from Intel in printed form and online.[1]

To avoid some of the limitations of traditional architectures, IA-64 incorporates a unique combination of features, including an instruction format encoding parallelism explicitly, instruction predication, and speculative/advanced loads [4]. Nevertheless, it also offers full upwards-compatibility with IA-32 (x86) code.

1.1 The IA-64 Floating Point Architecture

The IA-64 floating point architecture has been carefully designed to allow high performance. Features include multiple floating-point status fields and special instructions for transferring data between integer and floating point registers. The centerpiece of the architecture is the `fma` (floating point multiply-add or fused multiply-accumulate) instruction. This computes $xy + z$ from inputs x, y and z with a single rounding error. Except for subtleties over signed zeros, floating point addition and multiplication are just degenerate cases of `fma`, $1y + z$ and $xy + 0$, so do not need separate instructions. Variants of the `fma` switch signs of operands: `fms` computes $xy - z$ while `fnma` computes $z - xy$.

---

[1] See http://developer.intel.com/design/ia64/downloads/adag.htm.

J. Harrison and M. Aagaard (Eds.): TPHOLs 2000, LNCS 1869, pp. 233–251, 2000.

The IA-64 architecture supports several different floating point formats compatible with the IEEE 754 Standard for Binary Floating-Point Arithmetic [10]. For the four most important formats, we give the conventional name, the precision, and the minimum and maximum exponents. Thus, numbers in a format with precision p and minimum and maximum exponent E_{min} and E_{max} are those representable as:

$$\pm d_0 . d_1 d_2 d_3 \cdots d_{p-1} \times 2^e$$

with the $d_i \in \{0, 1\}$ and $E_{min} \le e \le E_{max}$.

Format name	p	E_{min}	E_{max}
Single	24	-126	127
Double	53	-1022	1023
Double-extended	64	-16382	16383
Register	64	-65534	65535

The single and double formats are mandated and completely specified in the Standard. The double-extended format (we will often just call it 'extended') is recommended and only partially specified by the Standard. The register format has the same precision as extended, but allows greater exponent range, helping to avoid overflows and underflows in intermediate calculations. As well as these "scalar" formats, IA-64 features a SIMD format where two single-precision numbers are packed in a floating point register and the pair operated on in parallel. Numerically, this amounts to just two parallel copies of the single-precision format, but pragmatically it places different demands on the programmer since one can no longer use higher intermediate precision or range while maintaining the additional level of parallelism.

Most operations, including the fma, take arguments and return results in some of the 128 floating point registers provided for by IA-64, in which floating point numbers from all formats map onto a standard bit encoding. By a combination of settings in the multiple status fields and completers on instructions, the results of operations can be rounded in any of the four IEEE rounding modes (to nearest, towards positive or negative infinity, and towards zero) and into any of the supported floating point formats, whatever format the operands come from.

1.2 Division in Software

In most current computer architectures, in particular the Intel IA-32 (x86) architecture currently represented by the Pentium® III processor, instructions are specified for the floating point and integer division operations. In IA-64, the only instruction specifically intended to support division is the *floating point reciprocal approximation* instruction, frcpa. This merely provides an approximate reciprocal which software can use to generate a correctly rounded quotient. There are several reasons for relegating division to software.

- By implementing division in software it immediately inherits the high degree of pipelining in the basic fma operations. Even though these operations take several clock cycles, new ones can be started each cycle while others are in progress. Hence, many division operations can proceed in parallel, leading to much higher throughput than is the case with typical hardware implementations.
- Greater flexibility is afforded because alternative algorithms can be substituted where it is advantageous. It is often the case that in a particular context a faster algorithm suffices, e.g. because the ambient IEEE rounding mode is known at compile-time, or even because only a moderately accurate result is required (e.g. in some graphics applications).
- In typical applications, division is not an extremely frequent operation, and so it may be that die area on the chip would be better devoted to something else. However it is not so infrequent that a grossly inefficient software solution is acceptable, so the rest of the architecture needs to be designed to allow reasonably fast software implementations.

1.3   Formal Floating Point Theory

The formal verifications are conducted using the freely available[2] HOL Light prover [7]. HOL Light is a version of HOL [5], itself a descendent of Edinburgh LCF [6] which first defined the 'LCF approach' that these systems take to formal proof. LCF provers explicitly generate proofs in terms of extremely low-level primitive inferences, in order to provide a high level of assurance that the proofs are valid. In HOL Light, as in most other LCF-style provers, the proofs (which can be very large) are not usually stored permanently, but the strict reduction to primitive inferences in maintained by the abstract type system of the interaction and implementation language, which for HOL Light is CAML Light [16,3]. This language serves as a programming medium allowing higher-level derived rules (e.g. to automate linear arithmetic, first order logic or reasoning in other special domains) to be programmed as reductions to primitive inferences, so that proofs can be partially automated. In general, however, the user must describe the proof at a moderate level of detail.

The verifications described here draw extensively on a formalized theory of real analysis [8] and floating point arithmetic [9]. These sources should be consulted for more details, but we now summarize some of the main formal concepts used in the present paper.

HOL notation is generally close to traditional logical and mathematical notation. However, the type system distinguishes natural numbers and real numbers, and maps between them by &; hence &2 is the real number 2. The multiplicative inverse x^{-1} is written inv(x), the absolute value $|x|$ as abs(x) and the power x^n as x pow n.

Much of the theory of floating point numbers is generic. Formats are identified by triples of natural numbers fmt and the corresponding set of representable real

---

[2] See http://www.cl.cam.ac.uk/users/jrh/hol-light/index.html.

numbers, ignoring the upper limit on the exponent range, is iformat fmt. The second field of the triple, extracted by the function precision, is the precision, i.e. the number of significand bits. The third field, extracted by the ulpscale function, is N where 2^{-N} is the smallest nonzero floating point number of the format.

Floating-point rounding is performed by round fmt rc x which denotes the result of rounding the real number x into a floating point format fmt under rounding mode rc, neglecting the upper limit on exponent range. The predicate normalizes determines whether a real number is within the range of normal floating point numbers in a particular format, i.e. those representable with a leading 1 in the significand, while losing determines whether a real number will lose precision, i.e. underflow, when rounded to a given format.

An important concept in floating point arithmetic is a unit in the last place or *ulp*. Though widely used by floating point experts, there are a number of divergent definitions and care is needed in the formalization [9]. To understand the present paper, the following is adequate: if x is any real number and fmt identifies a floating point format, then ulp fmt x ('an ulp in x with respect to floating point format fmt') is the distance between the two closest floating point numbers straddling x.

The canonical sign, exponent and significand fields for a representable real number are extracted by functions decode_sign, decode_exponent and decode _fraction. Actual floating-point register bitstrings are distinguished from the real numbers they represent, and the mapping from bitstrings to reals is performed by a function Val. Whether a floating point number is normal is determined by a predicate normal.

2   Perfect Rounding

The IEEE Standard for Binary Floating-Point arithmetic [10] specifies that the result of division (as with other basic algebraic operations such as addition, multiplication and square root) should be as if the ideal mathematical result were calculated exactly then rounded in the appropriate rounding mode. Later we examine in detail how to make sure of this for division, but first some general discussion of perfect rounding and the related HOL proofs seems appropriate. Suppose x is the exact result of the operation, e.g. a/b in the case of division, and the calculated answer is z. Whatever the implementation, z will result from rounding an ideal mathematical answer, say y, to some operation. Anticipating later examples, suppose the final step of a division algorithm computes the final quotient from three arguments q, r and y by means of the fma operation:

$$\text{fma.}\,pc.\,sf\ \ q = r_3,\ y_3,\ q_3$$

Because the fma itself conforms to (the obvious extrapolation of) the IEEE Standard, the result q arises from rounding the exact mathematical value $q^* = r_3 y_3 + q_3$ in the intended rounding mode. We need to ensure that whatever the rounding mode, q^* and the exact quotient a/b round to the same floating point number.

2.1 Sufficient Conditions for Perfect Rounding

In the following diagram the longer markings denote floating point numbers and the shorter ones the midpoints between floating point numbers. Assuming we are in round-to-nearest mode, $\frac{a}{b}$ will round to the number below it, but q^* to the number above it.

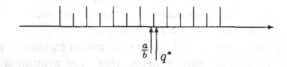

A little reflection shows that in order to ensure perfect rounding in the round-to-nearest mode, a sufficient condition is that q^* and a/b are never separated by a midpoint, for which in turn it suffices that for any midpoint m we have $|a/b - q^*| < |a/b - m|$. Quite generally, we can prove in HOL the following theorem:

```
⊢  ¬(precision fmt = 0) ∧
   (∀m. m ∈ midpoints fmt ⟹ abs(x - y) < abs(x - m))
   ⟹ (round fmt Nearest x = round fmt Nearest y)
```

Obviously this precondition cannot be satisfied if a/b is exactly a midpoint. However it is easy to prove that this cannot occur *provided the quotient is in the normal range*:

```
⊢  a ∈ iformat fmt ∧ b ∈ iformat fmt ∧
   ¬(b = &0) ∧ normalizes fmt (a / b)
   ⟹ ¬(a / b ∈ midpoints fmt)
```

For other rounding modes, an analogous property is required for floating point numbers rather than midpoints. To ensure correctness for all rounding modes, the following suffices.

```
⊢  ¬(precision fmt = 0) ∧
   (∀a. a ∈ iformat(exprange fmt,precision fmt + 1,ulpscale fmt + 1)
        ⟹ abs(x - y) < abs(x - a))
   ⟹ (round fmt rc x = round fmt rc y)
```

Note that we state the theorem in terms of a floating point format with one extra bit of precision, which is exactly the floating point numbers plus midpoints:

```
⊢  ¬(p = 0)
   ⟹ (midpoints(E,p,N) ∪ iformat(E,p,N) = iformat(E,p+1,N+1))
```

Since it is possible for the quotient to be exactly a floating point number, or the midpoint between denormal numbers (e.g. $1.11\cdots11\times2^{E_{min}}/2$), we need to deal with these special cases separately. As we shall see, these work automatically for the algorithms as they are structured here.

2.2   Flag Settings

We must ensure not only correct results in all rounding modes, but that the flags are set correctly. However, this essentially follows in general from the correctness of the result in all rounding modes (strictly, in the case of underflow, we need to verify this for a format with slightly larger exponent range). For the correct setting of the inexact flag, we need only prove the following HOL theorem:

```
⊢  ¬(precision fmt = 0) ∧
   (∀rc. round fmt rc x = round fmt rc y)
   ⟹ ∀rc. (round fmt rc x = x) = (round fmt rc y = y)
```

The proof is simple: if x rounds to itself, then it must be representable. But by hypothesis, y rounds to the same thing, that is x, in *all rounding modes*. In particular the roundings up and down imply x <= y and x >= y, so y = x. The other way round is similar.

2.3   Exclusion Zones

The theorems above show that provided q^* and a/b are closer to each other than a/b is to a floating point number or midpoint, correct rounding is assured. One approach to proving this for a given algorithm is to ask: how close can a/b be to a floating point number or midpoint? A little work allows us to provide an answer to that question [2], which we can formalize as the following HOL theorem:

```
⊢  a ∈ iformat(E,p,N) ∧
   b ∈ iformat(E,p,N) ∧
   c ∈ iformat(E,p+1,N+1) ∧
   &2 pow (p - 1) / &2 pow N <= abs(a) ∧
   ¬(b = &0)
   ⟹ (a / b = c) ∨
      abs(a / b - c) >= abs(a / b) / &2 pow (2 * p + 2)
```

It can be read as saying that every floating point number or midpoint c is surrounded by an 'exclusion zone' of size approximately $\frac{|c|}{2^{2p+2}}$ within which no floating point quotient can lie. This implies that if a/b is not exactly a floating point number, then having:

$$|q^* - a/b| < \frac{|a/b|}{2^{2p+2}}$$

would suffice for perfect rounding. By using higher intermediate precision together with the benefit of the fma, this kind of relative error can be achieved without trouble, and some of the Intel division algorithms can be verified using the above property. However, in the case of extended precision or SIMD operation, we have no higher intermediate precision available. Then even the `fma` does not quite allow us to guarantee getting q^* that close to a/b in a straightforward way, and we must prove more precise theorems, which we discuss below.

A refinement of the 'exclusion zone' approach is not only to identify the width of the exclusion zone but to isolate the inputs a and b where the quotients lie closest to floating point numbers or midpoints. Then one can get away with a worse error bound provided those special cases also work correctly, which one can verify by explicitly running through the algorithm. For the square root, this approach works well [2], and one can feasibly isolate a moderate number of 'difficult cases', allowing a uniform and effective way of verifying square root algorithms (which we have used in analogous verifications for square root). For division, there are too many solutions for a and b for this to be a feasible approach for verification. However, once either a or b is fixed — for example in the special case of finding reciprocals — the number of solutions is typically quite moderate.

3 Implementing Division on IA-64

The general form of the IA-64 assembly language `frcpa` instruction is:

```
frcpa.sf q, p = a, b
```

where q, a and b are floating point registers, p is a predicate register, and sf is a floating-point status field. Essentially, a and b are the dividend and divisor respectively, and q is the destination register for the result. The status field sf controls the behavior in exceptional cases, e.g. division by zero, and the predicate register p is set to `false` if the inputs were exceptional, e.g. if a or b was zero. In the exceptional cases, q is set to the IEEE-correct quotient, either directly by the hardware or via a SWA (software assistance) trap, and no further action is necessary. Otherwise p is set to `true` and q is set to an approximation of $1/b$ with a guaranteed relative error:

$$|q - 1/b| \leq 2^{-8.86}|1/b|$$

(In fact, the ISA specifies the details of the approximation more precisely, so that the particular value, which by the way has at most 11 significant bits, is predictable on all IA-64 processors.) Software is then expected to use this to arrive at the IEEE-correct quotient, i.e. the result that would be obtained if the quotient were calculated exactly then rounded using the ambient IEEE rounding mode. Moreover, the six IEEE flags must be set correctly, e.g. the inexact flag is set if and only if the quotient is not exactly a floating point number.

3.1 Intel-Provided Algorithms

It is not immediately obvious that without tricky and time-consuming bit-twiddling, it is possible to produce an IEEE-correct result and set all the IEEE flags correctly via ordinary software. Remarkably, however, fairly short straight-line sequences of fma operations (or negated variants), suffice to do so. This approach to division was pioneered by Markstein [11] on the IBM RS/6000[3] family. It seems that the ability to perform both a multiply and an add or subtract without an intermediate rounding is essential to this, but besides its utility here, the fma has many other benefits in improving floating point performance and accuracy.

Intel provides a number of recommended division and square root algorithms, in the form of short sequences of straight-line code written in IA-64 assembly language. The intention is that these can be inlined by compilers, used as the core of mathematical libraries, or called on as macros by assembly language programmers. The algorithms are available for download from:

http://developer.intel.com/software/opensource/numerics.htm

All the Intel-provided algorithms have been carefully designed to provide IEEE-correct results and trigger IEEE flags and exceptions appropriately. Subject to this correctness constraint, they have been written to maximize performance on the Itanium™ processor. However, they are also likely to be the most appropriate algorithms for future IA-64 processors, even those with significantly different hardware characteristics.

Separate algorithms are provided for the main IA-64 floating point formats (single, double, extended and SIMD), since faster algorithms are usually possible when the required precision is lower. As well as the multiplicity of formats, most algorithms have two separate variants, one of which is designed to minimize latency (i.e. the number of clock cycles between starting the operation and having the result available), and the other to maximize throughput (the number of operations executed per cycle, averaged over a large number of independent instances). Which variant is best to use depends on the kind of program within which it is being invoked.

3.2   Refining Approximations

First we will describe in general terms how we can use fma operations to refine an initial reciprocal approximation towards a better reciprocal or quotient approximation. For clarity of exposition, we will ignore rounding errors at this stage, and later show how they are taken account of in the formal proof. In the next subsection we cover the subtler issue of guaranteeing correct rounding.

Consider determining the reciprocal of some floating point value b. Starting with a reciprocal approximation y with a relative error ϵ:

$$y = \frac{1}{b}(1 + \epsilon)$$

we can perform just one fnma operation:

---

[3] All other trademarks are the property of their respective owners.

$$e = 1 - by$$

and get:

$$
\begin{aligned}
e &= 1 - by \\
&= 1 - b\frac{1}{b}(1 + \epsilon) \\
&= 1 - (1 + \epsilon) \\
&= -\epsilon
\end{aligned}
$$

Now observe that:

$$
\begin{aligned}
\frac{1}{b} &= \frac{y}{(1 + \epsilon)} \\
&= y(1 - \epsilon + \epsilon^2 - \epsilon^3 + \cdots) \\
&= y(1 + e + e^2 + e^3 + \cdots)
\end{aligned}
$$

This suggests that we might improve our reciprocal approximation by multiplying y by some truncation of the series $1 + e + e^2 + e^3 + \cdots$. The simplest case using a linear polynomial in e can be done with just one more fma operation:

$$y' = y + ey$$

Now we have

$$
\begin{aligned}
y' &= y(1 + e) \\
&= \frac{1}{b}(1 + \epsilon)(1 + e) \\
&= \frac{1}{b}(1 + \epsilon)(1 - \epsilon) \\
&= \frac{1}{b}(1 - \epsilon^2)
\end{aligned}
$$

The magnitude of the relative error has thus been squared, or looked at another way, the number of significant bits has been approximately doubled. This, in fact, is exactly a step of the traditional Newton-Raphson iteration for reciprocals. In order to get a still better approximation, one can either use a longer polynomial in e, or repeat the Newton-Raphson linear correction several times. Mathematically speaking, repeating Newton-Raphson iteration n times is equivalent to using a polynomial $1 + e + \cdots + e^{2^n - 1}$, e.g. since $e' = \epsilon^2 = e^2$, two iterations yield:

$$y'' = y(1 + e)(1 + e^2) = y(1 + e + e^2 + e^3)$$

However, whether repeated Newton iteration or a more direct power series evaluation is better depends on a careful analysis of efficiency and the impact of rounding error. The Intel algorithms use both, as appropriate.

Now consider refining an approximation to the quotient with relative error ϵ; we can get such an approximation in the first case by simply multiplying a reciprocal approximation $y \approx \frac{1}{b}$ by a. One approach is simply to refine y as much as possible and then multiply. However, this kind of approach can never guarantee getting the last bit right; instead we also need to consider how to refine q directly. Suppose

$$q = \frac{a}{b}(1 + \epsilon)$$

We can similarly arrive at a remainder term by an **fnma**:

$$r = a - bq$$

when we have:

$$
\begin{aligned}
r &= a - bq \\
&= a - b\frac{a}{b}(1 + \epsilon) \\
&= a - a(1 + \epsilon) \\
&= -a\epsilon
\end{aligned}
$$

In order to use this remainder term to improve q, we also need a reciprocal approximation $y = \frac{1}{b}(1 + \eta)$. Now the **fma** operation:

$$q' = q + ry$$

results in, ignoring the final rounding:

$$
\begin{aligned}
q' &= q + ry \\
&= \frac{a}{b}(1 + \epsilon) - a\epsilon\frac{1}{b}(1 + \eta) \\
&= \frac{a}{b}(1 + \epsilon - \epsilon(1 + \eta)) \\
&= \frac{a}{b}(1 - \epsilon\eta)
\end{aligned}
$$

3.3   Obtaining the Final Result

While we have neglected rounding errors hitherto, it is fairly straightforward to place a sensible bound on their effect. To be precise, the error from rounding is at most half an ulp in round-to-nearest mode and a full ulp in the other modes.

```
⊢  ˜(precision fmt = 0)
⟹ (abs(error fmt Nearest x) <= ulp fmt x / &2) ∧
   (abs(error fmt Down x) < ulp fmt x) ∧
   (abs(error fmt Up x) < ulp fmt x) ∧
   (abs(error fmt Zero x) < ulp fmt x)
```

where

```
⊢  error fmt rc x = round fmt rc x - x
```

It turn, we can easily get fairly tight lower and upper bounds on an ulp in x in terms of the magnitude of x, the upper bound assuming normalization:

```
⊢  abs(x) / &2 pow (precision fmt) <= ulp fmt x
```

and

```
⊢  normalizes fmt x ∧ ˜(precision fmt = 0) ∧ ˜(x = &0)
⟹ ulp fmt x <= abs(x) / &2 pow (precision fmt - 1)
```

Putting these together, we can easily prove simple relative error bounds on all the basic operations, which can be propagated through multiple calculations by simple algebra. It is easy to see that while the relative errors in the approximations are significantly above 2^{-p} (where p is the precision of the floating point format), the effects of rounding error on the overall error are minor. However, once we get close to having a perfectly rounded result, rounding error becomes highly significant. How the algorithm is designed and verified now depends radically on whether we have higher precision available. If we do, then we can usually rely on a simple 'exclusion zone' proof. Otherwise, we need more precise theorems, the central one being the following due to Markstein [11]:

Theorem 1. *If q is a floating point number within 1 ulp of the true quotient a/b of two floating point numbers, and y is the correctly rounded-to-nearest approximation of the exact reciprocal $\frac{1}{b}$, then the following two floating point operations:*

$$r = a - bq$$
$$q' = q + ry$$

using round-to-nearest in each case, yield the correctly rounded-to-nearest quotient q'.

This is not too difficult to prove in HOL. First we observe that because the initial q is a good approximation, the computation of r cancels so much that no rounding error is committed. (This is intuitively plausible and stated by Markstein without proof, but the formal proof was surprisingly messy.)

```
⊢  2 <= precision fmt ∧
   a ∈ iformat fmt ∧ b ∈ iformat fmt ∧ q ∈ iformat fmt ∧
   normalizes fmt q ∧ abs(a / b - q) <= ulp fmt (a / b) ∧
   &2 pow (2 * precision fmt - 1) / &2 pow (ulpscale fmt) <= abs(a)
   ⟹ (a - b * q) ∈ iformat fmt
```

Now the overall proof given by Markstein is quite easily formalized. However, we observed that the property actually used in the proof is in general somewhat weaker than requiring y to be a perfectly rounded reciprocal. The theorem actually proved in HOL is:

Theorem 2. *If q is a floating point number within 1 ulp of the true quotient a/b of two floating point numbers, and y approximates the exact reciprocal $\frac{1}{b}$ to a relative error $< \frac{1}{2^p}$, where p is the precision of the floating point format concerned, then the following two floating point operations:*

$$r = a - bq$$
$$q' = q + ry$$

using round-to-nearest in each case, yield the correctly rounded-to-nearest quotient q'.

The formal HOL statement is as follows:

```
⊢  2 <= precision fmt ∧
   a ∈ iformat fmt ∧ b ∈ iformat fmt ∧
   q ∈ iformat fmt ∧ r ∈ iformat fmt ∧
   ¬(b = &0) ∧
   ¬(a / b ∈ iformat fmt) ∧
   normalizes fmt (a / b) ∧
   abs(a / b - q) <= ulp fmt (a / b) ∧
   abs(inv(b) - y) < abs(inv b) / &2 pow (precision fmt) ∧
   (r = a - b * q) ∧
   (q' = q + r * y)
   ⟹ (round fmt Nearest q' = round fmt Nearest (a / b))
```

Although in the worst case, the preconditions of the original and modified theorem hardly differ (recall that $|x|/2^p \leq ulp(x) \leq |x|/2^{p-1}$), it turns out that in many situations the relative error condition is much easier to satisfy. In Markstein's original methodology, one needs first to obtain a perfectly rounded reciprocal, which he proves can be done as follows:

Theorem 3. *If y is a floating point number within 1 ulp of the true reciprocal $\frac{1}{b}$, then one iteration of:*

$$e = 1 - by$$
$$y' = y + ey$$

using round-to-nearest in both cases, yields the correctly rounded reciprocal, except possibly when the mantissa of b consists entirely of 1s.

If we rely on this theorem, we need a very good approximation to $\frac{1}{b}$ before these two further serial operations and one more to get the final quotient using the new y'. However, with the weaker requirement on y', we can get away with a correspondingly weaker y. In fact, we prove:

Theorem 4. *If y is a floating point number that results from rounding a value y_0, and the relative error in y_0 w.r.t. $\frac{1}{b}$ is $\leq \frac{d}{2^{2p}}$ for some natural number d (assumed $\leq 2^{p-2}$), then y will have relative error $< \frac{1}{2^p}$ w.r.t. $\frac{1}{b}$, except possibly if the mantissa of b is one of the d largest. (That is, when scaled up to an integer $2^{p-1} \leq m_b < 2^p$, we have in fact $2^p - d \leq m_b < 2^p$.)*

Proof. For simplicity we assume $b > 0$, since the general case can be deduced by symmetry from this. We can therefore write $b = 2^e m_b$ for some integer m_b with $2^{p-1} \leq m_b < 2^p$. In fact, it is convenient to assume that $2^{p-1} < m_b$, since when b is an exact power of 2 the main result follows easily from $d \leq 2^{p-2}$. Now we have:

$$\frac{1}{b} = 2^{-e}\frac{1}{m_b}$$

$$= 2^{-(e+2p-1)}\left(\frac{2^{2p-1}}{m_b}\right)$$

and $ulp(\frac{1}{b}) = 2^{-(e+2p-1)}$. In order to ensure that $|y - \frac{1}{b}| < |\frac{1}{b}|/2^p$ it suffices, since $|y - y_0| \leq ulp(\frac{1}{b})/2$, to have:

$$|y_0 - \frac{1}{b}| < (\frac{1}{b})/2^p - ulp(\frac{1}{b})/2$$

$$= (\frac{1}{b})/2^p - 2^{-(e+2p-1)}/2$$

$$= (\frac{1}{b})/2^p - (\frac{1}{b})m_b/2^{2p}$$

By hypothesis, we have $|y_0 - \frac{1}{b}| \leq (\frac{1}{b})\frac{d}{2^{2p}}$. So it is sufficient if:

$$(\frac{1}{b})d/2^{2p} < (\frac{1}{b})/2^p - (\frac{1}{b})m_b/2^{2p}$$

Canceling $(\frac{1}{b})/2^{2p}$ from both sides, we find that this is equivalent to:

$$d < 2^p - m_b$$

Consequently, the required relative error is guaranteed except possibly when $d \geq 2^p - m_b$, or equivalently $m_b \geq 2^p - d$, as claimed.

The HOL statement is as follows. Note that it uses $e = d/2^{2p}$ as compared with the statement we gave above, but this is inconsequential.

```
⊢   2 <= precision fmt ∧
    b ∈ iformat fmt ∧
    y ∈ iformat fmt ∧
    ¬(b = &0) ∧
    normalizes fmt b ∧
    normalizes fmt (inv(b)) ∧
    (y = round fmt Nearest y0) ∧
    abs(y0 - inv(b)) <= e * abs(inv(b)) ∧
    e <= inv(&2 pow (precision fmt + 2)) ∧
    &(decode_fraction fmt b) <
    &2 pow (precision fmt) - &2 pow (2 * precision fmt) * e
    ⟹ abs(inv(b) - y) < abs(inv(b)) / &2 pow (precision fmt)
```

4   HOL Algorithm Verifications

We will now give two examples of actual IA-64 division algorithms and describe their HOL verification. Both algorithms are for single precision arithmetic, but one is a scalar algorithm that uses higher precision internally, and the other is a SIMD algorithm that uses only single precision operations. The two verifications thus present interesting contrasts.

4.1   Scalar Single Precision Algorithm

The following algorithm is for single precision computation, but makes clever use of the availability of higher intermediate precision. The steps of the algorithm are grouped into six stages which may be executed in parallel if the particular IA-64 machine allows this, as the Itanium™ processor does. The last column indicates the floating point format into which the result of that operation is rounded. Note that in all the algorithms we consider, all steps but the last are done in round-to-nearest mode, and the last in the ambient rounding mode.

1. $y_0 = \frac{1}{b}(1 + \epsilon)$ frcpa

2. $e_0 = 1 - by_0$ Register
   $q_0 = ay_0$ Register

3. $q_1 = q_0 + e_0 q_0$ Register
   $e_1 = e_0 e_0$ Register

4. $q_2 = q_1 + e_1 q_1$ Register
   $e_2 = e_1 e_1$ Register

5. $q_3 = q_2 + e_2 q_2$ Registerdouble

6. $q = q_3$ Single

The algorithm forms an initial reciprocal approximation y_0 and a quotient approximation q_0, then refines them both by two stages of Newton-Raphson iteration. The subtlety is in the last two lines, where q_3 is rounded to 'register double' (double precision but with a wider exponent range) and subsequently rounded again to single precision, in order to obtain a perfectly rounded result. We now turn to the formal verification.

As detailed in [9], we have written derived rules that can automatically propagate forward known upper and lower ranges on the size of arguments to the result of fma-type operations, automatically verifying that the result neither overflows nor loses precision and hence that we can express the result as a relative perturbation of the exact result. HOL's programmability is vital here; these proofs would be extraordinarily tedious to orchestrate by hand.

We do this for all steps of the algorithm, though we then have to reexamine some of them more precisely to make the proof work. Results of later lines have accumulated many errors from previous ones, and again we use an automatic HOL rule to bound these. The bounds derived automatically in this way are naive. For example, if we know $|\epsilon| < 2^{-24}$, the automatic rule can deduce that $y_0(1 + \epsilon)(1 - \epsilon) = y_0(1 + \epsilon')$ with $|\epsilon'| \le 2^{-24} + 2^{-24} + 2^{-24}2^{-24}$. Of course, with a little intelligence, a human can derive $|\epsilon'| \le 2^{-48}$. This kind of intelligence has to be injected sometimes, but generally, the automated process is enough to do the donkey work of keeping track of the dozens (hundreds in some other verifications) of ultimately negligible error terms. The first important relative error is in q_3 before rounding, i.e. $q_3^* = q_2 + e_2 q_2$. We find that $q_3^* = \frac{a}{b}(1 + e)$ with $|e| \le 197509/2^{80}$.

Now we distinguish two cases according to whether a/b is actually representable in the 'register single' format. (The use of register single rather than single simplifies the later argument, which is otherwise complicated by the possibility that a/b could be exactly the midpoint between two denormal numbers.)

If a/b is in the register single format, then it is a fortiori in the register double format. Since $q_3^* = \frac{a}{b}(1 + e)$ with $|e| \le 2^{-62}$, it is clear that $q_3 = a/b$ exactly, and so q is certainly the IEEE correct answer since it literally results from rounding a/b to single precision.

If a/b is not in the register single format, then we still have a respectable relative error for q_3 after rounding because rounding was into a format with more than twice single precision. In fact, we have $q_3 = \frac{a}{b}(1 + e)$ with $|e| \le 2^{-52}$, and examining the exclusion zone theorem, we need only $|e| < 2^{-(2 \times 24 + 2)}$. Consequently, correctness is proved.

4.2   SIMD Single Precision Algorithm

The following algorithm is for SIMD single precision computation. It can also be grouped in 6 parallel stages, though on a machine capable of issuing fewer than

3 floating point operations per cycle, some instructions may need to be offset by a cycle.

1. $y_0 = \frac{1}{b}(1 + \epsilon)$ **frcpa**

2. $d = 1 - by_0$ Single
   $q_0 = ay_0$ Single

3. $y_1 = y_0 + dy_0$ Single
   $r_0 = a - bq_0$ Single

4. $e = 1 - by_1$ Single
   $y_2 = y_0 + dy_1$ Single
   $q_1 = q_0 + r_0y_1$ Single

5. $y_3 = y_1 + ey_2$ Single
   $r_1 = a - bq_1$ Single

6. $q = q_1 + r_1y_3$ Single

Once again we can use the automated tools to produce simple relative error bounds for the intermediate stages. In this case, however, more human intervention in the proofs is necessary, since for extreme inputs the intermediate steps, which have no additional exponent range, *can* overflow or underflow. However, the parallel version of **frcpa** indicates this possibility by clearing a predicate register, triggering the use of a different algorithm. We simply need to verify that the condition tested ensures that no overflow or underflow occurs here, which is easily done.

First, suppose that a/b is exactly, or is very close to, a single precision floating point number c. In this case, the semi-automatic error analysis indicates that $q_1^* = q_0 + r_0y_1 = \frac{a}{b}(1+\epsilon)$ with $|\epsilon| \leq 2^{-25.9}$, close enough to ensure that $q_1 = c$. As before, this ensures that the exact cases work correctly, and allows us to dispose also of the directed rounding mode cases, since these are the only problematic ones for a simple exclusion zone proof. For the more difficult case of round-to-nearest and where the quotient is not close to a floating point number, the critical relative error result is for y_3 before rounding, which is indicated in the HOL goal by the following derived assumptions:

```
['Val e * Val y_2 + Val y_1 = inv(Val b) * (&1 + e16)']
['abs e16 <= &657 / &2 pow 50']
```

In other words, $y_3^* = \frac{1}{b}(1 + e_{16})$ with $|e_{16}| \leq 657/2^{50}$. Since $657/2^{50} \leq 165/2^{2 \times 24}$, we can now apply Theorem 4 to show that y_3 will satisfy the relative error criterion needed for Theorem 2, except possibly when the mantissa of b is one of the 165 largest. For these cases, HOL is programmed to evaluate the result of the y_3 computation on them explicitly (dealing with the arbitrary exponent scaling is the only slight difficulty), and it automatically confirms that the criterion is always attained in these cases too. (Note that if this fails, we may still be able to show the overall quotient result will be correct, but it needs somewhat more work and has never arisen in practice so far.) Consequently, we can now apply Theorem 2 and deduce that the final result is correctly rounded and all flags set (subject to the criterion identified for the intermediate results not to overflow or underflow, which matches the cases indicated by the parallel frcpa).

A more complicated analysis (which has not been formalized in HOL) suggests that while y_3 always satisfies the relative error criterion, it fails to be perfectly rounded for precisely 12 of the possible 2^{24} input b significands. Consequently, this algorithm could not be justified based only on Markstein's theorems in their original form.

Another situation where the new theorems allow us to justify faster algorithms is extended precision division. Using Markstein's original theorems, it seems the best that can be achieved is the following:

1. $y_0 = \frac{1}{b}(1 + \epsilon)$ [frcpa]
2. $e_0 = 1 - by_0$ $q_0 = ay_0$
3. $y_1 = y_0 + e_0 y_0$ $e_1 = e_0^2$
4. $y_2 = y_1 + e_1 y_1$ $r_0 = a - bq_0$
5. $e_2 = 1 - by_2$
6. $y_3 = y_2 + e_2 y_2$
7. $e_3 = 1 - by_3$ $q_1 = q_0 + r_0 y_3$
8. $y_4 = y_3 + e_3 y_3$ $r_1 = a - bq_1$
9. $q_2 = q_1 + r_1 y_4$

However, using the new theorems, we can justify the following, which is faster by one fma latency.

1. $y_0 = \frac{1}{b}(1 + \epsilon)$ [frcpa]
2. $d = 1 - by_0$ $q_0 = ay_0$
3. $d_2 = dd$ $d_3 = dd + d$
4. $d_5 = d_2 d_2 + d$ $y_1 = y_0 + y_0 d_3$
5. $y_2 = y_0 + y_1 d_5$ $r_0 = a - bq_0$
6. $e = 1 - by_2$ $q_1 = q_0 + r_0 y_2$
7. $y_3 = y_2 + ey_2$ $r = a - bq_1$
8. $q = q_1 + ry_3$

5   Conclusions and Related Work

We have outlined an approach to the formal verification of classes of division algorithms which is a formalization and improvement of standard theoretical approaches [11,2]. The approach has been successfully applied to a large number of division algorithms that Intel is distributing to help IA-64 programmers, helping to give greater confidence in the correctness of these subtle algorithms. Moreover, the verification effort has led to some stronger theorems on which to base algorithms of this type, and so directly to some efficiency improvements.

The verification is conducted on a detailed abstract model of the application programmer's view of the IA-64 ISA, and naturally relies on the IA-64 processor on which the code is run accurately implementing the ISA. Moreover, formal verification cannot completely guard against simple transcription errors in utilized versions of the code, a danger particularly significant since they may be inlined by various compilers and software development tools. For the purpose of isolating such errors as well as providing additional levels of assurance, Intel has also developed extensive validation suites. Formal verification can never completely eliminate the need for such precautions, but it can allow us to focus testing on more productive areas. (Indeed, a particularly attractive feature of the 'exclusion zone' approach [2] is that the difficult cases are not only used in a formal proof but are also good test cases to exercise the algorithm and its practical realization.)

As well as the floating point division work reported here, we have verified various analogous square root algorithms using a formalization of the refined exclusion zone approach [2]. In addition, we have formally verified several integer divide algorithms, which use a specialized floating-point division algorithm as a core. For an overview of the implementation of integer division on IA-64 and proofs of correctness, see [1]. Much more detail about the IA-64 implementation of division, square root and other mathematical functions are given in [12].

The closest related work to that described here is the formal verification of division algorithms reported in [13] and [15]. Although these are respectively for microcode and hardware RTL, and the present work is for software, this difference is not as significant as it may seem, since all these implementations seem to be modeled at a similar level. The major difference is that our work covers algorithms written using the standard resources available to the application programmer, based on a high-level specification that the underlying operations are IEEE-correct. Other work on formal verification of division hardware using a combined theorem prover and model checker [14] is also closely related, but in this work the verification is taken down to a lower level (the implementation in terms of logic gates), and closely integrated with the overall design flow, helping to reduce the chance of transcription errors.

References

1. Marius Cornea, Cristina Iordache, Peter Markstein, and John Harrison. Integer divide and remainder operations in the Intel IA-64 architecture. In Jean-Claude Bajard, Christiane Frougny, Peter Kornerup, and Jean-Michel Muller, editors, *RNC4, the fourth international conference on Real Numbers and Computers*, pages 161–184, 2000.
2. Marius Cornea-Hasegan. Proving the IEEE correctness of iterative floating-point square root, divide and remainder algorithms. *Intel Technology Journal*, 1998-Q2:1–11, 1998. See http://developer.intel.com/technology/itj/q21998/articles/art_3.htm.

3. Guy Cousineau and Michel Mauny. *The Functional Approach to Programming*. Cambridge University Press, 1998.
4. Carole Dulong. The IA-64 architecture at work. *IEEE Computer*, 64(7):24–32, July 1998.
5. Michael J. C. Gordon and Thomas F. Melham. *Introduction to HOL: a theorem proving environment for higher order logic*. Cambridge University Press, 1993.
6. Michael J. C. Gordon, Robin Milner, and Christopher P. Wadsworth. *Edinburgh LCF: A Mechanised Logic of Computation*, volume 78 of *Lecture Notes in Computer Science*. Springer-Verlag, 1979.
7. John Harrison. HOL Light: A tutorial introduction. In Mandayam Srivas and Albert Camilleri, editors, *FMCAD'96*, volume 1166 of *Lecture Notes in Computer Science*, pages 265–269. Springer-Verlag, 1996.
8. John Harrison. *Theorem Proving with the Real Numbers*. Springer-Verlag, 1998. Revised version of author's PhD thesis.
9. John Harrison. A machine-checked theory of floating point arithmetic. In Yves Bertot, Gilles Dowek, André Hirschowitz, Christine Paulin, and Laurent Théry, editors, *TPHOLs'99*, volume 1690 of *Lecture Notes in Computer Science*, pages 113–130, 1999. Springer-Verlag.
10. IEEE. Standard for binary floating point arithmetic. ANSI/IEEE Standard 754-1985, The Institute of Electrical and Electronic Engineers, Inc.
11. Peter Markstein. Computation of elementary functions on the IBM RISC System/6000 processor. *IBM Journal of Research and Development*, 34:111–119, 1990.
12. Peter Markstein. *IA-64 and Elementary Functions: Speed and Precision*. Prentice-Hall, 2000.
13. J Strother Moore, Tom Lynch, and Matt Kaufmann. A mechanically checked proof of the correctness of the kernel of the $AMD5_K86$ floating-point division program. *IEEE Transactions on Computers*, 47:913–926, 1998.
14. John O'Leary, Xudong Zhao, Rob Gerth, and Carl-Johan H. Seger. Formally verifying IEEE compliance of floating-point hardware. *Intel Technology Journal*, 1999-Q1:1–14, 1999. http://developer.intel.com/technology/itj/q11999/articles/art_5.htm.
15. David Rusinoff. A mechanically checked proof of IEEE compliance of a register-transfer-level specification of the AMD-K7 floating-point multiplication, division, and square root instructions. *LMS Journal of Computation and Mathematics*, 1:148–200, 1998. Available on the Web via http://www.onr.com/user/russ/david/k7-div-sqrt.html.
16. Pierre Weis and Xavier Leroy. *Le langage Caml*. InterEditions, 1993. See also the CAML Web page: http://pauillac.inria.fr/caml/.

Fast Tactic-Based Theorem Proving [*]

Jason Hickey[1] and Aleksey Nogin[2]

[1] Department of Computer Science
Caltech 256-80
Pasadena, CA 91125
jyh@cs.caltech.edu
[2] Department of Computer Science
Cornell University
Ithaca, NY 14853
nogin@cs.cornell.edu

Abstract. Theorem provers for higher-order logics often use *tactics* to implement automated proof search. Tactics use a general-purpose meta-language to implement both general-purpose reasoning and computationally intensive domain-specific proof procedures. The generality of tactic provers has a performance penalty; the speed of proof search lags far behind special-purpose provers. We present a new modular proving architecture that significantly increases the speed of the core logic engine. Our speedup is due to efficient data structures and *modularity*, which allows parts of the prover to be customized on a domain-specific basis. Our architecture is used in the MetaPRL logical framework, with speedups of more than two orders of magnitude over traditional tactic-based proof search.

1 Introduction

Several provers [8,9,3,11,12,15,18] use higher-order logics for reasoning because the expressivity of the logics permits concise problem descriptions, and because meta-principles that characterize entire classes of problems can be proved and reused on multiple problem instances. In these provers, proof automation is coded in a *meta-language* (often a variant of ML) as *tactics*. Automation speed has a direct impact on the level of reasoning. If proof search is slow, more interactive guidance is needed to prune the search space, leading to excessive detail in the tactic proofs.

We present a proving architecture that addresses the problem of speed and customization in tactic provers. We have implemented this architecture in the MetaPRL logical framework, achieving more than two orders of magnitude speed-up over the existing NuPRL-4 implementation. We obtain the speedup in two parts: our architecture is modular, allowing components to be replaced with domain-specific implementations, and we use efficient data structures to implement the proving modules.

[*] Support for this research was provided by DARPA grants F30602-95-1-0047 and F30602-98-2-0198

J. Harrison and M. Aagaard (Eds.): TPHOLs 2000, LNCS 1869, pp. 252–267, 2000.

In this paper, we explain this modular architecture. We show that the logic engine can be broken into three modules: a *term* module that implements the logical *language*, a term *rewriter* that applies primitive inferences, and a *proof* module that manages proofs and defines tactics. The computational behavior of proof search is dominated by term rewriting and operations on terms, and we present implementations of the modules for domains with frequent applications of substitution (like type theory), and for domains with frequent applications of unification (like first-order logic).

MetaPRL, our testbed, is implemented in Objective Caml [19]. It includes logics like first-order logic, the NuPRL type theory, and Aczel's CZF set theory [1]. We include performance measurements that compare MetaPRL's performance with NuPRL-4 on the NuPRL type theory. In our measurements, we also show how particular module implementations change the performance in the different domains.

One might think that the comparison between MetaPRL and NuPRL-4 is not very fair since NuPRL-4 uses interpreted ML and MetaPRL is implemented in OCaml. But in fact only very high-level code uses interpreted ML in NuPRL-4 while most of the time is spent performing low-level operations such as term operations and primitive rule applications. And in NuPRL-4 all the low-level operations are implemented in Lisp and are compiled by a modern Lisp compiler. This should make the comparisons relatively fair, especially when we are talking about two orders of magnitude speed difference.

It should also be noted that MetaPRL is a *distributed* prover [14], leading to additional speedups if multiple processors are used. Distribution is implemented by inserting a scheduling and communication layer between the refiner and the tactic interface. For this paper, we describe operation and performance without this additional scheduling layer.

The organization of the paper is a follows. In Section 2, we give an overview of tactic proving, and present the high-level architecture. In Sections 3, 4, and 5, we explore the proving modules in more detail, and develop their implementations. In Section 6, we compare the performance of the different implementations, and in Section 7 we summarize our results, and present the remaining issues. This work builds on the efforts of many systems over the last decade, and in Section 8 we present related work.

2 Architectural Overview

We consider a general architecture of a tactic prover consisting of three parts, as shown in Figure 1. A *logic* contains the following kinds of objects:

1. *Syntax definitions* define the *language* of a logic,
2. *Inference rules* define the primitive inferences of a logic. For instance, the first-order logic contains rules like MODUS_PONENS in a sequent calculus.

$$\frac{}{\Gamma, A \vdash A} \text{ AXIOM} \qquad \frac{\Gamma \vdash A \Rightarrow B \quad \Gamma \vdash A}{\Gamma \vdash B} \text{ MODUS\_PONENS}$$

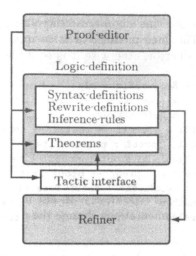

Fig. 1. General tactic prover architecture

3. *Rewrites* define computational equivalences. For example, the type theory defines functions and application, with the equivalence $(\lambda x.b)\ a \longleftrightarrow b[a/x]$.
4. *Theorems* provide proofs for derived inference rules and axioms.

The *refiner* [5] performs two basic operations. First, it builds automation procedures from the parts of a logic.

1. Syntax definitions are compiled to functions for constructing logical formulas.
2. Rewrite primitives (and derived rewrite theorems) are compiled to *conversions* that allow computational reductions to be applied during a proof.
3. Inference rules and theorems are compiled to primitive *tactics* for applying the rule, or instantiating the theorem.

The second refiner operation is the *application* of conversions and tactics, producing justifications from the proofs. The major parts of the refiner interface are shown below.[1] It defines abstract types for data structures that implement terms, tactic and rewrite definitions, proofs, and logics. Proof search is performed in a backward-chaining goal-directed style. The `refine` function takes a `logic` and a `tactic` search procedure, and applies it to a *goal* term to produce a *partial* proof. The goal and the resulting *subgoals* can be recovered with the `sub/goal_of_proof` projection functions. Proofs can be composed with the `compose proof subproofs` function, which requires that the goals of the `subproofs` correspond to the subgoals of the `proof`, and that both derivations occurred in the same logic. If an error occurs in any of the refiner functions, the `RefineError` exception is raised. The `tactic_of_conv` function creates a tactic from a rewrite definition. The final two functions, called *tacticals*, are the primitives for implementing proof search. Operationally, the `andthen tac1 tac2`

---

[1] Throughout this paper we will use a simplified OCaml syntax to give the component descriptions.

tactic applies `tac1` to a goal and immediately applies `tac2` to all the subgoals, composing the result. The `orelse tac1 tac2` is equal to `tac1` on goals where `tac1` does not produce an error, otherwise it is equivalent to `tac2`.

```
module type RefinerSig = sig
      type term, tactic, conv, proof, logic
      exception RefineError
      val refine : logic → tactic → term → proof
      val goal_of_proof : proof → term
      val subgoals_of_proof : proof → term list
      val compose : proof → proof list → proof
      val tactic_of_conv : conv → tactic
      val andthen : tactic → tactic → tactic
      val orelse : tactic → tactic → tactic
end
```

The `logic` data type is the concrete representation of a logic. The MetaPRL logical framework defines multiple logics in an inheritance hierarchy (partial order) where if L_{child}: `logic` inherits from L_{parent}: `logic`, all the theorems of L_{parent} are valid (and provable) in L_{child}. In contrast, the NuPRL-4 prover has a single global logic containing the syntax and rules of the NuPRL type theory.

In a prover like NuPRL-4, the refiner can be characterized as *monolithic*. There is no well-defined separation of the refiner into components, and there is no well-defined interface like the `RefinerSig` we defined above—there is *one* built-in refiner. This has made it difficult to customize and maintain NuPRL-4, and our choice in MetaPRL has been to partition the refiner into several small well-defined parts.

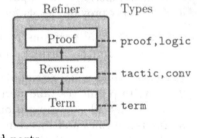

This modular structure has an additional benefit: if we partition the refiner into abstract parts, we can create domain-specific implementations of its parts. While the whole refiner is a part of a trusted code base, we do not need to worry about introducing bugs while doing domain-specific optimization. When we need to be extra sure, that everything is correct, we can do proof development using the domain-specific code and later double-check the proof using the reference implementation. And for some parts of the system we even have a debugging mode that runs two implementations side-by-side and notifies the user if they behave differently. This not only protects us from bugs introduced by the domain-specific code, but also helps us to debug the reference implementation as well.

The choice of partitioning we use is guided by the *type* definitions, producing the layered architecture shown at the right. The lowest layer, the *term* module, defines the logical language; the *rewriter* module implements applications of primitive tactics and conversions using term rewriting; and the *proof* module defines the `logic` and `proof` data types. We present specifications and implementations of these modules in the following section.

3 The *Term* Module

All logical terms, including goals and subgoals, are expressed in the language of *terms*, implemented by the *term* module. The general syntax of all terms has three parts. Each term has 1) an operator-name (like "sum"), which is a unique name indicating the logic and component of a term; 2) a list of parameters representing constant values; and 3) a set of subterms with possible variable bindings. We use the following syntax to describe terms, based on the NuPRL definition [2]:

$$\underbrace{opname}_{operator\ name}\ \underbrace{[p_1;\cdots;p_n]}_{parameters}\ \underbrace{\{v_1.t_1;\cdots;v_m.t_m\}}_{subterms}$$

A few examples are shown at the right. Variables are terms with a string parameter for their name; numbers have an integer parameter. The lambda term contains a binding occurrence: the variable x is bound in the subterm b.

Displayed form	Term
1	`number[1]{}`
$\lambda x.b$	`lambda[]{x. b}`
$f(a)$	`apply[]{f; a}`
v	`variable["v"]{}`
$x+y$	`sum[]{x; y}`

The term module implements several basic term operations: substitution ($b[a/x]$) of a term (a) for a variable (x) in a term (b), free-variable calculations, α-equivalence, etc. When a logic defines a rule, the refiner compiles the rule pattern into a sequence of term operations. The term interface is shown below. The abstract types opname, param, term, and bound_term represent operator names, constant parameters, terms, and bound terms (the subterms of a term). The major operations include destructors to decompose terms and bound-terms, as well as a substitution function subst, free variable calculations, and term equivalence.

```
module type TermSig = sig
    (* Types and constructors: *)
    type opname, param, term, bound_term
    val mk_opname : string list → opname
    val mk_int_param : int → param
    val mk_string_param : string → param
    val mk_term : opname → param list → bound_term list → term
    val mk_bterm : string list → term → bound_term

    (* Destructors and other operations: *)
    val dest_term : term → opname * param list * bound_term list
    val dest_bterm : bound_term → string list * term
    val subst : (string * term) list → term → term
    val free_vars : term → string list
    val alpha_equal : term → term → bool
end
```

3.1   Naive Term Implementation (Term_std)

The most immediate implementation of terms is the naive "standard" implementation, which builds the term with tupling.

```
type opname = string list
and param = Int of int | String of string
and term = opname * param list * bound_term list
and bound_term = string list * term
```

While this structure is easy to implement, it suffers from poor substitution performance. The following pseudo-code gives an outline of the substitution algorithm.

```
let rec subst sub t =
    if t is a variable then
        if (t, t') ∈ sub then t' else t
    else let (opname, params, bterms) = t in
        (opname, params, List.map (subst_bterm sub) bterms)
and subst_bterm sub (vars, t) =
    let sub' = remove (v, t') from sub if v ∈ vars in        ①
    let vars', sub'' = rename binding variables to avoid capture in   ②
    (vars', subst sub'' t)
```

The sub argument is a list of **string/term** pairs that are to be simultaneously substituted into the term in the second argument. The main part of the substitution algorithm is in the part for substituting into bound terms. In step ①, the substitution is modified by removing any **string/term** pairs that are freshly bound by the binding list **vars**, and in step ②, the binding variables are renamed if they intersect with any of the free variables in the terms being substituted.

Roughly analyzed, this algorithm takes time at least linear in the size of the term on which the substitution is performed. Furthermore, each substitution performs a full copying of the term. Substitution is a very common operation in MetaPRL — each application of an inference rule involves at least one substitution.[2] The next implementation performs lazy substitution, useful in domains like type theory.

3.2   Delayed Substitution (Term_ds)

If substitution is frequent, it is often more efficient to save computations for use in multiple substitution operations. We use three main optimizations: we save free-variable calculations, we perform lazy substitution, and we provide special representations for commonly occurring terms.

When a substitution is performed on a term for the first time, we compute the set of free variables of that term, and save them for later use. When a

---

[2] Testing for α-equivalence also takes linear time. One way to decrease the cost would be to use a normalized representation (such as a DeBruijn representation). However, term *destruction* on the normalized representation can be expensive because of the need to rename variables that become free (what are the subterms of $\lambda x.\lambda y.xy$ and $\lambda x.\lambda y.yx$?). These renamings can be delayed, as the next Section shows, but the cost of equivalence testing will increase.

substitution is applied, the free-variables set is used to discard the parts of the substitution for variables that do not occur free in the term. This saves time, and it also saves space by reusing subterms where the substitution has no effect instead of unnecessarily copying them. Memory savings, in turn, further improve performance by improving the CPU cache efficiency and reducing the GC time.

During proof search, most tactic applications fail, and only a part of the substitution result is usually examined in the proof search. In this common case, it is more efficient to delay the application of a substitution until the substitution results are actually requested by the dest_term function.

We also optimize two commonly-occurring terms: *variables* and *sequents*. Rather than using the term encoding of variables, we provide a custom representation using a string. The *sequent* optimization uses a custom data structure to give constant-time access to the hypotheses, instead of the usual linear-time encoding. These "custom" terms are abstract optimizations—they do not change the Term interface definition. For each custom term, we add special-case handlers to each of the generic term functions.

The following definition of terms uses all of these optimizations (the definitions for the bound_term, opname and param types are unchanged). The definition of sequents, which we omit, uses arrays to represent the hypotheses and conclusions of the sequent.

```
type term = { free_vars :   VarsDelayed
                         | Vars of string set;
              core :   Term of (opname * param list * bound_term list)
                     | Subst of (subst * term)
                     | Var of string
                     | Sequent of sequent }
and subst = (string * term) list
and sequent = ···
```

The free_vars field caches the free variables of the term, using VarsDelayed as a placeholder until the variable set is computed. The core field stores the term value, using the Term variant to represent values where a substitution has been expanded, the Subst variant to represent delayed substitutions, and the Var and Sequent variants for custom terms. We maintain the following invariants on Subst: substitution lists are never empty, and the domain of the substitution is included in the free-variables of the term.

The free-variables computation is one of the more complex operations on this data structure. When the free variables are computed for a term, there are three main cases: if the free variables have already been computed, they are returned; if the core is a Term, the free variables are computed from the subterms; and if the core is a delayed substitution, the substitution is used to modify the free variables of the inner term.

```
let rec free_vars = function
      { free_vars = Vars fv } → fv
  | { core = core } as t →
      let fv = match core with
            Term (_, _, bterms) → Set.map_list free_vars_bterm bterms
          | Subst (sub, t) → free_vars_subst sub (free_vars t)
```

```
            | Var v → Set.singleton v
            | Sequent seq → free_vars_sequent seq
        in (t.free_vars ← Vars fv); fv and free_vars_bterm (bvars, t) =
    Set.subtract_list (free_vars t) bvars
and free_vars_subst sub fv =
    Set.union
        (Set.subtract_list fv (List.map fst sub))
        (Set.map_list free_vars (List.map snd sub))
```

If the free variables haven't already been computed, the free_vars function computes them, and assigns the value to the free_vars field of the term. In the Term case, the free variables are the union of the free variables of the subterms, where any new binding occurrences have been removed. In the Subst (sub, t) case, the free variables are computed for the inner term t, then the variables being replaced are removed from the resulting set, and then the free variables of the substituted terms are added.

The subst function has a simple implementation: eliminate parts of the substitution that have no effect (in order to maintain the invariant), and save the result in a Subst pair if the resulting substitution is not empty.

```
let subst sub t =
    let fv = free_vars t in
        match remove (v, t') from sub if v ∉ fv with ①
        [] → t (* substitution has no effect *)
        | sub' → { free_vars = VarsDelayed; core = Subst (sub', t) }
```

The set implementation determines the complexity of substitution. If the set lookup takes $O(1)$, then pruning ① takes time linear in the number of variables in sub.

The effect of the substitution is delayed until the term is destructed. The dest_term function is required to expand the substitution by one step. We use the get_core function, shown below, to expand the toplevel substitutions in the term. If the substitution was applied to a Term, get_core will push it down to the immediate subterms. After the substitution is expanded, get_core will store the result in the core field to save time on the next get_core invocation. As usual, we omit the code for sequents.

```
let rec get_core = function
    { core = Subst (sub, t') } as t →
        let core' = match get_core t' with
            Var v → get_core (List.assoc v sub) (* always succeeds *)
            | Term (opname, params, bterms) →
                Term (opname, params, List.map (do_bterm_subst sub) bterms)
            | Sequent seq → Sequent (sequent_subst sub seq)
        in (t.core ← core'); core'
    | { core = simple_core } → simple_core
and do_bterm_subst sub (vars, t) =
    let sub' = remove (v, t) from sub if v ∈ vars in
    let vars', sub'' = rename binding variables to avoid capture in
        (vars', subst sub'' t)
```

Note that the List.assoc in the Var case will never fail, due to our invariants.

The dest_term function first uses get_core to expand the top-level substitution (if any), and then it returns the parts of the term. To preserve the external interface of the term module, it is also required to convert the custom terms back to their original form.

```
let rec dest_term t = match get_core t with
    Term (opname, params, bterms) → (opname, params, bterms)
    Var v → (mk_opname ["variable"], [String v], [])
    Sequent s → dest_sequent s
```

4 The *Rewriter* Module

The rewriter performs term manipulations for rule applications. Inference rules and computational rewrites are both expressed using second-order patterns. For example, the rewrite for beta-reduction is expressed with the following pattern:

$$(\lambda x.b_x)\, a \to b_a$$

In this rewrite, the variable a is a *pattern* variable, representing the "argument" term. The variable b_x is a *second-order pattern* variable, representing a term with a free variable x. The pattern b_a represents a *substitution*, with a substituted for x in b. The $(\lambda x.b_x)\, a$ is called the *redex*, and the substitution b_a is called the *contractum*.

```
module Rewrite (Term : TermSig) : sig
    type redex_prog, con_prog, state
    exception RewriteError
    val compile_redex : term → redex_prog
    val apply_redex : redex_prog → term → state
    val compile_contractum : redex_prog → term → con_prog
    val build_contractum : con_prog → state → term
end
```

In NuPRL-4 the computation and inference engines are implemented as separate interpreters that are parameterized by the rewriting patterns. In MetaPRL we combine these functions and improve performance by compiling to a rewriting virtual machine. The MetaPRL rewriter module provides four major functions. The compile_redex function takes a redex pattern, expressed as a term, and it compiles it to a redex *program*. The apply_redex function applies a pre-compiled program to a specific term, raising the RewriteError exception if the pattern match fails, or returning a state that summarizes the result. The compile_contractum compiles a contractum pattern against a particular redex program, and the build_contractum function takes the contractum program and the result of a redex application, and produces the final contractum term.

Currently, the rewrite module compiles redices to bytecode programs that perform pattern matching, storing the parts of the term being matched in several register files. Contracta are also compiled to bytecode programs that construct the contractum term using the contents of the register file. The virtual machine has the four parts shown in Figure 2:

1. a *program* store and program counter for the rewrite program,
2. a *term/bterm stack* with a stack pointer to manage the current term being rewritten,
3. a *term/bterm* register file,
4. a *parameter* register file for each type of parameter.

The instructions for the machine are shown in Figure 3. The matching instruction **dest_term** checks if the term at the top of the term stack has the operator name **opname**, and if it has the right number of bound terms and parameters of the given types. If it succeeds, the parameters are saved in the parameter registers, the term is popped from the term stack, and the bound terms are pushed onto the stack. The **mk_term** instruction does the opposite: it retrieves the parameter values from the register file, pops bc bound terms from the stack, adds the **opname** and pushes the resulting term onto the stack. The **dest_bterm** and **mk_bterm** functions are used to save and restore binding variables for the term at the top of the stack.

The **so_var** instruction pops a term from the term stack and saves it in term register r, along with the free variables in $v_1, \ldots, v_n$. The corresponding constructor **so_subst** pops bc terms from the stack, substitutes them for the variables $v_1, \ldots, v_n$ in term r, and pushes the result onto the stack. The **match_term** instruction is used during matching for redices like $(x + x) \to 2x$ that contain common subterms.

The example in the Figure gives the code for a beta-reduction. The first **dest_term** instruction matches the outermost **apply** term and pushes the function and argument onto the stack. The **dest_bterm** operations remove the binding variables of the subterms, and the **so_var** instructions stores the results to the register file. At the end of a match against the term $(\lambda x.b)\ a$, register r_1

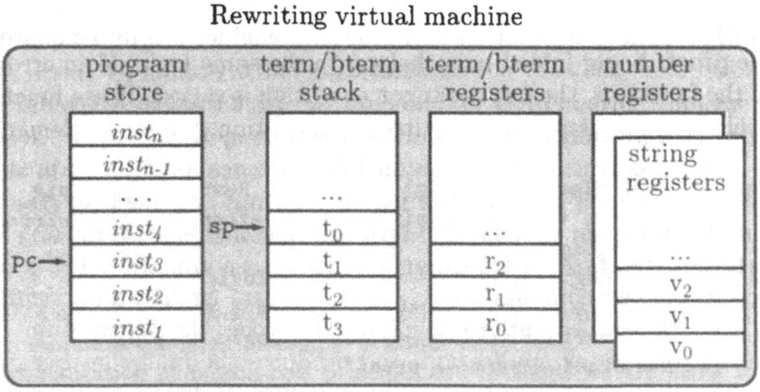

Rewriting virtual machine

Fig. 2. Rewrite virtual machine

Instructions		Example: $(\lambda x.b_x)\, a \longrightarrow b_a$	
Matching:		Redex:	
dest_term	$opname[p_1; \cdots ; p_n].bc$	dest_term	apply[].2
dest_bterm	$v_1, \ldots , v_n$	dest_bterm	
match_term	$r[t_1; \cdots ; t_n]$	dest_term	lambda[].1
so_var	$r[v_1; \cdots ; v_n]$	dest_bterm	v_1
Constructors:		so_var	$r_1[v_1]$
mk_term	$opname[p_0; \cdots ; p_n].bc$	dest_bterm	
mk_bterm	$v_1, \ldots , v_n$	so_var	$r_2[]$
so_subst	$r.bc$	Contractum:	
p_i: parameter register		so_subst	$r_2.0$
v_i: string register		so_subst	$r_1.1$
r: term register			
t_i: literal term			
bc: arity of bterm			

Fig. 3. Virtual machine instructions

contains b, register r_2 contains a, and register v_1 contains x. When the contractum is constructed, the first instruction pushes a onto the stack; and the second instruction pops a, substitutes it for x in b, and pushes the result.

5   The *Proof* Module

The third part of the refiner manages validity in logics as well as maintaining proof trees for theorems. The proof module exports the interface shown below. The empty_logic is the logic without any rules/rewrites. The join_logics function builds the union of two logics, and the add_rule and add_rewrite function add rules/rewrites from their syntactical description as terms. The proof type represents a partial proof tree [7], which may be modified by applying a tactic to the proof goal with the refine function. The compose function is used to stitch together partial proofs into larger proofs. Bookkeeping must be performed here—the proofs being joined must belong to the same logic. If an error occurs in any of the functions, the RefineError exception is raised. These functions are not difficult to implement, and we skip the description of their implementations.

```
module Proof (Term : TermSig) (Rewrite : RewriteSig) : sig
    type logic, tactic, rewrite, proof   exception RefineError
    val empty_logic : logic
    val join_logics : logic → logic → logic
    val add_rule : logic → term → logic * tactic
    val add_rewrite : logic → term → logic * rewrite
    val new_proof : term → proof
    val refine : proof → tactic → proof
    val compose : proof → proof list → proof
```

```
            val proof_goal : proof → term
            val proof_subgoals : proof → term list
end
```

6   Performance

We group the performance measurements into two parts. All measurements were done on a Linux 400MHz Pentium machine, with 512MB of main memory, and all times are in seconds. For the first part, we compare the speed of the Meta-PRL prover (using the modular refiner) with the NuPRL-4 prover. For the first example, we perform pure evaluation based on the following definition of the factorial function:

$$\text{rewrite } fact\{i\} \longleftrightarrow \textit{if } i = 0 \textit{ then } 1 \textit{ else } i * fact\{i-1\}$$

We used the following evaluation algorithm: recursively traverse the term top-down, performing beta-reduction, unfolding the `fact` definition (taking care to evaluate the argument first), etc. This algorithm stresses search during rewriting. Roughly speaking, evaluation should be quadratic in the factorial argument: each term traversal is linear in the size of the term, and the size of the term grows linearly with each traversal (rewriting does not use tail-recursion), until the final base case is reached and the value is computed. The following table lists the performance numbers.

	Argument value			
Configuration	100	250	400	650
Term_std	0.35	2.05	5.42	16.0
Term_ds	0.42	2.41	6.32	18.4
NuPRL-4	55	330	>1800	>1800

On this example, the NuPRL-4 took between 125 and 160 times longer on the problems where it finished within 30 minutes. On the two larger problems, we terminated the computation after 30 minutes.[3] In MetaPRL, the largest problem performs about 14 million attempted rewrites.

This table also shows a difference between the term module implementations. The "naive" term module performs better on this example because the recursive traversals of the term expand most of the delayed substitutions.

The next example also compares MetaPRL with NuPRL-4, on the pigeonhole problem stated in propositional logic[4]. The pigeonhole problem of size i proves that $i + 1$ "pigeons" do not fit into i "holes." The `pigeonT` tactic performs

---

[3] NuPRL-4 *can* evaluate these terms. The built-in term evaluator, which bypasses the refiner, evaluates the largest example in about 22 seconds.

[4] This formalization of pigeon-hole principle and methods we are using to prove it are obviously highly inefficient. However this formalization provided us with a nice way of comparing the performance of simple propositional proof search in the two systems.

a search customized to this domain, and the `propDecideT` tactic is a generic decision procedure for *intuitionistic* propositional logic (based on Dyckoff's algorithm [10]). Both search algorithms use only propositional reasoning and both explore an exponential number of cases in i.

Configuration	Tactic	Problem size			Memory
		2	3	4	(Max MB)[5]
`Term_std`	`pigeonT`	<0.1	2.53	94.0	126
`Term_ds`	`pigeonT`	<0.1	0.71	17.0	20.8
NuPRL-4	`pigeonT`	0.5	89	>1800	
`Term_std`	`propDecideT`	0.3	238	>1800	
`Term_ds`	`propDecideT`	0.13	55.0	>1800	
NuPRL-4	`propDecideT`	21.9	>1800	>1800	

In this example, NuPRL-4 works between 125 and 170 times slower than `Term_ds`. And the delayed-substitution implementation of terms performs significantly better than the naive implementation, partly because of the efficient substitution in the application of the rules for propositional logic, and also because the `Term_ds` module preserves a great deal of sharing of common subterms. On the largest problem the `pigeonT` tactic performs about 1.57 million primitive inference steps.

For the last examples, we give a few comparisons between the MetaPRL modules in two additional domains. The GEN problems is a heredity problem in a large first-order database. The NUPRL problem is an automated rerun of all proof transcripts in the NuPRL type theory. The transcripts contain a mix of low-level proof steps, such as lemma application and application of inductive reasoning, to higher-level steps that include verification-condition automation and proof search. The transcripts contain about 2,500 interactive proof steps.

We don't include performance measurements for NuPRL-4 on these examples, because the system differences require a porting effort (for instance, NuPRL-4 does not currently implement a generic first-order proof search procedure). In

Configuration	Problem	
	GEN	NUPRL
`Term_std`	20.4	39.3
`Term_ds`	14.4	36.6

our experience with NuPRL-4, proofs with several hundred steps tend to take several minutes to replay.

Once again, the `Term_ds` module performs better than the naive terms, due to the frequent use of substitution in applications of the rules of these theories. The times for proof replay include the time spent loading the proof transcripts and building the tactic trees. This cost is similar for both term implementations, and the performance numbers are comparable. The first-order problem, GEN, performs proof search by resolution, using the refiner to construct a primitive proof tree only when a proof is found. This final step is expensive, because each

---

[5] This does not include the space that the system occupied after the initial loading — 19 MB with `term_std` and 20.5 MB with `term_ds`

resolution step has to be justified by the refiner. The final successful proof in this problem performs about 41 thousand primitive inference steps.

7 Summary

We have achieved significant speedups for tactic proving. Our new prover design shows consistent speedups of more than two orders of magnitude over the NuPRL-4 system. Most of this speedup is due to efficient implementations of the prover components, but an additional part is due to the modular design, which allows the prover to be customized with domain-specific implementations. In addition, the MetaPRL system is programmed in OCaml, an efficient modular language. In contrast, NuPRL-4 tactics are programmed in *classic* ML, which is compiled to Common Lisp, and the NuPRL-4 refiner is implemented in Common Lisp.

In first-order logics, we estimate that an order of magnitude speed factor remains between MetaPRL and provers like ACL2 [17]. Some of this difference can be addressed with a specific refiner modules: a first-order term module would contain custom representations for terms in disjunctive normal form and sequents (sequents provide particularly poor representations for large first-order problems), and the rewrite module would optimize inference by resolution. However, a better solution would be to integrate first-order provers into the logical framework using translation modules that provide a tactic interface through encapsulation of the external functions.

There are a few avenues left to explore. Since we compile rewrites to bytecode, it is natural to wonder what the effect of compiling to native code would be. Also, while we currently do not optimize the proof module, there is significant overhead in composing and saving the primitive proof trees. In some domains, we may be able to perform proof compression, or delay the composition of proofs.

8 Related Work

Harrison's HOL-Light [13] shares some common features with the MetaPRL implementation. Harrison's system is implemented in Caml-Light, and both systems require fewer computational resources than their predecessors. Howe [16] has taken another approach to enhancing speed in NuPRL-4. The programming language defined by the NuPRL type theory is *untyped*, leading to frequent production of well-formedness (verification) conditions. Using type annotations, Howe was able to speed up rewriting in NuPRL-4 by a factor of 10. We haven't attempted to apply Howe's ideas to MetaPRL implementation of NuPRL type theory, but we believe that MetaPRL performance can be further improved using these ideas.

Basin and Kaufmann [4] give a comparison between the NuPRL-3 system and NQTHM [6] (the predecessor of the ACL2 [17] system). The NQTHM prover uses a quantifier-free variant of Peano arithmetic. Basin and Kaufmann's measurements showed that NQTHM was roughly 15 times faster than NuPRL-3 for *different formalizations* of Ramsey's theorem. It is likely that ACL2 and NuPRL-4 have a larger gap in speed.

References

1. Peter Aczel. The type theoretic interpretation of constructive set theory: Inductive definition. In *Logic, Methodology and Philosophy of Science VII*, pages 17–49. Elsevier Science Publishers, 1986.

2. Stuart F. Allen, Robert L. Constable, Douglas J. Howe, and William Aitken. The semantics of reflected proof. In *Proceedings of the Fifth Symposium on Logic in Computer Science*, pages 95–197. IEEE, June 1990.

3. Bruno Barras, Samuel Boutin, Cristina Cornes, Judicaël Courant, Jean-Christophe Filliâtre, Eduardo Giménez, Hugo Herbelin, Gérard-Mohring, Amokrane Saïbi, and Benjamin Werner. *The Coq Proof Assistant Reference Manual*. INRIA-Rocquencourt, CNRS and ENS Lyon, 1996.

4. David A. Basin and M. Kaufmann. The Boyer-Moore prover and Nuprl: An experimental comparison. In Gérard Huet and Gordon Plotkin, editors, *Logical Frameworks*, pages 89–119. Cambridge University Press, 1991.

5. J. L. Bates. *A Logic for Correct Program Development*. PhD thesis, Cornell University, 1979.

6. R. S. Boyer and J. S. Moore. *A Computational Logic*. Academic Press, New York, 1979.

7. Robert L. Constable, T. Knoblock, and J.L. Bates. Writing programs that construct proofs. *J. Automated Reasoning*, 1(3):285–326, 1984.

8. Thierry Coquand, Bengt Nordström, Jan M. Smith, and Björn von Sydow. Type Theory and Programming. *EATCS*, February 1994. bulletin no 52.

9. Judy Crow, Sam Owre, John Rushby, Natarajan Shankar, and Mandayam Srivas. A Tutorial Introduction to PVS. In *WIFT '95: Workshop on Industrial-Strength Formal Specification Techniques*, April 1995. http://www.csl.sri.com/sri-csl-fm.html.

10. R. Dyckhoff. Contraction-free sequent calculi for intuitionistic logic. In *The Journal of Symbolic Logic*, pages Vol. 57, Number 3, September 1992.

11. R.L. Constable et.al. *Implementing Mathematics in the NuPRL Proof Development System*. Prentice–Hall, 1986.

12. M.J.C. Gordon and T.F. Melham. *Introduction to HOL*. Cambridge University Press, 1993.

13. John Harrison. HOL Light: A tutorial introduction. In *Formal Methods in Computer-Aided Design (FMCAD'96)*, pages 265–269. Springer LNCS 1166, 1996.

14. Jason Hickey. Fault-tolerant distributed theorem proving. In Harald Ganzinger, editor, *Automated Deduction – CADE-16, 16th International Conference on Automated Deduction*, LNAI 1632, pages 227–231, Trento, Italy, July 7–10, 1999. Springer-Verlag.

15. Jason J. Hickey. Nuprl-Light: An implementation framework for higher–order logics. In *14th International Conference on Automated Deduction*. Springer, 1997.

16. Douglas J. Howe. A type annotation scheme for Nuprl. In *Theorem Proving in Higher-Order Logics*. Springer, 1998.

17. Matt Kaufmann and J. Moore. An industrial strength theorem prover for a logic based on common lisp. *IEEE Transactions on Software Engineering*, 23(4):203–213, April 1997.

18. Lawrence C. Paulson. *Isabelle: A Generic Theorem Prover*. Springer LNCS 828, 1994.

19. Pierre Weis and Xavier Leroy. *Le langage Caml*. Dunod, Paris, 2nd edition, 1999. In French.

Implementing a Program Logic of Objects in a Higher-Order Logic Theorem Prover

Martin Hofmann and Francis Tang*

Laboratory for Foundations of Computer Science
Division of Informatics
University of Edinburgh
Scotland, UK

Abstract. We present an implementation of a program logic of objects, extending that (AL) of Abadi and Leino. In particular, the implementation uses higher-order abstract syntax (HOAS) and—unlike previous approaches using HOAS—at the same time uses the built-in higher-order logic of the theorem prover to formulate specifications. We give examples of verifications, extending those given in [1], that have been attempted with the implementation. Due to the mixing of HOAS and built-in logic the soundness of the encoding is nontrivial. In particular, unlike in other HOAS encodings of program logics, it is not possible to directly reduce normal proofs in the higher-order system to proofs in the first-order object logic.

1 Introduction

The object-oriented (henceforth abbreviated as "OO") style of programming has shown to be exceptionally popular for developing large systems in a modular fashion. Despite its popularity, it is still lacking with regards to formal methods for verification.

This article is a foundational contribution towards the development of formal tools verification for OO languages. We have implemented a program logic for an object calculus, based on the logic from [1,2]. We have used the proof assistant LEGO[6] for historic reasons, though the techniques can be applied to other existing theorem provers, for example PVS and Isabelle/HOL. The encoding is notable for using:

- HOAS for encoding program syntax; and
- a direct embedding of the object logic into the metalogic.

The use of HOAS simplifies the encoding since we inherit variable scoping rules and alpha-conversion from the metalogic. Using the metalogic itself allows us to use the built-in features of the theorem prover. As a consequence of these two implementation decisions, soundness is non-trivial.

---

* Studentship funded by the EPSRC, UK.

J. Harrison and M. Aagaard (Eds.): TPHOLs 2000, LNCS 1869, pp. 268–282, 2000.

We give examples that have been attempted with the implementation. We considered the examples from Abadi and Leino as presented in [2]. Furthermore we extend their work with a new example based on the dining philosophers scenario.

Hereafter, the article is organised as follows. We first present a summary of the program logic from [2], giving the syntax of the object calculus and the verification axioms. We then present our implementation. Though the actual implementation is in LEGO, for expository purposes, we take as our metalanguage the fragment without universes, dependent and inductive types. We then give a selection of examples we have verified. A statement of the soundness property as well as the idea behind the proof are given in Section 5 but the details will be given elsewhere. Finally we conclude the article by giving some subjective views which have arisen from the work, and give a survey of related work.

2   The Abadi-Leino Logic

In [2], we are presented with an imperative, typed object language with subtyping but not recursive types. The language is given a syntax-directed operational semantics and also a Hoare-style verification logic for program correctness, which we will refer to simply as AL. The verification logic is proved to be sound but is also shown to be incomplete.

Objects are records of fields and methods. The only other types apart from objects are booleans and natural numbers. Each field is of primitive type or object type. Each method has exactly one bound variable denoting "self". The methods do not have any other formal parameters but arguments can be indirectly passed to them by first assigning to the fields in the object. There is no data abstraction nor an inheritance mechanism.

One record is a *subtype* of another if the one contains all fields of the other and for each method m in the other, a method whose return type is a subtype of that of m. The subtyping relation is said to be covariant with respect to method return values and invariant with respect to fields.

Method bodies are of the form $\varsigma(s)b$ where b is a program typically with free occurrences of s. Programs are built-up using constants (booleans and natural numbers), variables, and constructors for objects, let statements, conditional statements, field lookup, method invocation and field update. For field names $f_0, \ldots, f_k$, variables $x_0, \ldots, x_k$, method names $m_0, \ldots, m_l$, and method bodies $\varsigma(s)b_0, \ldots, \varsigma(s)b_l$, we have the program

$$[f_0=x_0, \ldots, f_k=x_k, m_0=\varsigma(s)b_0, \ldots, m_l=\varsigma(s)b_l]$$

which evaluates to a reference to an object with fields f_i and methods m_j. For a variable x and programs a and b, where b typically contains free occurrences of x, we have the program

let x=a in b .

The remaining constructions are standard and written *if x then a_0 else a_1*, *x.f*, *x.m* and *x.f:=y*, where a_0 and a_1 are programs, *x* and *y* are variables, *f* is a field identifier and *m* is a method identifier.

The program *let x=a in b* introduces the variable *x*. Execution of this program evaluates *a*, then *b* with occurences of *x* replaced with the previous result of evaluating *a*. Variables cannot be assigned to. However, a result can be an *object name* which does have state, and in this way mutable storage cells can be encoded as objects with one field. Since *a* is executed before *b*, we can define sequential composition *a; b* in the usual way.

For arbitrary programs *a* with object type and field *f*, it is, in general, not possible to write *a.f* with the intention to mean "evaluate *a* then look up *f* in the result." Such a program has to be encoded via the let construction as *let x=a in x.f*. Similarly, it is in general not possible to write *a.f:=b* nor *a.m*. This restriction simplifies the rules since evaluation of a variable is not side-effecting. Evaluation of an arbitrary program *a* is possibly side-effecting.

Since object terms evaluate to references, we also have the phenomenon of aliasing. For example, in the program

let x=a in (let y=x in b) ,

the variables *x* and *y* both refer to the same object during the excution of *b*: changes to *x* through field updates and method invocations also change *y*.

The semantics is given in terms of an abstract machine with a *stack* and a *store*. All terminating programs evaluate to a *result* in $\mathcal{R}$ which is the set of references (referred to as *object names* $\mathcal{H}$) and constants. An evaluation relation is introduced, written

$$S, \sigma \vdash a \rightsquigarrow v, \sigma' ,$$

meaning program *a* evaluated with stack *S* and initial store σ terminates with result *v* and final store σ'. We also have the set $\mathcal{F}$ of fieldnames and $\mathcal{M}$ of methodnames. A stack is a partial mapping from variables to *results*. A store is a mapping from object names to a pair of records: one of results indexed by field names, and one of method closures indexed by method names.

The verification logic is used for deriving judgements of the form

$$\Gamma \Vdash a : A :: T$$

where Γ is a *context*, *a* is a program, *A* a *specification* and *T* is a *transition relation*. A context is a sequence $x_0:A_0, \dots, x_k:A_k$ of variable/specification pairs. Transition relations describe the behaviour of executing a program. They play the rôle of the assertions *p* and *q* in a Hoare triple $\{p\}S\{q\}$ and use the pseudo-variables $(\grave{\sigma}, all\grave{o}c)$ and $(\acute{\sigma}, all\acute{o}c)$ to refer, respectively, to the store before and after execution, and *r* to refer the result. As a pair, $(\sigma, alloc)$ can be considered as a (curried) partial function of type $\mathcal{H} \rightharpoonup (\mathcal{F} \cup \mathcal{M}) \rightharpoonup \mathcal{R}$. Formally σ is a total function of type $(\mathcal{H} \times (\mathcal{F} \cup \mathcal{M})) \rightarrow \mathcal{R}$ and *alloc* is a predicate over $\mathcal{H}$ that defines the domain of the partial function. A specification describes what a result from executing a program can potentially do. It can be thought of as the *interface* of an object. Specifications are necessary because a result can be an object with methods which are in essence "thunked" functions in the sense of suspended computations. For compositionality of these verification judgements, it is important that we can deduce what potential behaviour an object has.

We follow [2] and introduce the abbreviation *Res* for creating transition relations, defined by

$$Res(e) \stackrel{\text{def}}{=} r = e \wedge (\forall x, y).(\acute{\sigma}(x,y) = \grave{\sigma}(x,y) \wedge (a\acute{l}loc(x) \equiv a\grave{l}loc(x)))\ .$$

The predicate *Res(e)* is used to describe an execution where the result of evaluation is *e* and the store is not changed. For example, we have the constant rule

$$\frac{E \Vdash \diamond}{E \Vdash \textit{false} : \textit{Bool} :: \textit{Res(false)}}$$

(where the judgement $E \Vdash \diamond$ simply means that E is a welldefined environment.) This rule states that evaluating a constant does not change the store and the result of evaluation is the constant itself. Another easy rule is that for field lookup:

$$\frac{E \Vdash x : [f{:}A] :: Res(x)}{E \Vdash x.f : A :: Res(\grave{\sigma}(x, f))}\ .$$

Note that in the premise, we have the simple judgement $E \Vdash x : [f{:}A] :: Res(x)$. To apply this rule to variables that have more fields or even methods, we must apply the subsumption rule that is defined below.

By allowing transition relations to be strengthened in a subspecification, the subtype relation is straight-forwardly extended to specifications to give a subspecification relation $<:$. The formal definition can be found in Sec. 3.3 of [2].

Using the subspecification relation, we have the important rule of subsumption for verification judgments:

$$\frac{\Vdash A <: A' \quad \Vdash_{fol} T \Rightarrow T' \quad E \Vdash a : A : T}{E \Vdash a : A' : T'}$$

provided A' and T' are wellformed. Here $\Vdash_{fol} \phi$ denotes provability in first-order logic augmented with the standard axioms for equality.

We also have the let rule. This rule is defined

$$\frac{\begin{array}{l} E \Vdash a : A :: T \quad E, x{:}A \Vdash b : B :: T' \\ E \Vdash B \quad E \Vdash T'' \text{ is a transition relation} \\ \Vdash_{fol} T[\grave{\sigma}/\acute{\sigma}, a\grave{l}loc/a\acute{l}loc, x/r] \wedge T'[\grave{\sigma}/\grave{\sigma}, a\grave{l}loc/a\grave{l}loc] \Rightarrow T'' \end{array}}{E \Vdash \textit{let } x{=}a \textit{ in } b : B :: T''}$$

where the judgement $E \Vdash B$ means that B is a wellformed specification. Intuitively, we have $E \Vdash \textit{let } x{=}a \textit{ in } b : B :: T''$ provided T'' is a consequence of T and T'. The substitutions $[\grave{\sigma}/\acute{\sigma}, a\grave{l}loc/a\acute{l}loc, x/r]$ and $[\grave{\sigma}/\grave{\sigma}, a\grave{l}loc/a\grave{l}loc]$ handle the intermediate state that exists after executing a but before executing b and also the assignment of the result of a to variable x.

With the exception of the subsumption rule, the let rule is the only other rule that cannot be applied backwards. This is because the premise contains the following formula

$$\Vdash_{fol} T[\breve{\sigma}/\acute{\sigma}, a\breve{l}loc/a\acute{l}loc, x/r] \wedge T'[\breve{\sigma}/\grave{\sigma}, a\breve{l}loc/a\grave{l}loc] \Rightarrow T''$$

and the formulae on the left of the connective do not appear in the conclusion of the rule. This formula is necessary because

$$T[\breve{\sigma}/\acute{\sigma}, a\breve{l}loc/a\acute{l}loc, x/r] \wedge T'[\breve{\sigma}/\grave{\sigma}, a\breve{l}loc/a\grave{l}loc]$$

is not a transition relation since it possibly has free occurences of $\breve{\sigma}$, $a\breve{l}loc$) and x. In a higher-order setting, we can use existential quantification to bind such free variables. Note that this problem is not present in Hoare logic because the intermediate state is existentially quantified in the metalogic.

3 Implementation

We implement a logic that is based on that presented in [2]. In the implementation we: encode the language syntax using HOAS; and use the meta-logic itself as the logic for writing transition relations.

Since our meta-logic is higher-order, our logic differs from that of [2] in that transition relations are now higher-order formulae. We appropriately modify the premises in the subsumption and let rules to take into account this difference.

A convenient consequence of our use of higher-order logic is that we can derive new rules that are often easier to use.

3.1 Metalanguage

We now introduce the metalanguage which is used to present the implementation of the program logic. The metalanguage is based on a higher-order simply-typed lambda calculus.

For base types, we have the natural numbers nat, booleans bool, variables VV, fieldnames FN, methodnames MN, results EE, specifications SS and program terms PP. We have the usual type formers: propositions Prop, function space $\tau_1 \to \tau_2$, product space $\tau_1 \times \tau_2$, τ_1-indexed record $\mathsf{Rcd}_{\tau_1}^{\tau_2}$ with entries from τ_2, variables x, application $e_1 \, e_2$ and abstraction $\lambda x^\tau . e_1$. The type of transition relations TR is defined to be $\mathsf{EE} \to (\mathsf{EE} \to \mathsf{FN} \to \mathsf{EE})^2 \to (\mathsf{EE} \to \mathsf{Prop})^2 \to \mathsf{Prop}$, where we write $\cdots \to A^2 \to \cdots$ as shorthand for $\cdots \to A \to A \to \cdots$.

We define a higher-order classical logic using the constants $\forall_\tau : (\tau \to \mathsf{Prop}) \to \mathsf{Prop}$ and $\supset: \mathsf{Prop} \to \mathsf{Prop} \to \mathsf{Prop}$ for universal quantification and implication respectively. We take the standard classical higher-order logic encodings of conjunction ($\wedge$), disjunction ($\vee$), negation ($\neg$), existential quantification ($\exists$) and Leibniz equality $=^\tau: \tau \to \tau \to \mathsf{Prop}$.

For predicates $P, Q : \tau \to$ Prop, we write $P \subseteq Q$ as shorthand for $\forall_\tau x. P(x) \supset Q(x)$. In particular, for sets A and B, the formula $A \subseteq B$ simply means than A is a subset of B, as expected. We define composition of $T :$ TR and $U :$ EE $\to$ TR, written $T; U$ by

$$(T; U)(r, \breve{\sigma}, \acute{\sigma}, a\breve{l}loc, a\acute{l}loc) \stackrel{\text{def}}{=} \exists \breve{r}, \breve{\sigma}, a\breve{l}loc. T(\breve{r}, \grave{\sigma}, \breve{\sigma}, a\grave{l}loc, a\breve{l}loc) \wedge$$
$$U(\breve{r}, r, \breve{\sigma}, \acute{\sigma}, a\breve{l}loc, a\acute{l}loc) \quad .$$

We have for constants: the normal constants for natural numbers (0, succ, $+, \dots$); booleans (**ff**, **tt**, **and**, $\dots$); product types ($\pi_1^{\tau_1, \tau_2} \pi_2^{\tau_1, \tau_2}$, $\langle -, - \rangle_{\tau_1, \tau_2}$; the record manipulation constants:

$$\text{lookup}_{\tau_1, \tau_2} : \text{Rcd}_{\tau_1}^{\tau_2} \to \tau_1 \to \tau_2 \quad \text{update}_{\tau_1, \tau_2} : \text{Rcd}_{\tau_1}^{\tau_2} \to \tau_1 \to \tau_2 \to \text{Rcd}_{\tau_1}^{\tau_2}$$
$$\text{empty}_{\tau_1, \tau_2} : \text{Rcd}_{\tau_1}^{\tau_2} \quad \text{domain}_{\tau_1, \tau_2} : \text{Rcd}_{\tau_1}^{\tau_2} \to \tau_1 \to \text{Prop} \ .$$

We omit type annotations whenever possible, use parentheses with commas for (possibly) repeated application of terms, and infix notation where appropriate. We use the more succinct notation $[f_1=a_1, \dots, f_k=a_k]$ for records, and for a of type $\text{Rcd}_{\tau_1}^{\tau_2}$, we write a_e for $\text{lookup}(a, e)$. We write $f \in \text{dom}(r)$ for $\text{domain}_{\tau_1, \tau_2}(r, f)$.

We have two types of judgements: typing judgements $\Gamma \vdash e : \tau$ and validity judgements $\Gamma \vdash \phi$ provided $\Gamma \vdash \phi :$ Prop. We take the standard typing rules of simply typed lambda calculus and the standard logical rules and axioms of classical higher-order logic with Leibniz equality.

The intended interpretation of elements of record types are partial functions with finite domain. Thus equality over record types is the standard equality of partial functions, namely equality on their graphs. Thus we have a number of axioms on records that delineate this interpretation.

3.2   Program Logic

The remaining constants are those for the program logic: specification constructors nat : SS, bool : SS and obj : $\text{Rcd}_{\text{FN}}^{\text{EE} \to \text{SS}} \to \text{Rcd}_{\text{MN}}^{\text{EE} \times \text{EE} \to \text{TR}} \to$ SS; specification subsumption $<:$: SS $\to$ SS $\to$ Prop; program term constructors false : PP, true : PP, let : PP $\to$ (VV $\to$ PP) $\to$ PP, obj : $\text{Rcd}_{\text{FN}}^{\text{VV}} \to \text{Rcd}_{\text{MN}}^{\text{VV} \to \text{PP}} \to$ PP, if : VV $\to$ PP $\to$ PP $\to$ PP, var : VV $\to$ PP, fsel : VV $\to$ FN $\to$ PP, minv : VV $\to$ MN $\to$ PP and fupd : VV $\to$ FN $\to$ VV $\to$ PP; the value constructors bool$_\text{EE}$: bool $\to$ EE and nat$_\text{EE}$: nat $\to$ EE; and the formal symbol that represents the stack var$_\text{EE}$: VV $\to$ EE. The constants bool$_\text{EE}$, nat$_\text{EE}$, and var$_\text{EE}$ can be seen as coercion functions and will therefore be omitted in this presentation.

Constant let gives our encoding of syntax its higher-order nature. As an illustration: program

$\qquad$ *let x=true in if x then false else true*

has encoding

$\qquad$ let(true, $\lambda x.$if(x, false, true)) .

We generalise the encoding procedure and write $\ulcorner a \urcorner$ for the encoding of a.

Most important of all, we have the constant $[- : - :: -] : \mathsf{PP} \to \mathsf{SS} \to \mathsf{TR} \to \mathsf{Prop}$ and we encode the rules so that if

$$x_1{:}A_1, \ldots, x_n{:}A_n \Vdash a : A :: T$$

then we have

$$\vdash \forall x_1, \ldots x_n.[x_1 : \ulcorner A_1 \urcorner] \supset \cdots \supset [x_n : \ulcorner A_1 \urcorner] \supset [\ulcorner a \urcorner : \ulcorner A \urcorner :: \ulcorner T \urcorner]$$

where $[- : -]$ is defined by $[x : A] \overset{\text{def}}{=} [\mathsf{var}(x) : A :: \mathsf{Res}(x)]$.

Hereafter, unless explicitly typed otherwise, (meta-)variables and decorated variants of: n have type nat, x and y have type VV; f have type FN; m have type MN; a have type PP; b have type VV $\to$ PP; A have type SS; B have type EE $\to$ SS; T have type TR; and U have type EE $\to$ TR.

Subsumption axioms. The following axioms are for the subsumption relation.

$$\forall_{\mathsf{Rcd}^{\mathsf{SS}}_{\mathsf{FN}}} A, A'.\forall_{\mathsf{Rcd}^{(\mathsf{EE}\to\mathsf{SS})\times(\mathsf{EE}\to\mathsf{TR})}_{\mathsf{MN}}} B, B'.$$

$$\begin{aligned}
&(\mathsf{dom}(A') \subseteq \mathsf{dom}(A)) \supset \\
&(\forall f \in \mathsf{dom}(A').A_f = A'_f) \supset \\
&(\mathsf{dom}(B') \subseteq \mathsf{dom}(B)) \supset \\
&(\forall m \in \mathsf{dom}(B').\pi_1(B_m) <: \pi_1(B'_m)) \supset \\
&(\forall m \in \mathsf{dom}(B').\forall y.\pi_2(B_m)(y) \subseteq \pi_2(B'_m)(y)) \supset \\
&\quad \mathsf{obj}(A, B) <: \mathsf{obj}(A', B')
\end{aligned} \tag{ss\_obj}$$

$$\mathsf{bool} <: \mathsf{bool} \tag{ss\_bool}$$

$$\mathsf{nat} <: \mathsf{nat} \tag{ss\_nat}$$

Program axioms. The remaining axioms are those of the program logic. They are encoded as follows.

$$\begin{aligned}
&\forall a.\forall A'.\forall T'.\forall A.\forall T. \\
&\quad (A <: A') \supset \\
&\quad (T \subseteq T') \supset \\
&\quad [a : A :: T] \supset [a : A' :: T']
\end{aligned} \tag{ws\_subs}$$

$$[\mathsf{false} : \mathsf{bool} :: \mathsf{Res}(\mathtt{ff})] \tag{ws\_constf}$$

$$[\mathsf{true} : \mathsf{bool} :: \mathsf{Res}(\mathtt{tt})] \tag{ws\_constt}$$

$$\forall n.[\mathsf{nat}(n) : \mathsf{nat} :: \mathsf{Res}(n)] \tag{ws\_nat}$$

As an example of functions over constants, for any binary natural number operation op, we have

$$\begin{aligned}
&\forall x_0, x_1. \\
&\quad [x_0 : \mathsf{nat}] \supset [x_1 : \mathsf{nat}] \supset \\
&\quad [op(x_0, x_1) : \mathsf{nat} :: \mathsf{Res}(op(x_0, x_1))]
\end{aligned} \tag{ws\_natop}$$

$\forall x.\forall a_0, a_1.\forall B.\forall U.\forall B_0, B_1.\forall U_0, U_1.$
$[x : \text{bool}] \supset$
$[a_0 : B_0(x) :: U_0(x)] \supset$
$(B_0(\mathbf{tt}) = B(\mathbf{tt}) \wedge U_0(\mathbf{tt}) \equiv U(\mathbf{tt})) \supset$ $\hspace{2cm}$ (ws_cond)
$[a_1 : B_1(x) :: U_1(x)] \supset$
$(B_1(\mathbf{ff}) = B(\mathbf{ff}) \wedge U_1(\mathbf{ff}) \equiv U(\mathbf{ff})) \supset$
$[\text{if}(x, a_0, a_1) : B(x) :: U(x)]$

$\forall a.\forall b.\forall A'.\forall T''.\forall A.\forall T.\forall U.$
$[a : A :: T] \supset$
$(\forall x.[x : A] \supset [b(x) : A' :: U(x)]) \supset$ $\hspace{2cm}$ (ws_let)
$(T; U \subseteq T'') \supset$
$[\text{let}(a, b) : B :: T'']$

$\forall x.\forall m.\forall B.\forall U.$
$[x : \text{obj}([], [m=\langle B, U\rangle])] \supset$ $\hspace{2cm}$ (ws_minv)
$[\text{minv}(x, m) : B(x) :: U(x)]$

$\forall x.\forall f.\forall A.\forall T.$
$[x : \text{obj}([f=A], [])] \supset$
$(\forall r.\forall \grave{\sigma}, \acute{\sigma}.\forall alloc, al\acute{l}oc.$ $\hspace{4cm}$ (ws_fsel)
$\quad T(r, \grave{\sigma}, \acute{\sigma}, al\grave{l}oc, al\acute{l}oc) \equiv \text{Res}(\acute{\sigma}(x, f), r, \grave{\sigma}, \acute{\sigma}, al\grave{l}oc, al\acute{l}oc)) \supset$
$[\text{fsel}(x, f) : A :: T]$

$\forall_{\text{Rcd}_{\text{FN}}^{\text{VV}}} x.\forall_{\text{Rcd}_{\text{MN}}^{\text{VV} \rightarrow \text{PP}}} b.\forall_{\text{Rcd}_{\text{FN}}^{\text{SS}}} A.\forall_{\text{Rcd}_{\text{MN}}^{(\text{EE} \rightarrow \text{SS}) \times (\text{EE} \rightarrow \text{TR})}} B.\forall T.$
$(\text{dom}(x) = \text{dom}(A) \wedge \text{dom}(b) = \text{dom}(B)) \supset$
$(\forall f \in \text{dom}(x).[\text{var}(x_f) : A_f]) \supset$
$(\forall m \in \text{dom}(b).\forall y.[y : \text{obj}(A, B)] \supset [b_m(y) : \pi_1(B_m)(y) :: \pi_2(B_m)(y)]) \supset$
$$\left(\begin{array}{l} \forall r.\forall \grave{\sigma}, \acute{\sigma}.\forall al\grave{l}oc, al\acute{l}oc. \\ \quad T(r, \grave{\sigma}, \acute{\sigma}, al\grave{l}oc, al\acute{l}oc) \equiv (\forall z.z \neq r \supset al\grave{l}oc(z) \equiv al\acute{l}oc(z)) \wedge \\ \hspace{3.5cm} (\forall f \in \text{dom}(x).\acute{\sigma}(r, f) = x_f) \wedge \\ \hspace{3.5cm} (\forall z.\forall w.z \neq r \supset \grave{\sigma}(z, w) = \acute{\sigma}(z, w)) \end{array} \right) \supset$$
$[\text{obj}(x, b) : \text{obj}(A, B) :: T]$

$\hspace{10cm}$ (ws_obj)

$\forall x, y.\forall f.\forall_{\text{Rcd}_{\text{FN}}^{\text{SS}}} A.\forall_{\text{Rcd}_{\text{MN}}^{(\text{EE} \rightarrow \text{SS}) \times (\text{EE} \rightarrow \text{TR})}} B.\forall T.$
$[x : \text{obj}(A, B)] \supset$
$[y : A_f] \supset$
$$\left(\begin{array}{l} \forall r.\forall \grave{\sigma}, \acute{\sigma}.\forall al\grave{l}oc, al\acute{l}oc. \\ \quad T(r, \grave{\sigma}, \acute{\sigma}, al\grave{l}oc, al\acute{l}oc) \equiv r = x \wedge \acute{\sigma}(x, f) = y \wedge \\ \hspace{3cm} (\forall z.\forall w.\neg(z = x \wedge w = f) \supset \\ \hspace{4cm} \grave{\sigma}(z, w) = \acute{\sigma}(z, w)) \wedge \\ \hspace{3cm} al\grave{l}oc = al\acute{l}oc \end{array} \right) \supset$$
$[\text{fupd}(x, f, y) : \text{obj}(A, B) :: T]$

$\hspace{10cm}$ (ws_fupd)

4 Examples

We have attempted several examples in our implementation. Initially, we followed the development in [2] and introduced some abbreviations to make our programs more succinct. Furthermore we derived, using the existing axioms, theorems (or equivalently, derivable rules) for these syntactic abbreviations.

For example, in the pure language, field selection strictly has the form $x.f$ where x is a variable. We introduce an abbreviation so that for an arbitrary program a, the program $a.f$ is an abbreviation for *let $x=a$ in $x.f$*, for x not free in a. This is encoded into our formal system by defining

$$\mathsf{fsel}'(a, f) \stackrel{\text{def}}{=} \mathsf{let}(a, \lambda x.\mathsf{fsel}(x, f)) \ .$$

We shall simply overload our existing notation and write fsel for fsel'. Crucially, we then prove the following theorem.

$$\vdash \forall a.\forall f.\forall A.\forall T', T.$$
$$[a : \mathsf{obj}([f{=}A], []) :: T] \supset$$
$$(\forall r.\forall \grave{\sigma}, \acute{\sigma}.\forall alloc, a\grave{l}loc.$$
$$T'(r, \grave{\sigma}, \acute{\sigma}, alloc, a\acute{l}loc) \equiv$$
$$\exists \breve{r}, \breve{\sigma}, a\grave{l}loc.T(\breve{r}, \grave{\sigma}, \breve{\sigma}, a\grave{l}loc, alloc) \wedge \mathsf{Res}(\acute{\sigma}(\breve{r}, f), r, \breve{\sigma}, \acute{\sigma}, a\grave{l}loc, a\acute{l}loc)) \supset$$
$$[\mathsf{fsel}(a, f) : A :: T']$$

(Note the use of the existential quantification in T' to account for the intermediate store and result of evaluating a.) This theorem allows us to directly derive judgments about programs using fsel without expanding its definition.

We continue to extend and overload the remaining program constructors and derive corresponding "higher-level" rules. Using these rules, we successfully prove the examples given in Sec. 4.1–2 of [2]. We then derive an easier-to-use let rule before attempting two larger examples: the greatest common divisor program (Sec. 4.3 in [2]), and an original example based on the dining philosophers scenario. We consider these two examples in more detail after the new let rule.

4.1 Reversible Let Rule

As mentioned in Sec. 2 the let rule is not reversible. In particular, whenever we apply the let rule, we must decide on what information to lose. Since most programs use the let constructor extensively, this quickly becomes cumbersome.

Using our implementation, we can derive the following substitute for the let rule.

$$\forall a.\forall b.\forall A'.\forall T''.\forall A.\forall T.\forall U.$$
$$[a : A :: T] \supset$$
$$(\forall x.[x : A] \supset [b(x) : A' :: U(x)]) \supset \qquad\qquad (\mathsf{wsq\_let})$$
$$(T; U \equiv T'') \supset$$
$$[\mathsf{let}(a, b) : B :: T'']$$

This rule does not lose any information. In proof derivations, it is particularly useful because information loss can be postponed until later using an explicit application of the subsumption axiom.

4.2   Greatest Common Divisor

The gcd program from [2], can be written using notation closer to that of popular OO languages, as follows. It is a simple exercise to translate this program into our formal language.

$$\text{calc\_gcd} \overset{\text{def}}{=} \lambda y.$$

$$\begin{array}{lll} \texttt{if} & (y.f < y.g) & \{y.g = y.g - y.f; y.m()\} \\ \texttt{else if} & (y.g < y.f) & \{y.f = y.f - y.g; y.m()\} \\ \texttt{else} & & \{y.f\} \end{array}$$

$$\text{gcd} \overset{\text{def}}{=} \text{obj}([f{=}\text{nat}(1), g{=}\text{nat}(1)], [m{=}\text{calc\_gcd}])$$

This program creates an object with one method m, such that if the fields have nonzero values a and b, invoking m will reduce both fields to the gcd of a and b. This is the intuition behind the formal specification given in [2]. To prove the formal specification statement in our logic, we strengthen the transition relation given in [2]. We can then prove that gcd satisfies the stronger specification. The subsumption axiom can be used to return to the original statement. We introduce the constant gcd : $\mathsf{EE} \to \mathsf{EE} \to \mathsf{EE}$ and add axioms consistent with its interpretation as the gcd function over natural numbers. And so we define

$$U_{\text{gcd}}(y) \overset{\text{def}}{=} \lambda r.\lambda \acute{\sigma}, \acute{\sigma}.\lambda alloc, alloc.$$
$$(1 \leq \acute{\sigma}(y, f) \wedge 1 \leq \acute{\sigma}(y, g)) \supset$$
$$r = \acute{\sigma}(y, f) \wedge r = \acute{\sigma}(y, g) \wedge$$
$$r = \text{gcd}(\acute{\sigma}(y, f), \acute{\sigma}(y, g)) \wedge$$
$$1 \leq \acute{\sigma}(y, f) \wedge 1 \leq \acute{\sigma}(y, g)$$

$$\text{Spec}_{\text{gcd}} \overset{\text{def}}{=} \text{obj}([f = \text{nat}, g = \text{nat}], [m = \langle \text{nat}, U_{\text{gcd}} \rangle]) \ .$$

Using these definitions, we can prove

$$\vdash [\text{gcd} : \text{Spec}_{\text{gcd}} :: T_{\text{triv}}]$$

where T_{triv} is a trivial transition relation.

4.3   Dining Philosophers

Object oriented languages have shown to be particularly suitable for writing simulations. In the next example, we consider a simulation in an OO language for a formalisation of the dining philosophers scenario. The formalisation we choose is based on that presented in Roscoe's book [9], where a general description of the scenario can be found. Our implementation follows Roscoe's observation that the important events that we should model are when the forks get picked up and put down. To make the example more managable, we only consider the case for three philosophers at the table.

We simulate the scenario by creating an object for each fork, and an object for each philosopher. The philophers interact with the forks by invoking their methods. In our example, two of the philosphers pick up their forks "left then right" and one picks up his forks "right then left." The resulting system is known not to deadlock. We prove this using a suitable formalisation of "does not deadlock."

Here is code to create a fork object.

$$\text{Fork} \stackrel{\text{def}}{=} \text{obj}([\text{on\_table}=\text{true}],$$

```
          [try_pick_up=λs. if  (s.on_table) {s.on_table = false; true}
                           else {false}
           put_down=λs.s.on_table = true; false])
```

A philosopher object invokes the try_pick_up method to pick up a fork. The method returns true after updating the fork object's state if this is possible. It returns false if the fork is not on the table.

We introduce the following definitions for creating the two types of philosophers.

```
phil_tick  def= λs. if  (s.n_forks == 0 and s.hungry) {
                    if  (s.fork1.try_pick_up()) {s.n_forks = 1; false}
                    else  {false}
                } else if  (s.n_forks == 1 and s.hungry) {
                    if  (s.fork2.try_pick_up())
                       {s.n_forks = 2; s.hungry = false; false}
                    else  {false}
                } else if  (s.n_forks == 2) {
                    s.fork2.put_down(); s.n_forks = 1; false
                } else {
                    s.fork1.put_down(); s.n_forks = 0; s.hungry = true; false
                }
```

$\text{LRPhil} \stackrel{\text{def}}{=} \lambda fork_l, fork_r.\text{Phil}(fork_l, fork_r)$

$\text{RLPhil} \stackrel{\text{def}}{=} \lambda fork_l, fork_r.\text{Phil}(fork_r, fork_l)$

$\text{Phil} \stackrel{\text{def}}{=} \lambda fork_1, fork_2.$
```
          obj([hungry=true, n_forks=nat(0),
              fork1=var(fork1), fork2=var(fork2)],
              [tick=phil_tick])
```

A philospher has four internal states: (1) he is hungry and is holding no forks; (2) he is hungry and he is holding one fork; (3) he is no longer hungry[1] and is holding two forks; and (4) he is not hungry and holding one fork. Each state transition corresponds exactly to a fork being either picked up or put down.

---

[1] Here we assume that the philosopher instantaneously eats as soon as he picks up the second fork and so is no longer hungry. The point is that the event corresponding to a philosopher eating is not important with respect to deadlock considerations.

Finally, we put the whole system together as follows by creating a "table" object.

$$
\begin{aligned}
\text{Table} \stackrel{\text{def}}{=}\ & \text{let}(fork_1 = \text{Fork}, fork_2 = \text{Fork}, fork_3 = \text{Fork}, \\
& phil_1 = \text{LRPhil}(fork_1, fork_2), \\
& phil_2 = \text{LRPhil}(fork_2, fork_3), \\
& phil_3 = \text{RLPhil}(fork_3, fork_1), \\
& \text{obj}(\\
& \quad [\text{f1}{=}fork_1, \text{f2}{=}fork_2, \text{f3}{=}fork_3, \\
& \quad \text{p1}{=}phil_1, \text{p2}{=}phil_2, \text{p3}{=}phil_3], \\
& \quad [\text{tick1}{=}\lambda s.s.\text{p1.tick}(), \\
& \quad \ \text{tick2}{=}\lambda s.s.\text{p2.tick}(), \\
& \quad \ \text{tick3}{=}\lambda s.s.\text{p3.tick}()]))
\end{aligned}
$$

The table should be considered as a "black box" with three buttons, one for each of the tick methods. To complete the simulation, one must compose this program with another program that plays out the possible traces of the system.

With the dining philosopher scenario simulated by these code fragments, we can prove that this system does not deadlock, which we will now formalise. We say that a philosopher is *blocked* whenever he needs to pick up a fork to perform a state transition but cannot (exactly when the fork in question is not on the table.) The system is *deadlocked* precisely when all the philosophers on the table are blocked.

Given the store σ, we can determine whether any particular philosopher is blocked by inspecting the values of the fields of the philosopher and its forks. To assist our intuitions, we define the following predicates. "Philosopher p is holding fork *fork*",

$$
\begin{aligned}
\text{is\_holding} \stackrel{\text{def}}{=}\ \lambda p.\lambda fork.\lambda\sigma.\ & \sigma(p, \text{n\_forks}) = 1 \wedge fork = \sigma(p, \text{fork1}) \vee \\
& \sigma(p, \text{n\_forks}) = 2 \wedge fork = \sigma(p, \text{fork1}) \vee \\
& \sigma(p, \text{n\_forks}) = 2 \wedge fork = \sigma(p, \text{fork2})
\end{aligned}
$$

"Philosopher p is waiting for fork *fork*,"

$$
\begin{aligned}
\text{waiting\_for} \stackrel{\text{def}}{=}\ \lambda p.\lambda fork.\lambda\sigma. \\
& (\sigma(p, \text{n\_forks}) = 0 \wedge \sigma(\sigma(p, \text{fork1}), \text{on\_table}) = \texttt{ff} \\
& \quad \wedge\ fork = \sigma(p, \text{fork1})) \\
& \vee\ (\sigma(p, \text{n\_forks}) = 1 \wedge \sigma(\sigma(p, \text{fork2}), \text{on\_table}) = \texttt{ff} \\
& \quad \wedge\ fork = \sigma(p, \text{fork2}))\ .
\end{aligned}
$$

Assuming that $F(t)$ is the set of forks, and $P(t)$ the set of philosophers on table t, for $p \in P(t)$, the predicate "philosopher p is blocked,"

$$
\text{blocked} \stackrel{\text{def}}{=} \lambda t.\lambda p.\lambda\sigma.\exists_{F(t)} fork.\text{waiting\_for}(p, fork, \sigma)
$$

and "all philosophers are blocked,"

$$\text{all\_blocked} \stackrel{\text{def}}{=} \lambda t.\lambda\sigma.\forall_{P(t)}p.\text{blocked}(p,\sigma) \ .$$

One way to prove that our system does not deadlock is to use the following fact. Let $\prec$ be a total order such that $fork_1 \prec fork_2 \prec fork_3$. It is the case that the order in which the philosophers pick up their forks respects $\prec$. It is then straightforward to prove that the system does not deadlock[2].

For table t, order relation $orel$ and store σ, if we define InvTable by

$$
\begin{aligned}
\text{InvTable}(t, orel, \sigma) \stackrel{\text{def}}{=} \ &\forall_{P(t)}p.\text{InvPhil}(p, orel, \sigma) \wedge \\
&(\forall_{F(t)}f.\sigma(f, \text{on\_table}) = \text{ff} \supset \\
&\quad \exists_{P(t)}p.\text{is\_holding}(p, f, \sigma)) \wedge \\
&\text{f\_p\_relationship} \wedge \text{f\_distinct} \wedge \text{p\_distinct}
\end{aligned}
$$

where f_p_relationship states that the fork fields of the philosophers point to the intended forks, f_distinct and p_distinct state that the fork and philosopher objects are pairwise distinct and

$$
\begin{aligned}
\text{InvPhil}(p, orel, \sigma) \stackrel{\text{def}}{=} \ &orel\,(\sigma(p, \text{fork1}), \sigma(p, \text{fork2})) \wedge \\
&(\text{state}_0(p) \vee \text{state}_1(p) \vee \text{state}_2(p) \vee \text{state}_3(p))
\end{aligned}
$$

where each $\text{state}_j(p)$ states the values of the n_forks and hungry fields of philosopher p at the corresponding state. It follows that if we define

$$
\begin{aligned}
\text{Spec}_{\text{Table}} \stackrel{\text{def}}{=} \ \text{obj}(\ &[\text{f1}=\text{Spec}_{\text{Fork}}, \text{f2}=\text{Spec}_{\text{Fork}}, \text{f3}=\text{Spec}_{\text{Fork}}, \\
&\text{p1}=\text{Spec}_{\text{Phil}}, \text{p2}=\text{Spec}_{\text{Phil}}, \text{p3}=\text{Spec}_{\text{Phil}}], \\
&[\text{tick1}=\text{TR}_{\text{tick}}, \text{tick2}=\text{TR}_{\text{tick}}, \text{tick3}=\text{TR}_{\text{tick}}])
\end{aligned}
$$

and

$$\text{TR}_{\text{tick}} \stackrel{\text{def}}{=} \lambda s, r.\lambda\acute{\sigma}, \acute{\sigma}.\lambda alloc, alloc.\text{InvTable}(s, \acute{\sigma}) \supset \text{InvTable}(s, \acute{\sigma})$$

we can prove in our logic,

$$\vdash [\text{Table} : \text{Spec}_{\text{Table}} :: \lambda r.\lambda\acute{\sigma}, \acute{\sigma}.\lambda alloc, alloc.\text{InvTable}(r, \prec, \acute{\sigma})] \ .$$

That is, InvTable is an *invariant* of the system. It is an invariant in the sense that it holds immediately after the table object is created, and it is invariant with respect to the actions of the three "buttons." Of course, $\text{Spec}_{\text{Fork}}$ and $\text{Spec}_{\text{Phil}}$ are specifications that are strong enough to describe the behaviour of fork and philosopher objects respectively.

Furthermore, we can prove, for table t, philosopher p, forks $fork$, $fork'$ and store σ,

$$\text{blocked}(p, \sigma) \supset \text{is\_holding}(p, fork, \sigma) \supset \sigma(p, \text{fork1}) = fork \tag{1}$$

$$\text{is\_holding}(p, fork, \sigma) \supset \text{waiting\_for}(p, fork', \sigma) \supset \sigma(p, \text{fork2}) = fork' \tag{2}$$

$$
\begin{aligned}
&\text{InvTable}(t, orel, \sigma) \supset \forall_{F(t)}fork. \\
&\quad \sigma(fork, \text{on\_table}) = \text{ff} \supset \exists_{P(t)}p.\text{is\_holding}(p, fork, \sigma)
\end{aligned}
\tag{3}
$$

---

[2] This is in fact a special case of Roscoe's rules for avoiding deadlock in [9].

and

$$\mathsf{InvTable}(t, orel, \sigma) \supset \forall_{P(t)} p.\ orel\ (\sigma(p, \mathsf{fork1}), \sigma(p, \mathsf{fork2}))\ . \tag{4}$$

Assuming this, it is straight forward to prove the corollary

$$\mathsf{InvTable}(t, orel, \sigma) \supset \neg\mathsf{all\_blocked}(t, \sigma)\ , \tag{5}$$

as required.

5 Soundness

Similar to AL we have the following soundness property.

Theorem 1. *Assume that $\emptyset, \emptyset \vdash a \rightsquigarrow v, \sigma'$ is provable. For boolean b, if*

$$\vdash [\ulcorner a \urcorner : \boldsymbol{bool} :: \lambda r.\lambda \hat{\sigma}, \acute{\sigma}.\lambda alloc, alloc.r = b]$$

then $v = b$.

We prove this, or rather an appropriate generalisation involving open programs and assumptions of the form $[x_i : A_i]$ where x_i are free program variables, by induction on the operational semantics, along the lines of the soundness proof in [2]. Complication arises from the fact that the predicates $[- : -]$ and $[- : - :: -]$ can appear in the transition relations, as can the constants for program constructions and specifications. We overcome this by assigning trivial meanings to these when they appear in transition relations. For example, $[- : - :: -]$ can be interpreted as constant true. The details will appear in an expanded version of this article.[3]

6 Conclusions and Related Work

Our implementation differs from other work not only because we use HOAS but also because we embed the logic in the metalogic directly. Primarily for the purpose of "language analysis," Nipkow et al.[4] have encoded an OO language in Isabelle/HOL[5] using a "deep embedding" for the syntax. Similarly, Honsell in [3] encodes the syntax of Dynamic Logic in a first-order style. Such encodings allow justification arguments to be given by induction over the syntax. In [7], Reddy presents an OO, Algol-like language IA$^+$ based on Reynold's Idealized Algol[8] and its specification logic. Language IA$^+$ uses HOAS and its specification logic is higher-order but programs can only create objects on the stack, not in the heap. In contrast, the language of AL creates objects in the heap (global store).

Our design decision to use HOAS has allowed us to quickly and succinctly implement a verification system since we inherit scoping rules and alpha conversion

---

[3] The originally submitted version of this article indicated a semantical soundness proof. In the meantime, we have realised that this more direct approach is possible.

from the metalanguage. Directly embedding the logical connectives results in a system that can take full advantage of the features of the underlying theorem prover.

The use of a theorem prover has shown to be invaluable for keeping track of the many assumptions that occur during the verification of nontrivial examples. However, in practice, it is still difficult to verify, using LEGO, even small examples such as those presented in this article. One often gets too involved trying to prove "trivial" subgoals. Since our implementation does not use any specific features of LEGO nor constructive type theory, we may find that using a theorem prover with more automation, such as PVS or Isabelle/HOL, would result in a more usable verification tool.

Acknowledgements

The authors would like to thank David von Oheimb, Jan Jürjens and anonymous referees for their comments on earlier versions of this article.

References

[1] Martín Abadi and Rustan Leino. A logic of object-oriented programs. In Michel Bidoit and Max Dauchet, editors, *TAPSOFT '97: Theory and Practice of Software Development, 7th International Joint Conference CAAP/FASE, Lille, France*, volume 1214 of *Lecture Notes in Computer Science*, pages 682–696. Springer-Verlag, New York, N.Y., 1997.

[2] Martín Abadi and Rustan Leino. A logic of object-oriented programs. SRC Research Reports SRC-161, Compaq SRC, September 1998. Revised version of [1].

[3] F. Honsell and M. Miculan. A natural deduction approach to dynamic logic. *Lecture Notes in Computer Science*, 1158, 1996.

[4] Tobias Nipkow, David von Oheimb, and Cornelia Pusch. μJava: Embedding a programming language in a theorem prover. In F.L. Bauer and R. Steinbrüggen, editors, *Foundations of Secure Computation*. IOS Press, 2000.

[5] Lawrence C. Paulson. *Isabelle: A Generic Theorem Prover*. Springer-Verlag LNCS 828, 1994.

[6] Robert Pollack. *The Theory of LEGO: A Proof Checker for the Extended Calculus of Constructions*. PhD thesis, University of Edinburgh, 1994.

[7] U. S. Reddy. Objects and classes in algol-like languages. In *Foundations of Object-oriented Languages*, January 1998.

[8] John C. Reynolds. Idealized algol and its specification logic. In Danielle Néel, editor, *Tools and Notions for Program Construction*, pages 121–161. Cambridge University Press, 1982.

[9] A. W. Roscoe. *The Theory and Practice of Concurrency*. Prentice Hall, 1997.

A Strong and Mechanizable Grand Logic*

M. Randall Holmes

Boise State University

Abstract. The purpose of this paper is to describe a "grand logic",
that is, a system of higher order logic capable of use as a general purpose foundation for mathematics. This logic has developed as the logic
of a theorem proving system which has had a number of names in its
career (EFTTP, Mark2, and currently Watson), and the suitability of
this logic for computer-assisted formal proof is an aspect which will be
considered, though not thoroughly. A distinguishing feature of this system is its relationship to Quine's set theory *NF* and related untyped
λ-calculi studied by the author.

1 Introduction

The theory we develop here will be referred to as W, after the current name
"Watson" of the theorem prover in which it is implemented (for a more through
discussion of this prover see [8]). The notation of the system will be presented
just as it is presented to (and by) the theorem prover.

The roots of this logical system are in Quine's set theory "New Foundations"
(*NF*) of [10], but it cannot be described simply as an implementation of *NF*.
NF is not known to be consistent; the grand logic presented here is (partly)
based on the variation *NFU* of *NF* presented by Jensen in [9], which is known
to be consistent and suitable for applications (see [7] for a development). *NF*
and *NFU* are set theories; W is an untyped λ-calculus. *NF* and *NFU* are usually
presented using standard first-order logic; this system interprets the notions of
propositional and predicate logic in terms of its own rather different primitives.

2 Syntax

The formal theory W presented here is an equational theory. All statements of W
are equations between terms (intended for use as rewrite rules) and the focus of
the theory is on the structure of terms rather than on the structure of propositions. Terms representing truth values stand in for propositions, and the usual
notions of propositional and predicate logic are expressed as operations on terms
representing truth values.

This section is devoted to the syntax of the language of W. First of all, if A
and B are terms, A = B is an equation (as statement of W); but the = operator

---

* The author gratefully acknowledges the support of US Army Research Office grant
DAAG55-98-1-0263

J. Harrison and M. Aagaard (Eds.): TPHOLs 2000, LNCS 1869, pp. 283–300, 2000.

also occurs as a term constructor with the natural meaning (A = B is a term which is equal to true if A = B holds and equal to false if A = B is false). The overloading of = should always be easily disambiguated in what follows.

Any string of positive length consisting of characters taken from the sets of letters, digits, and the special characters ? and _ is an atomic term.

Atomic terms are of four kinds:

numerals: Any atomic term consisting only of digits is a numeral. (This category may be regarded as subsumed under "constants" below: it is not of special logical interest).

bound variables: An atomic term consisting of ? followed by a non-zero-initial numeral is a bound variable.

free variables: An atomic term beginning with ? and containing another non-numeric character is a free variable.

constants: An atomic term not beginning with ? and containing a non-numeric character is a constant.

Before constructions of composite terms are introduced, a preliminary discussion of kinds of operator is needed.

operators: A string of special characters (not listed, but excluding all characters found in atomic constants and excluding paired forms such as quotes, braces, brackets, and parentheses) is an operator. In particular, @ and @! are operators representing two different kinds of function application, and , is the ordered pair constructor. Also, a string of alphanumerics preceded by a backquote ' is an operator.
It is important to note that an operator is not itself a term. We oversimplify by stipulating that each operator is either prefix or infix, but not both (there is some overloading in the prover). (Operators are declared infix or prefix in particular theories.)

We now present the constructions of composite terms.

prefix terms: A prefix term consists of a (prefix) operator followed by a term.
abstraction terms: An abstraction term (a function) consists of a term enclosed in brackets. (Abstraction terms implement λ-terms, and standard λ-notation will sometimes be used).
parenthesized term: A term enclosed in parentheses.
infix terms: An infix term consists of a atomic, abstraction, or parenthesized term, followed by an (infix) operator, followed by a term.
case expressions: A case expression consists of a parenthesized term, followed by | |, followed by a parenthesized term, followed by ,, followed by a term. The special operator | | may only occur in terms of this form.
reduction of parentheses: Parentheses around an atomic term or abstraction term may always be removed. Parentheses around an infix term or case expression may be removed except when it is the left subterm of an infix term or one of the two leftmost subterms of a case expression. If a term is obtained from another term by reduction of parentheses (or by the addition of parentheses for clarity), it is regarded as being the same term.

completeness of description: The class of terms is the intersection of all sets containing all atomic terms and closed under the term constructions given above.

This description of the syntax is based on the default order of precedence of the Watson prover, in which all operators have the same precedence and group to the right.

3 Equational Logic

The bedrock of the logic of W is equational logic. All statements in the language of W are equations, understood to be implicitly universally quantified over the free variables occurring in them. All free variables are untyped, with an exception described below (in the discussion of class abstraction).

In this section we restrict ourselves to the sublanguage of the language of W which excludes bound variables. (Abstraction terms without bound variables may occur; these represent constant functions.)

We define substitution for the restricted language without bound variables: if A, T are terms and ?x is any variable, we define $A\{T/?x\}$ as the result of replacing all occurrences of the variable ?x with (T). (Of course, the parentheses may then often be reduced away).

The basic rules of the equational logic of W are as follows:

reflexivity: For any term A, A = A is a theorem.
symmetry: If A = B is a theorem, then B = A is a theorem.
transitivity: If A = B is a theorem and B = C is a theorem, then A = C is a theorem.
localization: If A = B is a theorem and C is a term then $C\{A/?x\} = C\{B/?x\}$ is a theorem. (?x being any free variable).
specification: If A = B is a theorem and C is a term then $A\{C/?x\} = B\{C/?x\}$ is a theorem. (?x being any free variable).

These rules will need to be refined when bound variables are introduced.

4 The Logic of Terms Defined by Cases

We now consider the first part of the grand logic W, corresponding to propositional logic and the logic of identity.

We introduce the predeclared constants **true** and **false**, representing the truth values.

In a case expression T || U , V, we refer to the subterm T as the *hypothesis* of the case expression and to the subterms U and V as its *branches*. The intended meaning of the term (T = U) || V , W is "if T = U then V else W"; when T is not an equation, T || U, V is intended to have the same meaning as (true = T) || U , V.

We introduce axioms governing the behavior of the special term construction of "case expressions".

The basic axioms are the following:

P1: ((?x = ?x) || ?y , ?z) = ?y
P2: ((true = false) || ?y , ?z) = ?w
HYP: ((?a = ?b) || (A{?a/?x}) , B) =
    ((?a = ?b) || (A{?b/?x}) , B)
DIST: (A{((?a = ?b) || ?c , ?d)/?x}) =
    (?a = ?b) || A{?c/?x} , A{?d/?x}

The axioms **P1** and **P2** implement special cases of our preformal understanding that a case expression will be equal to its first branch when the hypothesis is true and to its second branch when the hypothesis is false. In an expression (A = B) || T , U, it should be clear that we can freely replace A with B or vice versa in the context T without affecting the value of the term: this is captured by the axiom **HYP**. The name is taken from the idea that this implements "reasoning under hypotheses". The axiom **DIST** allows the "distribution" of the hypothesis of a subterm over a larger context.

It should be noted that **HYP** and **DIST** are axiom schemes rather than single axioms (thanks to a referee for pointing out that I needed to say this!) They could in principle be replaced in almost all applications by single axioms of the form

*HYP: ((?a = ?b) || (?A @! ?a) , ?B) =
    ((?a = ?b) || (?A @! ?b) , ?B)
*DIST: (?A @! ((?a = ?b) || ?c , ?d) =
    (?a = ?b) || (?A @! ?c) , (?A @! ?d)

where (as noted above) @! is a function application operator. In earlier versions of the prover, axioms of the latter forms were actually used; applying such axioms to get each instance of the full schemes involved λ-abstraction and β-reduction. In the current version of the prover, there is built-in support for the application of the schemes, not involving any use of the function machinery of the prover, so it seems more natural to present the schemes.

The axiom set actually built into Watson is slightly larger, but we want to emphasize the extreme simplicity of the logic of case expressions presented here. The additional content provided by Watson can be presented as the pair of axioms:

EQ: (?a = ?b) = (?a = ?b) || true , false
GH: ((true = ?x) || ?y , ?z) = ?x || ?y , ?z

These can be regarded as providing implicit definitions of terms with the operator = and of case expressions with hypotheses which are not equations. Though these are useful constructions, it is worth noting that they are not an essential part of the underlying theory.

The following propositions are easy consequences of the six axioms given so far:

E1: (?a = ?a) = true
E2: (true = false) = false
B1: (true || ?x , ?y) = ?x
B2: (false || ?x , ?y) = ?y

Watson has **E1** and **B1-2** as built-in assumptions instead of **P1-2**; **E2** is provable from these and **EQ**, **GH**, as are **P1-2**.

The axiom **HYP** allows substitutions to be made in the left branch of the hypothesis under the locally valid assumption that the hypothesis is true; it may seem that we have neglected similar things one can do in the right branch using the assumption that the hypothesis is false, but this is not the case! We present three theorems, the last of which captures the use of negative hypotheses:

T0: ((?a = ?b) || ?x , ?x) = ?x
T1: ((?a = ?b) || A{((?a = ?b) || ?x, ?y)/?v} , ?z) =
    (?a = ?b) || A{?x/?v} , ?z
T2: ((?a = ?b) || ?x, A{((?a = ?b) || ?y , ?z)/?v}) =
    (?a = ?b) || ?x , A{?z/?v}

While the axiom **HYP** allows us to rewrite only in the left branch of a case expression, the theorems **T1** and **T2** allow rewriting of into both the left and right branches of case expressions, though of a more restricted nature.

We omit the easy proofs of **T0** and **T1**. We do prove **T2**.

(?a = ?b) || ?x, A{((?a = ?b) || ?y , ?z)/?v} = (EQ)

((?a = ?b) || true , false) || ?x ,
  A{(((?a = ?b) || true , false) || ?y , ?z)/?v} = (substitution)

(?u || ?x , A{(?u || ?y , ?z)/?v})
  {((?a = ?b) || true , false)/?u} = (DIST)

(?a = ?b) ||
  ((?u || ?x , A{(?u || ?y , ?z)/?v}){true/?u}),
  (?u || ?x , A{(?u || ?y , ?z)/?v}){false/?u} = (substitution)

(?a = ?b) ||
  (true || ?x , A{(true || ?y , ?z)/?v}) ,
  (false || ?x , A{(false || ?y , ?z)/?v}) = (B1 and B2)

(?a = ?b) || ?x , A{(false || ?y , ?z)/?v} = (B2)

(?a = ?b) || ?x , A{?z/?v}

which completes the proof of **T2**.

Though we regard the formulation using **DIST** and **HYP** as more mathematically elegant, it should be noted that taking **HYP** and **T0-2** as primitive assumptions is equivalent, and this is the axiomatization which is effectively hard-wired into the prover. We omit the short proof of **DIST** from **T0-2**.

Propositional connectives are readily defined using expressions defined by cases. We give only the definition of negation as an example.

Definition: ~T is defined as T || `false, true`

It is worth remarking that in case T is neither `true` nor `false`, this definition treats it in the same way as `false` (and so ~T is equal to `true` in this case). Similar considerations apply to the other propositional connectives.

We now prove a completeness theorem for the logic of case expressions in its intended interpretation.

A theory in the language of W is an set of equations between terms in the language of W (with some fixed set of constants and constant operators), closed under the application of the rules of equational logic (reflexivity, symmetry, transitivity, localization and specification).

Definition: If M is a set with more than one element, an environment for M relative to a theory is a map from the free variables of the language of W to elements of M.

An interpretation of the theory M is a map which takes any pair consisting of an environment for M and a term to an element of M.

An interpretation I is said to be sound for a theory if the following conditions hold:

1. If σ is an environment and **v** is a free variable, then $I(\sigma, v) = \sigma(v)$.
2. If t and u are terms such that $t = u$ is an equation in the theory, and σ is any environment, then $I(\sigma, t) = I(\sigma, u)$.
3. $I(\sigma, \text{true}) \neq I(\sigma, \text{false})$ for any σ.
4. If t is a term containing no free variables, then $I(\sigma, t) = I(\sigma', t)$ for any environments σ and σ'.

We now prove a

Completeness Theorem: Any theory which does not have **true** = **false** as an element has a sound interpretation in a set M which is at most countably infinite.

Proof: We construct an interpretation whose range is the set of equivalence classes of variable-free terms of the language of the theory under a suitable equivalence relation.

Terms T and U will be equivalent if they are provably equal in the theory. This is not sufficient to define the desired equivalence relation, because the theory may not be complete (it may not allow the decision of all equations). To define the complete theory, enumerate all equations between variable-free terms in its language. Consider the first equation T = U on this list with the property that neither T = U nor ((T = U)||true,false) = false is a theorem. It is straightforward to establish that T = U is a theorem iff $((T = U) || true , false) = true$ is a theorem, and so that $((T = U)||true,false) = false$ cannot both be theorems (because symmetry and transitivity of equality would force $true = false$ to be a theorem, contrary to hypothesis).

We claim that adding $T = U$ to the theory and closing under the application of the rules of equational logic will still produce a consistent theory ($true = false$ will not belong to the extended theory). Suppose otherwise: then we would have a proof

$$true = V1 = \ldots = Vn = false$$

with each step justified by an element of our theory or the equation $T = U$ (possibly combined with an application of the rule of localization).

We could then modify this proof to the following form:

$(T=U)||true,false =$
$(T=U)||V1,false =$
$\ldots$
$(T=U)||Vn,false =$
$(T=U)||false,false = (T0)$
$false$

Each step of this proof would be valid in the original theory: steps using equations of the original theory obviously remain valid and the steps using $T = U$ would be justified by applications of the axiom **HYP** of the logic of case expressions. So the original theory would prove $((T=U)||true,false) = false$, which we have seen is impossible.

We can then repeat this process to obtain a complete theory (one which decides every equation). The resulting complete theory allows us to define a sound interpretation I in the set of equivalence classes of variable-free terms of the language; $I(\sigma, t)$ will be the equivalence class of the term obtained from the term t by replacing each free variable v occurring in t with some element of the equivalence class of terms $\sigma(v)$. Since the language itself is no more than countably infinite, any partition of the set of terms of the language is likewise no more than countably infinite. The proof is complete.

It follows from the Completeness Theorem and the definability of notions of propositional logic and the logic of identity in the logic of case expressions given here that this logic codes all valid reasoning in propositional logic and the logic of identity (as claimed above). Complete implementations of propositional logic reasoning in several styles have been made in Watson, using the principles described here.

The definition of another version of this logic of case expressions and the proof of its completeness are found in our unpublished [4].

We are well aware that the use of an `if ... then... else ...` construction as a primitive in the definition of logical connectives is not novel. We have not seen it widely advertised that the four basic axioms (which we repeat here in standard notation for emphasis) together with rules of equational logic are sufficient to provide a basis for propositional logic and the logic of identity in an untyped context.

P1: $(\text{if } x = x \text{ then } y \text{ else } z) = y$
P2: $(\text{if } \text{true} = \text{false} \text{ then } y \text{ else } z) = z$
HYP: $(\text{if } a = b \text{ then } F(a) \text{ else } c) = (\text{if } a = b \text{ then } F(b) \text{ else } c)$
DIST: $F(\text{if } a = b \text{ then } c \text{ else } d) = (\text{if } a = b \text{ then } F(c) \text{ else } F(d))$

5 Bound Variables and Substitution

We introduce the notation for variable binding used in the prover, which is a system of the sort introduced by de Bruijn (in [2]) with "nameless dummies", though it is not the usual scheme of "de Bruijn indices". We also introduce the formal definition of substitution for this system and extend the rules of equational logic to the language as extended with bound variables.

The construction of functions is the only variable binding construction in the logic of Watson. There are two different kinds of function application, set function application, represented by the infix operator ⊙, and class function application, represented by the infix operator ⊙!. The same variable binding construction builds both set and class functions; there is a syntactical constraint on permitted occurrences of ⊙! in functions, but no corresponding restriction on permitted occurrences of ⊙. The application of the β-reduction rule is more restricted for the ⊙ operator than for ⊙!, as will be discussed in the next section.

We recall that an atomic term consisting of ? followed by a non-zero-initial numeral is a bound variable.

An occurrence of a term in Watson is said to have "level n" if it occurs as a subterm of n abstraction terms (if it is enclosed in n pairs of brackets, on a typographical level). The bound variable ?n cannot occur sensibly at a level lower than n (where the two occurrences of "n" in different type faces represent a positive integer and its numeral). The intended semantics is that an abstraction term [T] occurring at level $n - 1$ represents a λ-term (a function) in which the bound variable is ?n: so for example the term [?1] at level 0 stands for the function $(\lambda x.x)$: the term [[?1]] (at level 0) is $(\lambda x.(\lambda y.x))$, the map which sends x to the constant function of x (the K combinator) while [[?2]] is $(\lambda x.(\lambda y.y))$, the constant function whose value is the identity function. The term [[?3]] has no semantics at level 0 except as a subterm of a larger term; we cannot see the bracket that binds the bound variable ?3.

We formally qualify the notion of term to facilitate discussion of subterms of nontrivial level: a "level n term" is a term in which each bound variable ?m occurs enclosed in at least $m - n$ brackets. Note that any level n term is also a term of level m for each $m > n$, though the semantics of typographically identical terms may be different at different levels. Level 0 terms are the terms which have sensible semantics in a top-level term; level n terms are those terms which can appear in a level 0 term inside n enclosing brackets. In a term being considered as a level n term, we will speak of subterms enclosed in m brackets as occurring at level $m + n$ (tacitly assuming that there are n more brackets somewhere in a larger context).

This scheme is closer to the usual variable binding scheme than the familiar scheme of "deBruijn indices" (we have seen the scheme we use referred to as "deBruijn levels"): a term in the usual λ-calculus can be converted to this form by renaming the outermost bound variables to ?1, the next-to-outermost bound variables to ?2, etc., then replacing all the binders ($\lambda x. \ldots$) with brackets. An advantage of this scheme over deBruijn indices is that instances of the same bound variable always look the same; a disadvantage is that terms with bound variables will have to have the bound variables renumbered when they are substituted into a context at a different level.

Practical experience with using this system suggests that as long as brackets are not too deeply nested the notation is intelligible. In the current Watson theory package, an operator . is provided with the defining axiom (?x.?y) = ?y (ignore the first argument); a tactic is provided which converts every bracket term [T] in the current context to the form [?n.T], where ?n is the appropriate bound variable. There is a converse tactic to get rid of such annotations. The development of a tactic of this kind under Watson is easy, and it restores the advantages of the usual variable binding notation with a binder at the head of the term (if one doesn't mind having the names of one's bound variables chosen for one). Note that the introduction and removal of such annotations is automated; if a user introduces incorrect annotations by hand, they are easily checked and corrected; it is exactly the fact that the semantics of the annotations are trivial which makes it possible for prover tactics (which are not allowed to change a term in a way which affects its reference) to correct the annotations where necessary.

On a formal level, the introduction of variable binding requires a change in the definition of substitution and an extension of the rules of equational logic.

If A and B are terms of the same level n and ?x is a free variable, we define a term A{B/?x} of the same level n. Where m and n are numerals with $m > n$ and B is a level n term, we define B{m/n} as the term which results when each bound variable ?i in B with index $i > n$ is replaced by ?j with index $j = i + m - n$. (A variable which is bound by a bracket in B (a ?i with $i > n$) will no longer be associated with the correct bracket if the term B is substituted into a context enclosed in m brackets instead of n brackets: it will need to have its numbering shifted by $m - n$.) The refinement in the definition of A{B/?x} is that each occurrence of ?x needs to be replaced with (B{m/n}) rather than simply (B), where m is the level of that occurrence of ?x.

The definition of A{B/?x} can be extended to the case where the level n of B is greater than the level l of A, just in case no occurrence of the variable ?x in A is at a level less than n. The form of the definition is exactly the same in this case; this extension is needed for the formalization of the rule of localization.

We present extended axioms of equational logic for W, defining notions of theorem at each level n. Of course, our true theorems are the level 0 theorems.

reflexivity: For any level n term A, A $=$ A is a level n theorem.

symmetry: If A $=$ B is a level n theorem, then B $=$ A is a level n theorem.

transitivity: If A $=$ B is a level n theorem and B $=$ C is a level n theorem, then A $=$ C is a level n theorem.

localization: If A $=$ B is a level n theorem and C is a level m term in which all occurrences of ?x are at level n or higher (so $n \geq m$) then C$\{$A/?x$\}$ $=$ C$\{$B/?x$\}$ is a level m theorem. (?x being any free variable). (notice that the definition of substitution handles any needed renumbering of bound variables in the equation A $=$ B that is applied).

specification: If A $=$ B is a level n theorem and C is a level n term then A$\{$C/?x$\}$ $=$ B$\{$C/?x$\}$ is a level n theorem. (?x being any free variable).

level conversion: If A $=$ B is a level n theorem and $m > n$, then A$\{$m/n$\}$ $=$ B$\{$m/n$\}$ is a level m theorem.

The harmonization of this system with the logic of case expressions given above amounts to recognizing that the new definition of substitution needs to be used. There is no essential change in the proof of completeness; it goes the same way mod renumbering of bound variables in the equation T $=$ U mentioned in that proof when used at different levels.

We now develop the defining axiom of the class map application operator @!. Where ?n is a bound variable, T is a level n term and U is a level $n - 1$ term, we define T$\{$U/?n$\}$ as the level $n - 1$ term which results if all occurrences of ?n in T are replaced by (U) and all occurrences of bound variables ?i with $i > n$ in T are replaced by ?j with $j = i - 1$. We can then state the rule of β-reduction in the very natural form:

(class) β-reduction: ([T] @! U) $=$ T$\{$U/?n$\}$ is a level $n - 1$ theorem for each level n term T and level $n - 1$ term U.

Another form in which this could be stated (without introducing new notation, but that is its only merit!) is "([T$\{$n/(n-1)$\}\{$?n/?x$\}$] @! U) $=$ T$\{$U/?x$\}$ is a level $n - 1$ theorem for any level $n - 1$ terms T and U".

So far we appear to have axiomatized untyped λ-calculus, which is incompatible with the presence of functions without fixed points, such as negation, which we can already define. Paradox is avoided by a restriction on the formation of abstraction terms containing the operator @!. We define the head of a term and its number of arguments as follows: if a term T is not of the form U @! V, then it is its own head and has 0 arguments; if a term T is of the form U @! V, then its head is the head of U and it has one more argument than U. We define an n-function as follows: a term not of the form [T] is a 0-function and a term of the form [T] is an $(n + 1)$-function iff T is an n-function. The restriction on the formation of abstraction terms is that if a term with n arguments appears as a subterm of an abstraction term, its head must be either an n-function or a free variable. Notice that under this condition any heads of subterms of abstraction terms which are n-functions for $n > 0$ can be eliminated by β-reductions. For example, this restriction forbids the formation of fixed points of arbitrary operators F by self-application of abstraction terms [F @! (?1 @! ?1)], because ?1 @! ?1 is prevented from occurring as a subterm of an abstraction term.

6   The Theory of Class Abstraction

We have seen above that the operations of propositional logic can be interpreted in the logic of case expressions. We now use the class function machinery of Watson to interpret quantification.

The essential idea is that the universal quantifier can be interpreted as the function **forall** defined as [?1 = [true]] (i.e., $(\lambda x.(x = (\lambda y.\text{true})))$; there is nothing new about this idea!). If a formula ϕ is represented by a term T, then the formula $(\forall x.\phi)$ will be represented (mod technicalities about the variable binding) by [T] = [true] = forall @! [T]. If the formula ϕ is represented by a term T, the formula $(\exists x.\phi)$ will be represented by the term $\sim$([T] = [false]). So we define **forsome** as [$\sim$(?1=[false])]. (the definition of **forsome** is not quite as nice as that of **forall**, because it does not mean quite what one would like when T takes on values which are not truth-values). In any event, **forall** @ [T] and **forsome** @ [T] will code the intended quantified statements when T codes a formula (and so has boolean value).

We now demonstrate that first order logic with equality on infinite domains is captured exactly by the logic of case expressions augmented with our scheme of class functions. The precise sense in which this is true is as follows: we can take any countably infinite model of a first order theory and introduce a definition of the class function abstraction and application operations which will satisfy the formal rules of this system and under which the internal definitions of the quantifiers will succeed.

Take any first order theory T (with equality) with a finite or countably infinite set of primitive predicates, constants and function symbols and having a countably infinite model M. We indicate how to represent the machinery of class abstraction within M in such a way that the definitions of the quantifiers in terms of class abstraction succeed.

We partition the countably infinite set M into a sequence of countably infinite subsets M_i indexed by the natural numbers.

We need to translate the language of T into the language of W. Select two distinct elements of the model M as referents of the terms **true** and **false**. Propositions of the language of T will be interpreted as terms with values **true** or **false**. Introduce constants (in the sense of W) translating each constant of T. Introduce operators translating each predicate and function symbol of T (equality is translated by =). Unary predicates or function symbols will correspond to prefix operators, and binary predicates or function symbols will correspond to infix operators. If there are operators of ternary or higher arity, these can be accomodated by introducing the pair operator (,); for example, an atomic sentence with a ternary predicate symbol like $Rxyz$ would have the translation x 'R y , z. The pair operator can represent any injection from $M \times M$ into M.

We define a class L_0 of terms in the language of W containing interpretations of all terms and quantifier-free propositions of the language of T. L_0 contains all free variables and translated constants of T, plus **true** and **false**. It is closed under the construction of terms with (translated) predicates and function symbols of T (plus = and ,) and the construction of case expressions (used to handle propositional connectives). It is the smallest class of terms satisfying these closure conditions.

For each term T in L_0 which contains no free variable other than a fixed variable ?x, construct the abstraction term [T{1/0}{?1/?x}] (after this point, we abbreviate this as [T{?1/?x}]). These abstraction terms are permitted in W, because no such term T will contain any occurrence of @!; this will remain true throughout the iterative construction we are about to carry out. Each such abstraction term corresponds in a natural way to a function from M to M; we assign an element of M_0 as the referent of each such abstraction term, assigning the same referent to terms which correspond to the same function. This will succeed because there are clearly no more than countably infinitely many such terms.

Our intention is now to augment our language by adding all the abstraction terms we have just constructed as new constants. We extend the language L_0 to include all abstractions over terms of L_0 (notice that this is not the same as taking the closure of L_0 under the abstraction term construction!); we call this extended language L_1 (it is clearly harmless to allow free variables in abstraction terms; the reference of an abstraction term with free variables in it will be determined once the reference of each free variable is determined). Notice that for each term T of L_0 which codes a proposition ϕ, we have [T{?1/?x}] = [**true**], which codes $(\forall x.\phi)$, as a term of L_1; the language L_1 allows us to express some quantified sentences.

We then proceed in the same way through steps indexed by the natural numbers. When the language L_n has been constructed, we consider the set of all terms T of L_n which contain no free variable other than ?x. We construct abstraction terms [T{?1/?x}] for each such term. Each such abstraction term corresponds to a function from M to M. Some of these terms will correspond to functions with the same extension as an abstraction term already defined; assign these the same referent as the term(s) with which they are coextensional. Assign to each term which has a "new" extension a referent in M_n (none of whose elements will have been used yet as referents for abstraction terms), assigning terms with the same extension the same referent. It will be possible to do this because the class of abstraction terms being considered is no more than countably infinite. We extend the language L_n with all abstraction terms [T{?1/?x}] for T a term of L_n, obtaining the language L_{n+1}; we are able to determine the reference of any term of L_{n+1} once the reference of any free variables in the term is given. Notice that if any proposition ϕ is coded by a term T of L_n, the proposition $(\forall x.\phi)$ will be coded by the term [T{?1/?x}] = [**true**] in L_{n+1}.

We consider the language L_ω, the union of all the languages L_n. We augment L_ω with the class application operator @!, using the β-reduction scheme to determine the meaning of terms [T] @! U and assigning a default value to each term T @! U where the referent of T is not the referent of any abstraction term. L_ω allows us to abstract freely over terms which do not contain @! (this should be clear from the construction); abstraction over terms with a subterm with n arguments and head an n-function makes sense because the occurrences of @! in such subterms can be eliminated by repeated β-reduction, obtaining an abstraction term provided by L_ω; abstraction over terms with a subterm with n arguments and head a free variable makes sense as long as we stipulate that such free variables are implicitly typed as n-functions (the prover enforces this). So the abstraction terms allowed by W are all interpretable, since the abstraction terms in L_ω are interpretable. Note further that L_ω, although we have only directly interpreted quantfier-free sentences of T, actually provides indirect interpretations for all quantified sentences of T.

This discussion establishes that the notions of class abstraction can be added harmlessly (as a conservative extension) to any first-order theory with an infinite model. It further needs to be shown that the deductive machinery of the theory of class abstraction is strong enough to recover the usual properties of quantifiers. This is best seen by pointing out that both of the usual rules for universal quantifiers can be emulated in the theory of class abstraction:

```
(forall @ [T]) = true         premise
([T] = [true]) = true         definition of forall
[T] = [true]                  simple case expression reasoning
([T] @ ?x) = [true] @ ?x      localization
T{?x/?1} = true               beta-reduction on both sides
```

demonstrates universal instantiation.

```
T = true                      level 0 theorem (premise)
T{1/0} = true                 level 1 theorem,
                              by level conversion
T{1/0}{?1/?x} = true          level 1 theorem, by specification
[T{1/0}{?1/?x}] = [true]      level 0 theorem, by localization
forall @ [T{1/0}{?1/?x}]      definition of forall
```

demonstrates universal generalization.

Universal generalization and universal instantiation, combined with propositional logic which we know we can interpret using the logic of case expressions, is enough to verify the rules for the existential quantifier.

Generalized predicates can be represented by free variables in this system (free variables appearing as heads of application terms) but such free variables cannot be replaced with bound variables, which prevents the representation of quantification over predicates: there is no second-order logic here.

7 Higher Order Logic via Stratified Abstraction

The "λ-calculus" described in the previous section is a late innovation in the logic of Watson. It is a quite weak system. Watson incorporates another much stronger λ-calculus, equivalent in strength and expressive power to a safe variant of Quine's set theory "New Foundations", on which it is based. It is also equivalent in strength to Church's simply typed λ-calculus with an axiom of infinity (with refinements introduced below, it is somewhat stronger). It differs from the Church system in being untyped. It can be noted here that the entire logic W is untyped (except for the implicit typing of free variables appearing as heads of curried class application terms). The stronger λ-calculus is called "stratified λ-calculus", and is discussed at length in [5], [6], and [7]. Here our treatment will be briefer.

The stratified λ-calculus is best understood initially via a related typed system, a fragment of the simple type theory of Church (see [1]). The fragment has types indexed by the natural numbers: type 0 is the type ι of individuals (of unspecified character), and type $n + 1$, for each n is the type $(n \to n)$ of functions from type n to type n. In addition, type 0 has at least two distinct elements and each type satisfies the type identity $(n \times n) = n$: i.e., each type supports an ordered pair (Watson actually assumes $(n \times n) \subseteq n$; surjectivity of the pair is not assumed).

This type system shares a characteristic with Russell's type theory of sets which Church's simple type theory does not have: all the types look the same in a certain sense. If one raises each type index in an axiom of this typed λ-calculus, one obtains another axiom; it is easy to see from this fact that the same holds for theorems. This suggests that it is reasonable to suppose that the whole structure consisting of types $0, 1, 2 \ldots$ is isomorphic to the structure consisting of types $1, 2, 3 \ldots$ – or even that the type distinctions can be collapsed completely. This is the same as the motivation for the modification of Russell's theory of types for sets which gives Quine's set theory "New Foundations".

It turns out that the ability to safely collapse a type theory using polymorphism in this way is sensitive to details of its axiomatization. If one assumes full extensionality (that every object is a λ-term) it is an open question whether the collapse can be carried out (equivalent to the open question of the consistency of NF). If one does not assume extensionality, one obtains a theory which is known to be consistent and essentially equivalent to Jensen's variation $NFU +$ Infinity of "New Foundations", which has the same consistency strength and expressive power as Russell's theory of types or Church's simple theory of types (with infinity). This collapsing process is discussed in detail in [6].

The theory obtained when the type structure is collapsed is one-sorted – objects of the theory are not typed – but a notion of "relative type" still plays an important role in the theory. The point is that when the type distinctions are collapsed one still has only those instances of the scheme of β-reduction [T]@U = T{U/?1} which make sense in terms of the type scheme. This is vitally important: one does not want to acquire instances of β-reduction like [~?1@?1]@?x = ~?x@?x, from which, if one defines R as [~?1@?1], one can deduce the disastrous theorem RₒR = ∼RₒR. But the abstraction term [∼?1ₒ?1] is in some sense illicit, because there is no way to type it sensibly in terms of the typed system described above.

We now describe the way that these ideas are implemented in the logic W of Watson. Each operator is supplied with "relative types" for its arguments (called the left type and right type): if an operator % (infix for the sake of the example) has left type i and right type j, this tells us that if a term T % U were of type n in the typed system, then T would be type $n + i$ and U would be type $n + j$. For example, the function application operator ₒ has left type 1 and right type 0, because a type $n + 1$ function is applied to a type $n + 0$ argument to get a type n term. It should be noted that negative relative types are possible: for example, a singleton set operator would have type -1 for its sole argument.

There is an additional option: some operators (such as the class application operator ₒ!) are "opaque"; abstraction into an opaque context is not allowed in stratified abstraction terms.

The machinery of relative types is used to identify function abstracts which are allowed in the function abstraction scheme for the application operator ₒ. Such abstraction terms are said to be "stratified" by analogy with terminology used in "New Foundations" and related set theories for formulas permitted in set abstracts.

Formal definitions of relative type and stratification follow:

Definition: Occurrences of subterms of a term (with exceptions in opaque contexts) are said to have "relative type" in that term. Relative type is defined recursively:

1. The relative type of a term in itself is 0.
2. If the relative type of an occurrence of the term A in a term T is n, and the left (resp. right) type of the operator % is i, then the relative type of the analogous occurrence of A in the obvious occurrence of T in T % U (resp U % T or % T (in the case of a unary operator)) is $n + i$. If % is opaque, then the relative type of the analogous occurrence of A in the obvious occurrence of T in any of these terms is undefined.
3. If the relative type of an occurrence of the term A in a term T is n, then the relative type of the analogous occurrence of A in the occurrence of T in [T] is $n - 1$.
4. The relative type of an occurrence of A in T || U , V is the same as the relative type of its occurrence in the appropriate one of T, U, V.

Definition: An abstraction term [T] is "stratified" if the relative type in T of each occurrence (there need not be any occurrences) of the variable ?n bound by the brackets is defined and equal to 0, and if each abstraction term appearing as a proper subterm of [T] is stratified.

Axiom scheme (stratified β-reduction): [T]ₒU = T{U/?n} is a level n axiom, when [T] is a stratified abstraction term.

Note that a term like [∼?1ₒ?1] is actually well-formed, and we do have ([∼?1ₒ?1] ₒ! U) = ∼UₒU, but we do not have the disastrous ([∼?1ₒ?1] ₒ U)

= ∼U@U, because [∼?1@?1] is not stratified. Notice also that because the class application operator @! is "opaque", one cannot define functions in the higher order logic which depend in any nontrivial way on facts about class application.

An important note here is that it might be thought to be dangerous that we have made set function application and class function application coincide for stratified abstraction terms. This turns out not to be a problem as long as one provides enough non-functions (terms T not equal to [T @ ?1]). The only real curiosity here is that one can prove that set function application is nonextensional by considering class abstractions like [∼?1 @ ?1] which would be paradoxical if they were also set abstractions.

8   Experience with Watson

It is possible to develop the theory of quantification using the machinery of the stratified λ-calculus alone (and this is how it was done originally). If the class application operator were not used, unstratified abstraction terms would be treated as ill-formed (there is a current release of Watson which still takes this approach). The representation of (∀x.φ) as forall @ [T] and the verification of instantiation and generalization would still work, with the restriction that we would only consider formulas represented by stratified terms. It is known that all stratified theorems of systems like "New Foundations" or *NFU* have proofs which involve only stratified sentences, and most sentences of mathematical interest are stratified; this restriction did not initially seem to be a problem in practical work with the prover, except for a technical problem detailed below.

There is a technical difficulty with the implementation of first-order logic using stratified λ-calculus which must be noted. A sentence like (∀x.(∃y.x = y)), which is regarded as "stratified" in the context of a set theory like "New Foundations", is represented in the language of Watson by a term forall @ [forsome @ [?1 = ?2]] which is not on the face of it stratified! If the whole term is assigned type 0, the subterm forall gets type 1 and the subterm [forsome @ [?1 = ?2]] gets type 0; thus the subterm forsome @ [?1 = ?2] gets type −1, from which we see that forsome gets type 0 and [?1=?2] gets type 0. We then see that ?1 = ?2, and so both ?1 and ?2, get type −2. The rules of stratification require that the type of ?1 (−2) be the same as the type of the body forsome @ [?1 = ?2] of the abstraction term in which it is bound, and this is not the case: the term forsome @ [?1 = ?2] has type −1.

This is a merely technical problem because one can show that the relative type of a term with a boolean value (like forsome @ [?1 = ?2]) can be freely raised or lowered by any desired amount to recover stratification. The equations ((P || [true] , [false])) @ 0 = P and ([P] = [true]) = P hold when P is replaced by either **true** or **false**; these equations can be used to freely raise or lower the type of a term whose value is known to be boolean. Of course, no one wants to carry out manipulations of this kind explicitly in a theorem proving system! The solution of this problem was to enable the prover to recognize for itself subterms belonging to classes on which type raising or lowering is possible and exploit this information to recognize a more general class of terms as stratified. With this generalization of stratification, the technical problem outlined above became entirely invisible to the user.

Classes on which type-raising and lowering is possible (called "strongly cantorian sets", abbreviated s.c.) are of considerable interest in set theories like *NF*. If it is assumed that the set of natural numbers is s.c., it follows that most sets of interest in mathematics and certainly all sets of interest in computer science applications are s.c. The relaxation of stratification restrictions for natural number values and values belonging to common data types proves useful in practice; it has the side-effect of making the logic somewhat stronger than the simple theory of types with infinity. It is beyond the scope of this paper, but it is worth noting briefly that a theme of our research is the study of an analogy between the notion of "s.c. set" and the notion of "data type", and that practical experience with Watson seems to indicate that this can be a useful analogy.

The problems with the treatment using stratified λ-calculus which caused us to introduce the class application operator were subtler, having to do with uniform treatment of quantifiers over variables of different relative types in formal rules for first-order logic. For example, the addition of the class machinery makes it possible to handle the logical principle $(\forall xy.\phi) \leftrightarrow (\forall yx.\phi)$ uniformly; if quantification were implemented using set abstraction, it would be necessary to take the difference in relative type between x and y into account in each such equivalence. The introduction of class application and abstraction increases the ability of the prover to apply limited forms of higher-order matching as well.

The representation of mathematical constructions in this higher-order logic is very similar to the representation in the fragment of Church's type theory described above. Since the latter system is not usually used, some remarks are in order. The lack of types like $((\iota \to \iota) \to \iota)$ and $(\iota \to (\iota \to \iota))$ in this fragment of simple type theory does not create significant problems with expressive power: both of these types are readily represented in type $2 = ((\iota \to \iota) \to (\iota \to \iota))$ by exploiting the coding of any type or subcollection of a type in the linear type scheme using a collection of constant functions in the next higher type. The same device works in general to handle types outside the linear type scheme. Mathematics as implemented in Watson tends to look very much like mathematics implemented in a typed λ-calculus, except for this kind of occurrence of the constant function operator to adjust relative types. The declaration of "data types" as s.c. often allows such occurrences of the constant function operator to be omitted.

9   Conclusions and Relations to Other Work

The main purpose of this paper is to document the mathematical underpinnings of the Watson theorem prover. We have been more attentive to the features which are not documented elsewhere (the logic of case expressions and the new class abstraction machinery) than to the higher order logic embodied in the stratified λ-calculus. We feel that this system has certain features of independent interest, however. The use of the logic of case expressions as a foundation for propositional logic seems interesting to us; certainly the axiomatization is economical. It is less novel to identify the abstraction implicit in quantification with the abstraction which constructs functions, and in fact the latest version with class application as well as set application retreats from such an identification. The development of Watson has been an outgrowth of our interest in the application of the untyped set theories in the style of Quine and the related λ-calculi, and we believe that untyped grand logics ought to be of interest in theorem proving in general.

We are aware that there is other work using deBruijn indices and related schemes (including the one given here) which would be technically similar to our formal development of substitution, especially by researchers in the area of "explicit substitution". We can only make up for our lack of references by pleading ignorance of this work; our development is independent, though certainly not original.

We do not believe that any theorem proving system is very close in its details to Watson, and in any event the details of the theorem prover are not relevant to this paper. The closest system in terms of its underlying mathematical framework is probably HOL ([3]), which implements Church's classical simple type theory of functions.

References

1. A. Church. A formulation of the simple theory of types. *Journal of Symbolic Logic*, 5, 1940.
2. N. deBruijn, "Lambda-calculus with nameless dummies, a tool for automatic formula manipulation, with application to the Church-Rosser theorem", in Nederpelt, *et. al.*, eds., *Selected Papers on Automath*, North Holland, 1994.
3. M. Gordon. A proof generating system for higher-order logic. Technical Report 103, University of Cambridge Computer Laboratory, January 1987.
4. M. Randall Holmes, "A functional formulation of first-order logic 'with infinity' without bound variables", preprint, available at the Watson web page http://math.boisestate.edu/~holmes/proverpage.html
5. M. Randall Holmes, "Systems of combinatory logic related to Quine's 'New Foundations' ", *Annals of Pure and Applied Logic*, 53 (1991), pp. 103-33.
6. M. Randall Holmes, "Untyped λ-calculus with relative typing", in *Typed Lambda-Calculi and Applications* (proceedings of TLCA '95), Springer, 1995, pp. 235-48.
7. M. Randall Holmes, *Elementary Set Theory with a Universal Set*, Academia-Bruylant, Louvain-la-Neuve, 1998.
8. M. Randall Holmes, "The Watson Theorem Prover", preprint, available as part of the online documentation at the Watson web page http://math.boisestate.edu/~holmes/proverpage.html
9. Ronald Bjorn Jensen, "On the consistency of a slight (?) modification of Quine's 'New Foundations' ", *Synthese*, 19 (1969), pp. 250-63.
10. W. V. O. Quine, "New Foundations for Mathematical Logic", *American Mathematical Monthly*, 44 (1937), pp. 70-80.

Inheritance in Higher Order Logic: Modeling and Reasoning

Marieke Huisman and Bart Jacobs

Computing Science Institute, University of Nijmegen
Toernooiveld 1, 6525 ED Nijmegen, The Netherlands
{marieke,bart}@cs.kun.nl

Abstract. This paper describes a way of modeling inheritance (in object-oriented programming languages) in higher order logic. This particular approach is used in the LOOP project for reasoning about JAVA classes, with the proof tools PVS and ISABELLE. It relies on nested interface types to capture the superclasses, fields, methods, and constructors of classes, together with suitable casting functions incorporating the difference between hiding of fields and overriding of methods. This leads to the proper handling of late binding, as illustrated in several verification examples.

1 Introduction

This paper reports on a particular aspect of the semantics of object-oriented languages, like JAVA, used in the "LOOP" verification project [23]. It concentrates on inheritance. A companion paper [3] explains the underlying memory model.

Inheritance is a key feature of object-oriented languages. It allows a programmer to model his/her application domain according to a natural "is-a" relationship between classes of objects. One can use inheritance, for instance, to say that a lorry is-a vehicle by making a class of lorries a subclass (or "child" or "descendant") of a superclass (or "ancestor") of vehicles. Important aspects of inheritance are re-use of code, and polymorphism. The latter is sometimes called subtype polymorphism (to distinguish it for example from parametric polymorphism). Its effect is that the particular implementation that is used in a method call is determined by the actual (run-time) type of the receiving object, which tells to which class the object belongs. This mechanism is often referred to as dynamic method look-up or late binding. It is precisely this dynamic aspect of object-oriented languages which is difficult to capture in a static logical setting. Therefore, the semantics of inheritance—as a basis for reasoning about classes—is a real challenge, see *e.g.* [5,17,21,6,12,8,18]. There is a whole body of research on encodings of classes using recursive or existential types, in a suitably rich polymorphic type theory (like $F^\omega_{\leq:}$ or $F_{<:}$). Four such (functional) encodings are formulated and compared in a common notational framework in [4]. But they all use quantification or recursion over type variables, which is not available in the higher order logic (the logics of PVS and ISABELLE/HOL) that

J. Harrison and M. Aagaard (Eds.): TPHOLs 2000, LNCS 1869, pp. 301–319, 2000.
© Springer-Verlag Berlin Heidelberg 2000

will be used here. Quantification and/or recursion over type variables is available in LEGO and COQ, but since much proving power is required for verifying non-trivial properties about actual JAVA programs, we prefer to use tools like PVS and ISABELLEbecause they do not have the overhead of explicit proof-objects. The setting of the encoding in [18] is higher order logic with "extensible records". This framework is closest to what we use (but is still stronger). Also, an experimental *functional* object-oriented language, without references and object identity is studied there. This greatly simplifies matters, because the subtle late binding issues involving run-time types of objects (which may change through assignments, see Section 7) do not occur. Indeed, it is a crucial aspect of *imperative* object-oriented programming languages that the declared type of a variable may be different from—but must be a supertype of—the actual, run-time type of an object to which it refers. This property is called type-safety. Our semantics of inheritance works for an existing object-oriented language, namely JAVA, with all such semantical complications.

The explanations below only describe a small part of the denotational semantics of JAVA used in the LOOP project. Due to space limitations, many aspects have to be left unexplained. We intend to concentrate on the main ideas underlying the handling of inheritance, using paradigmatic examples. Many related issues, like inheritance from multiple interfaces (which mainly involves proper name handling), method overloading, or object creation via constructor chaining, are not covered in the present paper.

For our JAVA verification work a special purpose compiler, called LOOP, for *Logic of Object-Oriented Programming*, has been developed. It works as a front-end to a proof tool, for which both PVS [19] and ISABELLE [20] can be used, as suggested by the following diagram.

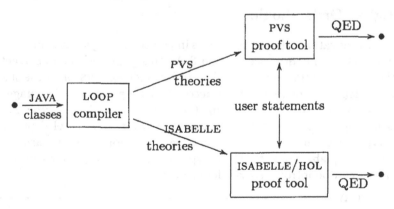

The LOOP tool translates JAVA classes into logical theories, containing definitions (embodying the semantics of the classes) plus special lemmas that are used for automatic rewriting. The tool works on classes which are accepted by a standard JAVA compiler. It handles almost all of sequential JAVA. The generated logical theories can be loaded into the back-end proof tool, together with the so-called semantical prelude, which contains basic definitions, like in Section 3 below. Subsequently, the user can state desired properties about the original JAVA classes and prove these on the basis of the semantical prelude and the generated theories. For example, a user may want to prove that a method terminates, returning a certain value; see Section 8 for several examples.

The semantics that is used is based on so-called coalgebras (see [14,13]). In general, a coalgebra is a function with type $X \to F(X)$, where F describes the interface, or access points, and X the state space, or set of states. Coalgebras give rise to a general theory of behaviour for dynamical systems, involving useful notions like invariance and bisimilarity, but we shall not make use of it here. In this paper, coalgebras are only used to conveniently combine all the ingredients of a class, *i.e.* the fields, methods and constructors, in a single function. Specifically, n functions $f_1 \colon \mathsf{Self} \to \sigma_1, \ldots, f_n \colon \mathsf{Self} \to \sigma_n$ with a common domain can be combined in one function $\mathsf{Self} \to [\, f_1 \colon \sigma_1, \ldots, f_n \colon \sigma_n \,]$ with a labeled product type as codomain[1], forming a coalgebra. Thus, the combined representations of fields, methods and constructors of a class form a coalgebra that is used as implementation of the class. The use of coalgebras in this paper is mostly organisational and remains fairly superficial; it is not essential for what happens[2].

The paper is organised as follows. It starts with two preliminary sections: one on the type-theoretic notation that will be used, and one about some basic aspects of JAVA semantics. Then, Section 4 introduces interfaces types as labeled products to capture the ingredients of classes, and shows how these are nested to incorporate superclasses. Section 5 discusses hiding and overriding at the level of these interface types, via special cast functions, and Sections 6 and 7 show how these functions realise the appropriate late binding behaviour. Finally, Section 8 describes two example verifications, one in PVS and one in ISABELLE/HOL, involving small but non-trivial JAVA programs.

2   Higher Order Logic

The actual verifications of JAVA programs in the LOOP project are done using either[3] PVS or ISABELLE/HOL, see Section 8. In this paper we shall abstract away from the specific syntax for the higher order logic of PVS or ISABELLE/HOL, and use a (hopefully more generally accessible) type-theoretic language. It involves types which are built up from: type variables $\alpha, \beta, \ldots$, type constants nat, bool, string (and some more), exponent types $\sigma \to \tau$, labeled product (or record) types $[\mathsf{lab}_1 \colon \sigma_1, \ldots, \mathsf{lab}_n \colon \sigma_n]$ and labeled coproduct (or variant) types $\{\, \mathsf{lab}_1 \colon \sigma_1 \mid \ldots \mid \mathsf{lab}_n \colon \sigma_n \,\}$, for given types $\sigma, \tau, \sigma_1, \ldots, \sigma_n$. New types or type constructors can be introduced via definitions, as in:

─ TYPE THEORY ────────────────────────────────────

$$\mathsf{lift}[\alpha] \;:\; \mathsf{TYPE} \;\stackrel{\mathrm{def}}{=}\; \{\, \mathsf{bot} \colon \mathsf{unit} \mid \mathsf{up} \colon \alpha \,\}$$

───

[1] Alternatively, one can combine these n functions into elements of a "trait type" $\{\, f_1 \colon \mathsf{Self} \to \sigma_1, \ldots, f_n \colon \mathsf{Self} \to \sigma_n \,\}$, like in [1, §§8.5.2].

[2] As a side-remark, all the encodings discussed in [4] implicitly also use coalgebras.

[3] Translating to both PVS and ISABELLE/HOL offers the verifier a choice which proof tool to use.

where unit is the empty labeled product type []. This lift type constructor adds a bottom element to an arbitrary type, given as type variable α.

For exponent types we shall use the standard lambda abstraction $\lambda x : \sigma . M$ and application $N \cdot L$ notation. For terms $M_i : \sigma_i$, we have a labeled tuple ($\mathsf{lab}_1 = M_1, \ldots, \mathsf{lab}_n = M_n$) inhabiting the labeled product type $[\mathsf{lab}_1 : \sigma_1, \ldots, \mathsf{lab}_n : \sigma_n]$. For a term $N : [\mathsf{lab}_1 : \sigma_1, \ldots, \mathsf{lab}_n : \sigma_n]$ in this product, we write $N.\mathsf{lab}_i$ for the selection term of type σ_i. Dually, for a term $M : \sigma_i$ there is a labeled or tagged term $\mathsf{lab}_i\, M$ in the labeled coproduct type $\{\mathsf{lab}_1 : \sigma_1 \mid \ldots \mid \mathsf{lab}_n : \sigma_n\}$. And for a term $N : \{\mathsf{lab}_1 : \sigma_1 \mid \ldots \mid \mathsf{lab}_n : \sigma_n\}$ in this coproduct type, together with n terms $L_i(x_i) : \tau$, possibly containing a free variable $x_i : \sigma_i$, there is a case term CASES N OF $\{\mathsf{lab}_1\, x_1 \mapsto L_1(x_1) \mid \ldots \mid \mathsf{lab}_n\, x_n \mapsto L_n(x_n)\}$ of type τ. These introduction and elimination constructions for exponents and labeled (co)products are required to satisfy standard (β)- and (η)-conversions.

In this paper we do not use any formulas in higher order logic—which are of course terms of type bool—and work exclusively in the underlying type theory. This is possible because we describe only a limited part of the semantics of JAVA.

3   Semantics of Java Statements and Expressions

In this paper we shall use Self as a type variable representing a global state space. Later, Self will be instantiated with the type OM, describing a concrete state space. But as long the details from OM are not needed, the type variable Self shall be used, for abstraction. JAVA statements and expressions will be modeled as state transformer functions (or coalgebras) acting on Self. Statements and expressions in JAVA may either hang, terminate normally, or terminate abruptly. These different output options are captured by two output types StatResult[Self], and ExprResult[Self, α], in:

$$\mathsf{Self} \longrightarrow \mathsf{StatResult[Self]} \qquad\qquad \mathsf{Self} \longrightarrow \mathsf{ExprResult[Self,}\, \alpha]$$

where α is a type variable for the result type of the JAVA expression. These output types are defined as labeled coproducts:

— TYPE THEORY —————————————————————————

$$\mathsf{StatResult[Self]} : \mathsf{TYPE} \stackrel{\mathrm{def}}{=} \qquad\qquad \mathsf{ExprResult[Self,}\, \alpha] : \mathsf{TYPE} \stackrel{\mathrm{def}}{=}$$

StatResult[Self]	ExprResult[Self, α]
{ hang : unit	{ hang : unit
| norm : Self	| norm : [ns : Self, res : α]
| abnorm : StatAbn[Self] }	| abnorm : ExprAbn[Self] }

——

The types StatAbn[Self] and ExprAbn[Self] capture the various abnormalities that can occur for JAVA statements and expressions (like exceptions, returns, breaks and continues). Their precise structure is not relevant for this paper—but can be found in [10,3,9].

On the basis of this representation, the denotational semantics of all of JAVA's language constructs, like while, catch *etc.*, can be defined, closely following the JAVA language specification [7]. For instance, the composition $s;t$ of two statements s,t: Self $\rightarrow$ StatResult[Self] is defined as:

─ TYPE THEORY ────────────────────────────────────

$$s;t : \text{Self} \rightarrow \text{StatResult[Self]} \stackrel{\text{def}}{=} \lambda x: \text{Self. CASES } s \cdot x \text{ OF } \{$$
$$| \text{ hang} \mapsto \text{hang}$$
$$| \text{ norm } y \mapsto t \cdot y$$
$$| \text{ abnorm } a \mapsto \text{abnorm } a \}$$

──

We do not describe all these details here, as they are not necessary to understand inheritance. What we do need in the sequel is a special type RefType for references. It is defined as either a null-reference null or a non-null-reference ref x, where x consists of a pointer to a memory location, where the object that is being referred to resides (see [3] for details), a string, indicating the run-time type of the object, and a third field that is used if the reference points to an array to give its dimension and length:

─ TYPE THEORY ────────────────────────────────────

$$\text{RefType} : \text{TYPE} \stackrel{\text{def}}{=}$$
$$\{ \text{null: unit } | \text{ ref: } [\text{ objpos: MemLoc},$$
$$\text{clname: string},$$
$$\text{dimlen: lift}[[\text{dim: nat, len: nat}]]] \}$$

──

Recall that in object-oriented languages one must keep track of the run-time type of an object, because it may differ from its declared type. All references in JAVA (both to objects and to arrays) are translated in type theory to values of type RefType. Thus, if we have an object a in a class A and an object b in a subclass B of A, then the translation of an assignment a = b involves a replacement of the reference to a by the reference to b. Since both are inhabitants of RefType, this is well-typed. If b has run-time type B, then so will a after the assignment.

4   Nested Labeled Product Types for Interfaces

JAVA has classes and interfaces. Interfaces only contain the headers of methods (their names and the types of their parameters and results, if any), but not their implementations (given by what are usually called method bodies). The latter can only occur in classes. In this section we do not make a distinction between classes and interfaces, because method bodies do not play a rôle. Therefore, class can also mean interface at this stage. What we describe is how certain labeled product types (in type theory) are extracted from JAVA classes. These product types describe the superclasses, fields (or instance variables) with associated

assignment operations, methods, and constructors of a class. They form the basis
for the type-theoretic formalisation of JAVA classes. Below, we first describe how
an appropriate labeled product type is extracted for a single isolated class, and
then how inheritance is handled—involving several related classes.

It is easiest to proceed via an example of a JAVA class:

```
– JAVA
   class MyClass {
     int i;
     int k = 3;
     void m (byte a, int b) { if (a > b) i = a; else i = b; }
     MyClass () { i = 6; }
   }
```

Ignoring the implicit superclass Object, the following interface type is extracted.

```
– TYPE THEORY

              MyClassIFace[Self] : TYPE ≝
                [...      // for the superclass, see below
                 i : int,
                 i_becomes : int → Self,
                 k : int,
                 k_becomes : int → Self,
                 m : byte → int → StatResult[Self],
                 MyClass : ExprResult[Self, RefType] ]
```

There are several things worth noticing here.

– The field declaration int i gives rise not only to a label i : int for field
  lookup in the product type but also to an associated assignment operation,
  with label i_becomes. This assignment operation takes an integer as input,
  and produces a new state in Self, in which the i field is changed to the
  argument of the assignment operation (and the rest is unchanged). Similarly
  for k. Variable initialisers (like k = 3) are ignored at this stage, since they
  are irrelevant for the interface type (just as method bodies).
– The method m, which is a void method, is modeled as an entry m in the
  labeled product of type StatResult[Self][4]. Similarly, methods with a return
  value are modeled with ExprResult, e.g. int n () {return 3;} would give
  rise to a label n with type ExprResult[Self, int].

---

[4] To prevent name clashes, the LOOP compiler does more. For example, overloading of
labels usually is not allowed in labeled product types. Therefore the LOOP compiler
does not use m but m_byte_int as translation of m in JAVA. Here we shall ignore such
bureaucratic aspects, and simply assume that no such name clashes occur.

– The type of the constructor MyClass is implicit in the JAVA code, but is made explicit in the type-theoretic formalisation. Since a constructor returns a reference to a newly created object, it is modeled as an entry with type ExprResult[Self, RefType]. Constructors are often left implicit in JAVA code, as so-called default constructors. These are added explicitly to interface types.

Thus, a labeled product term in the interface type MyClassIFace contains all the operations (*i.e.* field access, field assignment, method calls and object construction) that can be applied to instances of MyClass.

The types occurring in the interface type MyClassIFace above describe the "visible" signatures of the fields, methods and constructors in the JAVA class MyClass. But in object-oriented programs there is always an implicit argument to a field/method/constructor, namely the current state of the object on which the field/method/constructor is invoked. This is made explicit by modeling classes as *coalgebras* for interface types, *i.e.* as functions of the form:

$$\text{Self} \longrightarrow \text{MyClassIFace[Self]}$$

Such a coalgebra actually combines the fields, methods and constructors of the class in a single function. The individual operations are made explicit, using the isomorphism $\text{Self} \to [\, f_1 \colon \sigma_1, \dots, f_n \colon \sigma_n \,] \cong [\, f_1 \colon \text{Self} \to \sigma_1, \dots, f_n \colon \text{Self} \to \sigma_n \,]$, via what we call "extraction" functions:

– TYPE THEORY ──

Assuming a variable $c \colon \text{Self} \to \text{MyClassIFace[Self]}$,

$$\vdash \text{i}(c) \colon \text{Self} \to \text{int} \stackrel{\text{def}}{=} \lambda x \colon \text{Self}. \, (c \cdot x).\text{i}$$

$$\vdash \text{i\_becomes}(c) \colon \text{Self} \to \text{int} \to \text{Self} \stackrel{\text{def}}{=} \lambda x \colon \text{Self}. \, (c \cdot x).\text{i\_becomes}$$

$$\vdash \text{k}(c) \colon \text{Self} \to \text{int} \stackrel{\text{def}}{=} \lambda x \colon \text{Self}. \, (c \cdot x).\text{k}$$

$$\vdash \text{k\_becomes}(c) \colon \text{Self} \to \text{int} \to \text{Self} \stackrel{\text{def}}{=} \lambda x \colon \text{Self}. \, (c \cdot x).\text{k\_becomes}$$

$$b \colon \text{byte}, j \colon \text{int} \vdash \text{m}(b)(j)(c) \colon \text{Self} \to \text{StatResult[Self]} \stackrel{\text{def}}{=} \lambda x \colon \text{Self}. \, ((c \cdot x).\text{m}) \cdot b \cdot j$$

$$\vdash \text{MyClass}(c) \colon \text{Self} \to \text{ExprResult[Self, RefType]} \stackrel{\text{def}}{=} \lambda x \colon \text{Self}. \, (c \cdot x).\text{MyClass}$$

──

Note that we use a form of overloading: the i in $(c \cdot x).$i is a label from a product, whereas the i in i(c) is the extraction function that is being defined. Note also that for fields like i, besides the look-up function i, an additional update function i_becomes is defined. The coalgebra $c \colon \text{Self} \to \text{MyClassIFace[Self]}$ above thus combines all the operations of the class MyClass. In the remainder of this paper, we shall always describe operations—fields (with their assignments), methods, constructors—of a class, say A, using extraction functions as above, with respect to a coalgebra of type AIFace.

4.1 Inheritance and Nested Interface Types

Now that we have seen the basic idea of how to build an interface type from the fields, methods and constructors of a JAVA class, we proceed to incorporate superclasses. This will be done via nesting of interface types. Again, it is easiest to use an example.

```
— JAVA —————————————————————————————————
   class MySubClass extends MyClass {
     int j;
     int n (byte b) { m(b, 3); return i; }
   }
```

This new class `MySubClass` inherits the field i and method m of `MyClass`, and it declares its own field j and method n. As can be seen in the body of the method n, the methods and fields from the super class are immediately available, *i.e.* the method m and field i are called without any further reference to `MyClass`. This should also be possible in our formalisation.

This class gives rise to the following interface type MySubClassIFace in type theory. In this labeled product type the first entry MyClassIFace is the interface type defined earlier for the class `MyClass`, thus formalising the inheritance relationship. In a similar way, the type MyClassIFace contains an entry super_Object: ObjectIFace[Self], formalising the implicit inheritance from Object by `MyClass`.

```
— TYPE THEORY —————————————————————————————
```

$$\text{MySubClassIFace[Self] : TYPE} \stackrel{\text{def}}{=}$$

$$[\,\text{super\_MyClass} : \text{MyClassIFace[Self]},$$
$$\quad \text{j} : \text{int},$$
$$\quad \text{j\_becomes} : \text{int} \to \text{Self},$$
$$\quad \text{n} : \text{byte} \to \text{ExprResult[Self, int]},$$
$$\quad \text{MySubClass} : \text{ExprResult[Self, RefType]}\,]$$

As before, we shall consider a coalgebra $c: \text{Self} \to \text{MySubClassIFace[Self]}$ as representation of the class `MySubClass`. For such a coalgebra we can again define extraction functions, giving us access to all ingredients of `MySubClass`, but also of `MyClass`, via the nesting of interfaces. This goes as follows.

```
— TYPE THEORY —————————————————————————————
```

Assuming a variable $c: \text{Self} \to \text{MySubClassIFace[Self]},$

$$\vdash \text{j}(c) : \text{Self} \to \text{int} \stackrel{\text{def}}{=} \lambda x : \text{Self}. (c \cdot x).\text{j}$$

$$\vdash \text{j\_becomes}(c) : \text{Self} \to \text{int} \to \text{Self} \stackrel{\text{def}}{=} \lambda x : \text{Self}. (c \cdot x).\text{j\_becomes}$$

$$b : \text{byte} \vdash \text{n}(b)(c) : \text{Self} \to \text{StatResult[Self]} \stackrel{\text{def}}{=} \lambda x : \text{Self}. ((c \cdot x).\text{n}) \cdot b$$

$$\vdash \mathsf{MySubClass}(c)\colon \mathsf{Self} \to \mathsf{ExprResult}[\mathsf{Self}, \mathsf{RefType}] \stackrel{\mathrm{def}}{=}$$
$$\lambda x\colon \mathsf{Self}.\,(c \cdot x).\mathsf{MySubClass}$$

// continue with the superclass MyClass

$$\vdash \mathsf{i}(c)\colon \mathsf{Self} \to \mathsf{int} \stackrel{\mathrm{def}}{=} \lambda x\colon \mathsf{Self}.\,(c \cdot x).\mathsf{super\_MyClass.i}$$

$$\vdash \mathsf{i\_becomes}(c)\colon \mathsf{Self} \to \mathsf{int} \to \mathsf{Self} \stackrel{\mathrm{def}}{=} \lambda x\colon \mathsf{Self}.\,(c \cdot x).\mathsf{super\_MyClass.i\_becomes}$$

$$b\colon \mathsf{byte}, j\colon \mathsf{int} \vdash \mathsf{m}(b)(j)(c)\colon \mathsf{Self} \to \mathsf{StatResult}[\mathsf{Self}] \stackrel{\mathrm{def}}{=}$$
$$\lambda x\colon \mathsf{Self}.\,((c \cdot x).\mathsf{super\_MyClass.m}) \cdot b \cdot j$$

// etc.

The repeated extraction functions, like i, i_becomes and m, thus give immediate access to all ingredients of superclasses. Note how this involves overloading in type theory, because for instance $\mathsf{i}(c)$ is defined both for coalgebras $c\colon \mathsf{Self} \to \mathsf{MyClassIFace}[\mathsf{Self}]$ and for coalgebras $c\colon \mathsf{Self} \to \mathsf{MySubClassIFace}[\mathsf{Self}]$ representing the classes MyClass and MySubClass.

5 Overriding and Hiding

In the previous section we have seen an example of inheritance where the subclass MySubClass simply adds an extra field and method to the superclass. But the same fields and methods may also be repeated in subclasses. In JAVA this is called *hiding* of fields, and *overriding* of methods. Different names are used, because the mechanisms are different: field selection is based on the static type of receiving objects, whereas method selection is based on the dynamic (or run-time) type of an object. The latter mechanism is often referred to as dynamic method lookup, or late binding. Consider the following example.

— JAVA ————————————————————————————————

```
class A {
  int i = 1;
  int m() { return i * 100; }
}
class B extends A {
  int i = 10;
  int m() { return i * 1000; }
}
class Test {
  int test1() { A[] ar = { new A(), new B() };
    return ar[0].i + ar[0].m() + ar[1].i + ar[1].m(); }
}
```

The field i in the subclass B hides the field i in the superclass A, and the method m in B overrides the method m in A. In the test1 method of class Test a local variable ar of type 'array of As' is declared and initialised with length 2 containing a new A object at position 0, and a new B object at position 1. Note that at position 1 there is an implicit conversion from B to A to make the new B object fit into the array of As. Interestingly, the test1 method will return ar[0].i + ar[0].m() + ar[1].i + ar[1].m(), which is 1 + 1 * 100 + 1 + 10 * 1000 = 10102, because: when new B() is converted to type A the hidden field becomes visible again—so that the field ar[1].i is statically bound to i in A—but the overriding method replaces the original method—so that the method ar[1].m() leads to execution of m in B (which uses the field i from B). See [2, §§3.4], or also [7, §§8.4.6.1]:

> Note that a qualified name or a cast to a superclass is not effective in attempting to access an overridden method; in this respect, overriding of methods differs from hiding of fields.

This difference in binding for redefined fields and methods is typical for JAVA. For example in EIFFEL [16] it is not allowed to redefine fields in subclasses.

It is a challenge to provide a semantics for this behaviour. We do so by using a special cast function between coalgebras, which performs appropriate replacements of methods and fields. We shall illustrate this in the above JAVA example. The interface types for classes A and B are defined as follows.

— TYPE THEORY —————————————————————————

AIFace[Self] : TYPE $\overset{\text{def}}{=}$ BIFace[Self] : TYPE $\overset{\text{def}}{=}$

[super_Object : ObjectIFace[Self],   [super_A : AIFace[Self],
  i : int,   i : int,
  i_becomes : int → Self,   i_becomes : int → Self,
  m : ExprResult[Self, int],   m : ExprResult[Self, int],
  A : ExprResult[Self, RefType]]   B : ExprResult[Self, RefType]]

————————————————————————————————————

Notice that the interface type BIFace[Self] contains m and i twice: once directly, and once inside the nested interface type AIFace[Self]. Thus we define two extraction functions to access the individual operations for each of them:

— TYPE THEORY —————————————————————————

Assuming a variable c: Self → BIFace[Self],

$$\vdash i(c): \text{Self} \to \text{int} \overset{\text{def}}{=} \lambda x: \text{Self}.\,(c \cdot x).i$$

$$\vdash A\_i(c): \text{Self} \to \text{int} \overset{\text{def}}{=} \lambda x: \text{Self}.\,(c \cdot x).\text{super}\_A.i$$

$$\vdash m(c): \text{Self} \to \text{ExprResult}[\text{Self}, \text{int}] \overset{\text{def}}{=} \lambda x: \text{Self}.\,(c \cdot x).m$$

$$\vdash A\_m(c): \text{Self} \to \text{ExprResult}[\text{Self}, \text{int}] \overset{\text{def}}{=} \lambda x: \text{Self}.\,(c \cdot x).\text{super}\_A.m$$

————————————————————————————————————

The extraction functions A_i and A_m are used for **super** invocations.

What we want is a way of "casting" a B coalgebra c: Self $\to$ BIFace[Self] to an A coalgebra $B2A(c)$: Self $\to$ AIFace[Self] which incorporates the differences between hiding and overriding. Just taking the super_A entry is not good enough because then we get fields *and* methods from the superclass: we need additional updates, which select the fields of the superclass A, but the methods of the subclass B. Therefore, we use a record update on the entry super_A, which updates the method entries to the methods of B, defining:

– TYPE THEORY ———————————————————————

$$c: \text{Self} \to \text{BIFace[Self]} \vdash$$

$$B2A(c) : \text{ Self} \to \text{AIFace[Self]} \overset{\text{def}}{=}$$

$$\lambda x: \text{Self.} (c \cdot x).\text{super\_A WITH } (m := m(c) \cdot x)$$

As a result, $m(B2A(c)) = m(c)$, and $i(B2A(c)) = i(\text{super\_A}(c))$.

In general, all overriding methods from a subclass replace the methods from its superclass. Hidden fields reappear after casting because they are not replaced.

These cast operations are always defined for all cases of inheritance between the JAVA classes that are considered. Notice that the cast operations work "transitively", in the sense that given class C extending class B, and class B extending class A, the generated functions C2B, B2A and C2A are such that:

$$B2A(C2B(c)) = C2A(c).$$

6 Handling Late Binding

The example in the previous section involves late binding: $ar[1]$ has static type A, but invoking $ar[1].m()$ results in the execution of m from B, because $ar[1]$ has *run-time* type B. We shall study this mechanism in more detail. First, in this section we concentrate on late binding within the current object (on **this** if you like), and later, in the next section, we concentrate on method invocations on different objects.

Suppose for now that the class A from the previous section also contains a method n which simply calls m, and is used in B, as in:

– JAVA ————————————————————————————

```java
class A {
  ... // as before
  int n() { return i +  m(); }
}
```

```
class B extends A {
   ... // as before
   int test2() { return n(); }
}
```

Again due to late binding, test2 returns the value of the field i from A plus the result from the method m in B, since, as explained earlier, field selection is based on the static type and method selection is based on dynamic types. Since the run-time type of the object in which test2 is executed is B, late binding ensures the execution of m from B. Thus, test2 returns the value of i from A + 1000 × the value of i from B.

This behaviour is realised in our semantics by using the method bodies of A, in particular the body of n, with appropriate casts from a B coalgebra to an A coalgebra. Before we can see how this works, we need to know a bit more about method bodies.

6.1 Formalisation of Method Bodies

Space restrictions prevent us from explaining the details about the translation of JAVA method bodies into type theory, as performed by the LOOP tool. Therefore we concentrate on what is relevant here, necessarily leaving many things unexplained. More details may be found in [15,10,3,9]. So far we have used a type variable Self for the state space. In the actual translation, a fixed type OM is used. It represents the underlying memory model, see [3]. It consists of three parts: a heap, a stack, and a static part, each with an infinite series of memory cells and a 'top' position indicating the next unused cell. Several 'put' and 'get' operations are defined for writing and reading from this memory, at various locations.

The type-theoretic translation of the body of the method n from A looks as follows.

─ TYPE THEORY ─────────────────────────────────

c: OM $\to$ AIFace[OM] $\vdash$

   nbody(c) : OM $\to$ ExprResult[OM, int] $\overset{\text{def}}{=}$

   λx: Self. LET ret_n: OM $\to$ int $=$ get_int(stack(stacktop(x), 0)),
         ret_n_becomes: OM $\to$ int $\to$ OM $=$
            put_int(stack(stacktop(x), 0))
      IN (CATCH-EXPR-RETURN(stacktop_inc;
            E2S(A2E(ret_n_becomes(F2E(i(c)) + m(c))));
            RETURN)(ret_n) @@ stacktop_dec)(x)

───

The reader is not expected to understand all details about the translation of this method body, as that is not really needed at this stage. We briefly explain the basics: first, a special local variable ret_n is declared, together with an associated assignment operation, and is bound to a particular position on the stack. This variable ret_n is used to temporarily hold the result of the computation. At the end it is read by the CATCH-EXPR-RETURN function. But first, the stacktop is incremented, so that later method calls do not interfere with the values in the cell used for this method (where the value for ret_n is stored). The actual body return i + m() gets translated into an assignment of $F2E(i(c)) + m(c)$ to the return variable via ret_n_becomes, followed by the return statement RETURN— where F2E is an auxiliary function used to turn a field access function into an expression, and similarly E2S and A2E produce expression with appropriate types. At the very end, the stacktop is decremented again, freeing the used cell at the stack. Hopefully, this explanation does convey the main idea of what is going on, namely:

$$\text{nbody}(c) = \boxed{\quad \cdots i(c) + m(c) \cdots \quad}$$

The important thing to note is that the definition of nbody is parameterised[5] by an A coalgebra $c: \text{OM} \to \text{AIFace}[\text{OM}]$. In the translation of A, the call $n(c)$ rewrites to $\text{nbody}(c)$. The whole trick in getting late binding to work correctly is to have the (repeated) extraction function $n(d)$ for a B coalgebra $d: \text{OM} \to \text{BIFace}[\text{OM}]$ rewrite to the method body $\text{nbody}(\text{B2A}(d))$, which is the body as in A, but with a casted coalgebra. The effect is summarised in the following table.

Class	binding	m in nbody	i in nbody
A with coalgebra $c: \text{OM} \to \text{AIFace}[\text{OM}]$	$n(c)$ to $\text{nbody}(c)$	$m(c)$	$i(c)$
B with coalgebra $d: \text{OM} \to \text{BIFace}[\text{OM}]$	$n(d)$ to $\text{nbody}(\text{B2A}(d))$	$m(\text{B2A}(d))$ $= m(d)$	$i(\text{B2A}(d)) =$ $i(\text{super\_A}(d))$

This is precisely what we want, namely that the method call to m in n in B, i.e. m in $\text{nbody}(\text{B2A}(d))$, is m from B, whereas i in $\text{nbody}(\text{B2A}(d))$ is i from A. The coalgebra by which nbody is parametrised thus formalises the method lookup table of the current object.

In conclusion, late binding is realised by binding in subclasses the repeated extraction functions of methods from superclasses to the bodies from the superclasses, but with casted coalgebras.

7 Method Calls to Other Objects

In this section we consider method calls of the form o.m(), where o is a "receiving" or "component" object. Field access o.i is not discussed explicitly, but is handled similarly. Examples occurred in Section 5, where o was an array access ar[0] or ar[1].

---

[5] In reality it is even more complicated, since the method body has more parameters than are mentioned here.

So far we have been using coalgebras with type OM → AlFace[OM] to capture the ingredients of a class A. These coalgebras actually have two more parameters, namely a memory position, of type MemLoc, and a string. The memory position points to the location in memory where the values of the fields of the object are stored. The string can be the name of the class that the coalgebra itself represents (like "A"), or the name of one of its subclasses, representing the run-time type of an object. Thus, we use parametrised coalgebras of type string → MemLoc → OM → AlFace[OM].

For each class, say A, a specific coalgebra A_clg : string → MemLoc → OM → AlFace[OM] is assumed, with requirement:

$$A\_clg(``A")(p) \text{ implements } A.$$

This implementation requirement expresses that fields, methods and constructors in A_clg("A") behave as described, for example, in their method bodies. If A has a subclass B, then additional requirements are imposed, namely,

$$A\_clg(``B")(p) = B2A(B\_clg(``B")(p)) \quad \text{and} \quad B\_clg(``B") \text{ implements } B$$

(And similarly, for further subclasses.) The first of these requirements expresses that the implementation of A on an object with run-time type B behaves like the implementation of B, casted to A.

Why is this relevant? Consider a JAVA method invocation expression o.m(), where the receiving object o has static type A, say, and m is non-void (i.e. has a return type). This expression is translated via an auxiliary function CE2E[6], namely as $[\![o.m()]\!] = CE2E(A\_clg)([\![o]\!])(m)$. This function CE2E first evaluates $[\![o]\!]$; if $[\![o]\!]$ terminates normally, this produces a value in RefType, see the end of Section 3. In case this result is a null-reference, a NullPointerException will be thrown; if it is a non-null-reference, it contains a memory location p and a string s (describing o's run-time type). The method $m(A\_clg \cdot s \cdot p)$ will then be evaluated, corresponding to execution of m by the receiving object o—stored at location p in OM—with the run-time type of o determining the implementation of m that is chosen. Using the implementation requirements on coalgebras from the previous paragraph and the coalgebra-cast functions, the appropriate body for m is found. All this is in accordance with the explanation of method invocation in the JAVA language specification [7, §§15.11].

The function CE2E is defined as follows.

---

[6] CE2E stands for "Component-Expression-to-Expression".

─ TYPE THEORY ──

c: string $\to$ MemLoc $\to$ OM $\to$ IFace,
o: OM $\to$ ExprResult[OM, RefType],
m: (OM $\to$ IFace) $\to$ OM $\to$ ExprResult[OM, α] $\vdash$

$\quad$ CE2E$(c)(o)(m)$: OM $\to$ ExprResult[OM, α] $\overset{\text{def}}{=}$

$\qquad \lambda x$: OM. CASES $o \cdot x$ OF {
$\qquad\qquad$ | hang $\mapsto$ hang
$\qquad\qquad$ | norm $y \mapsto$
$\qquad\qquad\qquad$ CASES y.res OF {
$\qquad\qquad\qquad\qquad$ | null $\mapsto$ "NullPointerException"
$\qquad\qquad\qquad\qquad$ | ref $r \mapsto m(c \cdot (r.$clname$) \cdot (r.$objpos$)) \cdot (y.$ns$)$ }
$\qquad\qquad$ | abnorm $a \mapsto$ abnorm a }

──

Notice that such a method invocation hangs, or terminates abruptly if the receiving object o does, and also that the possible side-effect of evaluating o is passed on to the method m, via the state y.ns. The details of how exceptions are thrown are not relevant here, and are omitted.

The main point is: if we have an object **a** in a class **A** and an object **b** in a subclass **B** of **A**, both with a method **m**, then after an assignment **a** = **b** the run-time type of **a** (given by the clname label) is equal to the run-time type of **b**, and so a method invocation **a.m()** will have the same effect as **b.m()**, since

$$\text{m}(\text{A\_clg}("B")(p)) = \text{m}(\text{B2A}(\text{B\_clg}("B")(p))) = \text{m}(\text{B\_clg}("B")(p)).$$

where p is the memory location of **a** (and **b**). But note that a field access expression **a.i** may yield a different result from **b.i**!

8   Example Verifications

Next it will be described how the semantics, as sketched in the previous sections, is used for tool-supported reasoning about JAVA classes. Actually, no explicit reasoning principles are needed for handling inheritance, because automatic rewriting takes care of proper method selection. Therefore, inheritance requires no special attention in verification—but remains difficult in specification. This is of course very convenient, and a good reason for using this particular semantics.

We shall describe two example verifications, based on translations of JAVA programs by the LOOP tool. The first verification is in PVS, and the second one in ISABELLE/HOL. Here we shall no longer use the type-theoretic syntax of earlier sections, but use PVS and ISABELLE syntax. The first verification is about the JAVA classes in Section 5, and establishes the properties mentioned there. The PVS statements that have been proved are:

```
– PVS ──────────────────────────────────────────────

    IMPORTING ...  % code generated by the LOOP tool is loaded

    test1 : LEMMA  p < heap?top(x) IMPLIES
        norm??(test1?(Test?clg("Test")(p))(x))
           AND
        res?(test1?(Test?clg("Test")(p))(x)) = 10102

    test2 : LEMMA  p < heap?top(x) IMPLIES
        norm??(test2?(B?clg("B")(p))(x))
           AND
        res?(test2?(B?clg("B")(p))(x)) =
           i(B?2?A(B?clg("B")(p)))(x) + i(B?clg("B")(p))(x) * 1000
──────────────────────────────────────────────────────
```

The first lemma **test1** states that evaluation of **test1** terminates normally, returning **10102**. The second lemma states that evaluation of **test2** also terminates normally, and the return value equals the value of **i** from **A**, plus 1000 times the value of **i** from **B**.

The PVS code contains lots of question marks '?', which are there only to prevent possible name clashes with JAVA identifiers (which cannot contain '?'). Both lemmas have a technical assumption p < heap?top(x) requiring that the position **p** of the receiving object is in the allocated part of the heap memory. The proofs of both these lemmas proceed entirely by automatic rewriting[7], and the user only has to tell PVS to load appropriate rewrite rules, and to start reducing. The functions **CE2E** and **B2A** play a crucial rôle in this verification. Hopefully the reader appreciates the semantic intricacies involved in the proof of the first lemma: array creation and access, local variables, object creation, implicit casting, and late binding.

The second verification deals with the following JAVA program.

```
– JAVA ─────────────────────────────────────────────

    class C {
      void m() throws Exception { m(); }
    }
    class D extends C {
      void m() throws Exception { throw new Exception(); }
      void test() throws Exception { super.m(); }
    }
──────────────────────────────────────────────────────
```

---

[7] To give an impression, the proof of **test1** involves 790 rewrite steps, taking about 67 sec., on a 450 Mhz. Pentium III with 128 MB RAM under Linux.

At a first glance, one might think that evaluation of the method `test` will not terminate, but on the contrary, it throws an exception. In the body of `test` the method `m` of `C` is called. This method calls `m` again, but—due to late binding—this results in execution of `m` in `D`. However, if `m` is called on an instance of class `C` directly, this will not terminate. The ISABELLE/HOL statements that have been proved are the following.

```
─ ISABELLE ──────────────────────────────────────────────────
  (* Code generated by the LOOP tool is loaded *)
  Goal "p < heap_top x ==> \
  \       case DInterface.test_ (D_clg ''D'' p) x of \
  \         Hang       => False\
  \        |Norm y     => False\
  \        |Abnorm a => True";
  (* Simplifier *)
  qed "m_in_D_Abnorm";

  Goal "p < heap_top x ==> \
  \       case CInterface.m_ (C_clg ''C'' p) x of \
  \         Hang       => True\
  \        |Norm y     => False\
  \        |Abnorm a => False";
  (* Proof *)
  qed "m_in_C_hangs";
```

These lemmas state that evaluation of `m` on an object with run-time type `D` will terminate abnormally, while evaluation of `m` on an object with run-time type `C` will not terminate, *i.e.* will hang.

In the ISABELLE code the full name (including the theory name) is used for the extraction functions. This is to prevent name clashes, due to overloading. Again, the technical assumption `p < heap_top x` is used. The proof of the first lemma proceeds entirely by automatic rewriting[8], after the user has added appropriate rewrite rules to the simplifier. The crucial point in this verification is the binding of the extraction function for `super.m` on a D coalgebra d: OM → DIFace[OM] to the method body C_mbody(D2C(d)).

The verification of the second lemma requires some more care, since it can not be done via automatic rewriting (as this would loop). To prove non-termination, several unfoldings and an appropriate induction are necessary.

9   Conclusions

We have described the main ideas of the inheritance semantics in the LOOP project for reasoning about JAVA classes, and shown the practical usability of

---

[8] On a Pentium II 266 Mhz with 96 MB RAM, running Linux, this takes about 71 sec, involving 5070 rewrite steps—including rewriting of conditions.

this semantics in two example verifications, where late binding was handled by automatic rewriting, both in PVS and in ISABELLE/HOL.

For more complicated examples, a Hoare logic can be used for reasoning [10]. The largest case study that have been done so far, is the verification of a non-trivial class invariant for JAVA's **Vector** class [11]. This verification gives an impression of the size of JAVA programs that can be handled. Currently, this approach is also applied to the JavaCard API, see also [22].

Acknowledgements

Thanks are due to to Hans Meijer and Erik Poll for their useful feedback on the manuscript, and to Joachim van den Berg for suggesting the JAVA example in the second verification in Section 8.

References

1. M. Abadi and L. Cardelli. *A Theory of Objects*. Monographs in Comp. Sci. Springer, 1996.
2. K. Arnold and J. Gosling. *The Java Programming Language*. Addison-Wesley, 1996.
3. J. van den Berg, M. Huisman, B. Jacobs, and E. Poll. A type-theoretic memory model for verification of sequential Java programs. Techn. Rep. CSI-R9924, Comput. Sci. Inst., Univ. of Nijmegen, 1999.
4. K.B. Bruce, L. Cardelli, and B.C. Pierce. Comparing object encodings. In M. Abadi and T. Ito, editors, *Theoretical Aspects of Computer Software*, number 1281 in Lect. Notes Comp. Sci., pages 415–438. Springer, Berlin, 1997.
5. L. Cardelli. A semantics of multiple inheritance. *Inf. & Comp.*, 76(2/3):138–164, 1988.
6. W. Cook and J. Palsberg. A denotational semantics of inheritance and its correctness. *Inf. & Comp.*, 114(2):329–350, 1995.
7. J. Gosling, B. Joy, and G. Steele. *The Java Language Specification*. Addison-Wesley, 1996.
8. M. Hofmann, W. Naraschewski, M. Steffen, and T. Stroup. Inheritance of proofs. *Theory & Practice of Object Systems*, 4(1):51–69, 1998.
9. M. Huisman. *Reasoning about Java Programs in Higher-Order Logic, using PVS and Isabelle/HOL*. PhD thesis, Univ. Nijmegen, 2000. Forthcoming.
10. M. Huisman and B. Jacobs. Java program verification via a Hoare logic with abrupt termination. In T. Maibaum, editor, *Fundamental Approaches to Software Engineering*, number 1783 in Lect. Notes Comp. Sci., pages 284–303. Springer, Berlin, 2000.
11. M. Huisman, B. Jacobs, and J. van den Berg. A case study in class library verification: Java's Vector class. Techn. Rep. CSI-R0007, Comput. Sci. Inst., Univ. of Nijmegen. (An earlier version appeared in: B. Jacobs, G.T. Leavens, P. Müller, and A. Poetzsch-Heffter (eds.), Formal Techniques for Java Programs. Proceedings of the ECOOP'99 Workshop. Technical Report 251, Fernuniversität Hagen, 1999, pages 37–44), 2000.
12. B. Jacobs. Inheritance and cofree constructions. In P. Cointe, editor, *European Conference on Object-Oriented Programming*, number 1098 in Lect. Notes Comp. Sci., pages 210–231. Springer, Berlin, 1996.

13. B. Jacobs. Objects and classes, co-algebraically. In B. Freitag, C.B. Jones, C. Lengauer, and H.-J. Schek, editors, *Object-Orientation with Parallelism and Persistence*, pages 83–103. Kluwer Acad. Publ., 1996.
14. B. Jacobs and J. Rutten. A tutorial on (co)algebras and (co)induction. *EATCS Bulletin*, 62:222–259, 1997.
15. B. Jacobs, J. van den Berg, M. Huisman, M. van Berkum, U. Hensel, and H. Tews. Reasoning about classes in Java (preliminary report). In *Object-Oriented Programming, Systems, Languages and Applications (OOPSLA)*, pages 329–340. ACM Press, 1998.
16. B. Meyer. *Object-Oriented Software Construction*. Prentice Hall, 2nd rev. edition, 1997.
17. J.C. Mitchell. Toward a typed foundation for method specialization and inheritance. In *Principles of Programming Languages*, pages 109–124. ACM Press, 1990.
18. W. Naraschewski and M. Wenzel. Object-oriented verification based on record subtyping in higher-order logic. In J. Grundy and M. Newey, editors, *Theorem Proving in Higher Order Logics*, number 1479 in Lect. Notes Comp. Sci., pages 349–366. Springer, Berlin, 1998.
19. S. Owre, J.M. Rushby, N. Shankar, and F. von Henke. Formal verification for fault-tolerant architectures: Prolegomena to the design of PVS. *IEEE Trans. on Softw. Eng.*, 21(2):107–125, 1995.
20. L.C. Paulson. Isabelle: The next 700 theorem provers. In P. Odifreddi, editor, *Logic and computer science*, pages 361–386. Academic Press, London, 1990. The APIC series, vol. 31.
21. B.C. Pierce and D.N. Turner. Simple type theoretic foundations for object-oriented programming. *Journ. Funct. Progr.*, 4(2):207–247, 1994.
22. E. Poll, J. van den Berg, and B. Jacobs. Specification of the JavaCard API in JML. In *Fourth Smart Card Research and Advanced Application Conference (CARDIS)*. Kluwer Acad. Publ., 2000, to appear. Available as Techn. Rep. CSI-R0005, Comput. Sci. Inst., Univ. of Nijmegen.
23. Loop Project. http://www.cs.kun.nl/~bart/LOOP/.

Total-Correctness Refinement for Sequential Reactive Systems

Paul B. Jackson*

Division of Informatics
University of Edinburgh
Edinburgh EH9 3JZ, UK
pbj@dcs.ed.ac.uk

Abstract. We introduce a coinductively-defined refinement relation on sequential non-deterministic reactive systems that guarantees total correctness. It allows the more refined system to both have less non-determinism in its outputs and to accept more inputs than the less refined system. Data reification in VDM is a special case of this refinement.
Systems are considered at what we have called *fine* and *medium* levels of granularity. At the fine-grain level, a system's internal computational steps are described. The fine-grain level abstracts to a medium-grain level where only input/output and termination behaviour is described. The refinement relation applies to medium grain systems.
The main technical result of the paper is the proof that refinement is respected by contexts constructed from fine grain systems. In other words, we show that refinement is a precongruence.
The development has been mechanized in PVS to support its use in case studies.

1 Introduction

Refinement. Refinement is a fundamental verification methodology and has a strong conceptual appeal. It takes a black-box view of systems, characterizing them by their observable interface behaviour.

Let A be an abstract system, C a concrete system, and assume that it has been shown that A *refines to* C, written $A \sqsubseteq C$. A good definition of $\sqsubseteq$ and theory of refinement then provide a guarantee that we can substitute C for A in any environment with no observable consequences.

Formally one way to give evidence for substitutivity is to show a *precongruence* property:

$$\vdash A \sqsubseteq C \Rightarrow \mathcal{E}[A] \sqsubseteq \mathcal{E}[C]$$

of $\sqsubseteq$ for a class of contexts or environments $\mathcal{E}$.

This paper introduces a new definition of a refines-to relation for sequential non-deterministic systems that addresses weaknesses of previously proposed relations. The main technical result is to prove this refines-to relation to be a precongruence for a general class of environments.

---

* Also affiliated with the Institute for System Level Integration, Livingston, UK

J. Harrison and M. Aagaard (Eds.): TPHOLs 2000, LNCS 1869, pp. 320–337, 2000.

Inclusion-Based Refinement. Many common definitions of a refinement relation involve inclusion. For example refinement might assert that a step transition relation of the concrete system is included in that of the abstract system, or that every trace of the concrete system is also a trace of the abstract system, a *trace* being a sequence of observable states or input/output values. Such definitions have several problems, as we explain in the next two subsections. We use trace inclusion as an example, but our remarks apply to other inclusion-based definitions too.

Contravariance of Inputs. A consequence of a trace-inclusion definition is that, if there is some step of behaviour in the concrete trace corresponding to the environment passing the system some input, there must be a similar step in the abstract trace. This is intuitively the wrong way round and allows a bad concrete system to inadvertently constrain environment behaviour and falsely appear to be correct. A variety of approaches have tried to deal with this. For example, the notion of *receptivity* is introduced [5].

Total Correctness. We consider it important that a refinement relation capture total correctness. Without totality, it is much harder to argue that a concrete system could replace an abstract system with no observable consequences.

Trace inclusion is a partial correctness rather than total correctness notion. It requires that when the concrete system makes some step of behaviour passing output to the environment, the abstract system must make some matching step. However it doesn't ever require that the concrete system make any output step in the first place.

As explained in [4], one adaptation for total correctness is to introduce an extra value $\perp$ into the state spaces of systems. If a system originally is not guaranteed to make an output step from some given state, a transition to $\perp$ is added, along with a transition to every other state. There is therefore no possibility for a system to be blocked from making a step, all systems are total. Furthermore, on starting from a $\perp$ state, a system must non-deterministically be able to transition to every possible state (including $\perp$ again). With this setup, trace inclusion requires that, whenever the abstract system is capable of making only controlled steps (i.e. not to a $\perp$ state), the concrete system also can only make controlled steps, and so inclusion now enforces total correctness.

The Proposed Refines-to Relation. We propose a *refines-to* relation that directly captures the desirable contravariant relationship between inputs of abstract and concrete systems, and that ensures total correctness without the complications of adding extra $\perp$ states. We define refines-to coinductively. See Sec. 4 for details.

Fine and Medium Grain Systems. We focus our attention on non-deterministic sequential systems that alternately accept an input value from some environment and return an output value back to the environment. We assume systems can modify some internal state and that this state is preserved between returning an output value and accepting some next input.

We use an automata-based *fine-grain* model for describing system implementations. See Sec. 5. This model represents atomic computation steps and can exhibit phenomena such as divergence and deadlock. Fine grain systems abstract to a *medium-grain* level where just the input/output and termination behaviour of systems is captured. The medium grain level is also appropriate for directly creating system specifications. See Sec. 3 for the medium grain system definition. This medium grain formalism uses precondition and transition relations and is very similar to the way systems are described in VDM [10], for example.

Refines-to is defined only on medium grain systems. It is independent of how we characterise systems at the fine grain. For example, for the fine grain model we could have used instead a structured operational semantics that captures total correctness. One advantage of an automata-based approach to fine grain systems is that the characterisation of when systems terminate is direct and obviously correct.

When showing that *refines-to* is a precongruence, we use a variation on fine-grain systems to construct the general class of environments that we show precongruence with respect to. See Sec. 6 for the definition of the variation and Sec. 7 for the precongruence proof.

Evaluating Goodness of Refines-to. A precongruence property is generally desirable for any refinement relation, but isn't sufficient by itself to justify the relation's definition. To take an extreme example, an always true refinement relation is indeed a precongruence, it but provides no substitutivity guarantees at all. We also must look at the environment beyond the boundaries of the system we model formally, and consider the expectations this environment has.

Sometimes, for example in the process algebra community, these expectations are formalized by developing a theory of *testing* [6] and showing (at least) that any more refined system passes all tests that a more abstract system passes. The hope is that it is more straightforward to agree that a testing theory adequately captures the expectations of an external environment than to agree that the refinement relation does.

We haven't developed a testing theory, and instead simply discuss the expectations we might reasonably have of sequential reactive systems. We do observe that the total-correctness proof obligations adopted in VDM for showing that one sequential program is a data reification of another are a consequence of our definition of *refines-to*. Also, it would be easy to derive the similar VDM obligations for showing an implementation meets a specification.

Use of a Theorem Proving System. We see all of the Pvs [13] formalization work described in this paper as being necessary support material for case studies in verifying actual systems.

It's worth mentioning too that we also found the use of Pvs a significant help in clarifying what definitions were necessary, how lemmas should be phrased, and how proofs should go. At the same time, we found the main proofs sufficiently intricate and the weight in the formal notation sufficiently high that in many cases it was necessary to be sketching proofs on paper before or at the same time as attempting the Pvs proofs.

An Illustrative Example. We show in Sec. 8 a specification of an abstract data type of sets as a medium grain system, and an implementation as a fine grain system.

2   Related Work

The use of coinduction to define refinement relations has been made popular by the process algebra community [12].

Jacobs in [9] characterises classes in object-oriented languages as coalgebraic categories, and uses a coinductive notion of refinement to specify correctness of implementations. His approach is more general than ours in that he allows for changes in the system interface in going from abstract to concrete. However, he takes a simpler view of systems: he models them using total functions so non-determinacy is not possible, and he doesn't take account of any input preconditions that might need to be satisfied for termination. We imagine it would be possible to adapt these extra features that we consider into his framework. This work is also being implemented in Pvs.

We originally considered a coinductive definition of a refinement relation that allows contravariance on inputs after seeing Abramsky discuss such a relation [1]. The relation he considers is on labelled transition systems with input and output labels on the transitions. He also has a game-theoretic version that applies to prefix-closed sequences of input/output behaviour. One limitation of his relation is that it captures partial, not total correctness.

A formalism for concurrent systems that allows contravariance on inputs and prevents restriction of environment behaviour by the system is that of alternating refinement relations [3]. This work also uses coinductive characterisation of refinement. To tackle concurrency issues, its definition is more elaborate than ours. For example, the nesting depth of alternations of quantifiers is four, compared to 2 in our case. In the reactive modules [2] formalism being pursued by a subset of the authors of [3], a notion of *temporal abstraction* is defined, much like our map from fine to medium grain systems, that can hide internal computation steps of system components.

In the literature on refinement of sequential programs (see [4] for a recent comprehensive survey), our approach is closest to that taken in VDM [10]. Our *medium grain systems* exactly correspond to the precondition and VDM post condition[1] style specifications.

Early work of Milner [11] looks at denotational semantics for *transducers* which are effectively the same as our medium grain systems. To our knowledge, Milner never proposed a coinductive definition of refinement for transducers, though he deployed coinductive definitions heavily in his concurrency theory

---

[1] relations on inputs and outputs, rather than just relations on outputs as in Hoare style specifications

work on labelled transition systems. There the distinction between inputs and outputs is erased at the level much of the semantics work is carried out, so the opportunity we take to treat them differently is lost.

3   Medium Grain Systems

A *medium grain system* is a full description of the behaviour of a non-deterministic sequential reactive system from an input/output and termination point of view. The intent is that both system specifications and implementations can be phrased as medium grain systems.

The type Med_gs of medium grain systems , parameterized by types I and O of input and output values and type Q of internal states, is defined as a subtype of a record type:

```
Med_gs[Q,I,O] : TYPE ≐
{s : ( pre ⊆ Q × I,
        trans ⊆ Q × I × O × Q  )
|
   ∀p,i. s.pre(p,i) ⇒ ∃q,o. s.trans(p,i,o,q)  }.
```

The notation 'fieldname ⊆ Type' abbreviates 'fieldname : $\mathcal{P}$(Type)' where $\mathcal{P}$ is the powerset (set of subsets) operator. Subsets of a type T are represented as functions of type T → bool, so membership of an element x in a subset s is expressed as function application s(x), a notation in keeping with the correspondence between subsets and predicates.

The field trans specifies what transitions the system can make. The relation trans(p,i,o,q) indicates that, starting from state p and presented with input value i, it is possible for the internal computations of the system to eventually terminate in state q and for the system to return output value o. Because of non-determinism there might be more than one q and o for given p and i. The field pre specifies a precondition. The relation pre(p,i) indicates that starting from state p and presented with input i, the internal computations of the system are guaranteed to terminate in some state from which output is generated. In general it is not equivalent to ∃q,o. trans(p,i,o,q) but stronger. Even if a system can reach q and output o from a given state p and input i, because of non-determinism, it might also deadlock or go into a divergent computation.

It would be convenient to include the type parameter Q as an initial field of the record type in the definition of Med_gs. However this is not possible in the Pvs specification language.

To fully describe in Pvs a medium grain system, we sometimes augment the presentation of the system as an element of Med_gs by identifying some element of Q as the system's initial state.

We imagine interactions between an environment and a medium grain system as a continuing dialogue: if the thread of control is with the environment, the environment can choose to provide the system with some input. The system then processes this input and possibly eventually generates some output. Control then passes back to the environment which is free is choose some further input for the system.

For some purposes, we make the assumption that the environment has no ability to access or modify the internal system state. The environment might only know that the system initially started off in some well-characterized state.

We imagine that a medium grain system being used as a specification will exhibit a range of possible behaviour on a given input that is only dependent on the initial state and the observed input/output behaviour inbetween. We consider a system with this property to be *coarse grain*. Coarse grainness is a desirable property for specifications. Coarse grainness corresponds to determinacy in the CCS process calculus [12]. We haven't yet made any use of coarse grainness in our work.

4 Definition of Refinement

Our definition of what it means for one system to be a refinement of another is in the style of the coinductive definition of bisimulation [12].

Fix on an abstract medium grain system sa and a concrete medium grain system sc with distinct internal states Qa and Qc and both over input type I and output type O: in Pvs, they have respective types Med_gs[Qa,I,O] and Med_gs[Qc,I,O].

A relation R $\subseteq$ Qa $\times$ Qc is a *refinement relation* from sa to sc iff it satisfies

$$R(pa,pc) \Rightarrow \tag{1}$$
$$\forall i. \ \text{sa.pre}(pa,i) \Rightarrow$$
$$\text{sc.pre}(pc,i)$$
$$\land \ \forall qc, \ o. \ \text{sc.trans}(pc,i,o,qc) \Rightarrow$$
$$\exists qa. \ \text{sa.trans}(pa,i,o,qa) \land R(qa,qc)$$

for any states pa and pc.

System sa in initial state inita *refines to* system sc in initial state initc, written

refines_to(sa,sc)(inita,initc),

iff there exists a refinement relation R such that R(inita,initc). The relation refines_to(sa,sc) is easily shown itself to be a refinement relation, and so by this definition it is the greatest refinement relation, adopting the usual ordering of relations by inclusion.

We realise the definition of refines_to in Pvs as the greatest fixed point of the appropriate functional. Pvs doesn't provide direct support for such coinductive definitions. However, we easily prove a lattice-theoretic version of the Tarski-Knaster fixed-point theorem and specialise it for the creation of coinductive definitions over the lattice of subsets of a type.

Trivially we show that refines_to is a preorder, that is, it is reflexive and transitive.

Why is this definition plausible? Assume we have found a refinement relation
R, system sa is in some state pa, system sc is in some state pc, and R(pa,pc)
holds. We then know for a start that

$$\forall i. \; \text{sa.pre(pa,i)} \; \Rightarrow \; \text{sc.pre(pc,i)}. \tag{2}$$

This is very reasonable: system sc is guaranteed to converge to an output on
every input that sa converges on. System sc might converge also on other inputs
too, but that doesn't matter here.

We also know

$$\forall i, \; qc, \; o. \; \text{sa.pre(pa,i)} \; \wedge \; \text{sc.trans(pc,i,o,qc)} \; \Rightarrow \tag{3}$$
$$\exists qa \; : \; \text{sa.trans(pa,i,o,qa)} \; \wedge \; \text{R(qa,qc)}.$$

Any output that the concrete system generates on an abstractly acceptable input
is also an abstractly acceptable output. The concrete system's output behaviour
is always what we might expect. The concrete system might exhibit less non-determinism, completely in line with the approach in specification of introducing
non-determinism, not because that non-determinism is expected in any one implementation, but in order to permit flexibility in implementation. However (2)
guarantees that there always is *some* output that the concrete system generates. Importantly too from (3) we know R(qa,qc) holds, so we also expect all
subsequent I/O behaviour of the concrete system to be in accordance with the
abstract system behaviour.

We make the assumption above that an environment would never want to
supply a system with input when there is not a firm expectation that the system
will eventually generate some output given that input. We are not trying to
define a notion of refinement that is to be used when thinking about the fault
tolerance of systems or about systems that have divergent computations in the
normal course of events.

Having said that, this definition of refinement should also be applicable if
only partial correctness were of interest. There is nothing intrinsic in the definition itself that refers to total correctness. However for partial correctness one
would want to discard the subtyping condition we have used in the definition of
the Med_gs type that requires at least one output value to exist whenever the
precondition is satisfied.

A common approach to establishing a refinement relationship between an
abstract and concrete system involves introducing a function rmap of type Qc
$\rightarrow$ Qa (sometimes known as a *refinement mapping, abstraction map* or *retrieve
function*) and an invariant on concrete states c_inv $\subseteq$ Qc. The function rmap
and predicate c_inv define a refinement relation:

$$\text{R(pa,pc)} \; : \; \text{bool} \; \doteq \; \text{c\_inv(pc)} \; \wedge \; \text{pa = rmap(pc)}.$$

Specialising (1), a predicate stating that rmap and c_inv form a refinement
relation is

$$\text{refmap\_step(sa,sc,c\_inv,rmap)} \; : \; \text{bool} \; \doteq$$

```
∀pc,i.
  c_inv(pc) ∧ sa.pre(rmap(pc),i) ⇒
  sc.pre(pc,i)
  ∧ ∀qc, o. sc.trans(pc,i,o,qc) ⇒
            sa.trans(rmap(pc),i,o,rmap(qc)) ∧ c_inv(qc),
```

and the coinduction principle that goes with refines_to specialises to the theorem refines_to_ind_with_refmap_a:

```
⊢ c_inv(initc) ∧ inita = rmap(initc)
  ∧ refmap_step(sa,sc,c_inv,rmap)
  ⇒
      refines_to(sa,sc)(inita,initc).
```

We observe that the antecedents of this theorem are exactly a strict subset of the proof obligations in VDM [10] for establishing a data reification relationship between an abstract data type and its implementation when there is also an invariant on the concrete type.

The extra proof obligation in [10] concerns *adequacy*. In our notation:

```
∀qa. ∃ qc. c_inv(qc) ∧ qa = rmap(qc).
```

This is usually desirable because it says that every abstract value has at least one concrete representation. However it is not necessary for showing

```
refines_to(sa,sc)(inita,initc).
```

If it so happens that in the abstract system sa starting from state inita we cannot access every abstract state by some sequence of input values, then adequacy needn't hold for the inaccessible states. This is unlikely to happen if the abstract system is an initial specification, but it could reasonably happen if it is a system at some intermediate level of refinement.

We also observe that if the preconditions sa.pre and sc.pre in refmap_step are always true, the theorem refines_to_ind_with_refmap_a reduces to the induction principle commonly used when refinement is defined as trace inclusion.

5   Fine Grain Systems

5.1   Definition of Fine Grain System

A *fine grain system* is a system description that allows the presentation of the individual computation steps that a system can perform. It is a suitable formalism for describing system implementations: see Sec. 8 where an example is given of describing the procedures in an imperative implementation of an abstract data type as a fine grain system.

We build on the definition of a fine grain system when defining later the contexts or environments that some medium grain system may be operating in. See Sec. 6 and Sec. 7.

We define a type `Fin_gs` of fine grain systems as

```
Fin_gs[Q,I,O] : TYPE ≐
  {s : ⟨ run ⊆ Q,
         input : (Q × I) → Q,
         step ⊆ Q × Q,
         output : Q → O,
         wbehaved ⊆ Q ⟩
  |
    ∀p,q. s.step(p,q) ⇒ s.run(p)  }
```

with parameters `Q`, `I`, and `O` as in the definition of the `Med_gs` type in Sec. 3.

Initially a fine grain system is in some state for which `run` is false. When an input value is presented to a fine grain system, the system uses `input` to transition to a new state. The system then uses `step` to repeatedly make non-deterministic internal transitions. As specified by the subtyping predicate, steps can only be taken from states that satisfy `run`. The system halts and uses `output` to generate an output value if and when it reaches a state for which `run` is false.

A system can *deadlock*, reach a state p for which `run` is true, but ¬∃q. `step(p,q)`. Deadlock might seem an unusual feature to have in a model of a sequential system, but it is a natural phenomenon for guarded transition systems to exhibit. Deadlock is one appropriate behaviour for handling exceptional situations without extra machinery in the formalism. And checks for its absence can reveal bugs in system descriptions.

A system can also *diverge*, perform steps ad-infinitum without ever reaching a state in which `run` is false.

Once halted, a system is then ready to be reactivated by a further input. The predicate `wbehaved` identifies those states from which any step by `step` is guaranteed to be well-behaved. A step might not be well-behaved if it involves interacting with a subsystem.

As with medium grain systems, to fully specify a fine grain system we often also identify some element of `Q` as the system's initial state.

5.2 Abstraction from Fine to Medium Grain

To form the input/output medium-grain view of a fine grain system s with type `Fin_gs[Q,I,O]`, we use the fine to medium grain map:

```
map_fm(s) : Med_gs[Q,I,O] ≐
  ⟨ pre := mgs_pre(s),
    trans := mgs_trans(s)
  ⟩,
```

where

```
mgs_pre(s)(p,i) : bool ≐
  progressive?(s)(s.input(p,i))
```

$\wedge\ \neg$inf_chain(s.step)(s.input(p,i))

mgs_trans(s)(p,i,o,q) : bool $\doteq$
  star(s.step)(s.input(p,i),q)
  $\wedge\ \neg$s.run(q)
  $\wedge$ o = s.output(q)

at_progressive?(s)(q) : bool $\doteq$
  s.run(q) $\Rightarrow$ s.wbehaved(q) $\wedge\ \exists$r. s.step(q,r)

progressive?(s)(q) : bool $\doteq$
  $\forall$r. star(s.step)(q,r) $\Rightarrow$ at_progressive?(s)(r).

Here we draw on an auxiliary development of properties of finite and infinite sequences of values where adjacent values are related by a binary relation R. The relation star(R) is the reflexive transitive closure of R. The predicate instance inf_chain(R)(x) indicates that there exists an infinite chain of R-linked values starting from x. If star(s.step)(q,r), then by the subtype property of fine grain systems, every state on any path from q up to but excluding r is a run state. A state is progressive? if every run state accessible by stepping through only run states is both well behaved and not deadlocked. The predicate name at_progressive? is an abbreviation for 'atomically progressive?'. The predicate mgs_pre identifies exactly those inputs of the fine grain system for which no divergence is possible and it is guaranteed that the system will eventually reach a halting state. It might be difficult when reasoning with actual systems to work with this definition of mgs_pre, and simpler to use instead some predicate known to be stronger than that given here. The predicate mgs_trans specifies what outputs the fine grain system might generate for each input.

With the typing of the map_fm definition, the PVS type checker automatically generates a TCC (type correctness condition) that requires us to check that the subtype predicate in the Med_gs definition is satisfied.

6 Parameterized Fine Grain Systems

6.1 Definition of Parameterized Fine Grain System

A *parameterized fine grain system* is an adaptation of a fine grain system that can feed inputs to and receive outputs from a medium grain subsystem. The use of it in this paper is as a general description of contexts that medium grain systems might operate in. The type of parameterized fine grain systems is:

Prm_fin_gs[Q,I,O,Ix,Ox] : TYPE $\doteq$
  {s : $\langle$ run $\subseteq$ Q,
       input : (Q $\times$ I) $\rightarrow$ Q,
       output : Q $\rightarrow$ O,
       i_step $\subseteq$ Q $\times$ Q,

```
        x_en ⊆ Q,
        x_input : x_en → Ix,
        x_output : (Q × Ox) → Q  )
  |
      ∀p. s.x_en(p) ∨ (∃q. s.i_step(p,q)) ⇒ s.run(p)  },
```

where the type parameters for `Prm_fin_gs` are Q for internal states, I for values
input from the environment, O for values output to environment, Ix for values
fed to the medium grain subsystem, and Ox for values received back from the
subsystem. The fields `run`, `input` and `output` are as for a fine grain system. The
relation `i_step` is for internal steps, and the predicate `x_en`, function `x_input`
and function `x_output` are for the interface to the subsystem. Their use will
become clear in the next subsection.

6.2   Instantiation of Parameterized Fine Grain System

Here we show how to combine a parameterized fine grain system s with a medium
grain system x to create an unparameterized fine grain system. There are several
options as to how the internal state spaces of s and x are related. In general
they might share some state and also each have some distinct private state. Our
immediate interest is in the situation where the only interaction can be via x's
input/output interface, so we choose to keep the state spaces distinct. Let Q
be the state space of s and Qx the state space of x. The type of states for the
combined system is Q × Qx.

Let the type parameters I, O, Ix, and Ox be defined as in Sec. 6.1. The
parameterised fine grain system s then has type `Prm_fin_gs[Q,I,O,Ix,Ox]` and
the medium grain system x has type `Med_gs[Qx,Ix,Ox]`. The map instantiating
s with subsystem x has definition:

```
  m_ipfd(s, x) : Fin_gs[(Q × Qx),I,O] ≐
    ⟨ run     := λ(q,qx). s.run(q),
       input := m_ipfd_input(s,x),
       step  := m_ipfd_step(s,x),
       output := λ(q,qx). s.output(q),
       wbehaved := m_ipfd_wbehaved(s,x)   ⟩,
```

where

```
  m_ipfd_step(s, x)(ppx,qqx) : bool ≐
    let (p,px) = ppx, (q,qx) = qqx in
    s.i_step(p,q) ∧ px = qx
    ∨ s.x_en(p) ∧ ∃ox. x.trans(px, s.x_input(p), ox, qx)
                    ∧ q = s.x_output(p,ox)

  m_ipfd_input(s, x)(qqx,i) : Q × Qx ≐
    let (q,qx) = qqx in s.input(q,i), qx
```

```
m_ipfd_wbehaved(s, x)(q,qx) : bool ≐
    s.x_en(q) ⟹ x.pre(qx, s.x_input(q)).
```

Here 'm_ipfd' stands for 'map instantiating parameterised fine grain system keeping states distinct'. In the definition of m_ipfd_step, we see how x_en is used to identify when calls to the subsystem are enabled. In most sensible systems, we expect that it will never be possible to take an i_step when x_en is true, but we haven't found a need yet to specify this requirement. The function x_input is used to feed inputs to the subsystem, and function x_output processes the resulting outputs from the subsystem.

When a system is modelled as the parameterized fine grain system s, we assume that the granularity of i_steps is chosen sufficiently finely that, within the system behaviour modelled by a single i_step, there is no possibility for divergence or deadlock. Therefore, in defining m_ipfd_wbehaved, we need only consider that bad behaviour of m_ipfd_step can result if x is called when x.pre is false.

The map mm_map combines m_ipfd with the fine to medium grain map defined previously:

```
mm_map (s : Prm_fin_gs[Q,I,O,Ix,Ox])(x : Med_gs[Qx,Ix,Ox])
       : Med_gs[(Q × Qx),I,O]
    ≐  map_fm(m_ipfd(s, x)).
```

7   Refinement is Precongruence

Let ps be a parameterized fine grain system of type Prm_fin_gs[Q,I,O,Ix,Ox] with initial state q, let sa be an abstract medium grain subsystem of type Prm_fin_gs[Qa,Ix,Ox] with initial state qa, and let sc be a more concrete medium grain subsystem of type Prm_fin_gs[Qc,Ix,Ox] with initial state qc. The lemma precong_lemma:

```
⊢ refines_to(sa,sc)(qa,qc) ⟹
    refines_to(mm_map(ps)(sa), mm_map(ps)(sc))((q,qa),(q,qc))
```

states that the refines_to relation is a precongruence.

The proof is by coinduction, using the 'refines_to candidate':

```
rt_cand(sa,sc)(qqa,qqc) : bool ≐
    qqa.1 = qqc.1 and refines_to(sa,sc)(qqa.2,qqc.2)
```

to instantiate the coinduction lemma. Key foundational lemmas in the proof are

$$
\begin{aligned}
&⊢ \texttt{rt\_cand(sa, sc)(qqa, qqc)} \quad\quad\quad\quad\quad\quad\quad\quad\quad (4)\\
&\quad ∧\ \texttt{at\_progressive?(m\_ipfd(ps,sa))(qqa)}\\
&\quad ∧\ \texttt{m\_ipfd(ps, sc).step(qqc, rrc)}\\
&\quad ⟹\\
&\quad\quad ∃\texttt{rra.}\ \ \texttt{m\_ipfd(ps, sa).step(qqa, rra)}
\end{aligned}
$$

$$\wedge \ \texttt{rt\_cand(sa, sc)(rra, rrc)}$$

```
⊢ rt_cand(sa,sc)(qqa,qqc)
  ∧ at_progressive?(m_ipfd(ps,sa))(qqa)
  ⇒
      at_progressive?(m_ipfd(ps,sc))(qqc).
```

Key intermediary lemmas are

```
⊢ rt_cand(sa,sc)(qqa,qqc)
  ∧ progressive?(m_ipfd(ps,sa))(qqa)
  ∧ ¬inf_chain(m_ipfd(ps,sa).step)(qqa)
  ⇒
      ¬inf_chain(m_ipfd(ps,sc).step)(qqc),
```

proven by coinduction on `inf_chain(m_ipfd(ps,sa).step)`, and

```
⊢ rt_cand(sa, sc)(qqa, qqc)
  ∧ progressive?(m_ipfd(ps,sa))(qqa)
  ∧ star(m_ipfd(ps, sc).step)(qqc, rrc)
  ⇒
      ∃rra. star(m_ipfd(ps, sa).step)(qqa, rra)
            ∧ rt_cand(sa, sc)(rra, rrc),
```

proven by induction on `star(m_ipfd(ps, sc).step)` using an inductive characterisation of `star(R)` with R steps successively added on the left, and use of lemma (4) above.

8   Example Specification

We give here an example of a specification of an ADT (abstract data type) of finite sets as a medium grain system, and an implementation as a fine grain system. We show the correctness statement for the implementation in terms of our *refines-to* relation.

8.1   Sets Specification

We consider the ADT to be parameterised by a type T of elements, to have operators:

```
bool empty ()       test if empty
void insert(T)      insert a possibly new element
void remove (T)     remove an existing element
T choose ()         choose an element
bool member (T)     test if an element is in the set
```

and to have a constructor null for the empty set.

We introduce datatypes for the input and outputs of both fine and medium grain systems.

```
IType [T:TYPE+] : DATATYPE
 BEGIN
   i_empty : i_empty?
   i_insert(i_insert_arg : T) : i_insert?
   i_remove(i_remove_arg : T) : i_remove?
   i_choose : i_choose?
   i_member(i_member_arg : T) : i_member?
 END IType

OType [T:TYPE+] : DATATYPE
 BEGIN
   o_empty(o_empty_val : bool) : o_empty?
   o_insert : o_insert?
   o_remove : o_remove?
   o_choose(o_choose_val : T) : o_choose?
   o_member(o_member_val : bool) : o_member?
 END OType
```

Such datatype statements in Pvs declare constructors, recognisers, and field selectors, and introduce various auxiliary definitions and property axioms.

The medium grain system for sets is:

```
a_sys : Med_gs[AState,IType,OType] ≐
   ⟨ pre := a_pre, trans := a_trans ⟩,
```

where

```
AState : TYPE ≐ P(T)
```

```
a_trans(p,ip,op,q) : bool ≐
   cases ip of
      i_empty :      q = p ∧ op = o_empty(empty?(p)),
      i_insert(x) :  q = add(x,p) ∧ op = o_insert,
      i_remove(x) :  member(x,p) ∧
                     q = remove(x,p) ∧ op = o_remove,
      i_choose :     nonempty?(p) ∧
                     q = p ∧ op = o_choose(choose(p)),
      i_member(x) :  q = p ∧ op = o_member(member(x,p))
   endcases
```

```
a_pre(p,ip) : bool ≐
   cases ip of
      i_empty :      true,
      i_insert(x) :  true,
      i_remove(x) :  member(x,p),
      i_choose :     nonempty?(p),
      i_member(x) :  true
   endcases.
```

An initial state for the empty set is:

```
a_null : AState ≐ emptyset[T].
```

Here we have employed definitions such as member, remove and emptyset from Pvs's standard sets-as-predicates library.

Note that we only specify that the remove operation be well behaved and terminate if it happens that that element we are trying to remove is indeed initially contained in the set.

We introduce a non-deterministic choose operation to pick some element from a set. It is defined in terms of the choose function on sets, which in turn makes use of the Hilbert epsilon operator in Pvs's type theory. No requirement is placed on the behaviour of choose if the set is empty.

8.2   Sets Implementation

We base our implementation on lists. We will require these lists to not contain duplicates when we come to proving the correctness statement we show in the next subsection.

The type of states is:

```
CFState : TYPE ≐
  ⟨ pc : nat,
    sys_input : IType,
    set : list[T],
    tvar : T,
    tsvar : list[T],
    bvar : bool  ⟩
```

When executing an operation, we keep the input value to the fine grain system stored in the field sys_input. This field not only holds the input value (if any) of the operation, but also indicates *which* operation is currently executing. We use the predicate:

```
at_proc(p : pred[IType])(u) : bool ≐ p(u.sys_input)
```

to indicate which procedure we are currently in.

The field pc is the program counter, field set holds the list representation of the set, and fields tvar, tsvar, and bvar are temporary variables intended for use within operations.

The system definition is:

```
cf_sys : Fin_gs[CFState,IType,OType] ≐
  ⟨ run     := cf_run,
    input   := cf_input,
    step    := cf_step,
    output  := cf_output,
    wbehaved := λu. true  ⟩.
```

The system is in a run state when the pc is non-zero:

```
cf_run(u) : bool ≐ u.pc > 0.
```

Operations always start with a pc of 1:

```
cf_input(u,ip) : CFState ≐ u with [sys_input := ip, pc := 1].
```

The step relation is composed from step relations for each operation:

```
cf_step(u,v) : bool ≐
   cases u.sys_input of
      i_empty      : cf_empty_step(u,v),
      i_insert(x)  : cf_insert_step(u,v),
      i_remove(x)  : cf_remove_step(u,v),
      i_choose     : cf_choose_step(u,v),
      i_member(x)  : cf_member_step(u,v)
   endcases.
```

Examples of step relations for operations are:

```
cf_remove_step(u,v) : bool ≐
   cf_remove_step_1(u,v)
   ∨ cf_remove_step_2(u,v)
   ∨ cf_remove_step_3(u,v)
   ∨ cf_remove_step_4(u,v)
   ∨ cf_remove_step_5(u,v)

cf_remove_step_2(u,v) : bool ≐
   at_pc(2)(u) ∧ cons?(u.set) ∧ v = u with [pc := 3]

cf_remove_step_4(u,v) : bool ≐
   at_pc(3)(u)
   ∧ cons?(u.set)
   ∧ car(u.set) = i_remove_arg(u.sys_input)
   ∧ v = u with [pc := 2, set := cdr(u.set)]

cf_choose_step(u,v) : bool ≐
   at_pc(1)(u)
   ∧ cons?(u.set)
   ∧ v = u with [pc := 0, tvar := car(u.set)]
```

Note how we implement choose by simply returning the head element of the list.

Selector functions on Pvs datatype are partial functions, only total on the relevant subtype of the datatype. For example, above, remove_step_2 is the only way of reaching at_pc(3), but to make remove_step_4 type check in Pvs, we have to again check the cons?ness of u.set. We could regard the possibility of deadlock that this repeated check implies as a way of modelling the exception that might be raised in actual code if we reached step 4 and u.set were not a cons.

The output function is:

```
cf_output(u) : OType ≐
  cases u.sys_input of
      i_empty :       o_empty(null?(u.set)),
      i_insert(x) : o_insert,
      i_remove(x) : o_remove,
      i_choose :     o_choose(u.tvar),
      i_member(x) : o_member(u.bvar)
  endcases.
```

The correctness of the output function relies on the preservation of the sys_input field from when an operation is started.

The initial state of the implementation is:

```
cf_null : CFState ≐
  ⟨ pc := 0,
    sys_input := i_empty,
    set := null[T],
    tvar := εx. true,
    tsvar := null[T],
    bvar := false ⟩.
```

The only important values here are for pc and set. The other values are just placeholders.

8.3   Correctness Statement

We construct a medium grain black-box abstraction of this system as follows:

```
CMState : TYPE ≐ CFState,
cm_sys : Med_gs[CMState,IType,OType] ≐ map_fm(cf_sys),
cm_null : CMState ≐ cf_null.
```

The theorem that our implementation is a correct implementation of the sets specification is then:

```
⊢ refines_to(a_sys, cm_sys)(a_null, cm_null).
```

9   Conclusions

We have introduced a refinement relation *refines-to* that can be used in correctness specifications for a very general class of programs. For example it is applicable to abstract data types, modules and classes in imperative and object oriented languages. The relation's merits include

- it captures total correctness requirements,
- it has a simple intuitive operational reading,
- it captures expectations about the covariant nature of outputs and the contravariant nature of inputs under refinement,
- it is a precongruence with respect to a general class of environments,
- standard proof obligations used for refinement in VDM can be derived from it.

While its use should make specifications significantly clearer than they might otherwise be, it doesn't make verification tasks any easier.

We are currently exploring the use of *refines-to* in specifying and verifying garbage collection algorithms. A refinement approach is appealing because it allows the use of black-box abstract data types for both the specification and implementation of garbage-collected heap memory. In previous work of ours in this area [8], we specified correctness using linear temporal logic assertions that had to refer to internal details of the garbage collection algorithm.

References

[1] Samson Abramsky. A note on reactive refinement. Personal Communication, May 19th 1999.

[2] Rajeev Alur and Thomas Henzinger. Reactive modules. *Formal methods in System Design*, 15:7–48, 1999.

[3] Rajeev Alur, Thomas A. Henzinger, Orna Kupfermann, and Moshe Y. Vardi. Alternating refinement relations. In *CONCUR '98*, LNCS. Springer Verlag, 1998.

[4] Willem-Paul de Roever and Kai Engelhardt. *Data Refinement: Model-oriented proof methods and their comparison*. Number 47 in Cambridge Tracts in Theoretical Computer Science. Cambridge University Press, 1998.

[5] David L. Dill. *Hierarchical Verification of Speed Independent Asynchonous Circuits*. MIT, 1988.

[6] Matthew Hennessey. *A theory of Testing*. MIT, 1989.

[7] Ulrich Hensel and Bart Jacobs. Coalgebraic theories of sequences in PVS. *Journal of Logic and Computation*, 9(4):463–500, 1999.

[8] Paul B. Jackson. Verifying a garbage collection algorithm. In Jim Grundy and Malcolm Newey, editors, *11th International Conference on Theorem Proving in Higher-Order Logics: TPHOLs'98*, volume 1479 of *Lecture Notes in Computer Science*, pages 225–244. Springer-Verlag, September 1998.

[9] Bart Jacobs. Behaviour-refinement of coalgebraic specifications with coinductive correctness proofs. In *Proceedings of TAPSOFT/FASE 1997*, LNCS. Springer Verlag, 1997.

[10] C. B. Jones. *Program Specification and Verification in VDM*. Prentice Hall, 2nd edition, 1990.

[11] R. Milner. Processes: a mathematical model of computing agents. In *Logic colloquium '73*, pages 157–173. North Holland, 1975.

[12] R. Milner. *Communication and Concurrency*. Prentice Hall, 1989.

[13] S. Owre, J.M. Rushby, and N. Shankar. PVS: A prototype verification system. In D. Kapur, editor, *11th Conference on Automated Deduction*, volume 607 of *Lecture Notes in Artificial Intelligence*, pages 748–752. Springer-Verlag, 1992. See http://www.csl.sri.com/pvs.html for up-to-date information on PVS.

Divider Circuit Verification with Model Checking and Theorem Proving

Roope Kaivola and Mark D. Aagaard

Intel Corporation, RA2-401, 2501 NW 229th Avenue, Hillsboro, OR 97124, USA

Abstract. Most industrial-size hardware verification problems are amenable to neither fully automated nor fully manual hardware verification methods. However, combinations of these two extremes, human-constructed proofs with automatically verified lower-level steps, seem to offer great promise. In this paper we discuss a formal verification case study based on such a combination of theorem-proving and model-checking techniques. The case study addresses the correctness of a floating-point divider unit of an Intel IA-32 microprocessor.

The verification was carried out in the Forte framework, which consists of a general-purpose theorem-prover, ThmTac, on top of a symbolic trajectory evaluation based model-checking engine. The correctness of the circuit was formulated and decomposed to smaller, automatically model-checkable, statements in a pre/postcondition framework. The other key steps of the proof involved relating bit vectors to integer arithmetic and general arithmetic reasoning.

1 Introduction

The size and complexity of industrial-scale circuits means that they are rarely amenable to fully automated verification, as in the traditional model-checking paradigm. On the other hand, the amount of detail in these circuits puts them beyond the reach of purely human-constructed proofs, as in the theorem-proving paradigm. Consequently, a fair amount of recent research has concentrated on combining the two approaches. The goal is to automate tedious low-level reasoning, while retaining the freedom for the human verifier to set the overall proof verification strategy.

In this paper we describe a verification of the input-output correctness of a floating-point divider unit from an Intel IA-32 microprocessor. The verification is based on human-constructed proofs with automatically verified lower-level steps. It was carried out using the Forte verification system [1,2]. Forte is a combined model-checking and theorem-proving system that we have built on top of the Voss system [14]. The interface language to Voss is FL, a strongly-typed functional language in the ML family [20]. Model checking in Voss is done via symbolic trajectory evaluation (STE) [23]. Theorem proving is done in the ThmTac[1] proof tool. ThmTac is written in FL and is an LCF-style implementation of a higher-order classical logic.

Since the widely publicized Pentium floating point erratum in 1995, a multitude of divider hardware verification case studies have been published [4,8,7,5,18,19,22]. Floating point dividers are particularly hard to verify due to the iterative nature of division

---

[1] The name "ThmTac" comes from "theorems" and "tactics".

J. Harrison and M. Aagaard (Eds.): TPHOLs 2000, LNCS 1869, pp. 338–355, 2000.

algorithms, the use of multiplication in the natural high-level correctness statements, and the range of data. No currently known model-checking technique is capable of directly verifying floating point division algorithms against a high level correctness statement. Usually the top-level correctness statement is decomposed into small portions, which are then verified by automated model-checking. The reasoning that justifies the deduction of the high-level correctness statement is then done as a pen-and-paper proof or with a theorem-proving or proof-checking tool.

We set out to perform a fully mechanized proof in a single, unified framework that would connect the top-level correctness statement all the way down to the actual register-transfer level description of the hardware. In some of the earlier case studies combining theorem-proving and model-checking techniques, model-checking is done in one system, and the results transferred to another system for theorem-proving purposes. In our opinion this approach still leaves room for error, as there may be unstated or poorly understood assumptions underlying the accuracy of translation of statements from one formalism and framework to another. A single, tightly integrated environment also helps in making the proof more manageable and understandable by allowing assumptions, qualifications and verified statements to be expressed in a uniform notation.

Carrying out the entire proof in a single environment set certain requirements on the verification system. First, it must contain a sufficiently powerful model-checking engine. Secondly, as the decomposition proofs will unavoidably involve many different flavors of reasoning, the environment should contain a reasonably general theorem-prover and enable the user to write her own application-specific extensions.

Although most of the discussion in the paper is applicable to all of the division-like operations supported by the hardware, we will concentrate on the (partial) remainder calculation in particular. According to the IEEE standard on floating-point arithmetic [15], the remainder operation is always expected to produce precise results, so this choice means that the present paper does not need to address the separate and largely orthogonal issue of specifying and verifying floating point rounding.

In Section 3 we review some basics of floating-point arithmetic, and examine a simple division algorithm and its implementation in hardware. In Section 4 we discuss the intuitive specification of the remainder operation and the main proof steps used in its verification. The following Sections 5, 6 and 7, deal with three general issues emerging in the proof: the principle of "proof by evaluation", general arithmetic reasoning and the relation of bit-vector statements and arithmetical statements, and reasoning about flow of computation in a pre-postcondition paradigm. Section 8 then returns to the main verification, and gives a more detailed view of the required proof steps.

2   The Forte System

Forte [1] is a combined model-checking and theorem-proving system based on Voss [14]. The interface and scripting language to Voss is FL, a strongly-typed functional language in the ML family [20]. Model checking in Voss is done via symbolic trajectory evaluation. Theorem proving is done in the ThmTac proof tool. ThmTac is written in FL and is an LCF-style implementation of a higher-order classical logic.

The Forte scripting language, FL, includes binary decision diagrams (BDDs) as first-class objects and trajectory evaluation as a built-in function. The principle aim of ThmTac is to enable seamless transitions between model checking, where we *execute* FL functions, and theorem proving, where we *reason* about the behavior of FL functions. This goal was achieved via a reflection-like mechanism named "lifted FL" [2]. In this section we give a brief overview of two of the underlying technologies in Forte: lifted FL and trajectory evaluation.

2.1   Lifted FL

Parsing an FL expression results in a conventional combinator graph [21] for evaluation purposes. Parsing a lifted FL expression results in both a combinator graph and an abstract syntax tree representing the text of the expression. The abstract syntax tree is available for FL functions to examine, manipulate, and evaluate.

FL expressions are lifted by enclosing them in ', as in '1 + 2'. If an FL expression has type α, the lifted version of that expression will have type α expr. An expression of type α expr can be evaluated to an expression of type α using the built-in function eval.

Forte uses lifted FL as the term language for ThmTac and FL as the specification language for model checking. Our link from theorem proving to model checking is via the evaluation of lifted FL expressions. Roughly speaking, any FL expression that evaluates to true can be turned into a theorem.

Figure 1 shows how we move between standard evaluation (*i.e.*, programming) and theorem proving. The left column illustrates lifting a Boolean expression. The right column illustrates evaluating a lifted expression and proving a theorem with evaluation.

```
fl> 1 + 4 - 2 > 2;               fl> eval '1 + 4 - 2 > 2';
it :: bool                       it :: bool
T                                T

fl> '1 + 4 - 2 > 2';             fl> Prove '1 + 4 - 2 > 2' Eval_tac;
it :: bool expr                  it :: Theorem
'1 + 4 - 2 > 2'                  |- '1 + 4 - 2 > 2'
```

Lifting FL expressions   Transition from evaluation to theorem proving

Fig. 1. Evaluation and theorem proving in lifted FL

To use lifted FL as the term language for theorem proving, we needed to add support for free variables and quantifiers. We supported free variables by modifying the FL parser to allow free variables in lifted FL expressions, but to complain about free variables in normal FL expressions. Evaluating a lifted FL expression that contains free variables will raise an exception. We implement quantifiers with regular FL functions that raise exceptions when evaluated and then axiomatize the behavior of the functions in ThmTac.

2.2 Trajectory Evaluation

Symbolic trajectory evaluation is based on traditional notions of digital circuit simulation and excels at datapath verification. Trajectory evaluation correctness statements are called *trajectory assertions* and are written as: $\models_{ckt} [ant \Longrightarrow\!\!\!> cons]$. The *antecedent* (*ant*) gives an initial state and input stimuli to the circuit *ckt*, while the *consequent* (*cons*) specifies the desired response of the circuit. Formally, $\models_{ckt} [ant \Longrightarrow\!\!\!> cons]$ means: all sequences that are in the language of the circuit and that satisfy the antecedent will also satisfy the consequent.

Two keys to the efficiency of trajectory evaluation are the restricted language of the temporal formulas and the built-in support for data abstraction via a lattice of simulation values. The core specification language for antecedents and consequences (trajectory formulas) is shown in figure 2. The specification language does not include negation and the only temporal operator is "next".

$$
\begin{aligned}
\textit{traj\_form} \equiv\ &node\ \textit{is}\ value \\
\mid\ &\textit{traj\_form}\ \textbf{when}\ guard \\
\mid\ &\text{N}\ \textit{traj\_form} \\
\mid\ &\textit{traj\_form}\ \textbf{and}\ \textit{traj\_form}
\end{aligned}
$$

The meaning of: $\text{N}^{t}(node\ \textit{is}\ value\ \textbf{when}\ guard)$ is: "if *guard* is true then at time t, *node* has value *value*"; where *node* is a signal in the circuit and *value* and *guard* are Boolean expressions (BDDs).

Fig. 2. Trajectory formulas

Fig. 3. The four valued lattice

The simulation model for trajectory evaluation extends the conventional Boolean domain to a lattice. The theory of trajectory evaluation supports general lattices. However, for gate-level hardware verification, the four valued lattice shown in Figure 3, which is used by Forte, suffices.

In conventional symbolic simulation, the value of a signal is either a scalar value (T or F) or a symbolic expression representing the conditions under which the signal is T. In trajectory evaluation, the value X denotes lack of information: the signal could be either T or F. Because of the restricted temporal logic of trajectory evaluation, if a trajectory assertion ($\models_{ckt} [ant \Longrightarrow\!\!\!> cons]$) holds when some signal has a value of X at some point in time, then the assertion will also hold when the signal has a value of either T or F. An essential result is that any assertion verified over a sequence containing Xs will hold for sequences with Xs replaced with either T or F [3,6]. It is important to note that the converse does not necessarily hold. That is, if a property holds both when a signal is T and when it is F, then it is not necessarily the case that the property will hold when the signal is X.

Figure 4 is an example of how the use of X over-approximates the possible behaviors of a circuit. When a is either T or F, c is T. If a is a variable v, then c is T. However, when a is a X, we do not have any information about the value of b. In particular, we do not know that b is the inverse of a. Hence, in the fourth line c cannot be anything except X.

The last line demonstrates the affects of the top element of the lattice, $\top$. The top element, $\top$, describes conditions under which a node has conflicting values. These situations arise when the antecedent is inconsistent or when the value calculated by the circuit differs from that in the antecedent. Because $\top$ is the highest value in the lattice, a signal that is $\top$ satisfies all consequents.

Assertion	Simulation values a b c			Assertion value
$\models_{ckt}$ [a is F$\Longrightarrow$c is T]	T F		T	T
$\models_{ckt}$ [a is T$\Longrightarrow$c is T]	F T		T	T
$\models_{ckt}$ [a is $v\Longrightarrow$c is T]	v $\neg v$		T	T
$\models_{ckt}$ [$\emptyset\Longrightarrow$c is T]	X X		X	F
$\models_{ckt}$ $\begin{bmatrix} a\,is\,T\,and \\ a\,is\,F \end{bmatrix}\Longrightarrow$f is F	$\top$ $\top$		$\top$	T

Fig. 4. Xs and approximation

Assertion	Assertion Value
$\models_{ckt}$ $\begin{bmatrix} d\,is\,F\,and \\ e\,is\,r \end{bmatrix}\Longrightarrow$f is F	T
$\models_{ckt}$ [d is F$\Longrightarrow$f is F]	T
$\models_{ckt}$ [d is $v\Longrightarrow$f is F]	$\neg v$

Fig. 5. Examples of assertion results

Figure 5 illustrates a variety of trajectory assertions about a simple AND gate and the resulting values of the assertions. Note in particular, the third line, which shows how the value of an assertion is symbolic if the assertion is only satisfied under certain circumstances.

3   Divider Circuit

The rest of the paper is dedicated to examining the application of the verification framework outlined above to a particular case study, a subcircuit of an Intel IA-32 microprocessor carrying out floating-point division and remainder calculation.

Let us first briefly recall some basics of binary floating-point numbers, a binary representation for a subset of real numbers. A typical representation is a triple $f = (s, e, m)$, where the *sign* s is a single bit, the *exponent* e a bit vector of some fixed length *expln*, the *mantissa* m another bit vector of some fixed length *manln*. The real number $r(f)$ encoded by the triple is $(-1)^{\widehat{s}} * 2^{\widehat{e} - bias} * \widehat{m} * 2^{-manln+1}$, where $\widehat{x}$ is the natural number encoded by the bit vector x in the usual fashion and *bias* is some fixed *exponent bias*. Here the mantissa m has intuitively $manln - 1$ fraction bits and one bit to the left of the binary point, so m always encodes a value strictly less than 2.

The IEEE standard [15] defines several different representations for floating-point numbers, differing on details, but all adhere to the general idea described above. The standard also defines special encodings for zeros, infinities and various other such exceptional values, but in the current paper we do not need to be concerned with these. We call a floating-point number *normal* iff it is not one of these special cases and if the mantissa bit to the left of the binary point is 1, i.e. if m encodes a value that is at least 1.

Since only a small subset of the reals are representable as floating-point numbers, not all results of arithmetic operations on floating-point numbers can necessarily be expressed precisely as floating-point numbers themselves. Therefore the IEEE standard defines the concept of *rounding*: determining which sufficiently close representable number should be used, if the accurate result is not representable.

input: two normal floating-point numbers $N = (N_s, N_e, N_m)$ and $D = (D_s, D_e, D_m)$
       (we view abstractly N_e and D_e as natural numbers and N_m and D_m as fractions below)
variables: floating-point numbers $Q = (Q_s, Q_e, Q_m)$ and $R = (R_s, R_e, R_m)$, integers $imax$ and i

$i := 0;\ \ imax := div\_iteration\_count;$
$Q_m[0] := 0;\ \ R_m[0] := N_m;$
while $i < imax$ **do**
      /* determine quotient bit $q_i \in \{0,1\}$ */
      if $R_m[i] < D_m$ **then** $q_i := 0$ **else** $q_i := 1$ **fi**
      /* update quotient and remainder accordingly */
      $Q_m[i+1] := Q_m[i] + 2^{-i} * q_i;\ \ R_m[i+1] := 2 * (R_m[i] - q_i * D_m);\ \ i := i+1$
od
$Q_s := N_s$ **xor** $D_s;\ \ Q_e := N_e - D_e;\ \ Q_m := Q_m[imax];$
$R_s := N_s;\ \ R_e := N_e - imax;\ \ R_m := R_m[imax];$

if DIV then output (**round**(Q_s, Q_e, Q_m));
if REM then output (R_s, R_e, R_m);

Fig. 6. Simple iterative division-remainder algorithm

To illustrate the principles of the approach we used for verifying the divider circuit, consider the simple iterative division-remainder algorithm sketched in Figure 6. It takes two normal floating-point numbers N and D as input, and produces either the rounded quotient Q or the remainder R of N divided by D. This algorithm is essentially the same as the one taught in school for pen-and-paper division, although in binary instead of decimal. The value of $div\_iteration\_count$ depends on the required precision of result.

The primary purpose of the algorithm is division computation, and it could be argued that the remainder is simply a by-product of this. Nevertheless, here we concentrate on the remainder calculation, as this allows us to ignore the largely orthogonal issue of specifying formally what correct rounding means. The techniques discussed here are applicable to division, as well, so the choice is merely a matter of presentation.

To be more accurate, the remainder operation is expected to produce a floating-point number W such that $r(W) = r(N) - \lfloor r(N)/r(D) \rfloor * r(D)$, where $\lfloor x \rfloor$ is the function rounding x down to the preceding integer for positive x, and up to the following integer for negative x. In other words, the operation should produce the remainder after computing an integer quotient, which corresponds to defining $imax$ as $N_e - D_e + 1$ above.

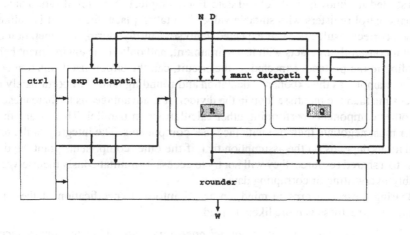

Fig. 7. Simple divider-remainder hardware

To illustrate a hardware implementation of the division algorithm, Figure 7 depicts a simplified division circuit. The circuit has inputs for the dividend N and the divisor D, and it also has some control signal inputs, at least a 'start operation' signal and signals specifying whether a division or remainder operation is to be performed. Mantissa calculation is done in a feedback loop, one iteration per clock cycle, and exponent calculation is done in a separate subunit. As output, the circuit produces the result W of the required calculation and some control information, such as various flags.

Current industrial hardware implementations of division algorithms are many magnitudes more complex than the simple one above. For example, they may use redundant or multiple representations of Q and R, produce more than one quotient bit per iteration, or perform speculative calculations, for purposes of optimizing the speed of the circuit (see [9] for various options). The circuit we verified was no exception in this respect: it contains over 7000 latches and a print-out of the register-transfer level description of the circuit is about one inch thick. Nevertheless, the principles of the algorithm and the hardware are similar to the simple case above, and the verification of the circuit is structured much the same way as for the simple case.

4 Overview of Verification

At its face value, translating the correctness statement of the algorithm to the hardware implementation is easy: a natural formulation would be *IF 'start operation' signal is asserted, AND the circuit is instructed to perform a remainder operation, AND the input values are N and D, THEN at the time the circuit produces output W, the equation* $r(W) = r(N) - \lfloor r(N)/r(D) \rfloor * r(D)$ *holds*. However, in the context of an actual microprocessor, this statement is overly optimistic and is unlikely to be true for several reasons. First, usually not all values of data are handled by hardware alone: to reduce the size of the circuit, atypical cases such as division by zero, tiny or huge results etc. are often handled partially by microcode routines. Secondly, the circuit is likely to function correctly only when started at a known, well-defined state. For example, before initialization of various internal control registers with suitable values has taken place, the circuit is unlikely to produce correct results, nor is it expected to do so. Thirdly, during the operation of the circuit it constantly interacts with its environment, and only if the environment behaves according to the protocol expected by the circuit, can the circuit itself function correctly. For example, as the exponent calculation and rounding take a proportionately much shorter time than the mantissa loop in the divider, it is advantageous to share these parts with other components performing other calculations in parallel. This means that the divider must negotiate their use with the other components. The integrity of the divider calculations depends on the assumption that, if the other components grant the divider access to a shared resource, they will not try to access it simultaneously themselves, thus possibly overwriting or corrupting data.

Bearing these concerns in mind, an actual informal specification of the circuit's functional correctness is more likely to read:

> *IF the circuit is internally in a normal operating state, AND the environment behaves according to the expected protocol, AND 'start execution' signal is asserted, AND the circuit is instructed to perform a remainder operation, AND the input values N and D are within the range handled by hardware,*
> *THEN at the time the circuit produces output W, the equation*
> $r(W) = r(N) - \lfloor r(N)/r(D) \rfloor * r(D)$ *holds.*

In the context of the complete microprocessor we can strengthen this statement by proving separately that *whenever 'start execution' signal can be asserted, the divider circuit is internally in normal operating state*, which allows us to discharge the first conjunct of the antecedent in the statement above. The proof can be carried out in a fairly traditional temporal-logic-based model-checking framework, but as it is largely separate from the main proof examined in the current paper, we shall not discuss it any further here.

Let us then have a brief overview of the main steps in verifying this functional correctness statement. As the algorithm and the hardware are iterative in nature, it is reasonable to start by looking for a loop invariant for the mantissa calculation. At the high level there is a natural loop invariant that relates the quotient and remainder mantissas $Q_m[i]$ and $R_m[i]$ to the input numbers D and N, derived from the fundamental defining equation of division:

$$(N_m = Q_m[i] * D_m + 2^{-i} * R_m[i]) \wedge (R_m[i] < 2 * D_m)$$

The multiplication operator in this high-level invariant means that verifying the property by direct model-checking is difficult. Hence, we decompose the problem by introducing two lower-level properties. The first is a bit-vector invariant that is optimized for model checking efficiency. The second property is the recurrence relation that the loop is supposed to compute, i.e., an equation relating current and previous loop values.

This divides the verification task into seven parts:

A Use model checking to show that the circuit satisfies a low-level bit-vector invariant.
B Prove that the low-level bit-vector invariant implies a numerical recurrence relation.
C Prove that the numerical recurrence relation maintains a high-level invariant.
D Prove that the high-level invariant guarantees that the final result emerging from the loop is the correct unrounded result.
E Use model-checking to show that a correct bit-vector relation holds between the loop output and the final output emerging from the rounder.
F Prove that the bit vector relation between loop output and final output implies a correct numerical relation between these.
G Prove that the correctness of the loop output and the correct numerical relation between loop output and final output implies the top-level correctness statement.

Different types of reasoning are required for the different parts: steps A and E involve only plain model-checking, steps B and F require reasoning about the correspondence between bit-vector operations and their arithmetic counterparts, step C relies on pure arithmetic reasoning, and steps D and G mainly apply reasoning about the flow of computation with some additional doses of arithmetic reasoning.

In the following three Sections we first look at some general technical issues emerging in the proof: the concept of proof by evaluation, in particular in relation to quantified statements; the transition from bit vectors to true arithmetic; and the formulation of and reasoning about statements concerning flow of computation. In Section 8 we shall return to the main proof in more detail, and see how these general techniques fit in.

5   Proof by Evaluation

As described in Section 2.1, eval is an FL function of type α expr $\rightarrow \alpha$. Evaluation is available to the ThmTac user in rewriting and in tactic application. Eval_rw is a rewrite that evaluates a term and substitutes the result in for the original term (*e.g.,* replace 1+2 with 3). Eval_tac evaluates the goal of the sequent. It solves the goal if the goal evaluates to true and raises an exception otherwise.

We have concentrated ThmTac on verifying *implementation specific* properties, that is, properties about specific circuits. This means that we tend to encounter many concrete values (*e.g.,* a specific list of BDD variables in an STE run) and relatively few term variables (*e.g.,* a list variable a of an unknown length). We originally intended for Eval_tac to be used just for carrying out symbolic trajectory evaluation runs. However, we have found that many subgoals that would normally require instantiating general theorems (*e.g.,* properties of lists), are concrete and are most easily solved by evaluation. For example, proving $[1, 2, 3]@[4, 5, 6] = [1, 2, 3, 4, 5, 6]$ could be done either by instantiating a theorem about the associativity of @ or by evaluating the goal.

One of the critical distinctions between theorem proving and BDD-based model checking is that in theorem proving, variables are terms, while in model checking, variables are BDDs. An important feature of ThmTac is the ability to use BDD evaluation as a means to prove theorems about Boolean variables. In an earlier paper [2], we briefly described our initial technique for moving between term and BDD variables. As we have continued to use ThmTac, our technique has evolved. In this section we provide a relatively detailed description of the enhanced techniques.

	Term	BDD
variable in FL	*NONE*	`variable "x"`
variable in lifted FL	`VAR "x"`	`APPLY (LEAF variable) (LEAF (STRING "x"))`
quantifier usage	$\forall x.\ T \implies x$	`Quant_forall ["x"] (T ==> (variable "x"))`

Table 1. Variables and quantification for terms and BDDs

Table 1 shows variables and quantification for terms and BDDs in FL and lifted FL. A term variable is a lifted FL construct that has no representation in "normal" FL. In FL, a BDD variable is created from a string using the function `variable`. In lifted FL a term variable is created with the `VAR` construct and a BDD variable is the application of the function `variable` to a string. Because Booleans are a finite domain, we can implement functions to quantify over Boolean variables and can translate term quantifiers over Boolean variables to BDD quantification. The universal BDD quantifier, `Quant_forall`, is implemented as shown in Figure 8.

```
let Quant_forall var body =
            bdd_substitute (var, T) body
        AND bdd_substitute (var, F) body;
```

Fig. 8. Universal quantification over BDDs

Transforming an expression from term quantifiers and term variables to BDD quantifiers and BDD variables is complicated by both performance and soundness issues. A naive, but sound, method would be to have ThmTac provide a new and unique name for each BDD variable. This is infeasible for performance reasons though, because the variable would not be placed in an optimal location in the all-important BDD-variable order defined by the user. Additionally, increasing the number of BDD variables slows down some BDD operations. Thus, for performance reasons, we needed to allow users to specify the mapping from term variables to BDD variables.

However, giving users complete freedom to choose BDD variable names would introduce soundness problems. Users could inadvertently prove contradictions if they chose BDD variables that were already used within the proof. Large verifications typically use hundreds of different BDD variables, which makes it relatively easy to lose track of where each variable is used. Thus, for correctness purposes, we have given ThmTac the burden of ensuring that users provide valid mappings of term variables to BDD variables.

Replacing term quantifiers and variables with BDD quantifiers and variables is implemented by the rewrite Term2BDD. Users provide a variable mapping to Term2BDD that specifies the BDD variables to use in place of each term variable. The term variables are allowed to be of type bool or bool list.

In order to rewrite $\forall x.P$ with Term2BDD [("x", vs)], where x may be free in P and where vs is of type string list, the following conditions must hold:

1. x must be of type bool or bool list.
2. If x is of type bool, then vs must be a singleton list.
3. The names in vs must be disjoint from the BDD variables that appear in P.

If these conditions are met, then Term2BDD:

1. replaces the term quantifier $\forall x$ with the BDD quantifier Quant_forall vs
2. substitutes all occurrences of VAR "x" in P with map variable vs

One subtlety in the above conditions is that term quantification over a list is for lists of all lengths, while BDD quantification is for fixed-length lists. To be completely rigorous, we should require that each term quantifier restrict the bound variable to a specific list, such as: $\forall x.$ (length $x = 32$) $\implies P$. We plan to address this shortcoming in the near future. So far, we have not encountered any theorems in our normal work that would be true if instantiated with a list of incorrect length and false if presented with a list of correct length.

Gordon [10] has an alternative method for transforming from terms to BDDs in HOL. The principle distinction between his work and ours is that his transformations go from a purely term world to a purely BDD world. In HOL, term expressions do not contain BDD variables. In contrast, a lifted FL expression might contain BDD variables, and so we require an additional safety check before carrying out the transformation.

6   Arithmetic Reasoning

The top-level input-output correctness statement and the high-level loop invariant of the divider are naturally expressed in terms of mathematical entities and operations. Much of the reasoning related to the preservation of the high-level invariant is also most naturally expressed in terms of arithmetics and general arithmetical rules. On the other hand, model-checking techniques using symbolic values and BDD-based representations cannot deal with statements involving integer or real operations. Instead, the model-checked statements need to be expressed in terms of bit-vectors and bit-vector arithmetics.

Bridging the semantic gap between bit vectors and numbers brings about several issues. Assume for the moment being that we are dealing with natural numbers on the abstract level, and n-bit vectors on the concrete level, and consider a simple combinational circuit with two n-bit inputs a and b, and one n-bit output c. If the circuit is expected to compute the numeric operation $\hat{\oplus}$ (e.g. addition, subtraction etc), its natural correctness statement would be expressed by $\hat{c} = \hat{a}\hat{\oplus}\hat{b}$, where, as before, $\hat{x}$ denotes the usual conversion of a bit vector to a natural number. For model-checking, we would reformulate this statement as $c = a \oplus b$, where $\oplus$ is the bit-vector counterpart of $\hat{\oplus}$. Deducing the natural correctness statement from the model-checkable one depends then on a general correspondence theorem relating $\hat{\oplus}$ and $\oplus$:

$$\forall x. \forall y. \; \widehat{x \oplus y} = \hat{x} \hat{\oplus} \hat{y}$$

Effectively this states that the concrete bit-vector operation implements correctly the abstract mathematical operation.

However, the general correspondence theorem is unlikely to be universally true. Due to the representation of values by n bits, it is far more likely that the equality only holds modulo 2^n; if the bit-vector operation $\oplus$ wraps over, it no longer corresponds directly to $\hat{\oplus}$, which causes various complications. First, reasoning in arithmetic modulo 2^n is harder and requires more care than in ordinary integer arithmetic. Secondly, as the main correctness statement is still formulated in ordinary arithmetic, we somehow must regain that from arithmetic modulo 2^n. This means that usually we must keep track of side conditions guaranteeing that the bit-vector operation does not wrap over. In simple cases these side conditions can be manageable, although an extra burden, but in more involved cases, with nested expressions, keeping track of all the necessary side conditions becomes extremely cumbersome.

To alleviate this problem, we wrote a library of routines for bit-vector integer arithmetic operations in which each vector and operation is augmented with an extra flag-bit detecting wrap-around, loss of precision or other such event. So, instead of just bit vectors, the basic entities handled by the new library are (bit vector, exactness bit) pairs. Using these routines, a user can build expressions in bit-vector arithmetics in the usual fashion, and by checking the value of the exactness bit determine whether the bit-vector operation corresponds to its integer arithmetic counterpart.

For example, the addition operation is this library is defined as shown in Figure 9, where ADD_bv_bv is the plain bit-vector addition operation, and msb a function returning the most significant bit of its argument. Intuitively the definition states that the result is exact iff both of the operands are exact and no wrap-around occurs. Other supported operations are subtraction, negation, multiplication by a power of 2, modulus by a power of 2, and equality and magnitude comparisons.

```
let +@ (bv1,e1) (bv2,e2) =
    let bv = ADD_bv_bv bv1 bv2 in
    let e = e1 AND e2 AND
          ((msb bv1 != msb bv2) OR (msb bv1 = msb bv))
    in
    (bv, e);
```

Fig. 9. Bit-vector addition with exactness test

For each of these operations the library contains a formally derived correspondence theorem. For example, for the addition operation above, this theorem states that for all $bv1$, $e1$, $bv2$, $e2$ and bv, if $(bv1, e1) + @ (bv2, e2) = (bv, T)$, then $\widehat{bv1} + \widehat{bv2} = \hat{bv}$. where

+ is regular integer addition. Using the theorem, the user can lift model-checked results stated in terms of +@ to statements formulated in terms of + without manually keeping track of the side conditions. Analogous correspondence theorems exist for the other operations.

Once the model-checked results have been lifted to the level of integer arithmetics, all the usual machinery for reasoning about them is at our disposal: laws of associativity, distributivity, cancellation etc, various rewriting rules for simplification of expressions, and so on. This part of the verification was a fairly straightforward task, given the relatively well-developed support for arithmetic reasoning in ThmTac. Notice, however, that all the proofs were carried out in terms of integers and not real numbers, although the latter would be the most natural choice for reasoning about floating-point operations. Ideally we would like to operate in terms of real number arithmetic as e.g. in [12], but as support libraries for this are not in place in ThmTac yet, integers were chosen as a pragmatic compromise.

7 Reasoning about Flow of Computation

In the arithmetic reasoning described in previous section, we are relating statements about bit-vector arithmetic and logical relations to statements about relations between integers. This is a mathematically well-understood area, and it is easy to find the right conceptual level for the proofs.

However, when we are deducing the correctness of the loop output from the preservation of the loop invariant we are reasoning about the temporal progress of computation in the circuit. Here it is not quite as clear what the appropriate framework for expressing the proof is, and what general principles of reasoning are at stake. To bring in some conceptual machinery to structure the proof, we chose to formulate these temporal aspects of the proof in a variant of the traditional pre-postcondition framework.

The theory of pre-postcondition triples is a standard framework for specification and pen-and-paper verification of traditional sequential programs (see [11,17] for introduction). In this approach, statements about programs are of the form $\{P\}S\{Q\}$, where P and Q are logical properties, and S is a program. Such a triple formalizes the statement *precondition P guarantees postcondition Q after running S*, or more accurately *for any possible execution of program S, if the execution starts in a situation satisfying P, then it terminates in a finite time and leads to a situation satisfying Q*.

To relate the pre-postcondition approach to circuits, consider a circuit ckt, and assume trajectory $tr_{in}(x)$ binds a vector x of Booleans to input signals at the time the input is intuitively read, and that a vector y is similarly bound to some output signals by trajectory $tr_{out}(y)$. If a formula $\phi_{in}(x)$ expresses the precondition the input is supposed to meet, and $\phi_{out}(x,y)$ the postcondition the circuit is supposed to produce, the statement *precondition ϕ_{in} guarantees that the postcondition ϕ_{out}* can be expressed by the formula

$$\forall in.\phi_{in}(in) \Rightarrow (\exists out.(\models_{ckt}[tr_{in}(in)\Longrightarrow\!\!\gg tr_{out}(out)])) \;\wedge$$
$$(\forall out.(\models_{ckt}[tr_{in}(in)\Longrightarrow\!\!\gg tr_{out}(out)]) \Rightarrow \phi_{out}(in,out))$$

In the following, we write $\{\phi_{in}\}(tr_{in},ckt,tr_{out})\{\phi_{out}\}$ as a shorthand for this.

To see that this formula indeed captures the intuition described above, recall from Section 2 that if the expression $\models_{ckt} [tr_{in}(x) \Longrightarrow\!\!\!\gg tr_{out}(y)]$ is true, where x and y are Boolean vectors of appropriate lengths, then for every execution e of the circuit ckt, or every sequence in the language of the circuit, if $tr_{in}(x)$ is true of e, then so is $tr_{out}(y)$. So, the formula states that for any vector x satisfying the precondition $\phi_{in}(x)$,

1. there is some output vector y such that for every execution e, if $tr_{in}(x)$ is true of e, then so is $tr_{out}(y)$, and
2. for every vector y for which 1 holds, the postcondition property $\phi_{out}(x, y)$ holds.

Notice that 2 alone does not suffice, since if 1 fails, 2 would hold vacuously for all conditions ϕ_{out}. Our formulation is slightly different from that of [13], although equivalent under natural assumptions. The current formulation makes it easier to derive some of the reasoning rules discussed below, in particular the postcondition conjunction rule.

Given a pre-postcondition statement in the form above, we can, in principle, compute the validity of it directly using Forte: the universal and existential quantifications can be replaced by BDD-quantification over symbolic values as explained in Section 5, the validity of $\models_{ckt} [tr_{in}(in) \Longrightarrow\!\!\!\gg tr_{out}(out)]$ can be evaluated by STE using symbolic values, and the rest just consists of evaluation of standard logical operations, again using symbolic values. Whether direct evaluation is feasible in practice depends on the formulae ϕ_{in} and ϕ_{out}, the computation the circuit performs on the input values, and whether these are efficiently representable using BDDs. In reality, we can directly compute the validity of a pre-postcondition statement only in very limited circumstances, and we need inference rules to combine model-checkable statements to larger ones.

As a part of our verification infrastructure, we wrote a set of FL routines which allow the user to work directly on the pre-postcondition level and abstract away from the details of evaluation. In addition to arguments corresponding to ϕ_{in}, ϕ_{out}, tr_{in}, ckt and tr_{out}, these routines have some additional parameters, such as STE weakening lists, which are used to guide the evaluation without affecting the semantics.

The main reason for introducing the pre-postcondition framework was to enable reasoning about the flow of computation in a well-structured manner. To this purpose, we defined and proved a set of general reasoning rules for pre-postcondition statements (Figure 10). These rules are closely related to the ones commonly used for traditional sequential programs. All these reasoning rules were formally derived from a set of simple axioms regarding STE [13] with some general first-order logic reasoning. The most conspicuous absence from this list is a general proof rule for iteration: as in our case all loops have a fixed upper bound for number of iterations, the weaker bounded induction rule below suffices.

Since the formulae in the pre-postcondition statements are parametrized with the vectors in and out, we need some additional notation to express the rules succinctly. If f and g are two-argument functions, we write $f \wedge'' g$ for $\lambda x.\lambda y.f(x, y) \wedge g(x, y)$, and analogously for other propositional connectives. If f is a one-argument function, we write f' for the function $\lambda x.\lambda y.f(y)$.

Precondition
strengthening

$$\frac{\{\phi_{in}\}(tr_{in}, ckt, tr_{out})\{\phi_{out}\} \qquad \forall x.\psi_{in}(x) \Rightarrow \phi_{in}(x)}{\{\psi_{in}\}(tr_{in}, ckt, tr_{out})\{\phi_{out}\}}$$

Postcondition
weakening:

$$\frac{\{\phi_{in}\}(tr_{in}, ckt, tr_{out})\{\phi_{out}\} \qquad \forall x.\forall y.\phi_{out}(x,y) \Rightarrow \psi_{out}(x,y)}{\{\phi_{in}\}(tr_{in}, ckt, tr_{out})\{\psi_{out}\}}$$

Pre- to
postcondition
transfer:

$$\frac{\{\phi_{in}\}(tr_{in}, ckt, tr_{out})\{\phi_{out}\} \qquad \forall x.\forall y.\phi_{in}(x) \wedge \phi_{out}(x,y) \Leftrightarrow \psi_{out}(x,y)}{\{\phi_{in}\}(tr_{in}, ckt, tr_{out})\{\psi_{out}\}}$$

Postcondition
conjunction:

$$\frac{\{\phi_{in}\}(tr_{in}, ckt, tr_{out})\{\phi_{out1}\} \qquad \{\phi_{in}\}(tr_{in}, ckt, tr_{out})\{\phi_{out2}\}}{\{\phi_{in}\}(tr_{in}, ckt, tr_{out})\{\phi_{out1} \wedge'' \phi_{out2}\}}$$

Sequential
composition:

$$\frac{\{\phi_{in}\}(tr_{in}, ckt, tr_{mid})\{\phi'_{mid}\} \qquad \{\phi_{mid}\}(tr_{mid}, ckt, tr_{out})\{\phi_{out}\}}{\{\phi_{in}\}(tr_{in}, ckt, tr_{out})\{\phi_{out}\}}$$

Bounded induction:

$$\frac{\forall i.(0 \le i < n) \Rightarrow \{\phi_i\}(tr_i, ckt, tr_{i+1})\{\phi'_{i+1}\}}{\{\phi_0\}(tr_0, ckt, tr_n)\{\phi'_n\}}$$

Fig. 10. Pre-post condition inference rules

8   Main Proof

Returning to the main verification task, let us now see how the technical machinery discussed in previous Sections can be used to formulate key steps of the proof.

We need to address first a general pragmatic issue: proliferation of quantifiers. When introducing the pre-postcondition formalism above, we were discussing circuits as if they had single input and outputs. In reality, though, we are dealing with verification tasks with tens of input and output vectors. If we introduce a separate term for each vector the number of quantified terms quickly becomes unmanageable. Consequently, we took another approach, and used a single term, denoting a very long vector, for quantification, and access routines for extracting slices out of that. For example, instead of writing $\forall x.\forall y.\forall z.\phi(x,y,z)$, where each of x, y and z ranges over bit vectors of length 16, we would write $\forall w.\phi(x(w), y(w), z(w))$, where w ranges over all bit-vectors of length 48, and x, y and z are routines extracting the first, middle or last 16 bits out of their argument, respectively. This is similar to techniques used by Joyce [16] and Windley [24], where a *representation variable*, typically denoting the state of the system being verified, is threaded through a verification. In the following definitions, let D_s, D_e, D_m, N_s, N_e, N_m, W_s, W_e, W_m, R_m, Q_m and ctl be functions extracting disjoint slices of appropriate lengths out of an argument vector, define $D(x) = D_s(x)@D_e(x)@D_m(x)$ where @ is the append-operation, and define $N(x)$ and $W(x)$ similarly.

We define the input-output correctness relation OUT in terms of integer operations as follows:

$$OUT(x,y) \equiv_{df} \exists Q.(ri(N(x)) = Q * ri(D(x)) + ri(W(y))) \ \wedge \ |ri(W(y))| < |ri(D(x))|$$

where the floating-point to integer conversion is: $ri((s,e,m)) = (-1)^{\widehat{s}} * 2^{\widehat{e}} * \widehat{m}$. Now the top-level correctness statement (goal of proof step G) can be formalized as

$$\{IN\}(tin, ckt, tout)\{OUT\}$$

where

$$IN(x) \equiv_{df} normal(N(x)) \ \wedge \ normal(D(x)) \ \wedge \ in\_range(N(x), D(x)) \ \wedge$$
$$remainder\_op\_executed(ctl(x)) \ \wedge$$
$$internal\_state\_ok(ctl(x)) \ \wedge \ environment\_ok(ctl(x))$$

where the intuitive meanings of the conjuncts of IN correspond to their names, and where $tin(x)$ is a trajectory binding $N(x)$ and $D(x)$ to the corresponding input signals and $ctl(x)$ to relevant control signals at the time the operation is started, and $tout(x)$ is a trajectory binding $W(x)$ to the output signals at the time the circuit is expected to produce output.

When expressed in terms of integer operations, the high-level mathematical loop invariant MI, the recurrence relation MR the mantissa loop is expected to compute, and the relation LO between loop output and final output can be defined as follows:

$$MI_i(x) \equiv_{df} (\widehat{N_m(x)} * 2^{manln} = \widehat{Q_m(x)} * \widehat{D_m(x)} + 2^{manln-i} * \widehat{R_m(x)}) \ \wedge$$
$$(\widehat{R_m(x)} < 2 * \widehat{D_m(x)})$$
$$MR_i(x,y) \equiv_{df} (\widehat{Q_m(y)} = \widehat{Q_m(x)} \ \wedge \ \widehat{R_m(y)} = 2 * \widehat{R_m(x)}) \ \vee$$
$$(\widehat{Q_m(y)} = \widehat{Q_m(x)} + 2^{manln-i} \ \wedge \ \widehat{R_m(y)} = 2 * (\widehat{R_m(x)} - \widehat{D_m(x)})))$$
$$LO(x,y) \equiv_{df} W_s(y) = N_s(x) \ \wedge \ W_e(y) = D_e(x) \ \wedge \ W_m(y) = R_m(x)$$

The lower-level bit vector invariant BI can be expressed as

$$BI_i(x) \equiv_{df} IN(x) \ \wedge \ loop\_data\_in\_range(x) \ \wedge \ loop\_data\_consistent(x)$$

The single most complex issue in the entire verification is determining the invariant BI exactly: some parts of it are easy, like the expected ranges of data values in the loop, but some are extremely low-level and implementation-dependent. In the actual verification the formula $loop\_data\_in\_range$ has four conjuncts and $loop\_data\_consistent$ seven, but nailing down the last few of these precisely took several weeks. The bit-vector recurrence relation BR_i is simply the bit-vector counterpart of MR_i, using the exactness-checking operations discussed in Section 6.

Let then $tloop_i(x)$ be a trajectory binding $R_m(x)$, $Q_m(x)$ and other data items manipulated by the mantissa loop to the corresponding signals at the loop at the time iteration i is being performed, and define $tl_i(x) \equiv_{df} tin(x)$ and $tloop_i(x)$. In terms of these definitions, proof step A consists of model-checking the following statements:

$$\{IN\}(tin, ckt, tl_0)\{BI'_0 \wedge'' MI'_0\}$$
$$\forall 0 \le i < imax. \ \{BI_i\}(tl_i, ckt, tl_{i+1})\{BI'_{i+1} \wedge'' BR_i\}$$

Due to the fact that BI really is a loop invariant, no major performance issues arose in the model-checking; the largest BDDs involved in the verification had only about 20 million nodes, using a rather obvious variable ordering.

Proof steps B and C then consist of proving the following statements:

$$\forall x. \forall y. BI_i(x) \wedge BR_i(x,y) \Rightarrow MR_i(x,y)$$
$$\forall x. \forall y. MI_i(x) \wedge MR_i(x,y) \Rightarrow MI_{i+1}(y)$$

Since BR_i is defined as the bit-vector counterpart of MI_i, the first of these is easy, and the second involves some routine arithmetic reasoning. Now the loop output correctness statement (goal of proof step D) can be formulated as

$$\{IN\}(tin, ckt, tl_{imax})\{BI'_{imax} \wedge'' MI'_{imax}\}$$

and proved from A, B and C by pre-postcondition reasoning.

Since the remainder operation does not involve any rounding, proof steps E and F, verifying the correctness of the rounder, are easy. Both can be formulated by the statement

$$\{BI'_{imax}\}(tl_{imax}, ckt, tout)\{LO\}$$

In operations with rounding, the goal of step E would consist of a bit-vector level specification and F of a mathematical specification of correct rounding. Finally, the main proof goal G can be derived from D and F by sequential composition, and some straightforward arithmetic reasoning.

One detail that has been glossed over in the description of the verification above is that the value of $imax$ varies according to the input values. This means that we have to show the statements above for all the potential values of $imax$, under the assumption that $imax = \widehat{N_e(in)} - \widehat{D_e(in)} + 1$. As there are only a restricted range values handled by the hardware, this can be done by enumeration. In practice large parts of the proof are independent of $imax$ and only need to be verified once.

9   Conclusion

We have described a formal verification case study of a floating-point divider circuit, using a combination of theorem-proving and model-checking techniques. To our knowledge, this is currently one of the most complex floating-point circuits that has been formally verified; the verification described here took about eight person-months. The advantages of the chosen approach were the safety of a mechanically verified proof combined with the freedom of complete control over the proof approach and details, which allowed us to use a wide variety of technical and conceptual machinery to tackle the complexity of the verification.

Acknowledgments

We thank John Harrison for mechanizing the original hand proofs of FDIV and FSQRT, John O'Leary for contributing to this work during discussions on rounding and division verification, and Bob Brennan for the opportunity to perform this work.

References

1. M. D. Aagaard, R. B. Jones, K. R. Kohatsu, R. Kaivola, and C.-J. H. Seger. Formal verification of iterative algorithms in microprocessors. In *DAC*, June 2000.
2. M. D. Aagaard, R. B. Jones, and C.-J. H. Seger. Lifted-fl: A pragmatic implementation of combined model checking and theorem proving. In L. Thery, editor, *Theorem Proving in Higher Order Logics*. Springer Verlag; New York, Sept. 1999.
3. M. D. Aagaard, T. F. Melham, and O. J. W. Xs are for trajectory evaluation, Booleans are for theorem proving. In *CHARME*. Springer Verlag; New York, Oct. 1999.
4. R. E. Bryant. Bit-level analysis of an SRT divider circuit. In *DAC*, pages 661–665, New York, June 1996. ACM.
5. Y.-A. Chen, E. Clarke, P.-H. Ho, Y. Hoskote, T. Kam, M. Khaira, J. O'Leary, and X. Zhao. Verification of all circuits in a floating-point unit using word-level model checking. In M. Srivas and A. Camilleri, editors, *Formal Methods in CAD*, volume 1166 of *LNCS*, pages 19–33, Palo Alto, CA, USA, Nov. 1996. Springer Verlag; New York.
6. C.-T. Chou. The mathematical foundation of symbolic trajectory evaluation. In *CAV*. Springer Verlag; New York, 1999.
7. E. M. Clarke, S. M. German, and X. Zhao. Verifying the SRT division algorithm using theorem proving techniques. In Rajeev Alur and Thomas A. Henzinger, editors, *CAV*, volume 1102 of *LNCS*, pages 111–122, New Brunswick, NJ, USA, July/Aug. 1996. Springer Verlag; New York.
8. E. M. Clarke, M. Khaira, and X. Zhao. Word level model checking-avoiding the Pentium FDIV error. In *DAC*, pages 645–648, New York, June 1996. ACM.
9. M. D. Ercegovac and T. Lang. *Division and Square Root, Digit-Recurrence Algorithms and Implementations*. Kluwer Academic, 1994.
10. M. Gordon. Programming combinations of deduction and BDD-based symbolic calculation. Technical Report 480, Cambridge Comp. Lab, 1999.
11. D. Gries. *The Science of Programming*. Springer-Verlag, 1981.
12. J. Harrison. A machine-checked theory of floating point arithmetic. In Y. Bertot, G. Dowek, A. Hirschowitz, C. Paulin, and L. Thery, editors, *Theorem Proving in Higher Order Logics*, pages 113–130. Springer Verlag; New York, Sept. 1999.
13. S. Hazelhurst and C.-J. H. Seger. A simple theorem prover based on symbolic trajectory evaluation and BDDs. *IEEE Trans. on CAD*, Apr. 1995.
14. S. Hazelhurst and C.-J. H. Seger. Symbolic trajectory evaluation. In T. Kropf, editor, *Formal Hardware Verification*, chapter 1, pages 3–78. Springer Verlag; New York, 1997.
15. IEEE. *IEEE Standard for binary floating-point arithmetic*. ANSI/IEEE Std 754-1985, 1985.
16. J. Joyce. Generic specification of digital hardware. In G. Jones and M. Sheeran, editors, *Designing Correct Circuits*, pages 68–91. Springer Verlag; New York, Sept. 1990.
17. A. Kaldewaij. *Programming: The Derivation of Algorithms*. Prentice-Hall, 1990.
18. J. S. Moore, T. W. Lynch, and M. Kaufmann. A mechanically checked proof of the AMD K-5 86 floating point division program. *IEEE Trans. on Comp.*, 47(9):913–926, Sept. 1998.
19. J. O'Leary, X. Zhao, R. Gerth, and C.-J. H. Seger. Formally verifying IEEE compliance of floating-point hardware. *Intel Technology Journal*, Q1, Feb. 1999.
20. L. Paulson. *ML for the Working Programmer,*. Cambridge University Press, 1996.
21. S. L. Peyton Jones. *The Implementation of Functional Programming Languages*. International Series in Computer Science. Prentice Hall, New York, 1987.
22. D. M. Russinoff. A mechanically checked proof of IEEE compliance of the floating point multiplication, division and square root algorithms of the AMD-K7 processor. *J. of Comp. Math.*, 1:148–200, 1998. London Math. Soc.
23. C.-J. H. Seger and R. E. Bryant. Formal verification by symbolic evaluation of partially-ordered trajectories. *Formal Methods in System Design*, 6(2):147–189, Mar. 1995.
24. P. J. Windley and M. Coe. A correctness model for pipelined microprocessors. In R. Kumar and T. Kropf, editors, *Theorem Provers in Circuit Design*, pages 32–51. Springer Verlag; New York, 1994.

Specification and Verification of a Steam-Boiler with Signal-Coq

Mickaël Kerbœuf[1], David Nowak[2], and Jean-Pierre Talpin[1]

[1] Inria-Rennes – Irisa, Campus de Beaulieu, Rennes, France
[2] Oxford University Computing Laboratory, Wolfson Building, Oxford, England

Abstract. Over the last decade, the increasing demand for the validation of safety critical systems has led to the development of domain-
specific programming languages (e.g. synchronous languages) and automatic verification tools (e.g. model checkers). Conventionally, the verification of a reactive system is implemented by specifying a discrete model
of the system (i.e. a finite-state machine) and then checking this model
against temporal properties (e.g. using an automata-based tool). We investigate the use of a synchronous programming language, SIGNAL, and
of a proof assistant, COQ, for the specification and the verification of
co-inductive properties of the well-known steam-boiler problem.
By way of this large-scale case-study, the SIGNAL-COQ formal approach,
i.e. the combined use of SIGNAL and COQ, is demonstrated to be a well-
suited and practical approach for the validation of reactive systems. Indeed, the deterministic model of concurrency of SIGNAL, for specifying
systems, together with the unparalleled expressive power of the COQ
proof assistant, for verifying properties, enables to disregard any compromise incurred by any limitation of either the specification and the
verification tools.
Keywords: synchronous programming, theorem proving, the steam-
boiler problem.

1 Introduction

In recent years, the verification of safety critical systems has become an area
of increasing importance for the development of softwares in sensitive fields:
medicine, telecommunication, transportation, energy.

The notion of *reactive system* has emerged to focus on the issues related
to the control of interaction and of response-time in mission-critical systems.
This has led to the development of specific programming languages and related
verification tools for reactive systems.

Conventionally, the verification of a reactive system is implemented by, first,
elaborating a *discrete* model of the system (i.e. an approximation of its behaviour
by a finite-state machine) specified in a dedicated language (e.g. a synchronous
programming language) and, then, by checking a property against the model
(i.e. model checking).

Synchronous languages (such as ESTEREL [5], LUSTRE [9], SIGNAL [4], STATE-
CHARTS [10]) have proved to be well adapted to the verification of safety and

J. Harrison and M. Aagaard (Eds.): TPHOLs 2000, LNCS 1869, pp. 356–371, 2000.
© Springer-Verlag Berlin Heidelberg 2000

liveness properties of reactive systems. For instance, model checking has been used at an industrial scale on SIGNAL programs to check properties such as liveness, invariance, reachability and attractivity.

Whereas model checking efficiently decides discrete properties of finite state systems, the use of formal proof systems enables to prove *numerical and parameterized properties* about *infinite state systems*. Using a proof system, we can not only prove the safety and liveness of a reactive system but also its *correctness* and *completeness*.

Such a proof is of course not automatic and requires interaction with he user to direct its strategy. The prover can nonetheless automate he most tedious and mechanical parts of the proof. In general, formal roofs of programs are difficult and time-consuming. In the very case of modeling a reactive system using a declarative synchronous language, however, this difficulty is milded thanks to the elegant stylistic combination of declarative programming and relational modeling.

We investigate the combined use of the synchronous language SIGNAL and of the proof assistant COQ for specifying and verifying properties of a large-scale case study, namely, the steam-boiler problem.

2   The Signal-Coq Formal Approach

Synchronous languages assume that computation takes no time (this is the so-called *"synchronous hypothesis"*). Actually, this means that the duration of computations is negligible in comparison to the time of reaction of the system. This *synchronous* hypothesis is particularly well adapted to verify safety and some forms of liveness properties. SIGNAL is a synchronous, declarative, data-flow oriented programming language. It is built around a simple paradigm: a process is a system of equations on signals; and a minimal kernel of primitive operators. A signal represents an infinite flow of data. At every instant, it can be absent or present with a value. The instants when values are present are determined by its associated *clock*. Interested reader may find more about SIGNAL in [4].

COQ [7] is a proof assistant for higher-order logic. It allows the development of computer programs that are consistent with their formal specification. The logical language used in COQ is a variety of type theory, the *Calculus of Inductive Constructions* [15]. It has been extended with *co-inductive types* (types defined as greatest fixed points rather than as least fixed points [8]) to handle infinite objects, It is thus well suited to represent signals.

In [14], we have introduced a co-inductive semantics for the kernel of the language SIGNAL and formalized it in the proof assistant COQ. In this section, we summarize the COQ definitions given for the primitive operators of SIGNAL. Interested reader may find the generalization to the complete language in [13].

A signal X is defined as a stream of $\bot$ and values v. Let $\mathcal{D}$ be a set of values. The set of signals $\mathcal{S}_\mathcal{D}$ is the largest set such that:

$$\mathcal{S}_\mathcal{D} = \{\bot.X \mid X \in \mathcal{S}_\mathcal{D}\} \cup \{v.X \mid v \in D, X \in \mathcal{S}_\mathcal{D}\}$$

Instantaneous Relation. The relation R_P^n is used in SIGNAL to specify an instantaneous relation between n signals. At each instant, these signals satisfy the predicate P. In COQ, according to the Curry-Howard isomorphism, a pair proof-specification is represented by a pair term-type. The type of non-well-founded proofs of R_P^n is introduced as a co-inductive type. Co-induction is needed to deal with infinite signals. For instance, R_P^2 is introduced as follows:

```
CoInductive Relation2 [U,V:Set; P:U->V->Prop] :
  (Signal U)->(Signal V)->Prop :=
  relation2_a: (X:(Signal U))(Y:(Signal V))
    (Relation2 P X Y)->
    (Relation2 P (Cons (absent U) X) (Cons (absent V) Y))
| relation2_p: (X:(Signal U))(Y:(Signal V))(u:U)(v:V)
    (P u v)->(Relation2 P X Y)->
    (Relation2 P (Cons (present u) X) (Cons (present v) Y)).
```

Down-Sampling. The SIGNAL equation $Z := X$ **When** Y states that the signal Z down-samples X when X is present and when Y is present with the value *true*. **When** is the least fixpoint of the following continuous functional:

$$F_{\textbf{When}}(f) =_{\text{def}} \begin{cases} (\bot.X, \bot.Y) \longmapsto \bot.f(X,Y) \\ (\bot.X, b.Y) \longmapsto \bot.f(X,Y) \\ (v.X, \bot.Y) \longmapsto \bot.f(X,Y) \\ (v.X, false.Y) \longmapsto \bot.f(X,Y) \\ (v.X, true.Y) \longmapsto v.f(X,Y) \end{cases}$$

Deterministic Merge. The SIGNAL equation $Z := X$ **Default** Y states that X and Y are merged in Z with the priority to X. **Default** is the least fixpoint of the following continuous functional:

$$F_{\textbf{Default}}(f) =_{\text{def}} \begin{cases} (\bot.X, \bot.Y) \longmapsto \bot.f(X,Y) \\ (\bot.X, v.Y) \longmapsto v.f(X,Y) \\ (u.X, \bot.Y) \longmapsto u.f(X,Y) \\ (u.X, v.Y) \longmapsto u.f(X,Y) \end{cases}$$

Delay. The SIGNAL function **Pre** is used to access to the previous value of a signal. **Pre** is the least fixpoint of the following continuous functional:

$$F_{\textbf{Pre}}(f) =_{\text{def}} \begin{cases} (u, \bot.X) \longmapsto \bot.f(u,X) \\ (u, v.X) \longmapsto u.f(v,X) \end{cases}$$

Using the previously defined denotations of primitive processes, we can derive the denotations of the derived operators of SIGNAL. The parallel composition is denoted by the logical *and* of the underlying logic and the introduction of local signals is denoted by an existential quantifier.

This co-inductive trace semantics of SIGNAL has been implemented with the proof assistant COQ (see [12] for details). Many lemmas are proved to ease the correctness proof of a reactive system specified with SIGNAL. The case study introduced in this paper confirms that our co-inductive approach is a natural, simple and efficient way to prove correctness of reactive systems.

3   Steam-Boiler Control Specification Problem

In order to compare the strengths and weaknesses of different design formalisms for reactive systems, the steam-boiler case study has been suggested by J.-R. Abrial, E. Börger and H. Langmaack. In this section, we briefly recall its original specification (see [2] for more details), and the additional precisions we bring (see [11] for more details).

3.1   Physical Environment

The physical environment is composed of several units (Fig. 1). Each one is characterized by physical constants and some of them provide data.

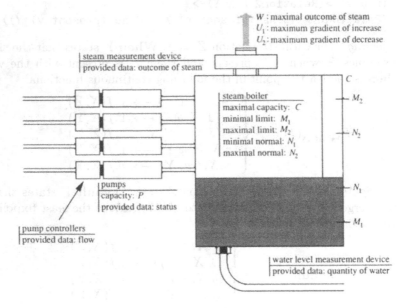

Fig. 1. Physical environment

3.2   Behaviour of the Steam-Boiler

The program has to control the level of water in the steam-boiler. This quantity should not be too low or too high. Otherwise, the system might be affected. The program also has to manage the possible failure of physical units. For that purpose, at every instant, it takes into account the global state of the physical environment which is denoted by an *operation mode*. The program follows a *cycle* which takes place each five seconds. A cycle consists of the reception of messages coming from the units, the analysis of the received informations, and the transmission of messages to the units. According to the operation mode, the program decides at each cycle if the system must stop or not. If not, it activates or deactivates pumps in order to keep the level of water in the middle of the steam-boiler.

The specification also gives additional information regarding the physical behaviour of the steam-boiler. Namely, new values, called adjusted and calculated values, are proposed. They enable a sustained control of the system, by providing a vision of its dynamic, when a measurement device is defective.

At each cycle, adjusted variables contain either real measurements or extrapolated values which are calculated during the preceding cycle. An adjusted variable contains a real measurement when the corresponding device works properly. Otherwise, it contains an extrapolated value.

Calculated variables provide, at each cycle, extrapolated values of measurements for the following cycle. They contain the extreme values that are possibly reachable from the current adjusted values.

3.3   Precisions and Decisions about the Original Specification

Because of the flexibility with which the original specification of the steam-boiler can be interpreted, we first need to make some details more precise, on the physical behaviour of the steam-boiler, and on the logical behaviour of its implementation in SIGNAL. Different items are concerned by our decisions. Namely:

Distinction between pump failures and pump controller failures. We cannot rely on the fact that controllers always provide a reliable information about their associated pumps. Indeed, according to the specification, failures of controllers have to be taken into account and thus, we have to consider them as being fallible. Consequently, how could pump failures and pump controller failures be distinguished ?

We first could try to detect the real throughput of each pump with an analysis of water-level variations in the boiler. But such a method presupposes a too restrictive set of conditions about the physical characteristics of pumps and their controllers. Moreover, it actually makes controllers useless.

We have therefore chosen to determinate what the real state of each pump and controller should be, for each possible combination of values. This solution, which seems to be the most reasonable and intuitive one, was proposed in [6] (a solution of the steam-boiler problem in LUSTRE).

Message occurrences. In order to have more flexibility for controlling the steam-boiler, each pump and each controller is connected to the main program by its own communication line. Thus, each pump can be managed simultaneously and independently.

Moreover, some incoming messages from pumps essential are not always relevant for the system at every instant. For example, a pump should not necessarily provide its state if it did not receive a command during the preceding cycle. But it can still provide its state at each cycle as specified in the original text. Only the presence of compulsory messages will be checked.

In addition to these messages, we introduce a new message H. This message is a pure signal and stands for the main clock of the program. All involved signals in the program have a clock which is a sub-clock of H. This signal is supposed to be reliable. It enables to detect the absence of compulsory messages.

Activation, deactivation of the pumps, and stop of the system. The decisions concerning the activation or the deactivation of the pumps, and the decision of stopping the system, are made according to the adjusted and calculated values. At first, a specific decision is made for each pair of extremum level, adjusted and calculated. Then, the program globally decides if the system shall stop or not. If not, the program decides how the level shall move (up or down), if necessary, and by taking into account each specific decision.

We calculate the best quantity of water to be provided, rather than just opening or closing all the pumps. Thus, at each cycle, the program calculates the optimal combination of open and closed pumps, in order to have an optimal progression of the level of water toward the middle of the boiler, taking into account failures of pumps and controllers.

3.4 Design and Architecture

The steam-boiler controller in SIGNAL is composed of four main processes (fig. 2).

- The IO_MANAGER process detects transmission failures. It implements a filter that guarantees the presence of the outgoing data, necessary to the processing. This process also provides a signal which announces the manual stop of the system.

- The FAILURE_MANAGER process is in charge of managing the dialogue between the physical units and the program regarding failure detections and repair indications. It detects failures and provides a global vision of the state of the physical system.

- The DYNAMIC process directly implements the equations suggested in the specification according to the detected failures and the values provided by the measurement devices.

- The CONTROL process is the main program. Starting from the global vision of the state of the system, and from the adjusted measurements provided by the preceding process, it manages the operation modes, makes the decision to stop the system or not, and finally delivers activation and deactivation commands to the pumps.

3.5 Motivation for the Choice of This Case Study

This case study is well adapted to our aim, i.e. to show the interest of the SIGNAL-COQ formal approach. Indeed, the program has to handle several physical parameters and it may use non linear numerical values (e.g. extrapolated values of the level which take into account gradients of increase and decrease of the steam throughput, i.e. typically non linear numerical terms). Thus, safety properties cannot be simply and directly proved with a standard model checker.

4   Verification of the Steam-Boiler with Coq

Proofs of program properties are built on the co-inductive trace semantics of SIGNAL which has been implemented with COQ [13].

This axiomatization is a set of COQ libraries which gathers the modeling of signals, the modeling of the primitives of the kernel language, and a number of functions, predicates and theorems about signals. These COQ libraries, as well as the proofs of the properties that are stated in the rest of this article, are available at [12].

4.1   Safety Obligations

A global safety property can be informally stated in the following way:

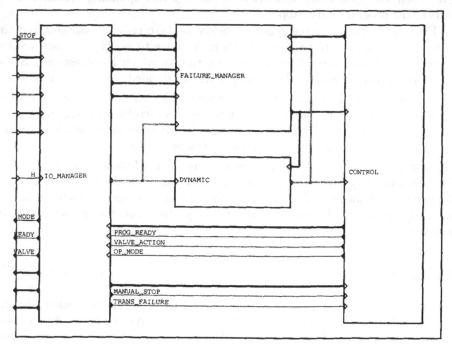

Fig. 2. SIGNAL processes of the steam-boiler controller

When a stop condition is satisfied, the system stops indeed, i.e. the program enters the emergency stop mode.

This statement implies several sub-properties. Our aim is to emphasize the interest of using COQ for their verification. Thus, in the sequel of this article, we concentrate our work especially on safety sub-properties that cannot be directly and simply proved by a standard model checker.

Since four stop conditions are specified, the global safety property has to be proved for each one:

1. *Manual stop.* The program received consecutively the required number of STOP messages from the user for manually stopping the system.

2. *Critical level.* The system is in danger because the water level is either too low or too high.

3. *Transmission failure.* The program detected a transmission failure.

4. *Initialization.* The water level measurement device is defective in the initialization mode.

In our SIGNAL specification, these situations are associated with critical messages. When one of these signals carries a value, the corresponding condition holds and so, the program must stop.

First of all, the expected relations between these critical messages and the operation mode have to be checked. Then, we have to verify that each critical message is actually present when the condition to which it corresponds holds. For that purpose, the implied sub-properties are divided into two main classes:

– A first class gathers properties that specify the correct behaviour of critical messages, regarding the critical situations to which they correspond.
– The second class gathers properties that justify some simplifications or specify the use of some internal signals in the processing.

We now only consider sub-properties coming from *Manual Stop* and *Critical level* because they involve parameters and non linear numerical values, unlike *Transmission failure* and *Initialization*. So, they are convincing examples to illustrate our approach. Moreover, *Critical level* gathers essential properties of our solution.

4.2   Manual Stop

The problem of manual stop is generalized, using a parameter called *nb_stop*, which stands for the number of STOP messages required for manually stopping the program, instead of the fixed value "3" initially suggested in the specification.

Since we are using a proof assistant, we do not need to instantiate this parameter with a particular value. First, A predicate that denotes the right behaviour of a counter of the successive synchronous instants between two signals is co-inductively defined in CoQ. Then, we prove that our SIGNAL process provides indeed a signal (called CPT) that behaves like a counter of the successive synchronous instants between the STOP signal (well called ... STOP) and the main clock (called H).

Instead of using a co-inductive predicate that denotes the expected behaviour of CPT, we define a co-recursive function that specifies CPT. This function is the least fixpoint of the following continuous functional:

$$F : (\mathbb{N} \times \mathcal{F}_{(U \cup \{\perp\})} \times \mathcal{F}_{(V \cup \{\perp\})} \to \mathcal{F}_{(\mathbb{N} \cup \{\perp\})})$$
$$\longrightarrow (\mathbb{N} \times \mathcal{F}_{(U \cup \{\perp\})} \times \mathcal{F}_{(V \cup \{\perp\})} \to \mathcal{F}_{(\mathbb{N} \cup \{\perp\})})$$

$$f \longmapsto \begin{cases} (n, \mathrm{Cons}(\perp, X), \mathrm{Cons}(\perp, Y)) \mapsto \mathrm{Cons}(\perp, f(n, X, Y)) \\ (n, \mathrm{Cons}(x, X), \mathrm{Cons}(\perp, Y)) \mapsto \mathrm{Cons}(0, f(0, X, Y)) \\ (n, \mathrm{Cons}(\perp, X), \mathrm{Cons}(y, Y)) \mapsto \mathrm{Cons}(0, f(0, X, Y)) \\ (n, \mathrm{Cons}(x, X), \mathrm{Cons}(y, Y)) \mapsto \mathrm{Cons}(n+1, f(n+1, X, Y)) \end{cases}$$

Let $cssm$, the least fixpoint of F. The CoQ definition of $cssm$ is the following:

```
CoFixpoint cssm :
(U,V:Set)nat->(Signal U)->(Signal V)->(Signal nat) :=
[U,V:Set] [n:nat] [X:(Signal U)] [Y:(Signal V)]Cases X Y of
 (Cons absent X')          (Cons absent Y')
   => (Cons (absent nat)    (cssm n X' Y'))
|(Cons (present _) X')  (Cons absent Y')
   => (Cons (present 0)     (cssm 0 X' Y'))
|(Cons absent X')          (Cons (present _) Y')
   => (Cons (present 0)     (cssm 0 X' Y'))
|(Cons (present _) X')  (Cons (present _) Y')
   => (Cons (present (S n)) (cssm (S n) X' Y'))
 end.
```

Using this function, the predicate that denotes the expected behaviour of CPT can now be stated:

$$\mathsf{CPT} = cssm(0, \mathsf{STOP}, \mathsf{H})$$

We open in CoQ a *section* in which hypotheses are stated. Those hypotheses correspond to the SIGNAL equations which are concerned by the property to be proved:

```
(|
...
| CPT ^= H
| CPT := ((ZCPT+1) when STOP) default (0 when H)
| ZCPT := CPT$1 init 0
| MANUAL_STOP := when (CPT=nb_stop)
...
|)
```

Those equations use constant signals. We first have to define them explicitly. Then, we have to state the hypothesis regarding H, the main clock of the program. In particular, the clock of STOP is a sub-clock of H.

This yields to the following equations:

```
0 | STOP ^< H
1 | CPT ^= H
2 | Cst0 := 0
3 | Cst0 ^= H
4 | CPT := ((ZCPT+1) when STOP) default (Cst0 when H)
5 | ZCPT := CPT$1 init 0
6 | A := (CPT=nb_stop)
7 | Csttrue := true
8 | Csttrue ^= A
9 | MANUAL_STOP := Csttrue when A
```

Using the co-inductive axiomatization of SIGNAL in COQ [13], this system of equations is translated into the following COQ hypotheses:

```
Variable nb_stop : nat.
Variables CPT,ZCPT,Cst0 : (Signal nat).
Variables H,STOP,MANUEL_STOP,Csttrue : Clock.
Variable A : (Signal bool).

Hypothesis Equation0 : (OrderClock STOP H).
Hypothesis Equation1 : (Synchro CPT H).
Hypothesis Equation2 : (Constant 0 Cst0).
Hypothesis Equation3 : (Synchro Cst0 H).
Hypothesis Equation4 :
    CPT = (SignalAA_to_SignalA
                (default (when (fonction1 [n:nat](plus n (S 0)) ZCPT)
                               (Clock_to_Signal_bool STOP))
                         (when Cst0
                               (Clock_to_Signal_bool H))) ).
Hypothesis Equation5 : ZCPT = (pre 0 CPT).
Hypothesis Equation6 : A = (fonction1 [n:nat](beq_nat n nb_stop) CPT).
Hypothesis Equation7 : (Constant tt Csttrue).
Hypothesis Equation8 : (Synchro Csttrue A).
Hypothesis Equation9 : MANUAL_STOP = (when Csttrue A).
```

In this environment, we aim at proving the following lemma:

```
Lemma 11 : CPT = (cssm 0 H STOP).
```

This property is too general for a model-checker because of the involved *nb_stop* parameter. It is also too restrictive for an inductive proof because of the instantiated parameters (values "0") involved in the cssm predicate and in the SIGNAL pre term. A more general property must be stated with non instantiated parameters. Additional hypotheses about these formal parameters can also be stated. For that purpose, the fifth SIGNAL equation of the previous specification is preferred the following, more general, one:

```
Variable ni : nat.
Hypothesis Equation5 : ZCPT = (pre ni CPT).
```

Then, the following lemma can be proved:

    Lemma 11b : CPT = (cssm ni H STOP).

In particular, the initial property is verified. This is the first part of the property. Using the same method, we also prove that MANUAL_STOP provides a value when CPT reaches the *nb_stop* value. Finally, we prove that the program enters the emergency stop mode in this case.

    An important feature of the method outlined in this section is that it does not at all impact the programming style because of verification constraints. SIGNAL processes are naturally translated into COQ objects (without, e.g., any variable instantiation).

4.3   Critical Water Level

The property concerning the water level can be divided into several sub-properties which correspond to the different cases of critical level. Those properties involve parameters like the boiler capacity, the extremal limits of the level, or the nominal capacity of each pump. Moreover, the processing depends on the adjusted values. Thus, those properties are parameterized and concern non linear numerical values. It is therefore not possible to verify them simply and directly with a standard model checker.

    At first, a set of preliminary lemmas that justify some simplifications in the program have to be proved. For instance, the following statements allow to eliminate some cases in the processing:

$$\forall t \in \mathbb{N}, \qquad qc_1(t) < qc_2(t) \tag{1}$$

$$\forall t \in \mathbb{N}, 0 \leq qa_1(t) \leq qa_2(t) \leq C \tag{2}$$

where $qa_1(t)$ and $qa_2(t)$ (resp. $qc_1(t)$ and $qc_2(t)$) stand for the minimal and maximal adjusted (resp. calculated) values of the level at instant t, and where C stands for the maximal capacity of the boiler. Indeed, the process in charge of making a decision about activations of the pumps relies on a list of the different possible interleavings of extrapolated and adjusted levels. But some of them are omitted because of the statements (1) and (2). So they have to be proved.

    The adjusted values $qa_1(t)$ and $qa_2(t)$ depend on calculated values $qc_1(t)$ and $qc_2(t)$, which are defined as follows:

$$\forall t \in \mathbb{N}^*, qc_1(t) = qa_1(t-1) - va_2(t-1)\Delta t - \frac{1}{2}U_1\Delta t^2 + pa_1(t-1)\Delta t \tag{3}$$

$$\forall t \in \mathbb{N}^*, qc_2(t) = qa_2(t-1) - va_1(t-1)\Delta t + \frac{1}{2}U_2\Delta t^2 + pa_2(t-1)\Delta t \tag{4}$$

where $va_1(t)$ and $va_2(t)$ stand for the adjusted values of the outcome of steam, and $pa_1(t)$ and $pa_2(t)$ stand for the adjusted values of the cumulated throughput of the pumps. The parameters U_1 and U_2 denote the maximum gradients of increase and decrease of the outcome of steam.

    In order to prove a property equivalent to the statement (1) with a model checker, the processing would have to be changed radically. For instance, the interval of possible values could be divided into several sub-levels and then, new boolean properties about the reachability of those levels could be defined. And in every case, all parameters like U_1, U_2 or C should be instantiated. With our SIGNAL-COQ approach, we do not consider those verification problems during the design of the program. Calculated values are textually stated (cf. (3) and (4)) in SIGNAL:

```
  ...
| QC1 ^= QC2
| QC1 := QA1 - (VA2*Dt) - (0.5*U1*Dt*Dt) + (PA1*Dt)
| QC2 := QA2 - (VA1*Dt) + (0.5*U2*Dt*Dt) + (PA2*Dt)
| VC1 ^= VC2
| VC1 := VA1-(U2*Dt)
| VC2 := VA2+(U1*Dt)
  ...
```

Note that the calculated values concern the following cycle. The definition of adjusted values are naturally given from the calculated values of the preceding cycle:

```
  ...
| ZQC2 := QC2$1 init C
| ZQC1 := QC1$1 init 0.0
| QA2 := (Q when J_OK) default ZQC2
| QA1 := (Q when J_OK) default ZQC1
| ZVC2 := VC2$1 init 0.0
| ZVC1 := VC1$1 init 0.0
| VA2 := (V when U_OK) default ZVC2
| VA1 := (V when U_OK) default ZVC1
  ...
```

Signals Q and V carry the values coming from the measurement devices. Signals J_OK and U_OK provide at each cycle a boolean information about the physical state of the measurement devices. We just have to translate these SIGNAL equations into COQ hypotheses and we prove the properties (1) and (2) using coinduction. COQ offers a natural syntax for manipulating such numerical objects. For instance, consider the following statement:

$$(\forall x, y \in \mathbb{Z})(0 \leq x) \Rightarrow (0 < y) \Rightarrow (0 < x + y)$$

Using the ZArith library of COQ, the definition of this statement is the following:

```
(x,y:Z)(Zle ZERO x)->(Zlt ZERO y) -> (Zlt ZERO (Zplus x y))
```

Meanwhile, the ZArith library also provides syntactical facilities. Thus, we have an equivalent way to define this statement:

```
(x,y:Z)'0 <= x'->'0 < y'->'0 < x+y'
```

Such a syntax is more intuitive and so, proving equations or inequations on $\mathbb{Z}$ in COQ is much easier.

The following first lemma is very simple to prove:

```
Lemma I_N : (a,b,c,d,e:Z) 'a <= b' -> 'c <= d' ->
'0 < 2*(b-Dt*c+Dt*e)+U2*(Dt*Dt) - 2*(a-Dt*d+Dt*e)-U1*(Dt*Dt)'.
```

And then it is used to prove the statement (1):

```
CoInductive Globally2 [U,V:Set;P:(Stream U)->(Stream V)->Prop]:
(Stream U)->(Stream V)->Prop :=
   globally2 : (X:(Stream U))(Y:(Stream V))(P X Y)
                  ->(Globally2 P (tl X) (tl Y))->(Globally2 P X Y).
```

This COQ statement defines a co-inductive predicate which implements the "□" connector for temporal logic. Indeed, in our co-inductive semantics of SIGNAL, we cannot handle explicit temporal indexes (see [13] for more details).

```
Definition ltSt := [X:(Signal Z)][Y:(Signal Z)]
(x,y:Z)(hd X)=(present x)->(hd Y)=(present y)->(Zlt x y).
```

This statement defines the predicate that will be applied to the Globally2 connector.

```
Theorem QA1_lt_QA2 : (Globally2 ltSt QC1 QC2).
```

This statement is equivalent to the statement (1)

The decision concerning the stop of the system because of a critical level is founded on the adjusted levels. Using the preceding theorem, it is very simple to prove the following property:

$$\forall t \in \mathbb{N}, qa_1(t) \leq q(t) \leq qa_2(t) \tag{5}$$

where q stands for the real level in the boiler. It means that even if a measurement device is defective, the program always knows the interval of possible current levels. Moreover, the program knows the interval of possibly reachable levels for the next cycle. Regarding these intervals, we have to check that the level is never likely to reach a critical value. For instance we have:

$$\forall t \in \mathbb{N}, (qa_1(t) \leq M_1 \wedge qc_1(t) \leq M_1) \Rightarrow \mathsf{Critical\_Level}(t) = T \tag{6}$$

It means that the program will stop (the critical message Critical_Level carries a value T) if the minimal next level is below M_1 (which is the minimal level under which the system is in danger after one cycle) while the current level is possibly already below M_1.

We also prove properties like the following one:

$$\forall t \in \mathbb{N}, (qc_1(t) \leq M_1 \wedge qc_2(t) \geq M_2) \Rightarrow \mathsf{Critical\_Level}(t) = T \tag{7}$$

It means that if the interval of possibly reachable levels for the next cycle is too wide for making a safe decision, the program stops.

These examples emphasize an important advantage of our approach. The statements of the expected safety properties are especially clear. Moreover, the programmer does not need to have in mind what kind of property checkable or not during the design phase. Thus, specifying, programming and verifying a problem are more natural and intuitive operations.

Unlike a model checker, a proof assistant, and more generally a theorem prover cannot provide a counter-example when the check fails. But COQ gives a strong logical framework in which the user acquires a great confidence in the conformity of the program to the specification. Moreover, if the program is erroneous, the proof progression will stop on an impossible sub-goal which is often explicit enough to understand the mistake.

Nevertheless, theorem proving is often less efficient and often more tedious than model checking. Then, even if we could check all properties with only a proof assistant like COQ, the optimal solution for verification consists in using a model checker as much as possible and in using a theorem prover when a property is out of the scope of the model checker.

5   Related Works

The steam-boiler problem has become a classical case study for testing and comparing formal methods. It has been entirely specified and proved with the B tool approach ([1]). In [6], a steam-boiler has been implemented in the synchronous data-flow language LUSTRE (quite similar to SIGNAL) and verified with its model-checker LESAR that allows verification of safety properties. This approach enables to prove boolean safety properties but cannot deal with numerical and parameterized properties. In [3], the semantics of LUSTRE has been formalized in the theorem prover PVS but co-induction is not used to represent infinite signals. The solution proposed in the LUSTRE-PVS approach consists of viewing signals as infinite sequences. In this setting, a signal is represented by a function which associates any instant i (a natural number) with the value v of the signal (if it is present) or with $\perp$ (if it is absent). The declarative and equational style of SIGNAL is similar to LUSTRE. However, LUSTRE programs always have a unique reference of logical time: they are *endochronous*. SIGNAL specifications differ from LUSTRE programs in that they can be *exochronous* (i.e. they can have many references of logical time). For instance, the process x:=1 | y:=2 does not constrain the clocks of x and y to be equal. Hence, had we used functions over infinite sequences to represent signals, we would have faced the burden of having to manipulate several, possibly unrelated, indexes of time i.

6   Conclusion

The axiomatization of the trace semantics of SIGNAL within the proof assistant COQ offers a novel approach for the validation of reactive systems.

We demonstrate the benefits of this formal approach for specifying and verifying properties of reactive systems by considering a large-scale case study, the steam-boiler controller problem.

Disregarding any compromise between the modeling tools and the modeled system, we augmented the original specification of the steam-boiler of [2] with a more precise description of the physical environment.

This case study shows to be well adapted to the evaluation of the SIGNAL-COQ formal approach, allowing the modeling of parameterized strong safety property with non-linear numerical constraints. In spite of the strong implication for the user during the proof-checking process, it appears that the use of a proof assistant like COQ has many advantages.

In addition to the facts that the approach alleviates any limitation in the expression of properties, it makes it possible to acquire a strong confidence in the system being specified. Moreover, it is noticeable that experiences at using COQ allowed to develop libraries which improved the efficiency of latter proofs.

However, this approach is interesting only with properties that cannot be directly proved by a model checker. It is thus advisable to use a proof assistant in complement to more classical approaches to check these particular (e.g. parameterized, co-inductive, non-linear) properties. In conclusion, the integration of model-checking and theorem-proving within a unified framework seems to be a promising prospect.

References

1. J.-R. Abrial. *The B-Book*. Cambridge University Press, 1995.
2. J.-R. Abrial, E. Börger, and H. Langmaack. Formal Methods for Industrial Applications: Specifying and Programming the Steam Boiler Control. *Lecture Notes in Computer Science*, 1165, October 1996.
3. S. Bensalem, P. Caspi, and C. Parent-Vigouroux. Handling Data-flow Programs in PVS. Research report (draft), Verimag, May 1996.
4. A. Benveniste and P. Le Guernic. Synchronous Programming with Events and Relations: the SIGNAL Language and its Semantics. *Science of Computer Programming*, 16(2):103–149, 1991.
5. G. Berry and G. Gonthier. The ESTEREL Synchronous Programming Language: Design, Semantics, Implementation. *Science of Computer Programming*, 19:87–152, 1992.
6. T. Cattel and G. Duval. The Steam-Boiler Problem in LUSTRE. *Lecture Notes in Computer Science*, 1165:149–164, 1996.
7. B. Barras et al. *The Coq Proof Assistant Reference Manual - Version 6.2*. INRIA, Rocquencourt, May 1998.
8. E Giménez. *Un Calcul de Constructions Infinies et son Application à la Vérification des Systèmes Communicants*. PhD thesis, Laboratoire de l'Informatique du Parallélisme, Ecole Normale Supérieure de Lyon, December 1996.
9. N. Halbwachs, P. Caspi, P. Raymond, and D. Pilaud. The Synchronous Dataflow Programming Language LUSTRE. *Proc. of the IEEE*, 79(9):1305–1320, September 1991.
10. D. Harel. Statecharts: A Visual Formalism for Complex Systems. *Science of Computer Programming*, 8:231–274, 1987.
11. M. Kerbœuf, D. Nowak, and J.-P. Talpin. The Steam-boiler Controller Problem in SIGNAL-COQ. Research Report 3773, INRIA, Campus universitaire de Beaulieu, 35042 RENNES Cedex (France), October 1999.

12. http://www.irisa.fr/prive/Mickael.Kerboeuf/gb/SBGB.htm.
13. D. Nowak. *Spécification et preuve de systèmes réactifs*. PhD thesis, IFSIC, Université Rennes I, October 1999.
14. D. Nowak, J.-R. Beauvais, and J.-P. Talpin. Co-inductive Axiomatization of a Synchronous Language. In *Proceedings of Theorem Proving in Higher Order Logics (TPHOLs'98)*, number 1479 in LNCS, pages 387–399. Springer Verlag, September 1998.
15. B. Werner. *Une Théorie des Constructions Inductives*. PhD thesis, Université Paris VII, May 1994.

Functional Procedures in Higher-Order Logic

Linas Laibinis and Joakim von Wright

Åbo Akademi University and Turku Centre for Computer Science (TUCS),
Lemminkäisenkatu 14, FIN-20520 Turku, Finland,
{linas.laibinis,jockum.wright}@abo.fi

Abstract. In this paper we present an approach for modelling functional procedures (as they occur in imperative programming languages) in a weakest precondition framework. Functional procedures are called inside expressions, but the body of a functional procedure is built using standard specification/programming syntax, including nondeterminism, sequential composition, conditionals and loops. We integrate our theory of functional procedures into the existing mechanisation of the refinement calculus in the HOL system. To make formal reasoning possible, we derive correctness rules for functional procedures and their calls. We also show how recursive functional procedures can be handled according to our approach. Finally, we provide a nontrivial example of reasoning about a recursive procedure for binary search.

1 Introduction

A procedure is a parameterised piece of code that can be called from another program. In imperative programming two kinds of procedures are encountered, which differ mainly in the way in which they are called. A call to an ordinary procedure is itself a program statement, while a call to a *functional procedure* is an expression. Thus, calls to functional procedures occur inside other expressions (in the right-hand side of an assignment or in the guard of a conditional or a loop). Many languages support functional procedures, but still they have been ignored in most theories of programming, such as Hoare logic or the refinement calculus. These theories typically do not treat expressions at all, assuming that the underlying logic handles them sufficiently.

In this paper we describe how functional procedures can be handled in a weakest-precondition framework, where programs are identified with predicate transformers. The existing mechanisation of predicate transformers in higher-order logic [12,3] provides a foundation for our work, and we have integrated our theory of functional procedures into the existing mechanisation in the HOL system. Thus we have a framework for reasoning in a mechanised logic about imperative programs that contain definitions of and calls to functional procedures. To make such reasoning possible in practice, we derive rules that reduce reasoning about the calling program to correctness reasoning about the body of the functional procedure. Special emphasis is put on retaining the original weakest precondition framework, where the semantics of expressions is compatible with the assignment axiom of Hoare Logic.

J. Harrison and M. Aagaard (Eds.): TPHOLs 2000, LNCS 1869, pp. 372–387, 2000.

We model functional procedures in their full generality; thus the body of a functional procedure can be built using standard specification syntax in the style of Dijkstra's guarded commands [4], including nondeterminism, sequential composition, conditionals and loops. Recursive procedures constitute a special challenge, but we show how they can be handled, and provide a nontrivial example of reasoning about a recursive procedure for binary search. Our framework assumes that functional procedures have no side-effects or reference parameters, and mutual recursion is not supported.

2   Predicate Transformer Semantics in Higher-Order Logic

This section briefly reviews the background to the paper, i.e., the formalisation of a weakest-precondition semantics in the higher-order logic of the HOL theorem proving system. For more details, we refer to earlier work [12].

2.1   Predicate Transformers

The program state can be modelled as a polymorphic type variable α or β which for concrete programs can be instantiated in different ways. At this point we do not assume that states have any specific internal structure, though we introduce some assumptions later, in connection with program variables.

A state predicate is a boolean function on states (i.e., it has type $\alpha \to bool$; we identify predicates with sets of states). A predicate transformer is a function that maps predicates to predicates. The intended interpretation is that of a predicate transformer $S : (\beta \to bool) \to (\alpha \to bool)$ as a weakest precondition. This means that if q is a predicate (a *postcondition*) and σ is a state then $\sigma \in S\,q$ if and only if execution of a program statement modeled by S from initial state σ is guaranteed to terminate in some final state σ' in q.

We do not assume any specific syntax for program statements. What we develop is a framework that can be used for any programming notation with a weakest precondition semantics. In examples, we will use a notation with assignments (deterministic and nondeterministic), sequential composition, conditionals, while-loops and blocks. The weakest precondition semantics for this notation has been embedded as described in [12]. For example, sequential composition and conditional composition are defined as follows:

$\vdash_{def} \forall c1\ c2\ q.\ (c1\ \textbf{seq}\ c2)\ q = c1\ (c2\ q)$
$\vdash_{def} \forall g\ c1\ c2\ q.\ \textbf{cond}\ g\ c1\ c2\ q = (\lambda s.\ g\ s \to c1\ q\ s \mid c2\ q\ s)$

The embedding of the programming notation is *shallow*, so it can be extended whenever we want to add new features, as long as these can be given a weakest precondition semantics (see Section 3.5).

The predicate transformers that model (demonically) nondeterministic program satisfy the following two *healthiness conditions*:

$\vdash_{def}$ strict c = (c false = false)
$\vdash_{def}$ conjunctive c = $\forall$P. c (glb P) = glb(λp. $\exists$q. P q $\wedge$ p = c q)

where false is the everywhere false predicate λu.F and glb is the greatest low er bound (intersection) operator on predicates:

$\vdash_{def}$ $\forall$P. glb P = (λs. $\forall$p. P p $\Rightarrow$ p s)

For a given program (predicate transformer), these healthiness conditions are easily proved automatically by a structural argument. *Correctness* (i.e., total correctness in the weakest-precondition sense) is formalised as follows:

$\vdash_{def}$ correct p c q = p implies (c q)

where implies models the implication (subset) ordering on predicates. Thus, correct p c q holds if any execution of c from an initial state in p is guaranteed to terminate in a final state in q.

2.2   Modelling Assignments

One of the basic statements of any imperative language is the assignment sta-tement which models a deterministic state change. It can be represented using state (update) function e of type $\alpha \rightarrow \beta$ where α is the type of initial state and β is the type of final state. The assignment statement is then defined (according to its weakest precondition semantics) as:

$\vdash_{def}$ $\forall$e q. assign e q = (λv. q (e v))

Note that the initial and final states can be of different types. This will be cruc al when modelling functional procedures.

A *nondeterministic assignment* (specification) statement describes a sta.e change where the result may not be uniquely determined. All we know is that the relationship P between initial and final state should be established. The definition of nondeterministic assignment is the following:

$\vdash_{def}$ $\forall$P q. nondass P q = (λv. $\forall$v'. P v v' $\Rightarrow$ q v')

In a concrete program, the state is a tuple (i.e., of product type) where every component corresponds to a program variable. We can use tupled λ-abstraction to make programs readable. In a state space with three variables $x:num, b:bool, y:num$, the assignment $x := x + y$ is described as

assign λ(x,b,y).(x+y,b,y)

rather than the equivalent but less readable

assign λu.(FST u + SND(SND u),FST(SND u),SND(SND u))

For details about this way of modelling program variables, we refer to [3].

3   Functional Procedures

The general purpose of a procedure is to abstract a certain piece of a code, giving it a name and then adapting it (through parameters) in different places of the program. Since procedures are program fragments, they can be modelled in the usual way, i.e., as predicate transformers [5].

The effect of calling an ordinary procedure is that the procedure body (adapted as described by the parameters) is executed in place of the procedure call. However, the effect of calling a functional procedure is that a value is returned, and calls to functional procedures appear inside expressions in assignments and guards. Thus, a call to a functional procedures cannot be replaced by the procedure body.

3.1   The Function Call Operator

Since a functional procedure is really a program fragment, we want to model it as a predicate transformer. Predicates map predicates to predicates, but intuitively they stand for program statements which transform (initial) states into (final) states. Because a state is a tuple, we can interpret a state as a value. Since the formalisation furthermore allows the initial and final states to be of different types, we can interpret the final state of an execution of a functional procedure as the return value, to be substituted for the call.

To make this work, we have to find a way of extracting the state function from the procedure body (the predicate transformer). Operationally we can see the body as modelling backward execution – we supply a set of final states we are interested in (postcondition), and calculate the biggest possible set of initial states (weakest precondition) from which we guaranteed to reach the final states described by the postcondition. State functions, however, model forward execution – for a given initial state they calculate the final state that is the result of the state change. We need to find a translation that reverses execution modelled by the functional procedure body.

For a given initial state we consider all possible sets of reachable final states (postconditions). We then calculate the intersection of all such sets of states (the minimal set of reachable final states), and finally we select a value from this minimal set as the result of our state function.

This intuition is formalised in the following definition:

$$\vdash_{def} \forall c.\ \mathtt{fcall}\ c\ =\ (\lambda u.\ \varepsilon v.\ \mathtt{glb}\ (\lambda q.\ c\ q\ u)\ v)$$

where c is the body of the functional procedure, u is the initial state (the arguments), and v is the result state (the value).

Note the use of the choice operator ε in the definition of fcall. It means that the result value of a function call is an arbitrary (but fixed) element from the set glb $(\lambda q.\ c\ q\ u)$. If this set is empty, then we have no information whatsoever about the value that is returned. However, conjunctivity and strictness (the two healthiness conditions that we generally require) together guarantee that the set is nonempty.

As an example, we define a very simple functional procedure that squares a natural number as follows:

$\vdash_{def}$ **sqfun** = **assign** (λ u. u*u)

Note that the assignment in the definition of **sqfun** plays the role of a *return* statement. To make this association explicit we introduce **return** as an alternative name for **assign**, to be used as the last statement to be executed in the body of a functional procedure.

In a Pascal-like syntax this corresponds to something like the following:

func *sqfun*(x : num) : num =
    return $x * x$

A call to this functional procedure can then be as follows:

assign λ (x,y). (x,y + **fcall sqfun** (x+1))

corresponding to an assignment of the form

$$y := y + sqfun(x + 1)$$

Note that we make no assumption about the syntax of expressions; any HOL-expression can be used as the right-and side of an assignment and (because our embedding is shallow) if new types and constants are defined, these can also be used without changing the theory described here.

3.2   Basic Properties

We shall now discuss a number of basic properties of the function call operator that we have proved as HOL theorems. We start with a basic soundness property: if the body of the functional procedure is an assignment statement then the function call extracts the state change function from it:

```
fcall_assign =
⊢ ∀e. fcall (assign e) = e
```

The proof rests on the fact that in this case, the intersection $glb(\lambda q. (assign\,e)\,q\,u)$ is the singleton set $\{e\,u\}$ where u is the initial (argument) state of the functional procedure. Therefore, the choice operator actually has no choice but to select e u as the result value of the function call.

Implicitly the same property holds for any deterministic and terminating functional procedure body, since such a statement is semantically equivalent to a single **assign** statement.

Next, we have a property that allows us show that a functional procedure in fact implements a specific function.

```
fcall_thm =
⊢ ∀c f. conjunctive c ∧ strict c ∧
        (∀u0. correct (λu. u = u0) c (λv. v = f u0)) ⇒
        (fcall c = f)
```

Here, c is the body of the functional procedure and f is (the HOL formalisation of) the function that the procedure implements. The implementation property is reduced to a corresponding correctness property of the procedure body, which can then be proved using standard (Hoare logic) methods.

Finally, we have two theorems that show how the function call operator can be propagated past an initial assignment and distributed into a conditional:

```
fcall_seq =
  ⊢ ∀c e. fcall (assign e seq c) s = fcall c (e s)
fcall_cond =
  ⊢ ∀g c1 c2 s.
        fcall (cond g c1 c2) s = (g s → fcall c1 s | fcall c2 s)
```

These theorems will be important when proving properties of concrete implementations. They could also support a kind of partial evaluation using the actual parameters of a function call.

3.3   Example: Implementation Proofs

Consider the very simple task of finding the minimum of two numbers. In HOL we can formalise the minimum function in the following way:

$$\vdash_{def} \forall m\ n.\ \text{MIN(m,n)}\ =\ (m < n \to m\ |\ n)$$

In the imperative programming notation we now code a (slightly different) functional procedure minfun

$$\vdash_{def}\ \textbf{minfun} =$$
```
            cond (λ(x,y). x ≤ y)
                 (return λ(x,y). x)
                 (return λ(x,y). y)
```

The two arguments of the functional procedure minfun form the initial state (pair). The variables here are explicitly modelled as projection functions FST and SND. In a Pascal-style programming notation this would translate to

```
func minfun(x : num, y : num) : num =
    if x ≤ y then
        return x
    else
        return y
    endif
```

Now we can prove that minfun actually implements the HOL function MIN.

```
⊢ ∀x y. fcall minfun = MIN
```

The proof is straightforward: first we use the theorem fcall_cond to distribute fcall into the conditional statement, then we eliminate fcall using the basic property fcall_assign. After this follows a case split and then the proof is finished off by arithmetic reasoning. Note that this kind of implementation theorem is very strong: when reasoning about a program that contains a function call, we can replace the function call with the mathematical function that it corresponds to. Thus, we never have to refer to the definition of minfun after this.

3.4   Nontermination

It is natural to expect functional procedures in our framework to be deterministic and terminating, since they typically implement (total) functions. The theorem fcall_assign shows that in this case the function call extracts the implemented function.

However, our formalisation of functional procedures is more general than this, because it allows function bodies that are nondeterministic and/or nonterminating. An obvious question is now: what do we know about the value that a functional procedure returns in these cases?

Since all expressions in HOL are total, a nonterminating function body does not lead to a nonterminating function call, but we get a return value about which we know absolutely nothing (apart from type information). This is obviously a shortcoming (although it is close to the view generally taken in systems based on partial correctness). The weakest precondition semantics identifies aborting and nonterminating behaviour, and one could argue that our implementation is compatible with such a view, when aborting behaviour is interpreted as behaviour about which we have (and can have) no information.

A way of avoiding this problem is to interpret an assignment $x := e$ as implicitly preceded by an assertion $\{\text{dom}(e)\}$ which aborts if e contains any nonterminating (aborting) function calls. One step even further away from what we are trying to model would be to treat functional procedures simply as ordinary procedures with a result parameter and to interpret the assignment as a block with a local variable for each function call and the return values computed and stored before the assignment itself is executed. However, then we would definitely not be modeling functional procedures in the way that we set out to do.

3.5   Nondeterminism

Now consider the case when the function body is (demonically) nondeterministic (but terminating). A simple case is when the procedure body consists of a single nondeterministic assignment statement nondass R. In this case, if for some given initial state (function parameters) u the set R u is not empty, then some selected element from the set R u is returned by the function call:

$$\vdash \forall R\ u.\ (\exists v.\ R\ u\ v) \Rightarrow R\ u\ (\text{fcall}\ (\text{nondass}\ R)\ u)$$

A similar argument can also be used when the body of the nondeterministic functional procedure is more complex, since it is then equivalent to some nondeterministic assignment.

Thus, (demonic) nondeterminism models *underspecification* (implementation-time nondeterminism rather than run-time nondeterminism). In fact, we could also permit *angelic* nondeterminism in the procedure body; this would correspond to having an oracle make decisions about the execution [1].

4   Correctness Reasoning with Functional Procedures

The usual way to prove that a program (or some program fragment) is correct with respect to a given precondition-postcondition pair is to decompose the global correctness property into correctness properties for the program components, using Hoare logic.

4.1   Correctness Proofs with Functional Procedures

When proving correctness of a program containing function calls, we use Hoare logic to decompose the proof in the ordinary way. When we get to the bottom level, we are faced with proving verification conditions that come from guards and assignments (e.g., conditions of the form $P \Rightarrow Q[x := E]$ that come from the assignment rule of Hoare logic). When function calls are present, such a condition expresses a relationship between the calling state, the argument to the function, and the result returned by the function call. The following theorem can then be used to reduce the condition to a correctness condition on the function body:

```
fcall_property =
 ⊢ ∀c R e u0.
     conjunctive c ∧ strict c ⇒
     correct (λu. u = e u0) c (λres. R u0 res) ⇒
         R u0 (fcall c (e u0))
```

Here c is the function body, and R expresses the relationship between the state from which the function is called (u0) and the function result (e is the function that says how the function argument is constructed from the calling state). Note also that `fcall_property` is a generalisation of `fcall_thm` (see Section 3.2). Since conjunctivity and strictness can be proved automatically, it gives a way of reducing a general property of a function call to a correctness property for the body of the functional procedure in question.

Let us use the squaring function to show how this is used in practice. Recall that it was defined to satisfy

```
⊢ sqfun = return (λu. u * u)
```

Suppose that we want to prove the following correctness assertion for the assignment statement with the function call:

```
⊢ correct (λ (x,y). T)
         (assign λ (x,y).(x,fcall sqfun (x + 1) − 1))
         (λ (x,y). y ≥ x)
```

Here the tupled abstraction makes clear the correspondence with the intended Hoare logic formula

$$\{T\}\ y := \mathtt{square\_fun}(x+1) - 1\ \{y \geq x\}$$

After applying the Hoare logic rule for assignment and simplifying, the goal is reduced to the following:

```
⊢ fcall sqfun (x + 1) − 1 ≥ x
```

We can now specialise the theorem fcall_property with the following: sqfun for c, with $(\lambda(x,y)\,r.\,r - 1 \geq x)$ for R, with $(\lambda(x,y).\,x + 1)$ for e, and with x for u0. This theorem reduces our goal (after the conjunctivity and strictness conditions have been automatically discharged) to

```
⊢ correct (λu. u = x+1) (return (λu. u * u)) (λr. r−1 ≥ x)
```

Now we apply the Hoare logic rule (recall that the return statement is an assignment) and the goal is reduced to

```
⊢ (x + 1) * (x + 1) − 1 ≥ x
```

which is a standard verification condition (and obviously true).

The functional procedure sqfun was very simple, but the same strategy works for more complex procedure bodies (that include, e.g., loops) and more complex correctness conditions as well. The example shows how the verification conditions that arise from program correctness proofs lead to new correctness proofs, when function calls are present. Since the body of one function may contain calls to another function, new correctness conditions may appear, and so on. Eventually, however, all function calls have been handled and we reach the ground level where only basic verification conditions remain (unless there is recursion; see Section 5).

4.2   Contextual Correctness Reasoning

A function call can occur in a situation where a context (i.e., a restriction on the possible values of variables) is known to hold. If this contextual knowledge can be expressed in the form of a predicate p that holds for the arguments at a call to c, then we can assume p as a precondition when reasoning about the body of the functional procedure c.

The theorem that captures this intuition is the following, in the case of an implementation proof:

```
fcall_thm_pre =
  ⊢ ∀c p f.
```

```
        conjunctive c ∧ strict c ∧
        (∀u0. correct (λu. (u = u0) ∧ p u) c (λv. v = f u0)) ⇒
        (∀u. p u ⇒ (fcall c u = f u))
```

A simple example of a situation where this property can be useful is when the function call occurs inside the guard of a conditional, e.g.,

```
    cond (λ(x,y). x>0 ∧ fcall foo x) ...
```

In this case, we may instantiate p to $(\lambda u.u > 0)$ when using fcall_thm_pre to reason about the call to foo.

A similar argument can also be used when proving some general property of a function call (e.g., when reducing correctness conditions):

```
fcall_property_pre =
⊢ ∀c p R e u0.
        conjunctive c ∧ strict c ∧
        correct (λu. (u = e u0) ∧ p u) c (λv. R u0 v)) ⇒
        p (e u0) ⇒ R u0 (fcall c (e u0))
```

This is a direct generalisation of fcall_property (Section 4).

5   Recursive Functions

Recursion in the context of (ordinary) procedures can be defined using the least fixpoint (with respect to the refinement ordering on predicate transformers) of a functional that corresponds to the recursively defined procedure. This method cannot be used directly with functional procedures, since the fcall operator is not monotonic with respect to the refinement ordering (nor any other suitable ordering).

5.1   A Constructor for Recursion

As a first step towards defining recursion we define an iterator.

```
⊢def (∀f. iter 0 f = assign (λs. εs'. T)) ∧
     (∀n f. iter (SUC n) f = f (iter n f))
```

Since there is no bottom (or undefined) element to start the iteration from, we choose to start it from some element selected by the choice operator. This means that we have to be careful when defining the recursion operator: it is not sufficient that two consecutive iterations give the same result (the selection operator may cause this to happen "by accident"). However, if from some point on all further iterations give the same result, then the iteration has stabilised. This justifies the following definition

```
⊢def ∀f. fmu f =
     assign (λs. εa. ∃m. ∀n. n > m ⇒ (fcall (iter n f) s = a))
```

Of course, the problem of nontermination is the same as before: a potentially infinite sequence of recursive calls is modelled as terminating and returning a result about which we know nothing.

The following example shows how fmu is used when defining a recursive functional procedure (recursion occurs inside a fcall). We define

```
⊢def Factfun = λ Z.
         cond (λx. x=0)
              (assign λx. 1)
              (assign λx. x * fcall Z (x−1))
⊢def factfun = fmu Factfun
```

This corresponds to a Pascal-style function definition of the following form:

$$\text{func } factfun(x : \text{num}) : \text{num} =$$
$$\text{if } x = 0 \text{ then}$$
$$\quad \text{return } 1$$
$$\text{else}$$
$$\quad \text{return } x * factfun(x - 1)$$
$$\text{endif}$$

5.2   Basic Properties

The most important property of the recursion operator fmu is that it gives the stabilisation point of iter, if such a point exists, for the arguments in question:

```
fmu_thm =
 ⊢ ∀f s k.
     (∀n. fcall (iter (k + n) f) s = g s) ⇒
     (fcall (fmu f) s = g s)
```

This property may not seem very informative, but it gives us the tools we need to prove properties of functional procedures defined with fmu. The argument k is crucial; it corresponds to a *termination argument* (an upper bound on the number of iterations needed to reach stability).

As an example, we briefly describe how one proves that factfun really implements the (built-in) FACT function of the HOL system.

According to fmu_thm it is sufficient to prove the following lemma

⊢ ∀x n. fcall (iter (SUC x + n) Factfun) x = FACT x

We have chosen SUC x as termination argument (which is reasonable when we are computing the factorial of x).

The proof of this lemma follows a fairly simple routine, involving only induction and rewriting with basic arithmetic facts. As a result, we immediately get the implementation theorem

⊢ ∀s. fcall factfun = FACT

5.3   Example: Binary Search

The factorial example illustrates the fmu operator and it shows that it is possible to prove properties of a recursive functional procedure. However, it can be argued that factfun merely encodes the standard recursive definition of the factorial function into imperative form, and that the proof really only performs the corresponding decoding. In order to show that more realistic functional procedures can be handled, we now consider an example where the procedure does not correspond to an encoding of a standard recursive function definition.

Our example is a binary search, which in standard syntax is as follows:

> func $binfind(f : \text{num} \to \text{num}, l : \text{num}, r : \text{num}, x : \text{num}) : \text{bool} =$
>> if $r \leq l$ then
>>> return F
>>
>> else
>>> [var $m := (l + r)$ div 2;
>>>> if $f\ m < x$ then
>>>>> return $binfind(f, m + 1, r, x)$
>>>>
>>>> else if $f\ m = x$ then
>>>>> return T
>>>>
>>>> else
>>>>> return $binfind(f, l, m, x)$
>>>>
>>>> endif endif
>>>
>>>]
>>
>> endif

The aim is to show that if the first argument f is a monotonic function (i.e., sorted), then $binfind(f, l, r, x)$ returns T if exists i such that $l \leq i < r$ and $f\ i = x$, and it returns F otherwise. Here we assume that the values handled are natural numbers, but we could obviously handle any total order. However, since HOL does not have type classes, a generic search algorithm would make the example more complicated, without improving the illustration of the main idea: reasoning about functional procedures.

We define a constant Binfind standing for the functional procedure of which the procedure binfind is the least fixpoint:

```
⊢ Binfind = λZ.
   cond (λ(f,l,r,x). r ≤ l)
    (return λ(f,l,r,x). F)
    ((assign λ(f,l,r,x). ((l + r) DIV 2,f,l,r,x)) seq
    (cond (λ(m,f,l,r,x). f m < x)
      (return λ(m,f,l,r,x). fcall Z (f,SUC m,r,x))
      (cond (λ(m,f,l,r,x). f m = x)
```

```
        (return λ(m,f,l,r,x). T)
        (return λ(m,f,l,r,x). fcall Z (f,l,m,x))
  )))
```

⊢ binfind = fmu Binfind

This corresponds exactly to the standard syntax above. The assignment

assign λ(f,l,r,x). ((l + r) DIV 2,f,l,r,x)

corresponds to the block entry, adding the new variable (m) as a first state component. No explicit block exit is needed; it is taken care of by the return statement.

The correctness of the binary search depends on the first argument being sorted. Thus, the theorem that we want to prove is the following:

⊢ ∀f x.
    (∀i j. i < j ⇒ f j ≤ f j) ⇒
    (∀l r. fcall binfind (f,l,r,x) =
        (∃i. l ≤ i ∧ i < r ∧ (f i = x)))

Exactly as for the simple example in Section 5.2, the crucial lemma shows that iteration of Binfind is guaranteed to terminate with a correct answer. The lemma has the following form:

⊢ ∀f:num→num. ∀x:num.
    (∀i j. i < j ⇒ f i ≤ f j) ⇒
    (∀d k l. fcall (iter (SUC d + k) Binfind) (f,l,l+d,x) =
        (∃i. l ≤ i ∧ i < l + d ∧ (f i = x)))

The critical part of the proof is an induction over d (the length of the search interval), which is also the termination argument. Since the termination argument is (approximately) halved rather than decreased by one, we must use general well-founded induction:

⊢ ∀P. (∀n. (∀m. m < n ⇒ P m) ⇒ P n) ⇒ (∀n. P n)

rather than standard induction over the natural numbers. The proof strategy is essentially the same as in the factorial example, but here we need to push fcall both into conditionals and past assignments (see Section 3.2). The proof then reduces to basic arithmetic facts (including tedious details about integer division) and to simple properties of monotonic functions. The following two are typical examples of lemmas used in the proof:

⊢ (∀i j. i < j ⇒ f i ≤ f j) ∧ (f i = x) ∧ f j < x ⇒ j < i
⊢ m > 0 ⇒ m DIV 2 < m

This proof follows a general strategy that can be used in similar proofs. However, automating this strategy does not seem feasible, at least not when general well-founded induction is used. In this example finding the right instantiations for d, k, and l in the lemma required elaborate equation solving. Furthermore, assumptions about the state (such as the monotonicity assumption on f) may be used in nontrivial ways.

The proof also depends on pushing fcall into the structure of the functional procedure, and this only works going into conditionals and past assignments. Thus, the same strategy cannot be used if nondeterministic constructs are involved, or if there are assignments after a recursive call. It is not clear whether there exists a useful proof strategy in these situations.

6 Conclusions

We have presented an approach for modelling functional procedures in a weakest precondition framework. We are explicitly interested in functional procedures as they occur in Pascal-like programs, i.e., where the procedure is described as an imperative program even though the call is used as an expression. Thus we cannot use existing theories of functional programs (e.g., [2,10]). Instead, functional procedures are handled through the link between assignments and state transforming functions. To our knowledge, they have not treated in this way before.

Our aim was not to develop a calculus for expressions and functional procedures. Instead, we developed a framework that stays within the weakest precondition tradition with simple (total) expressions, but allows function calls to appear inside expressions and function bodies to be written using any suitable programming notation with a weakest precondition semantics. The shallow embedding allows syntax to be flexible, so that any construct that can be given a weakest precondition semantics can be added without changing the theory (it also means that certain meta-level questions, such as completeness, cannot be asked in a meaningful way).

We integrated this approach into the mechanised version of the refinement calculus in HOL system. The HOL formalisation of the refinement calculus contains support for correctness reasoning about programs, and we reuse it for correctness reasoning where calls to functional procedures occur.

Two ways of proving (correctness) properties of function calls were described. If the functional procedure is characterised by an implementation theorem then the function call can be replaced directly by a reference to the corresponding (mathematical) function. In other cases, the proof leads to correctness proofs for the body of the functional procedure.

Our approach for modelling functional procedures allows function bodies to be nondeterministic and/or nonterminating. Since functions in HOL are always total, the result of a function call is always a well-defined value. In the nondeterministic case, the result returned by the function call is an arbitrary but fixed value of the form εP (where P is some nonempty set). Thus the value returned by the function call is deterministic, but the only information we can ever get about it is that it belongs to the set P. In this sense our approach differs significantly from *expression refinement* in a weakest precondition framework [6,7,

9] where the aim is to introduce nondeterminism into the expression language using choice operators. In our framework, a refinement of the body of a functional procedure does not lead to a refinement of the calling program (but proofs of properties of the calling program can generally be reused, since they are unlikely to make essential use of the selected element εP).

The approach presented here also differs significantly from Laibinis' work on (ordinary) procedures in HOL [5], although both are based on the same formalisation of weakest precondition semantics. Both are shallow embeddings based on the same underlying theory, which means that procedures in one framework could call procedures from the other. However, in our theory of functional procedure the main effort goes into modelling and reasoning about procedure calls, while the main focus of Laibinis' work is on modelling parameterisation and reasoning about refinement of procedure bodies.

The main drawback of our approach is the simplistic handling of nonterminating function calls, which (through the use of the choice operator ε) return a value about which we know nothing. This reflects an inherent feature of the HOL logic; an expressions like 5 DIV 0 (division by zero) also returns a fixed value about which we have no information. This can be avoided in a deep embedding of the expression language (Norrish [8] handles correctness reasoning for a model of the C language in this way, starting from an operational semantics), but then we could not reuse the HOL expression language and we would lose the simple handling of expressions in traditional Hoare logic and weakest precondition semantics that we set out to model.

An obvious continuation to this work would be an investigation of possible semi-automated strategies for proofs of implementation and correctness, both for simple and recursive functional procedures, and adding functional procedures to the HOL-based Refinement Calculator tool [3], in order to provide a more user-friendly interface for reasoning about imperative programs with functional procedures.

References

1. R.J. Back and J. von Wright Refinement Calculus: A Systematic introduction. Springer-Verlag, 1998.
2. G. Collins. A Proof Tool for Reasoning about Functional Programs. In *Proc. 1996 International Workshop on Higher Order Logic Theorem Proving,* Lecture Notes in Computer Science 1125, Turku, Finland, August 1996. Springer–Verlag.
3. M.J. Butler and J. Grundy and T. Långbacka and R. Rukšėnas and J. von Wright The Refinement Calculator: Proof Support for Program Refinement. Proc. FMP'97 – Formal Methods Pacific, Wellington, New Zealand, July 1997. Springer-Verlag.
4. E.W. Dijkstra A Discipline of Programming. Prentice-Hall international, 1976.
5. L. Laibinis. Mechanising procedures in HOL. Technical Report No.253, Turku Centre for Computer Science, 1999.
6. B. Mahony. Expression Refinement in Higher Order Logic. In Proc. 1998 International Refinement Workshop and Formal Methods Pacific, Discrete Mathematics and Theoretical Computer Science, Springer–Verlag, 1998.

7. J.M. Morris. Non-deterministic expressions and predicate transformers. *Information Processing Letters*, 61(5):241–246, 1997.
8. M. Norrish. C formalised in HOL. PhD thesis, University of Cambridge, 1998.
9. M. Schwenke and K. Robinson. What If? In Second Australian Refinement Workshop, 1992.
10. K. Slind. Function Definition in Higher-Order Logic. In *Proc. 1996 International Workshop on Higher Order Logic Theorem Proving*, Lecture Notes in Computer Science 1125, Turku, Finland, August 1996. Springer–Verlag.
11. J. von Wright. Verifying Modular Programs in HOL. Technical Report No.324, Computer Laboratory of University of Cambridge, 1994.
12. J. von Wright. Program Refinement by Theorem Prover. Proc. 6th Refinement Workshop, London, January 1994. Springer–Verlag.

Formalizing Stålmarck's Algorithm in Coq

Pierre Letouzey[1] and Laurent Théry[2]

[1] École Normale Supérieure, 45 rue d'Ulm, 75230 Paris France
Pierre.Letouzey@ens.fr
[2] INRIA, 2004 route des Lucioles, 06902 Sophia Antipolis France
Laurent.Thery@sophia.inria.fr

Abstract. We present the development of a machine-checked implementation of Stålmarck's algorithm. First, we prove the correctness and the completeness of an abstract representation of the algorithm. Then, we give an effective implementation of the algorithm that we prove correct.

1 Introduction

When formalizing an algorithm inside a prover, every single step has to be justified. The result is a presentation of the algorithm where no detail has been omitted. Mechanizing the proofs of correctness and completeness is the main goal of this formalization. Whenever such proofs are intricate and involve a large amount of case exploration, mechanized proofs may be an interesting complement to the ones on paper. Also, there is often a gap between an algorithm and its actual implementation. Bridging this gap formally and getting a reasonably efficient certified implementation is a valuable exercise.

In this paper we explain how this has been done for Stålmarck's algorithm [10] using the Coq prover [6]. This algorithm is a tautology checker. It is patented and has been successfully applied in industry. As it includes a number of heuristics, what we formalize is an abstract version of the algorithm. We prove different properties of the algorithm including correctness and completeness. We also cover two ways of ensuring that the result of an implementation is correct. We define execution traces and prove that these traces can be used to check that a formula is a tautology in a more elementary way. We also derive a certified implementation.

The paper is structured as follows. The algorithm is presented in Section 2. The formalization of the algorithm is described in Section 3. The notion of trace is introduced in Section 4. Finally the implementation is given in Section 5.

2 The Algorithm

Stålmarck's algorithm is a tautology checker. It deals with boolean formulae, i.e. expressions formed with the two constants $\top$ (true), $\bot$ (false), the unary symbol $\neg$ (negation), the binary symbols & (conjunction), # (disjunction), $\mapsto$

J. Harrison and M. Aagaard (Eds.): TPHOLs 2000, LNCS 1869, pp. 388–405, 2000.

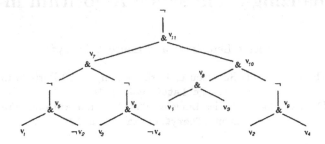

Fig. 1. Annotated tree-like representation of the formula

(implication), $=$ (equivalence), and a set of variables $(v_i)_{i \in \mathbb{N}}$. For example, the following formula is a boolean expression containing four variables v_1, v_2, v_3 and v_4:

$$((v_1 \mapsto v_2) \,\&\, (v_3 \mapsto v_4)) \mapsto ((v_1 \,\&\, v_3) \mapsto (v_2 \,\&\, v_4))$$

It is also a tautology. This means that the formula is valid (true) for any value of its variables. The first step of the algorithm is to reduce the number of binary symbols using the following equalities:

$$A \,\#\, B = \neg(\neg A \,\&\, \neg B)$$
$$A \mapsto B = \neg(A \,\&\, \neg B)$$
$$\neg\neg A = A$$

With this transformation, we obtain an equivalent formula containing only conjunctions, equalities and negations. By applying this transformation on our example, we get:

$$\neg((\neg(v_1 \,\&\, \neg v_2) \,\&\, \neg(v_3 \,\&\, \neg v_4)) \,\&\, ((v_1 \,\&\, v_3) \,\&\, \neg(v_2 \,\&\, v_4)))$$

The algorithm manipulates data structures called *triplets*. To handle negation, variables are *signed*: $\pm v_i$. A triplet is a group of three signed variables and a connector (either $\&$ or $=$), meaning that the first variable has the value of the result of applying the connector to the other two variables. The two kinds of triplets are written as $v_i := \pm v_j \,\&\, \pm v_k$ and $v_i := \pm v_j = \pm v_k$. Every reduced boolean expression has a corresponding list of triplets. If we consider the tree representation of the formula and annotate every binary tree with a fresh new variable as in Figure 1, taking every binary node of the annotated tree to form a triplet gives us the list of triplets representing the formula. In our example, we get the following list:

$$
\begin{array}{rclcll}
v_5 & := & v_1 & \& & -v_2 & \quad (1)\\
v_6 & := & v_3 & \& & -v_4 & \quad (2)\\
v_7 & := & -v_5 & \& & -v_6 & \quad (3)\\
v_8 & := & v_1 & \& & v_3 & \quad (4)\\
v_9 & := & v_2 & \& & v_4 & \quad (5)\\
v_{10} & := & v_8 & \& & -v_9 & \quad (6)\\
v_{11} & := & v_7 & \& & v_{10} & \quad (7)
\end{array}
$$

The value of the formula is the value of $-v_{11}$. The algorithm works by refutation. It assumes that the formula is false and tries to reach a contradiction by propagation. There is a set of rules for each kind of triplets that defines how to do this propagation. For the triplet $v_i := v_j \& v_k$ we have nine rules:

$$
\begin{array}{llllllll}
\textit{if} & v_i = -v_j, & \textit{propagate} & v_j = \top & \textit{and} & v_k = \bot & & \&_{i-j}\\
\textit{if} & v_i = -v_k, & \textit{propagate} & v_j = \bot & \textit{and} & v_k = \top & & \&_{i-k}\\
\textit{if} & v_j = v_k, & \textit{propagate} & & v_i = v_k & & & \&_{jk}\\
\textit{if} & v_j = -v_k, & \textit{propagate} & & v_i = \bot & & & \&_{j-k}\\
\textit{if} & v_i = \top, & \textit{propagate} & v_j = \top & \textit{and} & v_k = \top & & \&_{i\top}\\
\textit{if} & v_j = \top, & \textit{propagate} & & v_i = v_k & & & \&_{j\top}\\
\textit{if} & v_j = \bot, & \textit{propagate} & & v_i = \bot & & & \&_{j\bot}\\
\textit{if} & v_k = \top, & \textit{propagate} & & v_i = v_j & & & \&_{k\top}\\
\textit{if} & v_k = \bot, & \textit{propagate} & & v_i = \bot & & & \&_{k\bot}
\end{array}
$$

For the triplet $v_i := v_j = v_k$ we have twelve rules:

$$
\begin{array}{lllll}
\textit{if} & v_i = v_j, & \textit{propagate} & v_k = \top & =_{ij}\\
\textit{if} & v_i = -v_j, & \textit{propagate} & v_k = \bot & =_{i-j}\\
\textit{if} & v_i = v_k, & \textit{propagate} & v_j = \top & =_{ik}\\
\textit{if} & v_i = -v_k, & \textit{propagate} & v_j = \bot & =_{i-k}\\
\textit{if} & v_j = v_k, & \textit{propagate} & v_i = \top & =_{jk}\\
\textit{if} & v_j = -v_k, & \textit{propagate} & v_i = \bot & =_{j-k}\\
\textit{if} & v_i = \top, & \textit{propagate} & v_j = v_k & =_{i\top}\\
\textit{if} & v_i = \bot, & \textit{propagate} & v_j = -v_k & =_{i\bot}\\
\textit{if} & v_j = \top, & \textit{propagate} & v_i = v_k & =_{j\top}\\
\textit{if} & v_j = \bot, & \textit{propagate} & v_i = -v_k & =_{j\bot}\\
\textit{if} & v_k = \top, & \textit{propagate} & v_i = v_j & =_{k\top}\\
\textit{if} & v_k = \bot, & \textit{propagate} & v_i = -v_j & =_{k\bot}
\end{array}
$$

In our case, this simple mechanism of propagation is sufficient to establish that the formula is a tautology. We start with the state where $v_{11} = \top$ ($-v_{11} = \bot$)

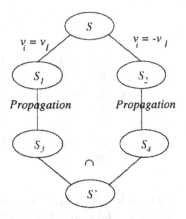

Fig. 2. The dilemma rule

and apply the following rules:

$$
\begin{array}{llllllll}
v_{11}{=}\mathsf{T}, & we\ get & v_7 = \mathsf{T} & and & v_{10} = \mathsf{T} & by & \&_{i\mathsf{T}} & on & (7) \\
v_7 = \mathsf{T}, & we\ get & v_5 = \bot & and & v_6 = \bot & by & \&_{i\mathsf{T}} & on & (3) \\
v_{10}{=}\mathsf{T}, & we\ get & v_8 = \mathsf{T} & and & v_9 = \bot & by & \&_{i\mathsf{T}} & on & (6) \\
v_8 = \mathsf{T}, & we\ get & v_1 = \mathsf{T} & and & v_3 = \mathsf{T} & by & \&_{i\mathsf{T}} & on & (4) \\
v_1 = \mathsf{T}, & we\ get & & & v_5 = -v_2 & by & \&_{j\mathsf{T}} & on & (1) \\
v_2 = \mathsf{T}, & we\ get & & & v_9 = v_4 & by & \&_{j\mathsf{T}} & on & (5) \\
v_3 = \mathsf{T}, & we\ get & & & v_6 = -v_4 & by & \&_{j\mathsf{T}} & on & (2)
\end{array}
$$

The last equation is a contradiction since we know that $v_6 = \bot$ and $v_4 = v_9 = \bot$. Note that the order in which propagation rules are selected is arbitrary.

Most of the time the propagation alone is not sufficient to conclude. In that case the *dilemma rule* can be applied. This rule works as depicted in Figure 2. Given a state S, it takes two arbitrary variables v_i and v_j and creates two separates branches. In one branch, it adds the equation $v_i = v_j$ to get S_1. In the second branch it adds the equation $v_i = -v_j$ to get S_2. On each of these branches, the propagation is applied to obtain S_3 and S_4 respectively. Then the result of the dilemma rule is the intersection S' of S_3 and S_4 that contains all the equations that are valid independently of the relation between v_i and v_j. If one of the branches gives a contradiction, the result is the final state of the other branch. If we obtain a contradiction on both branches, a contradiction is reached. The dilemma rule is iterated on all pairs of variables taking the state resulting from the previous application as the initial state of the next one, till no new information is gained or a contradiction is reached. If no contradiction is reached, the same process is applied using four variables creating four branches $(v_i = v_j, v_k = v_l)$, $(v_i = v_j, v_k = -v_l)$, $(v_i = -v_j, v_k = v_l)$ and $(v_i = -v_j, v_k = -v_l)$. If the iteration on four variables is not sufficient to conclude, we can proceed using 6 then 8, ..., then $2 * n$ variables. This gives us a generalized schema of the dilemma rule as depicted in Figure 3. The nice

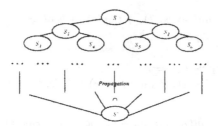

Fig. 3. The generalized dilemma rule

property of this algorithm is that the dilemma rule with four variables v_i, v_j, v_k and v_l with the restriction that $v_j = v_l = \top$ is sufficient to find most of the tautologies occurring in formal verification.

3   Formalization of the Algorithm

3.1   Triplets

To define triplets in Coq we first need a notion of signed variables. For this, we introduce the type rZ with two constructors on *nat*: + and -. We also take the convention that $\top$ is represented by +0 and $\bot$ by -0. On rZ, we define the usual operations: complement $(-)$, absolute value $(|\,|)$ and an order $<$ such that $i < j$ if and only if $|i| < |j|$.

A triplet is a set of three signed variables and a binary operation. We define the new type *triplet* with the only constructor `Triplet`:

Inductive *triplet* : *Set* :=
    `Triplet` : $rBoolOp \rightarrow rZ \rightarrow rZ \rightarrow rZ \rightarrow triplet$

where $rBoolOp$ is an enumerate type containing the two elements `rAnd` and `rEq`. In the following we use the usual pretty-printing convention for triplets: (`Triplet rAnd` i j k) and (`Triplet rEq` i j k) are written as $i := j \,\&\, k$ and $i := j = k$ respectively.

In order to define an evaluation on triplets, we first need to define an evaluation on rZ as:

Definition *rZEval* : $(nat \rightarrow bool) \rightarrow rZ \rightarrow bool$:=
    λf: $nat \rightarrow bool.\ \lambda r$: rZ.
       Cases r **of**
          $(+\ n) \Longrightarrow (f\ n)$
          $|\ (-\ n) \Longrightarrow \neg(f\ n)$
       end.

For the triplet we simply check that the first variable is equal to the result of applying the boolean operation to the other two variables:

Definition $tZEval: (nat \rightarrow bool) \rightarrow triplet \rightarrow bool :=$
$\quad \lambda f: nat \rightarrow bool. \lambda t: triplet.$
$\quad\quad$ **Cases** t **of**
$\quad\quad\quad$ (**Triplet** $r \; v_1 \; v_2 \; v_3$) $\Longrightarrow$
$\quad\quad\quad\quad (rZEval \; v_1) = ((rBoolOpFun \; r) \; (rZEval \; v_2) \; (rZEval \; v_3))$
$\quad$ **end**.

where the function $rBoolOpFun$ maps elements of $rBoolOp$ into their corresponding boolean operation.

As the algorithm manipulates a list of triplets, we introduce the notion of
realizability: a valuation realizes a list of triplets if the evaluation of each triplet
in the list gives true:

Definition $realizeTriplets: (nat \rightarrow bool) \rightarrow (list \; triplet) \rightarrow Prop :=$
$\quad \lambda f: (nat \rightarrow bool). \lambda L: (list \; triplet). \forall t: triplet. \; t \; in \; L \Rightarrow (tZEval \; f \; t) = \top.$

Another interesting notion is the one of valid equation with respect to a list of
triplets. An equation $i = j$ is valid if for every valuation f that realizes a list of
triplets L, f gives the same value for i and j:

Definition $validEquation: (list \; triplet) \rightarrow rZ \rightarrow rZ \rightarrow Prop :=$
$\quad \lambda L: (list \; triplet). \lambda p, q: rZ. \forall f: (nat \rightarrow bool).$
$\quad (realizeTriplets \; f \; L) \Rightarrow (f \; 0) = \top \Rightarrow (rZEval \; f \; p) = (rZEval \; f \; q).$

The condition $(f \; 0) = \top$ is here to keep the convention that $(+\,0)$ represents $\top$.

Not every list of triplets corresponds to a boolean expression. To express the
notion of tautology on triplets we simply ask for the top variable of the generated
list to be evaluated to true:

Definition $tTautology: Expr \rightarrow Prop :=$
$\quad \lambda e: Expr.$
$\quad\quad$ **Cases** ($makeTriplets \; e$) **of**
$\quad\quad\quad (l, s) \Longrightarrow (validEquation \; l \; s \; \top)$
$\quad$ **end**.

where $Expr$ is the type representing boolean expressions and $makeTriplets$ is the
function that computes the list of triplets corresponding to a given expression
and its top variable. With this definition, we have the following theorem:

Theorem $TautoEquivtTauto:$
$\quad \forall e: Expr. (tautology \; e) \Longleftrightarrow (tTautology \; e).$

where the predicate $tautology$ defines the usual notion of tautology on boolean
expressions.

3.2   States

All the operations of checking and adding equations are done with respect to a
state. We have chosen to represent states as lists of pairs of signed variables.

Definition $State: Set := (list \; rZ * rZ).$

The inductive predicate $\sim$ defines when two variables are equal:

Inductive $\sim : State \to rZ \to rZ \to Prop :=$
$\quad \sim\!Ref : \forall a\colon rZ.\,\forall S\colon State.\,a \sim_S a$
$\mid \quad \sim\!In : \forall a, b\colon rZ.\,\forall S\colon State.\,(a, b)\,in\,S \Rightarrow a \sim_S b$
$\mid \quad \sim\!Sym : \forall a, b\colon rZ.\,\forall S\colon State.\,a \sim_S b \Rightarrow b \sim_S a$
$\mid \quad \sim\!Inv : \forall a, b\colon rZ.\,\forall S\colon State.\,a \sim_S b \Rightarrow -a \sim_S -b$
$\mid \quad \sim\!Trans : \forall a, b, c\colon rZ.\,\forall S\colon State.\,a \sim_S b \Rightarrow b \sim_S c \Rightarrow a \sim_S c$
$\mid \quad \sim\!Contr : \forall a, b, c\colon rZ.\,\forall S\colon State.\,a \sim_S -a \Rightarrow b \sim_S c.$

The logic of Coq is constructive. This means that the theorem $\forall P\colon Prop.\,P \vee \neg P$ is not valid. However, instances of this theorem can be proved. For example we have:

Theorem $stateDec\colon \forall S\colon State.\,\forall a, b\colon rZ.\,a \sim_S b \vee \neg(a \sim_S b).$

The property of being a contradictory state is defined as:

Definition $contradictory\colon State \to Prop := \lambda S\colon State.\,\exists a\colon rZ.\,a \sim_s -a.$

Note that from the definition of $\sim$, it follows that in a contradictory state all equalities are valid. Inclusion and equality on states are defined as:

Definition $\subset : State \to State \to Prop :=$
$\quad \lambda S_1, S_2\colon State.\,\forall a, b\colon rZ.\,a \sim_{S_1} b \Rightarrow a \sim_{S_2} b.$

Definition $\equiv : State \to State \to Prop := \lambda S_1, S_2\colon State.\,S_1 \subset S_2 \wedge S_2 \subset S_1.$

A valuation realizes a state if all the equations of the state are valid:

Definition $realizeState : (nat \to bool) \to State \to Prop :=$
$\quad \lambda f\colon nat \to bool.\,\lambda S\colon State.\,\forall a, b\colon rZ.\,(a, b)\,in\,S \Rightarrow (rZEval\,f\,a) = (rZEval\,f\,b).$

We also need to define two basic functions on states: union and intersection. The union of two states is simply the state given by the concatenation of the two lists. In the following we use the notation $(a, b)+S$ to denote $[(a, b)] \cup S$.

The intersection of two states is not the intersection of their lists[1]. The function that computes the intersection of S_1 and S_2 first generates the list L_1 of all non-trivial equations of S_1, i.e. all pairs (a,b) such that $a \sim_{S_1} b$ and $a \neq b$. Then, it removes the equations that are not valid in S_2 from L_1. The resulting list represents $S_1 \cap S_2$.

3.3 One-Step Propagation

We formalize the one-step propagation as an inductive predicate $\to$ whose definition is given in Appendix A. Note that $S_1 \to_t S_2$ only means that there exists a rule that produces S_2 from S_1 using the triplet t. Because $\to$ is defined as a predicate, no particular strategy of rule application is assumed. The relation $\to$ is compatible with the equality as defined in Section 3.2:

---

[1] For example, given the lists $[(1, 2); (2, 3)]$ and $[(1, 3)]$, their intersection as states is $[(1, 3)]$ while their intersection as lists is $[]$.

Theorem $\rightarrow \equiv Ex$:
$\quad \forall S_1, S_2, S_3$: *State*. $\forall t$: *triplet*.
$\quad\quad S_1 \rightarrow_t S_2 \Rightarrow S_1 \equiv S_3 \Rightarrow \exists S_4$: *State*. $S_3 \rightarrow_t S_4 \wedge S_4 \equiv S_2$.

Also a propagation only adds equations:

Theorem $\rightarrow \cup Ex$:
$\quad \forall S_1, S_2$: *State*. $\forall t$: *triplet*. $S_1 \rightarrow_t S_2 \Rightarrow \exists S_3$: *State*. $S_2 \equiv S_3 \cup S_1$.

A corollary of this last theorem is that a progatation always produces a bigger state:

Theorem $\rightarrow Incl$:
$\quad \forall S_1, S_2$: *State*. $\forall t$: *triplet*. $S_1 \rightarrow_t S_2 \Rightarrow S_1 \subset S_2$.

In a similar way we can prove that the relation behaves as a congruence:

Theorem $\rightarrow Congruent\,Ex$:
$\quad \forall S_1, S_2, S_3$: *State*. $\forall t$: *triplet*.
$\quad\quad S_1 \rightarrow_t S_2 \Rightarrow \exists S_4$: *State*. $(S_3 \cup S_1) \rightarrow_t S_4 \wedge S_4 \equiv (S_3 \cup S_2)$.

This gives us as a corollary that the relation is monotone:

Theorem $\rightarrow Monotone\,Ex$:
$\quad \forall S_1, S_2, S_3$: *State*. $\forall t$: *triplet*.
$\quad\quad S_1 \rightarrow_t S_3 \Rightarrow S_1 \subset S_2 \Rightarrow \exists S_4$: *State*. $S_2 \rightarrow_t S_4 \wedge S_3 \subset S_4$.

Another interesting property is that the relation is confluent:

Theorem $\rightarrow ConflEx$:
$\quad \forall t_1, t_2$: *triplet*. $\forall S_1, S_2, S_3$: *State*. $S_1 \rightarrow_{t_1} S_2 \Rightarrow S_1 \rightarrow_{t_2} S_3 \Rightarrow$
$\quad\quad \exists S_4, S_5$: *State*. $S_2 \rightarrow_{t_2} S_4 \wedge S_3 \rightarrow_{t_1} S_5 \wedge S_4 \equiv S_5$.

Note that to establish these properties we do not use the particular equations that are checked or added. All relations with a shape similar to the one of $\rightarrow$ would have these properties.

The first semantic property that we have proved is that preserving the realizability for the one-step propagation is equivalent in some sense to evaluating the triplet to $\top$:

Theorem *realizeStateEvalEquiv*:
$\quad \forall f$: *nat* $\rightarrow$ *bool*. $\forall S_1, S_2$: *State*. $\forall t$: *triplet*.
$\quad\quad (f\ 0) = \top \Rightarrow (realizeState\ f\ S_1) \Rightarrow S_1 \rightarrow_t S_2$
$\quad\quad\quad \Rightarrow ((realizeState\ f\ S_2) \iff (tEval\ f\ t) = \top)$.

Another key semantic property is that no matter which rule is applied, the resulting state is the same:

Theorem $\rightarrow Eq$:
$\quad \forall t$: *triplet*. $\forall S_1, S_2, S_3$: *State*. $S_1 \rightarrow_t S_2 \Rightarrow S_1 \rightarrow_t S_3 \Rightarrow S_2 \equiv S_3$.

Moreover, a triplet is essentially useful only once:

Theorem $\rightarrow Invol$:

$\forall t$: *triplet.* $\forall S_1, S_2, S_3, S_4$: *State.*
$\quad S_1 \rightarrow_t S_2 \Rightarrow S_2 \subset S_3 \Rightarrow S_3 \rightarrow_t S_4 \Rightarrow S_3 \equiv S_4.$

The proofs of the above theorems are not very deep and mostly involve exploring the twenty-one possible rules of one-step propagation.

3.4   Propagation

The propagation consists in iterating the one-step propagation. We take the reflexive transitive closure of $\rightarrow_t$:

Inductive $\rightarrow^*$: *State* $\rightarrow$ *(list triplet)* $\rightarrow$ *State* $\rightarrow$ *Prop* :=
$\quad \rightarrow^* Ref : \forall S_1, S_2$: *State.* $\forall L$: *(list triplet).* $S_1 \equiv S_2 \Rightarrow S_1 \rightarrow_L^* S_2$
$\mid \quad \rightarrow^* Trans : \forall S_1, S_2, S_3$: *State.* $\forall L$: *(list triplet).* $\forall t$: *triplet.*
$\qquad\qquad t\ in\ L \Rightarrow S_1 \rightarrow_t S_2 \Rightarrow S_2 \rightarrow_L^* S_3 \Rightarrow S_1 \rightarrow_L^* S_3.$

All the properties of the one-step propagation can be lifted to the propagation. The exception is the theorem about realizability which has a simple implication since the propagation might use a strict subset of the list of triplets:

Theorem *realizeStateEval**:

$\forall f$: *nat* $\rightarrow$ *bool.* $\forall S_1, S_2$: *State.* $\forall L$: *(list triplet).*
$\quad (f\ 0) = \top \Rightarrow (realizeState\ f\ S_1) \Rightarrow S_1 \rightarrow_L^* S_2$
$\qquad \Rightarrow (realizeTriplets\ f\ L) \Rightarrow (realizeState\ f\ S_2).$

Finally the property that a triplet is useful only once is captured by:

Theorem $\rightarrow^* TermEx$:

$\forall L$: *(list triplet).* $\forall S_1, S_2$: *State.* $S_1 \rightarrow_L^* S_2 \Rightarrow$
$\quad (S_1 \equiv S_2) \vee (\exists t$: *triplet.* $\exists S_3$: *State.* $t\ in\ L \wedge S_1 \rightarrow_t S_3 \wedge S_3 \rightarrow_{L-[t]}^* S_2).$

where $L - [t]$ denotes the list obtained by removing t from L.

3.5   The Dilemma Rule

As we did for propagation, the dilemma rule is non-deterministic and modeled by a predicate. Also, we allow an arbitrary (but finite) number of splits:

Inductive $\rightarrow^d$: *State* $\rightarrow$ *(list triplet)* $\rightarrow$ *State* $\rightarrow$ *Prop* :=
$\quad \rightarrow^d Ref : \forall S_1, S_2$: *State.* $\forall L$: *(list triplet).* $S_1 \rightarrow_L^* S_2 \Rightarrow S_1 \rightarrow_L^d S_2$
$\mid \quad \rightarrow^d Split : \forall a, b$: *rZ.* $\forall S_1, S_2, S_3, S_4$: *State.* $\forall L$: *(list triplet).* $\forall t$: *triplet.*
$\qquad (a, b)+S_1 \rightarrow_L^d S_2 \Rightarrow (a, -b)+S_1 \rightarrow_L^d S_3 \Rightarrow S_2 \cap S_3 \equiv S_4 \Rightarrow S_1 \rightarrow_L^d S_4.$

The relation $\rightarrow^d$ is compatible with the equality:

Theorem $\rightarrow^d \equiv$:

$\forall S_1, S_2, S_3, S_4$: *State.* $\forall L$: *(list triplet).*
$\quad S_1 \rightarrow_L^d S_2 \Rightarrow S_3 \equiv S_1 \Rightarrow S_4 \equiv S_2 \Rightarrow S_3 \rightarrow_L^d S_4.$

The same theorems about inclusion also hold:

Theorem $\rightarrow^d \cup Ex$:

$\quad \forall S_1, S_2\text{: State.}\, \forall L\text{: (list triplet).}\, S_1 \rightarrow^d_L S_2 \Rightarrow \exists S_3\text{: State.}\, S_2 \equiv S_3 \cup S_1.$

Theorem $\rightarrow^d Incl$:

$\quad \forall S_1, S_2\text{: State.}\, \forall L\text{: (list triplet).}\, S_1 \rightarrow^d_L S_2 \Rightarrow S_1 \subset S_2.$

Unfortunately as we only have $(S_1 \cap S_2) \cup S_3 \subset (S_1 \cup S_3) \cap (S_2 \cup S_3)$ and not $(S_1 \cap S_2) \cup S_3 \equiv (S_1 \cup S_3) \cap (S_2 \cup S_3)$, the relation is not a congruence. A simple way to recapture this congruence would be to define $\rightarrow^d$ as:

Inductive $\rightarrow^d : State \rightarrow (list\ triplet) \rightarrow State \rightarrow Prop :=$

$\quad \rightarrow^d Ref : \forall S_1, S_2\text{: State.}\, \forall L\text{: (list triplet).}\, S_1 \rightarrow^*_L S_2 \Rightarrow S_1 \rightarrow^d_L S_2$

$\mid \quad \rightarrow^d Split : \forall a, b\text{: } rZ.\, \forall S_1, S_2, S_3, S_4\text{: State.}\, \forall L\text{: (list triplet).}\, \forall t\text{: triplet.}$

$\quad\quad (a, b)\text{+}S_1 \rightarrow^d_L S_2 \Rightarrow (a, -b)\text{+}S_1 \rightarrow^d_L S_3 \Rightarrow S_1 \subset S_4 \subset (S_2 \cap S_3) \Rightarrow S_1 \rightarrow^d_L S_4.$

but this would mean considering the merging of the two branches as a non-deterministic operation, so we prefer our initial definition. Even though the relation is not a congruence, it is monotone:

Theorem $\rightarrow^d Monotone$:

$\quad \forall L\text{: (list triplet).}\, \forall S_1, S_2, S_3\text{: State.}$

$\quad S_1 \rightarrow^d_L S_3 \Rightarrow S_1 \subset S_2 \Rightarrow \exists S_4\text{: State.}\, S_2 \rightarrow^d_L S_4 \wedge S_3 \subset S_4.$

and it is also confluent:

Theorem $\rightarrow^d Confluent$:

$\quad \forall L\text{: (list triplet).}\, \forall S_1, S_2, S_3\text{: State.}$

$\quad S_1 \rightarrow^d_L S_2 \Rightarrow S_1 \rightarrow^d_L S_3 \Rightarrow \exists S_4\text{: State.}\, S_2 \rightarrow^d_L S_4 \wedge S_3 \rightarrow^d_L S_4.$

The last property we have proved about the dilemma rule is that it preserves realizability:

Theorem $realizeStateEval^d$:

$\quad \forall f\text{: } nat \rightarrow bool.\, \forall S_1, S_2\text{: State.}\, \forall L\text{: (list triplet).}$

$\quad\quad (f\ 0) = \top \Rightarrow (realizeState\ f\ S_1) \Rightarrow S_1 \rightarrow^d_L S_2$

$\quad\quad\quad \Rightarrow (realizeTriplets\ f\ L) \Rightarrow (realizeState\ f\ S_2).$

3.6   Stålmarck's Algorithm

Stålmarck's algorithm is the reflexive transitive closure of the dilemma rule:

Inductive $\rightarrow^s : State \rightarrow (list\ triplet) \rightarrow State \rightarrow Prop :=$

$\quad \rightarrow^s Ref : \forall S_1, S_2\text{: State.}\, \forall L\text{: (list triplet).}\, S_1 \equiv S_2 \Rightarrow S_1 \rightarrow^s_L S_2$

$\mid \quad \rightarrow^s Trans : \forall S_1, S_2, S_3\text{: State.}\, \forall L\text{: (list triplet).}$

$\quad\quad\quad S_1 \rightarrow^d_L S_2 \Rightarrow S_2 \rightarrow^s_L S_3 \Rightarrow S_1 \rightarrow^s_L S_3.$

As for $\rightarrow^d$ we get the standard properties:

Theorem $\rightarrow^s \equiv$:

$\quad \forall S_1, S_2, S_3, S_4\text{: State.}\, \forall L\text{: (list triplet).}$

$\quad S_1 \rightarrow^s_L S_2 \Rightarrow S_3 \equiv S_1 \Rightarrow S_4 \equiv S_2 \Rightarrow S_3 \rightarrow^s_L S_4.$

Theorem $\to^s \cup Ex$:

   $\forall S_1, S_2$: *State*. $\forall L$: (*list triplet*). $S_1 \to^s_L S_2 \Rightarrow \exists S_3$: *State*. $S_2 \equiv S_3 \cup S_1$.

Theorem $\to^s Incl$:

   $\forall S_1, S_2$: *State*. $\forall L$: (*list triplet*). $S_1 \to^s_L S_2 \Rightarrow S_1 \subset S_2$.

Theorem $\to^s Monotone$:

   $\forall L$: (*list triplet*). $\forall S_1, S_2, S_3$: *State*.

     $S_1 \to^s_L S_3 \Rightarrow S_1 \subset S_2 \Rightarrow \exists S_4$: *State*. $S_2 \to^s_L S_4 \wedge S_3 \subset S_4$.

Theorem $\to^s Confluent$:

   $\forall L$: (*list triplet*). $\forall S_1, S_2, S_3$: *State*.

     $S_1 \to^s_L S_2 \Rightarrow S_1 \to^s_L S_3 \Rightarrow \exists S_4$: *State*. $S_2 \to^s_L S_4 \wedge S_3 \to^s_L S_4$.

Theorem $realizeStateEval^s$:

   $\forall f$: *nat* $\to$ *bool*. $\forall S_1, S_2$: *State*. $\forall L$: (*list triplet*).

     $(f\ 0) = \top \Rightarrow (realizeState\ f\ S_1) \Rightarrow S_1 \to^s_L S_2$

       $\Rightarrow (realizeTriplets\ f\ L) \Rightarrow (realizeState\ f\ S_2)$.

Only the last property is relevant for the correctness of the algorithm. From the theorem *realizeStateEval*^{s}, the following property is easily derived:

Theorem *stålmarckValidEquation*:

   $\forall L$: (*list triplet*). $\forall a, b$: *rZ*. $\forall S$: *State*.

     $[(a, -b)] \to^s_L S \Rightarrow (contradictory\ S) \Rightarrow (validEquation\ L\ a\ b)$.

Once we have this theorem, we can glue together all the theorems about tautology to get the correctness:

Theorem *stålmarckCorrect*:

   $\forall e$: *Expr*. $\forall S$: *State*.

     Cases (*makeTriplets e*) **of**

       $(l, s) \Longrightarrow [(s, \bot)] \to^s_l S \Rightarrow (contradictory\ S) \Rightarrow (Tautology\ e)$

     end.

Another property that has been formalized is the completeness of the algorithm:

Theorem *stålmarckComplete*:

   $\forall e$: *Expr*. (*Tautology e*) $\Rightarrow \exists S$: *State*.

     Cases (*makeTriplets e*) **of**

       $(l, s) \Longrightarrow [(s, \bot)] \to^s_l S \wedge (contradictory\ S)$

     end.

This is proved by showing that if e is a tautology, we obtain a contradiction by applying the dilemma rule on all the variables in the list of triplets. The program extracted from the constructive proof of the theorem *stålmarckComplete* would thus be comparable to the one that computes the truth table.

4   Trace

Our relation $\to^s$ contains all possible execution paths. The choice of the rules, the choice of the triplets and the choice of the variables for the dilemma rule are not explicitly given. A natural question arises on what an explicit implementation should produce to provide a certificate that it has reached a contradiction. Of course, a complete trace of the execution (states, rules, triplets, variables) is a valid certificate. In fact, we can do much better and keep only the triplets that have been used and the variables on which the dilemma rule has been applied. We define our notion of trace as:

Inductive *Trace*: *Set* :=
    emptyTrace : *Trace*
| tripletTrace : *triplet* → *Trace*
| seqTrace : *Trace* → *Trace* → *Trace*
| dilemmaTrace : *rZ* → *rZ* → *Trace* → *Trace* → *Trace*.

The semantics is given by the following predicate that evaluates a trace:

Inductive *evalTrace*: *State* → *Trace* → *State* → *Prop* :=
    emptyEval : $\forall S_1, S_2$: *State*. $S_1 \equiv S_2 \Rightarrow$ (*evalTrace* S_1 emptyTrace S_2)
| *tripletEval* : $\forall S_1, S_2$: *State*. $\forall t$: *triplet*.
    $S_1 \rightarrow_t S_2 \Rightarrow$ (*evalTrace* S_1 (tripletTrace t) S_2)
| *seqEval* : $\forall S_1, S_2, S_3$: *State*. $\forall T_1, T_2$: *Trace*.
    (*evalTrace* S_1 T_1 S_2) $\Rightarrow$ (*evalTrace* S_2 T_2 S_3)
    $\Rightarrow$ (*evalTrace* S_1 (seqTrace T_1 T_2) S_3)
| *dilemmaEval* : $\forall S_1, S_2, S_3, S_4$: *State*. $\forall a, b$: *rZ*. $\forall T_1, T_2$: *Trace*.
    (*evalTrace* (a, b)+S_1 T_1 S_2) $\Rightarrow$ (*evalTrace* $(a, -b)$+S_1 T_2 S_3)
    $\Rightarrow S_2 \cap S_3 \equiv S_4 \Rightarrow$ (*evalTrace* S_1 (dilemmaTrace a b T_1 T_2) S_4).

The fact that a trace determines a unique computation up to state equality is asserted by the following theorem:

Theorem *evalTraceEq*:
  $\forall S_1, S_2, S_3, S_4$: *State*. $\forall T$: *Trace*.
  (*evalTrace* S_1 T S_2) $\Rightarrow$ (*evalTrace* S_3 T S_4) $\Rightarrow S_1 \equiv S_3 \Rightarrow S_2 \equiv S_4$.

Conversely it is possible to get a trace from any non-deterministic computation:

Theorem *stålmarckExTrace*:
  $\forall S_1, S_2$: *State*. $\forall L$: (*list triplet*).
  $S_1 \rightarrow_L^s S_2 \Rightarrow \exists T$: *Trace*. (*evalTrace* S_1 T S_2) $\wedge T$ *in* L.

The second condition requires all the triplets in the trace T to be in L.

5 Implementation

Because of space limitation, we are only going to sketch the different components of the implementation. In particular, we do not make explicit the rules of sign using the notation $\pm v$ to denote either +v or -v.

5.1 Memory

We represent non-contradictory states using functional arrays. Appendix B lists the different axioms we are using in our development. The size of the array is

$maxN$, the natural number that exceeds by at least one all the variables in the list of triplets. The type of the elements of the array is defined as follows:

Inductive vM: Set :=
    ref : $rZ \rightarrow vM$
    class : $(list\ rZ) \rightarrow vM$

The value of the location i depends on the smallest element a such that $+i \sim a$. If $i \neq |a|$, the location i contains the value (**ref** a). Otherwise, it contains the value (**class** L), where L is the ordered list of the elements b such that $+i \sim b$ and $|b| \neq i$. All the constraints about the different values of the array are concentrated in the predicate *WellFormed*:

Definition Mem: Set := $\{r : (Array\ maxN\ vM)|\ (WellFormed\ maxN\ r)\}$.

Checking equality Given a memory m, it is easy to build a function min_m that returns for any element a of rZ the smallest b such that $a \sim_m b$. To check the equality between a and b in m, it is then sufficient to compare $(min_m\ a)$ and $(min_m\ b)$.

Adding an equation Given a memory m, it is also easy to build a function l_m that returns for any element a of rZ the ordered list of all the elements b such that $a \sim_m b$. The result of an addition to a memory is a triple $(Mem, bool, (list\ rZ))$. Since a memory can only represent a non-contradictory state, the boolean is set to true if the addition of the equation gives a contradiction, to false otherwise. The absolute values of the elements of the list are the locations of the arrays that have been modified by the update. To perform the addition of $a = b$ to m, we first compare $(min_m\ a)$ and $(min_m\ b)$. If $(min_m\ a) = (min_m\ b)$, the result is $(m, \bot, [])$. If $(min_m\ a) = -(min_m\ b)$, the result is $(m, \top, [])$. If $(min_m\ a) < (min_m\ b)$, the result is $(m', \bot, [(min_m\ a)] \cup (l_m\ b))$ where m' is obtained from m by setting the locations corresponding to the elements of $(l_m\ b)$ to (**ref** $\pm (min_m\ a)$) and the location $|(min_m\ a)|$ to (**class** $(\pm(l_m\ a) \cup \pm(l_m\ b))$). The case where $(min_m\ b) < (min_m\ a)$ is symmetric to the previous one.

Intersection The function that computes the intersection takes three memories m_1, m_2, m_3 and two lists d_1, d_2 under the hypothesis that $m_1 \subset m_2$, $m_1 \subset m_3$, d_1 is the difference list between m_1 and m_2, and d_2 is the difference list between m_1 and m_3. It returns a 4-tuple (m_1', m_2', m_3', d') such that $m_1' = m_2 \cap m_3$, $m_1' \equiv m_2' \equiv m_3'$ and d' is the difference list between m_1 and m_1'. It proceeds by successive additions to m_1 of equations $a_i = b_i$ where the a_i are the elements of $d_1 \cap d_2$ and the b_i are the smallest element such that $a_i \sim_{m_2} b_i$ and $a_i \sim_{m_3} b_i$.

5.2   Propagation

The implementation of the one-step propagation is a composition of checking equalities and adding equations. It has the type $Mem \rightarrow triplet \rightarrow (Mem, bool, (list\ rZ))$. To do the propagation, we need to define a way to select triplets. As the difference lists give the variables whose values have been modified, triplets containing these variables are good candidate for applying one-step propagation. The type of the propagation function is $Mem \rightarrow (list\ rZ) \rightarrow (Mem, bool, (list\ rZ))$. The difference lists resulting from the application of the one-step propagation are then recursively used for selecting triplets. This way of propagating terminates since we cannot add infinitely many equations to a memory.

5.3   Dilemma

We have implemented only the instances of the dilemma rule that are of practical use: *dilemma1*, the dilemma with $(a, \top)$ for an arbitrary a, and *dilemma2*, the dilemma with $((a,\ \top), (b,\ \top))$ for arbitrary a and b. To perform the first one, we use three memories, one for each branch and one to compute the intersection. For the second one we use an extra memory. The first memory m_1 is used to compute each branch iteratively. The intermediate result is stored in the second memory m_2. At the end of each iteration we compute the intersection of m_1 and m_2 using the third memory m_3. We then switch m_2 and m_3 and use the last memory to reset m_1 and m_3 before proceeding to the next branch. Note that a dilemma with any number of variables could be implemented in the same way using four memories.

5.4   Stålmarck

At this stage, we have to decide the strategy to pick up variables for the application of the dilemma rules. Our heuristics are very simple and could be largely improved. We first add the initial equation and propagate. If no contradiction is reached, we iterate the application of the function *dilemma1* using minimal variables starting from +1 to $+maxN$. We perform this operation till a contradiction is reached or no more information is gained. In the second case, we do a double iteration with a, b such that $0 < a < b < maxN$ using the function *dilemma2*. Implementing this naïve strategy is straightforward and gives us the function *doStal* for which we have proved the following property:

Theorem *doStalCorrect*:
  $\forall e: Expr. (doStal\ e) = \top \Rightarrow (Tautology\ e)$.

Note that it is the only property that we have proved for our implementation and clearly it is not sufficient. An algorithm that always returns $\bot$ would satisfy the above property. While our implementation is not complete since we use dilemma rules only up to four variables, we could prove some liveness property. This is feasible and would require to formalize the notion of n-hard formulae as described in [10].

Problem	dilemma	variables	connectives	hand-coded	balanced trees	tagged arrays
puz030_1	1	25	221	0.04 s	0.07 s	0.05 s
syn072_1	1	30	518	0.04 s	0.17 s	0.14 s
dk17_be	1	63	327	1.58 s	2.76 s	1.89 s
ssa0432_003	1	435	2363	6.38 m	47 s	42 s
jnh211	1	100	3887	9.47 m	9.36 m	9.14 m
aim50.1.6no.1	2	50	238	2.38 m	31.98 s	21.55 s
counter_be	2	18	290	11.62 s	6.76 s	4.24 s
misg_be	2	108	279	1.07 m	1.18 m	52.74 s
dubois20	2	60	479	7.59 m	7.95 s	5.98 s
add2_be	2	144	407	4.00 m	1.44m	1.13 m

Fig. 4. Some benchmarks on a Pentium 450

5.5   Benchmark

Once the implementation has been proved correct in Coq, the extraction mechanism [9] enables us to get a functional Ocaml [8] program. The result is 1400 lines long. To be able to run such a program, we need to provide an implementation of the arrays that satisfies the axioms of Appendix B. A first possibility is to use balanced trees to implement functional arrays. A second possibility is to use tagged arrays, since we have taken a special care in the implementation in order to be able to use destructive arrays. The tag in the array prohibits illegal accesses. For example, the set function for such arrays looks like:

```
let set tar m v = match tar with
  (ar,tag) -> if ((!tag) = true) then
                (tag := false; Array.set ar m v;(ar,ref(true)))
              else raise Prohibited_access;;
```

If the program terminates without exception, the result is correct. Table 4 gives some execution times on standard examples taken from [5]. For each problem, we give which level of dilemma rules is needed, the number of variables, the number of connectives and compare three versions of the algorithm: the algorithm is directly hand-coded in Ocaml with slightly different heuristics, our certified version with balanced trees and with tagged arrays. The time includes parsing the formula and generating triplets. Even though the performance of an implementation largely depends on the heuristics, our certified version seems comparable with the hand-coded one and the one presented by John Harrison in [5]. However, we are aware that in order to get a realistic implementation, much more work on optimizations and heuristics has to be done. Prover 4.0, the propositional prover of Prover Technology, takes at most two tenth of a second to conclude on the examples given in Table 4.

6   Conclusion

We hope that what we have presented shows that current theorem proving technology can be effectively used to reason about algorithms and their implementations. We have presented a formalization of Stålmarck's algorithm that includes formal proofs of the main properties of the algorithm. Then, we have proposed a format of execution traces and proved that it is adequate. Such certificates are important in practice. They represent a simple way of increasing the confidence in the correctness of specific results. Prover Technology commercializes the Prover Plug-In product for integration into CASE and EDA tools. Prover Plug-In is based on the Stalmarck's method, and supports a trace format [7] and an associated trace/proof checker. John Harrison [5] also presents a tactic based on Stålmarck's method for HOL [4] using traces: the search is handled by a program that generates traces, then, the prover uses these traces to build safe derivations of theorems. Finally, the effort for deriving a certified implementation is orthogonal to the one on traces since the correctness of results is ensured once and for all.

From the point of view of theorem proving, the most satisfying aspect of this work is the formalization of the algorithm. It is a relatively concise development of 3200 lines including 80 definitions and 200 theorems. The proof of correctness of the implementation is less satisfying. Proving the basic operations (addition and intersection) took 2/3 of the effort and represents more than 6000 lines of Coq. This does not reflect the effective difficulty of the task. The main reason why deriving these basic operations has been so tedious is that most of the proofs involves a fair amount of case-splitting. For example, proving properties of the addition often requires to take into account the signs and the relative value of the components of the equation. We have neither managed to abstract our theorems enough nor got enough automation so that we do not have to operate on the different cases manually. Moreover, the fact that we handle imperative features such as arrays in a functional way is a bit awkward. We plan in a near future to use improvements such those presented in [3] to reason directly on imperative programs inside Coq. Finally while the overall experience is quite positive, we strongly believe that for this kind of formalization to become common practice, an important effort has to be done in order to make proofs scripts readable by non-specialists. In that respect, recent efforts such as [2,11,12,13] seem very promising.

References

1. Yves Bertot, Gilles Dowek, André Hirschowitz, Christine Paulin, and Laurent Théry, editors. *Theorem Proving in Higher Order Logics: 12th International Conference, TPHOLs'99*, number 1690 in LNCS, Nice, France, 1999. Springer-Verlag.
2. Yann Coscoy, Gilles Kahn, and Laurent Théry. Extracting text from proofs. In *Typed Lambda Calculus and its Applications*, volume 902 of *LNCS*, pages 109–123. Springer-Verlag, 1995.

3. J.-C. Filliâtre. Proof of Imperative Programs in Type Theory. In *International Workshop, TYPES '98, Kloster Irsee, Germany*, volume 1657 of *LNCS*. Springer-Verlag, March 1998.

4. Michael J. C. Gordon and Thomas F. Melham. *Introduction to HOL : a theorem proving environment for higher-order logic*. Cambridge University Press, 1993.

5. J. Harrison. Stålmarck's algorithm as a HOL derived rule. In Joakim von Wright, Jim Grundy, and John Harrison, editors, *Theorem Proving in Higher Order Logics: 9th International Conference, TPHOLs'96*, number 1125 in LNCS, pages 221–234, Turku, Finland, August 1996. Springer-Verlag.

6. Gérard Huet, Gilles Kahn, and Christine Paulin-Mohring. The Coq Proof Assistant: A Tutorial: Version 6.1. Technical Report 204, INRIA, 1997.

7. Arndt Jonasson. Proof logging, definition of the log format. Prover Technology, December 1997.

8. Xavier Leroy. Objective Caml. Available at http://pauillac.inria.fr/ocaml/, 1997.

9. Christine Paulin-Mohring and Benjamin Werner. Synthesis of ML programs in the system Coq. *Journal of Symbolic Computation*, 15(5-6):607–640, 1993.

10. Mary Sheeran and Gunnar Stålmarck. A tutorial on Stålmarck's proof procedure for propositional logic. In *FMCAD '98*, volume 1522 of *LNCS*. Springer-Verlag, November 1998.

11. Don Syme. Three Tactic Theorem Proving. In Bertot et al. [1], pages 203–220.

12. Markus Wenzel. A Generic Interpretative Approach to Readable Formal Proof Documents. In Bertot et al. [1], pages 167–184.

13. Vincent Zammit. On the Implementation of an Extensible Declarative Proof Language. In Bertot et al. [1], pages 185–202.

A   The Predicate for One-Step Propagation

$\textbf{Inductive} \to = : State \to triplet \to State :=$

$\to_{\&_{p-q}} : \forall p, q, r: rZ. \forall S: State. \, p \sim_S -q \Rightarrow S \to_{p:=q\,\&\,r} (q, \top) + (r, \bot) + S$

$| \quad \to_{\&_{p-r}} : \forall p, q, r: rZ. \forall S: State. \, p \sim_S -r \Rightarrow S \to_{p:=q\,\&\,r} (q, \bot) + (r, \top) + S$

$| \quad \to_{\&_{qr}} : \forall p, q, r: rZ. \forall S: State. \, q \sim_S r \;\;\Rightarrow S \to_{p:=q\,\&\,r} (p, r) + S$

$| \quad \to_{\&_{q-r}} : \forall p, q, r: rZ. \forall S: State. \, q \sim_S -r \Rightarrow S \to_{p:=q\,\&\,r} (p, \bot) + S$

$| \quad \to_{\&_{p\top}} : \forall p, q, r: rZ. \forall S: State. \, p \sim_S \top \;\Rightarrow S \to_{p:=q\,\&\,r} (q, \top) + (r, \top) + S$

$| \quad \to_{\&_{q\top}} : \forall p, q, r: rZ. \forall S: State. \, q \sim_S \top \;\Rightarrow S \to_{p:=q\,\&\,r} (p, r) + S$

$| \quad \to_{\&_{q\bot}} : \forall p, q, r: rZ. \forall S: State. \, q \sim_S \bot \;\Rightarrow S \to_{p:=q\,\&\,r} (p, \bot) + S$

$| \quad \to_{\&_{r\top}} : \forall p, q, r: rZ. \forall S: State. \, r \sim_S \top \;\Rightarrow S \to_{p:=q\,\&\,r} (p, q) + S$

$| \quad \to_{\&_{r\bot}} : \forall p, q, r: rZ. \forall S: State. \, r \sim_S \bot \;\Rightarrow S \to_{p:=q\,\&\,r} (p, \bot) + S$

$| \quad \to_{=_{pq}} : \forall p, q, r: rZ. \forall S: State. \, p \sim_S q \;\;\Rightarrow S \to_{p:=q=r} (r, \top) + S$

$| \quad \to_{=_{p-q}} : \forall p, q, r: rZ. \forall S: State. \, p \sim_S -q \Rightarrow S \to_{p:=q=r} (r, \bot) + S$

$| \quad \to_{=_{pr}} : \forall p, q, r: rZ. \forall S: State. \, p \sim_S r \;\;\Rightarrow S \to_{p:=q=r} (q, \top) + S$

$| \quad \to_{=_{p-r}} : \forall p, q, r: rZ. \forall S: State. \, p \sim_S -r \Rightarrow S \to_{p:=q=r} (q, \bot) + S$

$| \quad \to_{=_{qr}} : \forall p, q, r: rZ. \forall S: State. \, q \sim_S r \;\;\Rightarrow S \to_{p:=q=r} (p, \top) + S$

$| \quad \to_{=_{q-r}} : \forall p, q, r: rZ. \forall S: State. \, q \sim_S -r \Rightarrow S \to_{p:=q=r} (p, \bot) + S$

$\mid \quad \to_{=_p\top} \; : \forall p, q, r\text{:}\ rZ.\ \forall S\text{:}\ State.\ p \sim_S \top \;\Rightarrow\; S \to_{p:=q=r} (q,r)\text{)}+S$

$\mid \quad \to_{=_p\perp} \; : \forall p, q, r\text{:}\ rZ.\ \forall S\text{:}\ State.\ p \sim_S \perp \;\Rightarrow\; S \to_{p:=q=r} (q,-r)+S$

$\mid \quad \to_{=_q\top} \; : \forall p, q, r\text{:}\ rZ.\ \forall S\text{:}\ State.\ q \sim_S \top \;\Rightarrow\; S \to_{p:=q=r} (p,r)+S$

$\mid \quad \to_{=_q\perp} \; : \forall p, q, r\text{:}\ rZ.\ \forall S\text{:}\ State.\ q \sim_S \perp \;\Rightarrow\; S \to_{p:=q=r} (p,-r)+S$

$\mid \quad \to_{=_r\top} \; : \forall p, q, r\text{:}\ rZ.\ \forall S\text{:}\ State.\ r \sim_S \top \;\Rightarrow\; S \to_{p:=q=r} (p,q)+S$

$\mid \quad \to_{=_r\perp} \; : \forall p, q, r\text{:}\ rZ.\ \forall S\text{:}\ State.\ r \sim_S \perp \;\Rightarrow\; S \to_{p:=q=r} (p,-q)+S.$

B   Axioms for Arrays

Parameter *get*: $\forall n\text{:}\ nat.\ \forall A\text{:}\ Set.\ \forall Ar\text{:}\ (Array\ n\ A).\ \forall m\text{:}\ nat.\ \forall H\text{:}\ m < n.\ A.$

Parameter *set*: $\forall n\text{:}\ nat.\ \forall A\text{:}\ Set.\ \forall Ar\text{:}\ (Array\ n\ A).\ \forall m\text{:}\ nat.\ \forall H\text{:}\ m < n.$
$\forall v\text{:}\ A.\ (Array\ n\ A).$

Parameter *gen*: $\forall n\text{:}\ nat.\ \forall A\text{:}\ Set.\ \forall f\text{:}\ nat \to A.\ (Array\ n\ A).$

Axiom $setDef_1$: $\forall n\text{:}\ nat.\ \forall A\text{:}\ Set.\ \forall Ar\text{:}\ (Array\ n\ A).\ \forall m\text{:}\ nat.\ \forall H\text{:}\ m < n.$
$\forall v\text{:}\ A.\ (get\ n\ A\ (set\ n\ A\ Ar\ m\ H\ v)\ m\ H) = v.$

Axiom $setDef_2$: $\forall n\text{:}\ nat.\ \forall A\text{:}\ Set.\ \forall Ar\text{:}\ (Array\ n\ A).\ \forall m_1, m_2\text{:}\ nat.$
$\forall H_1\text{:}\ m_1 < n.\ \forall H_2\text{:}\ m_2 < n.\ \forall H\text{:}\ m < n.\ \forall v\text{:}\ A.\ m_1 \neq m_2 \Rightarrow$
$(get\ n\ A\ (set\ n\ A\ Ar\ m_1\ H_1\ v)\ m_2\ H_2) = (get\ n\ A\ Ar\ m_2\ H_2).$

Axiom *genDef*: $\forall n\text{:}\ nat.\ \forall A\text{:}\ Set.\ \forall m\text{:}\ nat.\ \forall f\text{:}\ nat \to A.\ \forall H\text{:}\ m < n.$
$(get\ n\ A\ (gen\ n\ A\ f)\ m\ H) = (f\ m).$

Axiom *getIrr*: $\forall n\text{:}\ nat.\ \forall A\text{:}\ Set.\ \forall Ar\text{:}\ (Array\ n\ A).\ \forall m_1, m_2\text{:}\ nat.$
$\forall H_1\text{:}\ m_1 < n.\ \forall H_2\text{:}\ m_2 < n.\ m_1 = m_2 \Rightarrow$
$(get\ n\ A\ Ar\ m_1\ H_1) = (get\ n\ A\ Ar\ m_2\ H_2).$

Axiom *setIrr*: $\forall n\text{:}\ nat.\ \forall A\text{:}\ Set.\ \forall Ar\text{:}\ (Array\ n\ A).\ \forall m_1, m_2\text{:}\ nat.$
$\forall H_1\text{:}\ m_1 < n.\ \forall H_2\text{:}\ m_2 < n.\ \forall v\text{:}\ A.\ m_1 = m_2 \Rightarrow$
$(set\ n\ A\ Ar\ m_1\ H_1\ v) = (set\ n\ A\ Ar\ m_2\ H_2\ v).$

TAS — A Generic Window Inference System

Christoph Lüth[1] and Burkhart Wolff[2]

[1] FB 3 — Mathematik und Informatik, Universität Bremen
cxl@informatik.uni-bremen.de
[2] Institut für Informatik, Albert-Ludwigs-Universität Freiburg
wolff@informatik.uni-freiburg.de

Abstract. This paper presents work on technology for transformational proof and program development, as used by window inference calculi and transformation systems. The calculi are characterised by a certain class of theorems in the underlying logic. Our transformation system TAS compiles these rules to concrete deduction support, complete with a graphical user interface with command-language-free user interaction by gestures like drag&drop and proof-by-pointing, and a development management for transformational proofs. It is *generic* in the sense that it is completely independent of the particular window inference or transformational calculus, and can be instantiated to many different ones; three such instantiations are presented in the paper.

1 Introduction

Tools supporting formal program development should present proofs and program developments in the form in which they are most easily understood by the user, and should not require the user to adapt to the particular form of presentation as implemented by the system. Here, a serious clash of cultures prevails which hampers the wider usage of formal methods: theorem provers employ presentations stemming from their roots in symbolic logic (e.g. Isabelle uses natural deduction), whereas engineers are more likely to be used to proofs by transformation as in calculus. As a way out of this dilemma, a number of systems have been developed to support *transformational development*. However, many of these systems such as CIP [3], KIDS [21] or PROSPECTRA [12] suffered from a lack of proof support and proven correctness. On the other hand, a variety of calculi have been developed which allow formal proof in a transformational way and are proven correct [8,9,10,28,11,2], some even with a graphical user interface [14,6]. However, what has been lacking is a systematic, generic and reusable way to obtain a user-friendly tool implementing transformational reasoning, with an open system architecture capable of coping with the fast changes in technology in user interfaces, theorem provers and formal methods. Reusability of components is crucial, since we hope that the considerable task of developing appropriate GUIs for formal method tools can be shared with other research groups.

In [15], we have proposed an open architecture to build graphical user interfaces for theorem provers in a functional language; here, we instantiate this

J. Harrison and M. Aagaard (Eds.): TPHOLs 2000, LNCS 1869, pp. 406–423, 2000.

architecture with a generic transformation system which implements transformational calculi (geared towards refinement proofs) on top of an LCF-like prover.
By *generic*, we mean that the system takes a high-level characterisation of a
refinement calculus and returns a user-friendly, formally correct transformation
or window inference system. The system can be used for various object logics
and formal methods (a property for which Isabelle is particularly well suited as
a basis). The instantiation of the system is very straightforward once the formal
method (including the refinement relation) has been encoded. Various aspects
of this overall task have been addressed before, such as logical engines, window-
inference packages and prototypical GUIs. In contrast, TAS is an *integrated*
solution, bringing existing approaches into one technical framework, and filling
missing links like a generic pretty-printer producing markups in mathematical
text.

This paper is structured as follows: in Sect. 2 we give an introduction to window inference, surveying previous work and presenting the basic concepts. We
explain how the formulation of the basic concepts in terms of ML theorems leads
to the implementation of TAS. We demonstrate the versatility of our approach
in Sects. 3, 4 and 5 by showing examples of classical transformational program
development, for process-oriented refinement proofs and for data-oriented refinement proofs. Sect. 6 finishes with conclusions and an outlook.

2   A Generic Scheme of Window Inference

Window inference [18], structured calculational proof [8,1,2] and transformational hierarchical reasoning [11] are closely related formalisations of proof by
transformation. In this paper, we will use the format of [1], although we will
refer to it as window inference.

2.1   An Introduction to Window Inference

As motivating example, consider the proof for $\vdash (A \wedge B \Rightarrow C) \Rightarrow (B \wedge A \Rightarrow C)$.
In natural deduction, a proof would look like (in the notation of [27]; we assume
that the reader is roughly familiar with derivations like this):

$$
\cfrac{\cfrac{\cfrac{[B \wedge A]^1}{A} \wedge E \quad \cfrac{[B \wedge A]^1}{B} \wedge E}{A \wedge B} \wedge I \quad [A \wedge B \Rightarrow C]^2}{\cfrac{\cfrac{C}{B \wedge A \Rightarrow C} \Rightarrow I_1}{(A \wedge B \Rightarrow C) \Rightarrow (B \wedge A \Rightarrow C)} \Rightarrow I_2} \Rightarrow E
\tag{1}
$$

The following equivalent calculational proof is far more compact. We start
with $B \wedge A \Rightarrow C$. In the first step, we open a *subwindow* on the sub-expression
$B \wedge A$, denoted by the markers. We then transform the sub-window and obtain

the desired result for the whole expression:

$$\llcorner B \wedge A \lrcorner \Rightarrow C \qquad (2)$$
$$\Leftarrow \quad \{\text{focus on } B \wedge A\}$$
$$\bullet \; B \wedge A$$
$$= \{\wedge \text{ is commutative}\}$$
$$A \wedge B$$
$$\bullet \; \ulcorner A \wedge B \urcorner \Rightarrow C$$

The proof profits from the fact that we can replace equivalent subexpressions. This is formalised by *window rules* [11]. In this case the rule has the form

$$\frac{\Gamma \vdash A = B}{\Gamma \vdash E[A] \Rightarrow E[B]} \qquad (3)$$

where the second-order variable E stands for the unchanged *context*, while the subterm A (the *focus* of the transformation) is replaced by the transformation.

Comparing this proof with the natural deduction proof, we see that in the latter we have to decompose the context by applying one rule per operator, whereas the calculational proof employs second-order matching to achieve the same effect directly. Although in this format, which goes back to Dijkstra and Scholten [8], proofs tend to be shorter and more abstract, there are known counterexamples such as proof by contradiction.

In Grundy's work [11], window inference proofs are presented in terms of natural deduction proofs. By showing every natural deduction proof can be constructed using window inference rules, completeness of window inference for first-order logic is shown. This allows the implementation of window inference in a theorem prover. A similar technique underlies our implementation: the system constructs Isabelle proofs from window inference proofs.

As was shown in [11,1], window inference proofs are not restricted to first-order logic or standard proof refinement, i.e. calculational proofs based on the implication and equality. It is natural to admit a family $\{R_i\}_{i \in I}$ of reflexive and transitive binary relations that enjoy a generalised form of monotonicity (in the form of (3) above).

Extending the framework of window inference in these directions allows to profit from its intuitive conciseness not only in high-school mathematics and traditional calculus, which deals with manipulating equations, but also in formal systems development, where the refinement of specifications is often the central notion. However, adequate user interface support is needed if we want to exploit this intuitive conciseness; the user interaction to set a focus on a subterm should be little more than marking the subterm with the mouse (point&click), otherwise the whole beneficial effect would be lost again.

2.2   The Concepts

Just as equality is at the heart of algebra, at the heart of window inference there is a family of binary preorders (reflexive and transitive relations) $\{\sqsubseteq_i\}_{i \in I}$. These preorders are called the *refinement relations*. Practically relevant examples of refinement relations in formal system development are impliedness $S \Leftarrow P$ (used for algebraic model inclusion, see Sect. 3), process refinement $S \sqsubseteq_{FD} P$ (the process P is more defined and more deterministic than the process S, see Sect. 4), set inclusion (see Sect. 5), or arithmetic orderings for numerical approximations [29]. An example for an infinite family of refinement relations in HOL is the Scott-definedness ordering for higher-order function spaces (where the indexing set I is given by the types):

$$f \sqsubseteq_{(\alpha \to \beta) \times (\alpha \to \beta) \to Bool} g \equiv \forall x.\, f\, x \sqsubseteq_{\beta \times \beta \to Bool} g\, x \tag{4}$$

The refinement relations have to satisfy a number of properties, given as a number of theorems. Firstly, we require reflexivity and transitivity for all $i \in I$:

$$a \sqsubseteq_i a \qquad\qquad\qquad\qquad [\text{Refl}_i]$$
$$a \sqsubseteq_i b \wedge b \sqsubseteq_i c \Rightarrow a \sqsubseteq_i c \qquad\qquad [\text{Trans}_i]$$

The refinement relations can be ordered. We say $\sqsubseteq_i$ is *weaker* than $\sqsubseteq_j$ if $\sqsubseteq_i$ is a subset of $\sqsubseteq_j$, i.e. if $a \sqsubseteq_i b$ implies $a \sqsubseteq_j b$:

$$a \sqsubseteq_i b \Rightarrow a \sqsubseteq_j b \qquad\qquad\qquad [\text{Weak}_{i,j}]$$

The ordering is optional; in a given instantiation, the refinement relations may not be related at all. However, because of reflexivity, equality is weaker than any other relation, i.e. for all $i \in I$, the following is a derived theorem:[1]

$$a = b \Rightarrow a \sqsubseteq_i b \tag{5}$$

The main device of window inferencing are the window rules shown in the previous section:

$$(A \Rightarrow a \sqsubseteq_i b) \Rightarrow F\, a \sqsubseteq_j F\, b \qquad\qquad [\text{Mono}_{i,j}^F]$$

Here, F can either be a meta-variable[2], or a constant-head expression, i.e. a term of the form $\lambda y_1 \ldots y_m.c x_1 \ldots x_n$ with c a constant. Note how there are different refinement relations in the premise and conclusion of the rule. Using a family of rules instead of one monotonicity rule has two advantages: firstly, it allows us to handle, on a case by case basis, instantiations where the refinement relations are not congruences, and secondly, by allowing an additional assumption A in the monotonicity rules, we get more assumptions when refining inside a context. These *contextual assumptions* are crucial, many proofs depend on them.[3]

---

[1] In order to keep our transformation system independent of the object logic being used, we do not include any equality per default, as different object logics may have different equalities.

[2] In Isabelle, meta-variables are variables in the meta-logic, which are subject to unification. Users of other theorem provers can think of them just as variables.

[3] They already featured in the pioneering CIP-S system [3] in 1984.

Dependencies between refinement relations can be more complicated than the restricted form of weakening rules [Weak$_{i,j}$] above may be able to express; for example, (4) cannot be expressed by a weakening rule in either direction because of the outermost quantor on the right side. For this reason, there is a further need for *refinement conversions*, i.e. tactical procedures that attempt to rewrite one refinement proof goal into another.

To finish off the picture, we consider transformation rules. A transformation rule is given by a *logical core theorem* of the form

$$A \Rightarrow (I \sqsubseteq_j O) \tag{6}$$

where A is the *application condition*, I the *input pattern* and O the *output pattern*. In other words, transformation rules are theorems the conclusion of which is a refinement relation.

2.3 Parameters

The *parameters* for a transformation rule given by core theorem schema (6) are meta-variables occuring in the output pattern O but not in the input pattern I. After applying the transformation, a parameter occurs as a free meta-variable in the proof state. This is not always useful, hence parameters enjoy special support. In particular, in transformational program development (see Sect. 3) we have rather complex transformations with a lot of parameters and their instantiation is an important design decision. As a simple example, consider the theorem

$$t \Leftrightarrow \textbf{if } b \textbf{ then } t \textbf{ else } t$$

which as a transformation rule from the left to the right introduces a case distinction on b. This is not very helpful unless we supply a concrete value for b which helps us to further develop t in the two different branches of the conditional expression under the respective assumption that b holds, or does not.

TAS supports parameters by when applying a transformation checking whether it contains parameters, and if so querying for their instantiation. It further allows parameter instantiations to be stored, edited and reused. This avoids having to retype instantiations, which can get quite lengthy, and makes TAS suitable for transformational program development as well as calculational proof.

2.4 The Trafos Package

The **Trafos** package implements the basic window inferencing operations as Isabelle tactics, such as:

- opening and closing subwindows,
- applying transformations,
- searching for applicable transformations,
- and starting and concluding developments.

In general, our implementation follows Staples' approach [23], for example in the use of the transitivity rules to translate the forward chaining of transformation steps into backwards proofs on top of Isabelle's goal package, or the reflexivity rules to close subwindows or conclude developments.The distinctive features of our implementation are the subterm and search functionalities, so we concentrate on these in the following.

In order to open a subwindow or apply a transformation at a particular subterm, Trafos implements an abstract datatype path and operations apply_trafo, open_sub taking such a path (and a transformation) as arguments. To allow direct manipulation by point&click, we extend Isabelle's powerful syntax and pretty-printing machinery by *annotations* [15]. Annotations are markup sequences containing a textual representation of the path, which are attached to the terms. They do not print in the user interface, but instead generate a binding which invokes the respective operations with the corresponding path as argument. In general, users do not need to modify their theories to use the subterm selection facilities, they can be used as they are, including user-defined pretty-printing.[4]

The operations apply_trafo and open_sub analyse the context, and for each operation making up the context, the most specific $[\text{Mono}_i^F]$ rule is selected, and a proof step is generated. In order to speed up this selection, the monotonicity rules are indexed by their head symbol, so we can discard rules which cannot possibly unify; still, the application of the selected rules may fail, so a tactic is constructed which tries to apply any combination of possibly fitting rules, starting with the most specific.

Further, for each refinement relation $\sqsubseteq_i$, we try to find a rule $[\text{Mono}_{i,i}^F]$ where F is just a meta-variable and the condition A is void — this rule would state that $\sqsubseteq_i$ is a congruence. If we can find such a rule, we can use it to handle, in one step, large parts of the context consisting of operations for which no more specific rule can be found. If no such congruence rule can be found, we do not construct a step-by-step proof but instead use Isabelle's efficient rewriter, the simplifier, with the appropriate rules to break down larger contexts in one step.

As an example why the more specific rules are applied first, consider the expression $E = x + (\texttt{if } x = 0 \texttt{ then } u + x \texttt{ else } v + x)$. If we want to simplify $u + x$, then we can do so under the assumption that $x = 0$, and we have $x + 0 \Rightarrow u + x = u$ because of the theorem

$$(B \Rightarrow x = y) \Rightarrow (\texttt{if } B \texttt{ then } x \texttt{ else } z = \texttt{if } B \texttt{ then } y \texttt{ else } z) \qquad [\text{Mono}_=^{\text{If}}]$$

But if we had just used the congruence rule for equality $x = y \Rightarrow f\,x = f\,y$ we would have lost the contextual assumption $x = 0$ in the refinement of the if-branch of the conditional.

When looking for applicable transformations, performance becomes an issue, and there is an inherent trade-off between the speed and accuracy of the search.

---

[4] Except if Isabelle's freely programmable so-called *print translations* are used (which is rarely the case). In this case, there are facilities to aid in programming markup-generation analogously to these print-translations.

In principle, we have to go through all theorems in Isabelle's database and check whether they can be considered as transformation rule, and if so if the input pattern of the rule matches. Many theorems can be excluded straight away since their conclusion is not a refinement. For the rest, we can either superficially check whether they might fit, which is much faster but bears the risk of returning rules which actually do not fit, or we can construct and apply the relevant tactic. We let users decide (by setting a search option) whether they want fast or accurate search. Another speed-up heuristic is to be able to specify that rules are only collected from certain theories (called *active theories*). Finally, users can exclude expanding rules (where the left-hand side is only a variable), because most (but not all) of the time these are not really helpful. In this way, users can guide the search for applicable transformations by selecting appropriate heuristics.

When instantiating the functor Trafos, the preprocessing of the monotonicity rules as described above takes place (calculation of the simplifier sets, head constants etc.) Further, some consistency checks are carried out (e.g. that there are transitivity and reflexivity rules for all refinement relations).

2.5   Genericity by Functors

In Standard ML (SML), modules are called *structures*. *Signatures* are module types, describing the interface, and *functors* are parameterised modules, mapping structures to structures. Since in LCF provers theorems are elements of an abstract SML datatype, we can describe the properties of a window inference calculus as described in Sect. 2.2 above using SML's module language, and implement TAS a functor, taking a structure containing the necessary theorems, and returning a transformation or window inferencing system complete with graphical user interface built on top of this:

```
funtor TAS(TrfThy: TRAFOTHY) = ...
```

The signature TRAFOTHY specifies a structure which contains all the theorems of Sect. 2.2. Abstracted a little (by omitting some parameters for special tactical support), it reads as follows:

```
signature TRAFOTHY =
    sig val topthy   : string
        val refl     : thm list
        val trans    : thm list
        val weak     : thm list
        val mono     : thm list
        val ref_conv : (string* (int-> tactic)) list
        ...
    end
```

To instantiate TAS, we need to provide a theory (named topthy) which encodes the formal method of our choice and where our refinement lives, theorems describing the transitivity, reflexivity and monotonicity of the refinement relation(s), and a list of refinement conversions, which consist of a name, and a tactic when when applied to a particular subgoal converts the subgoal into another refinement relation.

When applying this functor by supplying appropriate arguments, we obtain a structure which implements a window inferencing system, complete with a graphical user interface. The graphical user interface abstracts from the command line interface of most LCF provers (where functions and values are referred to by names) by implementing a *notepad*, on which objects (theorems, theories, etc.) can be manipulated by drag&drop. It provides a *construction area* where the current on-going proof is displayed, and which has a *focus* to open subwindows, apply transformations to subterms or search the theorem database for applicable transformations. We can navigate the *history* (going backwards and forwards), and display the history concisely, or in detail through an active display, which allows us to show and hide subdevelopments. Further, the user interface provides an active *object management* (keeping track of changes to external objects like theories), and a *session management* which allows to save the system state and return to it later. All of these features are available for *any* instance of TAS, and require no additional implementation; and this is what we mean by calling TAS *generic*.

The implementation of TAS consists of two components: a kernel transformation system, which is the package `Trafos` as described in Sect. 2.4, and a graphical user interface on top of this. We can write this simplified as

```
functor TAS(TrfThy : TRAFOTHY) = GenGUI(Trafos(TrfThy : TRAFOTHY))
```

The graphical user interface is implemented by the functor `GenGUI`, and is independent of `Trafos` and Isabelle. For a detailed description, we refer to [15], but in a nutshell, the graphical user interface is implemented entirely in SML, using a typed functional encapsulation of Tcl/Tk called `sml_tk`. Most of the GUI features mentioned above (such as the notepad, and the history, object and session management) are implemented at this more general level.

The division of the implementation into a kernel system and a generic graphical user interface has two major advantages: firstly, the GUI is reusable for similar applications (for example, we have used it to implement a GUI `IsaWin` to Isabelle itself); and secondly, it allows us to run the transformation system without the graphical user interface, e.g. as a scripting engine to check proofs.

3   Design Transformations in Classical Program Transformation

In the design of algorithms, certain schemata can be identified [7]. When such a schema is formalised as a theorem in the form of (6), we call the resulting transformation rule a *design transformation*. Examples include *divide and conquer* [20], *global search* [22] or *branch and bound*. Recall from Sect. 2.2 that transformation rules are represented by a logical core theorem with an input pattern and an output pattern. Characteristically, design transformations have as input pattern a *specification*, and as output pattern a *program*. Here, a specification is given by a pre- and a postcondition, i.e. a function $f : X \to Y$ is specified by an implication $Pre(x) \longrightarrow Post(x, f(x))$, where $Pre : X \to Bool, Post : X \times Y \to Bool$. A program is given by a recursive scheme, such as well-founded recursion; the proof of the logical core theorem must accordingly be based on the corresponding induction principles, i.e. here well-founded induction. Thus, a function $f : X \to Y$ can be given as

$$\texttt{let fun } f(x) = E \texttt{ in } f \texttt{ end measure } < \qquad (7)$$

where E is an expression of type Y, possibly containing f, and $< \subseteq X \times X$ is a well-founded relation, the *measure*, which must decrease with every recursive call of f. The notational proximity of (7) to SML is intended: (7) can be considered as a functional program.

As refinement relation, we will use model-inclusion — when refining a specification of some function f, the set of possible interpretations for f is reduced. The logical equivalent of this kind of refinement is the implication, which leads to the following definition:

$$\sqsubseteq : Bool \times Bool \to Bool \qquad P \sqsubseteq Q \stackrel{def}{=} Q \longrightarrow P$$

Based on this definition, we easily prove the theorems $\texttt{ref\_trans}$ and $\texttt{ref\_refl}$ (transitivity and reflexivity of $\sqsubseteq$). We can also prove that $\sqsubseteq$ is monotone for all boolean operators, e.g.

$$s \sqsubseteq t \Rightarrow s \wedge u \sqsubseteq t \wedge u \qquad\qquad \texttt{ref\_conj1}$$

Most importantly, we can show that

$$(B \Rightarrow s \sqsubseteq t) \Rightarrow \texttt{if } B \texttt{ then } s \texttt{ else } u \sqsubseteq \texttt{if } B \texttt{ then } t \texttt{ else } u \qquad \texttt{ref\_if}$$
$$(\neg B \Rightarrow u \sqsubseteq v) \Rightarrow \texttt{if } B \texttt{ then } s \texttt{ else } u \sqsubseteq \texttt{if } B \texttt{ then } s \texttt{ else } v \qquad \texttt{ref\_then}$$

which provides the contextual assumptions mentioned above. When instantiating the functor, we also have to specify equality as a refinement relation. Since we can reuse the relevant definitions for all theories based on HOL, they have been put in a separate functor $\texttt{functor HolEqTrfThy(TrfThy : TRAFOTHY) : TRAFOTHY}$ In particular, this functor proves the weakening theorems (5) for all refinement relations, and appends them to the list $\texttt{weak}$. Thus, the full functor instantiation reads

```
structure HolRefThy =
  struct val name  = "HolRef"
         val trans = [ref_trans]
         val refl  = [ref_refl]
         val weak  = []
         val mono  = [ref_if, ref_else, ref_conj1, ref_conj2,
```

```
                    ref_disj1, ref_disj2, ...]
        val ref_conv = []
            ...
    end
structure TAS = TAS(HolEqTrfThy(HolRefThy))
```

The divide and conquer design transformation [20] implements a program $f : X \to Y$ by splitting X into two parts: the termination part of f, which can be directly embedded into the codomain Y of f, and the rest, where the values are divided into smaller parts, processed recursively, and reassembled. The core theorem for divide and conquer based on model-inclusion refinement and well-founded recursion reads:[5]

$$A \longrightarrow (Pre(x) \longrightarrow Post(x, f(x)))$$
$$\sqsubseteq$$
$$Pre(x) \longrightarrow f = \texttt{let fun } F(x) = \texttt{if } isPrim(x) \texttt{ then } Dir(x) \qquad (8)$$
$$\texttt{else } Com(\langle G, F \rangle(Decom(x)))$$
$$\texttt{in } F \texttt{ end measure } <)$$

As explained above, the parameters of the transformation are the meta-variables appearing in the output pattern but not in the input pattern of the logical core theorem (8). Here, these are

- the termination criterion $isPrim : X \to Bool$;
- the embedding of terminal values $Dir : X \to Y$;
- the decomposition function of input values $Decom : X \to Z \times X$;
- a function $G : Z \to U$ for those values which are not calculated by recursive calls of F;
- the composition function $Com : U \times Y \to Y$ that joins the subsolutions given by G and recursive calls of F;
- and the measure $<$ assuring termination.

We will now apply this transformation to synthesise a sorting algorithm in the theory of lists. We start with the usual specification of *sort*, as shown on the left of Fig. 1. We can see the notepad, on which the transformation object **Divide & Conquer** is represented by an icon. The workspace shows the current state of the already started development. The highlighting indicates the focus set by the user. Now we drag the transformation onto the focus; TAS interprets this gesture as application of the transformation at the focus. In this case, TAS infers that there are parameters to be provided by the user, who is thus guided to the necessary design decisions. The parameter instantiations are fairly simple: the termination condition is the empty list, which is sorted (hence *Dir* is the identity). The decomposition function splits off the head and the tail; the tail is sorted recursively, and the head is inserted into the sorted list (hence, *G* is the identity). Finally, the measure relates non-empty lists to their tails (since the

---

[5] $\langle f, g \rangle$ is the pairing of functions defined as $\langle f, g \rangle(x, y) \stackrel{def}{=} (f(x), f(y))$.

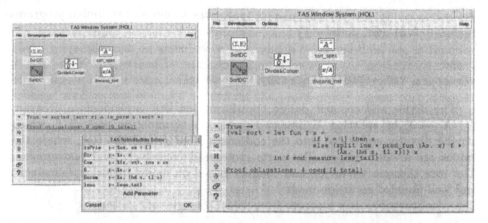

Fig. 1. TAS and its graphical user interface. To the left, the initial stage of the development, and the parameters supplied for the transformation; to the right, the development after applying the divide and conquer transformation. On the top of the window, we can see the notepad with the theory SortDC, the transformation Divide&Conquer, the specification sort_spec, the ongoing development (shaded) and the parameter instantiation divconq_inst.

recursive call always passes the tail of the argument; a relation easily proven to be well-founded).

This transformation step readily produces the desired program (right of Fig. 1). However, this step is only valid if the application conditions of the transformation hold. When applying a transformation, these conditions turn into proof obligations underlying a special bookkeeping. The proof obligations can be proven with a number of proof procedures. Typically, these include automatic proof via Isabelle's simplifier or classical reasoner and interactive proof via IsaWin. Depending on the particular logic, further proof procedures may be at our disposal, such as specialised tactics or model-checkers integrated into Isabelle.

Another well-known scheme in algorithm design is *global search* which has been investigated formally in [22]. It represents another powerful design transformation which has already been formalised in an earlier version of TAS [13].

4   Process Modelling with CSP

This section shows how to instantiate TAS for refinement with CSP [19], and will briefly present an example how the resulting system can be used. CSP is a language designed to describe systems of interacting components. It is supported by an underlying theory for reasoning about their equivalences, and in particular their refinements. In this section, we use the embedding HOL-CSP [26] of CSP into Isabelle/HOL. Even though shortage of space precludes us the set out the basics of CSP here, a detailed understanding of CSP is not required in the following; suffice it to say that CSP is a language to model distributed programs as communicating processes.

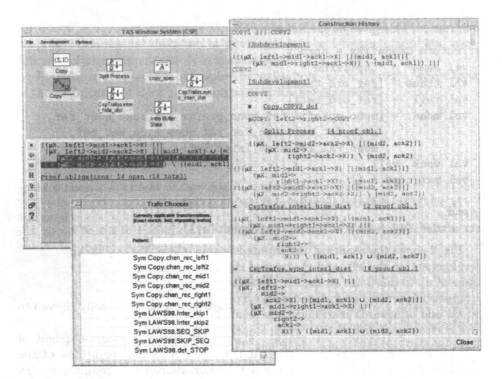

Fig. 2. TAS in the CSP instance. On the right, the construction history is shown. The development proceeded by subdevelopments on COPY1 and COPY2, which can be shown and hidden by clicking on [Subdevelopment]. Similarly, proof obligations can be shown and hidden. In the lower part of the main window, the focus is set on a subterm, and all applicable transformations are shown. By clicking on the name of the transformations, their structure can be displayed (not shown).

CSP is interesting in this context because it has three refinement relations, namely trace refinement, failures refinement and failures-divergence refinement. Here, we only use the third, since it is the one most commonly used when developing systems from specifications, but e.g. trace refinement can be relevant to show security properties.

Recall from Sect. 2.5 that to instantiate TAS we need a theory encoding our formal method, and theorems describing the refinement relation. The relevant theory is called CspTrafos, which contains the core theorems of some (simple) transformations built on top of Csp, the encoding of CSP into Isabelle/HOL.

For brevity, we only describe instantiation with failure-divergence refinement; the other two refinements would be similar. The theorems stating transitivity and reflexivity of failure-divergence refinement are called `ref_ord_trans` and `ref_ord_refl`, respectively. For monotonicity, we have a family of theorems describing monotonicity of the operators of CSP over this relation, but since the relation is monotone only with respect to the CSP relations it is not a proper congruence. This gives us the following functor instantiation:

```
structure CspRefThy = struct
  val name  = "CspTrafos"
  val trans = [ref_ord_trans]
  val refl  = [ref_ord_refl]
  val mono  = [mono_mprefix_ref,mono_prefix_ref,mono_ndet_ref,
               mono_det_ref,mono_Ren_ref,mono_hide_set_ref,
               mono_PaI_ref,mono_Inter_ref]
  val weak  = []
  val ref_conv = []
  ...
end
structure TAS = TAS(HolEqTrfThy(CspRefThy))
```

Fig. 2 shows the resulting, instantiated system in use. We can see an ongoing development on the left, and the opened construction history showing the development up to this point on the left. As we see, the development started with two processes in parallel; we focussed on both of these in turn to develop them separately, and afterwards rearranged the resulting process, using algebraic laws of CSP such as **sync_interl_dist** which states the distributivity of synchronisation over interleaving under some conditions. The development does not use powerful design transformations as in Sect. 3, but just employs a couple of the algebraic laws of CSP, showing how we can effectively use previously proven theorems for transformational development. Finding design transformations like divide and conquer for CSP is still an open research problem.

If we restrict ourselves to finite state processes (by requiring that the channels only carry finite messages), then we can even check the development above with the CSP model checker FDR [19], connected to Isabelle as a so-called *oracle* (a trusted external prover). This speeds up development at the cost of generality and can e.g. be used for rapid prototyping.

5   Data Refinement in the Refinement Calculus

In this section, we will emphasise a particular aspect of the genericity of TAS and demonstrate its potential for reuse of given logical embeddings. As we mentioned, TAS is generic with respect to the underlying refinement calculus, which in particular means that it is generic with respect to the underlying object logic. In the previous examples, we used higher-order logic (as encoded in Isabelle/HOL); in this example, we will use Zermelo-Fränkel set theory (as encoded in Isabelle/ZF). On top of Isabelle/ZF, Mark Staples has built a substantial theory for imperative program refinement and data refinement [24,25] following the lines of Back's Refinement Calculus RC [2].

RC is based on a weakest precondition semantics, where predicates and predicate transformers are represented as sets of states and functions taking sets of states to sets of states respectively. The distinctive feature of Staples' work over previous implementations of refinement calculi is the use of sets in the sense of ZF based on an open type universe. This allows derivations where the types of program variables are unknown at the beginning, and become more and more concrete after a sequence of development steps.

In order to give an idea of Staples' formalisation, we very briefly review some of the definitions of Back's core language in his presentation:[6]

$$\mathtt{Skip_A} \stackrel{def}{=} \lambda q : \mathbb{P}(\mathtt{A}).q$$

$$a \; ; \; b \stackrel{def}{=} \lambda q : dom(b).a \; ` \; b \; ` \; q$$

$$\mathtt{if} \; g \; \mathtt{then} \; a \; \mathtt{else} \; b \; \mathtt{fi} \stackrel{def}{=} \lambda q : dom(a) \cup dom(b).$$
$$(g \cap a \; ` \; q) \cup ((\bigcup(dom(a) \cup dom(b)) - g) \cap b \; ` \; q)$$

$$\mathtt{while} \; g \; \mathtt{do} \; c \; \mathtt{od} \stackrel{def}{=} \lambda q : \mathbb{P}(A). lfp_A \, N.(g \cap c \; ` \; N) \cup ((A - g) \cap q)$$

$$\cdots$$

This theory could be used for an instantiation of TAS, called TAS/RC. The instantiation follows essentially the lines discussed in the previous sections; with respect to the syntactic presentation, the configuration for the pretty-printing engine had to provide special support for 5 print-translations comprising 100 lines of code, and a particular set-up for the tactics providing reasoning over well-typedness, regularity and monotonicity. (We omit the details here for space reasons). As a result, a larger case study in [24] for the development of an BDD-related algorithm as a data-refinement from truth tables to decision trees can be represented *inside* TAS.

6   Conclusions and Outlook

This paper has presented the transformation system TAS. TAS is generic in the sense that it takes a set of theorems, describing a refinement relation, and turns them into a window inference or transformation system, complete with an easy-to-use, graphical user interface. This genericity means that the system can be instantiated both to a transformation system for transformational program development in the vein of traditional transformation systems such as CIP, KIDS or PROSPECTRA, or as system for window inference. We have demonstrated this versatility by showing instantiations from the provenance of each the two areas just mentioned, complemented with an instantiation from a different area, namely reasoning about processes using CSP.

The effort required for the actual instantiation of TAS is very small indeed, since merely the values for the parameters of the functor need to be provided.

---

[6] Note that the backquote operator ` is infix function application in Isabelle/ZF.

(Only rarely will tactical programming be needed, such as mentioned in Sect. 5, and even then it only amounts to a few lines of code.) It takes far more effort to set up the logical encoding of the formal method, in particular if one does so conservatively.

TAS' graphical user interface complements the intuitiveness of transformational calculi with a command-language-free user interface based on gestures such as drag&drop and proof-by-pointing. It further provides technical infrastructure such as development management (replay, reuse, history navigation), object management and session management.

TAS is implemented on top of the prover Isabelle, such that the consistency of the underlying logics and its rules can be ensured by the LCF-style architecture of Isabelle and well-known embedding techniques. It benefits further from the LCF architecture, because we can use SML's structuring mechanisms (such as functors) to implement reusable, generic proof components across a wide variety of logics.

Internally, we spent much effort to organise TAS componentwise, easing the reuse of as much code as possible for completely different logical environments. The GUI and large parts of TAS (except the package Trafos) are designed to work with a different SML-based prover, and are readily available for other research groups to provide GUI support for similar applications. On the other hand, the logical embeddings (such as HOL-CSP) which form the basis of the transformation calculi do not depend on TAS either. This allowed the easy integration of Staples' encoding of the refinement calculus into our system, as presented in Sect. 5.

6.1   Discussion and Related Work

This work attempts to synthesise previous work on transformational program development [3,21,12] which developed a huge body of formalised developments and design schemes, but suffered from ad-hoc, inflexible calculi, correctness problems and lack of proof support, with the work on window inferencing [18,11] and structured calculational proof [2,1], which provides proven correctness by LCF design and proof support from HOL or Isabelle.

PRT [6] is a program refinement tool (using window inference) which is built on top of the Ergo theorem prover. It offers an interface based on Emacs, which allows development management and search functionalities. However, the Tk-WinHOL system [14] comes closest to our own system conception: it is based on Tcl/Tk (making it platform independent), and offers focusing with a mouse, drag&drop in transformational goals, and a formally proven sound calculus implemented by derived rules in HOL. On the technical side it uses Tcl directly instead of an encapsulation (which in our estimate will make it much harder to maintain). On the logical side, it is also generic in the sense that it can be used with different refinement relations, but requires more work to be adapted to a new refinement relation; for example, users need to provide a pretty-printer which generates the correct mark-up code to be able to click on subterms. In contrast, TAS extends Isabelle's infrastructure (like the pretty-printer) into the graphical user interface, leaving the user with less work when instantiating the system.

The essential difference between window inferencing and structured calculational proof [1] is that the latter can live with more than one transformational goal. This difference is not that crucial for TAS since it can represent more than one transformational development on the notepad and is customisable for appropriate interaction between them via drag&drop operations.

Another possible generalisation would be to drop the requirement that all refinement relations be reflexive. However, this would complicate the tactical programming considerably without offering us perceivable benefit at the moment, so we have decided against it.

6.2   Future Work

Future work can be found in several directions. Firstly, the user interaction can still be improved in a variety of ways. Although in the present system, the user can ask for transformations which are applicable, this can considerably be improved by a best-fit strategy and, for example, stronger matching algorithms like AC-matching. The problem here is to help the user to find the few interesting transformations in the multitude of uninteresting (trivial, misleading) ones. Supporting design decisions at the highest possible user-oriented level must still count as an open problem, in particular in a generic setting.

Secondly, the interface to the outside world can be improved. Ideally, the system should interface to a variety of externally available proof formats, and export web-browsable proof scripts.

A rather more ambitious research goal is the reuse and abstraction of transformational developments. A first step in this direction would be to allow to cut&paste manipulation of the history of a proof.

Thirdly, going beyond classical hierarchical transformational proofs the concept of *indexed window inferencing* [29] appears highly interesting. The overall idea is to add an additional parameter to the refinement relation that allows to calculate the concrete refinement relation on the fly during transformational deduction. Besides the obvious advantage of relaxing the requirements to refinement relations to irreflexive ones (already pointed out in [23]), indexed window inferencing can also be used for a very natural representation of operational semantics rules. Thus, the system could immediately be used as an animator for, say, CSP, given the operational semantics rules for this language.

Finally, we would like to see more instances for TAS. Transformational development and proof in the specification languages Z and CASL should not be too hard, since for both embeddings into Isabelle are available [13,16]. The main step here is to formalise appropriate notions of refinement. A rather simple different instantiation is obtained by turning the refinement relation around. This amounts to *abstracting* a concrete program to a specification describing aspects of its behaviour, which can then be validated by a model-checker. For example, deadlock checks using CSP and FDR have been carried out in this manner, where the abstraction has been done manually[4,5,17]. Thus we believe that TAS represents an important step towards our ultimate goal of a transformation system which is similarly flexible with respect to underlying specification languages and refinement calculi as Isabelle is for conventional logical calculi.

Acknowledgements We would like to thank Mark Staples and Jim Grundy for providing us with the sources for their implementations of window inference and the refinement calculus respectively, and the anonymous referees for threir constructive criticism. Ralph Back pointed out several weaknesses of a previous version of TAS and made suggestions for improvements.

References

1. R. Back, J. Grundy, and J. von Wright. Structured calculational proof. *Formal Aspects of Computing*, 9:467–483, 1997.
2. R.-J. Back and J. von Wright. *Refinement Calculus*. Springer Verlag, 1998.
3. F. L. Bauer. *The Munich Project CIP. The Wide Spectrum Language CIP-L*. Number 183 in LNCS. Springer Verlag, 1985.
4. B. Buth, J. Peleska, and H. Shi. Combining methods for the deadlock analysis of a fault-tolerant system. In *Algebraic Methodology and Software Technology AMAST'97*, number 1349 in LNCS, pages 60–75. Springer Verlag, 1997.
5. B. Buth, J. Peleska, and H. Shi. Combining methods for the livelock analysis of a fault-tolerant system. In *Algebraic Methodology and Software Technology AMAST'98*, number 1548 in LNCS, pages 124–139. Springer Verlag, 1999.
6. D. Carrington, I. Hayes, R. Nickson, G. Watson, and J. Welsh. A Program Refinement Tool. *Formal Aspects of Computing*, 10(2):97–124, 1998.
7. T. H. Cormen, C. E. Leiserson, and R. L. Rivest. *Introduction to Algorithms*. The MIT Press and New York: McGraw-Hill, 1989.
8. E.W. Dijkstra and C.S. Scholten. *Predicate Calculus and Program Semantics*. Texts and Monographs in Computer Science. Springer Verlag, 1990.
9. D. Gries. *A Science of Programming*. Springer Verlag, 1981.
10. D. Gries. Teaching calculation and discrimination: A more effecticulum. *Communications of the ACM*, 34:45–54, 1991.
11. J. Grundy. Transformational hierarchical reasoning. *Computer Journal*, 39:291–302, 1996.
12. B. Hoffmann and B. Krieg-Brückner. *PROSPECTRA: Program Development by Specification and Transformation*. Number 690 in LNCS. Springer Verlag, 1993.
13. Kolyang, T. Santen, and B. Wolff. Correct and user-friendly implementations of transformation systems. In M. C. Gaudel and J. Woodcock, editors, *Formal Methods Europe FME'96*, number 1051 in LNCS, pages 629–648. Springer Verlag, 1996.
14. T. Långbacka, R. Rukšėna, and J. von Wright. TkWinHOL: A tool for doing window inferencing in HOL. In *Proc. 8th International Workshop on Higher Order Logic Theorem Proving and Its Applications*, number 971 in LNCS, pages 245–260. Springer Verlag, 1995.
15. C. Lüth and B. Wolff. Functional design and implementation of graphical user interfaces for theorem provers. *Journal of Functional Programming*, 9(2):167–189, March 1999.

16. T. Mossakowski, Kolyang, and B. Krieg-Brückner. Static semantic analysis and theorem proving for CASL. In *Recent trends in algebraic development techniques. Proc* 13th *International Workshop*, number 1376 in LNCS, pages 333–348. Springer Verlag, 1998.

17. R. S. Lazić. *A Semantic Study of Data Independence with Applications to Model Checking*. PhD thesis, Oxford University, 1999.

18. P. J. Robinson and J. Staples. Formalizing a hierarchical structure of practical mathematical reasoning. *Journal for Logic and Computation*, 14(1):43–52, 1993.

19. A. W. Roscoe. *The Theory and Practice of Concurrency*. Prentice Hall, 1998.

20. D. Smith. The design of divide and conquer algorithms. *Science of Computer Programming*, 5:37–58, 1985.

21. D. R. Smith. KIDS — a semi-automatic program development system. *IEEE Transactions on Software Engineering*, 16(9):1024–1043, 1991.

22. D. R. Smith and M. R. Lowry. Algorithm theories and design tactics. *Science of Computer Programming*, 14:305–321, 1990.

23. M. Staples. Window inference in Isabelle. In *Proc. Isabelle Users Workshop*. University of Cambridge Computer Laboratory, 1995.

24. M. Staples. *A Mechanised Theory of Refinement*. PhD thesis, Computer Laboratory, University of Cambridge, 1998.

25. M. Staples. Representing wp semantics in isabelle/zf. In G. Dowek, C. Paulin, and Y. Bertot, editors, *TPHOLs: The 12th International Conference on Theorem Proving in Higher-Order Logics*, number 1690 in lncs. springer, 1999.

26. H. Tej and B. Wolff. A corrected failure-divergence model for CSP in Isabelle/HOL. In J. Fitzgerald, C. B. Jones, and P. Lucas, editors, *Formal Methods Europe FME '97*, number 1313 in LNCS, pages 318–337. Springer Verlag, 1997.

27. D. van Dalen. *Logic and Structure*. Springer Verlag, 1994.

28. A. J. M. van Gasteren. On the shape of mathematical arguments. In *Advances in Software Engineering and Knowledge Engineering*, number 445 in LNCS, pages 1–39. Springer Verlag, 1990.

29. J. von Wright. Extending window inference. In *Proc. TPHOLs '98*, number 1497 in LNCS, pages 17–32. Springer Verlag, 1998.

Weak Alternating Automata in Isabelle/HOL

Stephan Merz

Institut für Informatik, Universität München
merz@informatik.uni-muenchen.de

Abstract. Thomas has presented a novel proof of the closure of ω-regular languages under complementation, using weak alternating automata. This note describes a formalization of this proof in the theorem prover Isabelle/HOL. As an application we have developed a certified translation procedure for PTL formulas to weak alternating automata inside the theorem prover.

1 Introduction

The close relationship between ω-automata and temporal logic [10,8] is one of the cornerstones of the theory that underlies model checking. Traditionally, ω-regular languages have been defined via Büchi automata [1,7,8], a straightforward extension of standard finite automata, but operating on infinite words. One of the fundamental results about ω-regular languages establishes their closure under complementation. It was first proven non-constructively by Büchi [1], relying on Ramsey's theorem. Over a period of 25 years, the result has been reproved several times, using variants of Büchi automata to obtain effective constructions, culminating in a paper by Safra [5] that gives an essentially optimal, exponential construction.

An alternative definition of ω-regular languages due to Muller, Saoudi, and Schupp [3] is based on (weak) alternating automata, for which several states can be simultaneously active during a run over a given word. In this framework, complementation can simply be achieved by dualizing the transition relation of the original automaton, avoiding the exponential blowup of Büchi automata. Although the construction is simple, its correctness proof is far from obvious. Thomas [9] has recently given a beautiful presentation of this proof in terms of winning strategies for the class of games associated with weak alternating automata, isolating the complexity of the proof in three independent subproblems. We have formalized Thomas' proof in the interactive theorem prover Isabelle/HOL and believe that this formalization constitutes an interesting case study in formalizing mathematics because it involves fairly advanced mathematical concepts such as logical games and strategies, offering a mix of combinatorial reasoning and of linear and modulus arithmetic that exercise the power of automated proof strategies.

As an application, we have then verified a simple, linear, and compositional construction [11,2] that associates a weak alternating automaton $\mathcal{A}_\varphi$ with a given

J. Harrison and M. Aagaard (Eds.): TPHOLs 2000, LNCS 1869, pp. 424–441, 2000.

formula φ of propositional temporal logic. Because this construction is defined as a set of recursive functions, we may use Isabelle's rewriting machinery to actually evaluate these functions and in this way obtain a certified translation of LTL formulas to automata within the theorem prover.

2   Isabelle/HOL

Isabelle is a generic interactive theorem prover which can be instantiated with different object logics. One popular and well-developed instance has been developed for higher-order logics, based on Church's version of Higher Order Logic. From now on, Isabelle means Isabelle/HOL. Extensive documentation can be found on the Web at http://isabelle.in.tum.de; we only highlight some of the syntax required for understanding the remainder of the paper.

We use types constructed by function application ($\Rightarrow$), products ($*$) or records (i.e., tuples with named components). Isabelle also supports inductive definitions of data types.

The syntax for formulas is standard. Isabelle distinguishes between object-level ($\Rightarrow$) and meta-level ($\Longrightarrow$) implication, and similarly for universal quantification, but that distinction is unimportant for our purposes. The notation $[\![A_1; \ldots; A_n]\!] \Longrightarrow A$ is short-hand for the nested meta-level implication $A_1 \Longrightarrow \ldots A_n \Longrightarrow A$.

Definitions of types and operators are collected in theories. Non-recursive operators are defined via the meta-level equality ($\equiv$), recursive operators can be introduced by primrec and recdef constructs.

We do not present any proofs, because Isabelle proof scripts are not intelligible for human readers, but we usually indicate their complexity in terms of how many interactions were necessary. Besides low-level proof commands such as resolution and instantiation, Isabelle provides higher-level search procedures (tactics) based on rewriting and the classical reasoner, which implements a tableau-based prover for predicate logic and sets. These automatic tactics must be supplied with information about which definitions to expand and which lemmas to use, which requires some expertise and experimentation.

3   Automata, Games, and Strategies

We describe the concepts of the theory of weak alternating automata and their associated games that are used in Thomas' proof as well as their formalization in Isabelle. The Isabelle definitions have been copied verbatim from the input files, except for some pretty-printing to improve readability.

3.1   Positive Boolean Formulas

The transition relation of an alternating automaton is conveniently defined via positive Boolean combinations of its states, represented by the following inductive data type parameterized by type σ.

```
datatype σ pboolean =
    Atomic σ
  | And     (σ pboolean) (σ pboolean)
  | Or      (σ pboolean) (σ pboolean)
```

Straightforward recursive functions compute the set of atoms that occur in a positive Boolean formula, and its models.

```
atoms :: σ pboolean ⇒ σ set
atoms (Atomic s) = {s}
atoms (And p q)  = (atoms p) ∪ (atoms q)
atoms (Or f g)   = (atoms f) ∪ (atoms g)

models :: σ pboolean ⇒ σ set set
models (Atomic s) = { M | s ∈ M }
models (And p q)  = (models p) ∩ (models q)
models (Or p q)   = (models p) ∪ (models q)
```

We will mainly be interested in "small" models that are subsets of the atoms contained in a formula.

```
smodels :: σ pboolean ⇒ σ set set
smodels p ≡ (models p) ∩ 𝒫(atoms p)
```

The *dual formula* $\tilde{p}$ of a positive Boolean formula p is obtained by exchanging conjunctions and disjunctions.

```
dual_form (Atomic s) = Atomic s
dual_form (And p q)  = Or (dual_form p) (dual_form q)
dual_form (Or p q)   = And (dual_form p) (dual_form q)
```

We can prove a number of preliminary lemmas about positive Boolean formulas and their models. For example, every formula has a model, and small models are finite sets. A set M is a model of $\tilde{p}$ iff it contains an element of every model of p

$$M \in models\ (dual\_form\ p) \equiv \forall R \in models\ p.\ \exists s.\ s \in M \cap R$$

and a similar relation holds for the small models of p and $\tilde{p}$ (Thomas considers minimal models, his "Remark 3" asserts a similar relationship). All of these lemmas are proved by induction, followed by invocations of Isabelle's automated tactics.

3.2   Automata and Runs

A weak alternating automaton $\mathcal{A} = (S, s_0, \delta, \rho)$ over alphabet B is given by a set S of states, an initial state $s_0 \in S$, a transition function δ that associates a positive Boolean formula $\delta(s, b)$ with every state $s \in S$ and input symbol $b \in B$, and a ranking function $\rho : S \to \mathbb{N}$ such that $\rho(t) \leq \rho(s)$ whenever t occurs in some formula $\delta(s, b)$ (this restriction is what makes $\mathcal{A}$ "weak"). We represent automata via a record type (σ, β) waa and a well-formedness predicate is_waa.

```
record (σ,β) waa =
  states    :: σ set
  initial   :: σ
  trans     :: [σ, β] ⇒ σ pboolean
  rank      :: σ ⇒ nat
```

```
is_waa :: (σ,β) waa ⇒ bool
is_waa auto ≡ initial auto ∈ states auto
            ∧ ∀ s ∈ states auto. ∀b.
                  atoms(trans auto s b) ⊆ states auto
            ∧ ∀ t ∈ atoms(trans auto s b).
                  rank auto t ≤ rank auto s
```

Runs of alternating automata over ω-words are often represented as infinite trees of states where the successors of a state s and input symbol b are given by some model of $\delta(s, b)$. Thomas suggests instead to represent runs as infinite dags, which can be formalized as a record that contains the root state and a function that returns the set of successor states for state s at a given depth in the dag. We also define two type synonyms that will be used to represent ω-words and other infinite sequences.

```
record σ dag =
  root     :: σ
  succs    :: [nat, σ] ⇒ σ set
types
  β word = nat ⇒ β
  σ seq  = nat ⇒ σ
```

The following definitions introduce the set of run dags of an automaton $\mathcal{A}$ over a given word w and the set of paths through an infinite dag:

```
run_dags :: [(σ,β) waa, β word] ⇒ σ dag set
run_dags auto w ≡
  {dg | root dg = initial auto
      ∧ ∀i s. succs dg i s ∈ smodels (trans auto s (w i))}
paths :: σ dag ⇒ (σ seq) set
paths dg ≡ {pi | pi 0 = root dg
              ∧ ∀i. pi (i+1) ∈ succs dg i (pi i)}
```

It remains to define the acceptance condition. Because ranks are decreasing along any path in a run dag, they must eventually stabilize. Now, the run of a weak alternating automaton is accepting iff for every path through the dag, this "limit rank" is even. Equivalently, the least rank assumed along any path through the dag must be even.[1]

```
ranks :: [σ seq, σ ⇒ nat] ⇒ nat set
```

---

[1] o denotes function composition; the range of a function f is denoted by **range** f.

```
ranks pi f ≡ range (f ∘ pi)

least_rank :: [σ seq, σ ⇒ nat] ⇒ nat
least_rank pi f ≡ LEAST i. i ∈ ranks pi f

acc_path   :: [σ seq, (σ,β) waa] ⇒ bool
acc_path pi auto ≡ (least_rank pi auto) mod 2 = 0

is_accepting :: [(σ,β) waa, σ dag] ⇒ bool
is_accepting auto dg ≡ ∀pi ∈ paths dg. acc_path pi auto
```

Finally, the language defined by an automaton is the set of words for which there exists some accepting run dag.

```
language :: (σ,β) waa ⇒ β word set
language auto ≡ {w | ∃dg ∈ run_dags auto w. is_accepting auto dg}
```

3.3   Games and Strategies

Logical games have become popular tools in semantics as well as in automata theory. The word problem for a weak alternating automaton $\mathcal{A}$ and an ω-word w can be visualized as a two-person game between A(utomaton) and P(athfinder) where A tries to demonstrate the existence of an accepting run, while P tries to spoil A's efforts. Every draw in the game consists of a move by A, followed by a move of P. For his i'th move, player A sees a state s of the automaton and chooses some (small) model M of $\delta(s, w_i)$, exploiting the non-determinism of automaton $\mathcal{A}$. Player P, trying to find some path in the run whose minimum rank is odd, then chooses some state $t \in M$ for the next round of the game. The outcome of the game is a path through a run dag of $\mathcal{A}$ for input w.

We start by defining type synonyms for the positions of the two players. A game is represented as an ω-sequence of pairs of positions.

```
types
  σ Apos = σ
  σ Ppos = σ set
  σ play = (σ Apos * σ Ppos) seq
```

These definitions differ from those used by Thomas in that he defines positions as pairs (i, s) resp. (i, M) where i gives the index of the current round. Doing so would pollute our terms with projection functions, so we provide i as an extra parameter whenever necessary. The following functions define the set of legal moves of either player at any position, as well as the initial position.

```
Amoves :: [(σ,β) waa, β word, nat, σ Apos] ⇒ σ Ppos set
Amoves auto w i s ≡ smodels (trans auto s (w i))

Pmoves :: [(σ,β) waa, β word, nat, σ Ppos] ⇒ σ Apos set
Pmoves auto w i M ≡ M
```

```
init_pos :: (σ,β) waa ⇒ σ Apos
init_pos auto ≡ initial auto
```

A draw sequence is an ω-sequence of alternating positions that correspond to legal moves; a play is a draw sequence that starts at the initial position. The outcome of a play is its projection on the positions of player A, i.e. on the states of the automaton.[2]

```
drawseqs :: [(σ,β) waa, β word, σ Apos] ⇒ σ play set
drawseqs auto w s ≡
  { pl | fst (pl 0) = s
    ∧ ∀i. snd (pl i) ∈ Amoves auto w i (fst (pl i))
    ∧ ∀i. fst (pl (i+1)) ∈ Pmoves auto w i (snd (pl i))}

plays :: [(σ,β) waa, β word] ⇒ σ play set
plays auto w ≡ drawseqs auto w (init_pos auto)

outcome :: σ play ⇒ σ seq
outcome pl ≡ fst ∘ pl

outcomes :: [(σ,β) waa, β word] ⇒ σ seq set
outcomes auto w ≡ outcome '' (plays auto w)
```

Player A wins if the least rank among the states in the outcome of the play is odd, otherwise P wins.

```
Awins :: [(σ,β) waa, σ play] ⇒ bool
Awins auto pl ≡ acc_path (outcome pl) auto

Pwins :: [(σ,β) waa, σ play] ⇒ bool
Pwins auto pl ≡ ¬ (Awins auto pl)
```

The question of interest is whether either player can force a win in the play for the given automaton and input word by following a strategy. It turns out that for weak alternating automata, it suffices to consider local (i.e., memoryless) strategies, where the next move is determined from the current position alone. We introduce types and well-formedness predicates for strategies to Isabelle.[3]

```
types
  σ Astrat = [nat, σ Apos] ⇒ σ Ppos
  σ Pstrat = [nat, σ Ppos] ⇒ σ Apos

isAstrat :: [σ Astrat, (σ,β) waa, β word] ⇒ bool
isAstrat strat auto w ≡ ∀i s. strat i s ∈ Amoves auto w i s
```

---

[2] fst and snd denote the projection functions. The expression f''S denotes the image of set S under f.

[3] These definitions will be revised in section 5.

```
isPstrat :: [σ Pstrat, (σ,β) waa, β word] ⇒ bool
isPstrat strat auto w ≡ ∀i M. strat i M ∈ Pmoves auto w i M
```

A strategy is a winning strategy for either player if it guarantees a win provided the player adheres to the strategy. We give the definitions for player A; those for player P are similar.

```
Aadheres :: [σ play, σ Astrat] ⇒ bool
Aadheres pl strat ≡ ∀i. snd (pl i) = strat i (fst (pl i))

isAwinStrat :: [(σ,β) waa, β word, σ Astrat] ⇒ bool
isAwinStrat auto w strat ≡
        isAstrat strat auto w
     ∧ ∀pl ∈ plays auto w. Aadheres pl strat ⇒ Awins auto pl
```

We have now assembled enough definitions to test them by proving some theorems. More constructions will be given as we go along.

4   Acceptance and Winning Strategies

The first subgoal is to establish the following lemma, reproduced from [9]:

Proposition 2. *The weak alternating automaton A accepts w iff player A has a local winning strategy in the game associated with A and w.*

The proof of the "only if" part requires the definition of a winning strategy for player A, given an accepting run (dag) of A over w. The idea is to let A force the outcome of the play to be a path in the given dag by choosing, for any given position, the successors of that state in the dag. Formally, we enter the goal

```
[ dg ∈ run_dags auto w; is_accepting auto dg ]
⟹ ∃ strat. isAwinStrat auto w strat
```

For the proof, we simply provide the "witness" term `succs dg` for the existential quantifier. Isabelle's automatic tactics are able to solve the resulting subgoal by expanding the necessary definitions.

For the other direction we must construct an accepting dag, given a winning strategy for player A. Again, we simply let the successors in the dag be defined by the strategy and prove that the dag

```
(| root = initial auto, succs = strat |)
```

is accepting if `strat` is a winning strategy for player A. The machine proof follows the same pattern outlined above. Note that the concise form of these statements and the natural proof pattern is possible because we are working in a higher-order setting.

5   Dualizing Automata and Strategies

Encouraged by the success of the proof of the first subproblem, we continue to follow Thomas' exposition. His second lemma connects strategies for an automaton A with those for its "dual" automaton $\tilde{A}$ obtained by dualizing the transition relation and incrementing the ranks.

```
dual :: (σ,β) waa ⇒ (σ,β) waa
dual auto ≡ (| states = states auto,
               initial = initial auto,
               trans   = λ s b. dual_form (trans auto s b),
               rank    = λ s. (rank auto s)+1 |)
```

It is easy to see (and proved automatically by Isabelle) that $\tilde{A}$ is well-formed if A is.

Our main goal is to show that winning strategies for player A in the game associated with automaton A give rise to winning strategies for P in the game for $\tilde{A}$ and vice versa, as asserted by the following proposition taken from Thomas' paper:

Proposition 4. *Player A has a local winning strategy in the game associated with A and word w iff player P has a local winning strategy in the game for $\tilde{A}$ and w.*

Looking at Thomas' proof, we find the following description (adapted to our notation) of how to construct a winning strategy for P in the game for $\tilde{A}$ from a given strategy for A in the game for A:

> Note that in fixing the strategy it suffices to consider only game positions (i, M) which are reachable [...] The set M of the game position (i, M) is produced by player A from a game position (i, s) such that $M \in \widetilde{\delta(s, w_i)}$. Player P chooses such a state s which could produce M via w_i. Now in the game associated with A at position (i, s), the given local winning strategy of A picks some $R \in \delta(s, w_i)$, and the definition of $\tilde{\delta}$ ensures that there is a state in $R \cap M$. For his move from the game position (i, M), player P chooses such a state [...]

The idea is that player P forces the outcome of the game to be a possible outcome of the game of A; since the minimum rank of that outcome must have been even with A's ranking function, it will now be odd. However, the construction described by Thomas requires P to take into account the position (i, s) from which player A determined his move in the current draw of the play, which is not allowed by our definition of a local strategy from section 3.3. The first sentence in the quote above might suggest to try an inductive definition, but this also fails. We therefore revise the definition of type Pstrat and the corresponding well-formedness predicate as follows:

```
types
  σ Pstrat = [nat, σ Apos, σ Ppos] ⇒ σ Apos
```

```
isPstrat :: [σ Pstrat, (σ,β) waa, β word] ⇒ bool
isPstrat strat auto w ≡
∀i s M. M ∈ Amoves auto w i s ⇒ strat i s M ∈ Pmoves auto w i M
```

With this revised definition, the construction becomes a direct transcription of Thomas' description: player P chooses some state that is both in the set of states chosen by A and in the set the original strategy would have chosen from $\mathcal{A}$'s transition function; such a state must exist by the relationship between the models of a positive Boolean formula and its dual. In Isabelle this construction is defined by the expression[4]

```
dualizeAstrat :: [(σ,β) waa, β word, σ Astrat] ⇒ σ Pstrat
dualizeAstrat auto w strat ≡ λi s M. εt. t ∈ (M ∩ strat i s)
```

Isabelle proves automatically that the dualized strategy is well-formed if the original strategy is. It remains to prove that it is a winning strategy for P in the game for $\tilde{\mathcal{A}}$ if the original strategy is a winning strategy for A in the game for $\mathcal{A}$. We state the goal

```
isAwinStrat auto w strat
⟹ isPwinStrat (dual auto) w (dualizeAStrategy auto w strat)
```

The main problem is to prove that for every outcome of the dualized strategy there is a play, obtained by applying the original strategy, on the original automaton with the same outcome; that play must therefore be won by A. This proof requires a little guidance and takes 10 interactions.

Thomas asserts that "the other direction is shown analogously, by exchanging the roles of $\mathcal{A}$ and $\tilde{\mathcal{A}}$". Isabelle of course requires an explicit construction, and after the revision of type Pstrat, the symmetry is even less obvious. Fortunately, the construction turns out to be quite simple, and there is no need for further modifications to our definitions.

```
dualizePStrat :: [(σ,β) waa, β word, σ Pstrat] => σ Astrat
dualizePStrat auto w strat ≡
      λi s. (strat i s) '' (smodels (trans auto s (w i)))
```

The proof that this construction yields a winning strategy for player A on $\tilde{\mathcal{A}}$ given a winning strategy for P on $\mathcal{A}$ is very similar to the proof described above.

6 Determinacy

The third subproblem in Thomas' proof consists in showing that all games are determined, assuming optimal play.

Proposition 5. *Let $\mathcal{A}$ be a weak alternating automaton. From any position in the game associated with $\mathcal{A}$ and word w, either player A or P has a local winning strategy.*

---

[4] ε denotes Hilbert's choice operator.

6.1   Attractor Sets and Associated Strategies

The central notion used in the proof is that of an *attractor set*. This is a set
of positions (for player A) from which either A or P can force, in finitely many
draws, a visit to a set of target positions. Attractor sets for player A are defined
inductively as follows:

$$attr_A^0(T) = T$$
$$attr_A^{d+1}(T) = attr_A^d(T)$$
$$\cup \{(i, s) \mid \text{for some A-move from } (i, s)$$
$$\text{all P-moves lead to } attr_A^d(T)\}$$

The set $attr_A(T)$ is defined as the union of all $attr_A^d(T)$. The definition of
$attr_P(T)$ is dual in that $attr_P^{d+1}(T)$ contains those positions for which every A-
move leads to a position such that P has some move towards $attr_P^d(T)$. We omit
reproducing the formalization of these definitions in Isabelle, which is straightforward.

Thomas writes: "From the positions in $attr_A(T)$ player A can force a decrease
of distance to T in each step (which defines a local strategy)". Let us make this
explicit:[5]

```
attrA_strat :: [(σ,β)waa, β word, (nat * σ Apos)set] ⇒ σ Astrat
attrA_strat auto w T ≡
λi s. εM. M ∈ Amoves auto w i s
        ∧ ∀d. (i,s) ∈ pick_ea (Amoves auto w) (Pmoves auto w)
                                    (attrAh d auto w T)
          ⇒ ∀t∈M. ∃e. e ≤ d
                ∧ (i+1,t) ∈ attrAh e auto w T
```

It is easy to prove that this is a well-defined strategy, although the quantifiers
are now nested deeply enough for Isabelle to require some guidance. It remains
to show that player A can force, via this strategy, a visit in the set T of target
positions:

```
⟦ pl ∈ drawseqs auto w s; (i, fst (pl i)) ∈ attrA auto w T;
    ∀j. i ≤ j ⇒ snd (pl j) = attrA_strat auto w T j (fst (pl j)) ⟧
⟹ ∃j. (i+j, fst (pl (i+j))) ∈ T
```

This assertion is proved by a rather straightforward induction on the distance d in the definition of $attr_A^d(T)$. More interesting is the formalization of
the next sentence in Thomas' proof: "Also note that for any game position outside $attr_A(T)$, player P will be able to avoid entering this set [...]; otherwise
the position would be already in $attr_A(T)$ itself. So from outside $attr_A(T)$, P can
avoid, by a local strategy, to enter this set and can hence avoid the visit of T."
We boldly formulate a strategy (for P) that avoids entering $attr_A(T)$:

---

[5] The auxiliary function `pick_ea` formalizes the body of the definition of $attr_A^{d+1}(T)$.

```
CattrA_strat :: [(σ,β) waa, β word, (nat * σ Apos) set]
                ⇒ σ Pstrat
CattrA_strat auto w T ≡
λi s M. εt. t ∈ M
        ∧ ((i,s) ∉ attrA auto w T ⇒ (i+1,t) ∉ attrA auto w T)
```

Why is this a well-defined strategy? Assume that $(i + 1, t) \in attr_A(T)$ holds for all possible moves t from M; that is, for every such t there exists some d such that $(i + 1, t) \in attr_A^d(T)$. Assuming that $M \neq \emptyset$ was a legal A-move from state s, we need to prove that this implies $(i, s) \in attr_A(T)$. It is here that we require M to be a finite set, for then there is some d such that $(i + 1, t) \in attr_A^d(T)$ for all $t \in M$, and therefore we obtain $(i, s) \in attr_A^{d+1}(T) \subseteq attr_A(T)$. Without this finiteness assumption, we would only be able to prove $(i, s) \in pick\_ea(attr_A(T))$, which need not be a subset of $attr_A(T)$.

It is only at this point in the proof (and in the similar proof for player P) where finiteness plays a role, and we therefore obtain a slight generalization of Thomas' result in that the set of states need not be finite, although the transition relations must be defined by finitary formulas.

With this observation, the required well-formedness and correctness conditions are not too hard to establish. In fact, their proofs are made more perspicuous by observing the following algebraic facts about attractor sets.

```
T ⊆ U ⟹ attrA auto w T ⊆ attrA auto w U
is_waa auto ⟹ attrA auto w (attrA auto w T) = attrA auto w T
```

The definitions and proofs for strategies forcing or avoiding visits to $attr_P(T)$ can mostly be obtained by cut-and-paste: the same tactics can also handle the dual quantifier combinations.

6.2   Proving Determinacy

Completing the proof of proposition 5, Thomas lets Q_i denote the set of states with rank i and Pos_0 the set of all positions in the game for automaton $\mathcal{A}$ and word w, and continues:

> Clearly, from the positions in $A_0 := attr_A(Q_0)$, Automaton can force, by a local strategy, to reach states of rank 0 and thus win. Consider the subgame whose set of positions is $Pos_1 := Pos_0 \setminus A_0$ (all of which have rank ≥ 1). From the positions in $A_1 := attr_P(Pos_1 \cap Q_1)$, Pathfinder can force, again by a local strategy to reach (and stay in) states of rank 1 and hence win. [...] In this way we continue: In the game with position set $Pos_2 := Pos_1 \setminus A_1$ (containing only states of rank ≥ 2) we form the attractor set $A_2 := attr_A(Pos_2 \cap Q_2)$, etc. Then the positions from which Automaton wins (by the local attractor strategies) are those in the sets A_i with even i. Similarly, Pathfinder wins from the positions in the set A_i with odd i (again by his local attractor strategies).

Instead of formalizing the induction principle based on "subgames" that this argument is based on, we give a direct recursive definition of the sets A_i:[6]

---

[6] Our definition ensures `determ_pos i ⊆ determ_pos (i+2)`, unlike Thomas' definition.

```
rankSet :: [σ ⇒ nat, nat] ⇒ (nat * σ) set
rankSet rk r ≡ { (i,s) | rk s = r }

determ_pos :: [nat, (σ,β) waa, β word] ⇒ (nat * σ Apos) set
recdef determ_pos "less_than"
  determ_pos 0 = λauto w. attrA auto w (rankSet (rank auto) 0)
  determ_pos 1 = λauto w. attrP auto w ((rankSet (rank auto) 1)
                                      \ (determ_pos 0 auto w))
  determ_pos (Suc (Suc k)) = λauto w.
    let pos = determ_pos k auto w
              ∪ ((rankSet (rank auto) (Suc (Suc k)))
                    \ (determ_pos (Suc k) auto w))

    in
    if (k mod 2 = 0) then attrA auto w pos else attrP auto w pos
```

We must also define the strategy player A should apply for positions in the set A_{2k}.

```
A_strat :: [nat, (σ,β) waa, β word] ⇒ σ Astrat
primrec
  A_strat 0 auto w =
  λi s. if (i,s) ∈ rankSet (rank auto) 0
        then εS. S ∈ Amoves auto w i s
        else attrA_strat auto w (rankSet (rank auto) 0) i s

  A_strat (Suc k) auto w =
  λi s. if (i,s) ∈ determ_pos (k+k) auto w
        then A_strat k auto w i s
        else if (i,s) ∈ rankSet (rank auto) (Suc (Suc (k+k)))
                        \ (determ_pos (Suc (k+k)) auto w)
        then CattrP_strat auto w (determ_pos(Suc(k+k)) auto w) i s
        else attrA_strat auto w
                (determ_pos (k+k) auto w
                 ∪ (rankSet (rank auto) (Suc (Suc (k+k)))
                      \ (determ_pos (Suc (k+k)) auto w))) i s
```

These definitions may look intimidating, but the idea is quite simple: given a position (i, s) in $A_0 = attr_A(Q_0)$, either the rank of s is already 0, in which case any continuation ensures that A wins. Otherwise, player A applies the attractor strategy that is known to force a visit in Q_0. Given a position $(i, s) \in A_{2k+2}$ there are three cases: either in fact $(i, s) \in A_{2k}$ holds, and A applies the strategy defined for positions in A_{2k}, which is already known by induction hypothesis. Second, if $(i, s) \in Q_{2k+2} \setminus A_{2k+1}$ (the "kernel" of A_{2k+2}) then A avoids positions in A_{2k+1}; this ensures that the ranks of subsequent positions will be even and $\leq 2k + 2$. Otherwise, player A applies the attractor strategy for A_{2k+2} to force an eventual visit in the kernel.

Continuing the formal development, we first prove that every position is contained in some A_i:

$$\exists k.\ k \le \text{rank auto } s \wedge (i,s) \in \text{determ\_pos k auto w}$$

The proof is by case distinction on whether the rank r of s is 0, 1, or $i+2$ for some $i \in \mathbb{N}$, expansion of the appropriate clause in the definition of A_r, and further case distinctions guided by the definitions, taking 13 interactions. More difficult is the proof of the following lemma, which asserts that strategy A_strat, applied to some position in A_{2k} forces the play to remain in some position in A_{2l}, for some $l \le k$.

```
[ is_waa auto; pl ∈ drawseqs auto w s;
  (i,fst (pl i)) ∈ determ_pos (k+k) auto w;
  snd (pl i) = A_strat k auto w i (fst (pl i)) ]
⟹ ∃l. l ≤ k ∧ (i+1,fst(pl(i+1))) ∈ determ_pos (l+l) auto w
```

The proof is essentially by induction on k, but requires 44 interactions, including many low-level instantiations. Of similar complexity is the proof of the overall correctness of the strategy, which takes 34 interactions.

```
[ is_waa auto; pl ∈ drawseqs auto w s;
  (i, fst (pl i)) ∈ determ_pos (k+k) auto w;
  ∀j. i ≤ j ⇒ snd (pl j) = A_strat k auto w j (fst (pl j)) ]
⟹ Awins auto pl
```

It remains to define a similar winning strategy for player P when starting from a position in A_{2k+1}, and reprove the analogous theorems. The basic ideas are the same, but due to the low-level nature of some of the proof scripts, they cannot be copied blindly. Since obviously there cannot be a winning strategy for both players for some position, it follows that the sets A_k form two disjoint hierarchies for k even or odd.

6.3 Complementation

We can now prove the complementation theorem:

```
is_waa auto ⟹ language (dual auto) = - language auto
```

The proof is simple, given the previous lemmas: automaton $\mathcal{A}$ does not accept input word w iff (by proposition 2) player A does not have a local winning strategy in the corresponding game iff (by proposition 4) player P does not have a local winning strategy in the game associated with $\tilde{\mathcal{A}}$ and w iff (by proposition 5) player A has a local winning strategy in that game iff (again by proposition 2) $\tilde{\mathcal{A}}$ accepts w.

7   From Temporal Logic to Weak Alternating Automata

As an application of our definitions and results, we now formalize a translation
of formulas of propositional temporal logic of linear time into weak alternating
automata [4,11]. In contrast to the standard translation of PTL to Büchi automata, this construction is compositional and of linear complexity; the hardest
step in the correctness proof is that for negation, which is based on the theorem
we have just proven.

7.1   Propositional Temporal Logic

We begin with the definition of a deep embedding of PTL (over a type α of
atomic propositions) in Isabelle:[7]

```
datatype α ptl =
     TRUE | Var α | NOT α ptl | OR (α ptl) (α ptl)
   | NEXT α ptl  | UNTIL (α ptl) (α ptl)
type α behavior = (α set) word

suffix :: [α behavior, nat] ⇒ α behavior
suffix ρ n ≡ λi. ρ(i+n)

holdsAt :: [α behavior, α ptl] ⇒ bool    ("_ ⊨ _")
ρ ⊨ TRUE
ρ ⊨ Var x      = (x ∈ ρ 0)
ρ ⊨ NOT f      = ¬(ρ ⊨ f)
ρ ⊨ f OR g     = ((ρ ⊨ f) ∨ (ρ ⊨ g))
ρ ⊨ NEXT f     = suffix ρ 1 ⊨ f
ρ ⊨ f UNTIL g = ∃n. suffix ρ n ⊨ g ∧ ∀ m<n. suffix ρ m ⊨ f

models :: α ptl ⇒ (α behavior) set
models f ≡ { ρ | ρ ⊨ f }
```

We will mainly restrict attention to *normal* formulas that do not contain
double negations; this predicate is easily defined as a recursive function, as is a
normalization function that removes any double negations. We can then prove
laws about PTL formulas such as

$$(\rho \models f \text{ UNTIL } g) = ((\rho \models g) \lor (\rho \models f \land \rho \models \text{NEXT}(f \text{ UNTIL } g)))$$

We inductively define the set of subformulas of a PTL formula. The *Fischer-
Ladner closure* $\mathcal{C}(\varphi)$ of a formula φ is the set that contains all subformulas of
φ and their complements. Observe that all formulas in $\mathcal{C}(\varphi)$ are normal if φ is
normal.

---

[7] We use infix syntax for the OR and UNTIL operators.

7.2   Definition of Automaton $\mathcal{A}_\varphi$

We associate a weak alternating automaton $\mathcal{A}_\varphi$ with every PTL formula φ. The set of states is given by the Fischer-Ladner closure of φ, with φ being the initial state. The transition relation and the ranks are defined by induction on the formula.[8]

```
ptl_trans :: [α ptl, α set] ⇒ (α ptl) pboolean
ptl_trans TRUE S = Atomic TRUE
ptl_trans (Var x) S =
    if x∈s then Atomic TRUE else Atomic(NOT TRUE)
ptl_trans (NOT f) S = subst complement (dual_form(ptl_trans f S))
ptl_trans (f OR g) S = Or (ptl_trans f S) (ptl_trans g S)
ptl_trans (NEXT f) S = Atomic f
ptl_trans (f UNTIL g) s =
    Or (ptl_trans g s)
        (And (Atomic (f until g)) (ptl_trans f S))

ptl_rank :: α ptl ⇒ nat
ptl_rank TRUE = 0
ptl_rank (Var x) = 1
ptl_rank (NOT f) = (ptl_rank f)+1
ptl_rank (f OR g) = max (ptl_rank f) (ptl_rank g)
ptl_rank (NEXT f) = ptl_rank f
ptl_rank (f UNTIL g) = let r = max (ptl_rank f) (ptl_rank g)
                        in  if r mod 2 = 0 then r+1 else r

ptl_waa :: α ptl ⇒ (α ptl, α set) waa
ptl_waa f ≡
    (| states  = fischer_ladner f, initial = f,
       trans   = ptl_trans,         rank    = ptl_rank |)
```

The definition of the transition relation for an automaton state corresponding to an **until** formula follows the recursive expansion law shown above. For a formula $\neg\varphi$, we take the dual of the Boolean combination associated with φ, but complement all atoms. Based on a few lemmas about the Fischer-Ladner closure, it is easy to prove that automaton $\mathcal{A}_\varphi$ is indeed well-formed if φ is a normal PTL formula.

```
normal f ⟹ is_waa (ptl_waa f)
```

Moreover, the automaton associated with the complement of φ is isomorphic to the dual automaton for φ modulo a renaming of all its states by complementation and possibly an adjustment of ranks that does not affect their parity.

---

[8] subst h p denotes the positive Boolean formula obtained from p by applying h to all atoms in p.

```
ren_auto  ::  [(σ,β) waa,  σ  ⇒  τ,  (τ,β) waa]  ⇒  bool
ren_auto src h tgt ≡
  states tgt = h''(states src)
∧ initial tgt = h(initial src)
∧ ∀s∈states src. ∀b. trans tgt (h s) b = subst h (trans src s b)
∧ ∀s∈states src. rank tgt (h s) mod 2 = rank src s mod 2


normal f ⟹
ren_auto (dual (ptl_waa f)) complement (ptl_waa (complement f))
```

7.3   Correctness of the Translation

We now prove that the automaton $\mathcal{A}_\varphi$ accepts precisely the models of φ, for any normal PTL formula φ. This requires proving that (i, ψ) is a winning position for player A in the game associated with $\mathcal{A}_\varphi$ and behavior ρ if and only if ψ holds of the i'th suffix of ρ, for any formula ψ in the Fischer-Ladner closure of φ. The only non-trivial cases are those for negation and **until**. For negation, the assertion follows by the complementation theorem for weak alternating automata, the observation that $\mathcal{A}_{\neg\psi}$ is obtained by renaming $\mathcal{A}_\psi$ via complementation, and the fact that complementation is injective for normal formulas. The most tedious part of the Isabelle proof is to show that an automaton obtained by renaming via a function that is injective on the states of the original automaton induces the same winning positions for either player. For a formula $\psi \equiv \psi_1$ **until** ψ_2, it suffices to observe that any draw sequence starting at ψ remains at ψ until it simulates a draw sequence for ψ_1 or ψ_2. Using the recursion law for the **until** operator, this justifies the definition of a winning strategy for player A.

Assembling the bits and pieces, we can now prove the correctness of the translation from PTL formulas to weak alternating automata:

```
language (ptl_waa (normalize f)) = models f
```

Isabelle's facility to state goals containing unknowns, which are instantiated during the proof, allows us to use this theorem to actually construct automata $\mathcal{A}_\varphi$ inside the theorem prover, based on Isabelle's built-in rewriting engine. In this way, we obtain a certified translation procedure from PTL formulas to weak alternating automata. The evaluation can actually be performed inside Isabelle because the construction is of linear complexity.

8   Conclusion

The work on this paper has been started by pure intellectual curiosity: Complementation of ω-automata has been one of the most celebrated problems of the field, and Thomas' streamlined presentation of the proof based on weak alternating automata and their associated games seemed to be the first one that could actually be carried out using an interactive theorem prover. The usefulness of such an endeavor may, however, be disputable. This case study has once again confirmed that at least part of the social process that leads to the acceptance of a proof can actually be replaced by machine certification, and that even well-polished hand proofs are still likely to contain errors such as the "type error" our formalization has revealed.

On the other hand, it cannot be disputed that it still takes some effort to convert even a very well-presented proof into machine-checkable form: our formalization of Thomas' proof took about three weeks, being reasonably familiar with both the subject matter and the tool. Still, this is perhaps not an inordinate amount of time for a reasonably complex proof.

It is obvious that formalization of mathematical proofs requires attention to details that are happily ignored in paper-and-pencil proofs. Still, if formalization in itself is to be of any value, the format of the documents produced by machine proofs is also important when discussing formalized mathematics. In this respect, our experience has been mixed. On the one hand, we found that the formalization of the underlying concepts was fairly natural and simple, due to the high expressiveness of the higher-order framework. Concerning the automation of proofs, the first part of the work reported here was carried out using Isabelle's standard tactic-based interface. We have found that the automatic tactics provided by Isabelle are incompatible with human reasoning capabilities: whereas complicated-looking subgoals may succumb to a single tactic invocation, other seemingly trivial goals (in particular those that involve arithmetic) need tedious low-level interaction. Moreover, small changes to the underlying definitions may render a tactic script obsolete. For the translation of PTL to automata, we have used Wenzel's recent Isar interface [12] that is based on an explicit proof language. This has been a very positive experience: although documents become much more verbose, the user has much more control of the interaction, and changes tend to be much easier to apply.

The main benefit of formalization, however, is exemplified by the certified translation of PTL formulas to automata presented in section 7 where effective computational procedures have been derived from the purely mathematical constructions arising from the proof. Our translation to automata constitutes the first step towards a formalized PTL decision procedure: having constructed the automaton, it remains to decide whether its language is empty or not in order to decide whether the formula is satisfiable or not. Deciding nonemptiness is rather easy using external tools ("oracles" in Isabelle terminology), for example based on BDD technology. In general, deciding nonemptiness of weak alternating automata is PSPACE-complete, and it is therefore less clear how to carry out this second step inside a theorem prover. Schneider [6] has presented a similar translation of PTL formulas to a symbolic representation of Büchi automata. His translation is also linear, and he also uses an external tool to decide nonemptiness. We believe that alternating automata may be preferable to Büchi automata because the translation is compositional, which may be an advantage for applications such as model checking. For example, one may want to apply minimizations during the construction of $\mathcal{A}_\varphi$, or pre-compute the product of the transition system under investigation with, say, certain fairness conditions.

References

1. J. R. Büchi. On a decision method in restricted second-order arithmetics. In *International Congress on Logic, Method and Philosophy of Science*, pages 1–12. Stanford University Press, 1962.
2. Orna Kupferman and Moshe Y. Vardi. Weak alternating automata are not so weak. In *5th Israeli Symposium on Theory of Computing and Systems*, pages 147–158. IEEE Press, 1997.
3. D. E. Muller, A. Saoudi, and P. E. Schupp. Alternating automata, the weak monadic theory of the tree and its complexity. In *13th ICALP*, volume 226 of *Lecture Notes in Computer Science*, pages 275–283. Springer-Verlag, 1986.
4. D.E. Muller, A. Saoudi, and P.E. Schupp. Weak alternating automata give a simple explanation of why most temporal and dynamic logics are decidable in exponential time. In *3rd IEEE Symposium on Logic in Computer Science*, pages 422–427. IEEE Press, 1988.
5. Shmuel Safra. On the complexity of ω-automata. In *29th IEEE Symposium on Foundations of Computer Science*, pages 319–327. IEEE Press, 1988.
6. Klaus Schneider and Dirk W. Hoffmann. A HOL conversion for translating linear time temporal logic to ω-automata. In Y. Bertot et al, editor, *TPHOLs'99: 12th International Conference on Theorem Proving in Higher Order Logics*, volume 1690 of *Lecture Notes in Computer Science*, pages 255–272, Nice, France, 1999. Springer-Verlag.
7. Wolfgang Thomas. Automata on infinite objects. In Jan van Leeuwen, editor, *Handbook of Theoretical Computer Science, volume B: Formal Models and Semantics*, pages 133–194. Elsevier, Amsterdam, 1990.
8. Wolfgang Thomas. Languages, automata, and logic. In G. Rozenberg and A. Salomaa, editors, *Handbook of Formal Language Theory*, volume III, pages 389–455. Springer-Verlag, New York, 1997.
9. Wolfgang Thomas. Complementation of Büchi automata revisited. In J. Karhumäki, editor, *Jewels are Forever, Contributions on Theoretical Computer Science in Honor of Arto Salomaa*, pages 109–122. Springer-Verlag, 2000.
10. Moshe Vardi. Verification of concurrent programs: The automata-theoretic framework. In *Proceedings of the Second Symposium on Logic in Computer Science*, pages 167–176. IEEE, June 1987.
11. Moshe Y. Vardi. *Computer Science Today*, volume 1000 of *Lecture Notes in Computer Science*, chapter Alternating Automata and Program Verification, pages 471–485. Springer-Verlag, 1995.
12. Markus Wenzel. Isar—a generic interpretative approach to readable formal proof documents. In Y. Bertot et al, editor, *TPHOLs'99: 12th International Conference on Theorem Proving in Higher Order Logics*, volume 1690 of *Lecture Notes in Computer Science*. Springer-Verlag, 1999.

Graphical Theories of Interactive Systems: Can a Proof Assistant Help?

Robin Milner

University of Cambridge Computer Laboratory,
New Museums Site, Pembroke Street,
Cambridge, CB2 3QG, England

Computer scientists are privileged, or doomed, to deal rigorously with large structures. This happens, of course, with hardware design and verification, and with programs and specifications. Considerable progress has been made with mechanised proof assistance for both. Going further into the back room, programming languages are also big structures. It's very uncommon to have help from a proof assistant while actually designing a language, probably because the very formalism for writing down what a language means is changing under our feet, so it's asking too much for those who build proof assistants to keep up with these developments enough to help the designers in real time. All the same, it has been encouraging to see plenty of post hoc verification of properties of Standard ML using its semantic formalism. Perhaps a future language design using "big step structure operational semantics" could be done using proof assistance to check out the sanity of a large set of inference rules before they are frozen into a design.

Going still further into the back room, some computation theories are also big structures. We would like to have a model of mobile interactive systems, in the form of a calculus in which one can really verify, say, that certain invariants are preserved by all activity; an example would be a security assertion. I have been developing action calculi – which is such a model – for many years, often changing notation and definitions, wanting to see whether a theorem survives the changes, wanting to visualise an embedding of one graph in another (since action calculi have a graphical presentation), and so on. A proof assistant would be a great help if I could keep it up to date with my changes of mind. It's a very hard challenge to ask for tools to help theory development; but it was also hard to get machine-assisted proof off the ground at all, and that has been done. In my talk I would like to provoke thinking about how this challenge can be addressed incrementally. Computer scientists developing theories are probably to the best guinea pigs for pilot studies.

J. Harrison and M. Aagaard (Eds.): TPHOLs 2000, LNCS 1869, p. 442, 2000.
© Springer-Verlag Berlin Heidelberg 2000

Formal Verification of the Alpha 21364 Network Protocol

Abdel Mokkedem and Tim Leonard

Compaq Computer Corporation
Alpha Development Group
334 South Street,
Shrewsbury, MA 01545-4112
Abdel.Mokkedem@Compaq.com, Tim.Leonard@Compaq.com

Abstract. We describe our formal verification that the Alpha 21364's network protocol guarantees delivery and maintains necessary message ordering. We describe the protocol and its formalization, and the formalization and proof of deadlock freedom and liveness. We briefly describe our experience with using three tools (SMV, PVS, and TLA+/TLC), with the cost effectiveness of formal methods, and with software engineering of formal specs.

1 Introduction

Compaq's Alpha 21364 microprocessor[Ban98] includes features that are hard to verify with traditional simulation-based methods – particularly glueless multiprocessor support. Simulation of a large multiprocessor is a challenge[BBJ+95,KN95,TQB+98], and though the project leaders felt that simulation would adequately verify that the RTL correctly implemented the multiprocessor protocols, it wouldn't adequately prove the absence of deadlock and livelock.

We describe our formal verification that the 21364's network (transport) protocol guarantees delivery and maintains necessary message ordering. (We also formally verified the coherence protocol, but don't describe that here.) We relate our experiences with three tools (SMV, PVS, and TLA+/TLC), with the cost effectiveness of formal methods, and with software engineering of formal specs.

Sections 2 and 3 describe the network protocol and its formalization. Sections 4 and 5 present the formalization and proofs of deadlock freedom and liveness. Section 6 discusses the results and what we learned.

2 The Protocol

The Alpha 21364 includes glueless multiprocessor support – each processor has four direct processor-to-processor network links (plus an I/O interface and a Rambus interface). In a multiprocessor system, each processor links to its neighbors north, south, east, and west, with the ends wrapped around to form a 2D torus, as shown in Figure 1.

A network protocol provides point-to-point message transport within the torus. It guarantees message delivery, maintains ordering of I/O traffic for each source-sink pair, and can route around some failures. It is used for message delivery by a cache-coherence protocol.

J. Harrison and M. Aagaard (Eds.): TPHOLs 2000, LNCS 1869, pp. 443–461, 2000.

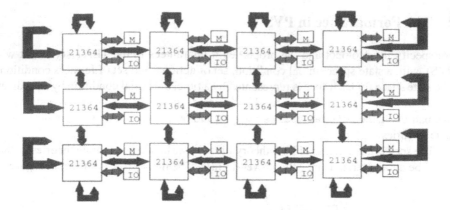

Fig. 1. A 12-processor 21364-based multiprocessor.

Though we verified the real protocol, the protocol and spec fragments shown are unverified excerpts and do not represent the protocol's actual details. In the rest of the paper, "the network" and "the protocol" refer to the example rather than the 21364's design. All the points we make are true of both.

The network uses a store-and-forward protocol, with messages buffered at intermediate nodes as they hop toward their destinations. Without some mechanism to prevent it, a deadlock cycle could appear, with buffers in every node in the cycle full of packets waiting for buffer space in the node ahead. An "intra-dimensional" deadlock runs all the way around the torus in a single direction (and thus in a single row or column). Other deadlocks are "inter-dimensional," and may have complex looping paths.

The network protocol avoids intra-dimensional deadlock by providing two virtual channels (that is, two buffers) for each direction [DS87]. For each virtual channel ("VC"), use of one link in each row or column is prohibited, so no deadlock cycle can form in a single VC. Packets travelling in a row or column use one VC or the other for the whole trip, so no inter-VC cycle can form in a single row or column.

Inter-dimensional deadlock is avoided by dimension-order routing [DS87]. One axis (north-south, for example) is primary and the other is secondary. Packets complete their travel in the primary axis before beginning travel in the secondary. This divides each route into two segments, each limited to a single row or column. Deadlock cycles are avoided in each segment by the intra-dimensional mechanism, and though packets travelling in the primary axis may depend on packets travelling in the secondary, the reverse is not true, so no cycle can form between them.

These mechanisms provide deadlock freedom for the network protocol, but deadlock problems reappear in the cache coherence protocol. To avoid them, coherence protocol messages are grouped into six classes. Each message can be completed using messages only from lower classes. The network protocol provides separate sets of buffers for each coherence-protocol message class, in effect providing independent networks.

3   The Formal Spec in PVS

We specify the protocol and the properties it guarantees in the TLA+ style (but with PVS), with a state space, initial condition, set of actions, and set of fairness conditions. The state space for each spec is represented by a type, the initial condition by a predicate saying whether or not a state is a legal initial state, actions by predicates over state pairs (the pair being the before and after states), and fairness conditions by predicates over state histories.

The spec is a collection of PVS theory files. Some had to be separate theories so they could be parameterized and called several times. The theory tree is shown in Figure 2.

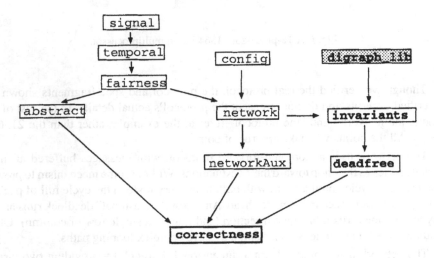

Fig. 2. Theory hierarchy.

The protocol's type definitions (config) define the space of legal network configurations and states, which need no notion of time. The initial conditions, actions, and fairness conditions are in a separate theory (network). These use signals, histories, temporal logic operators, and fairness, and PVS doesn't provide those as built-in libraries, so we wrote the pieces we needed (signals, temporal, and fairness). Many lemmas about the protocol (invariants) are used in the proof of deadlock freedom (deadfree), which itself is expressed using the built-in PVS [BS97] graph-theory library (digraph_lib).

The signals, temporal, and fairness theories are re-used to express the protocol's top-level guarantees (abstract). The abstract and concrete protocol specs have different notions of state (and in an earlier version, had different notions of time). We need to augment the concrete spec with "auxilliary variables" (networkAux), and then use a rather complex refinement mapping to extract an abstract history from the concrete protocol history before we can say that it must satisfy the abstract spec (correctness).

3.1 Signals, Histories, Temporal Logic, and Fairness

Signals (`signal`) and temporal-logic operators (`temporal`) are trivial, and are shown in $\boxed{1}$ and $\boxed{2}$.

```
signal[T: TYPE]: THEORY                                              1
BEGIN
     Signal: TYPE = [nat -> T]
END signal
```

```
temporal: THEORY                                                    2
BEGIN
IMPORTING signal[bool]

Eventually(signal: Signal[bool]): Signal[bool] =
  LAMBDA(t1: nat): EXISTS(t2: nat): t2 >= t1 AND signal(t2)

Always(signal: Signal[bool]): Signal[bool] =
  LAMBDA(t1: nat): FORALL(t2: nat): t2 >= t1 IMPLIES signal(t2)
END temporal
```

Theory $\boxed{3}$ introduces types `Action` and `History` and defines weak and strong fairness. `State` is an arbitrary parameter of the theory. Given an action, `IsEnable` returns a state predicate that says whether the action is enabled in a given state. The action is enabled if there exists a next state such that the action occurs between the current state and the next state. Given an action and a history, `Occurs` returns a signal saying at what times the action occured. `MapPredicate` maps a state predicate over a state history, returning a signal saying at what times in the history the predicate is satisfied. An action is weakly fair if it prohibits histories in which the event is forever enabled yet never occurs. An action is strongly fair if it prohibits histories in which the event is enabled infinitely often yet never occurs.

```
fairness[State: TYPE]: THEORY                                       3
BEGIN
IMPORTING temporal, signal[State], signal[bool]

Action : TYPE = [State, State -> bool]
History: TYPE = Signal[State]

IsEnabled(action: Action) : [State -> bool] =
  LAMBDA (state: State) : EXISTS (next_state: State) : action(state, next_state)

Occurs(action: Action, history: History) : Signal[bool] =
  LAMBDA (t: nat) : action(history(t), history(t+1))

MapPredicate(predicate:[State -> bool], history: History): Signal[bool] =
  LAMBDA (t: nat) : predicate(history(t))

IsWeaklyFair(action: Action, history: History): bool =
  Eventually(Always(MapPredicate(IsEnabled(action), history)))(0)
    IMPLIES Always(Eventually(Occurs(action, history)))(0)

IsStronglyFair(action: Action, history: History): bool =
  Always(Eventually(MapPredicate(IsEnabled(action), history)))(0)
    IMPLIES Always(Eventually(Occurs(action, history)))(0)
END fairness
```

3.2 The Abstract Spec (The Protocol's Guarantees)

The protocol's guarantees are easy to get roughly right: all sent messages must be delivered, and I/O messages from a particular source to a particular destination must be delivered in order. A few details tighten it up: *only* sent messages may be delivered. The destination of a message may not always be ready to accept deliveries, but we can assume it will always eventually be ready. Given that assumption, the network must always eventually be ready to accept new sent messages.

Actually, the network must guarantee that each message class accepts and delivers messages even if all other classes are blocked, so our assumption about the eventual readiness of destinations is expressed per class.

We made the formal spec of the protocol's guarantees as simple and abstract as possible, limited mostly by having to express the I/O-ordering constraint. We abstracted away most of the rest by parameterizing the theory.

In the hardware, messages aren't uniquely identifiable. We need to prohibit the protocol from throwing away or duplicating a message in flight even when an identical one is also in flight. We avoid the problem in the property spec by giving each message a unique ID. As it happens, we also need a time stamp so we can express in-order delivery, so we use the message UID for both purposes. The UID doesn't exist in the hardware implementation, and how we have deal with that in the proof is explained in Section 5.

The theory `abstract` has several parameters. `Source` is the set of processor interfaces that can present the network with messages for delivery. `Sink` is the set of interfaces to which those messages are delivered. `Class` is an attribute of messages; we assume that `Class` contains at least two distinct classes (`RDIO`, `WRIO`). The type `State` represents the network with an unordered set of tuples (source ID, destination ID, message content), the counter value to express ordering between I/O messages, `CanSource` which says whether the network is ready to receive new messages from a source port, and `CanSink` which says whether a sink port is ready to receive a delivered message.

```
abstract[PID: TYPE+, Source: TYPE+, Sink: TYPE+, Class: TYPE+,              4
         MessageBody: TYPE+, ... more parameters ...]: THEORY
BEGIN
ASSUMING RDIO: Class
         WRIO: Class
         rw_distinct: ASSUMPTION RDIO /= WRIO
ENDASSUMING

fset_lib: LIBRARY "/usr/share/pvs-2.3/lib/finite_sets"

SourceID    : TYPE = [# proc: PID, port: Source #]
SinkID      : TYPE = [# proc: PID, target: Sink #]
...
Message     : TYPE = [# class: Class, body: MessageBody, counter: nat #]

IMPORTING fset_lib@finite_sets[[SourceID, SinkID, Message]]

State : TYPE = [# Network : finite_set[[SourceID, SinkID, Message]],
                  Counter   : nat,
                  CanSource : [SourceID, Class -> bool],
                  CanSink   : [SinkID,   Class -> bool]   #]
IMPORTING fairness[State]

Action : TYPE = fairness[State].Action
History : TYPE = fairness[State].History
```

The abstract network has five possible actions, shown in `5` and described below. `NewMessage` puts a specified new message into the network for delivery from a specified source port to a specified destination port. After `NewMessage`, `CanSource` may be false for that class at that port. The action `AssertCanSource` sets it back to true to let more messages be sent. DeliverMessage delivers a specified message to the specified destination. AssertCanSink lets more messages of that class be delivered to that port. StutterStep does nothing, and is the abstraction of actions in the implementation that have no visible effect at the abstract level.

```
NewMessage(src: SourceID, dst: SinkID, m: Message): Action =           5
  LAMBDA (s, s_n:State):
      CanSource(s)(src, m'class)
  AND m'counter = Counter(s)
  AND CanSometimesSink(dst'target, m'class)
  AND src'proc = dst'proc IMPLIES LocalRouteAllowed(src'port, dst'target)
  AND Network(s_n) = add((src, dst, m), Network(s))
  AND Counter(s_n) = Counter(s)+1
  AND (   CanSource(s_n) = CanSource(s)
      OR CanSource(s_n) = CanSource(s) WITH [(src, m'class) := FALSE] )
  AND CanSink(s_n) = CanSink(s)

DeliverMessage(dst: SinkID, m: Message): Action =
  LAMBDA (s, s_n:State):
      CanSink(s)(dst, m'class)
  AND EXISTS (src: SourceID) :
        member((src, dst, m), Network(s))
      AND ( ( m'class=RDIO OR m'class=WRIO )
          IMPLIES FORALL (m2: IOMessage) :
                          member((src, dst, m2), Network(s))
                          IMPLIES m2'counter >= m'counter  )
      AND Network(s_n) = remove((src, dst, m), Network(s))
      AND Counter(s_n) = Counter(s)
      AND (   CanSource(s_n) = CanSource(s)
          OR CanSource(s_n) = CanSource(s) WITH [(src, m'class) := TRUE]
          )
      AND (   CanSink(s_n) = CanSink(s) WITH [(dst, m'class) := FALSE]
          OR CanSink(s_n) = CanSink(s)
          )

AssertCanSource(src: SourceID, class: Class): Action =
  LAMBDA (s, s_n:State):
      CanSometimesSource(src'port, class) = TRUE
  AND CanSource(s)(src, class) = FALSE
  AND CanSource(s_n) = CanSource(s) WITH [(src, class) := TRUE]
  AND Network(s_n) = Network(s)
  AND Counter(s_n) = Counter(s)
  AND CanSink(s_n) = CanSink(s)

AssertCanSink(dst: SinkID, class: Class): Action =
  LAMBDA (s, s_n:State):
      CanSometimesSink(dst'target, class) = TRUE
  AND CanSink(s)(dst, class) = FALSE
  AND CanSink(s_n) = CanSink(s) WITH [(dst, class) := TRUE]
  AND Network(s_n) = Network(s)
  AND Counter(s_n) = Counter(s)
  AND CanSource(s_n) = CanSource(s)

StutterStep: Action =   LAMBDA (s, s_n:State): s = s_n
```

NewMessage for some source, destination, and message occurs between an initial and after state iff

- the network is initially ready to accept a message of this class at this port, and
- the message is stamped with the initially current time, and
- the destination port accepts messages of this class, and
- if the message is local, this source port may send to this target, and
- the network afterward has its initial contents plus the message, and
- the timer afterward is one greater than it was initially, and

- the network may or may not be able to accept such messages from that port afterward, but the status of other input ports is unchanged, and
- the status of output ports is unchanged.

Note that the first two clauses depend only on the initial state, and the second two depend on the parameters and are independent of the state. These four together are the action's enabling condition. The others relate the result state to the initial state. Actions are predicates, not functions, to allow nondeterminism, and the value of CanSource after NewMessage shows how that's used. Finally, it's easy to forget to put in the last clause, but omitting it allows unintended nondeterminism – the status of output ports afterward could be anything. With it, the abstract actions are mutually exclusive. The implementation may do several actions at once because our mapping of time allows us to observe the abstract state intermittently.

DeliverMessage is enabled iff

- the environment is ready to accept that message class at this port, and
- an in-flight message has the specified destination and content, and
- if the message is RDIO or WRIO, it is the oldest I/O message in the net from its source to its destination

and actually occurs between an initial and after state iff

- the network afterward has its initial contents minus the message, and
- the network may be able to accept such messages from the source port afterward but the status of other input ports is unchanged, and
- the destination port may or may not be able to accept the delivery of such messages afterward but the status of other output ports is unchanged.

AssertCanSource (at some port and class) is enabled if CanSource is currently false there, and if that port is ever allowed to source such messages. The action occurs if CanSource becomes true there and all other system state is unchanged. AssertCanSink is the equivalent action for destination ports. A StutterStep does nothing.

The action AbstractNetworkNext (shown in ⌐6⌐) is an action that is one of the five allowed actions.

```
AbstractNetworkNext: Action =                                              6
  LAMBDA (s,s_n:State):
  EXISTS (src: SourceID, dst: SinkID, cl: Class, m: Message) :
    NewMessage(src, dst, m)(s, s_n)      OR
    DeliverMessage(dst, m)(s, s_n)       OR
    AssertCanSource(src, cl)(s, s_n)     OR
    AssertCanSink(dst, cl)(s, s_n)       OR
    StutterStep(s, s_n)
```

The fairness requirement (shown in ⌐7⌐) guarantees that every message that enters the network will be delivered. The first clause says that if a destination port is available often enough and there is a message in flight to it, the message will eventually be delivered to it. The second clause says that if all destination ports are eventually ready to sink packets in a class, then all ports will eventually be ready to accept messages in that class.

```
AbstractNetworkFairness(h: History): bool =                                  7
 ( FORALL (dst: SinkID, m: Message) :
          IsStronglyFair(DeliverMessage(dst, m), h)
 ) AND
 ( FORALL (class: Class) :
     (FORALL (dst: SinkID) : IsWeaklyFair(AssertCanSink(dst, class), h))
     IMPLIES
     (FORALL (src: SourceID): IsStronglyFair(AssertCanSource(src, class),h))
 )
```

In the initial condition, the set of in-flight messages is empty, the time stamp is zero, and all ports that can potentially accept messages are ready.

AbstractNetworkSpec (8) specifies the set of allowed behaviours. The initial state must satisfy the initial condition, all subsequent states in the behaviours are obtained by executing one of the possible actions, and the fairness requirements should hold.

```
AbstractNetworkInit(s: State): bool =                                        8
 s = (# Network   := emptyset,
        Counter   := 0,
        CanSource := LAMBDA (src: SourceID, class: Class) :
                            CanSometimesSource(src'port, class),
        CanSink   := LAMBDA (dst: SinkID,   class: Class) :
                            CanSometimesSink(dst'target, class) #)

AbstractNetworkSpec(h: History): bool =
  AbstractNetworkInit(h(0)) AND
  Always(Occurs(AbstractNetworkNext,h))(0) AND
  AbstractNetworkFairness(h)
```

3.3   The Concrete Spec (How the Protocol Works)

The concrete spec says how the protocol works. It describes a 2D torus with possibly failing links, legal configurations, and the routing algorithm. The basic theory axis (9) defines the two dimensions East-West and North-South, the four compass-point directions, the primary axis, non-negative cartesian coordinates for those axes, and few additional constants.

```
axis : THEORY                                                               9
BEGIN
Axis : TYPE = NS, EW
PrimaryAxis: Axis

OppositeAxis(axis:Axis): Axis = CASES axis OF NS: EW, EW: NS ENDCASES
SecondaryAxis :           Axis = OppositeAxis(PrimaryAxis)
Direction :               TYPE = {N, S, E, W}
NonnegCoordinates :       TYPE = [Axis -> nat]

OppositeDirection(d:Direction):Direction =
  CASES d OF  N : S, S : N, E : W, W : E ENDCASES
IsPositive (d:Direction):bool = d = N OR d = E
DirectionsOfAxis(a:Axis) : TYPE =
  { d : Direction | IF a = NS THEN d = N or d = S ELSE d = E or d = W ENDIF }
AxisOfDirection(d:Direction): Axis =
  CASES d OF N: NS, S: NS, E: EW, W: EW ENDCASES
END axis
```

The theory config (10) describes legal configurations of the network and its static control registers.

```
config [(IMPORTING axis) PhantomCorner: NonnegCoordinates,          10
        (IMPORTING coordinates[PhantomCorner]) InnerCorner: CoordInRect,
        Source: TYPE+, Sink: TYPE+, Class: TYPE+, ... ] : THEORY
BEGIN
...
BrokenLinks : [Pid, Direction -> bool]
Coordinate(a:Axis): TYPE = { n : nat | n <= PhantomCorner(a) }
BufferID : TYPE = [# proc: Pid, port: InputPort, cl: Class, ch: Channel #]
IPBufferID : TYPE = { bid: BufferIDRep | is_internal(port(bid)) }
EPBufferID : TYPE = { bid: BufferIDRep | is_external(port(bid)) }
SinkID : TYPE = [# proc: Pid, port: Sink, cl: Class #]

RouteType : TYPE = [# dir       : [a:Axis -> DirectionsOfAxis(a)],
                      val        : [a:Axis -> Coordinate(a)],
                      FirstAxis  : Axis,
                      ... more fields ...                     #]
RoutingTable: TYPE = [Pid -> [Pid -> RouteType ] ]
VCSelect : TYPE =
  [Pid -> [d:Direction -> [Coordinate(AxisOfDirection(d)) -> VirtChannel]]]
Neighbors : TYPE =
  [Pid -> [Direction -> [[# proc: Pid, port: Direction, working: bool #]]]]

Network : TYPE = [# RoutingTable: RoutingTable, VCSelect: VCSelect #]
```

The theory network (11) has several parameters, including the routing tables, the assignment of virtual channels (VC), and their respective datelines. The assumptions restrict these parameters to have legal values. For instance, one VCSelectAllowed assumption prevents switches from VC0 to VC1 to avoid intra-dimension deadlock.

The network state is described with a record that contains the value of each buffer, the number of free buffer entries at each input port, the wires through which a node receives deallocs from neighbors, the wires through which a node receives packets from neighbors, and the wires CanSink through which the environment asserts its readiness to accept message delivery.

```
network [Source: TYPE+, Sink: TYPE+, Message: TYPE+, Class: TYPE+,         11
         RoutingTable: RoutingTable, VCSelect: VCSelect,
         LocalRouteAllowed: [Source, Sink -> bool],... ] : THEORY
BEGIN

ASSUMING
VCSelectAllowed(vc_select:VCSelect,rt:RoutingTable): bool = ...
GoodRoutingTable : ASSUMPTION RoutingTableAllowed(RoutingTable)
GoodVCSelect     : ASSUMPTION VCSelectAllowed(VCSelect,RoutingTable)
ENDASSUMING

Header: TYPE = [# dir       : [a:Axis -> DirectionsOfAxis(a)],
                  val       : [a:Axis -> Coordinate(a)],
                  VC        : VirtChannel,
                  ... more fields ...                     #]
Packet: TYPE = [# route : Header, dest : Sink, class : Class, msg : Message #]
BufferEntry: TYPE = [# pkt : Packet,
                       wait: finseq[bool],
                       outports : finite_set[[OutputPort,Channel]] #]
State: TYPE = [# Buffers : [BufferID -> [# Packets   : finseq[BufferEntry],
                                           Deallocs  : nat #]],
                 FreeBufferEntries : [EPBufferID -> nat],
                 DeallocsIn        : [Pid -> [Direction -> finseq[Dealloc]]],
                 PacketsIn         : [Pid -> [Direction -> finseq[Packet]]],
                 CanSink           : [SinkID -> bool]                    #]

IMPORTING fairness[State]
Action : TYPE = fairness[State].Action
History : TYPE = fairness[State].History
```

The protocol allows these actions:

- NewMessage: A node accepts a new message from an internal port for delivery to a destination port. It builds a new packet and constructs the set of port/channel pairs that this packet can route through next. The source and destination classes must match, and the destination must be able to receive packets.
- ReceivePacket: A node moves a packet from a specified external port to an input buffer, adding info about legal next hops.
- RoutePacket A node moves a packet from a specified internal or external port buffer to a specified external port, updates the wait-bitvector if it's an IO packet, and decrements the count of free buffer entries.
- SendDealloc: A node sends a buffer-deallocation message (a dealloc) to a neighbor saying that a specified buffer has free entries.
- ReceiveDealloc: A node receives a dealloc from a neighbor, and increases its count of free buffer entries.
- AssertCanSink: A specified destination port signals that it is ready for the delivery of messages of a specified class.
- DeliverMessage: A specified message is moved from a specified buffer to a specified destination port. The destination may or may not be ready to accept more.

The code for two actions is shown in $\boxed{12}$, with NetworkNext.

```
ReceivePacket(i:Pid, d:Direction): Action =  LAMBDA(s,s_n: State):      ┌────┐
length(PacketsIn(s)(i)(d)) > 0  AND                                     │ 12 │
LET                                                                     └────┘
    newPkt = Head(PacketsIn(s)(i)(d)),
    newPktCh = VC(route(newPkt)),
    inBuff = (# proc := i, port := d, cl := class(newPkt),  ch := newPktCh #),
    wrioBuffer = inBuff WITH [(cl) := WRIO],
    outPorts = OutPorts(i, DirectionToInputPort(d), newPkt),
    WRIOQueue = Packets(Buffers(s)(wrioBuffer)),
    wait_bv = ...
IN s_n = s WITH [(Buffers)(inBuff)(Packets):=
                    Append(Packets(Buffers(s)(inBuff)),
                      (# pkt:= newPkt, wait := wait_bv, outports:= outPorts #)),
                  (PacketsIn)(i)(d) := Tail(PacketsIn(s)(i)(d))       ]

ReceiveDealloc(i:Pid, d:Direction): Action =  LAMBDA(s,s_n: State):
       length(DeallocsIn(s)(i)(d)) > 0
  AND LET newD = Head(DeallocsIn(s)(i)(d)),
          freeClass = PROJ_1(newD),
          freeChannel = PROJ_2(newD),
          freeBuffer = (# proc:= i,  port:= DirectionToInputPort(d),
                           cl:= freeClass, ch:= freeChannel #)
     IN s_n = s WITH [(FreeBufferEntries)(freeBuffer) :=
                        FreeBufferEntries(s)(freeBuffer) + 1,
                      (DeallocsIn)(i)(d) := Tail(DeallocsIn(s)(i)(d))  ]
... other actions ...

NetworkNext : Action =
 LAMBDA (s,s_n: State):
  EXISTS (i,j: Pid, ip: Sink, ep: Direction, srcBuf: BufferID, epBuf: EPBufferID,
          ipBuf: IPBufferID, dstBuf: SinkID, m: Message, dstCh:Channel,
          srcEntryIndex: below[length(Packets(Buffers(s)(srcBuf)))]) :
      NewMessage(ipBuf, dstBuf, m)(s,s_n) OR ReceivePacket(i,ep)(s,s_n)
   OR RoutePacket(srcBuf, ep, srcEntryIndex, dstCh)(s,s_n)
   OR SendDealloc(epBuf)(s,s_n) OR ReceiveDealloc(i,ep)(s,s_n)
   OR DeliverMessage(srcBuf, ip, m, srcEntryIndex)(s,s_n)
   OR AssertCanSink(dstBuf)(s,s_n) OR StutterStep(s,s_n)
```

`InternalActionsAreFair` (13) prohibits histories with unfair behavior. The actions `RoutePacket` and `DeliverMessage` need to be strongly fair because the output ports and the sink ports are shared by packets coming from several directions. Weak fairness is sufficient for the other actions.

```
InternalActionsAreFair(h:History): bool =                                  13
  FORALL (i:Pid, epBuffer:EPBufferID, srcBuffer:BufferID, dstPort:Sink,
          d:Direction, m:Message, destChannel:Channel, srcIndex:nat):
    IsStronglyFair( RoutePacket(srcBuffer, srcIndex, destChannel),   h ) AND
    IsWeaklyFair   ( ReceivePacket(i, d),                            h ) AND
    IsWeaklyFair   ( SendDealloc(epBuffer),                          h ) AND
    IsWeaklyFair   ( ReceiveDealloc(i, d),                           h ) AND
    IsStronglyFair( DeliverMessage(srcBuffer, dstPort, m, srcIndex), h )
```

The initial state considers the network empty and the sink ports available. The predicate `NetworkProtocolAllows` (14) ties together the initial condition, the state-transition function, and the fairness constraint.

```
NetworkInit(s: State):bool =                                               14
  FORALL (bid : BufferID, epbid : EPBufferID, ipbid : SinkID, i:Pid, d:Direction):
          Buffers(s)(bid) = (# (Packets) := empty_seq, (Deallocs) := 0 #)
      AND FreeBufferEntries(s)(epbid) = BufferSize(epbid)
      AND CanSink(s)(ipbid) = CanSometimesSink(ipbid'port, ipbid'cl)
      AND DeallocsIn(s)(i)(d) = empty_seq AND PacketsIn(s)(i)(d)  = empty_seq

NetworkProtocolAllows(h:History): bool =
        NetworkInit(h(0))
    AND Always(Occurs(NetworkNext,h))(0)
    AND InternalActionsAreFair(h)
```

4 Formalization and Proof of Deadlock Freedom

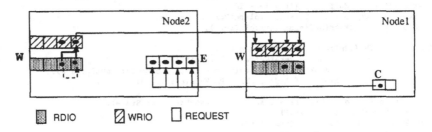

Fig. 3. Graph of dependencies between the packets.

Our first verification step consists of proving that the network protocol implementation is free of deadlock. Actually, we prove that a dependency graph is free of cycles, rather than that an action is always eventually enabled. We will see in Section 5 how the same dependency graph is re-used to prove the liveness property. We used a similar technique in a previous work [MHJG00]. Dependency graphs are represented using the PVS directed-graphs library. Vertices are buffer entries (type VCNode in 15). An entry nd1 depends on another entry nd2 if the packet in nd2 is blocking the packet in nd1. Figure 3 shows an example of a dependency between a packet in the C port buffer (L2-cache port) in Node1 and all packets in the East port buffer in Node2. It also shows intra-buffer dependencies between IO packets in Node2 (dashed lines) and dependencies between packets in the West port of Node2 and packets in the West port of Node1 (solid lines). Note that there is a non-IO dependency only when the destination buffer is entirely full. I/O packets depends on older I/O packets going to the same destination.

```
deadfree [...] : THEORY                                                    15
BEGIN
digraph_lib: LIBRARY "/usr/share/pvs-2.3/lib/digraphs"

IMPORTING invariants[...]

Node   : TYPE = [# buff_id : BufferID, index  : below[BufferSize(buff_id)] #]
VCNode : TYPE =  nd : Node | nd'buff_id'ch = VC0 or nd'buff_id'ch = VC1

IMPORTING digraph_lib@path_ops[VCNode], digraph_lib@path_lems[VCNode]

DepGraph(s:State) : digraph[VCNode] =
 (# vert  := LAMBDA (nd:VCNode): TRUE,
    edges := LAMBDA (nd1,nd2:VCNode):
       IF  is_internal(port(buff_id(nd2))) OR buff_id(nd1) = buff_id(nd2)
       THEN FALSE
       ELSE
         LET Buffer_nd1 = buff_id(nd1),
             Buffer_nd2 = buff_id(nd2),
             Packets_nd1 = Packets(Buffers(s)(Buffer_nd1)),
             Packets_nd2 = Packets(Buffers(s)(Buffer_nd2)),
             dstPort    = OppositeDirection(port(Buffer_nd2)),
             dstChannel = ch(Buffer_nd2),
             Deallocs_nd2 = Deallocs(Buffers(s)(Buffer_nd2)),
             DeallocsIn_nd1 = DeallocsIn(s)(proc(Buffer_nd1))(dstPort),
             dstBuf = Buffer_nd1 WITH [(port) := dstPort, (ch) := dstChannel ]
       IN % Non IO dependencies:
          % --------------------
          (   cl(Buffer_nd1) = cl(Buffer_nd2)
          AND index(nd1) < length(Packets_nd1)
          AND index(nd2) < length(Packets_nd2)
          AND Deallocs_nd2 = 0
          AND FreeBufferEntries(s)(dstBuf) = 0
          AND member(dstPort, dstChannel), outports(Packets_nd1(index(nd1))))
          AND NOT(EXISTS (k:below[length(DeallocsIn_nd1)]):
                         DeallocsIn_nd1(k) = (cl(Buffer_nd2),ch(Buffer_nd2)))
          AND Neighbors(Buffer_nd1'proc)(dstPort)'proc = Buffer_nd2'proc
          )
          OR
          % IO dependencies:
          % ----------------
          ( ... )
       ENDIF
 #)
```

Note that DepGraph does not include intra-buffer dependencies between I/O packets. We first prove the theorem NoDeadlockInv (16) which says that every walk (a sequence of vertices) in the dependency graph is a path (no vertex occurs twice). In other words, no cycle can be formed in any behaviour allowed by the implementation. Essentially, we prove that the invariant holds at the initial states and is preserved by every transition. The proof uses induction on the walk length and several invariants proved in the theory invariant. Some of these invariants assert that the state of a packet and its position in the network is consistent with its route information.

```
NoDeadlockInv : THEOREM FORALL (h:network.History):           16
  LET NoDeadlock(s:State): bool =
    FORALL (w:Walk(DepGraph(s))): path?(DepGraph(s),w)
  IN  NetworkProtocolAllows(h) IMPLIES Always(MapPredicate(NoDeadlock, h))(0)
```

Then we extend the dependency graph to include the intra-buffer dependencies (17):

```
% The following definition adds intra-buffer dependencies to the DepGraph.        17
DepGraph2(s:State) : digraph[VCNode] =
  (# vert   := LAMBDA (nd:VCNode): TRUE,
     edges := LAMBDA (nd1,nd2:VCNode):
                   edges(DepGraph(s))(nd1,nd2)
            OR (   buff_id(nd1) = buff_id(nd2)
               AND (buff_id(nd1)'cl = RDIO OR buff_id(nd1)'cl = WRIO)
               AND index(nd1) < index(nd2)
               AND LET Packets_nd1 = Packets(Buffers(s)(buff_id(nd1))),
                       Packets_nd2 = Packets(Buffers(s)(buff_id(nd2))),
                       Entry1 = Packets_nd1(index(nd1)),
                       Entry2 = Packets_nd1(index(nd2))
                    IN Entry1'pkt'route'val = Entry2'pkt'route'val
               )
  #)
```

We prove the theorem NoDeadlock2Inv (18) by showing that intra-buffer dependencies do not introduce cycles. This follows from the definition DepGraph2 and theorem NoDeadlockInv.

```
NoDeadlock2Inv : THEOREM FORALL (h:network.History):                    18
        LET NoDeadlock(s:State): bool =
                 FORALL (w:Walk(DepGraph2(s))): path?(DepGraph2(s),w)
        IN NetworkProtocolAllows(h) IMPLIES Always(MapPredicate(NoDeadlock, h))(0)
```

5   Formalization and Proof of the Liveness Property

In order to show that the network protocol satisfies its abstract correctness specification we construct a refinement mapping which maps every concrete history allowed by the implementation into an abstract history allowed by the abstract specification. In order to simplify the definition of the refinement map, we have extended the concrete state with an auxilliary variable to record the ID of the packet (from counter) and the node that sourced it (proc, port). We make sure the transitions never use the values of auxilliary variables, they only move them around (19). PVS allows us to do that in a clean way by creating an instance of the theory network with the new type Message (lines 1,2,3,4 in 19).

```
networkAux[...] : THEORY                                                19
BEGIN
Message: TYPE = [# body: MessageBody,                    % ------ line 1
                   source: [# proc: Pid, port: Source #], % ------ line 2
                   counter: nat #]                        % ------ line 3
IMPORTING network[...,Message,...]                        % ------ line 4

StateAux : TYPE = [# state : State, Counter : nat #]

IMPORTING fairness[StateAux]
Action : TYPE = fairness[StateAux].Action

NetworkAuxInit(s: StateAux):bool = NetworkInit(s'state) AND s'Counter = 0

NewMessageAux(srcBuffer:IPBufferID, dstBuffer:SinkID, m:Message): Action
  = LAMBDA (s,s_n: StateAux):
      m'source = (# proc := srcBuffer'proc, port := srcBuffer'port #)
      AND m'counter = s'Counter
      AND NewMessage(srcBuffer, dstBuffer, m)(s'state,s_n'state)
      AND s_n'Counter = s'Counter + 1
```

MapState (20) maps a concrete state from networkAux into an abstract state from abstract. A tuple e is in flight in the abstract network if there exists an entry in any buffer or wire in the concrete network holding a packet travelling from the source e'1 to the destination e'2 carrying the message e'3. CanSource is set in the abstract state iff the buffer of the input port in the corresponding concrete state is not full.

```
correctness[Source: TYPE+, Sink: TYPE+, ...] : THEORY                         20
BEGIN
c : THEORY = networkAux[PhantomCorner, InnerCorner, Source, ...]
a : THEORY = abstract[Pid, Source, Sink, MessageBody, Class, ...]

MapState(s:c.StateAux): a.State =
(# Network    := LAMBDA (e: [a.SourceID, a.SinkID, a.Message]):
    (EXISTS (srcBuffer:BufferID):
     EXISTS (k:below[length(s'state'Buffers(srcBuffer)'Packets)]):
        e'1 = s'state'Buffers(srcBuffer)'Packets(k)'pkt'msg'source
     AND e'2 = (#
        proc:= epsilon! (i:Pid): WhoAmI(i) =
                  s'state'Buffers(srcBuffer)'Packets(k)'pkt'route'val,
        target:= s'state'Buffers(srcBuffer)'Packets(k)'pkt'dest
                #)
     AND e'3'class = s'state'Buffers(srcBuffer)'Packets(k)'pkt'class
     AND e'3'body = s'state'Buffers(srcBuffer)'Packets(k)'pkt'msg'body
     AND e'3'counter = s'state'Buffers(srcBuffer)'Packets(k)'pkt'msg'counter)
 OR (EXISTS (i:Pid, d:Direction):
     EXISTS (k:below[length(s'state'PacketsIn(i)(d))]):
        e'1 = s'state'PacketsIn(i)(d)(k)'msg'source
     AND e'2 = (# proc := epsilon! (j:Pid): WhoAmI(j) =
                         s'state'PacketsIn(i)(d)(k)'route'val,
               target := s'state'PacketsIn(i)(d)(k)'dest
             #)
     AND e'3'class = s'state'PacketsIn(i)(d)(k)'class
     AND e'3'body = s'state'PacketsIn(i)(d)(k)'msg'body
     AND e'3'counter = s'state'PacketsIn(i)(d)(k)'msg'counter),
Counter    := s'Counter,
CanSource := LAMBDA (src:a.SourceID,cl:Class) :
      LET source = (# proc := src'proc, port := src'port, cl := cl #)
      IN length(s'state'Buffers(source)'Packets) < BufferSize(source),
CanSink   := LAMBDA (dst:a.SinkID,cl:Class) :
      LET sink = (# proc:= dst'proc, port:= dst'target, cl := cl #)
      IN s'state'CanSink(sink)
#)
```

Our goal is to prove the following theorem, where o denotes function composition:

```
networkSatisfiesabstract: THEOREM FORALL (c_history: c.History) :           21
    c.NetworkAuxProtocolAllows(c_history) IMPLIES
       a.AbstractNetworkSpec(MapState o c_history)
```

We have split the proof into three cases. First, we prove that concrete initial states map into abstract initial states. Second, we prove that for every action taken in the concrete history there exists a corresponding abstract action taken in the abstract history. Third, we prove that the implementation satisfies the fairness requirements described by the abstract specfication.

The proof of the two lemmas in 22 makes use of additional invariants we have proved in theory correctness.

```
networkSatisfiesabstractInit: LEMMA FORALL (s: StateAux):                    22
    NetworkAuxInit(s) IMPLIES AbstractNetworkInit(MapState(s))
networkSatisfiesabstractNext: LEMMA FORALL (h: c.History, n:nat):
      c.NetworkNextAux(h(n),h(n+1)) IMPLIES
         a.AbstractNetworkNext(MapState(h(n)), MapState(h(n+1)))
```

For instance, we needed the invariant saying that every packet in the concrete network has a distinct stamp (23).

```
                                                                              23
CounterIsUnique(s:c.StateAux): bool =
    FORALL (b1, b2:BufferID, index1:below[length(Packets(Buffers(s'state)(b1)))],
                             index2:below[length(Packets(Buffers(s'state)(b2)))]):
      ((b1 /= b2 OR index1 /= index2)
       IMPLIES  Buffers(state(s))(b1)'Packets(index1)'pkt'msg'counter  /=
                Buffers(state(s))(b2)'Packets(index2)'pkt'msg'counter
      ) AND
      FORALL (i:Pid,d:Direction,k:below[s'state'PacketsIn(i)(d)'length]):
               s'state'PacketsIn(i)(d)'seq(k)'msg'counter /=
               Buffers(state(s))(b1)'Packets(index1)'pkt'msg'counter

CounterIsUniqueInv: LEMMA FORALL (c_history: c.History) :
      c.NetworkProtocolAllows(h) IMPLIES
      Always(MapPredicate(CounterIsUnique, h))(0)
```

To prove $\boxed{24}$, we re-use the dependency graph and the theorem `NoDeadlock2Inv` which shows that there is no cycle in that graph.

```
                                                                              24
networkSatisfiesabstractFair: LEMMA FORALL (h: c.History):
        c.NetworkProtocolAllows(h) IMPLIES a.InternalActionsAreFair(h)
```

Essentially, we prove that every packet (buffer entry) eventually does not depend on any other packet. This means that the fanout of any node in the dependency graph eventually becomes zero ($\boxed{25}$), and consequently allows the packet to move a step forward using fairness.

```
                                                                              25
Unblocked(nd1:VCNode): [State -> bool] =
    LAMBDA (s:State): NOT(EXISTS (nd2:VCNode): edges(DepGraph2(s))(nd1,nd2))

every_edge_eventually_disappears : THEOREM
  FORALL (c_history: c.History) :
    c.NetworkAuxProtocolAllows(c_history) IMPLIES
  FORALL (nd:VCNode):
    Always(Eventually(MapPredicate(Unblocked(nd), c_history)))(0)
```

Then we use the fact that the distance of the packet to its destination decreases at each hop in order to prove that the packet eventually reaches its destination and is eventually delivered (by fairness of `c.DeliverMessage`).

Again, in order to decompose the proof, we prove several lemmas. `stability_lemma` ($\boxed{26}$) says that if an edge is permanent, at some point the path of permanent edges it depends on will saturate. The proof of this lemma uses the finiteness of the dependency graph and absence of cycles.

```
                                                                              26
stability_lemma : LEMMA FORALL (c_history:c.History, t:nat, nd0,nd1:VCNode):
        c.NetworkAuxProtocolAllows(c_history)
    AND Permanent((nd0,nd1),c_history,t)
    IMPLIES EXISTS (t2:nat, nd2:VCNode, w:Walk(DepGraph2(c_history(t2)'state))):
            from?(w,nd0,nd2)
        AND FORALL (i:below[l(w)]): Permanent((w(i),w(i+1)),c_history,t2)
        AND FORALL (nd3:VCNode): (edges(DepGraph2(c_history(t2)'state))(nd2,nd3)
                                 IMPLIES NOT(Permanent((nd2,nd3),c_history,t2)))
```

The next lemma ($\boxed{27}$) says that every individual edge that appears in the graph eventually disappears (though it may reappear again later).
It follows from `stability_lemma` and fairness conditions.

```
                                                                              27
every_edge_eventually_disappears : LEMMA
  FORALL (c_history: c.History) :
    NetworkAuxProtocolAllows(c_history) IMPLIES
    FORALL (c_t:nat, nd1,nd2: VCNode): Not(Permanent((nd1,nd2),c_history,c_t))
```

The next two lemmas (29) allow us to decouple I/O dependencies from normal dependencies. The first lemma says that if there is a dependency from nd1 to nd2 there should exist another dependency from nd1 to nd3 such that nd3 does not depend on any entry in a buffer within the same node (this can happen only between I/O buffers, by definition of DepGraph2). The second lemma says that the number of I/O dependency edges outgoing from a node decreases monotonically until it reaches zero, leaving only normal dependencies (that is, between buffers from different nodes).

```
Permanent(e:edgetype[VCNode],c_history:c.History,t:nat) : bool =        28
        edges(DepGraph2(c_history(t)'state))(e)
    AND FORALL (t2:nat):
        (t2 > t IMPLIES edges(DepGraph2(c_history(t2)'state))(e))

NoIODep(nd1:VCNode): [State -> bool] : bool = LAMBDA (s:State):
        FORALL (nd2:VCNode): ( edges(DepGraph2(s))(nd1,nd2)
                                IMPLIES buff_id(nd1)'proc /= buff_id(nd2)'proc )

NoIO_OR_Unblocked(nd:VCNode): [State -> bool] =
        LAMBDA (s:State): Unblocked(nd)(s) OR NoIODep(nd)(s)
```

The predicate Permanent (28) says whether an edge is permanent. NoIODep says that all the dependencies (edges) outgoing from a node are not I/O dependencies, that is, the entries they depend on are in a neighboring node.

```
delete_IO_dep : LEMMA FORALL (c_history:c.History, t:nat):       29
    c.NetworkAuxProtocolAllows(c_history)
    IMPLIES FORALL (nd1,nd2:VCNode):
        Permanent((nd1,nd2),c_history,t)
        IMPLIES (    NoIODep(nd2)(c_history(t))
            OR EXISTS (nd3:VCNode):
                (    Permanent((nd2,nd3),c_history,t)
                AND NoIODep(nd3)(c_history(t))
                )
            )
IO_disappears_monotonically : LEMMA FORALL (c_history: c.History):
    c.NetworkAuxProtocolAllows(c_history) IMPLIES
    FORALL (nd:VCNode):
        Always(Eventually(MapPredicate(NoIO_OR_Unblocked(nd), c_history)))(0)
```

The lemma delete_IO_dep (29) follows from the definition of DepGraph2. The proof of IO_disappears_monotonically uses induction on the number of I/O edges outgoing from a node, and lemmas delete_IO_dep and 27 .

6   Discussion

This was an engineering effort, not research, so our lessons are about what's cost effective rather than what's possible.

We've elided many details for the discussion, and also a major mode that made the spec somewhat more complex and added a third to the proof. We didn't learn anything from those parts worth talking about.

We didn't verify many things we wanted to. We would have liked to verify that the spec was satisfiable for many configurations, that its fault tolerance worked under certain classes of failure, and that the coherence protocol plus additional pieces, layered on top of the network protocol, implemented the Alpha memory model. But those weren't justified by a business need.

6.1   Experience with Different Verification Tools

We tried three verification systems. We started with model checking, but even with SMV's [McM99] scalar sets, induction, and other reductions, we couldn't reduce the state below 250 bits, mostly because of induction in two dimensions. Fortunately, it took very little time to figure that out. (We did use SMV successfully on the coherence protocol.)

We then used TLA+ [Lam99] and TLC [YML99]. TLA+ is a specification language based on the Temporal Logic of Actions. It uses set theory and is untyped. We started with English specs, a draft partial TLA+ spec (written by Josh Scheid), and access to the protocol architects and implementors, and we extended and then rewrote the spec over the course of several months. TLC is an explicit-state model checker for TLA+, and we used it to find many bugs in our spec, though because TLA+ is untyped it often took long runs to find bugs we considered type errors. We were beta-testers of TLC and found many bugs in it, but the developers fixed them so fast that it rapidly stabilized, and its bugs didn't slow us down. TLC added multithreading during our project, which let us run it 5-10 times faster. Even so we couldn't exhaustively cover any but the most extremely limited configurations. We had no other proof tools for TLA+.

Finally we translated the TLA+ spec into higher-order logic for PVS [SOR93] and started the proof there. The translation was trivial, and PVS type checking immediately found many more bugs, and in fact it found almost all the remaining ones. We also found and reported a variety of bugs in PVS itself, and those were not fixed during our project. Though we found ways of working around all of them, if we'd been using an open-source tool it would have been worth our effort to fix the bugs ourselves.

The organization of theories and files was surprisingly constrained by how PVS passes parameters to theories. What was shown in Figure 2 as the single "config" theory is in fact three theory files, so that some parts could be parameterized and reused.

6.2   Thoughts about Cost-Effectiveness

The design was largely debugged by simulation before we started. We could have found some of those bugs had we started earlier, but that wouldn't actually have saved any money; our "concrete" model is much more abstract than RTL, so simulation would have been necessary anyway. In theory, early formal specs and proof might have prevented bugs and so shortened our schedule, but that's entirely speculative. Our contribution was to verify what simulation couldn't: liveness and fairness.

The proof took the most effort (5 intense person months), but took less time than writing the specs (depending on how you count, 5-10 months of two people). Type checking found almost all the bugs in the spec. PVS type checking can require full interactive theorem proving, but in practice the type-checking proofs were automatic or pretty trivial. Formal specification and thinking through the formal proof in detail found the two bugs in the design. If the job had been to find bugs rather than to prove their absence, the mechanically checked proof would not have added much value – writing the formal specs, typechecking them, and thinking through the formal proof did most of it.

But we took on the verification to reduce risk; we didn't expect to find protocol bugs. We found that risks are much smaller in hindsight – it's harder to justify the effort after the fact, because risk reduction is unmeasurable. Partly because of that, we're now verifying things that are important, hard for simulation, *and* where we'll have lots of bugs to show for it afterward.

PVS, like most tools, is designed to use only a single processor, and there's an opportunity there. Even small groups now typically have lots of idle processors connected to a local net, and like many big organizations, we have literally hundreds of high-performance processors locally available. We distribute jobs among them to help simulation-based verification, and would have devoted them to help with the proof if we could have. Are there ways to use networked computers to ease theorem proving?

We can claim two bugs, neither in the protocol proper. The first was in the implementation rather than the protocol. The protocol designers had reversed a design decision repeatedly and the implementation had settled in an inconsistent state. We brought the confusion to light while formalizing the spec, and coincidentally, simulation independently discovered it the same day. The second was an unrecognized configuration constraint in the protocol. A mode for routing around failures conflicted with a mode for improving performance, and though each worked separately, together they allowed deadlock.

6.3   Thoughts about the Software Engineering of Formal Specs

The specs aren't large: 3 pages of library code, 6 pages of abstract spec, and 35 pages of network spec. The refinement map, deadlock-freedom property, liveness property, and 74 lemmas were another 25 pages. The deadlock-freedom proof was about 20,000 lines, and the fairness proof about another 6,000.

We used CVS for version control of the specs, but rather haphazardly. (CVS rather than another tool only because it was already being used for version control of the RTL.) Had there been more of us using the spec, version control would have been essential. Had there been more people doing the proof, version control of the proof would have been appropriate, too.

The formal protocol spec needed and got a code review by designers. A good display form would have been nice but wasn't necessary. Engineers and architects picked up the necessary higher-order logic, temporal logic, and obscure syntax without much effort. They could not have written in it without much practice, but understood it well enough to do very effective review. We should have reviewed more, and earlier.

We repeatedly changed types and parameterization of theories and functions. We found that giving actions as few parameters as possible makes spec maintenance easiest. We completely de-parameterized the actions when we realized that. Unfortunately, we did so before writing the fairness spec and learning that anything quantified outside a fairness operator in the fairness spec must be an action parameter. So we had to put those parameters back in. There are still constants that should be parameters because we didn't finish the changes. We would have benefited from software-engineering tools to help make such changes. Good browsing, outlining, and display tools would have been nice, too, both for us and during the code reviews. Had we been using SMV, we would have brought a machine to the reviews to check invariants in real time as they came up in discussion.

References

[Ban98]   Peter Bannon.   Alpha 21364: a scalable single-chip SMP.   In *Micropro-cessor Forum (Cahners MicroDesign Resources)*, pages 68–80, October 1998. http://www.digital.com/alphaoem/present/index.htm.

[BBJ+95]   M. Bass, T.W. Blanchard, D.D. Josephson, D. Weir, and D.L. Halperin. Design methodologies for the PA 7100LC microprocessor. *Hewlett-Packard Journal*, 1995.

[BS97]   Ricky W. Butler and Jon A. Sjogren. A PVS Graph Theory Library. Technical Report Memorandum, NASA Langly Research Center, December 1997. http://atb-www.larc.nasa.gov/ftp/larc/PVS-library.

[DS87]   W.J. Dally and C.L. Seitz. Deadlock-free message routing in multiprocessor inter-connection networks. *IEEE Transactions on Computers*, 1987.

[KN95]   Mike Kantrowitz and Lisa M. Noack. Functional verification of a multi-issue, pipe-lined, superscalar Alpha processor - the Alpha 21164 CPU chip. *Digital Technical Journal*, 1995.

[Lam99]   Leslie Lamport. Specifying concurrent systems with TLA+. In Manfred. Broy and Ralf Steinbrüggen, editors, *Calculational System Design*, pages 183–247. IOS Press, 1999.

[McM99]   K.L. McMillan. Getting started with SMV. Technical report, Cadence Berkeley Labs, December 1999. http://www-cad.eecs.berkeley.edu:80/˜kenmcmil/.

[MHJG00]   A. Mokkedem, R. Hosabettu, M.D. Jones, and G. Gopalakrishan. Formalization and analysis of a solution to the PCI 2.1 bus transaction ordering problem. *Formal Methods in System Design*, 2000.

[SOR93]   N. Shankar, S. Owre, and J. M. Rushby. *PVS Tutorial*. Computer Science Laboratory, SRI International, Menlo Park, CA, February 1993. Also appears in Tutorial Notes, *Formal Methods Europe '93: Industrial-Strength Formal Methods*, pages 357–406, Odense, Denmark, April 1993.

[TQB+98]   Scott A. Taylor, Michael Quinn, Darren Brown, Nathan Dohm, Scot Hildebrandt, James Huggins, and Carl Ramey. Functional verification of a multiple-issue, out-of-order, superscalar Alpha processor - the DEC Alpha 21264 microprocessor. In *Design Automation Conference, DAC '98*, pages 638–643, Moscone center, San Francisco, California, USA, June 1998. Association for Computing Machinery.

[YML99]   Yuan Yu, Panagiotis Manolios, and Leslie Lamport. Model checking TLA+ specifi-cations. In Laurence Pierre and Thomas Kropf, editors, *Correct Hardware Design and Verification Methods*, LNCS, pages 54–66. Springer-Verlag, September 1999.

Dependently Typed Records
for Representing Mathematical Structure*

Robert Pollack

Durham University, U.K.
rap@dcs.ed.ac.uk

1 Introduction

Consider a statement about groups *"For G a group, ..."*. A naive approach to formalize this is to unfold the meaning of group, so that every statement about groups begins with

$$\text{For } G \text{ a set, } + \text{ an operation on } G, + \text{ associative, } e \in G, \ldots \qquad (1)$$

This "unpackaged" approach can be improved by collecting all the parts of the meaning of group into a *context*, which need not be explicitly mentioned in every statement. A means of *discharging* some of the context is provided, so that statements made under that context can be instantiated with particular groups. However once the group context is discharged, all the parts of a group must be mentioned when using any general lemma about groups. Variations on this are supported by many proof tools, e.g. *Coq*'s `Section` mechanism [Coq99], *Lego*'s `Discharge` [LEG99], *Automath* contexts and *Isabelle* locales.

A significant refinement is achieved by giving names to bits of context as in *telescopes* [dB91], or first-class contexts as in Martin-Löf's framework with explicit substitutions [Tas97]. With these, we need not discharge a context to instantiate definitions and lemmas. But contexts or telescopes are "flat"; they don't show that structures are built from existing structures, sharing some parts, and inheriting some properties.

We informally define "packaging" as any approach to collecting the parts of mathematical structures, supporting more abstract manipulation of structures. Packaging is a two-edged sword: once structures are packaged to gain abstraction, we need more tools for manipulating them.

Overview In Sect. 2 we show well-known inductively definable packaging constructions, Sigma types and inductive records, pointing out some issues of efficiency and abstraction that are not so well-known. Section 3 presents true records, including treatment of labels. This presentation is inspired by the work of Betarte and Tasistro [BT98,Bet98,Tas97], but considerably simplifies and explains that work. One of our simplifications is removal of record subtyping from

---

* Supported by UK EPSRC grant GR/M75518

J. Harrison and M. Aagaard (Eds.): TPHOLs 2000, LNCS 1869, pp. 462–479, 2000.

the core description of records, in favor of the more general notion of *coercive subtyping*, which is briefly discussed in Sect. 4.

Sect. 5, about making signatures more precise, discusses *Pebble style sharing* and *manifest types* in signatures. The main novelty of the present paper is a simple treatment of manifest types in signatures. The main idea I wish to sell is that manifest signatures are necessary for the actual (in practice) formalization of mathematics.

Some notations I use $[x\colon A]M$ for lambda-abstraction, $(x\colon A)B$ for dependent function type, $(A)B$ for non-dependent function type and $M(N)$ for application. $[\_\colon A]M$ is a lambda-abstraction whose variable is not used in the body. Field labels are written r, p, to distinguish them from variables r, p.

Acknowledgement This paper owes much to discussion with my colleagues in the Computer Assisted Reasoning Group at Durham, especially Zhaohui Luo.

2 Definable Structures

We begin with some structuring techniques that are inductively definable in dependent type theory. These are first-class constructions, and as such can be parameterized using lambda-abstraction.

I will use partial equivalence relation (*PER*) as a running example. Let *sym* (resp. *trn*) express that R is a symmetric (resp. transitive) relation over S. *PER* is the telescope (2) or the informal record type (3)

$$[S\colon \mathsf{Set}][R\colon (S)(S)\mathsf{Prop}][sAx\colon sym(S)(R)][tAx\colon trn(S)(R)], \qquad (2)$$

$$\langle S\colon \mathsf{Set},\ R\colon (S)(S)\mathsf{Prop},\ sAx\colon sym(S)(R),\ tAx\colon trn(S)(R)\rangle. \qquad (3)$$

An object with the signature (or *fitting in to* the telescope) *PER* is informally

$$\langle S{=}T,\ R{=}Q,\ sAx{=}symQ,\ tAx{=}trnQ\rangle.$$

where $T\colon \mathsf{Set}$, $Q\colon (T)(T)\mathsf{Prop}$, $symQ\colon sym(T)(Q)$ and $trnQ\colon trn(T)(Q)$.

2.1 Sigma Types

It is clear from (1) that any approach to packaging must handle dependency of later parts on earlier parts of the package. The simplest dependent package is *pairs* with *Sigma types*. For our purposes it is best to use a *logical framework* presentation of Sigma types (Fig. 1), where dependency is handled by the dependent function type of the framework (see rule FORM). While I have written the computation rules as typed equality, they can be implemented by syntactic reduction.

$$\text{FORM} \;\frac{A:\mathsf{Type} \qquad P:(A)\mathsf{Type}}{\Sigma AP:\mathsf{Type}} \qquad\qquad \text{INTRO} \;\frac{\Sigma AP:\mathit{Type} \qquad a:A \qquad p:P(a)}{\langle a,p\rangle_{\Sigma AP}:\Sigma AP}$$

$$\text{ELIM1} \;\frac{p:\Sigma AP}{p.1:A} \qquad\qquad \text{ELIM2} \;\frac{p:\Sigma AP}{p.2:P(p.1)}$$

$$\text{COMP1} \;\frac{\langle a,p\rangle_{\Sigma AP}:\Sigma AP}{\langle a,p\rangle_{\Sigma AP}.1=a:A} \qquad\qquad \text{COMP2} \;\frac{\langle a,p\rangle_{\Sigma AP}:\Sigma AP}{\langle a,p\rangle_{\Sigma AP}.2=p:P(a)}$$

Fig. 1. LF presentation of Sigma types.

For type synthesis to be effective, the pairs, $\langle a,p\rangle_{\Sigma AP}$, must be *heavily typed*, i.e. carry the annotation ΣAP.[1] But then the type of the first component can be inferred, so I will write ΣP and $\langle a,p\rangle_{\Sigma P}$.

Sigma can be formalized in *Coq* (and similarly in *Lego*) as an inductively defined family with a single constructor:

```
Inductive sigT [A:Type; P:A->Type]: Type :=
            existT: (x:A)(P x) -> (sigT A P).
```

The constructor of (sigT A P) is (existT A P); i.e. the pairs are heavily typed, as in Fig. 1. The two projections are defined in terms of the inductive elimination rule (i.e. by case analysis); e.g. the first projection

```
projT1 [A:Type; P:A->Type; H:(sigT A P)]: A :=
            Cases H of (existT x _) => x end.
```

Unlike Fig. 1, definable projection is heavily typed, but that is an artifact of this functional presentation.

Example: right association We can represent *PER* by associating pairs to the right. This is usually written out directly

$$PER := \Sigma[S:\mathsf{Set}]\Sigma[R:(S)(S)\mathsf{Prop}]\Sigma[_-:sym(S)(R)]trn(S)(R). \qquad (4)$$

To clarify, this definition can be written incrementally

$$
\begin{aligned}
Inner\ [S:\mathsf{Set}][R:(S)(S)\mathsf{Prop}] &:= \Sigma[_-:sym(S)(R)]trn(S)(R),\\
Middle\ [S:\mathsf{Set}] &:= \Sigma[R:(S)(S)\mathsf{Prop}]Inner(S)(R), \qquad (5)\\
PER &:= \Sigma[S:\mathsf{Set}]Middle(S).
\end{aligned}
$$

Inside the signature, the fields are named and referred to by bound variables, S and R. However, these names are purely local; to refer to the fields of a *PER*

---

[1] For example, an un-annotated pair, $\langle a,p\rangle$, inhabits both ΣAP and $A\times P(a)$, which are not equal types.

object we must use the anonymous first and second projections. To help matters we can give names to field projectors. (I use informal *dot notation* for application of these defined projectors, although they are actually functions.)

$$
\begin{aligned}
S\,[P\colon PER] &: \text{Set} &&:= P.1 \\
R\,[P\colon PER] &: (P.S)(P.S)\text{Prop} &&:= P.2.1 \\
sAx\,[P\colon PER] &: sym(P.S)(P.R) &&:= P.2.2.1 \\
tAx\,[P\colon PER] &: trn(P.S)(P.R) &&:= P.2.2.2
\end{aligned}
$$

These defined field projectors are global, and cannot be reused globally (e.g. as projectors in other packages) without shadowing or other ad hoc solution.

Here is an inhabitant of the signature defined in (4)

$$
\langle T, \langle Q, \langle symQ, trnQ \rangle_{Inner(T)(Q)} \rangle_{Middle(T)} \rangle_{PER}. \tag{6}
$$

Example: left association An alternative is to associate pairs to the left.

$$
\begin{aligned}
Rel &:= \Sigma[S\colon \text{Set}](S)(S)\text{Prop}, \\
symRel &:= \Sigma[P\colon Rel]sym(P.1)(P.2), \\
PER &:= \Sigma[P\colon symRel]trn(P.1.1)(P.1.2).
\end{aligned} \tag{7}
$$

We do not get to use the local field names directly when defining this signature, but have to project the fields, e.g. $P.1.1$. As above, we can define top level names for field projectors of this tuple:

$$
S\,[P\colon PER] : \text{Set} \qquad := P.1.1.1
$$

$$
\vdots
$$

$$
tAx\,[P\colon PER] : trn(P.S)(P.R) := P.2
$$

Here is an inhabitant of the signature defined in (7)

$$
\langle \langle \langle T, Q \rangle_{Rel}, symQ \rangle_{symRel}, trnQ \rangle_{PER}. \tag{8}
$$

Ad hoc Association There are two other ways to build a 4-tuple out of pairs, and using Sigma types we are free to use any ad hoc association we choose. However, it seems that unitary rules for building records, to be discussed below, must choose left or right association uniformly.

Some Differences By giving both right and left associating definitions of *PER* incrementally I have emphasised the duality of these constructions. However this "symmetry" is broken because type dependency increases to the right. Here are three consequences.

The nested pairs of (6) and (8) are heavily typed, and there is duplication of type information in both cases, so an implementation may optimize structures by keeping only the outermost type annotation.[2] The inner annotations of (8) are

---

[2] *Lego* does this with built-in Sigma types.

subterms of outer annotations, so projection from left associating structures is cost-free using this optimization. However in (6), the inner annotations are substitution instances of outer annotations, so this optimization requires traversing types in order to project the second component.

If we want to add another field to a structure, (e.g. to make *PER* into *equivalence relation*), it must be added on the right, as it will, in general, depend on all the previous fields. Thus (7) can be extended directly and the structure will remain left associating and have *PER* as an immediate substructure. This property is called *extensibility*. On the other hand, extending (4) will either entail breaking the right-association or reorganizing the entire structure so that *PER* is no longer a substructure.

Suppose we want to specialize *PER* to the natural numbers. The data of definition (5) shows directly how the rest of the package depends on the first field; e.g. *Middle(nat)* is the structure we want. Such "application" of parameterized signatures is known as *Pebble style sharing*, and will be discussed further in Sect. 5. There is no obvious way to specialize definition (7) without reorganizing the entire structure. This point is evidently dual to the previous paragraph. The observation that "application" for sharing can be defined directly on nested Sigma types appears in [Kam99], without clear understanding that the tuples must be right associating.

2.2   Inductive Telescopes

The inductive definition of Sigma types as 2-tuples, with projections programmed in terms of inductive elimination, can be extended to arbitrary telescopes. If

$$\mathbb{T} \equiv [x_1 : A_1][x_2 : A_2(x_1)] \cdots [x_k : A_k(x_1, \ldots, x_{k-1})]$$

is a telescope, then there is an inductively defined type $\Sigma\mathbb{T}$, with a single constructor, given by the formation and introduction rules

$$\text{FORM} \quad \frac{\begin{aligned} & A_1 : \mathsf{Type} \\ & A_2 : (A_1)\mathsf{Type} \\ & \vdots \\ & A_k : (x_1 : A_1;\ x_2 : A_1(x_1);\ \ldots;\ A_{k-1}(x_1, \ldots, x_{k-2}))\mathsf{Type} \end{aligned}}{\Sigma\mathbb{T} : \mathsf{Type}} \tag{9}$$

$$\text{INTRO} \quad \frac{\Sigma\mathbb{T} : \mathsf{Type} \quad a_1 : A_1 \quad a_2 : A_2(a_1) \quad \cdots \quad a_k : A_k(a_1, \ldots, a_{k-1})}{\langle a_1, \ldots, a_k \rangle_{\Sigma\mathbb{T}} : \Sigma\mathbb{T}} \tag{10}$$

The premises of (9) say exactly that $\mathbb{T}$ is well-typed, and the premises of (10) say that $\langle a_1, \ldots, a_k \rangle$ fits in to $\mathbb{T}$. In *Coq* (and similarly in *Lego*) there is special syntax for inductive telescopes. For example, one can define *PER* as

```
Record PER: Type :=
      { S:Set; R:S->S->Prop; Sym:(sym S R); Trn:(trn S R) }.
```

which generates an inductive definition

```
Inductive PER : Type :=
    Build_PER : (S:Set; R:S->S->Prop)(trn S R)->(sym S R)->PER.
```

having one constructor, Build_PER. The field names, S, R, ..., are bound variables. To access the fields from outside the package, one must use the anonymous
eliminator Cases. For example, S is defined (approximately) as

```
S [x:PER]: Set := Cases x of (Build_PER S R _ _) => S.
```

Coq tries to automatically define these projectors, and name them with the
associated bound variable name, but this will fail if that name is already used
at top-level.

Uniform Packages For every k we can define the general telescope of length k.
Σ (Sect. 2.1) is the general 2-telescope. The general 4-telescope is programmed
in *Coq* as

```
Record Sig4 [A1: Type;
            A2: A1->Type;
            A3: (a1:A1)(A2 a1)->Type;
            A4: (a1:A1; a2:(A2 a1))(A3 a1 a2)->Type] : Type :=
    { a1:A1; a2:(A2 a1); a3:(A3 a1 a2); a4:(A4 a1 a2 a3) }.
```

This definition exactly captures rules, (9) and (10). *PER* can be defined as

```
Definition PER': Type :=
    (Sig4 Set
          [S:Set](S->S->Prop)
          [S:Set; R:S->S->Prop](sym S R)
          [S:Set; R:S->S->Prop; _:(sym S R)](trn S R)).
```

It is also possible to define general telescopes in terms of shorter general telescopes in various ways, as we defined *PER* in several ways in terms of pairs.

Some Differences. PER above is not heavily typed, since Build_PER can only
construct a PER. E.g. (Build_PER T Q symQ trnQ) inhabits PER. On the other
hand, PER' is heavily typed, and its constructor must be given type annotations.
   Name equality vs structure equality. Due to the way *Coq* and *Lego* create
inductive types, PER is different from any other type, so can be made abstract
by hiding its constructor, as is done in programming language module systems.
However PER' is definitionally equal to any type that is Sig4 applied to arguments that convert with those in the definition of PER'. To make PER' abstract
would require hiding the Sig4 constructor. Similarly, any structure defined by
specializing a more general package admits extra type equalities.

$$\text{FORM} \frac{L : \text{Type} \qquad A : (L)\text{Type}}{\langle L, \text{r}: A \rangle : \text{Type}} \qquad\qquad \text{INTRO} \frac{\langle L, \text{r}: A \rangle : \text{Type} \qquad l : L \qquad a : A(l)}{\langle l, \text{r}= a \rangle : \langle L, \text{r}: A \rangle}$$

Elimination: projection and restriction of the visible label.

$$\text{EL-TR} \frac{l : \langle L, \text{r}: A \rangle}{l|\text{r} : L} \qquad\qquad\qquad \text{EL-TP} \frac{l : \langle L, \text{r}: A \rangle}{l.\text{r} : A(l|\text{r})}$$

Elimination: passing the operations below top level.

$$\text{EL-LR} \frac{l : \langle L, \text{r}: A \rangle \qquad (l|\text{r})|\text{p} : P}{l|\text{p} : P} \text{r} \neq \text{p} \qquad \text{EL-LP} \frac{l : \langle L, \text{r}: A \rangle \qquad (l|\text{r}).\text{p} : P}{l.\text{p} : P} \text{r} \neq \text{p}$$

Computation rules.

$$\text{C-TR} \frac{\langle l, \text{r}= a \rangle : \langle L, \text{r}: A \rangle}{\langle l, \text{r}= a \rangle|\text{r} = l : L} \qquad\qquad \text{C-TP} \frac{\langle l, \text{r}= a \rangle : \langle L, \text{r}: A \rangle}{\langle l, \text{r}= a \rangle.\text{r} = a : A(l)}$$

$$\text{C-LR} \frac{l : \langle L, \text{r}: A \rangle \qquad (l|\text{r})|\text{p} : P}{(l|\text{r})|\text{p} = l|\text{p} : P} \text{r} \neq \text{p} \qquad \text{C-LP} \frac{l : \langle L, \text{r}: A \rangle \qquad (l|\text{r}).\text{p} : P}{(l|\text{r}).\text{p} = l.\text{p} : P} \text{r} \neq \text{p}$$

Fig. 2. Rules for left associating records.

3   Dependently Typed Records

Betarte and Tasistro [BT98,Bet98,Tas97] give an extension of Martin-Löf's framework to extensible, dependently typed records, with record subtyping. They had a prototype implementation, and worked interesting examples. However their presentation, in a complicated framework, with apparently essential use of subtyping, makes their system hard to understand. Here I give a simplified version of their system, without subtyping or explicit substitutions, which turns out to be straightforward left associating records. (I am informal about the difference between **Type** and **Set**.) Record subtyping will be treated orthogonally (using *coercive subtyping*) in Sect. 4. I also present right associating records, which are reasonable too.

3.1   Left Associating Records

A left associating record is a pair, with a labelled second component. It responds only to its own label, but passes any other label on to its first component. *Record types* (*signatures*) have syntax $\langle L, \text{r}: A \rangle$. *Records* (*structures*) have syntax $\langle l, \text{r}= a \rangle_{\langle L, \text{r}: A \rangle}$. I will henceforth omit type annotations on records, which are, however, necessary in this setting for type synthesis to be effective. The rules are shown in Fig. 2.

Labels do not bind, either in signatures or in records. In the notation $\langle l, \text{r}= a \rangle$, "$\text{r}= a$" is only syntax, not a local definition. It is more precise to say that the label is part of the signature, hence of the type annotation of a record.

Formation and Introduction In rules FORM and INTRO, L may be a record type, and may have a field r. Later fields shadow earlier fields with the same label. Allowing repeated labels in signatures is not completely satisfactory, but simplifies the presentation, while allowing signatures to be first-class.[3] Betarte and Tasistro use a kind, *record-type*, to enforce that if ρ : *record-type* is known, then all the labels of ρ are known, so side conditions about freshness of labels make sense. Our presentation could be modified to enforce fresh labels in a similar way.

Similarly, for us no empty record type is required; an informal notion of "pure record type" is obtained by starting from the unit type (which I write as $\langle \rangle$, although it is not a record).

Elimination and Computation There are two record eliminators, projection "*l*.r" and restriction "*l*|r". The side condition r $\neq$ p is needed to force the top-level rules to be used whenever possible, as r may be a field in *l*|r. In rules EL-LR (resp. EL-LP) we don't know that L is a record type, but *l*|p (resp. *l*.p) is only well typed if we already know that (*l*|r)|p (resp. (*l*|r).p) is well typed, which can only happen if L is (equal to) a record type with a field labelled p.

Betarte and Tasistro use record subtyping to explain projection: if $l : L$, and r: A is a field in L, they conclude *l*.r : $A(l)$. That is, the only use A can make of l is to project it at some fields that precede r in L, and l has at least those fields that precede r. Our restriction operation, which is not explicit for Betarte and Tasistro, allows us to write the elimination rules (e.g. EL-TP) prior to a notion of record subtyping.

The computation rules are as expected, given the elimination rules. I have written them as typed equality. While rules C-TR and C-TP can be implemented by syntactic reduction, rules C-LR and C-LP apparently require run-time type checking because of their second premises.

Records vs Sigma It is clear from our presentation that left associating signatures are just Sigma types carrying labels: erase "r" everywhere and read "|" and "." as ".1" and ".2" respectively. Thus they can be nested however you wish; we call them *left associating* because rule EL-LP searches from right to left. They could have an anonymous restriction operator (just drop rule EL-LR), but whenever we know that some object has record type, we already know its label.

Example: *PER* in left associating records In "official" syntax we write

$$set := \langle \langle \rangle, \text{S}: [\_: \langle \rangle]\text{Set} \rangle$$
$$Rel := \langle set, \text{R}: [x: set](x.\text{S})(x.\text{S})\text{Prop} \rangle$$
$$symRel := \langle Rel, \text{sAx}: [x: Rel]sym(x.\text{S})(x.\text{R}) \rangle$$
$$PER := \langle symRel, \text{tAx}: [x: symRel]trn(x.\text{S})(x.\text{R}) \rangle$$

Binding of variables for local field names is treated the same as in (7), although here, because of rules C-LR and C-LP, the depth of projections does not increase

---

[3] E.g. [L: Type, A: (L)Type]$\langle L$, r: $A \rangle$ is well-typed, although L may have label r.

$$\text{FORM} \; \frac{A : \text{Type} \qquad L : (A)\text{Type}}{\{r\colon A,\, L\} : \text{Type}}$$

$$\text{INTRO} \; \frac{\{r\colon A,\, L\} : \text{Type} \qquad a : A \qquad l : L(a)}{\{r = a,\, l\} : \{r\colon A,\, L\}}$$

$$\text{EL-TR} \; \frac{l : \{r\colon A,\, L\}}{l|r : L(l.r)}$$

$$\text{EL-TP} \; \frac{l : \{r\colon A,\, L\}}{l.r : A}$$

Signature abstraction:

$$\text{S-TR} \; \frac{\{r\colon A,\, L\} : \text{Type}}{\{r\colon A,\, L\}| = L : (A)\text{Type}}$$

$$\text{S-TP} \; \frac{\{r\colon A,\, L\} : \text{Type}}{\{r\colon A,\, L\}. = A : \text{Type}}$$

Fig. 3. Some rules for right associating records.

("$trn(x.\mathsf{S})(x.\mathsf{R})$" instead of "$trn(P.1.1)(P.1.2)$"). The field labels are new, but they do not interact with local names. This structure could be defined with three nested pairs, as in (7), but then the first field would not have a label; it would still be accessible as $l|\mathsf{R}$.

Writing this signature without intermediate definitions, and removing inner brackets and redundant type tags, we get a nearly acceptable notation:

$$PER := \langle \mathsf{S}\colon [\_]\mathsf{Set},\, \mathsf{R}\colon [x](x.\mathsf{S})(x.\mathsf{S})\mathsf{Prop},\, \mathsf{sAx}\colon [x]sym(x.\mathsf{S})(x.\mathsf{R}), \quad\quad (11)$$
$$\mathsf{tAx}\colon [x]trn(x.\mathsf{S})(x.\mathsf{R})\rangle.$$

An official inhabitant of (11) is $\langle\langle\langle\langle\star,\, \mathsf{S}{=}T\rangle,\, \mathsf{R}{=}Q\rangle,\, \mathsf{sAx}{=}\,symQ\rangle,\, \mathsf{tAx}{=}\,trnQ\rangle$, where $\star : \langle\rangle$. Omitting redundant information, we write

$$\langle \mathsf{S}{=}T,\, \mathsf{R}{=}Q,\, \mathsf{sAx}{=}\,symQ,\, \mathsf{tAx}{=}\,trnQ\rangle. \quad\quad (12)$$

3.2   Right Associating Records

I presented left associating records first, as they are close to the work of Betarte and Tasistro. However, from the viewpoint that records are just Sigma types with labels, right associating records are also natural. I guess that Betarte and Tasistro chose left association to achieve *extensibility*.

A right associating record is a pair, with a labelled first component. It responds only to its own label, but passes any other label on to its second component. *Record types* have syntax $\{r\colon A,\, L\}$. *Records* have syntax $\{r{=}a,\, l\}_{\{r\colon A,\, L\}}$. I will henceforth omit type annotations on records, which are, however, necessary for type synthesis to be effective. Again, "$r{=}a$" is not a local definition: r does not bind in l.

The rules are analogous to left associating records of Sect. 3.1, so I only present some of them in Fig. 3.

Signature abstraction We can define operations of projection and restriction on signatures (rules S-TR and S-TP of Fig. 3). Restriction, $\{r\colon A,\, L\}|$, takes a closed package, and shows how it functionally depends on its first field. This operation supports the *signature application* of [Kam99], and hence Pebble-style sharing (Sects. 1 and 5). This is the main reason to be interested in right associating records.

Example: *PER* in right associating records In "official" syntax we write

$$PER \; := \; \{S: \mathsf{Set}, [s: \mathsf{Set}]$$
$$\{R: (s)(s)\mathsf{Prop}, [r: (s)(s)\mathsf{Prop}]$$
$$\{sAx: sym(s)(r), [\_: sym(s)(r)]$$
$$\{tAx: trn(s)(r), [\_: trn(s)(r)]\langle\rangle\}\}\}\}.$$

Removing inferable type annotations and internal brackets, we can write

$$PER := \{S: \mathsf{Set}, [s]R: (s)(s)\mathsf{Prop}, [r]sAx: sym(s)(r), [\_]tAx: trn(s)(r)\}. \quad (13)$$

Binding of variables for local names is treated the same as in (4). An official inhabitant of (13) is $\{S{=}T, \{R{=}Q, \{sAx{=}\,symQ, \{tAx{=}\,trnQ, \star\}\}\}\}$. Omitting redundant information, we write $\{S{=}T, R{=}Q, sAx{=}\,symQ, tAx{=}\,trnQ\}$.

3.3 Labels and Variables

Labels are the global accessors for records, and hence cannot be alpha converted. Thus labels and variables cannot be the same syntactic class in dependent record types, or else how could we substitute y for x in $\langle y: \mathsf{Set}, z: x\rangle$. To my knowledge, the first satisfactory handling of this problem is in [HL94], where every field has both a label (that does not bind) and a variable (that does bind). *PER* would be written as

$$\langle S \triangleright s: \mathsf{Set}, R \triangleright r: (s)(s)\mathsf{Prop}, sAx \triangleright \_: sym(s)(r), tAx \triangleright \_: trn(s)(r)\rangle. \quad (14)$$

The approaches I give above, inspired by [BT98], are more parsimonious than [HL94] by using the existing dependent function type instead of introducing a new binding construct. Nonetheless, all three notations with labels and variables (i.e. (11), (13) and (14)) are heavy. Betarte and Tasistro point out that an informal notation, e.g.

$$\langle S: \mathsf{Set}, R: (S)(S)\mathsf{Prop}, sAx: sym(S)(R), tAx: trn(S)(R)\rangle, \quad (15)$$

can be translated mechanically to the formal notations. This is true, but some signatures cannot be represented in this informal manner, as an example from [HL94] shows:

left associating $\langle b: [\_: \langle\rangle]\mathsf{Type}, c: [x]\langle b: [\_: \langle\rangle]\mathsf{Type}, f: [y](y.b)x.b\rangle\rangle,$
right associating $\{b: \mathsf{Type}, [x: \mathsf{Type}]\{b: \mathsf{Type}, [y: \mathsf{Type}]f: (y)x\}\},$
Harper/Lillibridge $\langle b \triangleright x: \mathsf{Type}, c \triangleright \_: \langle b \triangleright y: \mathsf{Type}, f \triangleright \_: (y)x\rangle\rangle.$

Here, the variables x, y, are needed to disambiguate the two labels b. Thus it seems unlikely that a notation such as (15) could be a satisfactory formalization. Nonetheless, some well known proof tools (e.g. *PVS*) present dependent record types in this notation.

In the three formal approaches, left- and right- associating records, and Harper/Lillibridge style, labels and variables are distinct syntactic classes. But there can be no confusion, even if they are implemented with the same concrete type, as labels and variables only appear in different syntactic positions.

3.4 Dependent Records?

Both Harper/Lillibridge and Courant [Cou99] present structures that are *dependent* as well as *dependently typed*; i.e., field variables can be used in later fields as local definitions. For example, one could write $\langle \mathsf{n} \triangleright x = 3,\ \mathsf{m} \triangleright \_ = x \rangle$.[4] However, this record is definitionally equal to $\langle \mathsf{n} \triangleright x = 3,\ \mathsf{m} \triangleright \_ = 3 \rangle$, so no judgement can distinguish between the dependent presentation and the flattened one.

It is evident from rules INTRO of Figs. 2 and 3 that fields in my left and right associating records cannot depend on previous fields. But my records are equally expressive: I write $\langle \mathsf{n} = 3,\ \mathsf{m} = 3 \rangle$ at the same type as the example above. To preserve sharing, I might take $\langle \mathsf{n} = 3,\ \mathsf{m} = \mathsf{n} \rangle$ as syntactic sugar for *let* $n = 3$ *in* $\langle \mathsf{n} = \mathsf{n},\ \mathsf{m} = \mathsf{n} \rangle$, where n is a local variable that must be sufficiently fresh. Nonetheless, the dependency in Harper/Lillibridge structures does seem useful, even if I cannot say precisely what the difference is. I guess it is relevant here to mention that Harper/Lillibridge structures are not extensible: once a structure is closed there is no "potential" future use of its field variables.

4 Coercions

Presentations such as [HL94,BT98,Cou99] have a built-in notion of *structural subtyping*: roughly, any well-typed permutation of the fields of an extension of a signature is a subtype of that signature. Further, one allows corresponding fields themselves to be in the subtype relation. Whenever an object of a certain type is required, an object of a subtype is accepted: e.g. you can use a group wherever a monoid is expected. Below, I show how this approach is limited when structures are not "flat", but are constructed from substructures, as is desirable in practice.

Peter Aczel [Acz94] suggested a notion of *coercive subtyping* for type theory. Both *Coq* and *Lego* now support ad hoc, but very useful, notions of coercive subtyping [Sai97,Bai98]. Zhaohui Luo and colleagues [Luo99,LS99] have studied coercive subtyping foundationally, as an abbreviational mechanism which introduces definitional equalities at a logical framework level. This approach is more expressive in some ways than the implementations, but in other respects does not yet equal them. Also, we do not claim that all the usability and implementability issues of the logical framework (typed equality judgement, universes á la Tarski, etc.) are worked out.

---

[4] This style requires field variables in structures as well as in signatures.

As an example of coercive subtyping, reconsider equation (5), using coercions in *Coq* notation. Define `Inner` as a parameterized record, and use it as a field in a structure for `PER`

```
Record Inner [S:Set; R:S->S->Prop]: Type :=
  { Sym: (sym S R); Trn: (trn S R) }.
Record PER: Type := { S:>Set; R:>S->S->Prop; i:>(Inner S R) }.
```

The notation `S:>Set` means that `S:PER->Set` is treated as a coercion from `PER` to `Set`, so that if `p:PER` we can write `x:p` to mean `x` ranging over the carrier of `p`, i.e. `x:(S p)`, with the typechecker invisibly inserting the coercion `S`. Similarly `R:(p:PER)p->p->Prop` is a coercion from `p:PER` to relations over the carrier of `p`. (We can write `p` instead of `(S p)` in the type of `R`.) The statement about a particular `p:PER` that its relation is reflexive can be written as `(x:p)(p x x)`.

Similarly `i:>(Inner S R)` means that `i:(p:PER)(Inner (S p) (R p))` (which can be written as `i:(p:PER)(Inner p)`) is treated as a coercion from `PER` to `Inner`, so that whenever `p:PER`, the field projections `Sym` and `Trn` of `Inner` can be applied directly to p, with the typechecker invisibly inserting the coercion i. Thus `PER` appears to be a subtype of `Inner`.[5]

Structural subtyping cannot show `PER` as a subtype of `Inner`, because `PER` is not a permutation of an extension of `Inner`. In practice we often build new structures out of existing structures in this way (e.g. *ringSig* in Sect. 5). Structural subtyping depends on accidents of structure, and does not support natural mathematical definitions.

In this example the coercion i *opens* the `Inner` structure for users of the structure `PER`. This opening is transitive, in the sense that if we use `PER` in a larger structure, e.g.

```
Record ER: Type := { p:>PER; Rfl:(rfl p) }.
```

then we can still project the fields of `Inner` from an `ER` object. This also shows that extensibility is not very important, given coercive subtyping.

In practice we want *renaming* to support opening substructures with common labels; e.g. the additive and multiplicative monoids of a ring.

Subtyping Sigma Types Since records are constructed like nested Sigma types, it is useful to ask how subtyping propagates through Sigma. Suppose L is a subtype of L' by coercion $c : (L)L'$, and $A : (L')$Type. c can be lifted to a coercion $c_\Sigma : (\Sigma L\, A{\circ}c)\Sigma L'\, A$ showing that $\Sigma L\, A{\circ}c$ is a subtype of $\Sigma L'\, A$, defined by $c_\Sigma(\langle l, a\rangle) := \langle c(l), a\rangle$ [Luo99]. Note how the composition, $A{\circ}c$, is needed for the subtype to be well formed, as A expects an L'-object, not an L-object. This idiom will appear again in Sect. 5.3.

---

[5] The illusion is not complete, as `Inner` is parameterized, and the projections must be applied to the parameters: `(Trn (S p) (R p) p)`. However, with *implicit arguments*, we can write `(Trn p)`.

5   Manifest Signatures

Programming language designers have long recognized the need to see through the signatures of modules; [LB88,Mac86,Ler94,HL94] give a taste of the relevant literature. I assume the reader is familiar with the two basic approaches, *Pebble style sharing* which uses pure abstraction and application, and *manifest types* in signatures, which requires some new explanation. (I use the term *manifest types*, from [Ler94], informally, not referring to particulars of that paper.)

Expressive Theorems With any of the packages above, the lemma that the dual of a *PER* is also a *PER* could be stated as $(PER)PER$, but this formulation is too coarse to express our meaning. E.g. the identity function is also a proof of $(PER)PER$ but is not the duality construction.

We have seen the application of a parameterized signature (*Pebble-style* sharing) in Sect. 1. This is convenient for right associating structures [Kam99]. Using (5) as the definition of *PER*, the duality theorem can be stated as

$$(p: PER)Inner(p.\mathsf{S})(\mathrm{dual}(p.\mathsf{S})(p.\mathsf{R})).$$

This shows the duality explicitly, but doesn't actually return a *PER*, so operations on the *PER* package cannot be applied to the structure returned. E.g. we cannot use this theorem directly to prove that dualization is involutive.

A manifest signature expresses the intended meaning

$$(p: PER)\langle \mathsf{S}{=}\,p.\mathsf{S}\!: \mathsf{Set},\ \mathsf{R}{=}\,\mathrm{dual}(\mathsf{S})(p.\mathsf{R})\!: (\mathsf{S})(\mathsf{S})\mathsf{Prop},\ sAx\!: sym(\mathsf{S})(\mathsf{R}),\ \ldots\rangle \quad (16)$$

but forces us to rewrite the definition of *PER*, which is error prone and obscures the statement. (Since S is manifest in (16), we use S in place of its value in succeeding fields.)

What is needed is something like the *with* notation [Ler94] to add information about a signature. The duality lemma could be stated as

$$(p: PER)PER \ with \ \mathsf{S}{=}\,p.\mathsf{S} \ with \ \mathsf{R}{=}\,\mathrm{dual}(\mathsf{S})(p.\mathsf{R}). \quad (17)$$

This is often considered syntactic sugar for (16), but there are some details to make precise (Sect. 6).

This example shows that ordinary theorems involve functions from structures to structures. Thus I am interested in first-class records with manifest types, and guess that stratified module systems [Cou99] will be inadequate in practice.

Sharing Suppose *monSig* is the signature of monoids, and *grpSig* is the signature of groups. How can we define *ringSig* as an (additive) group and a (multiplicative) monoid, sharing the same carrier set, and having some axioms connecting the two operations? We might be satisfied with *Pebble-style* sharing, "applying" *monSig* to the carrier of the group. Although the objection still arises that in this approach no multiplicative monoid actually occurs as a substructure of a

$$\text{FORM} \frac{\Sigma LA : \textbf{Type} \qquad a : (l{:}L)A(l)}{\Psi LAa : \textbf{Type}} \qquad\qquad \text{INTRO} \frac{\Psi LAa : Type \qquad l : L}{\langle l \rangle_{\Psi LAa} : \Psi LAa}$$

Computation rules.

$$\text{COMP1} \frac{\langle l \rangle_{\Psi LAa} : \Psi Aa}{\langle l \rangle_{\Psi LAa}.1 = l : L} \qquad\qquad \text{COMP2} \frac{l : \Psi LAa}{l.2 = a(l.1) : A(l.1)}$$

Fig. 4. Some rules for manifest left associating Sigma.

ring, attempts to formalize some algebra in this way have made interesting progress [Pot99]. Nonetheless, *Pebble-style* sharing is heavy, and doesn't scale up in practice. What is needed is the *with* notation, allowing to write

$$ringSig := \langle G{:}\ grpSig,\ M{:}\ monSig\ with\ \mathsf{crr}{=}\ G.\mathsf{crr},\ \ldots \rangle.$$

5.1   Definable Manifest Signatures

Left Associating Using single constructor inductive definitions we can add a value specification to the right field of a Sigma type (Fig. 4). We call these *left associating* only because we intend to use them that way, as the example below shows. ΨAa doesn't say what the value of the second field is, but constrains it uniformly as a function of the first field. As before, I will write ΨAa instead of ΨLAa, and even more informally, $\langle l \rangle_a$ for $\langle l \rangle_{\Psi Aa}$.

In *Coq* notation this type is defined

```
Record Psi [L:Type; A:L->Type; a:(l:L)(A l)]: Type := { psi1:L }.
```

The first projection, rule COMP1, is defined by inductive elimination as before, but the second projection, rule COMP2, is defined using the heavy type annotations

```
Definition psi2 [L:Type; A:L->Type; a:(l:L)(A l); h:(Psi ?? a)]
     : (A (psi1 ??? h)) := (a (psi1 ??? h)).
```

This strong rule shows that ΨAa has its second field manifest.

From INTRO it is clear that ΨAa is isomorphic with L. From FORM, it is clear that ΨAa is a "subtype" of ΣA; there is a definable coercion that makes this subtyping implicit in *Coq*

```
Definition Psi_sigT [L:Type; A:L->Type; a:(l:L)(A l); h:(Psi ? A a)]
     : (sigT ? A) := (existT ?? (psi1 ??? h) (psi2 ??? h)).
Coercion Psi_sigT: Psi >-> sigT.
```

Example Surprisingly, although every ΨAa is uniformly typed (i.e. ΨAa : Type implies $A : (L)$Type), it is possible to construct non-uniform signatures. For example, although the informal signature $\langle K: \text{Type}, \ A: K, \ a: A \rangle$ is not well-typed (e.g. if $K = (\text{Set})\text{Set}: \text{Type}$), the manifest signature $\langle K = \text{Set}: \text{Type}, \ A: K, \ a: A \rangle$ is well-typed by the construction

$$
\begin{array}{lll}
L1 & := & \Psi([\_: \langle\rangle]\text{Type})([\_: \langle\rangle]\text{Set}) \\
L2 & := & \Sigma[x: L1]x.2 \\
L3 & := & \Sigma[x: L2]x.2
\end{array}
\qquad
\begin{array}{l}
\text{representing } \langle\langle\rangle, \ K = \text{Set}: \text{Type}\rangle, \\
\text{representing } \langle L1, \ A: K\rangle, \\
\text{representing } \langle L2, \ a: A\rangle.
\end{array}
$$

By rule COMP2, the occurrence of $x.2$ in the definition of $L2$ has value Set. $L3$ is inhabited by the tuple $\langle\langle\langle\star\rangle_{[\_: \langle\rangle]\text{Set}}, \ nat\rangle, \ 0\rangle$.

Other Definable Manifest Telescopes The same trick can be used to make fields manifest in any inductive telescope, and in practice this could be more convenient than building structures out of nested Σ and Ψ. However, as for Ψ, such manifest telescopes must be well-typed uniformly, so to construct non-uniform structures such as the last example, we must nest manifest telescopes. In this sense Ψ is the most general manifest telescope.

5.2   Subtyping Manifest Signatures

In the motivating example of *PER* duality, in order to view theorem (16) as returning a *PER*, I need a coercion that erases some manifest type information, so that the type of the structure returned in (16) can be seen as a subtype of *PER*. We have just seen the coercion `Psi_sigT` that does this for Ψ, returning the corresponding Σ. However there can be no coercion that allows viewing $\langle K = \text{Set}: \text{Type}, \ A: K, \ a: A \rangle$ as a subtype of $\langle K: \text{Type}, \ A: K, \ a: A \rangle$, since the latter is not even well typed. The usual rule for subtyping manifest signatures (e.g. [HL94,Cou99]) has a premise requiring the (less manifest) supertype to be well typed.

   In my presentation, the coercion forgetting a particular manifest field is constructed by applying `Psi_sigT` at that field (which actually forgets the manifest value, and is always well typed), then successively lifting the coercion through the following fields using c_Σ (Sect. 5). The typing of c_Σ checks at each stage that the supertype is well typed, and this approach can be seen as analysing the usual rule into two unitary rules `Psi_sigT` and c_Σ.

5.3   Manifest Left Associating Record Types

Just as we added labels to Σ in Sect. 3.1, so we add labels to Ψ. *Manifest* signatures have syntax $\langle L, \ r = a: A\rangle$. r is *opaque* in $\langle L, \ r: A\rangle$, and *manifest* in $\langle L, \ r = a: A\rangle$. Objects inhabiting manifest signatures officially have syntax $\langle l\rangle_{\langle L, \ r = a: A\rangle}$, but I will write them $\langle l, \ r = a(l)\rangle$.[6] Some rules are given in Fig. 5.

---

[6] An implementation might take this abuse of notation seriously, i.e. internalize the coercion $(\langle L, \ r = a: A\rangle)\langle L, \ r: A\rangle$.

$$\text{MFORM} \frac{\langle L, r\!:\!A\rangle : \textbf{Type} \quad a : (l\!:\!L)A(l)}{\langle L, r\!=\!a\!:\!A\rangle : \textbf{Type}} \qquad \text{MINTRO} \frac{\langle L, r\!=\!a\!:\!A\rangle : \textbf{Type} \quad l : L}{\langle l, r\!=\!a(l)\rangle : \langle L, r\!=\!a\!:\!A\rangle}$$

Manifest computation. $\text{C-MAN} \dfrac{l : \langle L, r\!=\!a\!:\!A\rangle}{l.r = a(l|r) : A(l|r)}$

Fig. 5. Some rules for manifest left associating records.

By inversion of MFORM, whenever $\langle L, r\!=\!a\!:\!A\rangle$ is well typed, so is $\langle L, r\!:\!A\rangle$. In general, however, well typedness of $\langle\langle L, r\!=\!a\!:\!A\rangle, s\!:\!B\rangle$ does not guarantee well typedness of $\langle\langle L, r\!:\!A\rangle, s\!:\!B\rangle$, as the typing of B in the former may depend on the value of r.

$\langle L, r\!=\!a\!:\!A\rangle$ is more informative than $\langle L, r\!:\!A\rangle$, so the elimination and computation rules of Sect. 3.1 also hold for $\langle L, r\!=\!a\!:\!A\rangle$. We can define the coercion $(\langle L, r\!=\!a\!:\!A\rangle)\langle L, r\!:\!A\rangle$ (Psi_sigT in Sect. 5.1) from the projection and restriction operations of $\langle L, r\!=\!a\!:\!A\rangle$. Thus $l : \langle L, r\!=\!a\!:\!A\rangle$ can be used as if it had type $\langle L, r\!:\!A\rangle$.

There is a new computation rule for the projection of a manifest field, C-MAN. It is admissible that rule C-MAN goes underneath the top constructor. For example, suppose $l : \langle L, \mathsf{p}\!=\!b\!:\!B, r\!:\!A\rangle$; we have

$$\dfrac{\dfrac{l : \langle L, \mathsf{p}\!=\!b\!:\!B, r\!:\!A\rangle}{l|r : \langle L, \mathsf{p}\!=\!b\!:\!B\rangle}\text{EL-TR}}{(l|r).\mathsf{p} = b((l|r)|\mathsf{p}) : B((l|r)|\mathsf{p})}\text{C-MAN} \qquad \dfrac{\begin{array}{c}l : \langle L, \mathsf{p}\!=\!b\!:\!B, r\!:\!A\rangle \\ \vdots\end{array}}{(l|r).\mathsf{p} = l.\mathsf{p}}\text{C-LP} \qquad \dfrac{\begin{array}{c}l : \langle L, \mathsf{p}\!=\!b\!:\!B, r\!:\!A\rangle \\ \vdots\end{array}}{(l|r)|\mathsf{p} = l|\mathsf{p}}\text{C-LR}$$

$$l.\mathsf{p} = b(l|\mathsf{p}) : B(l|\mathsf{p})$$

The *with* Notation "*with*" is explained in terms of manifest fields (Fig. 6). $\langle L, r\!:\!A\rangle$ *with* r=a is defined as $\langle L, r\!=\!a\!:\!A\rangle$ whenever the latter is well-typed (rule WITH-DEF). Having explained how to apply *with* to some record, L, we explain how to apply it to a longer record (rules WITH-RO and WITH-RM). Moving *with* to the right in a signature loses information: the typing of B in $\langle L$ *with* r=a, $\mathsf{p}\!:\!B\rangle$ may use that r=a, while in $\langle L, \mathsf{p}\!:\!B\rangle$ *with* r=a it may not.

Since L *with* r=a is constructed by *adding* manifest information to a well typed signature, L, the difficulty of forgetting manifest information (Sect. 5.2) does not arise. There is a uniform coercion $u_r^L : (L$ *with* $r=a)L$, which must be defined mutually with *with*, as it appears in the conclusions of rules WITH-RO and WITH-RM. The reason for this coercion in these rules is the lifting of subtyping through a signature, introduced in Sect. 5. The uniform definition of u_r^L shows that *with*-signatures are well behaved with respect to subtyping. E.g. (17) obviously returns a subtype of PER, while this fact about (16) requires checking. (The check is the computation showing (17) and (16) to be definitionally equal.) Conversely, $\langle K\!=\!\textbf{Set}\!:\!\textbf{Type}, A\!:\!K, a\!:\!A\rangle$ is not definitionally equal to any opaque signature followed by *with*s.

$$\text{WITH-DEF} \ \frac{\langle L, \ r= a: A \rangle : \textsf{Type}}{\langle L, \ r: A \rangle \ with \ r= a = \langle L, \ r= a: A \rangle : \textsf{Type}}$$

$$\text{WITH-RO} \ \frac{L \ with \ r= a : \textsf{Type} \qquad \langle L, \ \textsf{p}: B \rangle : \textsf{Type}}{\langle L, \ \textsf{p}: B \rangle \ with \ r= a = \langle L \ with \ r= a, \ \textsf{p}: Bou_r^L \rangle : \textsf{Type}} \ \textsf{p} \neq \textsf{r}$$

$$\text{WITH-RM} \ \frac{L \ with \ r= a : \textsf{Type} \qquad \langle L, \ \textsf{p}= b: B \rangle : \textsf{Type}}{\langle L, \ \textsf{p}= b: B \rangle \ with \ r= a = \langle L \ with \ r= a, \ \textsf{p}= bou_r^L: Bou_r^L \rangle : \textsf{Type}} \ \textsf{p} \neq \textsf{r}$$

Fig. 6. Rules for *with*. $u_r^L : (L \ with \ r= a)L$ is the coercion forgetting the manifest information $r= a$.

6   Ongoing Work and Conclusions

I have not directly developed the meta-theory of this approach, but manifest signatures can be expressed (i.e. programmed) in a logical framework such as that of Martin-Löf or Luo [Luo99] extended with inductive-recursive definition [Dyb97]. Thus, if the extended framework has good properties, as is informally believed, the system with manifest signatures preserves these properties. Here is an outline of this coding. Let *lbl* be a type having decidable equality, to be used for labels. *sign* : **Type** and *recd* : (*sign*)**Type** are defined by induction-recursion. *sign* has introduction rules

$$\text{UNIT} \ \frac{}{\langle \rangle : sign} \qquad \text{OPAQ} \ \frac{s : sign \quad \textsf{r} : lbl \quad A : (recd(s))\textsf{Type}}{\langle s, \ \textsf{r}: A \rangle : sign}$$

$$\text{MAN} \ \frac{s : sign \quad \textsf{r} : lbl \quad A : (recd(s))\textsf{Type} \quad a : (l{:}recd(s))A(l)}{\langle s, \ \textsf{r}= a: A \rangle : sign}$$

The actual types, computed by *recd*, are Σ types and Ψ types:

$$recd(\langle \rangle) = \langle \rangle \qquad recd(\langle s, \ \textsf{r}: A \rangle) = \Sigma \, A \qquad recd(\langle s, \ \textsf{r}= a: A \rangle) = \Psi \, A \, a.$$

Projection, restriction and *with* are programmed using *sign*-elimination.

It remains to experiment with this encoding, and develop its theory relative to the extended framework. This representation has first class labels with testable equality, which suggests possibilities for programmable renaming and opening.

Conclusions I have shown surprisingly simple first-class dependently typed records with manifest types. The manifest types are extended by a simple *with* notation. They have no built-in notion of subtyping, but coercive subtyping gives them a more flexible notion than the usual structural record subtyping. I have not developed any meta-theory, but these records are "interpretable" in type theory with inductive-recursive definitions. These records are suggested for formalizing mathematical structures, not necessarily as modules for separate checking or proof libraries. Further work remains on several important aspects of usability, such as efficiency and renaming of fields.

References

[Acz94]   P. Aczel. Simple overloading for type theories. Privately circulated notes, 1994.

[Bai98]   A. Bailey. *The Machine-checked Literate Formalisation of Algebra in Type Theory.* PhD thesis, Univ. of Manchester, 1998.

[Bet98]   G. Betarte. *Dependent Record Types and Formal Abstract Reasoning.* PhD thesis, Chalmers Univ. of Technology, 1998.

[BT98]   G. Betarte and A. Tasistro. Extension of Martin-Löf's type theory with record types and subtyping. In G. Sambin and J. Smith, editors, *Twenty Five Years of Constructive Type Theory.* Oxford Univ. Press, 1998.

[Coq99]   The Coq Project, 1999. http://pauillac.inria.fr/coq/.

[Cou99]   J. Courant. MC: A module calculus for Pure Type Systems. Technical Report 1217, CNRS Université Paris Sud 8623: LRI, June 1999.

[dB91]   N. G. de Bruijn. Telescopic mappings in typed lambda calculus. *Information and Computation*, 91(2):189–204, April 1991.

[Dyb97]   Peter Dybjer. A general notion of simultaneous inductive-recursive definition in type theory. *Journal of Symbolic Logic*, 1997. To appear.

[HL94]   R. Harper and M. Lillibridge. A type-theoretic approach to higher-order modules with sharing. In *POPL'94*. ACM Press, 1994.

[Kam99]   F. Kammüller. Modular structures as dependent types in isabelle. In T. Altenkirch, W. Naraschewski, and B. Reus, editors, *TYPES'98, Selected Papers*, volume 1657 of *LNCS*. Springer-Verlag, 1999.

[LB88]   B. Lampson and R. Burstall. Pebble, a kernel language for modules and abstract data types. *Information and Computation*, 76(2/3), 1988.

[LEG99]   The LEGO Proof Assistant, 1999. http://www.dcs.ed.ac.uk/home/lego/.

[Ler94]   X. Leroy. Manifest types, modules, and separate compilation. In *POPL'94*, New York, NY, USA, 1994. ACM Press.

[LS99]   Z. Luo and S. Soloviev. Dependent coercions. In *Category Theory in Computer Science, CTCS'99*, Electronic Notes in Theoretical Computer Science. Elsevier, 1999.

[Luo99]   Z. Luo. Coercive subtyping. *Journal of Logic and Computation*, 9(1), 1999.

[Mac86]   D. MacQueen. Using dependent types to express modular structure. In *POPL'86*, 1986.

[Pot99]   Loic Pottier. Algebra with Coq. See *User contributions* in Coq release [Coq99], 1999.

[Sai97]   A. Saibi. Typing algorithm in type theory with inheritance. *POPL'97*, 1997.

[Tas97]   A. Tasistro. *Substitution, Record Types and Subtyping in Type Theory, with Applications to the Theory of Programming.* PhD thesis, Chalmers Univ. of Technology, May 1997.

Towards a Machine-Checked
Java Specification Book

Bernhard Reus[1] and Tatjana Hein[2]

[1] School of Cognitive and Computing Sciences, University of Sussex at Brighton
bernhard@cogs.susx.ac.uk
[2] Fakultät für Mathematik und Informatik, Universität Passau
jana_h@gmx.net

Abstract. The semantics of the object-oriented, multi-threaded language Java is informally described in the Java Specification Book [5] where the memory model for concurrent threads is explained abstractly by means of asynchronous events and informal rules relating their occurrences. A formalization has been presented in [3] using certain posets of events (called event spaces) and a structural operational (small-step) semantics. Such an exact formal counterpart of the informal axiomatization of the Specification Book may not only serve as a reference semantics for different, possibly simplified, semantics, but also as a basis for language analysis. In this paper we present a machine-checked version of the formalization using Isabelle/HOL. Some proofs showing the redundancy of axioms in the Java Specification Book are discussed. As usual, by Isabelle's austerity some tacit assumptions and few minor mistakes were revealed.

1 Introduction

Java is an object-oriented programming language which offers a simple and tightly integrated support for concurrent programming. A concurrent program consists of multiple tasks that are or behave as if they were executed all at the same time. In Java tasks are implemented using *threads* (short for "threads of execution"), which are sequences of instructions that run independently within the encompassing program. Informal descriptions of this model can be found in several books (see e.g. [2], [7]). A precise description is given in the Java language specification [5]. In [3] a formal semantics of a non-trivial sublanguage of Java which includes dynamic creation of objects, blocks, error handling, and synchronization of threads has been presented. The semantics is given in the style of Plotkin's structural operational semantics (SOS) [12]. This technique has been used e.g. for the semantics of SML [9] and earlier for ADA [8].

Once having formalized the semantics, one can *prove* properties of the language mathematically. Corresponding work has already be carried out for the types system of (sequential) Java. In [4] it has been proved that the system for sequential Java is sound using big-step semantics, and a machine-checked proof in Isabelle/HOL has been given in [10].

J. Harrison and M. Aagaard (Eds.): TPHOLs 2000, LNCS 1869, pp. 480–497, 2000.
© Springer-Verlag Berlin Heidelberg 2000

The thread model, and in particular the interaction between threads via shared memory, is described in [3] in terms of structures called *event spaces*[1]. By using similar structures in operational semantics, an abstract "declarative" description of the Java thread model is obtained which is an exact formal counterpart of the informal language description [5] and which leaves maximal freedom for different implementations. Moreover, it can then be formally *proven* that a refinement of the semantics, e.g. using a concrete memory model, still fulfills the specification of [3].

The paper is organized as follows: First the abstract syntax is defined. The next section deals with the formalization of events and event spaces for the Java memory model. Then the axiomatization of stacks and stores is shortly discussed. In Section 5 the operational semantics is given as an inductively defined relation on configurations. Some remarks on the experiences with Isabelle and about ongoing and future work conclude the paper.

Isabelle/HOL We assume that the reader is familiar with Isabelle/HOL. But, even if this is not the case, the definitions – as they appear in the paper – should be readable for anyone with basic knowledge of predicate logic and functional languages. It should be emphasized that $[\![\ ]\!]$ enclose the context of assumptions of a goal or rule, and that $\Longrightarrow$ denotes meta-implication by contrast to $\longrightarrow$ denoting implication on the object level. Also, note that in HOL the total function space is denoted by a $\Rightarrow$ b whereas the partial function space is written a $\Rightarrow$ b option, where option is the usual lifting operator on types with constructors Some: 'a $\Rightarrow$ 'a option and None:'a option. Moreover, we define IsDefined(x) $\equiv$ x $\neq$ None and the is the partial inverse to Some.

Detailed information about Isabelle can be found, for example, one the web-page http://isabelle.in.tum.de or in [11].

Remark The Isabelle formalization strongly follows [3] which can be consulted for more detailed explanations on the subject.

2   Syntax

In this section the relevant subset of Java-syntax is introduced[2].

2.1   Primitive Syntactic Domains

We assume the following primitive types: left values, also called locations (lval), identifiers (identifier) and references different from null (nonnullobject):

```
types     nonnullobject
          lval
          identifier
```

---

[1] These correspond roughly to *configurations* in Winskel's *event structures*[13], which are used for denotational semantics of concurrent languages.

[2] It would have been nice to use the same definitions as [10] for the overlapping (sequential) part, but our axiomatization began independently of *loc.cit.*

Object references (`obj`), right values (results) (`rval`) and literals (`literal`) of basic Java-types (in our case just natural numbers and booleans) can then be defined inductively

```
datatype  obj     = Nullobj |
                    Nonnull nonnullobject

datatype  rval    = Oref obj |
                    Nval nat |
                    Bval bool

datatype  literal = NatLit   nat   |
                    BoolLit  bool  |
                    Null
```

Our formalization does not deal with typing problems (which are anyway considered in detail in [10]) but typing is still important for the operational semantics, so we have to model types. Any Java type (`jtype`) is either a class type (`classtype`) or a primitive type (`primitivetype`). How types are attributed to objects will be described later only abstractly (contrary to *loc.cit*).

```
type       classtype      = identifier

datatype   primitivetype = BoolType |
                           NatType  |
                           VoidType

datatype   jtype          = PrimType primitivetype |
                           ClType   classtype
```

Identifiers must come equipped with some types since for field identifiers there is a statically resolved overloading and method identifiers have to be resolved by dynamic lookup. Therefore, field identifiers carry the class type of declaration and method identifiers carry the static type of invocation needed for dynamic dispatch.

```
datatype  fieldidentifier  = FId identifier classtype
datatype  methodidentifier = MId fieldidentifier (jtype list) jtype
```

Moreover, we use type `throws` to represent exceptions that have been already thrown and thus need to be propagated through the context.

```
datatype throws = Throw  obj
types    thread = obj
```

The type `thread` is used to identify threads. As those are represented by objects in Java, one can simply use `obj`.

2.2   Environments

Environments are needed to keep the local variables of a block, e.g. a method body. We prefer to present all the semantic domains of our operational semantics by abstract datatypes instead of concrete definitions (see also Section 4), such that they can be replaced later by concrete implementations. Having proved that such an implementation satisfies the axioms, all the proofs based on those axioms will remain valid.

Environments consist of a set of declared variables (`identthis`) and a partial map from identifiers to values which is actually total for the subdomain of declared identifiers (`envmapping`). The special identifier `ThisExp`, representing the semantics of the keyword `this` of Java, has to be included in the set of identifiers. The abstract type of environments can thus be given by the following types and operations:

```
datatype  identthis = Ident    identifier |
                      ThisExp


types     envmapping =  (identthis ⇒ (rval option))


datatype  env = En (identthis set) envmapping


consts    Updenv ::  identthis ⇒ rval ⇒ env ⇒ env
          Mtenv  ::  env
          Lookup ::  identthis ⇒ env  ⇒ (rval option)
```

The empty environment is represented by `Mtenv`, updating of variables and variable lookup are defined as expected (cf. `Updenv` and `Lookup`, respectively).

2.3 Abstract Syntax

The abstract syntax is a slightly simplified version of the BNF-syntax given for Java. The number of syntactic categories is reduced w.r.t. table 1 of [3] We only distinguish *A-LeftHandSide* (`var`), *A-StatementExpression* (`stmexpr`), *A-Expression* (`expr`), *A-Block* (`block`), and *A-CatchClause* (`catch`).

```
datatype
    var   =
          Var        identifier                       |
          FieldVar   expr fieldidentifier
and
    stmexpr =
          NewC       classtype                        |
          Ass        var  expr                        |
          ValS       rval                             |
          MCall      expr methodidentifier (expr list)|
          AFrame     methodidentifier  block          |
          ThrowSE    throws                           |
          ReturnSE   (rval option)
and
    expr =
          StmtExp    stmexpr                          |
          Lit        literal                          |
          Acc        var                              |
```

```
            UnOp          (rval ⇒ rval) expr                        |
            BinOp         expr (rval ⇒ rval ⇒ rval) expr           |
            This
and
        stat =
            Nop                                                     |
            SemiCol                                                 |
            ThrowStmt     expr                                      |
            BlockStmt     block                                     |
            ExpStmt       stmexpr                                   |
            SyncStmt      expr   block                              |
            TryStmt       block catch (catch list)                 |
            TryFinStmt    block (catch list) block                 |
            ReturnStmt    (expr option)                            |
            CondStmt      expr stat                                 |
            VarDeclStmt   jtype identifier expr
and
        block =
            BlockIt       (stat list) env
and
        catch =
            CC            jtype identifier block
```

This mutually recursive type follows quite straightforwardly the syntax of Java, e.g. NewC stands for object creation[3] (aka new in Java), Ass stands for assignment (of program and field variables both represented by type var), ValS converts (right) values into expressions, MCall stands for method calls, activation frames are built using AFrame in order to interpret method calls and to determine the control flow in case of return-statements, ThrowSE is used to propagate an exception after it was thrown via the ThrowStmt-statement, ReturnSE propagates the result of a ReturnStmt which corresponds to Java's return; as well as return e; by alternatively using a None- or Some-term as argument. Acc stands for variable access. Expressions of type stmexpr can be turned into expressions via StmExpr but also into statements via ExprStm. Blocks are built from constructor BlockIt that takes a list of statements, so no explicit append-operator on statements (usually ;) is needed. The other constructors should be obvious.

In [3] there was no explicit analogue to ThrowSE throws, ReturnSE (rval option) and ValS rval. Without those, however, one cannot build a correct abstract term for the result of a statement expression e.g. an assignment. The formalization helped to keep syntactic categories in order.

3   Event Spaces

The execution of a Java program comprises many *threads* of computation running in parallel. Threads exchange information by operating on values and objects re-

---

[3] Note that we do not treat n−ary constructors with $n > 0$.

siding in a shared *main memory*. As explained in the Java language specification
[5], each thread also has a private *working memory* in which it keeps its own
working copy of variables that it must use or assign. As the thread executes a
program, it operates on these working copies. The main memory contains the
master copy of each variable. There are rules about when a thread is permitted or required to transfer the contents of its working copy of a variable into
the master copy or vice versa. Moreover, there are rules which regulate the
locking and *unlocking* of objects, by means of which threads synchronize with
each other. These rules are given in [5, Chapter 17] and formalized in this section
as "well-formedness" conditions for structures called *event spaces*. In the next
section event spaces are included in the configurations of multi-threaded Java to
constrain the applicability of certain operational rules.

Memory Actions are defined in accord with [5]:

```
datatype action =
    Lock    thread obj |
    Unlock thread obj |
    Use     thread lval rval |
    Assign thread lval rval |
    Load    thread lval rval |
    Store   thread lval rval |
    Read    thread lval rval |
    Write   thread lval rval
```

The terms Use, Assign, Load, Store, Read, Write, Lock, and Unlock are
used here to name actions which describe the activity of the memories during
the execution of a Java program. Use and Assign denote the above mentioned
actions on the private working memory. Read and Load are used for a loosely
coupled copying of data from the main memory to a working memory and dually
Store and Write are used for copying data from a working memory to the main
memory.

Events are instances of actions, which happen at different times during execution. Events are described abstractly without any commitment to a concrete
representation, in particular without any time stamps or other coding in terms
of natural numbers. We write e:Events(a) to indicate that an event e belongs
to the set of instances of action a. Moreover, Alpha, Beta, and Betal distinguish thread events, memory events, and memory events involving variables,
respectively.

```
types    event

consts   Events ::  action ⇒ (event set)
         Alpha  ::  thread ⇒ (event set)
         Beta   ::  obj    ⇒ (event set)
         Betal  ::  lval   ⇒ (event set)
```

The axioms forthose event sets are:

```
Alpha t ≡ { e. ∃p. (e ∈ (Events (Lock  t p))   ∨
                     e ∈ (Events (Unlock t p)))  ∨
```

```
( ∃1 v. e ∈ (Events (Use     t l v))  ∨
        e ∈ (Events (Assign t l v))  ∨
        e ∈ (Events (Load    t l v))  ∨
        e ∈ (Events (Store   t l v)) )}
```

```
Beta  p ≡ { e. ∃t. e ∈ (Events (Lock   t p )) ∨
              e ∈ (Events (Unlock t p ))  }
```

```
Betal l ≡ { e. ∃t v. e ∈ (Events (Write  t l v)) ∨
               e ∈ (Events (Read   t l v)) }
```

⟦ e ∈ Events a; e ∈ Events b ⟧ ⟹ a=b

∀ a S. ∃ e ∈ Events(a). e ∉ S

where the last axiom states that there are always enough events of any kind.

For instance, a rule about the interaction of locks and variables in the specification book [5, 17.6, p. 407] states – in English prose – for a thread θ, a variable V and a lock L:

"Between an *assign* action by $[\theta]$ on V and a subsequent *unlock* action by $[\theta]$ on L, a *store* action by $[\theta]$ on V must intervene; moreover, the *write* action corresponding to that *store* must precede the *unlock* action, as seen by the main memory. (Less formally: if a thread is to perform an *unlock* action on *any* lock, it must first copy *all* assigned values in its working memory back out to main memory.)"

We soon come back to the question how to formalize such a requirement. Before we must define appropriate relations on events.

An *event relation* is a relation

```
types    evtrelation =  (event × event) set
```

with a set of operations axiomatized below. An event is considered as "defined" or in the carrier (cf. **Carrier**) of an event relation if it is related to itself (compare this to partial equivalence relations) so the definition of the carrier set is already part of the event relation:

```
Carrier :: evtrelation ⇒ event set
Carrier E    ≡  { x. (x,x) ∈ E }
```

```
Down    :: evtrelation ⇒ event ⇒ event set
Down E e    ≡ { d. (d,e) ∈ E }
```

```
DownSet :: evtrelation ⇒ event ⇒ (event ⇒ bool) ⇒ event set
DownSet E e P ≡ { d. (d ∈ Down E e) ∧ P(d) }
```

```
TotalIn :: (event set) ⇒ evtrelation ⇒ bool
TotalIn A E   ≡ ∀x ∈ A. ∀y ∈ A. ((x,y) ∈ E ∨ (y,x) ∈ E)
```

```
Extends :: evtrelation ⇒ evtrelation ⇒ bool   (infixl 500)
```

```
X Extends Y    ≡
  Carrier Y ⊆ Carrier X ∧ Y ⊆ X ∧
  (∀a b. a ∈ (Carrier Y) ∧ b ∈ (Carrier Y) ∧ (a,b) ∈ X
  ⟶ (a,b) ∈ Y)
```

The predicate `TotalIn` yields true if the set of events A is totally ordered w.r.t. E. The set `Down E e` contains all events in E below e, and `DownSet E e P` is the intersection of `Down E e` with the elements fulfilling P.

The following maps are called "pairing" functions.

```
Read_of, Load_of, Store_of, Write_of, Lock_of, Unlock_of ::
  evtrelation ⇒ event ⇒ event option
```

The function `Read_of` e.g. matches the n-th occurrence of `Load(t,l,v)` in E with the n-th occurrence of `Read(t,l,v)` if such an event exists in E and is undefined otherwise. In other words `Read_of` is a monotone injective partial function with a partial inverse. This is expressed (without mentioning any natural numbers) by the following axioms:

```
e ∉ Events (Load t l r) ⟹ Read_of E e = None

⟦ Read_of E e = (Some f); e ∈ Events(Load t l r) ⟧
   ⟹  f ∈ Events (Read t l r) ∧ f ∈ Carrier E

⟦ L1 ∈ (Events (Load t l r));  L2 ∈ (Events (Load t l r));
    Read_of E L1 = Some R1; Read_of E L2 = Some R2; (L1,L2) ∈ E ⟧
   ⟹ (R1,R2) ∈ E

⟦ L1 ∈ (Events (Load t l r)); (Read_of E L1) = Some R1;
    R1 ∈ (Events (Read t l r)); R2 ∈ (Events (Read t l r));
    (R2,R1) ∈ E ⟧
   ⟹ ∃L2 ∈ (Events (Load t l r)). (Read_of E L2) = Some R2

⟦ Read_of E L1 = Read_of E L2; IsDefined (Read_of E L1) ⟧
   ⟹  L1 = L2

Read_of E e = Some f ⟹ Load_of E f = Some e
```

For `Store_of`, `Write_of`, `Lock_of`, `Unlock_of` analogous rules hold.

An *event space* is a poset of events (thought of as occurring in the given order), i.e. an event relation such that

```
(trans E) ∧ (antisym E) ∧ (ClosedDown E) ∧ (ClosedUp E)
```

where

```
(ClosedDown E)  ≡  ∀ (x,y) ∈ E. (x,x) ∈ E
(ClosedUp E)    ≡  ∀ (x,y) ∈ E. (y,y) ∈ E
```

in which every chain can be enumerated monotonically with respect to the arithmetical ordering $0 \leq 1 \leq 2 \leq \ldots$ of natural numbers or fulfilling the slightly stronger condition

```
FiniteHist E ≡
    ∀ e ∈ Carrier E. finite { d. d ∈ Carrier E ∧ (d,e) ∈ E }
```

which satisfies the conditions below that formalize directly the rules of [5, Chapter 17]. Contrary to [6] in `FiniteHist` we have chosen to avoid bijection with natural numbers and to use instead a condition that is nearer to configurations of event structures [13], namely that the history of any event is finite. The predicates `ClosedUp` and `ClosedDown` state reflexivity of the carrier of the argument relation.

Event space rules For every rule we include some short, informal explanations and refer to [5] for more detail. In the Isabelle code we usually write t instead of a thread name θ and l for (field) variable names l:

The actions performed by any one thread are totally ordered, and so are the actions performed by the main memory for any one variable [5, 17.2, 17.5].

```
Rule1 (E) ≡ ∀t. TotalIn ((Alpha t) ∩ (Carrier E)) E
Rule2 (E) ≡ ∀o. TotalIn ((Beta o)  ∩ (Carrier E)) E
           ∧ ∀l. TotalIn ((Betal l) ∩ (Carrier E)) E
```

A `Store` action by θ on l must intervene between an `Assign` by θ of l and a subsequent `Load` by θ of l. Less formally, a thread is not permitted to lose its most recent assign [5, 17.3]:

```
Rule3 (E) ≡    ∀ t l r s.
 ∀A ∈ (Events (Assign t l r)). ∀L ∈ (Events (Load t l s)).
    (A,L) ∈ E
 ⟶ ∃u. ∃S ∈ (Events (Store t l u)). (A,S) ∈ E ∧ (S,L) ∈ E
```

A thread is not permitted to write data from its working memory back to main memory for no reason [5, 17.3]:

```
Rule4 (E) ≡    ∀t l r s.
 ∀S1 ∈ (Events (Store t l r)). ∀S2 ∈ (Events (Store t l s)).
 S1 ≠ S2  ⟶  (S1,S2) ∈ E
 ⟶  ∃u. ∃A ∈ (Events(Assign t l u)). (S1,A) ∈ E ∧ (A,S2) ∈ E
```

Threads start with an empty working memory and new variables are created only in main memory and not initially in any thread's working memory [5, 17.3]:

```
Rule5 (E) ≡    ∀ t l r.
 ∀U ∈ (Events (Use t l r)). U ∈ (Carrier E)
 ⟶  (∃s. ∃A ∈ (Events (Assign t l s)). (A,U) ∈ E) ∨
    (∃s. ∃L ∈ (Events (Load t l s)). (L,U) ∈ E)
```

```
Rule6 (E) ≡    ∀ t l r.
 ∀S ∈ (Events (Store t l r)). S ∈ (Carrier E)
 ⟶  (∃s. ∃A ∈ (Events (Assign t l s)). (A,S) ∈ E)
```

A `Use` action transfers the contents of the thread's working copy of a variable to the thread's execution engine [5, §17.1]:

Rule7 (E) ≡   ∀ t l r s.
  ∀A ∈ (Events (Assign t l r)). ∀U ∈ (Events (Use t l s)).
    r ≠ s ⟶ (A,U) ∈ E
  ⟶ (∃u. ∃A1 ∈ (Events (Assign t l u)).
        (A,A1) ∈ E ∧ (A1,U) ∈ E ∧ A ≠ A1) ∨
      (∃w. ∃L ∈ (Events (Load t l w)). (A,L) ∈ E ∧ (L,U) ∈ E)

Rule8 (E) ≡   ∀ t l r s.
  ∀L ∈ (Events (Load t l r)). ∀U ∈ (Events (Use t l s)).
    r ≠ s ⟶ (L,U) ∈ E
  ⟶ (∃u. ∃A ∈ (Events (Assign t l u)). (L,A) ∈ E ∧ (A,U) ∈ E) ∨
      (∃w. ∃L1 ∈ (Events (Load t l w)). (L,L1) ∈ E ∧ (L1,U) ∈ E)

A `Store` action transmits the contents of the thread's working copy of a
variable to main memory [5, 17.1]:

Rule9 (E) ≡   ∀t l r s.
  ∀A ∈ (Events (Assign t l r)). ∀S ∈ (Events (Store t l s)).
    r ≠ s ⟶ (A,S) ∈ E
  ⟶ ∃u. ∃A1 ∈ (Events (Assign t l u)).
        (A,A1) ∈ E ∧ (A1,S) ∈ E ∧ A ≠ A1

Each `Load` or `Write` action is uniquely paired respectively with a matching
`Read` or `Store` action that precedes it [5, 17.2, 17.3]:

Rule10 (E) ≡   ∀t l r.
  ∀L ∈ (Events (Load t l r)). L ∈ (Carrier E)
  ⟶ ∃R ∈ (Events (Read t l r)).
        (Read_of E L) = (Some R) ∧ (R,L) ∈ E

Rule11 (E) ≡   ∀t l r.
  ∀W ∈ (Events (Write t l r)). W ∈ (Carrier E)
  ⟶ ∃S ∈ (Events (Store t l r)).
        (Store_of E W) = (Some S) ∧ (S,W) ∈ E

There are six more rules about locking and unlocking which are omitted due
to lack of space.

Discussion. Each of the above rules corresponds to one rule in [5]. Conversely,
some more rules of [5] can be derived in our axiomatization. In particular, we
can prove w.r.t. any event space E

⟦ ClosedUp E; ClosedDown E; trans E; antisym E;
  FiniteHist E; Rule1 E; Rule3 E; Rule4 E; Rule6 E;
  S ∈ Events(Store t l s); L ∈ Events(Load t l r);
  (L,S) ∈ E ⟧
⟹ ∃u. ∃A ∈ Events(Assign t l u). (A,S) ∈ E ∧ (L,A) ∈ E

stated as an axiom in [5, 17.3] which means that between a `Load` and a `Store`
for the same variable of the same thread there is an `Assign` for this thread and
variable in between.

In fact, by `Rule6` there must be some `Assign` action before the `Store`, even
a "maximal" such because of the following lemma:

⟦ ClosedUp E; ClosedDown E; trans E; FiniteHist E;
    Rule1 E; e ∈ Carrier E ⟧ ⟹
    (DownSet E e P ≠ {}) ⟶ (∃max. max ∈ (DownSet E e P) ∧
    (∀c. c ∈ (DownSet E e P) ⟶ (c,max) ∈ E))

by setting P = λe. ∃ t l v. (e = Assign t l v) ∧ e ∈ (Carrier E).
This maximal one must intervene between the Load and the Store, because
otherwise, from Rule1 and Rule3 there would be two Store events for the same
variable with no Assign in between, which contradicts Rule4.

Similarly, the following rule of [5, 17.3] can be derived from Rule10 and
Rule11:

⟦ ClosedDown E; ClosedUp E; antisym E; trans E; FiniteHist E;
    Rule2 E; Rule10 E; Rule11 E;
    L ∈ Events(Load t l r); S ∈ Events(Store t l s);
    (L,S) ∈ E; Write_of E S = Some W; ⟧
    ⟹
    ∃R. Read_of E L = Some R ∧ (R,W) ∈ E ;

The clause (Rule6) (as well as unspelled (Rule17)) simplify the corresponding
rules of [5, 17.3, 17.6] which include a condition Load(t,l,v) ≤ Store(t,l,v) to
the right of the implication. This extra condition is redundant, however, because
of the first lemma discussed above.

Note that the language specification requires any Read action to be completed
by a corresponding Load and similarly for Store and Write. We do not translate
such rules into well-formedness conditions for event spaces because the latter
must capture incomplete program executions.

```
IsEvtSpace E ≡
        ( (Rule1 E) ∧ (Rule2  E) ...
        ∧ (Rule16 E) ∧ (Rule17 E) ∧ (trans E) ∧ (antisym E)
        ∧ (ClosedDown E) ∧ (ClosedUp E) ∧ (FiniteHist E) )
```

Usage in operational semantics. Event spaces serve two purposes: First, they
provide all the information to reconstruct the current working memories of all
threads (which in fact do not appear in the configurations). Second, event spaces record the "historical" information on the computation which constrain the
execution of certain actions according to the language specification, and hence
the applicability of certain operational rules.

A *new event is adjoined* to an event space E by extending the execution order
as follows: If the event e is in Alpha t then it is above all other events in Alpha
t, and analogously for memory events.

```
AdjoinSet :: evtrelation ⟹ event ⟹ (evtrelation set)
AdjoinSet E a  ≡
  { R. IsEvtSpace R ∧
        (Carrier R = (Carrier E) Un {a}) ∧
        a ∉ (Carrier E)                    ∧
        (R Extends E)                      ∧
        (∀t q l.
```

```
    (if a ∈ (Alpha t) ∩ (Carrier E)
     then (∀a1 ∈ (Alpha t) ∩ (Carrier R). (a1,a) ∈ R)
     else (if a ∈ (Beta q) ∩ (Carrier E)
           then (∀a1 ∈ (Beta q) ∩ (Carrier R). (a1,a) ∈ R)
           else (if a ∈ (Beta1 l) ∩ (Carrier E)
                 then (∀a1 ∈ (Beta1 l) ∩ (Carrier R). (a1,a) ∈ R)
                 else True) }
```

The term E [+] e denotes the space thus obtained, provided it obeys the above rules, and it is otherwise undefined.

```
[+] :: evtrelation ⇒ event ⇒ (evtrelation option) (infixl 999)
E [+] a ≡ if (AdjoinSet E a = {})
            then None
            else Some (@F. F∈(AdjoinSet E a))
```

4   Stacks and Stores

Since the scope of local variables is determined by the block structure of the program, we keep them in a *stack* which grows and shrinks upon entering and exiting blocks. On the other hand, objects are permanent entities which survive the blocks in which they are created; therefore the collection of their *instance variables* (containing the values of their attributes) is kept in a separate structure: the *store*. Intuitively, stores can be thought of as mapping left-values (addresses of instance variables) to right-values (the primitive data of Java). Later on we shall see how different threads interact through the store. A formal description of stacks, stores and the configurations of the operational semantics is given below.

```
datatype  stack = Mtstack  |
                  Push       env stack


Pop            ::  stack ⇒ stack
Top            ::  stack ⇒ env
Bind           ::  identthis ⇒ rval ⇒ stack ⇒ (stack option)
Assig          ::  identthis ⇒ rval ⇒ stack ⇒ (stack option)
Lookup_stack   ::  identthis ⇒ stack ⇒ (rval option)
```

The (common) axioms are omitted. However, notice the difference between Bind and Assig. The former binds an identifier to a value in the top level environment, the latter searches in the stack for the first environment in which the identifier is declared and then updates it.

```
types   store


MtStore:: store
New    ::  classtype ⇒ store ⇒ (nonnullobj × store)
Upd    ::  lval ⇒ rval ⇒ store ⇒ store
Get    ::  lval ⇒ store ⇒ rval option
Init   ::  fieldidentifier ⇒ store ⇒ rval
```

Given a class and a store, New creates a new (nonnull) reference pointing to freshly allocated memory of the right size (depending on the class type) and initializes the fields of this newly created object with values specified by Init. This is axiomatized as follows:

```
IsDefined  (Get (Lval (fst (New C s)) (FId i C))  (snd (New C s)) )
   ⟹   the (Get (Lval (fst (New C s)) (FId i C)) (snd (New C s)) )
       =  Init   (FId i C) s
```

The axioms for Upd, Get, and MtStore are omitted as they simply denote update, retrieval, and empty store, respectively.

5   Semantic Rules for Multi-Threaded Java

Stores assume in multi-threaded Java a more active role than they have in sequential Java because of the way the main memory interacts with the working memories: a "silent" computational step changing the store may occur without the direct intervention of a thread's execution engine. Changes to the store are subject to the previous occurrence of certain events which affect the state of computation. Event spaces are included in the configurations to record such historical information.

Multi-threaded terms, stacks, and configurations. The type aterm serves as a supertype for statements, expressions and lists thereof.

```
datatype   aterm = ExprT      expr              |
                   ExprSeqT    (expr list)       |
                   StatT       stat              |
                   StatSeqT    (stat list)
```

In staterecord it is kept the information whether a thread is ready to execute (R), waits on an object having released a number of locks (W) or is in the state of being notified (N) still having to claim an amount of locks on an object.

```
datatype   staterecord = R          |
                         W obj nat |
                         N obj nat
```

An mterm is a set of 4-tuples consisting of a thread name, an abstract term to be executed, the state of the thread and a stack for the program variables. A configuration is a 4-tuple containing an mterm (i.e. all threads and their actual state), a set of objects which are bound to die (only relevant when explicit stopping of threads is allowed), an event space, and the main memory called store.

```
types mterm  = (thread × aterm × staterecord × stack) set
      config = (mterm × (obj set) × evtspace × store)
```

The one step reduction relation to_in_a_step is abbreviated ---> and the transitive closure to_in_n_steps is abbreviated to -*->.

```
to_in_a_step  :: (config × config) set
to_in_n_steps:: (config × config) set
in_a_step     :: [config,config] ⇒ bool  ( _ ---> _ )
in_n_steps    :: [config,config] ⇒ bool  ( _ -*-> _ )
c1 ---> c2 ≡ (c1,c2) ∈ to_in_a_step
c1 -*-> c2 ≡ (c1,c2) ∈ to_in_n_steps
```

The operation `WaitSet` computes the threads that are awaiting release of a certain object lock.

```
WaitSet       :: mterm ⇒ obj ⇒ (obj set)
WaitSet T p ≡ { t. ∃r n a.  (t,a,(W p n),r) ∈ T }
```

Frame is an auxiliary (partial) function that produces the right activation frame for a method call instantiating the list of formal parameters by the given list of actual values. The definition of `Frame` is not difficult and omitted. It makes use of `MethodBody` which is an abstract function (ie. it has no definition but has to be axiomatized appropriately if needed) that for a given identifier returns the definition body of the method together with its formal parameters.

```
Frame         :: obj ⇒ methodidentifier ⇒ (rval list)
                                  ⇒ store ⇒ (stmexpr option)
Methodbody    :: classtype ⇒ methodidentifier ⇒ store
                         ⇒ ( block × (identifier list) ) option
```

Moreover we use the following abbreviations for sets of `mterm`s:

```
MT    ::  mterm
||    ::  mterm ⇒ (thread × aterm × staterecord × stack)  ⇒ mterm
MT    ≡ {}
T || m ≡ insert m T
```

Let `Val v` abbreviate `StmtExpr (ValS v)` which is a value obtained as a result of an expression.

Spontaneous memory actions.

```
[ (t,a,R,r) ∈ T ; (Get l s) = Some v;
  (∃re ∈ (Events(Read t l v)). E [+] re = Some E1) ]
⟹
  (T,Q,E,s) ---> (T,Q,E1,s)
```

```
[ (t,a,R,r) ∈ T;
  (∃l v. ∃st ∈ (Event(Store t l v)). E [+] st = Some E1) ]
⟹
  (T,Q,E,s) ---> (T,Q,E1,s)
```

Note that the second rule "guesses" the value of the last `Assign` in order to perform a store action; axiom `Rule9` ensures that the guess is right. There are analogous rules for `Load` and `Write`.

The function for computing a left value out of a variable expression, if possible, is called `ExpLval` (we omit the definition):

```
ExpLval :: var ⇒(lval) option
IsLval  :: var ⇒ bool
IsLval e ≡ ExpLval e ≠ None
```

Assignment rules. First evaluate the variable on the left.

```
( (T1 || (t,(ExprT (Acc e1)),R,r1)), Q1, E1, s1 ) --->
( (T2 || (t,(ExprT (Acc e2)),z,r2)), Q2, E2, s2 )
==>
( (T1 || (t,(ExprT (StmtExp (Ass e1 e))),R,r1)), Q1, E1, s1 )
  --->
( (T2 || (t,(ExprT (StmtExp (Ass e2 e))),z,r2)), Q2, E2, s2 )
```

Next evaluate the expression on the right:

```
( (T1 || (t,(ExprT e1),R,r1)), Q1, E1, s1 ) --->
( (T2 || (t,(ExprT e2),z,r2)), Q2, E2, s2 )
==>
( (T1 || (t,(ExprT (StmtExp (Ass (Var i) e1))),R,r1)), Q1, E1, s1 )
  --->
( (T2 || (t,(ExprT (StmtExp (Ass (Var i) e2))),z,r2)), Q2, E2, s2 )

[ IsLval 1;
  ( (T1 || (t,(ExprT e1),R,r1)), Q1, E1, s1 ) --->
  ( (T2 || (t,(ExprT e2),z,r2)), Q2, E2, s2 ) ]
==>
( (T1 || (t,(ExprT (StmtExp (Ass 1 e1))),R,r1)), Q1, E1, s1 )
  --->
( (T2 || (t,(ExprT (StmtExp (Ass 1 e2))),z,r2)), Q2, E2, s2 )
```

If both sides are evaluated update the working memory for an assignment to a field variable (which involves the event space, update of the environment for a programm variable is similar). Nothing is said, so far, about a possible write-through to the store:

```
[ ExpLval le = Some 1;
    ∃as ∈ (Events(Assign t l v)). E [+] as = (Some E1)) ]
==>
  ( (T || (t, (ExprT (StmtExp (Ass le (Val v)))),R,r)), Q, E, s )
   --->
  ( (T || (t, (ExprT (Val v)),R,r)), Q, E1, s )
```

Rules can be applied only if the operation [+] is defined for the given arguments, that is, if the action being performed complies with the requirements of the language specification. By the above rules `Assign` (the same e.g. for `Use`) actions are only added to an event space, when dictated by execution of the current thread [5, 17.3]. There are 91 rules altogether, so we can only present some selected rules due to lack of space. Of course, some rules involving two threads are interesting:

Starting other threads. Let `IllegalThreadStateExcep:: classtype` and `Start, Run :: methodidentifier` be given constants. The precondition

```
Frame t2 Start [] s = None
```

of the following rules ensures that there is no overloading of **start** with a user-defined method. The first rule describes the standard case, the second covers the cases where the started thread is bound to die or there is no appropriate (user-defined) run()-method for it. The third rule is fired if one tries to start a thread that is already running. According to the Java specification this will result in an exception.

```
⟦  Frame t2 Start [] s = None;
        t2 ∉ Q; Frame t2 Run [] s = Some se ⟧
     ⟹
     ( (T || (t1,(StatT (ExpStmt (MCall (Val (Oref t2)) Start [])))),
              R,r1)), Q, E, s ) --->
     ( ((T || (t1,(StatT Nop),R,r1))
           || (t2,(StatT (ExpStmt se)),R,Mtstack)), Q, E, s )

⟦ Frame t2 Start [] s = None;
        (t2  ∈ Q ∨ (Frame t2 Run [] s) = None) ⟧
     ⟹
     ( (T || (t1,(StatT (ExpStmt(MCall (Val (Oref t2)) Start [])))),
              R,r1)), Q, E, s ) --->
     ( ((T || (t1,(StatT Nop),R,r1))
           || (t2,(StatT Nop),R,Mtstack)), Q - {t2}, E, s )

⟦ Frame t2 Start [] s = None; ((t2,a,z,r1) ∈ T ∨ t2 = t1);
        New IllegalThreadStateExcep s = (p,s1) ⟧
     ⟹
     ( (T || (t1,(StatT (ExpStmt(MCall (Val (Oref t2)) Start [])))),
              R,r)), Q, E, s ) --->
     ( (T || (t1,StatT(ExpStmt(ThrowSE (Throw (Nonnull p))))),
              R,r)), Q, E, s1 )
```

6   Why Doing It with Isabelle

It is well accepted meanwhile that a formalization by "paper and pencil" should be followed – if possible – by a thorough machine-checkable formalization. Theorem provers and proof checkers like Isabelle provide a corresponding tool for constructing and maintaining such a high and trustworthy level of formality. This claim has been once more sustained in the present case for the semantics of multi-threaded Java.

In the formalization [3] of the informal Java specification [5] some minor errors could be found regarding the "type" correctness of abstract syntax. The use of a tool often reveals gaps and hidden assumptions. In our case, it gave rise to the discussion how to express the fact that chains of events are well-founded.

Moreover, since terms of abstract syntax can become quite huge and clumsy, it comes in handy to dispose of a system that helps to manipulate such terms and to perform the bookkeeping. Syntax sugar (already supported by Isabelle) is important and its usage should be as easy as possible to obtain readable propositions (to say nothing of the proofs). One of the most striking and helpful features

of Isabelle, is the available stock of theories and theorems easily accessible on
the web.

To the Isabelle-novice, some behaviour of Isabelle may look quite confusing,
in particular error messages like "inner syntax error"[4]. Another problem with
error messages occurs in inductive definitions where they neither refer to the
name of the rule nor to line numbers.

A very tricky feature (especially if you have worked with other provers before) is the fact that Isabelle declares implicitly any unknown identifier as a
new variable. On one hand this is convenient as one is liberated from writing
many declarations. On the other hand already a misspelled constant may lead
to opaque effects later on. Nested datatypes with Isabelle-98 at least, produce
a memory overflow on a machine with 256 MB RAM (Isabelle-gurus probably
have more memory at hand[5]) and caused more problems that expected when
coding up the syntax.

7   Conclusions and Future Work

In this paper we have presented a machine-checked version of the structural
operational semantics of the concurrency model of Java in Isabelle. Our semantics covers a substantial part of the dynamic behaviour of the language. Most
notably type information (class, interface and method declarations) and some
control flow statements are missing. By using Isabelle several minor flaws mainly
regarding the abstract syntax and the syntactic well-definedness of terms on the
right hand side of reduction rules were discovered in the "paper-and-pencil"
specification of [3].

It would be nice to extend the multi-threaded semantics with a type-checking
result in the form of a subject reduction theorem as done in [10] for sequential
Java using big-step semantics. One should be able to reuse some parts of *loc.cit.*
adopting their notation.

On the basis of the presented Isabelle/HOL-theories we are currently trying to formalize more proofs about language analysis: The first is a correctness
theorem of so-called "prescient" store actions [5, 17.8]. These actions "allow optimizing Java compilers to perform certain kinds of code rearrangements that
preserve the semantics of properly synchronized programs [...]." ([3]). The
second theorem for "properly synchronized programs", i.e. those that change
and access shared variables only in synchronized blocks, states that it cannot
be observed by other threads whether read/load and store/write events happen
synchronously or asynchronously. This would mean a possible simplification of
the memory model.

---

[4] It can take e.g. a long time to detect that one is not allowed to use a variable name
o as it is already used for function composition. Moreover, trying `rewrite_tac` instead of `rewrite_goals_tac` one obtains the mysterious message "`proved different
goal`".

[5] Thanks to Markus Wenzel for pointing out to us the `quick_and_dirty` mode.

It seems a desirable and achievable goal to produce some Isabelle theories containing the type system and semantics of Java plus some characteristic meta properties of the language (including proofs). Those could not only serve as a "certificate" for Java, but may also contain material that can be reused for the semantics of other languages still awaiting definition.

Acknowledgment

The first author likes to thank Stephan Merz for discussions ans hints about the behaviour of Isabelle. The second author is indebted to Andy Mück for moral and scientific support.

References

1. J. Alves-Foss, editor. *Formal Syntax and Semantics of Java*, volume 1523 of *Lect. Notes Comp. Sci.* Springer, Berlin, 1999.
2. Ken Arnold and James Gosling. *The Java Programming Language.* Addison–Wesley, Reading, Mass., 1996.
3. P. Cenciarelli, A. Knapp, B. Reus, and M. Wirsing. An Event-Based Structural Operational Semantics of Multi-Threaded Java. In Alves-Foss [1], pages 157–200.
4. Sophia Drossopoulou and Susan Eisenbach. Java is Type Safe — Probably. In Mehmet Aksit, editor, *Proc. 11th Europ. Conf. Object-Oriented Programming*, volume 1241 of *Lect. Notes Comp. Sci.*, pages 389–418, Berlin, 1997. Springer.
5. James Gosling, Bill Joy, and Guy Steele. *The Java Language Specification.* Addison–Wesley, Reading, Mass., 1996.
6. Tatjana Hein. Formalisierung einer strukturierten operationellen Semantik für multi-threaded Java in Isabelle. Fakultät für Mathematik und Informatik, Universität Passau, 1999. Diploma-Thesis.
7. Doug Lea. *Concurrent Programming in Java.* Addison–Wesley, Reading, Mass., 1997.
8. Wei Li. An Operational Semantics of Multitasking and Exception Handling in Ada. In *Proc. AdaTEC Conf. Ada*, pages 138–151, New York, 1982. ACM SIGAda.
9. Robin Milner, Mads Tofte, Robert Harper, and David MacQueen. *The Definition of Standard ML (Revised).* MIT Press, Cambridge, Mass., 1997.
10. Tobias Nipkow and David von Oheimb. Machine-checking the Java Specification: Proving Type-Saftey. In Alves-Foss [1].
11. L.C. Paulson. *Isabelle: A Generic Theorem Prover*, volume 828 of *Lect. Notes in Comp. Sci.* Springer Verlag, 1994.
12. Gordon D. Plotkin. A Structural Approach to Operational Semantics (Lecture notes). Technical Report DAIMI FN–19, Aarhus University, 1981 (repr. 1991).
13. Glynn Winskel. An Introduction to Event Structures. In Jacobus W. de Bakker, Willem P. de Roever, and Grzegorg Rozenberg, editors, *Linear Time, Branching Time and Partial Order in Logics and Models for Concurrency*, volume 354 of *Lect. Notes Comp. Sci.*, pages 364–397. Springer, Berlin, 1988.

Another Look at Nested Recursion

Konrad Slind

Cambridge University Computer Laboratory

Abstract. Functions specified by nested recursions are difficult to define and reason about. We present several ameliorative techniques that use deduction in a classical higher-order logic. First, we discuss how an apparent circular dependency between the proof of nested termination conditions and the definition of the specified function can be avoided. Second, we propose a method that allows the specified function to be defined in the absence of a termination relation. Finally, we show how our techniques extend to nested program schemes, where a termination relation cannot be found until schematic parameters have been filled in. In each of these techniques, suitable induction theorems are automatically derived.

1 Introduction

Recursion equations specifying a function f are said to be *nested* when an argument to a recursive call of f contains another invocation of f. For example, the second clause in the following equations has a nested recursion:

$$\begin{aligned} \mathsf{g}\ 0 &\equiv 0 \\ \mathsf{g}\ (\mathsf{Suc}\ x) &\equiv \mathsf{g}\ (\mathsf{g}\ x). \end{aligned} \tag{1}$$

Nested recursion has traditionally posed problems for mechanization, especially in logics of total functions. The standard criterion in such a logic for accepting that recursion equations form a 'good' definition is that the arguments to recursive calls must decrease in a wellfounded relation. For our example, this means that for some wellfounded relation R, both $\forall x.\ R\ x\ (\mathsf{Suc}\ x)$ and $\forall x.\ R\ (\mathsf{g}\ x)\ (\mathsf{Suc}\ x)$ must be proved. Taking R to be the less-than relation ($<$), the first of these termination conditions is easy enough, but the second seems problematic. The trouble is that even *stating* $\forall x.\ \mathsf{g}\ x < \mathsf{Suc}\ x$ as a meaningful proposition seems to assume that g has been defined, but that is just the point of proving the termination conditions! Thus there seems to be a circular dependency between definition and termination proofs in the case of nested recursion.

We have found that working formally in a mechanized logic has helped to clarify some of the intricacies surrounding nested recursion. In our general approach, recursion equations (nested or not) are given meaning by deriving them

J. Harrison and M. Aagaard (Eds.): TPHOLs 2000, LNCS 1869, pp. 498–518, 2000.

from the following wellfounded recursion theorem:[1]

$$(f = \mathsf{WFREC}\ R\ \mathcal{F}) \wedge \mathsf{WF}(R) \supset \forall x.\ f(x) = \mathcal{F}\ (f \mid R, x)\ x. \qquad (2)$$

To derive the specified equations, the equations are first reduced, via a pattern matching translation similar to that used in compilation of functional programs, to a *functional* $\mathcal{F}$. The HOL constant definition mechanism is then used to define the constant as an application of WFREC:

$$\mathsf{f} \equiv \mathsf{WFREC}\ R\ \mathcal{F}. \qquad (3)$$

Subsequently, (2) is instantiated by (3). Further deductive steps are then required to (automatically) extract termination conditions and prove them. If all the termination conditions are proved, then the specified recursion equations may be used as unconstrained rewrite rules. This approach has been mechanized in the TFL system [17,19], which has been instantiated to Hol98 and Isabelle/HOL.

In TFL, every recursive definition is accompanied by an induction theorem, which is derived from the wellfounded induction theorem by an algorithm described in [18]. The style of such an induction theorem can be sloganized as '*the induction hypothesis holds for each argument to a recursive call*'. With this in mind, the following is the induction theorem *specified* by **g**:

$$\forall P.\ P\ 0\ \wedge\ (\forall x.\ P\ x \wedge P\ (\mathsf{g}\ x) \supset P\ (\mathsf{Suc}\ x)) \supset \forall v.\ P\ v. \qquad (4)$$

This general approach, of defining total functions by appeal to wellfounded recursion and reasoning using induction theorems based on the recursions of the functions has been taken by many systems, most notably that developed by Boyer and Moore [4].

In the remainder of the paper, we discuss two styles of treating nested functions and their induction theorems. In the first, the termination relation is supplied at the moment the function is defined. In the second, the termination relation is not given at function definition time; instead, it is represented by a variable, which can be instantiated at the user's convenience. Both of these styles circumvent the circularity problem described above, and both derive appropriate induction theorems.

2   Definitions with Termination Relations

This section is a detailed elaboration of work already reported in [17]. In a verification of McCarthy's 91 function, we defined 91 by supplying an appropriate termination relation at definition time and were subsequently able to prove the nested termination condition for 91. Somewhat surprisingly, the proof of termination for 91 was *self-contained*, in the sense that the specification of 91 was not needed; this provided a counterexample to the prevailing wisdom [10,14] which

---

[1] Notation: WFREC is a 'controlled' fixpoint operator, WF denotes wellfoundedness, and $f \mid R, x$ is a function restriction (none of these notions are explored in this paper).

held that proofs of termination and correctness for nested recursive functions must be intertwined.

We will use g to illustrate these points. After transforming the equations (1) into a functional $\mathcal{F}$ and making the definition $g \equiv WFREC\ (<)\ \mathcal{F}$, the following constrained equations are derivable, as explained in [17]:[2]

$$WF(<) \vdash g\ 0 = 0$$
$$[WF(<),\ x < \mathsf{Suc}\ x,\ g\ x < \mathsf{Suc}\ x] \vdash g(\mathsf{Suc}\ x) = g(g\ x).$$

It is simple to prove and eliminate $WF(<)$ and $x < \mathsf{Suc}\ x$, leaving

$$\vdash g\ 0 = 0$$
$$g\ x < \mathsf{Suc}\ x \vdash g(\mathsf{Suc}\ x) = g(g\ x). \tag{5}$$

To finish the termination proof of g requires showing the nested termination condition $\forall x.\ g\ x < \mathsf{Suc}\ x$. However, the proof seems problematic since, in any attempt to use the recursive clause of (5) in the proof, the hypothesis $g\ x < \mathsf{Suc}\ x$ must be eliminated. As already noted, the historical answer to this apparent circularity has been to assert that correctness and termination must be proved simultaneously for nested recursions, for then the correctness property can be used instead of attempting to unroll the function in the proof of the nested termination condition.

However, another approach emerged in the mid-1990's [8,17]: a strong enough inductive hypothesis allows the circularity to be avoided. For example, the nested termination condition for g can be proved by induction along $<$ (a case split and a lemma are needed, however). In fact, applying (4) seems to be exactly what is needed. The full rendering of (4) is actually

$$[WF(<),\ (\forall x.\ x < \mathsf{Suc}\ x),\ (\forall x.\ g\ x < \mathsf{Suc}\ x)]$$
$$\vdash \tag{6}$$
$$\forall P.\ P\ 0 \wedge (\forall x.\ P\ x \wedge P\ (g\ x) \supset P\ (\mathsf{Suc}\ x)) \supset \forall v.\ P\ v.$$

Notice that the termination conditions are fully quantified; this is necessary to make the derivation go through. As above, $WF\ (<)$ and $\forall x.\ x < \mathsf{Suc}\ x$ are trivial to prove and eliminate from the hypotheses, leaving us with

$$[\ \forall x.\ g\ x < \mathsf{Suc}\ x\ ] \vdash \forall P.\ P\ 0 \wedge (\forall x.\ P\ x \wedge P\ (g\ x) \supset P\ (\mathsf{Suc}\ x)) \supset \forall v.\ P\ v. \tag{7}$$

Attempting to apply this theorem to prove $\forall x.\ g\ x < \mathsf{Suc}\ x$ is obviously not going to work because application of the induction theorem presupposes that which is to be proved. However, a slight variant of (7) is usable: instead of quantifying the nested termination condition and moving it onto the hypotheses while deriving the induction theorem, the conditions on the use of the nested induction

---

[2] Unlike earlier work, termination condition extraction in this paper quantifies termination conditions as little as possible, i.e., only variables bound in the right hand side of an equation will become universally quantified in the extracted termination conditions.

hypothesis are left 'in place'. This yields the following induction theorem (where WF ($<$) and $\forall x.\ x <$ Suc x have already been eliminated from the hypotheses):

$$\vdash \forall P.\ P\ 0\ \wedge (\forall x.\ P\ x \wedge \underbrace{(g\ x < \text{Suc } x \supset P\ (g\ x))}_{\text{nested i.h.}}) \supset P\ (\text{Suc } x)) \supset \forall v.\ P\ v. \quad (8)$$

We call this the *provisional* induction theorem. TFL automatically derives the provisional induction theorem for nested recursive definitions that come with termination relations. In some cases, the provisional induction theorem can be useful for proving nested termination conditions, and after they have been proved (by whatever means), they can be eliminated from the provisional induction theorem to obtain the specified induction theorem. With that background, we return to our example.

$$\forall x.\ g\ x < \text{Suc } x. \quad (9)$$

Proof. Induct with (8). This leaves two goals: g $0 <$ Suc 0 (which is proved by unwinding (5) at 0) and the goal stemming from the recursive case:[3]

$$\frac{\text{g (Suc } x) < \text{Suc (Suc } x)}{\begin{array}{l} 0.\ \ \text{g } x < \text{Suc } x \supset \text{g (g } x) < \text{Suc (g } x) \\ 1.\ \ \text{g } x < \text{Suc } x \end{array}}$$

Rewrite with (5); this is allowed because the constraint on applying (5) is just assumption 1.

$$\frac{\text{g (g } x) < \text{Suc (Suc } x)}{\begin{array}{l} 0.\ \ \text{g } x < \text{Suc } x \supset \text{g (g } x) < \text{Suc (g } x) \\ 1.\ \ \text{g } x < \text{Suc } x \end{array}}$$

The hypotheses yield g $(g\,x) <$ Suc $(g\,x)$. The proof then completes by a chain of inequalities:

$$\text{g (g } x) \leq \text{g } x < \text{Suc } x < \text{Suc (Suc } x).$$

□

Now (5) and (8) can be freed of (9); after this, they can be applied to, *e.g.*, prove the specification of g: $\forall x.\ g\ x = 0$. Note that this property could also have been proven straightaway by use of (5) and mathematical induction. However, that doesn't invalidate our point: in many cases, termination and correctness can be proved separately, which is often simpler than a proof of the combined properties.

The general picture that this small example illustrates is that—in some cases—the constrained recursion equations for a nested function f and its provisional induction theorem can be used to prove totality of f. A crucial point in the proof will require f to be 'evaluated' at an argument a such that a nested call $f(b)$ results. The unrolling of $f(a)$ will be allowed on condition that $f(b)$ terminates. If the inductive hypotheses are strong enough, this condition can be shown without circularity.

---

[3] The goal is above the line and assumptions are below.

3   Example: First Order Unification

The nested unification algorithm we verify[4] in this section was first described, informally but in great detail, by Manna and Waldinger [10]. Larry Paulson later verified the algorithm using Cambridge LCF [14]. Sten Agerholm duplicated Paulson's work in a version of LCF built inside the HOL system [1]. The algorithm has also been verified using Type Theory [16,3,11].

Following Paulson, we define terms as binary trees instead of the more standard n-ary trees; this is not a significant limitation, as Paulson argues [14]. The following are the constructors of the term type:

$$\text{Var} : \alpha \to \alpha \text{ term}$$
$$\text{Const} : \alpha \to \alpha \text{ term}$$
$$\_\_ \cdot \_\_ : \alpha \text{ term} \to \alpha \text{ term} \to \alpha \text{ term} \quad \text{(infix, left associative)}$$

The variables of a term are denoted by vars_of, and can be defined by a simple recursion. Similarly, the occurs check is defined as follows:

$$\text{occ}(u, \text{Var } v) \equiv \text{False}$$
$$\text{occ}(u, \text{Const } c) \equiv \text{False}$$
$$\text{occ}(u, M \cdot N) \equiv (u = M) \vee (u = N) \vee \text{occ}(u, M) \vee \text{occ}(u, N)$$

This definition implies that the occurs check is actually a *proper* suboccurrence check: for example, it is not true that $\text{occ}(x, x)$.

Substitutions are represented by association lists and applied by the following definition.[5]

$$(\text{Var } v \triangleleft \theta) \equiv \text{assoc } v \ (\text{Var } v) \ \theta$$
$$(\text{Const } c \triangleleft \theta) \equiv \text{Const } c$$
$$((M \cdot N) \triangleleft \theta) \equiv (M \triangleleft \theta) \cdot (N \triangleleft \theta)$$

The equality of substitutions is defined as: $(\sigma =_s \theta) \equiv \forall t. \ t \triangleleft \sigma = t \triangleleft \theta$. Composition of substitutions is a left associative binary infix operator:

$$[\,] \bullet bl \equiv bl$$
$$((a, b) :: al) \bullet bl \equiv (a, b \triangleleft bl) :: (al \bullet bl)$$

Many standard facts about substitutions are required in the formalization; *e.g.*, composition of substitutions is associative: $\vdash (\gamma \bullet \sigma) \bullet \theta =_s \gamma \bullet (\sigma \bullet \theta)$ and that iterated substitutions can be composed: $(subst\_comp) \quad \vdash (t \triangleleft (r \bullet s)) = ((t \triangleleft r) \triangleleft s)$.

The unification algorithm returns a *most general unifier* of the input terms, when it succeeds. Unifiers are substitutions that make terms equal and a *most*

---

[4] The verification was performed in the Isabelle/HOL instantiation of TFL.

[5] The assoc function is defined as

$$\text{assoc } d \ x \ [\,] \equiv d$$
$$\text{assoc } d \ x \ ((p, q) :: t) \equiv \text{if } x = p \text{ then } q \text{ else assoc } d \ x \ t.$$

general unifier is a unifier that can be instantiated to get any unifier.

$$\text{Unifier } \theta \, t \, u \equiv (t \triangleleft \theta = u \triangleleft \theta)$$
$$\text{MGU } \theta \, t \, u \equiv \text{Unifier } \theta \, t \, u \wedge \forall \sigma. \text{ Unifier } \sigma \, t \, u \supset \exists \gamma. \, \sigma =_s \theta \bullet \gamma$$

The recursion equations specifying the unification algorithm are the following:

1. $\text{Unify}(\text{Const } m, M \cdot N)$ $= \text{None}$
2. $\text{Unify}(M \cdot N, \text{Const } x)$ $= \text{None}$
3. $\text{Unify}(\text{Const } m, \text{Var } v)$ $= \text{Some}[(v, \text{Const } m)]$
4. $\text{Unify}(M \cdot N, \text{Var } v)$ $= \text{if occ}(\text{Var } v, M \cdot N) \text{ then None else Some}[(v, M \cdot N)]$
5. $\text{Unify}(\text{Var } v, M)$ $= \text{if occ}(\text{Var } v, M) \text{ then None else Some}[(v, M)]$
6. $\text{Unify}(\text{Const } m, \text{Const } n) = \text{if } (m = n) \text{ then Some}[] \text{ else None}$
7. $\text{Unify}(M_1 \cdot N_1, M_2 \cdot N_2)$ $= \text{case Unify}(M_1, M_2)$
   $\quad\quad\quad\quad\quad\quad \text{of None} \Rightarrow \text{None}$
   $\quad\quad\quad\quad\quad\quad | \text{ Some } \theta \Rightarrow \text{case Unify}(N_1 \triangleleft \theta, N_2 \triangleleft \theta)$
   $\quad\quad\quad\quad\quad\quad\quad\quad\quad \text{of None} \Rightarrow \text{None}$
   $\quad\quad\quad\quad\quad\quad\quad\quad\quad | \text{ Some } \sigma \Rightarrow \text{Some}(\theta \bullet \sigma).$

$$(10)$$

As can be seen, the algorithm recurses only in clause 7. The termination of Unify is difficult to prove for two reasons: (1) the nested recursion and (2) the arguments in $\text{Unify}(N_1 \triangleleft \theta, N_2 \triangleleft \theta)$ can be larger than the arguments to $\text{Unify}(M_1 \cdot N_1, M_2 \cdot N_2)$, which means that a simple size-based relation won't work. The termination relation (named UTR) for Unify is essentially that given by Manna and Waldinger: UTR (M_1, M_2) (N_1, N_2) holds if

- vars_of $M_1 \cup$ vars_of M_2 is a proper subset of vars_of $N_1 \cup$ vars_of N_2; orelse
- vars_of $M_1 \cup$ vars_of $M_2 =$ vars_of $N_1 \cup$ vars_of N_2, and the size of M_1 is less than the size of N_1 and the size of M_2 is less than the size of N_2.

The formal details of the construction of UTR may be found in [19]. Only the base cases of the termination proof for Unify require unfolding the definition of UTR; in the induction step, we merely require that (1) UTR is transitive, and (2) that (loosely) UTR ignores a certain amount of term structure:

$$(X, \; (A \cdot (B \cdot C), \; D \cdot (E \cdot F))) \in \text{UTR}$$
$$\supset \quad\quad\quad (11)$$
$$(X, \; ((A \cdot B) \cdot C, \; (D \cdot E) \cdot F)) \in \text{UTR}.$$

When the recursion equations together with UTR are submitted to TFL, the following theorems are returned: a constrained set of equations, and a constrained induction principle. The returned equations 1 to 6, not being recursive, are just what was specified, and are constrained only by WF UTR. Equation 7 has the following 2 non-nested termination conditions attached: $((M_1, M_2), (M_1 \cdot N_1, M_2 \cdot N_2)) \in \text{UTR}$ and WF UTR, and also the nested termination condition. The two non-nested termination conditions are easy to prove and eliminate from the returned recursion equations and the provisional induction theorem, which is

$$\vdash \forall P. (\forall m\ n.\ P\ (\mathsf{Const}\ m, \mathsf{Const}\ n)) \land \tag{12}$$
$$(\forall m\ M\ N.\ P\ (\mathsf{Const}\ m, M \cdot N)) \land$$
$$(\forall m\ v.\ P\ (\mathsf{Const}\ m, \mathsf{Var}\ v)) \land$$
$$(\forall v\ M.\ P\ (\mathsf{Var}\ v, M)) \land$$
$$(\forall M\ N\ x.\ P\ (M \cdot N, \mathsf{Const}\ x)) \land$$
$$(\forall M\ N\ v.\ P\ (M \cdot N, \mathsf{Var}\ v)) \land$$
$$(\forall M_1\ N_1\ M_2\ N_2.$$
$$\left(\begin{array}{l} \forall \theta.\ \mathsf{Unify}(M_1, M_2) = \mathsf{Some}\ \theta \\ \quad \supset ((N_1 \lhd \theta, N_2 \lhd \theta), (M_1 \cdot N_1, M_2 \cdot N_2)) \in \mathsf{UTR} \\ \qquad \supset P\ (N_1 \lhd \theta, N_2 \lhd \theta) \\ \land\ P\ (M_1, M_2) \supset P\ (M_1 \cdot N_1, M_2 \cdot N_2)) \end{array}\right)$$
$$\supset$$
$$\forall v\ v_1.\ P\ (v, v_1).$$

Next we tackle the nested termination condition. Applying the provisional induction theorem (12) makes the proof relatively straightforward. Manna and Waldinger needed to use idempotence of the substitutions coming from Unify—a correctness property—at a crucial point in their termination proof. In contrast we need no such extra information.

$$\forall \theta.\ \mathsf{Unify}(M_1, M_2) = \mathsf{Some}\ \theta \supset \left(\begin{array}{c} (N_1 \lhd \theta,\ N_2 \lhd \theta), \\ (M_1 \cdot N_1,\ M_2 \cdot N_2) \end{array}\right) \in \mathsf{UTR}. \tag{13}$$

Proof. The first thing we do is shrink the scopes of N_1 and N_2 as much as possible. Thus it suffices to prove

$$\forall M_1\ M_2\ \theta.\ \mathsf{Unify}(M_1, M_2) = \mathsf{Some}\ \theta \supset$$
$$\forall N_1\ N_2.\ ((N_1 \lhd \theta, N_2 \lhd \theta), (M_1 \cdot N_1, M_2 \cdot N_2)) \in \mathsf{UTR}$$

We then induct with (12) and simplify with the rewrite rules for Unify. The base cases are all easy; for the recursive case, the following is to be shown:

$$\left(\begin{array}{l} \mathsf{case}\ \mathsf{Unify}(M_1, M_2) \\ \quad \mathsf{of}\ \mathsf{None}\texttt{=>}\mathsf{None} \\ \quad |\ \mathsf{Some}\ \theta_3\texttt{=>}\mathsf{case}\ (\mathsf{Unify}(N_1 \lhd \theta_3, N_2 \lhd \theta_3) \\ \qquad\qquad\qquad\quad \mathsf{of}\ \mathsf{None}\texttt{=>}\mathsf{None} \\ \qquad\qquad\qquad\qquad |\ \mathsf{Some}\ \sigma\texttt{=>}\mathsf{Some}(\theta_3 \bullet \sigma)) \end{array}\right) = \mathsf{Some}\ \theta$$
$$\supset$$
$$\forall P\ Q.((P \lhd \theta, Q \lhd \theta), (M_1 \cdot N_1) \cdot P, (M_2 \cdot N_2) \cdot Q) \in \mathsf{UTR}$$

The two inductive hypotheses are the *nested* i.h.

$$\vdash \forall \theta_0.\ \mathsf{Unify}(M_1, M_2) = \mathsf{Some}\ \theta_0 \supset$$
$$((N_1 \lhd \theta_0, N_2 \lhd \theta_0), (M_1 \cdot N_1, M_2 \cdot N_2)) \in \mathsf{UTR} \supset$$
$$\forall \theta_1.\ \mathsf{Unify}(N_1 \lhd \theta_0, N_2 \lhd \theta_0) = \mathsf{Some}\ \theta_1 \supset$$
$$\forall P\ Q.\ ((P \lhd \theta_1, Q \lhd \theta_1), ((N_1 \lhd \theta_0) \cdot P, (N_2 \lhd \theta_0) \cdot Q)) \in \mathsf{UTR} \tag{14}$$

and the *non-nested* i.h.

$$\vdash \forall \theta_2.\ \mathsf{Unify}(M_1, M_2) = \mathsf{Some}\ \theta_2 \supset \tag{15}$$
$$\forall N_1\ N_2.\ ((N_1 \vartriangleleft \theta_2, N_2 \vartriangleleft \theta_2), (M_1 \centerdot N_1, M_2 \centerdot N_2)) \in \mathsf{UTR}.$$

The proof proceeds by two case analyses on the results of applying Unify. We start by making a case analysis on $\mathsf{Unify}(M_1, M_2)$. The None case is vacuously true; alternatively, suppose that Some θ_3 is the result. We can use *modus ponens* on (15) to prove

$$\vdash \forall N_1\ N_2.\ ((N_1 \vartriangleleft \theta_3, N_2 \vartriangleleft \theta_3), (M_1 \centerdot N_1, M_2 \centerdot N_2)) \in \mathsf{UTR} \tag{16}$$

and therefore the nested i.h. (14) can be simplified (twice) to obtain

$$\vdash \forall \theta_1.\ \mathsf{Unify}(N_1 \vartriangleleft \theta_3, N_2 \vartriangleleft \theta_3) = \mathsf{Some}\ \theta_1 \supset \tag{17}$$
$$\forall P\ Q.\ ((P \vartriangleleft \theta_1, Q \vartriangleleft \theta_1), ((N_1 \vartriangleleft \theta_3) \centerdot P, (N_2 \vartriangleleft \theta_3) \centerdot Q)) \in \mathsf{UTR}.$$

The goal has also been reduced by the case analysis, yielding

$$\begin{pmatrix} \mathsf{case}\ \mathsf{Unify}(N_1 \vartriangleleft \theta_3, N_2 \vartriangleleft \theta_3) \\ \mathsf{of}\ \mathsf{None}{=}{>}\mathsf{None} \\ |\ \mathsf{Some}\ \sigma{=}{>}\mathsf{Some}(\theta_3 \bullet \sigma) \end{pmatrix} = \mathsf{Some}(\theta) \supset \begin{pmatrix} (P \vartriangleleft \theta, Q \vartriangleleft \theta), \\ ((M_1.N_1).P, (M_2.N_2).Q) \end{pmatrix} \in \mathsf{UTR}.$$

We now make a case analysis on $\mathsf{Unify}(N_1 \vartriangleleft \theta_3, N_2 \vartriangleleft \theta_3)$. Again, the None case is vacuously true, and so suppose that Some σ is the result. We are left with the goal

$$(\mathsf{Some}(\theta_3 \bullet \sigma) = \mathsf{Some}\ \theta) \supset \begin{pmatrix} (P \vartriangleleft \theta, Q \vartriangleleft \theta), \\ ((M_1 \centerdot N_1) \centerdot P, (M_2 \centerdot N_2) \centerdot Q) \end{pmatrix} \in \mathsf{UTR},$$

and hence the goal (by use of the injectivity of Some and also the theorem *subst_comp*)

$$\begin{pmatrix} (P \vartriangleleft \theta_3 \vartriangleleft \sigma, Q \vartriangleleft \theta_3 \vartriangleleft \sigma), \\ ((M_1 \centerdot N_1) \centerdot P, (M_2 \centerdot N_2) \centerdot Q) \end{pmatrix} \in \mathsf{UTR}.$$

This second case analysis allows the nested i.h. (17) to be further simplified, yielding

$$\vdash \forall P\ Q.\ \begin{pmatrix} (P \vartriangleleft \sigma, Q \vartriangleleft \sigma), \\ ((N_1 \vartriangleleft \theta_3) \centerdot P, (N_2 \vartriangleleft \theta_3) \centerdot Q) \end{pmatrix} \in \mathsf{UTR}. \tag{18}$$

We then instantiate (18) by $P \mapsto P \vartriangleleft \theta_3$ and $Q \mapsto Q \vartriangleleft \theta_3$ to prove

$$\vdash \begin{pmatrix} (P \vartriangleleft \theta_3 \vartriangleleft \sigma, Q \vartriangleleft \theta_3 \vartriangleleft \sigma), \\ ((N_1 \vartriangleleft \theta_3) \centerdot (P \vartriangleleft \theta_3), (N_2 \vartriangleleft \theta_3) \centerdot (Q \vartriangleleft \theta_3)) \end{pmatrix} \in \mathsf{UTR}. \tag{19}$$

All the conditions and quantifications of the nested i.h. have now been stripped away, but we still haven't used the nested i.h. By the definition of substitution, (19) is equal to

$$\vdash \begin{pmatrix} (P \vartriangleleft \theta_3 \vartriangleleft \sigma, Q \vartriangleleft \theta_3 \vartriangleleft \sigma), \\ ((N_1 \centerdot P) \vartriangleleft \theta_3, (N_2 \centerdot Q) \vartriangleleft \theta_3) \end{pmatrix} \in \mathsf{UTR}. \tag{20}$$

The fact that UTR is transitive plus (20) allow the goal to be reduced to

$$\left(\begin{array}{l} ((N_1 \bullet P) \triangleleft \theta_3, (N_2 \bullet Q) \triangleleft \theta_3), \\ ((M_1 \bullet N_1) \bullet P, (M_2 \bullet N_2) \bullet Q) \end{array} \right) \in \mathsf{UTR}.$$

The nested i.h. has now been used. The non-nested i.h. (16) can now be instantiated with $N_1 \mapsto N_1 \bullet P$ and $N_2 \mapsto N_2 \bullet Q$ to prove

$$\vdash \left(\begin{array}{l} ((N_1 \bullet P) \triangleleft \theta_3, (N_2 \bullet Q) \triangleleft \theta_3), \\ (M_1 \bullet (N_1 \bullet P), M_2 \bullet (N_2 \bullet Q)) \end{array} \right) \in \mathsf{UTR}. \tag{21}$$

By *modus ponens* with (11) and (21), the goal is proved.
□

Next we obtain unconstrained rules (not shown) and the specified induction theorem:

$\forall P.\ (\forall m\ n.\ P\,(\mathsf{Const}\ m, \mathsf{Const}\ n)) \wedge$
$\quad (\forall m\ M\ N.\ P\,(\mathsf{Const}\ m, M \bullet N)) \wedge$
$\quad (\forall m\ v.\ P\,(\mathsf{Const}\ m, \mathsf{Var}\ v)) \wedge$
$\quad (\forall v\ M.\ P\,(\mathsf{Var}\ v, M)) \wedge$
$\quad (\forall M\ N\ x.\ P\,(M \bullet N, \mathsf{Const}\ x)) \wedge$
$\quad (\forall M\ N\ v.\ P\,(M \bullet N, \mathsf{Var}\ v)) \wedge$
$\quad (\forall M_1\ N_1\ M_2\ N_2.$
$\qquad (\forall \theta.\ \mathsf{Unify}(M_1, M_2) = \mathsf{Some}\ \theta \supset P\,(N_1 \triangleleft \theta, N_2 \triangleleft \theta)) \wedge P\,(M_1, M_2)$
$\qquad \supset P\,(M_1 \bullet N_1, M_2 \bullet N_2))$
$\quad \supset \forall v\ v_1.\ P\,(v, v_1)$

$$\tag{22}$$

Now the correctness of Unify can be quite directly established.

$$\forall \theta.\ (\mathsf{Unify}(P, Q) = \mathsf{Some}\ \theta) \supset \mathsf{MGU}\ \theta\ P\ Q \tag{23}$$

Proof. By induction with (22), followed by expanding the definition of Unify. The base cases are all simple. In the recursive case, the failure branches are trivial. Thus assume that $\mathsf{Unify}(M_1, M_2) = \mathsf{Some}\ \theta$ and $\mathsf{Unify}(N_1 \triangleleft \theta, N_2 \triangleleft \theta) = \mathsf{Some}\ \sigma$ hold. The inductive hypotheses yield $\mathsf{MGU}\ \theta\ M_1\ M_2$ and $\mathsf{MGU}\ \sigma\ (N_1 \triangleleft \theta)\ (N_2 \triangleleft \theta)$. It remains to show $\mathsf{MGU}(\theta \bullet \sigma)\ (M_1 \bullet N_1)\ (M_2 \bullet N_2)$. It is immediate from the definitions of MGU and Unifier and *subst_comp* that $\theta \bullet \sigma$ unifies $(M_1 \bullet N_1)$ and $(M_2 \bullet N_2)$; we now show that $\theta \bullet \sigma$ is most general. Assume that γ unifies $(M_1 \bullet N_1)$ and $(M_2 \bullet N_2)$, i.e., $M_1 \triangleleft \gamma = M_2 \triangleleft \gamma$ and $N_1 \triangleleft \gamma = N_2 \triangleleft \gamma$. There is a δ such that $\gamma =_s \theta \bullet \delta$ because θ is most general; hence, $(N_1 \triangleleft \theta) \triangleleft \delta = (N_2 \triangleleft \theta) \triangleleft \delta$. There is a ρ such that $\delta =_s \sigma \bullet \rho$ because σ is most general. We wish to prove $\exists q.\ \gamma =_s \theta \bullet \sigma \bullet q$, and do so as follows:

$$\begin{array}{ll} & \exists q.\ \gamma =_s \theta \bullet \sigma \bullet q \\ \text{iff} & \exists q.\ \theta \bullet \delta =_s \theta \bullet \sigma \bullet q \\ \text{iff} & \exists q.\ \theta \bullet \delta =_s \theta \bullet (\sigma \bullet q) \\ \text{iff} & \exists q.\ \delta =_s \sigma \bullet q \\ \text{iff} & \exists q.\ \sigma \bullet \rho =_s \sigma \bullet q \\ \text{iff} & \exists q.\ \rho =_s q \end{array}$$

□

4   Deferring Termination

The *relationless* definition method of [17] provides a sound way to define recursive functions without having to supply a correct termination relation with the recursion equations. The termination relation occurs as a variable in the termination conditions of a function defined in this style; the termination conditions persist as constraints on the recursion equations and induction theorem until it is convenient to eliminate them. Thus the definition of a recursive function can be separated from the delivery of its termination relation and the proof of its termination conditions. The general idea is that a function f may be defined by computing its functional $\mathcal{F}$ and gathering its termination conditions $TC_1(R) \ldots TC_k(R)$, leaving the termination relation R variable. In the definition, a suitable termination condition is chosen via an indefinite description operator:

$$\mathsf{f} \equiv \mathsf{WFREC}\ (\varepsilon R.\mathsf{WF}\ R \wedge TC_1(R) \wedge \ldots \wedge TC_k(R))\ \mathcal{F}$$

Subsequent steps assume the termination conditions and derive the constrained equations and induction theorem.

This technique *fails* for nested functions, since the assembled termination conditions must mention the function being defined, and the attempted definition will therefore not be an abbreviation, with the result that the invocation of the primitive principle of definition will fail. In essence, the relationless technique depends on all functions occurring in an argument to a recursive call having already been defined.

Work on *program schemes* [20] suggests a new way to deal with this problem. The technique proceeds in two steps: first an *auxiliary* version of the function is defined in which the termination relation is treated as a parameter; subsequently, the desired function is defined in terms of the auxiliary. Following these two definitions, the specified recursion equations and induction theorem can be automatically derived. However one oddity remains: the termination conditions will be those of the auxiliary function.

To make the discussion more concrete, we return to the g function. The first step is to compute the functional $\mathcal{F}$ for the recursion equations, instantiate the recursion theorem, perform the 'case' reductions, and extract termination conditions:

$$[\mathsf{WF}\ R,\ G = \mathsf{WFREC}\ R\ \mathcal{F}] \vdash G\ 0 = 0$$

$$\left[\begin{array}{l} \mathsf{WF}\ R,\ R\ x\ (\mathsf{Suc}\ x), \\ R\ (G\ x)\ (\mathsf{Suc}\ x),\ G = \mathsf{WFREC}\ R\ \mathcal{F} \end{array} \right] \vdash G\ (\mathsf{Suc}\ x) = G\ (G\ x) \tag{24}$$

Then the auxiliary function aux is defined; in the definition the termination relation R simply becomes a parameter of aux:

$$\mathsf{aux}\ R \equiv \mathsf{WFREC}\ R\ \mathcal{F}. \tag{25}$$

Then (25) may be cancelled from (24):

$$[\text{WF } R] \vdash \text{aux } R\ 0 = 0$$

$$\begin{bmatrix} \text{WF } R, \\ R\ x\ (\text{Suc } x), \\ R\ (\text{aux } R\ x)\ (\text{Suc } x) \end{bmatrix} \vdash \text{aux } R\ (\text{Suc } x) = \text{aux } R\ (\text{aux } R\ x) \tag{26}$$

Now the second definition—the intended one—can be made by gathering the termination conditions for aux, quantifying them, and choosing a relation satisfying them. Thus, letting εTC stand for $\varepsilon R.\ \text{WF } R \wedge (\forall x.\ R\ x\ (\text{Suc } x)) \wedge (\forall x.\ R\ (\text{aux } R\ x)\ (\text{Suc } x))$, we define

$$\mathbf{g} \equiv \text{aux } (\varepsilon TC) \tag{27}$$

and also prove, by the Select Axiom,[6]

$$[\text{WF } R, (\forall x.\ R\ x\ (\text{Suc } x)), (\forall x.\ R\ (\text{aux } R\ x)\ (\text{Suc } x))]$$
$$\vdash$$
$$\text{WF } (\varepsilon TC) \wedge \tag{28}$$
$$(\forall x.\ (\varepsilon TC)\ x\ (\text{Suc } x)) \wedge$$
$$(\forall x.\ (\varepsilon TC)\ (\text{aux } (\varepsilon TC)\ x)\ (\text{Suc } x)).$$

Substituting εTC for R in (26), we get

$$[\,\text{WF } (\varepsilon TC)\,] \vdash \text{aux } (\varepsilon TC)\ 0 = 0$$

$$\begin{bmatrix} \text{WF } (\varepsilon TC), \\ (\varepsilon TC)\ x\ (\text{Suc } x), \\ (\varepsilon TC)\ (\text{aux } (\varepsilon TC)\ x)\ (\text{Suc } x) \end{bmatrix} \vdash \begin{array}{l} \text{aux } (\varepsilon TC)\ (\text{Suc } x) \\ \quad = \text{aux } (\varepsilon TC)\ (\text{aux } (\varepsilon TC)\ x) \end{array}$$

and from this we obtain, by use of (28) in the assumptions and (27) in the conclusions,

$$[\,\text{WF } R\,] \vdash \mathbf{g}\ 0 = 0$$

$$\begin{bmatrix} \text{WF } R, \\ \forall x.\ R\ x\ (\text{Suc } x), \\ \forall x.\ R\ (\text{aux } R\ x)\ (\text{Suc } x) \end{bmatrix} \vdash \mathbf{g}\ (\text{Suc } x) = \mathbf{g}\ (\mathbf{g}\ x).$$

Examining the result, one can see that the specified equations have been derived. Also, a termination problem involving only aux has been generated. Moreover, the choice of the termination condition is completely unconstrained in the termination problem. A formal description of this definition technique is given in Appendix A.

□

---

[6] The Select Axiom of the HOL logic is $\forall P\ x.\ P\ x \supset P(\varepsilon x.\ P\ x)$.

We have automatically derived the specified recursion equations for g, and generated an independent termination problem phrased in terms of the auxiliary function aux. The termination conditions of g and aux are identical. Two means of settling the termination problem have been derived fully automatically: the definition of the auxiliary function, and the provisional induction scheme for the auxiliary function.

One might worry that the ability to prove termination has somehow been tampered with in the derivation. We believe that no termination arguments have been lost in this series of transformations.

Proof sketch. Suppose a function f is defined by explicitly giving a termination relation TR, *i.e.*,

$$f \equiv \mathsf{WFREC}\ TR\ \mathcal{F}$$

In the extracted termination conditions, $\mathsf{WF}(TR), TC_1, \ldots, TC_n$, the nested conditions will have occurrences of f. Suppose that $\mathsf{WF}(TR), TC_1, \ldots, TC_n$ are proved. Now consider a relationless definition of the same equations; this defines the auxiliary function aux:

$$\mathsf{aux}\ \mathcal{R} \equiv \mathsf{WFREC}\ \mathcal{R}\ \mathcal{F}.$$

Termination condition extraction collects the same termination conditions as for f, except that occurrences of TR are instead a variable $\mathcal{R}$ and occurrences of f are instead applications aux $\mathcal{R}$. If we now substitute $\mathcal{R} \mapsto TR$ into these termination conditions, all the non-nested termination conditions are provable, since they are just the (non-nested) originals. That leaves the nested conditions, in which occurrences of aux $\mathcal{R}$ are now aux TR. It is trivial to show f = aux TR, and thus each nested termination condition is also provable.
□

4.1 Relationless Induction for Nested Functions

Producing the specified induction theorem for relationless nested definitions is straightforward. The derivation depends on the provisional induction theorem that is automatically derived for the auxiliary function. Returning to our running example, the provisional induction theorem derived for aux is

$[\mathsf{WF}\ R, \forall x.\ R\ x\ (\mathsf{Suc}\ x)]$
$\vdash$
$\forall P.\ P\ 0 \wedge (\forall x.\ P\ x \wedge (R\ (\mathsf{aux}\ R\ x)\ (\mathsf{Suc}\ x) \supset P\ (\mathsf{aux}\ R\ x)) \supset P\ (\mathsf{Suc}\ x)) \supset \forall v.\ P\ v.$

First, notice that the nested termination condition is not an assumption, but is instead embedded in the conclusion of the theorem. Therefore, we add the nested termination condition to the hypotheses, and then reduce the conclusion:

$[\mathsf{WF}\ R,\ \forall x.\ R\ x\ (\mathsf{Suc}\ x),\ \forall x.\ R\ (\mathsf{aux}\ R\ x)(\mathsf{Suc}\ x)]$
$\vdash$
$\forall P.\ P\ 0 \wedge (\forall x.\ P\ x \wedge P\ (\mathsf{aux}\ R\ x) \supset P\ (\mathsf{Suc}\ x)) \supset \forall v.\ P\ v.$

As before, let εTC stand for

$$\varepsilon R. \text{ WF } R \wedge (\forall x.\ R\ x\ (\text{Suc } x)) \wedge (\forall x.\ R\ (\text{aux } R\ x)\ (\text{Suc } x)).$$

Make the substitution $R \mapsto \varepsilon TC$ to obtain

$$[\text{WF } (\varepsilon TC), \forall x.\ (\varepsilon TC)\ x\ (\text{Suc } x), \forall x.\ ((\varepsilon TC)\ (\text{aux } (\varepsilon TC)\ x)\ (\text{Suc } x)]$$
$$\vdash$$
$$\forall P.\ P\ 0 \wedge (\forall x.\ P\ x \wedge P\ (\text{aux } (\varepsilon TC)\ x) \supset P\ (\text{Suc } x)) \supset \forall v.\ P\ v.$$

By use of (28) we can obtain

$$[\text{WF } R, \forall x.\ R\ x\ (\text{Suc } x), \forall x.\ R\ (\text{aux } R\ x)\ (\text{Suc } x)]$$
$$\vdash$$
$$\forall P.\ P\ 0\ \wedge (\forall x.\ P\ x \wedge P\ (\text{aux } (\varepsilon TC)\ x) \supset P\ (\text{Suc } x)) \supset \forall v.\ P\ v.$$

Simplifying with (27) then yields

$$[\text{WF } R, \forall x.\ R\ x\ (\text{Suc } x), \forall x.\ R\ (\text{aux } R\ x)\ (\text{Suc } x)]$$
$$\vdash$$
$$\forall P.\ P\ 0\ \wedge (\forall x.\ P\ x \wedge P\ (g\ x) \supset P\ (\text{Suc } x)) \supset \forall v.\ P\ v.$$

$\square$

The formal derivation of this class of induction theorems may be found in [19].

5 Example: Term Evaluation

Kapur and Subramaniam [9] pose the following induction challenge (we have slightly edited it for stylistic purposes). Consider a datatype of arithmetic expressions arith, having constructors for constants (C), variables (V), the addition of two expressions (Plus), and the Apply operator.

$$C : \text{num} \to \alpha \text{ arith}$$
$$V : \alpha \to \alpha \text{ arith}$$
$$\text{Plus} : \alpha \text{ arith} \to \alpha \text{ arith} \to \alpha \text{ arith}$$
$$\text{Apply} : \alpha \text{ arith} \to \alpha \text{ arith} \to \alpha \text{ arith} \to \alpha \text{ arith}$$

Two ways to evaluate expressions are given. The call-by-name strategy is a mutual and nested recursion with a 'helper' function:

$$\text{CBN } (C\ n, y, z) \equiv C\ n$$
$$\text{CBN } (V\ x, y, z) \equiv \text{if } x = y \text{ then CBNh } z \text{ else V } x$$
$$\text{CBN } (\text{Plus } a_1 a_2, y, z) \equiv \text{Plus } (\text{CBN } (a_1, y, z))(\text{CBN } (a_2, y, z))$$
$$\text{CBN } (\text{Apply } B\ v\ M, y, z) \equiv \text{CBN } (\text{CBN } (B, v, M), y, z)$$

$$\text{CBNh } (C\ n) \equiv C\ n$$
$$\text{CBNh } (V\ x) \equiv V\ x$$
$$\text{CBNh } (\text{Plus } a_1 a_2) \equiv \text{Plus } (\text{CBNh } a_1)(\text{CBNh } a_2)$$
$$\text{CBNh } (\text{Apply } B\ v\ M) \equiv \text{CBN } (B, v, M)$$

Apply $B \, v \, M$ can be thought of as a β-redex: $(\lambda v.B) \, M$. $\mathsf{CBN}(e, y, z)$ replaces y by z in e, and also reduces Apply nodes. The definition returns the specified rules and the specified induction theorem:

$\forall P_0 \, P_1.$
$\quad (\forall n \, y \, z. P_0 \, (\mathsf{C} \, n, y, z)) \, \wedge$
$\quad (\forall x \, y \, z.((x = y) \supset P_1 \, z) \supset P_0 \, (\mathsf{V} \, x, y, z)) \, \wedge$
$\quad (\forall a_1 \, a_2 \, y \, z. P_0 \, (a_2, y, z) \wedge P_0 \, (a_1, y, z) \supset P_0 \, (\mathsf{Plus} \, a_1 \, a_2, y, z)) \, \wedge$
$\quad (\forall B \, v \, M \, y \, z. P_0(\mathsf{CBN}(B, v, M), y, z) \wedge P_0(B, v, M) \supset P_0(\mathsf{Apply} \, B \, v \, M, y, z)) \wedge$
$\quad (\forall n. \, P_1 \, (\mathsf{C} \, n)) \, \wedge$
$\quad (\forall x. \, P_1 \, (\mathsf{V} \, x)) \, \wedge$
$\quad (\forall a_1 \, a_2 \, . P_1 \, a_2 \wedge P_1 \, a_1 \supset P_1 \, (\mathsf{Plus} \, a_1 \, a_2)) \, \wedge$
$\quad (\forall B \, v \, M. \, P_0 \, (B, v, M) \supset P_1 \, (\mathsf{Apply} \, B \, v \, M))$
$\quad \supset$
$\quad (\forall v_0. \, P_0 \, v_0) \wedge (\forall v_1. P_1 \, v_1)$

$$(29)$$

There are nine termination constraints, which we will abbreviate for clarity (occurrences of INL and INR arise because of the modelling of the mutual recursion as a 'union' function over a sum [2]; this will not occupy us here):

$\mathsf{CBN\_Terminates}(R) \equiv$
$\quad \mathsf{WF} \, R \, \wedge$
$\quad (\forall M \, v \, B. \, R \, (\mathsf{INL} \, (B, v, M)) \, (\mathsf{INR} \, (\mathsf{Apply} \, B \, v \, M))) \, \wedge$
$\quad (\forall a_1 \, a_2. \, R \, (\mathsf{INR} \, a_2) \, (\mathsf{INR} \, (\mathsf{Plus} \, a_1 \, a_2))) \, \wedge$
$\quad (\forall a_2 \, a_1. \, R \, (\mathsf{INR} \, a_1) \, (\mathsf{INR} \, (\mathsf{Plus} \, a_1 \, a_2))) \, \wedge$
$\quad (\forall z \, y \, M \, v \, B. \, R \, (\mathsf{INL} \, (\mathsf{auxCBN} \, R \, (\mathsf{INL} \, (B, v, M)), y, z))$
$\qquad\qquad\qquad (\mathsf{INL} \, (\mathsf{Apply} \, B \, v \, M, y, z))) \, \wedge$
$\quad (\forall z \, y \, M \, v \, B. \, R \, (\mathsf{INL} \, (B, v, M)) \, (\mathsf{INL} \, (\mathsf{Apply} \, B \, v \, M, y, z))) \, \wedge$
$\quad (\forall a_1 \, z \, y \, a_2. \, R \, (\mathsf{INL} \, (a_2, y, z)) \, (\mathsf{INL} \, (\mathsf{Plus} \, a_1 \, a_2, y, z))) \, \wedge$
$\quad (\forall a_2 \, z \, y \, a_1. \, R \, (\mathsf{INL} \, (a_1, y, z)) \, (\mathsf{INL} \, (\mathsf{Plus} \, a_1 \, a_2, y, z))) \, \wedge$
$\quad (\forall z \, y \, x. \, (x = y) \supset R \, (\mathsf{INR} \, z) \, (\mathsf{INL} \, (\mathsf{V} \, x, y, z))).$

Note how the nested invocation of CBN has been transformed into auxCBN in the termination constraints.

The call-by-value strategy (also a nested function) uses an environment of evaluated expressions, accessed by a simple lookup function:

$$\mathsf{lookup} \, x \, [] \equiv 0$$
$$\mathsf{lookup} \, x \, ((y, z) :: rst) \equiv \text{if } x = y \text{ then } z \text{ else } \mathsf{lookup} \, x \, rst$$

$$\mathsf{CBV} \, (\mathsf{C} \, n, env) \equiv n$$
$$\mathsf{CBV} \, (\mathsf{V} \, x, env) \equiv \mathsf{lookup} \, x \, env$$
$$\mathsf{CBV} \, (\mathsf{Plus} \, a_1 a_2, env) \equiv \mathsf{CBV} \, (a_1, env) + \mathsf{CBV} \, (a_2, env)$$
$$\mathsf{CBV} \, (\mathsf{Apply} \, B \, v \, M, env) \equiv \mathsf{CBV} \, (B, (v, \mathsf{CBV} \, (M, env)) :: env)$$

The following are the termination conditions of CBV; we again make a definition that encapsulates them:

$$CBV\_Terminates(R) \equiv$$
$$WF\ R \wedge$$
$$(\forall a_2\ env\ a_1.\ R\ (a_1, env)\ (\text{Plus}\ a_1\ a_2, env)) \wedge$$
$$(\forall a_1\ env\ a_2.\ R\ (a_2, env)\ (\text{Plus}\ a_1\ a_2, env)) \wedge$$
$$(\forall v\ B\ env\ M.\ R\ (M, env)\ (\text{Apply}\ B\ v\ M, env)) \wedge$$
$$(\forall env\ M\ v\ B.\ R\ (B, (v, \text{auxCBV}\ R\ (M, env)) :: env)$$
$$(\text{Apply}\ B\ v\ M, env))$$

With the definitions finished, correctness can be stated:

$$CBN\_Terminates(R) \wedge CBV\_Terminates(R_1)$$
$$\supset$$
$$\forall x\ y\ z\ env.$$
$$CBV\ (CBN\ (x, y, z), env)$$
$$=$$
$$CBV\ (x, (y, CBV\ (z, env)) :: env)$$

Proof. By induction with (29), where the following instantiations are made:

$$P_0 \mapsto \lambda(x, y, z).\ \forall env.\ CBV\ (CBN\ (x, y, z), env)$$
$$=$$
$$CBV(x, (y, CBV\ (z, env)) :: env)$$

$$P_1 \mapsto \lambda z.\ \forall env.\ CBV\ (CBNh\ z, env) = CBV\ (z, env).$$

The instantiation for P_0 just sets it to the goal at hand. The instantiation for P_1 however, has been suggested by Boulton's method [2] for finding induction predicates for mutual recursive functions. With these two instantiations, the remainder of the proof is an anticlimax: it is simply conditional rewriting with the induction hypotheses and the definitions of CBN, CBNh, CBV, and lookup. $\square$

The partial correctness proof was surprisingly easy, given a correctly instantiated induction theorem. What is more of interest from the perspective of the present paper is how simple the whole exercise was when termination became a background issue. It took the author very little time to type the definitions in and get the proof. In a setting where first a correct termination relation had to be provided and proved, things would have taken much longer and the point of the exercise—to see how the induction proof worked—would have been like a mirage: visible but not attainable without some sweat. Of course the termination proofs must still be completed;[7] what our approach allows is flexibility as to *when* they are tackled.

---

[7] Termination of CBV is easy since all recursions are on immediate sub-expressions. Termination of CBN comes from noticing that it removes all Apply nodes from an

6   Schemes

Recursion equations with extra free variables on the 'right hand side' are known as *schemes*. The definition algorithms and the derivation of induction for nested recursions are essentially unchanged for schemes. The only step requiring special treatment is the definition of the auxiliary function:

$$\text{aux } R \equiv \text{WFREC } R \; \mathcal{F}.$$

This must now take account of $X_1, \ldots, X_k$, the free variables of $\mathcal{F}$, as follows (for more background to our approach, see [20]):

$$\text{aux } R \equiv \lambda X_1 \ldots X_k. \; \text{WFREC } R \; \mathcal{F}.$$

As an example, in the book *ML for the Working Programmer*[15], a nested scheme is cited as an example (p. 225 in the first edition) which apparently requires domain theory for the proof of a property:

> *Our approach to program schemes is simpler than resorting to domain theory, but is less general. In domain theory it is simple to prove that any ML function of the form*
>
> $$\text{fun h } x \equiv \textit{if } p \, x \textit{ then } x \textit{ else } \text{h}(\text{h}(g \, x))$$
>
> *satisfies*
>
> $$\text{h (h } x) = \text{h } x$$
>
> *for all* x—*regardless of whether the function terminates. Our approach cannot easily handle this. What well-founded relation should we use to demonstrate the termination of the nested recursive call in* h*?*

Because our semantics is based on wellfoundedness, our system cannot admit instances of p and g that allow h to loop. However, Paulson's question can be given a partial answer, provided one is content to admit only instantiations of p and g that make h a total function. To see how this works out, we start by making the definition

$$\text{h } x \equiv \text{if } p \, x \text{ then } x \text{ else } \text{h (h } (g \, x)),$$

which yields the constrained theorem

$$\left[\begin{array}{l} \text{WF } R, \; \forall x. \; \neg p \, x \supset R \, (g \, x) \, x, \\ \forall x. \; \neg p \, x \supset R \, (\text{haux } R \, g \, p \, (g \, x))x \end{array}\right]$$
$$\vdash$$
$$\text{h } g \, p \, x = \text{if } p \, x \text{ then } x \text{ else } \text{h } g \, p \, (\text{h } g \, p \, (g \, x)),$$
(30)

expression; when there are none, it recurses on smaller expressions. An important part of the proof of termination of CBN is the use of the provisional induction theorem for auxCBN to prove that applying auxCBN to an expression removes all Apply nodes.

and the similarly constrained induction theorem

$$\left[\begin{array}{l} \text{WF } R, \; \forall x. \; \neg p \, x \supset R \, (g \, x) \, x, \\ \forall x. \; \neg p \, x \supset R \, (\text{haux } R \, g \, p \, (g \, x)) \, x \end{array}\right]$$
$$\vdash$$
$$\forall Q. \; (\forall x. \; (\neg p \, x \supset Q \, (g \, x)) \wedge (\neg p \, x \supset Q \, (h \, g \, p \, (g \, x)))) \supset Q \, x) \\ \supset \forall v. \; Q \, v.$$
(31)

With these to hand, it is indeed easy to prove the theorem

$$\left[\begin{array}{l} \text{WF } R, \; \forall x. \; \neg p \, x \supset R \, (g \, x) \, x, \\ \forall x. \; \neg p \, x \supset R \, (\text{haux } R \, g \, p \, (g \, x)) \, x \end{array}\right]$$
$$\vdash$$
$$\forall x. \; h \, g \, p \, (h \, g \, p \, x) = h \, g \, p \, x.$$
(32)

Proof. Induct with (31) and then expand with (30). The resulting goal yields to an automatic first order prover supplied with (30). ☐

In order to remove the constraints on (30),(31), or (32), instantiations for p and g must be found, then a suitable R must be found, and then the termination conditions can finally be proved, using the recursion equations and provisional induction theorem for haux.

7   Related Work

Boyer and Moore [5] require nested recursions to be first proved to satisfy non-nested recursion equations before being admittted as definitions.

PVS relies on its type system to support nested recursive definitions. Essentially, the specification of the function is used in proving termination: nested recursive calls are required to lie in the set of behaviours of the function by clever use of subtyping [13].

The paper [6] gives an external semantics via a fixpoint operator for the recursive functions, including nested recursions, of the LAMBDA logic. The implementation of LAMBDA automatically extracts termination conditions, but doesn't automatically derive induction theorems.

Giesl [8] also made the observation—independently but earlier—that termination and correctness need not be intertwined for nested functions. In [7], he shows that, if nested termination conditions can be proved by the specified induction theorem for a nested function, then such a proof is sound. In the same paper, he describes a powerful automated method for automatically proving termination of nested functions (it can prove the termination of the 91 function). Giesl's work is presented in the setting of first order logic and uses such notions as call-by-value evaluation on ground terms; in addition his theorems are justified meta-theoretically. In contrast, our definitions, being total functions in classical logic, are oblivious to evaluation strategy, and can moreover be higher order and schematic. Since our derivations all proceed by object-logic deduction in a sound logic, we need make no soundness argument.

Kapur and Subramaniam [9] show how the RRL proof system can use its cover set induction method to tackle the automation of nested and mutual induction.

Researchers in Type Theory have evolved several means of dealing with nested recursion; Nordstrom uses *accessibility* relations to increase the power of Martin-Löf Type Theory for expressing general recursions, including nested recursion[12]. Recently, the power of dependent types has been used to give a structural induction termination proof of the Unify function [11].

8   Conclusions and Future Work

In this paper, we have covered two main methods for dealing with nested recursion: the first requires termination relations to be given at definition time; the second allows the termination relation to be given at the user's convenience. We have shown how schematic equations, where the termination relation can't be given until the parameters are instantiated, reduces to the latter method.

We hope our techniques serve to de-mystify the delicate business of dealing with nested recursion. In particular, it is not always true that termination and correctness need to be proved together for such recursions; that practice is better viewed as an instance of the well-known phenomena of modifying the goal so as to have stronger inductive hypotheses.

The foundationally inclined reader may feel quite ill after our barrage of invocations of the Select Axiom. It would be interesting therefore, to try to find a way to make our definitions under the assumption that a satisfactory termination relation existed.

We regard our results on relationless definition of nested recursion as only partly satisfactory. The specified recursion equations and induction theorem are automatically derived, which is good; however, the termination proof using the provisional induction theorem and recursion equations for the auxiliary function is usually clumsy and hard to explain.

References

1. S. Agerholm. LCF examples in HOL. *The Computer Journal*, 38(2):121–130, July 1995.
2. Richard Boulton and Konrad Slind. Automatic derivation and application of induction schemes for mutually recursive functions. In *Proceedings of the First International Conference on Computational Logic (CL2000)*, London, UK, July 2000. To appear. Available at http://www.cl.cam.ac.uk/users/kxs/papers/mutual.html.
3. Ana Bove. Programming in Martin-Löf Type Theory. Unification: A non-trivial Example. Master's thesis, Chalmers University of Technology, 1999. Licentiate Thesis.
4. Robert S. Boyer and J Strother Moore. *A Computational Logic*. Academic Press, 1979.
5. Robert S. Boyer and J Strother Moore. *A Computational Logic Handbook*. Academic Press, 1988.

6. Simon Finn, Mike Fourman, and John Longley. Partial functions in a total setting. *Journal of Automated Reasoning*, 18(1):85–104, February 1997.

7. Juergen Giesl. Termination of nested and mutually recursive algorithms. *Journal of Automated Reasoning*, 19(1):1–29, August 1997.

8. Jürgen Giesl. *Automatisierung von Terminierungsbeweisen für rekursiv defininierte Algorithmen*. PhD thesis, Technische Hochshule Darmstadt, 1995.

9. Deepak Kapur and M. Subramaniam. Automating induction over mutually recursive functions. In *Proceedings of the 5th International Conference on Algebraic Methodology and Software Technology (AMAST'96)*, volume 1101 of *Lecture Notes in Computer Science*. Springer-Verlag, 1996.

10. Zohar Manna and Richard Waldinger. Deductive synthesis of the unification algorithm. *Science of Computer Programming*, 1:5–48, 1981.

11. Conor McBride. *Dependently Typed Functional Programs and their Proofs*. PhD thesis, University of Edinburgh, 1999.

12. Bengt Nordstrom. Terminating general recursion. *BIT*, 28:605–619, 1988.

13. S. Owre, J. M. Rushby, N. Shankar, and D.J. Stringer-Calvert. *PVS System Guide*. SRI Computer Science Laboratory, September 1998. Available at http://pvs.csl.sri.com/manuals.html.

14. Lawrence Paulson. Verifying the unification algorithm in LCF. *Science of Computer Programming*, 3:143–170, 1985.

15. Lawrence Paulson. *ML for the working programmer*. Cambridge University Press, second edition, 1996.

16. Joseph Rouyer. Développement d'algorithme d'unification dans le Calcul des Constructions avecs types inductifs. Technical Report 1795, INRIA-Lorraine, November 1992.

17. Konrad Slind. Function definition in higher order logic. In *Theorem Proving in Higher Order Logics*, number 1125 in Lecture Notes in Computer Science, Turku, Finland, August 1996. Springer-Verlag.

18. Konrad Slind. Derivation and use of induction schemes in higher order logic. In *Theorem Proving in Higher Order Logics*, number 1275 in Lecture Notes in Computer Science, Murrary Hill, New Jersey, USA, August 1997. Springer-Verlag.

19. Konrad Slind. *Reasoning about Terminating Functional Programs*. PhD thesis, Institut für Informatik, Technische Universität München, 1999. Accessible at http://www.cl.cam.ac.uk/users/kxs/papers.

20. Konrad Slind. Wellfounded schematic definitions. In David McAllester, editor, *Proceedings of the Seventeenth International Conference on Automated Deduction CADE-17*, volume 1831, Pittsburgh, Pennsylvania, June 2000. Springer-Verlag.

A   Relationless Nested Recursion: Derivation

Given a nested recursion

$$f(pat_1) \equiv rhs_1[f]$$
$$\vdots$$
$$f(pat_n) \equiv rhs_n[f]$$

the machinery of TFL performs the same initial steps as a non-nested relationless definition, *viz.*, translates patterns, instantiates the recursion theorem, performs

β-reduction, specializes the patterns, reduces the cases of the function, and finally performs termination condition extraction to arrive at

$$\begin{bmatrix} \mathsf{WF}(R), TC_{11}[f], \ldots, TC_{1k_1}[f], \\ f \equiv \mathsf{WFREC}\ R\ (\lambda f\ x.M) \end{bmatrix} \vdash f(pat_1) = rhs_1[f]$$

$$\vdots \tag{33}$$

$$\begin{bmatrix} \mathsf{WF}(R), TC_{n1}[f], \ldots, TC_{nk_n}[f], \\ f \equiv \mathsf{WFREC}\ R\ (\lambda f\ x.M) \end{bmatrix} \vdash f(pat_n) = rhs_n[f].$$

Note that R is a variable not occurring in the original equations. Now the auxiliary function is defined:

$$\mathsf{aux}\ R \equiv \mathsf{WFREC}\ R\ (\lambda f\ x.M). \tag{34}$$

Now the substitution $f \mapsto \mathsf{aux}\ R$ can be made in the theorems from (33), and the 'definitional assumption' can consequently be eliminated. Notice that the replacement of f takes place in the hypotheses as well, since the nested termination condition will be found there.

$$[\mathsf{WF}(R), TC_{11}[\mathsf{aux}\ R], \ldots, TC_{1k_1}[\mathsf{aux}\ R]] \vdash \mathsf{aux}\ R\ (pat_1) = rhs_1[\mathsf{aux}\ R]$$

$$\vdots \tag{35}$$

$$[\mathsf{WF}(R), TC_{n1}[\mathsf{aux}\ R], \ldots, TC_{nk_n}[\mathsf{aux}\ R]] \vdash \mathsf{aux}\ R\ (pat_n) = rhs_n[\mathsf{aux}\ R]$$

Now consider a relation chosen to meet the termination conditions of aux:

$$\begin{aligned} \varepsilon R.\ \mathsf{WF}(R) \land \forall(TC_{11}[\mathsf{aux}\ R]) \land \ldots \land \forall(TC_{1k_1}[\mathsf{aux}\ R]) \\ \land\ \forall(TC_{n1}[\mathsf{aux}\ R]) \land \ldots \land \forall(TC_{nk_n}[\mathsf{aux}\ R]) \end{aligned} \tag{36}$$

Call this term $\varepsilon R.TC$. Notice that this is a closed term. Now define the intended function:

$$\mathsf{f} \equiv \mathsf{aux}\ (\varepsilon R.TC). \tag{37}$$

We now bridge the gap between the auxiliary definition and the intended function by making the substitution $R \mapsto \varepsilon R.TC$ in the recursion equations for aux from (35):

$$\begin{bmatrix} \mathsf{WF}\ (\varepsilon R.TC), \\ [R \mapsto \varepsilon R.TC]\ (TC_{11}\ [\mathsf{aux}\ R]), \ldots, \\ [R \mapsto \varepsilon R.TC]\ (TC_{1k_1}\ [\mathsf{aux}\ R]) \end{bmatrix} \vdash \begin{aligned} \mathsf{aux}\ (\varepsilon R.TC)\ (pat_1) \\ = \\ [R \mapsto \varepsilon R.TC]\ (rhs_1[\mathsf{aux}\ R]) \end{aligned}$$

$$\vdots \tag{38}$$

$$\begin{bmatrix} \mathsf{WF}\ (\varepsilon R.TC), \\ [R \mapsto \varepsilon R.TC]\ (TC_{n1}\ [\mathsf{aux}\ R]), \ldots, \\ [R \mapsto \varepsilon R.TC]\ (TC_{nk_n}\ [\mathsf{aux}\ R]) \end{bmatrix} \vdash \begin{aligned} \mathsf{aux}\ (\varepsilon R.TC)\ (pat_n) \\ = \\ [R \mapsto \varepsilon R.TC]\ (rhs_n\ [\mathsf{aux}\ R]) \end{aligned}$$

Since R did not occur in any of the original right hand sides, and also because the definition of f has no free variables, it is valid to replace aux $(\varepsilon R.TC)$ by f on the right hand sides of (38):

$$
\begin{bmatrix}
\text{WF } (\varepsilon R.TC), \\
[R \mapsto \varepsilon R.TC]\,(TC_{11}\,[\text{aux } R]), \dots, \\
[R \mapsto \varepsilon R.TC]\,(TC_{1k_1}\,[\text{aux } R])
\end{bmatrix} \vdash \text{f}\,(pat_1) = rhs_1[\text{f}]
$$

$$
\vdots \tag{39}
$$

$$
\begin{bmatrix}
\text{WF } (\varepsilon R.TC), \\
[R \mapsto \varepsilon R.TC]\,(TC_{n1}\,[\text{aux } R]), \dots, \\
[R \mapsto \varepsilon R.TC]\,(TC_{nk_n}\,[\text{aux } R])
\end{bmatrix} \vdash \text{f}\,(pat_n) = rhs_n[\text{f}]
$$

It is important to abstain from performing this replacement in the assumptions. All that is required now is to finesse the assumptions, and that can be achieved by use of the Select Axiom:

$$
[\text{WF}(R), \forall(TC_{11}[\text{aux } R]), \dots, \forall(TC_{nk_n}[\text{aux } R])]
$$
$$
\vdash
$$
$$
\text{WF } (\varepsilon R.TC)\ \wedge
$$
$$
\forall([R \mapsto \varepsilon R.TC](TC_{11}[\text{aux } R]))\ \wedge \tag{40}
$$
$$
\vdots
$$
$$
\forall([R \mapsto \varepsilon R.TC](TC_{nk_n}[\text{aux } R]))
$$

By invoking the Cut rule with (39) and (40), the final result is obtained:

$$
\begin{bmatrix}
\text{WF}(R), \\
\forall(TC_{11}[\text{aux } R]), \\
\vdots \\
\forall(TC_{nk_n}[\text{aux } R])
\end{bmatrix} \vdash \text{f}\,(pat_1) = rhs_1[\text{f}]
$$

$$
\vdots
$$

$$
\begin{bmatrix}
\text{WF}(R), \\
\forall(TC_{11}[\text{aux } R]), \\
\vdots \\
\forall(TC_{nk_n}[\text{aux } R])
\end{bmatrix} \vdash \text{f}\,(pat_n) = rhs_n[\text{f}]
$$

□

Automating the Search for Answers to Open Questions*

Larry Wos[1] and Branden Fitelson[1,2]

[1] Mathematics and Computer Science Division, Argonne National Laboratory,
Argonne, IL 60439-4801,
wos@mcs.anl.gov
[2] University of Wisconsin, Department of Philosophy, Madison, WI 53706,
fitelson@facstaff.wisc.edu

Abstract. This article provides evidence for the arrival of automated reasoning. Indeed, one of its primary goals of the early 1960s has been reached: The use of an automated reasoning program frequently leads to significant contributions to mathematics and to logic. In addition, although not clearly an original objective, the use of such a program now plays an important role for chip design and for program verification. That importance can be sharply increased; indeed, in this article we discuss the possible value of automated reasoning to finding better designs of chips, circuits, and computer code. We also provide insight into the mechanisms—in particular, strategy—that have led to numerous successes. To complement the evidence we present and to encourage further research, we offer challenges and open questions for consideration. We include a glimpse of the future and some commentary on the possibly unexpected benefits of automating the search for answers to open questions.

1 An Unlikely But Realized Dream

In the late 1940s, researchers (including the logician Luukasiewicz) considered the possibility of *mechanically checking a proof* to be within reach. At the other end of the spectrum, some thought *mechanical proof finding* to be out of the question. For many, that view was still extant in the early 1960s, when an audacious effort seriously commenced whose objective was the design of a computer program that could make significant contributions to mathematics and to logic. In other words, some researchers (brave or foolish) embarked on a journey whose destination was proof finding of interesting theorems—and, if gold was found, the automated answering of open questions.

The search for answers to open questions is frequently thought to be the dominion of mathematics and logic. However, closely related are questions posed by the designers of circuits and chips and by the writers of computer programs.

---

* This work was supported in part by the Mathematical, Information, and Computational Sciences Division subprogram of the Office of Advanced Scientific Computing Research, U.S. Department of Energy, under Contract W-31-109-Eng-38.

J. Harrison and M. Aagaard (Eds.): TPHOLs 2000, LNCS 1869, pp. 519–525, 2000.

Such questions take various forms. Does a given design of a chip or circuit meet its specifications—is it free of bugs? Given a bit of computer code (or a given design), can one find an alternative that offers far more efficiency? In this article, we make a case for using a program to find better designs, where the methodologies are taken from our recent successful research in finding shorter proofs; see the Appendix, which takes the form of a whitepaper.

As for mathematics and logic, as the following list illustrates, open questions come in an even greater variety of flavors.

1. Is every Robbins algebra a Boolean algebra?
2. Is the formula XHN a single axiom for equivalential calculus?
3. Does there exist a circle of pure proofs for the Moufang identities?
4. Does a particular identity that holds in orthomodular lattices also hold in ortholattices?
5. Does the fragment of combinatory logic with basis consisting of B and M satisfy the strong fixed point property?
6. Is the formula XCB a single axiom for equivalential calculus?

Answers to the cited questions—and to many, many more of diverse types—can often be found by relying heavily on an automated reasoning assistant. Indeed, the first four have already been answered with the help of Argonne's powerful automated reasoning programs [3,7,6,1]; for a discussion of the two open questions, 5 and 6, see Sect. 3. A delightful bonus: To enlist the aid of a reasoning program in the search for answers, one need not be an expert. Today, various mathematicians only vaguely familiar with automated reasoning are using William McCune's reasoning program OTTER [2]—the program featured in this article—in their research. (If guidance is desired in the use of OTTER, if a fuller understanding of the elements of automated reasoning is the objective, or if one seeks open questions to attack, each is easily within reach through consulting the new book *A Fascinating Country in the World of Computing: Your Guide to Automated Reasoning* [7]; its included CD-ROM is a gold mine. If one wishes to browse in a dense forest of once-open questions answered with the use of OTTER, the monograph by McCune and Padmanabhan [4] is the choice.)

Complementing the use by mathematicians of automated reasoning and also contributing substantially to the realization of the dream of profitably using a reasoning program is the use by firms that include AMD and Intel. In particular, the cited firms each employ people whose assignment is to prove theorems in the context of correctness of various designs. The chief weapon is recourse to a reasoning program. Was part of the motivation the remarkable achievement of Boyer, Moore, and colleagues in their design and verification of a chip and language [5], a chip that was eventually manufactured and used?

1.1   The Source of Power

Although for many years OTTER was the fastest reasoning program, programs now exist that run faster. But (in our view), CPU speed is not the key. Indeed, an increase in CPU power of a factor of 4 (we conjecture) brings very few theorems in range that were previously out of range. The obstacle rests with the incredible size of the space of deducible conclusions.

And here is where the power resides that has led to so many recent successes: OTTER offers a variety of powerful strategies, some to restrict its reasoning, some to direct its reasoning, and some to permit the program to emphasize the role of certain designated information. We strongly conjecture that without access to various types of strategy, the vast majority of the successes of the past few years would not have been reached. For a glimpse of how all has changed, we note that, in contrast to two decades ago, our submission to OTTER of problems taken from various areas of logic is almost always met with a proof. (We intend to present many new proofs in print and on an included CD-ROM in a planned book entitled *Automated Reasoning and the Finding of Missing and Elegant Proofs in Formal Logic.*)

Rather than formal definitions, we give the following examples of strategy in terms of their objective.

1. The *set of support strategy* typically restricts a program from exploring the space of conclusions that follow from the axioms.
2. The *expression complexity strategy* restricts a program from considering terms, formulas, or equations conjectured to interfere with effectiveness because of their complexity.
3. The *variable richness strategy* restricts the program from considering formulas or equations whose number of distinct variables appears to make them unattractive.
4. The *term-avoidance strategy* prevents the program from retaining any newly deduced conclusion that contains a term in the class of those designated as unwanted; see Sect. 4 for a fuller discussion.

In contrast to the preceding four strategies that restrict a program's reasoning, the following useful strategies direct its reasoning.

5. The *resonance strategy* instructs a program to focus on conclusions that resemble any of a set designated by the researcher as appealing, in preference to all other available conclusions.
6. The *ratio strategy* instructs a program to choose k conclusions by complexity, 1 by first come first serve, then k, then 1, and the like, where k is assigned by the researcher.
7. The *weighting strategy* directs a program to focus on items whose complexity is smallest, where the complexity is in part determined by user-assigned values.

Among other factors, additional power is derived from a mechanism to simplify and canonicalize information and from a variety of inference rules, one of which treats equality as "understood". However, in contrast to so many reasoning programs, (we maintain that) OTTER's offering a veritable arsenal of strategies is the key.

2   Open Questions Detailed

At this point, we provide the promised details concerning questions 5 and 6 posed in Sect. 1. Each, as noted, remains open.

For the first of the two questions (5), we give the definitions of the combinators B and M and that of a fixed point combinator $\mathbf{F}$. (Expressions in combinatory logic are assumed to be left associated unless otherwise indicated.)

```
Bxyz = x(yz)
Mx = xx
Fx = x(Fx)
```

Does there exist a fixed point combinator $\mathbf{F}$ expressed purely in terms of the combinators B and M such that $\mathbf{F}x = x(\mathbf{F}x)$? To provide a small taste of the nature of this question, we note that BML is a fixed point combinator for the fragment whose basis consists solely of B, M, and L, where $Lxy = x(yy)$.

For the second question (6) that remains open, we give two definitions, the second of which is included for pedagogical reasons.

```
e(x,e(e(e(x,y),e(z,y)),z))   %  XCB
e(x,e(e(y,z),e(e(z,x),y)))   %  XHN
```

Is the formula XCB a single axiom for all of equivalential calculus? The formula XHN is a single axiom. If one were able to deduce some known single axiom, such as XHN, starting with XCB, then one would have established that XCB is also a single axiom. On the other hand, if the goal is to disprove the implied theorem, then an obvious approach is to find an appropriate counterexample in the form of a model.

3   From Mathematics and Logic to Design

Astounding to us, many researchers in the field do not share our enthusiasm for attacking open questions via automated reasoning. Our eagerness is of course based in part on the desire to *know* the answer: Is there a proof, or is there a counterexample in the form of a model? A glance at our research clearly establishes our preference for areas of mathematics and logic.

In addition to contributing to mathematics and to logic, however, our studies of the automation of an attack on open questions have two important benefits. First, because sometimes we fail in our early attempts, we are forced to formulate and then implement new approaches, methodologies, and strategies. We always aim at generality. Therefore, independent of finding an answer to an open question, we produce mechanisms that increase (in a significant manner) the power of reasoning programs. That increase in turn brings into range additional open questions, and the loop continues.

A second benefit is that some of the new approaches, methodologies, and strategies appear to offer much for design and verification. To show how this might be true, we note that another class of open questions exists, outside of the usually cited classes. That class can be termed *missing proofs*. For one example, if the only proofs of a given theorem are by induction or by some other metaargument, then an axiomatic proof is missing. For a second example, if a theorem is announced without proof by a master (which removes any doubt about its truth), then again a proof is missing. For a third example (of the many types we have identified)—and an example that is pertinent to design—if a proof is in hand and the conjecture is that a rather shorter proof exists but has not yet been found, then again a proof is missing.

In the past two years, we have devoted substantial effort to finding missing proofs, heavily emphasizing the search for shorter proofs. The term-avoidance strategy and the resonance strategy have played key roles in our numerous successes. Those studies, in our view, could be put to great use in design. Indeed, imagine that one has in hand a design of a chip, a circuit, or a computer program. Our approach would be to obtain a constructive proof with OTTER of the given design and then (in the context of the resonance strategy) use the deduced steps of that proof in search of a better design. Then, as part of our effort and for a tiny taste of what we would do next, we would instruct the program to avoid the use of each of the deduced steps (one at a time) to see whether a shorter proof could be found.

Although clearly nothing like an isomorphism or a guarantee, the shorter the proof, the simpler the constructed object—chip, circuit, or program. A simpler object (everything being equal) is easier to verify, is more reliable, makes better use of energy, and produces less heat. In other words (with almost all of the details omitted), we suspect that design and verification would benefit from adapting our recent research.

Important to note is an easily overlooked subtlety when a shorter proof is the goal. Imagine that the goal is to find a proof (shorter than that in hand) of Q **and** R **and** S. As the attack proceeds, shorter and still shorter proofs may be found of, say, S, which might lead one to the conclusion that ever-shorter proofs of the conjunction are in the making. Quite often, such is not the case. Indeed, a shorter proof of a member of the conjunction may be such that the omitted steps (from the longer proof) are useful in the total proof, where their replacements serve no other purpose than that of producing a shorter proof of the cited member. The situation in focus may be familiar to programmers or circuit designers. Reliance on a subroutine with fewer instructions or reliance on a subcircuit with fewer components does not necessarily add efficiency for the larger program or circuit. This amusing subtlety makes the finding of shorter proofs far more difficult than it might at first appear.

As part of our recent studies, we have also focused on term avoidance. The decision to employ the strategy might be based on mere curiosity (as so often occurs in mathematics and in logic), or it might be based on practical considerations (as frequently occurs in design and verification). Indeed, regarding the former, one might wonder about the existence of a proof in which nested negation is forbidden, a proof in which no deduced step contains a term of the form $n(n(t))$ for any term t where the function n denotes negation. As for the latter, because of economy or efficiency, one might wish to seek an object in which some type of component or instruction is absent. For example, one might wish to avoid the use of **NOR** gates.

In contrast to the just-cited motivations for use of the term-avoidance strategy, we find that its use markedly increases the likelihood of success in the context of automating the search for answers to open questions. The explanation is quite subtle; indeed, adding a constraint might on the surface make finding a proof much harder. Note that the space of deducible conclusions can grow exponentially as a program's attack proceeds. This property is directly addressed by (apparently arbitrarily) choosing a type of term to be avoided and then preventing the program from venturing into the subspace of deducible conclusions each of which contains one or more occurrences of such a term. Of course, depending on the type of term to be avoided, one's intuition might balk. For example, in the case of avoiding nested negation, one might understandably doubt that the objective can be reached. However, we have almost always succeeded in the presence of this constraint. Perhaps the explanation rests with (1) the existence of many, many more proofs than one might expect and (2) the removal of (apparently) distracting information. Put another way, by avoiding conclusions of a specified type, it appears that the density of good information within that which is retained is sharply increased.

In view of our recent successes, we conjecture that those involved in design and verification might benefit from our various methodologies focusing on finding proofs in which some class of terms is absent.

4   The Future

We have focused on how our recent successes in finding proofs with an automated reasoning program are potentially valuable to design and validation. In the near-term future, perhaps some firm will submit to us a design in the clause language OTTER employs. Also required is the property that OTTER can produce a constructive proof that the design meets the specifications. We would then attempt to simplify the proof, fewer steps, less complex expressions, and perhaps the avoidance of certain classes of term. If success were to occur, the firm might then have a better design.

We also envision in the future a rather odd use of a type of parallelism. Specifically, the likelihood of success regardless of the goal (we conjecture) would be sharply increased if one had access to a large network of computers. When the objective was identified, the set of computers (perhaps 10,000) would each separately attack the problem, each in a manner somewhat different from the rest. For example, each might employ a different bound on the complexity of retained information, a different value for the parameter that governs the actions of the ratio strategy, a different set of resonators, and the like. All members of the set of assigned computers would simultaneously attack the problem. Currently, we rely on a miniscule version of this approach, sometimes resulting in success.

In summary, we estimate the current state of automated reasoning to be fifty years ahead of what an optimist might have predicted but twenty years ago. The explanation rests mainly with the formulation of new and diverse strategies. For dramatically greater advances, we conjecture that strategy still holds the key.

References

1. McCune, W.: Automatic Proofs and Counterexamples for Some Ortholattice Identities, Information Processing Letters **65** (1998), 285–291
2. McCune, W.: Otter 3.0 Reference Manual and Guide. Technical report ANL-94/6. Argonne National Laboratory, Argonne, Illinois (1994)
3. McCune, W.: Solution of the Robbins Problem, J. Automated Reasoning **19**, no. 3 (December 1997) 263–276
4. McCune, M., and Padmanabhan, R.: Automated Deduction in Equational Logic and Cubic Curves. Lecture Notes in Computer Science, Vol. 1095. Springer-Verlag, New York (1996)
5. Moore, J S.: System Verification (special issue), J. Automated Reasoning **5**, no. 4 (December 1989) 409–544
6. Wos, L.: Otter and the Moufang Identity Problem, J. Automated Reasoning **17**, no. 2 (1996) 215–257
7. Wos, L., and Pieper, G. W.: A Fascinating Country in the World of Computing: Your Guide to Automated Reasoning. World Scientific, Singapore (1999)

Appendix: Conjectures Concerning Proof, Design, and Verification[*]

Larry Wos

Mathematics and Computer Science Division, Argonne National Laboratory,
Argonne, IL 60439-4801,
wos@mcs.anl.gov

1 Setting the Stage

This article focuses on an esoteric but practical use of automated reasoning that may indeed be new to many, especially those concerned primarily with verification of both hardware and software. Specifically, featured are a discussion and some methodology for taking an existing design—of a circuit, a chip, a program, or the like—and refining and improving it in various ways. (Although the methodology is general and does not require the use of a specific program, McCune's program OTTER does offer what is needed. OTTER has played and continues to play the key role in my research, and an interested person can gain access to this program in various ways, not the least of which is through the included CD-ROM in [3].) When success occurs, the result is a new design that may require fewer components, avoid the use of certain costly components, offer more reliability and ease of verification, and, perhaps most important, be more efficient in the contexts of speed and heat generation. Although I have minimal experience in circuit design, circuit validation, program synthesis, program verification, and similar concerns, (at the encouragement of colleagues based on successes to be cited) I present material that might indeed be of substantial interest to manufacturers and programmers.

I write this article in part prompted by the recent activities of chip designers that include Intel and AMD, activities heavily emphasizing the proving of theorems. As for my research that appears to me to be relevant, I have made an intense and most profitable study of finding proofs that are shorter [2,3], some that avoid the use of various types of term, some that are far less complex than previously known, and the like. Those results suggest to me a strong possible connection between more appealing proofs (in mathematics and in logic) and enhanced and improved design of both hardware and software. Here I explore diverse conjectures that elucidate some of the possibly fruitful connections.

The strongest argument opposed to what I discuss in this article rests on the great amount of money, time, energy, and expertise that has been devoted to design and related activities. Indeed, one might understandably suspect that

---

[*] This work was supported by the Mathematical, Information, and Computational Sciences Division subprogram of the Office of Advanced Scientific Computing Research, U.S. Department of Energy, under Contract W-31-109-Eng-38.

J. Harrison and M. Aagaard (Eds.): TPHOLs 2000, LNCS 1869, pp. 526–533, 2000.

such experts already know how to produce superb and often minimal design. (As a counterargument, I note that the proofs found by OTTER, applying the methodology that has been developed as part of my research, often are start- lingly unlike those a person might find. Perhaps more important, many of the proofs that are found are in various ways more appealing than the literature ofeers.) However, a test of what is featured here is inexpensive, and, if the result is positive, the reward might be immense. The test consists of some expert first supplying a set of graduated-in-complexity designs and the proofs that they meet specifications. Perhaps the designs supplied would already have been maximized for good properties. Second, if I am to be involved, part of the test requires sup- plying the proofs in the clause notation, the notation used by OTTER. Perhaps Mathematica could produce the needed translations. Then I would take the pro- ofs (in clause notation) and attempt to shorten them or improve them in some other aspect discussed here. If I found better proofs, which I have in Boolean algebra (quite related to circuit design), I would submit them for evaluation.

If I were not involved, one might consult the book [3], which offers the pro- gram and much of what is needed to use it. Such has indeed been the case for areas of mathematics and of logic. Therefore, perhaps a new type of design would emerge. Your cost is that of producing an OTTER input file, and it appears that might require but a few days of a person's time who knew about design; my cost is research time devoted to an attempt to improve a given design. Sometimes such research time and effort lead to a set of solutions, each of which could be evaluated by an expert for its properties.

Also addressed in this article is the concern of design from scratch, that case in which no design exists to be modified, extended, and improved upon. I conjec- ture that my research and that of colleagues that has culminated in answers to diverse open questions will prove pertinent. After all, producing a design from scratch answers the corresponding open question concerning its existence. In- deed, quite different from the task of finding "nicer" and more desirable proofs is the task of answering open questions.

I shall review without technical details various approaches I and colleagues take for finding "better" proofs and answering open questions, and I claim that many of the approaches will prove useful to manufacturing, at least eventually. The explicit and implicit claims and conjectures should be viewed most critically, in view of my lack of expertise in design and synthesis. I will be content with merely sketching diverse ideas. I will also include observations that might seem too obvious to state, but are included to remove ambiguity.

To complete the stage setting, I give a foretaste of what is to come. Consider the following circuit-design problem (known as the two-inverter puzzle) [3], one that I myself would not have solved, but McCune's program OTTER did solve.

Using as many AND and OR gates as you like, but using only two NOT gates, can you design a circuit according to the following specification? There are three inputs, i1, i2, and i3, and three outputs, o1, o2, and o3. The outputs are related to the inputs in the following simple way:

o1 = not(i1)   o2 = not(i2)   o3 = not(i3) .

Remember, you can use only two NOT gates!

The fact that an automated reasoning program was able to design the desired circuit hints at what might be possible in the context of synthesizing circuits from scratch; see Section 3.

In the context of finding better circuits (see Section 2), imagine that a person or a program succeeds in solving the two-inverter puzzle, but the solution absurdly contains as a subexpression the OR of i1 and i1. In other words, assume that the cited subexpression is not needed, that an unneeded OR gate is present. The methodology presented in this article might quickly enable a program, given the unwanted solution, to find a better one, omitting the extra OR gate.

Still with the focus on the two-inverter puzzle, in the context of term avoidance (see Section 4), imagine that the first solution that is offered contains NOT(NOT(i3)). Of course, a canonicalization rule could be applied to replace the apparently unnecessary cited expression with i3. Far better and in the spirit of the corresponding methodology to be touched upon, the program could be instructed to avoid retention of all expressions containing NOT(NOT(t)) for any term t. Possibly not obvious, such avoidance can contribute markedly to program effectiveness; indeed, unwanted conclusions can lead to much wandering—for a program, or for a person.

In contrast to the discussion focusing on combinational circuits, clearly a focus on sequential design in which time and delay are factors presents distinctly different and difficult problems to solve. Although I can at this moment offer little advice in that regard, in that my research has never dealt with this aspect, I nevertheless conjecture that the preceding discussion will, for some, suggest what is more than conceivable and perhaps promising.

2   Shorter Proofs in Relation to Improved Design

Although by no means does a one-to-one correspondence exist, it seems patently clear that (in the following sense) a strong correlation does exist between proof length and simplicity of design. Consider two proofs A and B, source unspecified, each intended to construct the same object (such as a circuit). Assume (in this hypothetical case) that the length of A is moderately to sharply less than the length of B. Finally, assume that the (automated reasoning) program in use offers an ANSWER literal (to display the constructed object) and that the program finds both proofs.

Quite often, although certainly not always, the object displayed when A is completed is preferable to that displayed when B is completed in the sense that it relies on fewer components. Therefore, it seems quite reasonable to conjecture that a methodology for finding shorter proofs might indeed be of interest in the design of circuits or chips or the synthesis of programs. Moreover, a simpler (in the sense under discussion) object in general is easier to verify, less difficult to show that the specifications are met. My research has produced such a methodology, one that has been applied successfully again and again in mathematics and in logic (although quite often no shorter proof is yielded). (Section 6.7 of

[3] discusses the latest methodology I have formulated for systematically seeking shorter proofs.)

In the context of finding shorter proofs in my own research, one of the more satisfying concerned finding a 100-step proof, where I was presented for a start with an 816-step proof. The theorem in focus was one from Boolean algebra, a field relevant in various ways to circuit design. The approach I took did indeed, at the beginning, rely on the supplied 816-step proof. Further, at each stage in the process aimed at finding a shorter and then still shorter proof, the program keyed on the completed proof at an earlier stage.

The notion I suggest that might be of interest asserts that a program could be given a design (circuit, chip, program) whose corresponding proof that the specifications were met was in hand. The cited approach emphasizes the role of the steps of the proof in hand, preferring formulas or equations that are similar to one of the steps. Indeed, with a strategy known as the *resonance strategy*, the proofs that are found along the way—shorter and shorter, if all is going well— play a vital role. Another aspect of the approach concerns blocking the use of various steps of a given proof with the intention that, not only will such blocked steps be absent, but a shorter proof will emerge. (My preferred approach to blocking the use of a step rests on the use of demodulation, a procedure normally used for simplification and canonicalization.)

Also of interest and quite curious is the fact that, occasionally, a shorter proof has the property that all of its steps are among those of the somewhat longer proof being used by the resonance strategy. The explanation rests with the fact that the program finds new ways of connecting already-used items, ignoring others totally, and succeeding in completing a proof. For example, sometimes the program can use the fifth step with the twelfth step to deduce the twentieth step, which in the longer proof was obtained from the eighteenth and nineteenth, and discover that the eighteenth and nineteenth steps can be ignored. The correspondence for design would be the use of some, but not all, of the components of an existing design with (so to speak) a rewiring, without the introduction of new components.

3   New Proofs in Relation to Radically New Designs

In contrast to the preceding section in which the object is to take an existing design and improve upon it, here the focus is on finding the desired object from scratch. In such a case, often, no clue exists concerning the nature of the corresponding proof whose ANSWER literal, if successful, will display the object. Starting from scratch, no surprise, is far more difficult than beginning with an existing object and its corresponding proof. Nevertheless, I and my colleague Branden Fitelson are very encouraged by our various successes with finding a proof where no clue concerning its nature was available [1].

As for the word "radically" occurring in the title of this section, it was not used lightly. The proofs yielded by applying the various methodologies relying on OTTER's arsenal of weapons are (so it strongly appears) sharply unlike what a person might produce. For example, in fields of logic, the literature steadfastly offers numerous proofs relying heavily on the use of terms of the form $n(n(t))$ for various terms t, where the function n denotes negation (**not**). In contrast to the literature and the implicit view that such double-negation terms are virtually required, I have found (through heavy use of OTTER) numerous proofs avoiding such terms. More important, the methodology is general—not tuned to any specific type of term, such as that involving negation.

For a second example, where a researcher might understandably shy away from considering a messy and complex formula, equation, or expression, a reasoning program finds little discomfort in its consideration. Indeed, equations with more than 700 symbols present no problem for OTTER. Simply put and without explanation, the attack taken by a powerful automated reasoning program often resembles that taken by an unaided researcher in few if any ways. Rather than a disadvantage, (it seems to me) this divergence in attack accounts for many marked successes. I conjecture (with some trepidation) that, if the goal were a radically new design, an expert might be greatly rewarded by adding as an assistant a program such as OTTER

One key aspect of the methodology OTTER applies when seeking a proof where none is in hand is reliance on the already-cited resonance strategy, but reliance in a slightly different manner. Specifically, what amounts to patterns corresponding to steps that proved useful in related proofs are included in the input. Often very few of those correspondents (resonators) are present in the proof that results when successful, and often not many more of its steps match one of the resonators. Naturally, the question then arises concerning how such inclusions help. With a new proof, I suspect that those few of its steps that are either one of the actual patterns or match a resonator (in a manner where variables are treated as indistinguishable) provide the keys to getting around narrow corners, over wide plateaus, and the like (speaking metaphorically). In other words, without the guidance offered by the included resonators, success would not occur. The idea is similar to the case in which a colleague provides a few vital hints, even if that colleague cannot solve the actual problem.

4   Term-Avoidance Proofs in Relation to Design

The avoidance of terms, such as those in the double-negation class, is somewhat reminiscent of avoiding the use of some component. Sometimes the desire is for minimal but nonzero use of some type of component—as was the case in the two-inverter puzzle—but, often, the intent is to never have present some type of term or component. For example, OR gates might come into play in some fashion during the exploration by person or by program, and yet their actual use might be unwanted. As commented earlier, a program such as OTTER can be instructed to completely avoid retaining any unwanted conclusion, thus reflecting the intent of the user.

5   Complexity of Proofs

In this section, in contrast to the preceding in which I was able to give hints about a concrete relation between properties of proofs and improvements in design, I simply discuss another aspect of my research concerned with proof betterment. In other words, I (at the moment) leave to the expert in design, verification, and synthesis the extrapolation to other areas.

One of the sometimes annoying properties of all proofs in hand is unwanted complexity of various types. The most obvious type concerns the length of the formulas or equations of the deduced proof steps. Simply put, the proofs in hand may each be far messier than preferred. Such messiness is not merely an aesthetic consideration; indeed, its presence can make the proof harder to follow and may suggest that key lemmas (that would reduce the complexity) have as yet not been discovered.

OTTER offers what is needed in the context of deduced-step length, namely, a parameter called max_weight. The user can assign a value to this parameter and can instruct the program to measure deduced-step complexity purely in terms of symbol count. When a new conclusion is drawn whose complexity exceeds the user-assigned value to max_weight, the conclusion is immediately discarded.

Further, by assigning a small value to max_weight and by including as resonators expressions corresponding to the steps of an existing proof with even smaller assigned values, the user can attempt to force the program to find a subproof with an intriguing property (discussed earlier). Specifically, to complete a proof, the program (in the case under discussion) sometimes finds a proof that is shorter than the one in focus such that all of the deduced steps of the shorter proof are among those of the proof whose steps are being used to guide the program's attack. In effect, if successful, the original proof has been (so to speak) rewired in a manner that reduces the number of components needed to achieve the objective.

Of a quite different nature in the context of proof complexity is that concerned with the maximum number of distinct variables found in the deduced steps. In particular, for each formula or equation from among the deduced steps, a number (integer) corresponding to it can be trivially computed that matches the corresponding number of distinct variables present. The formula $P(i(x,x))$, for example, has the number 1 associated with it, one distinct variable even though two variables (not distinct) are present. The maximum of the assigned numbers to the deduced steps (excluding those that correspond to the input or hypotheses) is the number of maximum distinct variables for the proof. Is that number (as a measure of complexity) in some important manner related to component use or instruction use?

Fortunately, OTTER offers the appropriate parameter, max_distinct_vars. The user can assign a value to this parameter. When a conclusion is deduced, before it is retained, the number of distinct variables in it is compared with the max_distinct_vars and, if it is strictly greater, the new item is immediately purged.

The use of this parameter can have some unexpected consequences for proof betterment and, perhaps, for design enhancement. Indeed, if i is the minimum of the various values of the maximum number of distinct variables for the known proofs, and if j is assigned to max_distinct_vars with j strictly less than i, then the program is forced to pursue a line of study that cannot produce, if successful, any of the known proofs. In other words, reminiscent of Section 3, the program might complete a radically new proof, find a radically new design.

Just as a note, other measures of complexity can be nicely and effectively studied with OTTER. For but one example, a measure of complexity concerns the level of a proof. By definition, the level of the input items that characterize the problem is 0, and the level of a deduced item is 1 greater than the maximum of the levels of the hypotheses from which it is deduced. This parameter is pertinent to tree depth, the tree of the proof.

6 Verification

In this article, I have begun to make a case for the use of automated reasoning in the context of design and verification. Mainly, I have focused on design (implicitly, of circuits, chips, and programs). However, all things being equal, the simpler the design, the greater the ease of verification. Therefore, what has been discussed has some relevance to verification. Explicit is the position that the properties of a proof that constructs some object are reflected in the nature of the object. For example, if the proof is strictly shorter than that in hand, then (quite often) the corresponding object rests on the use of fewer components (whatever they may be). For a second example, if the proof avoids the use of some type of term (such as double negation), then the constructed object avoids the use of some type of component.

As for additional topics that appear to merit mention, perhaps the following are among them. OTTER can be and has been used to show that one of a set of axioms is dependent on the remainder. For design, the parallel might be that of showing that some thought-to-be key property that must be studied, in addition to the rest, in fact is dependent on the rest. If the remaining properties are shown to hold, then the cited key property must, without verifying its presence. Fitelson and I have also succeeded in proving that a weakening of some well-recognized axiom system does the trick, suffices to axiomatize the area of discourse. The analogue might be that of showing that some key property can be replaced by a far weaker property, one that is easier to satisfy and easier to verify.

7 Review and Summary

The approach taken in this article is to merely sketch various notions, to provide hints or clues as to what I conjecture to be more than feasible. Although I claim no expertise in design, synthesis, and verification, my research has yielded some startling results in mathematics and in logic. Some of those results concern the answering of open questions, whose analogue might be the design of a radically new nature. Some of the results focus on proof betterment: shorter, less complex, term-avoidance, and the like. The analogues of those have been discussed, although not in the greatest depth.

The beauty of relying on a program such as McCune's OTTER is that its proofs are most detailed. Another charming and useful aspect of its proofs is that they very often differ sharply from the type of proof an unaided researcher finds. This program offers a veritable arsenal of weapons from which to choose when attacking a question or problem, as well as diverse mechanisms pertinent to powerful reasoning. The program runs with incredible speed and, in contrast to living creatures, tirelessly.

As discussed here, through the use of the resonance strategy, the presence of an actual design can be put to great use when the goal is to refine and improve it in some manner. However, if the various successes in answering open questions points in the right direction, the lack of a design does not prevent the finding of a desired object; indeed, one can start from scratch, as I and my colleague Branden Fitelson have done in areas of logic. Of course, starting from scratch presents a more difficult problem to solve, especially when no clues are offered of any type regarding the nature of a possible proof.

The material sketched here might be timely, in view of the current interest in theorem proving by members of industry that include Intel and AMD. I suspect that (perhaps) many of the items discussed here offer a new notion, even to those familiar with automated reasoning. I cannot measure at this time the practicality. Certainly, one obstacle is sequential design in contrast to combinational, that concerned with time and with delay, for example. Nevertheless, I await (with pleasure and anticipation) your examination of and comment on the ideas presented here. I conjecture that a program such as OTTER will provide a most valuable automated reasoning assistant for design and synthesis—it clearly has for us in mathematics and in logic.

References

1. Fitelson, B., and Wos, L.: Missing Proofs Found, preprint ANL/MCS-P816-0500, Argonne National Laboratory, Argonne, Illinois (2000)
2. Wos, L.: The Automation of Reasoning: An Experimenter's Notebook with OTTER Tutorial. Academic Press, New York (1996)
3. Wos, L., and Pieper, G. W.: A Fascinating Country in the World of Computing: Your Guide to Automated Reasoning. World Scientific Publishing, Singapore (1999)

Author Index

Lecture Notes in Computer Science

For information about Vols. 1–1781
please contact your bookseller or Springer-Verlag

Vol. 1824: J. Palsberg (Ed.), Static Analysis. Proceedings, 2000. VIII, 433 pages. 2000.

Vol. 1825: M. Nielsen, D. Simpson (Eds.), Application and Theory of Petri Nets 2000. Proceedings, 2000. XI, 485 pages. 2000.

Vol. 1826: W. Cazzola, R.J. Stroud, F. Tisato (Eds.), Reflection and Software Engineering. X, 229 pages. 2000.

Vol. 1829: C. Fonlupt, J.-K. Hao, E. Lutton, E. Ronald, M. Schoenauer (Eds.), Artificial Evolution. Proceedings, 1999. X, 293 pages. 2000.

Vol. 1830: P. Kropf, G. Babin, J. Plaice, H. Unger (Eds.), Distributed Communities on the Web. Proceedings, 2000. X, 203 pages. 2000.

Vol. 1831: D. McAllester (Ed.), Automated Deduction – CADE-17. Proceedings, 2000. XIII, 519 pages. 2000. (Subseries LNAI).

Vol. 1832: B. Lings, K. Jeffery (Eds.), Advances in Databases. Proceedings, 2000. X, 227 pages. 2000.

Vol. 1833: L. Bachmair (Ed.), Rewriting Techniques and Applications. Proceedings, 2000. X, 275 pages. 2000.

Vol. 1834: J.-C. Heudin (Ed.), Virtual Worlds. Proceedings, 2000. XI, 314 pages. 2000. (Subseries LNAI).

Vol. 1835: D. N. Christodoulakis (Ed.), Natural Language Processing – NLP 2000. Proceedings, 2000. XII, 438 pages. 2000. (Subseries LNAI).

Vol. 1836: B. Masand, M. Spiliopoulou (Eds.), Web Usage Analysis and User Profiling. Proceedings, 2000, V, 183 pages. 2000. (Subseries LNAI).

Vol. 1837: R. Backhouse, J. Nuno Oliveira (Eds.), Mathematics of Program Construction. Proceedings, 2000. IX, 257 pages. 2000.

Vol. 1838: W. Bosma (Ed.), Algorithmic Number Theory. Proceedings, 2000. IX, 615 pages. 2000.

Vol. 1839: G. Gauthier, C. Frasson, K. VanLehn (Eds.), Intelligent Tutoring Systems. Proceedings, 2000. XIX, 675 pages. 2000.

Vol. 1840: F. Bomarius, M. Oivo (Eds.), Product Focused Software Process Improvement. Proceedings, 2000. XI, 426 pages. 2000.

Vol. 1841: E. Dawson, A. Clark, C. Boyd (Eds.), Information Security and Privacy. Proceedings, 2000. XII, 488 pages. 2000.

Vol. 1842: D. Vernon (Ed.), Computer Vision – ECCV 2000. Part I. Proceedings, 2000. XVIII, 953 pages. 2000.

Vol. 1843: D. Vernon (Ed.), Computer Vision – ECCV 2000. Part II. Proceedings, 2000. XVIII, 881 pages. 2000.

Vol. 1844: W.B. Frakes (Ed.), Software Reuse: Advances in Software Reusability. Proceedings, 2000. XI, 450 pages. 2000.

Vol. 1845: H.B. Keller, E. Plöderer (Eds.), Reliable Software Technologies Ada-Europe 2000. Proceedings, 2000. XIII, 304 pages. 2000.

Vol. 1846: H. Lu, A. Zhou (Eds.), Web-Age Information Management. Proceedings, 2000. XIII, 462 pages. 2000.

Vol. 1847: R. Dyckhoff (Ed.), Automated Reasoning with Analytic Tableaux and Related Methods. Proceedings, 2000. X, 441 pages. 2000. (Subseries LNAI).

Vol. 1848: R. Giancarlo, D. Sankoff (Eds.), Combinatorial Pattern Matching. Proceedings, 2000. XI, 423 pages. 2000.

Vol. 1849: C. Freksa, W. Brauer, C. Habel, K.F. Wender (Eds.), Spatial Cognition II. XI, 420 pages. 2000. (Subseries LNAI).

Vol. 1850: E. Bertino (Ed.), ECOOP 2000 – Object-Oriented Programming. Proceedings, 2000. XIII, 493 pages. 2000.

Vol. 1851: M.M. Halldórsson (Ed.), Algorithm Theory – SWAT 2000. Proceedings, 2000. XI, 564 pages. 2000.

Vol. 1853: U. Montanari, J.D.P. Rolim, E. Welzl (Eds.), Automata, Languages and Programming. Proceedings, 2000. XVI, 941 pages. 2000.

Vol. 1854: G. Lacoste, B. Pfitzmann, M. Steiner, M. Waidner (Eds.), SEMPER — Secure Electronic Marketplace for Europe. XVIII, 350 pages. 2000.

Vol. 1855: E.A. Emerson, A.P. Sistla (Eds.), Computer Aided Verification. Proceedings, 2000. X, 582 pages. 2000.

Vol. 1857: J. Kittler, F. Roli (Eds.), Multiple Classifier Systems. Proceedings, 2000. XII, 404 pages. 2000.

Vol. 1858: D.-Z. Du, P. Eades, V. Estivill-Castro, X. Lin, A. Sharma (Eds.), Computing and Combinatorics. Proceedings, 2000. XII, 478 pages. 2000.

Vol. 1860: M. Klusch, L. Kerschberg (Eds.), Cooperative Information Agents IV. Proceedings, 2000. XI, 285 pages. 2000. (Subseries LNAI).

Vol. 1861: J. Lloyd, V. Dahl, U. Furbach, M. Kerber, K.-K. Lau, C. Palamidessi, L. Moniz Pereira, Y. Sagiv, P.J. Stuckey (Eds.), Computational Logic – CL 2000. Proceedings, 2000. XIX, 1379 pages. (Subseries LNAI).

Vol. 1862: P. Clote, H. Schwichtenberg (Eds.), Computer Science Logic. Proceedings, 2000. XIII, 543 pages. 2000.

Vol. 1863: L. Carter, J. Ferrante (Eds.), Languages and Compilers for Parallel Computing. Proceedings, 1999. XII, 500 pages. 2000.

Vol. 1864: B. Y. Choueiry, T. Walsh (Eds.), Abstraction, Reformulation, and Approximation. Proceedings, 2000. XI, 333 pages. 2000. (Subseries LNAI).

Vol. 1866: J. Cussens, A. Frisch (Eds.), Inductive Logic Programming. Proceedings, 2000. X, 265 pages. 2000. (Subseries LNAI).

Vol. 1868: P. Koopman, C. Clack (Eds.), Implementation of Functional Languages. Proceedings, 1999. IX, 199 pages. 2000.

Vol. 1869: M. Aagaard, J. Harrison (Eds.), Theorem Proving in Higher Order Logics. Proceedings, 2000. IX, 535 pages. 2000.

Vol. 1872: J. van Leeuwen, O. Watanabe, M. Hagiya, P.D. Mosses, T. Ito (Eds.), Theoretical Computer Science. Proceedings, 2000. XV, 630 pages. 2000.

Vol. 1880: M. Bellare (Ed.), Advances in Cryptology – CRYPTO 2000. Proceedings, 2000. XI, 545 pages. 2000.

Vol. 1893: M. Nielsen, B. Rovan (Eds.), Mathematical Foundations of Computer Science 2000. Proceedings, 2000. XIII, 710 pages. 2000.